Watch It Made in the U.S.A.

**A Visitor's Guide to the Companies
That Make Your Favorite Products**

D0731128

Praise for *Watch It Made in the U.S.A.*

"Ever wonder how Celestial Seasonings mixes all those herbs for their teas? Or how Hallmark comes up with those cute sayings for their cards? Here's your chance to find out."

—USA Today

"Unusual travel opportunities, and they're closer than you think..."

—Good Morning America

"This is a product that makes you proud to be an American: a guide to all the tourable places that make the products America loves best."

—Daily News, New York's Hometown Newspaper

"...a fascinating behind-the-scenes look at household names, names that many of us take for granted...."

—Chicago Tribune

"Factory tours are great value vacations."

—Sunday Boston Herald

"*Watch It Made in the U.S.A.* would be right up your assembly line....a wealth of information on tours and museums."

—The Philadelphia Inquirer

"...take time out to visit one of these factories—the whole family will enjoy the tour!"

—Good Housekeeping

"If the mystery of how the fortune gets into the fortune cookie keeps you up at night, thumb through *Watch It Made in the U.S.A....*"

—SELF

Watch It Made in the U.S.A.

A Visitor's Guide to the Companies That Make Your Favorite Products

Karen Axelrod & Bruce Brumberg

Foreword by Herman G. Rowland Sr., Jelly Belly Candy Co.

AVALON
TRAVEL

Watch It Made in the U.S.A.
A Visitor's Guide to the Companies That Make Your Favorite Products
Third Edition

Karen Axelrod and Bruce Brumberg

Published by
Avalon Travel Publishing
1400 65th Street, Suite 250
Emeryville, CA 94608

Text © 2002 by Karen Axelrod and Bruce Brumberg. All rights reserved.
Maps © 2002 by Avalon Travel Publishing, Inc.
All rights reserved.

ISBN: 1-56691-431-0
ISSN: 1540-3378

Editors: Ellen Cavalli, Angelique S. Clarke
Copy Editor: Emily McManus
Graphics Coordinator: Melissa Sherowski
Production and Design: Amber Pirker
Map Editor: Naomi Adler Dancis
Cartography: Mike Morgenfeld, Colby Barr
Factchecker and Indexer: Beth Polzin

Front cover photos: © Jelly Belly
Back cover photos: © Fenton © Herr's Snack Factory © Toyota
Photographs: © respective companies, unless otherwise noted.

Distributed by Publishers Group West

Printed in China through Colorcraft Ltd., Hong Kong

Please send all comments, corrections, additions, amendments, and critiques to:

WATCH IT MADE
IN THE U.S.A.
Third Edition
Avalon Travel Publishing
1400 65th Street, Suite 250
Emeryville, CA 94608, U.S.A.

email: atpfeedback@avalonpub.com
www.factorytour.com

Printing History
1st edition—1994
3rd edition—September 2002
5 4 3 2 1

Dedications

To the American workers, engineers, and managers who strive to make the best quality products in the world.

To our marriage and the love and times we share together.

To Hilary Dana and Gregory Seth, the best products we've made.

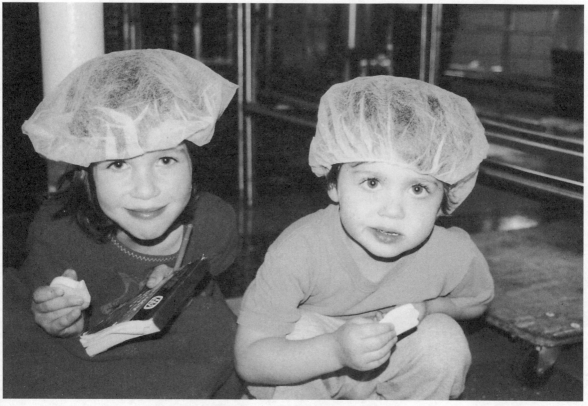

*Hilary and Gregory Brumberg enjoying candy making
at Hebert Candies in Shrewsbury, Massachusetts.*

Contents

Foreword

To visit a factory or company museum is to share, for that brief time, the fascinating, exciting, and sometimes tasty makings of products we know and love. Even with products we think we know, a factory tour reveals new wonders, undiscovered facts and an appreciation for the care and work that goes into American manufacturing.

We built our California plant in 1986 to make Jelly Belly beans and one hundred other candies. Then local civic groups called up to ask for a tour. We thought, well, why not? Those first tours took people on a walk inside the factory. Word-of-mouth in the neighboring communities grew and grew, and soon the local press got wind of the tours. We added displays to help visitors understand the process, and information about the five generations of candy makers who have created our history.

Soon the numbers of visitors grew so large we made an investment in an elevated walkway we call the Jelly Belly Trail. Then, in 1999 we built a large visitor center in California and three years later opened a warehouse tour in Wisconsin. These days thousands of visitors come through our doors each week arriving from all parts of the country, and now many are international travelers, too.

Throughout the years as we've steadily expanded our tours and amenities, the response from the public has been overwhelming enthusiasm. Local people bring out-of-town relatives and friends for the fun of it. One family who visited recently had arranged a family reunion around plans to visit our factory and arrived with 17 family members who had traveled from three states. Schoolteachers arrange field trips and send us their class projects. Seniors arrive by touring bus, and business travelers stop by to see American ingenuity at work.

Our employees and our family are proud of the confections we make. Every time someone takes our tour, they see first hand the knowledge and dedication it takes to make our candies. That is true for all the companies in this book. America produces an incredible array of products that are the best in the world, and factory tours allow visitors to learn how this happens by hearing, seeing, experiencing what it takes to make these products.

Readers of this book are in for adventures that stretch across the country and across many products. If your love is baseball or computers or teddy bears, there is a factory tour for you. The Tillamook Cheese factory in Oregon or the potato chips at Herr's in Pennsylvania will get your mouth watering. If it's a love of planes, trucks, and cars, the Boeing, Mercedes-Benz, and Mack Trucks factories offer an insider's view.

But sometimes the real eye opening experiences are those you don't expect. So I invite you to take a tour and prepare to be amazed.

The authors Karen Axelrod and Bruce Brumberg have searched out and compiled a practical and comprehensive guide to a world of factory touring. You will find everything you need to know to plan a visit, so I invite you to take a tour soon. And if you are planning a trip to Northern California or Wisconsin, I hope you will stop by and see us.

Herman G. Rowland, Sr.
Chairman of the Board
Jelly Belly Candy Company
Fairfield, California

Preface

When you were younger, you probably read *Charlie and the Chocolate Factory* or watched the movie version, *Willy Wonka and the Chocolate Factory*. As you may remember, Charlie won the opportunity to visit a chocolate factory by finding a special golden ticket in his Wonka Bar. His luck led to a fascinating journey.

This book is like that golden ticket in Charlie's chocolate bar. With this guide you can visit factory tours and company museums throughout the U.S.A. Whether you're with your family, traveling alone, or on a field or business trip, you'll have fun, discover how well-known products are made, and learn what these companies did to grow and prosper. Along the way, you will receive plenty of free samples and tastes.

Ours is a harried society that just wants to plug it in, mix it with milk, turn the ignition, or open the box. We want you to experience the excitement of watching people and machines make the food we eat, the cars we drive, the musical instruments we play, and the sporting goods we use.

After visiting (by foot or armchair) the more than 300 companies featured in this book, you'll marvel at the behind-the-scenes processes involved in producing the products we take for granted. You'll be proud of the hardworking American people and companies that make it all possible. We like to say that this book gives you the opportunity to go out and "kick the tires" of the American economy. Watch how American companies proudly maintain their competitive edge and are again perceived as the world leaders in many industries.

To compile the list of companies that offer tours, museums, and visitor centers, we followed many paths and traveled thousands of miles. The book focuses on recognized national or regional companies that make familiar products, whether they be chocolates, cars, clothes, toys, or beer. Each tour or museum either has regular hours or is open to the general public by reservation.

Enjoy the tours. But don't stuff yourself with the free samples like the guests did on the tour of Willy Wonka's chocolate factory!

Third Edition Thoughts

Now is the time to explore and take pride in what makes the U.S.A. special. We can no longer take our family, our security, or our economy for granted. Along with our people, history, culture, and natural beauty, our economy is a source of our national strength and patriotism.

We believe the third edition takes on greater importance than our other two editions. More than just a travel guide, *Watch It Made in the U.S.A.* will help you appreciate firsthand the products, companies, technology, and workers that inspire our economy. Plus, with the concerns about airplane travel, the book offers you new travel experiences close to home.

The first two editions sold very well and went into multiple printings. Throughout our numerous media interviews, including *Good Morning America* and CNN, we were asked why we wrote the book, and our responses still ring true for the third edition. We often answered that we're curious people—wondering about how the toothpaste gets into the toothpaste tube and how the tea gets into the tea bag. We explained in first edition interviews that there was no book out there like this one, it sparked our interest in business, and that we decided to write it before having children.

Along with the first two editions came our two children. They helped us see these tours through their curious eyes and to focus more on the needs of younger visitors and their parents. Our daughter, Hilary, earned her first frequent-flier points when she was three months old, traveling to The Creegan Company's "Animation Factory" in Ohio, her first official factory tour. She even went to meetings with us at such companies as Amway (now part of Alticor) and Binney & Smith (Crayola). For the third edition, our son, Gregory, also traveled with us, amused by the chocolate-making machines at Hebert Candies.

When asked about the best tours, we say that it depends on your interests. Some people like the craftsmanship required to make Fenton art glass and Martin guitars. Others enjoy the high speed of Coca-Cola bottling lines or the robots and welding at automobile plants. We like to mention tours that can easily be added onto an existing vacation. For example, if you're going skiing, hiking, or climbing in the Rockies, you can also watch the tea get into the tea bag at Celestial Seasonings in Boulder, Colorado.

The third edition includes hundreds of factory tours, company museums, and visitors centers to enjoy. We've completely updated all the existing write-ups and visited many more places. Highlights include a new Caribbean section covering four islands. In all, we've added full write-ups for 60 new sites! New factory tours in the book include Eli's Cheesecake World in Chicago, the Gibson guitar factory in Memphis, and National Vitamin in Las Vegas.

New, small company museums and exhibits include the Jell-O Gallery in New York, "Kool-Aid Discover the Dream" in Nebraska, and Frederick's of Hollywood Lingerie Museum in California. Large visitors centers include the Jelly Belly Center in Wisconsin, John Deere Pavilion in Illinois, Dole Pineapple Plantation in Hawaii, and Zippo/Case Visitors Center in Pennsylvania. We've added seven new sites in California, four in Illinois, and six in Pennsylvania. (Note: Since the last edition, York County in Pennsylvania has declared itself "factory tour capital.") Almost 60 percent of states have at least one new tour.

Unfortunately, we had to drop some sites from the book because facilities closed or moved, tours were discontinued, or companies didn't want the continued publicity. September 11, 2001, with its heightened physical security concerns, had its impact. Factory tours were curtailed—Hershey's, one of our all-time favorites, stopped offering tours in its Oakdale, California, plant. Many securities and commodities exchanges and mints that regularly gave tours have temporarily suspended tours. We even wrote features for some new tours but couldn't include them in the book because the company discontinued them before we submitted the manuscript. For example, Sunmaid Raisins, in California, discontinued its tour for security reasons because the tour was held so close to the production area. We were scheduled to visit the NASDAQ MarketSite in New York City on September 12, 2001, but the site is now open only for special events.

We hope you will take the opportunity to use this book to visit the companies that make your favorite products and keep our economy strong. When you cannot physically visit a company, our narrative description gives you a vicarious feel for the experience. In addition, companies may have virtual tours on their websites. However, nothing matches the true sights and sounds of actually visiting. Plus, because 90 percent of the tours in this book are free, and many give free samples, factory tours and company museums remain the best vacation value in America.

We sincerely hope that your adventures bring you as much enjoyment and wonder as we have experienced!

Acknowledgments

First and foremost, we want to thank the companies that provide tours and museums, and also the people at those businesses who met with us, answered our numerous questions, verified the accuracy of our information, and gave us encouragement. The firms that open their doors to the public have stories to tell about their place in America's heritage and in its economic future. Convention and visitors bureaus, state tourism boards, and chambers of commerce gave us information and materials, which we appreciated.

Twenty years ago this book wouldn't have been needed, as just about all companies gave public tours. Now many forces, including budget cuts, insurance rates, trade-secret protection, government regulations, and physical security concerns have caused companies to end them. Fortunately, a trend has emerged toward opening new visitors centers and company museums as an alternative to factory tours.

Since this was a very expensive book to research, write, and produce, we also specially thank those companies with photographs in the book. No company paid for its inclusion in *Watch It Made in the U.S.A.* or for our publishing its logo. Companies did pay a modest fee to include black-and-white or color photos. Without this small amount of funding the book either would not have been published or its purchase price would have been far beyond what the average person spends for a travel book.

We enjoyed the support from our parents, Elaine and Norman Brumberg (actually, Bruce's parents became supportive when we were researching the first edition after we gave his dad a Harley-Davidson T-shirt and his mom T-shirts from Ben & Jerry's and Wild Turkey), and Harriet and David Axelrod (Karen's mother's love of travel inspired us both to do this book; we wish she were alive to see it in print); strength from our grandmother Franziska Hirschhorn (we miss her dearly); and continued guidance and encouragement from our aunt and uncle, Erika and Larry Casler. Elaine Brumberg and Larry Casler set good examples for us, as they have written books of their own.

It took a team to make this book. Kristin Odmark provided pre-game scheduling and ongoing emotional support. Elizabeth Hunt independently pitched the first five innings, working full-time to update the information for most of the existing companies in the book and writing some of the new features. Willa Mueller came in for the last few innings, and diligently coordinated the new companies and the photographs along with the neverending details. Cheerfully Mariana Agathokolis and Johanna McKenzie pitched in with cheerful and thorough assistance to complete the manuscript and wrote a few features. Valerie Dumova provided consistent, steady writing support. Other people who helped write a few features are Kathryn Kaplan, Ilyse Kramer, and Mark Malseed.

Other folks who helped us (in alphabetical order) either with this edition or the prior ones include Harriet Brumberg, Andy Cavatorta, Scott Dimetrosky (who initially developed our website, at www.factorytour.com), Sam Donisi, Susan Koffman, Pam Kubbins, Jeanne Lothrop, Amy and Mark Seiden, Judith Woodruff, and Howard Zaharoff.

Unfortunately, we could not list all those friends, relatives, writers, and editorial assistants who helped with research, writing, editing, and word processing and who provided general advice, support, and ideas for all the editions—but we do express our heartfelt appreciation to all of them. We have funded all the travel ourselves, so we appreciated the help with accommodations provided by Radisson Waikiki Prince Kuhio in Honolulu, Hawaii (808-922-0811).

Finally, we thank the staff at Avalon Travel Publishing for sharing our vision for this book.

Tour
Tools

Safety Guidelines

Lawsuits are a product we make too many of in the U.S.A. During our research we discovered many companies that have discontinued their tours because of fears of lawsuits from injured guests and increases in liability insurance rates for allowing public visitors. Follow basic safety rules and your common sense to avoid injury.

The authors and publisher of *Watch It Made in the U.S.A.* **make no warranty, expressed or implied, regarding the safety of any of the tours in this book and assume no liability with respect to the consequences of using the information contained herein. If you have any special safety concerns, contact the companies directly before you decide to visit.**

The factories in this book are all working facilities, not full-time tourist attractions. While many of them provide the kind of space-age excitement you normally see only in the movies, these factories are the real thing, with potentially dangerous machines.

If you are injured, it is likely that the company will completely discontinue its public tours. Please listen to your tour guide and read any safety warnings. Remember the following rules:

1. Do not wander away from your tour guide or away from any specified tour path. Many factory tours have lines painted on the floor. You must stay between them.
2. Parents and adult group leaders should keep a close watch on children. Kids will be very curious about the sights, sounds, and smells, and may be tempted to wander off and touch things that could be dangerous.
3. Wear any protective equipment that you are provided with on your tour. These may include eyeglasses, earplugs, hard hats, or hair nets. If you have trouble wearing any of these items, tell your tour guide immediately.
4. Do not touch anything, including machines, products, parts, or boxes, unless your tour guide specifically hands something to you.
5. Wear closed-toe shoes with rubber soles that have good traction. Do not wear sandals or high heels (many companies will not allow you to go on the tour). Wear shoes that will provide protection against sharp objects and that are comfortable for walking. Floors can be slippery. For safety reasons, it is best not to wear shorts.

How Companies Were Selected

Our search for companies to include in *Watch It Made in the U.S.A.* began in stores where their products are sold. We went through supermarkets, department stores, car dealerships, and sporting goods stores, searching for the names of companies that make popular products in the U.S.A. Sometimes store owners thought we were competitors, as we would pick up a box, turn it over to see who made the product, and scribble down the company's address and phone number.

We also searched through directories and magazine ads, hunting down more manufacturers of U.S.A.-made products. We contacted state travel offices, local convention and visitors bureaus, and chambers of commerce looking for names of companies in their areas that gave tours. For the third edition, we did numerous Internet searches. Readers of the book and companies who had started tours also contacted us with suggested additions. These lists, which we continued making and updating throughout our writing and traveling, were only the start of our research.

Then we called...and called...and visited most of the sites in the book. We spoke with companies throughout the U.S.A., asking whether they gave tours or had a museum (often called a "visitors center"). We didn't hide the fact that we were writing a book. We wanted to include only those companies that accept public visitors and would talk with us about their history, tours, and products.

No company paid for its written feature in *Watch It Made in the U.S.A.* The companies had to meet the following criteria:

1. **Tours open to the general public.** Throughout our research we found companies that give tours only to buyers, to technical organizations, or upon special request. We did not include these companies or others that had too many requirements for visitors.

2. **Tours available to individuals and families.** Some companies will give tours only to local school groups, senior citizen clubs, Boy and Girl Scout troops, or bus tour companies. To be included in *Watch It Made in the U.S.A.,* a company had to at least allow individuals and families not affiliated with a group tour to visit. You may need to join a scheduled group tour (or the company may combine individual requests to form a group) and make reservations far in advance, but every facility in this book should be open to you.

3. **Products of general interest that are worth traveling to see made.** Unless you have a technical background or are in a specific industry, we thought that seeing how your favorite everyday products are made would hold the most fascination. In addition to tours of the icons of American business, we sought out small companies that have good products and interesting tours. Most of the companies in the book make consumer-related or widely recognized products. We also selected companies where you could watch the completion of the final product and therefore excluded parts manufacturers.

4. **Company did not object to being featured in this book.** Companies generally do not make money from their tours. They give tours as a public and community service, often pulling employees from their regular jobs to conduct the tours. We excluded companies that did not want the calls and tour requests that this widely distributed book would generate, if the tour was not already mentioned in other public sources. A small number of companies asked not to be included after we had visited them and written our extensive features. In most cases we were able to retain their features after modifying the tour information to meet the companies' concerns. In a few instances we had to drop tours of well-known companies.

continued on next page

We strove to select companies from diverse industries and all areas of the country. We wanted to capture the industries for which different regions are known, such as cheese in Wisconsin and Vermont, glass in West Virginia, movies in Southern California, bourbon in Kentucky, RVs in northern Indiana, Cajun hot sauces in Louisiana, and wood products in the Pacific Northwest. Certain high-tech industries, such as computer manufacturing and biotechnology, do not give regular public tours for proprietary reasons, so they are excluded by their choice. In other industries, such as beer brewing and newspaper publishing, tours are a standard practice; from this group we selected the most high-profile companies or those with interesting processes or histories.

We were surprised that companies in certain states, even though very industrial, do not seem interested in giving public tours. For example, while manufacturing-intensive states such as Pennsylvania, Wisconsin, and Ohio offer a variety of captivating tours, most New Jersey and Connecticut companies remain closed to the public. In contrast, companies in less industrial states such as Kentucky and Vermont have exhibited great pride in opening themselves to the public.

In addition to factory tours, we also included company museums or visitors centers devoted to one company's products and history. Some companies have replaced their public factory tours with educational and entertaining museums that explain how they started, succeeded, and make their products. The Crayola FACTORY at Two Rivers Landing in downtown Easton, Pennsylvania, is an example. Since Jelly Belly Candy Co.'s Fairfield, California, factory tours have become so popular, the company expanded in 2001, opening Jelly Belly Center in Pleasant Prairie, Wisconsin. More companies are now establishing museums to preserve their heritage, instill corporate culture, and tell their story to the public, new employees, and customers. We did not include company museums that are like art exhibits. The museums we selected, like the tours, give you a sense of what the companies are all about.

Going Beyond This Book

We excluded wineries, power plants, chemical factories, meat processors, most service industries, and tobacco manufacturers. The company tours in this book are the easiest ones to join—you either just show up or call in advance to reserve a space. If you are interested in visiting a company not featured here, contact the public affairs or human resources department at the corporate headquarters or local plant. With persistence, you can tour many firms if you're not a direct competitor. Explain your individual request and also ask if the company offers tours for specialized business and technical groups (often for a fee).

No book like this has ever been published before. Although we tried hard to find the public factory tours and company museums currently available, we do not claim that this guide contains all of them. Since we will update this book again, we would like your comments on the sites you visit from this guide and on tours we should consider for the next edition. Please write us at Avalon Travel Publishing, 1400 65th Street, Suite 250, Emeryville, CA 94608 and visit our website at www.factorytour.com. We hope this book's success will lead more companies to open their doors to the general public.

How to Use This Book

We wanted *Watch It Made in the U.S.A.* to be much more than a directory. Therefore, we *did not* write it by sending surveys out to companies and then publishing a compilation of the responses. We visited most of the companies included here. We took periodic breaks from our regular jobs to travel the U.S.A. in search of its economic soul. For those companies that time did not permit us to visit, we either hired writers to do so or conducted in-depth phone interviews that required companies to send us videos, articles, and tour scripts in addition to reviewing their websites. After we wrote each feature, we verified its accuracy with the company.

Each company tour or museum feature includes a narrative description and a practical information section. This book is organized alphabetically by state. The features appear in alphabetical order unless positioning of photographs necessitated slight alteration.

Narrative Description

Some of us are awed by fast-moving bottling machines and fascinated by robotic welders or giant presses, while others appreciate the artisanship of a glassblower, woodworker, or potter. The narrative description will help you determine which tours you and your family will enjoy.

Each feature has a three- to five-paragraph write-up that captures the highlights of the tour and some background on the company. The write-ups also provide a basic understanding of how different products are made. We try to give you a sense of being there—what you might see, hear, smell, taste, or even touch; if a company is big or small; and whether you actually visit the factory floor or watch production through glass windows. We wrote this part in a conversational tone so that even the armchair traveler would be able to vicariously experience the tour or museum.

Practical Information Section

The second part of the feature provides basic practical information on location, hours, admission charge, freebies, age and group requirements, disabled access, gift shop and outlet stores, and nearby attractions. The category titles in this section are self-explanatory. The following are some special notes on the different categories in this section:

Cost: Many company tours, visitors centers, and museums are free or have a nominal charge, which makes them a great vacation value. However, charges may change after this book's printing, so call ahead.

Freebies: Many tours give samples, ranging from beer and ice cream to miniature baseball bats. Remember—you're a guest, so be appreciative.

Video Shown: These are often interesting, informative, and even humorous. They provide a close-up view inside machines and show production steps not seen on the tour. If videos are optional, we suggest you view them before going on the tour. They help you understand what you will see.

Reservations Needed: If a company requires reservations, it is crucial to do so. *Do not just show up*—you will not get a tour. Make reservations as far in advance as possible. Some companies require individuals and families to join a scheduled group tour that has not reached its maximum size, which this section will note. For these companies, you need to be more flexible in scheduling your visit. Many companies produce a range of products; if you have certain favorites, call ahead to find out what will be in production on the day of your visit.

Days and Hours: These are the hours for the tour or museum, not for the gift shop or outlet store. Hours are subject to change, and factories may shut down (hopefully for expansion construction), so call before your visit to avoid disappointment. Automobile plants, for example, often temporarily discontinue their tours so assembly lines can be reconfigured for major model changes. Many of the companies with regular tour

continued on next page

schedules have voice-mail telephone numbers that answer common questions on schedule changes and directions. The hours listed here are the range during which tours are given, unless a frequency is specified. Holiday schedules vary by company. For example, some companies view the day after Thanksgiving as a holiday.

Plan to Stay: We included the amount of time needed for the basic visit, plus additional time for additions such as the gift shop. The length of time spent on self-guided tours depends on the level of your interest. A short recommended time provides an indication of the company size or the amount you'll see.

Minimum Age: Tours have minimum age restrictions because of safety and insurance requirements. Companies strictly enforce these limits.

Disabled Access: Almost all of the tours in this book are working factories first and not full-featured visitor attractions. They try to accommodate people with disabilities while focusing on the safety concerns of both visitors and workers. Few companies told us absolutely "no" for disabled access. Almost all plants, however, have some limited-access areas, which we tried to note, and some may require advance notice. We are not commenting on the restrooms or compliance with the Americans with Disabilities Act standards, only the ease with which people with disabilities can visit these companies.

Group Requirements: Advance reservations are almost always required for groups, and some companies have maximum group sizes. This section is useful for group tour planners.

Special Information: Re-read the safety rules at the beginning of the book, since we do not repeat them in this section. For worker safety and proprietary reasons, many tours do not allow photography (which includes snapshot and video cameras). "No photography" refers to factory production areas, not gift shops, museums, and display areas. If you or a family member are sensitive to noise, smells, or temperature changes, be aware of these conditions when selecting a tour. However, these shocks to the senses are part of the exciting realism of factory tours.

Gift Shop/Outlet Store: Most gift shops sell logoed items and company products. The real factory outlet stores offer great bargains. Hours are often longer than the tour hours.

Directions: While we have made our best efforts to give you accurate narrative directions (double-checked with the companies and often given from two possible directions), call the company for directions or check its website. At the top of each write-up is the street address of the factory or museum.

Nearby Attractions: To round out your day, we list some of the nearby parks, museums, and other activities. We also draw your attention to other nearby factory tours and company museums. These factory tours and museums, which are listed first, are within a larger radius from the plant than the other nearby attractions. In addition to the more than 300 full-page company features in the book, we list more than 150 additional factory tours in this section (phone numbers included). For reasons of variety, quality, tour restrictions, or time, we decided not to write full features on these other tours.

Trademarks

We have used the commonly known company name rather than the longer corporate name. To the best of our knowledge, all of the product names in this book are trademarks. Throughout the text, we capitalized the first letter of all words that are trademarks. When companies provided us with their logos, we included them at no charge. The logos in no way imply that a company is a sponsor of the book. These logos are also trademarks that cannot be reproduced without a company's express consent.

Advice for Business Travelers

These tours are not merely a new way to grab a free beer during a business trip to Milwaukee or St. Louis. At its core, *Watch It Made in the U.S.A.* is a travel guide to American business. Our business backgrounds led us to write this book. When we took a factory tour or visited a company museum, we discovered how that company makes and markets its products, how the company started and grew, and even whether it's a good stock investment.

From our visits, we developed ideas that we couldn't get from any newspaper, magazine, or business book. Sure, you can read a book about Ted Turner, Andy Grove, Mary Kay Ash, or Bill Gates—but *Watch It Made in the U.S.A.* tells you how to visit CNN, Intel, Mary Kay Cosmetics, or Microsoft to see the companies they founded in action. Visiting the sites in this book will spice up a business trip with new experiences that may help you in your own work.

Improve Your Understanding of Business News and Trends

The tours offer a new perspective on our economy, workplace productivity, and job creation. After visiting a few of the companies profiled, whether they be *Fortune* 500 corporations or typical small businesses making a quality product, you'll have a better filter for understanding business and economic news. The concepts of total quality management, re-engineering, just-in-time inventory, or *kaizen* (constant improvement), for example, which many companies in this book use in some form, have new meaning when you see how they are adapted to the production of baseball bats, cars, and chocolate. You'll also notice production and product trends before they are reported in the media and appear on store shelves.

Sources of Useful New Ideas

By visiting these companies you will not only experience firsthand how they operate but also expose yourself to new business techniques. You may even discover a company whose stock you want to own, as you have a chance to go beyond its financials, press releases, and annual report.

Don't think that these tours appeal only to people in manufacturing-related jobs! Many of the tours and museums show you much more than just how the company makes its products; they also reveal its marketing, management, and new-product development approach. To get the most from your visit, make it a point to look for and ask about innovative approaches and solutions that the company has developed, then think about how your business could adopt them. Try to discover what really makes the company successful and admired, then ponder how your firm can emulate it.

The companies' public relations departments may at times shape the tour scripts, but what you see, hear, sense, and ask cannot be totally controlled. The tour guides, especially those who are company retirees or volunteer line employees, can provide great insights and amusing anecdotes. However, while you want to be inquisitive, be careful not to sound like an industrial spy. Companies are very concerned about protecting what they view as proprietary technology, processes, or information, and, after September 11, 2001, their physical security.

These are not new worries. Kellogg's, for example, ended its cereal-factory tours in 1986 because of suspected spying by competitors. Because of these anxieties, some businesses have limited their tours, replaced them with museums or visitors centers (such as Kellogg's Cereal City USA in Battle Creek, Michigan), or asked us not to include them in the book (or even asked us to remove an existing write-up).

Don't confine yourself to visiting firms that make products similar to your company's. Trips outside your own industry can provide stimulus, inspiration, and new techniques. The cross-fertilization of ideas from other industries helps develop business creativity. To have a "Learning Organization," one of the training buzzwords popularized

continued on next page

by Peter Senge in *The Fifth Discipline,* you need to seek out new experiences. In *A Whack on the Side of the Head,* author Roger von Oech writes that "many good ideas have been discovered because someone poked around in an outside industry or discipline, and applied what he found to his own field." Follow von Oech's advice—be a business "explorer" and search for insights from companies outside your own industry.

In two of Tom Peters' best-selling business books, *In Search of Excellence* and *A Passion for Excellence,* he explains how the best managers practice a form of "management by walking around." Go out and walk around someone else's company—you'll be surprised at what you learn.

Business Only Tours

The public tours in *Watch It Made in the U.S.A.* are suitable for both family and business travelers. They are either free or inexpensive. However, we have discovered other companies that offer higher-priced, in-depth tours and seminars for visitors who want to know how they manage workers and operations. FedEx, for example, offers a glimpse into its Memphis package-handling and service quality operations (call 901-224-4919).

Advice for Family Travelers, Teachers, and Field-Trip Leaders

Our Hope

Touring factories anywhere in the country is a fun experience for children. It can also be highly educational. Children will remember the smell of crayons, the taste of breads right off the production line, the sight of car- and paper-making machinery. And because they are kids, they'll be curious about how it all works.

One of our hopes in writing this book is that more children will visit production facilities and company museums in the U.S.A. and be inspired to build things or go into business themselves. America needs entrepreneurs, factory workers, engineers, and business managers to keep its industries strong. By taking these tours, kids can develop a sense of pride in "Made in the U.S.A." products. They will see that we make many things in the U.S.A., and we make them well.

Before Your Visit

Whether you're a parent, trip leader, or teacher, there are a number of things you can do with your children to maximize the learning experience while still having fun. The more kids learn before they go on the tour, the more they will get out of it. For teachers, field trips can be an exciting part of an integrated unit.

Before you go, talk about the products you are about to see made. Examine your crayons, teddy bears, or the family car or piano. Ask your kids how they think those products are made. In the kitchen or classroom, try making your own batch of bread, fudge, or pretzels. This will give children a frame of reference for how the factory makes the same thing on a much larger scale.

Do a little background research with your children. Read about the tour or company museum in this book. If you are going on a local outing or a family trip, let the kids have some input as to which places you visit. Check the library for books telling the history of the baseball, or how corn flakes were invented. Some books include great drawings illustrating production of all sorts of products. Visit the company's website. (For easy reference, companies' websites are listed in this book.) Teenagers might be interested in looking at a company's investor relations information on the Web or in calling for its annual report.

Talk with your children about the things they want to learn on the field trip. What questions do they want answered? Think about the product, and the people, facilities, and materials that go into making it. Write down questions and bring them with you. Kids can make their own clipboards by stapling their questions onto a piece of cardboard and tying on a pencil. With questions in hand, the junior reporters are ready for the tour!

During the Tour

Tour guides are a great source for answers to your children's questions. But first, kids should try observing their surroundings. What happens first? Second? Third? How does the toothpaste get into the tube? What puts the windshield on the car? Watch the workers closely. Are they working together as a team to produce something, or are they working independently? Do they use machines or small hand tools? Why are the workers wearing aprons, hard hats, or goggles? Do you think the workers are proud of the products they make? Similar questions delving into the history of the company, its products, and its culture can be developed for company museums.

The most important thing to remember on the tour is to *follow the Safety Guidelines* we list in this book, as well as any special instructions the company gives you. Children must understand that factories can be dangerous places. Be sure to tell them that when they are on a tour, they must listen to the tour guide, wear any protective gear the guide gives them, and walk only where they are allowed.

continued on next page

After the Tour

After the tour or visit to a company museum, talk about which parts were most interesting, a great topic for long car rides during driving vacations. What did each person learn? Younger children can draw pictures of how products are made or of workers doing their jobs. They can discuss what they found "cool" and share their experiences with their classes at school.

Parents and teachers might also encourage teenagers to imagine being an integral part of a company. Companies need all sorts of people, the innovators and creators, the builders and writers, the people selling on the front line and the ones doing the work behind the scenes. Perhaps they will leave with a new job or career idea. (That goes for adults, too!)

Watch It Made in the U.S.A.

Martin Guitar

Basic Brown Bear Factory

444 DeHaro Street
San Francisco, CA 94107
(415) 626-0781
www.basicbrownbear.com

BEER

You'll enjoy playing teddy bear obstetrician on this tour. At this factory, discover how teddy bears are born and participate in their delivery. One of the few U.S. manufacturers of stuffed bears, Basic Brown Bear (BBB) lets you watch them handmake the cuddly creatures from start to finish.

In the cutting and sewing area, often the owner proudly explains her process. First, she draws each pattern on paper and makes a sample animal from the pattern. Workers use bandsaws to slice 24 layers of plush fabric into pattern pieces. Seamstresses sew together individual bear parts and outfits, stitching the sections inside out, then reaching inside to push out the bear legs, ears, and noses. Each seamstress can make about 35 baby bears or 10 grandparent bears a day, plus their clothes.

You learn that the first stuffed bears had shoe buttons for eyes. Now, grommets snap mushroom-shaped plastic eyes into place. A tour highlight is stuffing bears with polyester from a bright yellow machine used to fill life jackets during WWII. Now you can bring a bear to life by inflating it like a balloon. Wait on a line of yellow paw prints to push the filler's foot pedal. Out shoots a mixture of air and polyester. Another machine injects beans into bears. Once a bear is cuddly enough, its back is hand-sewn shut.

At the beauty parlor, workers smooth out bear seams with an electric wire brush. A pressurized-air "bear bath" or "bear shower" (depending on the critter's size) removes fur "fuzzies." Children (and adults) giggle when they too receive a "bear shower" or give a bear a "bath." Bears are dressed in their outfits, including company-made wire-rim glasses. Visitors leave with a special affection for the bears they brought to life.

Cost: Free tour. Prices for stuffing your own animal run from $12 to $300.

Freebies: No

Video Shown: 20-minute Emmy award–winning video, "The Teddy Bear Factory,"

with its catchy tune, tells how teddy bears are made.

Reservations Needed: No, except for groups of 8 or more people.

Days and Hours: Mon–Sun 10:00 AM–5:00 PM, on the hour. Last tour at 4:00 PM. Closed holidays.

Plan to Stay: 30 minutes, plus time for stuffing and showering your own bear, and the gift shop.

Minimum Age: 3

Disabled Access: Yes

Group Requirements: Groups of 8 or more people should call 2 weeks in advance. Maximum group size is 40.

Special Information: Can also stuff your own animals at BBB's other stores in The Cannery, near Fisherman's Wharf (call 888-900-2327), in Old Town San Diego (call 877-234-2327), and in the Mall of America in Bloomington, MN (call 800-396-2327).

Gift Shop: More than 30 styles of stuffed bears (and other animals) and bear clothes, all handmade by BBB, are sold exclusively at this location. Mon–Sun 10:00 AM–5:00 PM. Price list available from (800) 554-1910.

Directions: Westbound from the Bay Bridge, take 9th St./Civic Center exit and get into the immediate left-hand lane, which puts you onto 8th St. Stay on 8th St. until it ends at the traffic circle. Turn right onto Kansas St. Turn left onto Mariposa St. BBB is on the left-hand corner of Mariposa and DeHaro Sts. From the South Bay, take Hwy. 101 North. Take the Vermont St. exit and cross over Vermont St. onto Mariposa St. Stay on Mariposa St. until you reach DeHaro St. (about 4 blocks). BBB is on the left-hand corner.

Nearby Attractions: Scharffen Berger chocolate tour (see page 81); Anchor Brewery tour (across the street, call 415-863-8350); downtown San Francisco attractions are 10–20 minutes away, including Wells Fargo Bank Museum (call 415-396-2619).

▲ Visitors holding bears they stuffed during a tour of Basic Brown Bear Factory, in San Francisco, California.

▼ Kids observe as an energetic tour guide demonstrates how the plush fabric is cut for each bear's parts.

Jelly Belly Candy Co.

One Jelly Belly Lane
Fairfield, CA 94533
(707) 428-2838
www.jellybelly.com

JELLY BEANS, CHOCOLATES, AND GUMMI CANDIES

The original gourmet jelly bean.®

FEATURED TOUR

If you question whether former president Ronald Reagan's policies were good for the U.S. economy or for kids, then you should visit this factory that produces millions of jelly beans per day, or 14 billion beans annually. The publicity surrounding President Reagan's fondness for gourmet Jelly Belly jelly beans led to increased demand, round-the-clock shifts, a new factory, and amusing tours for children and adults. The company has been making candy since 1898, but it was the introduction of the Jelly Belly in 1976 that spurred its modern growth.

While you'll see how the company makes a variety of creative candies, such as its line of Pet Gummi candies, the highlight is watching how it makes the Jelly Belly beans in more than 40 flavors. At the tour's beginning, you'll stare at large mosaic portraits of famous faces and figures such as Ronald Reagan and the Statue of Liberty, each made of 14,000 jelly beans. Follow your tour guide along Jelly Belly Candy Trail, an elevated walkway inside the 215,000-square-foot factory. View the beans at different stages of their creation. Be prepared for intense aromas. Unlike standard jelly beans, Jelly Belly beans are flavored both in the center and in the shell. Machines pour the special bean-center mixture into cornstarch molds that hold 1,260 centers per tray. Guess the exotic flavors, like strawberry daiquiri or peanut butter, as the bean centers travel by in the distance.

After the centers harden overnight, mechanical arms flip the trays over, and the centers are placed into spinning, open stainless steel drums. Here, workers add four layers of flavored syrup and sugars to create the outer shells. Each bean is automatically checked for correct size and color before traveling through the bagging and boxing machines. You'll look down at a hopper filled with a colorful and flavorful sea of jelly beans. The correctly weighed amount of jelly beans drops into plastic packets below. However, workers hand-pack the Gummi candies, which are too sticky for machines.

Cost: Free

Freebies: 3-ounce bag of Jelly Belly beans with an official menu matching colors to flavors. Logoed paper hat to wear during the tour.

Videos Shown: Short videos show close-up view of candy making on weekends.

Reservations Needed: No

Days and Hours: Mon–Sun 9:00 AM–5:00 PM. No production on weekends, but see production video. Closed holidays and the last week in June through the first week of July.

Plan to Stay: 40 minutes, plus time for candy kitchen, café, and gift shop.

Minimum Age: None, with 1 adult for every 6 children.

Disabled Access: Yes

Group Requirements: None

Special Information: No photography. Jelly Belly Center in Wisconsin also gives tours (see page 356). In exhibition candy kitchen, view candy makers hand-dipping chocolates and making toffee and caramel apples.

Retail Store: Sells more flavors of jelly beans than you can imagine (not only exotic fruit tastes, but also unusual flavors like toasted marshmallow, buttered popcorn, and jalapeño). Look for 2-pound bags of Belly Flops, factory seconds. Open Mon–Sun 9:00 AM–5:00 PM. Jelly Belly Café serves Jelly Belly–shaped pizzas, hamburgers, and buns. Ice cream counter.

Directions: From the San Francisco/Oakland area, take I-80 East to Hwy. 12 East. Turn right onto Beck Ave., right onto Courage Dr., right onto North Watney Way, and right onto Jelly Belly Ln. From Sacramento, take Abernathy exit left to Hwy. 12 East, then follow the above directions.

Nearby Attractions: In the same industrial park, Anheuser-Busch (Budweiser) Brewery tour (call 707-429-7595), Thompson Candy self-guided tour (call 707-435-1140), and VG Buck Olive Oil tasting (call 800-865-4836); Marine World Africa U.S.A.; Seguin Moreau barrel making tour (see page 82), Napa Valley wineries, and Culinary Institute of America located 20 minutes away.

▲ In Fairfield, California, Jelly Belly beans travel into hoppers before they are weighed and packaged.

The entrance to the Jelly Belly Visitor Center leads to a patio where visitors can bring a picnic or dine
▼ al fresco on Jelly Belly bean-shaped burgers and pizza from the café.

Coors

13th and Ford Streets
Golden, CO 80401
(303) 277-BEER
www.coors.com

TEDDY BEARS

The world's largest single-site brewery sits at the base of the Colorado Rockies between two "tabletop" mountains. In addition to the distinctly nonindustrial setting, the brewery tour has other memorable sights. The "Coors Copper Kitchen" brewhouse observation area is bordered on two sides by 50 handmade copper kettles, each the size of an above-ground swimming pool. Each kettle's sides are white ceramic tile, while its top is a dome of shiny copper with a long, narrow, copper neck. The kettles have assigned roles in the brewing process, which your guide will gladly explain.

Founded in 1873, Coors claims it is the only brewer in the U.S.A. to do most of its malting on-site. Before barley can be used in the brewing process, its starch must be converted into malt. The barley steeps in two-story-deep stainless-steel tanks, which prepares it for growth. Next, the barley is spread out on long screens called "germination beds." After the seeds sprout, the barley is roasted for 14 hours in immense kilns, then aged and milled.

The stillness of the malting process contrasts with the speedy aluminum-can packaging machine area. Thousands of cans converge here every minute and then roll by in 6-, 12-, and 24-pack cartons.

Cost: Free

Freebies: 3 beer samples in Coors' hospitality lounge for visitors age 21 or older, with picture ID. Serves most Coors brands and assorted soft drinks.

Videos Shown: Peter Coors' welcome message, shown at tour entrance area. Another video shows can and bottle manufacturing, filling, packaging, shipping, and distributing.

Reservations Needed: No, except for groups of 20 or more people.

Days and Hours: Mon–Sat 10:00 AM–4:00 PM. Closed holidays. Call for schedule around holidays.

Plan to Stay: 40 minutes for brewery tour, plus time for beer sampling, gift shop, and shuttle-bus tour from Coors parking lot through Historic Golden. Coors grounds also have interesting features, including a 16-foot-high, 13-foot-wide original copper brew kettle used in the 1880s. (It stands at the main entrance.) Veterans' memorial salutes the "Defenders of Freedom."

Minimum Age: Under 18 must be accompanied by adult.

Disabled Access: Yes, an alternative route is available.

Group Requirements: Groups of more than 20 people should make reservations 1 week in advance (call 303-277-2552).

Special Information: For special-needs tours call 303-277-2552. Tours also offered at Coors' Memphis, TN, brewery (call 901-368-BEER).

Gift Shop: Coors & Co. sells a wide range of logoed clothes and beer souvenirs, including mugs, glasses, barstools, and tap handles. Look for the popular blinking bottle-cap buttons. Open Mon–Sat 10:00 AM–5:00 PM. Closed holidays.

Directions: From Denver, take I-70 West to Hwy. 58 West to Golden. Exit at Washington Ave. and turn left on Washington, then left onto 13th St. to Ford St. for visitors' parking. You're in Golden when you see the archway over the main street ("Howdy, Folks! WELCOME TO GOLDEN—Where the West Lives!") and smell the malted barley. Parking-lot shuttle takes you on a brief tour around Golden and then to brewery.

Nearby Attractions: Colorado Railroad Museum; Foothills Art Center; Buffalo Bill Memorial Museum and Grave; Rocky Mountain Quilt Museum; Golden Pioneer Museum; Heritage Square Village.

▲   Guests get to sample Coors' crisp, clear, refreshing beers at the hospitality bar, at Coors' brewery in Golden, Colorado.

▼   Located in the Colorado Rockies since 1873, Coors is the largest single-site brewery in the world.

Hammond's Candies Since 1920

4969 Colorado Boulevard
Denver, CO 80216
(888) CANDY-99
www.hammondscandies.com

CANDY

Ever wonder how candy canes or other hard candies get their stripes? At Hammond's you'll see how hard candy has been made by hand since the 1920s. First, step into the packing room, where workers pack lollipops or candy canes.

Next, through a wall of windows in the kitchen, you'll see large copper kettles. Inside, 50 pounds of sugar, water, and corn syrup heats to over 300°. Two men lift and carry a huge kettle and pour the bubbling, amber-colored liquid onto a metal table. Next you may see the candy maker adding different colors to areas of this sheet of candy: for a candy cane, he scoops out some red paste with a spatula and mixes it into one section, then adds green in another corner. Another section remains clear. Finally, the "scrap"—the crushed beginnings and ends of other candy—is melted into another section: this will become the candy canes' center.

Once the sheet has cooled, the candy maker cuts the color sections with giant scissors—these will become the candy canes' stripes. A clear section is placed on a taffy-puller-like machine. As the machine pulls, it adds air, turning the candy white. Next the red, white, and green sections are laid out on a heated table in a long, flat "blanket."

The cooks then place the center piece on the puller, to add air (so it will melt faster in your mouth) and flavoring, like cherry. Next this centerpiece, which is shaped like a big duffel bag, is placed on the blanket of stripes, and the blanket is wrapped around it. The candy makers put this roll on a heated canvas mat. The mat is on a machine that rotates the bundle. When the bundle is hot enough, a cook takes one end in his hands and pulls it to the width of a candy cane. As the cook pulls, the machine rolls the bundle. This motion creates the twist in the candy cane stripes. As the cook cuts the

strip into pieces, a worker takes each piece from him and puts a crook in it. Other workers place the canes on trays to cool, and then they roll the finished candy canes into the packaging room.

Cost: Free

Freebies: Candy samples

Video Shown: 10-minute segment about the tour, from a Food Network program.

Reservations Needed: No, except for groups over 10 people or special needs groups..

Days and Hours: Mon–Fri 9:00 AM–2:30 PM, every 30 minutes. Closed Easter, Memorial Day, July 4th, Labor Day, Thanksgiving, Christmas, and New Year's.

Plan to Stay: 30 minutes for tour and video, plus time for gift shop.

Minimum Age: None

Disabled Access: Yes, call a day ahead for reservations.

Group Requirements: Groups of 10 or more people should call in advance.

Special Information: Must wear hairnets. Very small children may wear a hat. Strollers do not fit in factory. Tour can be hot in the summer in the cooking area. Candy Cane Festival held in December. Call for dates.

Gift Shop: Sells factory seconds, a range of handmade candies, Christmas decorations, books on candy making, and T-shirts. Mon–Fri 9:00 AM–4:00 PM.

Directions: From I-70, take Colorado Blvd. exit. Go north on Colorado Blvd. and turn left onto 48th Ave. Take an immediate right onto the frontage road. The factory is one block down on the left side of the street.

Nearby Attractions: U.S. Mint tour (see page 94); Denver Zoo; Denver Museum of Natural History; Denver Museum of Miniature Dolls & Toys; City Park and Botanical Garden.

▲ Candy canes are placed on a tray to cool before being packaged.

When visiting Hammond's Candies Since 1920 in Denver, Colorado, you can watch the candy makers
▼ pull candy canes by hand.

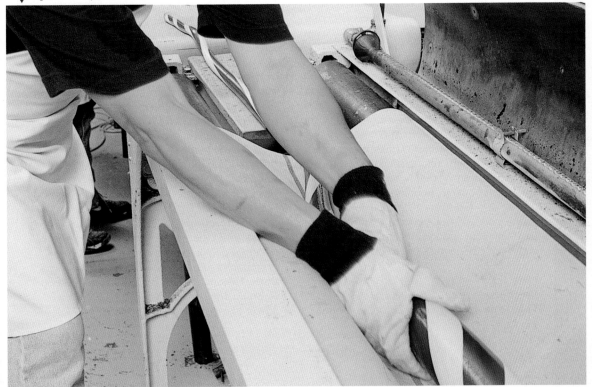

John Deere Pavilion

1400 River Drive
Moline, IL 61265
(309) 765-1000 / (800) 765-9588
www.johndeerepavilion.com

AGRICULTURAL EQUIPMENT

John Deere
PAVILION

Deere & Company's visitor center, the John Deere Pavilion, celebrates the past, present, and future of agriculture, as well as the history of the company. The 14,000-square-foot Pavilion is like one you'd see at a fairground, except the walls are made almost entirely of glass. Inside, stop at reception to request your own personal tour guide, likely a Deere retiree, who will happily customize your visit any way you like.

If you've never been on a farm, this is your chance to climb aboard a brand-new, shiny green tractor, combine, or cotton picker that sits on the Pavilion floor. How has equipment like the tractor changed over the years, since Deere made the 1918 Waterloo Boy model? To find out, compare the new machines to their antique counterparts, also on display at the Pavilion (but don't climb on the antiques—they're too fragile). To see a tractor or combine in action, take a virtual tour at one of the touch-screen displays. "Tour" the combine factory and watch employees assemble this boxy piece of machinery, then see the machine harvest wheat, soy, and corn. At another station the "tour" shows workers assembling tractors. Notice all the different attachments—each attachment performs a different task on the field.

"Cornucopia" is a touch-screen exhibit that takes you from the beginning of a product's life until it gets to market. Learn the life story of apples, pork, or cotton. Another interactive exhibit called "The Past" walks you through the history of agriculture, while "The Future" educates guests about how the world will feed its booming population, which may double in the next 40 years. Like many guests, you may find yourself returning to the Pavilion again and again simply to reminisce and share experiences of life on the farm.

Cost: Free
Freebies: No
Video Shown: 10-minute film, "The Bounty,"

about the challenges of farming from the planting season to the harvest.

Reservations Needed: No
Days and Hours: January–March: Mon–Fri 9:00 AM–5:00 PM, Sat 10:00 AM–5:00 PM, Sun 12:00 PM–4:00 PM. April–December: Mon–Fri 9:00 AM–6:00 PM, Sat 10:00 AM–5:00 PM, Sun 12:00 PM–4:00 PM. Closed Easter, Thanksgiving, Christmas, and New Year's.

Plan to Stay: 1 hour for tour and "The Bounty," plus time for store.
Minimum Age: None
Disabled Access: Yes
Group Requirements: Groups of 30 or more should call in advance if possible.
Special Information: No videotaping of "The Bounty." Visit John Deere factory tours in East Moline, IL (see page 132) and Waterloo, IA (see page 148).
Gift Shop: John Deere Store sells a variety of items emblazoned with the company logo, from baseball caps and towels to fishing lures and mailboxes. January–February: Mon–Sat 10:00 AM–5:00 PM, Sun 12:00 PM–4:00 PM. March–December: Mon–Fri 10:00 AM–6:00 PM, Sat 10:00 AM–5:00 PM, Sun 12:00 PM–4:00 PM.
Directions: From the east, take I-74 West into Moline. Take the 7th Ave. exit (last Illinois exit). Turn left on 7th Ave. Go 4 blocks and turn right on 15th St. Go 4 blocks. From the west, take I-80 to I-74 East. Follow I-74 East across the Mississippi River to Illinois. Take the River Dr. exit (the first exit). Turn left on River Dr. and go 4.5 blocks. John Deere Pavilion is on the corner of River Dr. and 15th St.
Nearby Attractions: John Deere Harvester Works tour (see page 132); Moline Tractor & Plow Co. half-block away on John Deere Commons (call 800-240-5265); Mississippi River; Historic Deere family homes; Deere & Company Administrative Center; Tournament Players Club at Deere Run.

FEATURED TOUR

▲ The John Deere Pavilion is a 14,000-square-foot glass-enclosed structure located in downtown Moline, Illinois. It is the world's most comprehensive agricultural exhibit.

▼ New products and fully restored antique equipment are featured on the floor of the John Deere Pavilion.

Winnebago Industries

1316 South 4th Street
Forest City, IA 50436
(641) 585-6936
www.winnebagoind.com

Winnebago Industries was born in 1958, when a group of local businesses, worried about Iowa's depressed farm economy, persuaded Modernistic Industries of California to build a travel-trailer factory in Forest City. Local businessmen soon bought the factory and, in 1960, named it Winnebago Industries, after the county in which it was located. Since 1966, when the company started making motor homes, the name Winnebago has become synonymous with "motor home."

You will not doubt Winnebago's self-proclaimed position as an industry leader after touring the world's largest RV production plant. The company prides itself on its interlocking joint construction and on the fact that it produces the majority of parts in-house, including fabric covers for its seats and sofas. The 200-acre factory includes the main assembly areas (which you'll see on the tour), metal stamping division, plastics facility, sawmill and cabinet shop, and sewing and design departments.

In the chassis prep building (not on tour), parts of the all-steel frame are stamped out on the "Dinosaur." Sparks fly as workers weld floor joints and storage compartments to the chassis. The completed RV (including windshield) will be set into this steel frame. The front end drops from a mezzanine onto the chassis and is aligned by laser beams.

The motor-home production lines are in a building employees affectionately call "Big Bertha." From your vantage point on the catwalk, you'll see the developing motor homes creep down three 1,032-foot-long assembly lines at 21 inches per minute. First, workers install a heat-resistant laminated floor. Next, they install the bathroom fixtures, then screw the Thermo-Panel sidewalls (made of block foam embedded with an aluminum frame and steel supports, interior paneling, and an exterior fiberglass skin) onto steel outriggers extending from the floor of the motor home. Further down the line, cabinets are installed.

Finally, the entire unit receives a one-piece, fiberglass-covered, laminated roof. The motor home is then driven to the company's stitchcraft building to receive its furniture and window coverings. The completed motor home is rigorously inspected in the test chambers, where it experiences severe "rainstorms." Select units also travel through a test track of road hazards.

Cost: Free

Freebies: Winnebago Industries product brochures

Video Shown: 22-minute "Winnebago Industries Factory Tour" video takes you through a detailed view of the world's largest motor-home factory. When no factory tours, visitors can watch this video as well as informative videos on individual Winnebago, Itasca, Rialta, and Ultimate motor homes.

Reservations Needed: No, except for groups larger than 6 people.

Days and Hours: April–October: Mon–Fri 9:00 AM and 1:00 PM; November–mid-December: Mon–Fri 1:00 PM. No tours mid-December–March 31. Closed holidays and 1 week in July.

Plan to Stay: 1.5 hours for video and tour, plus time for Visitors Center motor-home exhibits and wall displays.

Minimum Age: No, but small children must be accompanied by an adult.

Disabled Access: Yes, for Visitors Center. Factory tour includes 3 staircases.

Group Requirements: Groups larger than 6 people should make reservations 2 weeks in advance.

Special Information: Photography allowed in Visitors Center but not in plant.

Gift Shop: Winnebago-Itasca Travelers Club gift shop sells logoed items, including jackets, shirts, and caps. Open 8:30 AM–4:00 PM year-round. Closed holidays.

Directions: From I-35, exit at Hwy. 9 West. At junction of Hwy. 9 and Hwy. 69, take Hwy. 69 South. Turn right on B14 and immediately turn right on 4th St. in Forest City. Visitors Center is on right.

Nearby Attractions: Pammel RV Park; Pilot Knob State Park; Mansion Museum; Waldorf College; Heritage Park.

▲ The Winnebago Adventurer from Winnebago Industries in Forest City, Iowa, is the nation's top-selling motor home.

▼ Roof installation on one of Winnebago Industries' motor home–manufacturing assembly lines.

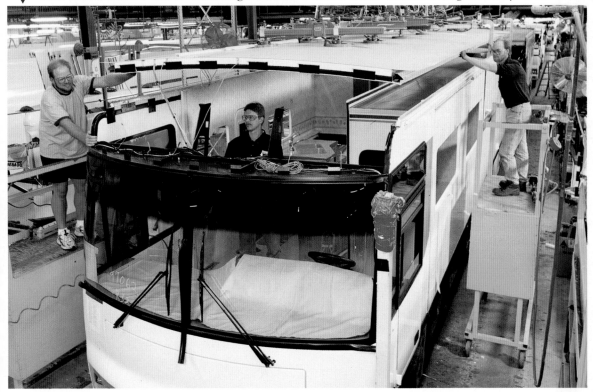

Rebecca-Ruth Candies

112 East 2nd Street
Frankfort, KY 40601
(502) 223-7475 / (800) 444-3766
www.rebeccaruth.com

CHOCOLATES AND BOURBON BALLS

FEATURED TOUR

Kentucky's famous 100-proof bourbon whiskeys—and a lot of local pride—are key ingredients in this family-owned company's world-renowned chocolates. These chocolates are as rich as the history surrounding the Rebecca-Ruth name itself. Founded in 1919 by two uncommonly courageous schoolteachers, Rebecca Gooch and Ruth Booe, the company's popularity grew as a result of the women's highly acclaimed chocolates and was aided by their creative sales techniques—which included loudly plugging their products on street corners. Ruth Booe originated the "Bourbon Ball." Made with real Kentucky bourbon and crowned with a Southern pecan, this confection has become the treat of the South.

The brightly striped awning shading this small, house-like store and factory creates an unpretentious atmosphere. The 10 to 15 employees (some of whom have been here for over 30 years) make about 100,000 pounds of confections a year.

In the cream-candy room are articles about Rebecca-Ruth from national magazines such as *Southern Living* and *Gourmet*. Workers pull candy cream on a hook by hand and then use a taffy-pull machine. When it's "just right," the rope of candy is cut into pieces and left to sit. It becomes very creamy, rich, and flaky. Pecan brittle and pecan butter are also made in this room.

In the kitchen, the cast-iron candy furnace and copper kettles emit the sweet scent of hand-stirred, melting sugars. In the production area, large mixers prepare rich fillings for their assembly-line journey down the enrobing line. First the candy dough is extruded onto a belt, and then it goes through a "chocolate waterfall." Two workers personally apply the finishing touches: a luscious southern pecan, sprinkles, or a swirled flourish on top.

A tour highlight is seeing "Edna's table." For close to 70 years, Edna Robbins handmade delicacies on the same marble table used by Rebecca and Ruth. (Ruth bought "Edna's table" for $10 in 1917.)

Cost: Free

Freebies: Samples of the original Bourbon Balls and other chocolates (children receive nonalcoholic samples only).

Video Shown: 8-minute video on candy production.

Reservations Needed: No, except for bus groups.

Days and Hours: January–October: Mon–Sat 9:00 AM–4:30 PM. Closed holidays.

Plan to Stay: 10–15 minutes, plus time in retail store.

Minimum Age: Young children should be accompanied by an adult.

Disabled Access: No

Group Requirements: Bus operators should call (800) 444-3766 to make reservations or obtain additional information.

Special Information: Video cameras not allowed. Production more likely in mornings, before candy holidays, and in September and October.

Retail Store: Sells a wide variety of liquor-cream chocolates (including Bourbon Balls, Kentucky Irish Coffees, and Kentucky Mint Juleps), and liquor-free chocolates, including nut clusters, butter creams, and Kentucky Creamed Pull Candy. Open year-round Mon–Sat 8:00 AM–5:30 PM, Sun 12:00 PM–5:00 PM. Closed Christmas, New Year's, and July 4th. Catalog available from 800 number above.

Directions: From Lexington, take I-64 West to Frankfort Exit 58, then take U.S. 60 West. Turn left onto Second St. Rebecca Ruth is on left. From Louisville, take I-64 East to Frankfort Exit 53. Take Rt. 127 North to U.S. 60 East, which becomes Second St. Stay on Second St. Cross over Capital Ave. Rebecca-Ruth is on left.

Nearby Attractions: Three Chimneys horse farm and Toyota tours (see pages 164 and 165); Buffalo Trace Distillery tour (call 502-223-7641).

▲ Owner Charles Booe enjoys a piece of Rebecca-Ruth Candies, based in Frankfort, Kentucky.

▼ At the decorating station, workers hand-place pecans on Rebecca-Ruth chocolates.

Toyota

1001 Cherry Blossom Way
Georgetown, KY 40324
(502) 868-3027 / (800) 866-4485
www.toyotageorgetown.com

VEHICLES

Toyota's largest vehicle manufacturing plant outside of Japan is located in this growing community in Kentucky's Bluegrass Region. Toyota Motor Manufacturing, Kentucky (TMMK), covers 7.5 million square feet of floor space, the equivalent of 156 football fields. But don't worry about your legs getting tired on the plant tour, because you'll be riding comfortably in one of their trams.

TMMK employs more than 7,000 team members who build nearly 2,000 quality vehicles each day. A "takt time" of 55 seconds on both of the vehicle assembly lines means that two new Toyota vehicles are built in Georgetown every 55 seconds!

TMMK began production in 1988 with the popular Toyota Camry sedan. The Avalon sedan was added in 1994. The Sienna minivan was produced from 1997 to 2002. Production of the Camry Solara coupe begins in 2003.

Toyota vehicles get their start in Stamping, taking shape from huge coils of cold-rolled steel. The steel is cleaned, straightened, and stamped into sheet-metal components that make up the vehicle bodies. With hundreds of tons of force, the automatic presses shape the steel into doors, hoods, roofs, and many other parts.

The sheet-metal components then move to Body Weld, where team members and computer-controlled robots perform the welding that results in a completed body shell. The new vehicle bodies then travel by overhead conveyors to Paint before moving on to the Trim, Chassis, and Final lines in Assembly.

As you tour TMMK, your guide points out the foundations of the world-renowned Toyota Production System. These will include examples of *kaizen,* or continuous improvement; just-in-time parts delivery; and the *andon* system, where team members can stop the line at any time to address quality concerns or any problems.

In the TMMK Visitor Center, you will see current models of the vehicles and engines built in Georgetown, plus the very first Camry produced by team members in May 1988. The Visitor Center also includes interactive video displays and exhibits on Quality, Teamwork, and the Toyota Production System.

Cost: Free

Freebies: Toyota vehicle (in the form of a refrigerator magnet!).

Video Shown: 10-minute video provides a brief plant overview, including sections not included on the tour.

Reservations Needed: Yes, but walk-ins will be accommodated as space permits.

Days and Hours: Plant tour: Mon–Fri 10:00 AM, 12:00 PM, and 2:00 PM, Thur also 6:00 PM. Closed holidays. *Toyota reserves the right to cancel or reschedule tours at any time.* Visitor Center: Mon–Fri 9:00 AM–4:00 PM, Thur until 7:00 PM.

Plan to Stay: 1.5–2 hours for plant tour, video, and exhibits.

Minimum Age: Plant tour: 1st grade for public tours and 4th grade for school tours. Visitor Center: none.

Disabled Access: Yes

Group Requirements: Maximum group size is 64 adults. Large groups must call several months in advance.

Special Information: Photographs and video and mechanical recordings are allowed in the Visitor Center but not during the plant tour.

Gift Shop: Sells logoed golf shirts, T-shirts, caps, etc. Open same hours as Visitor Center.

Directions: From Lexington, take I-75 North to Exit 126 (Georgetown/Cynthiana). Turn right onto U.S. 62 (Cherry Blossom Way). Drive exactly 2.5 miles and turn left at Visitor Entrance sign.

Nearby Attractions: Three Chimneys horse farm, Rebecca-Ruth Candies, and Old Kentucky Candies tours (see pages 164, 163, and 162); Kentucky Horse Park; Keeneland Racecourse; Calumet horse farm; Georgetown College.

FEATURED TOUR

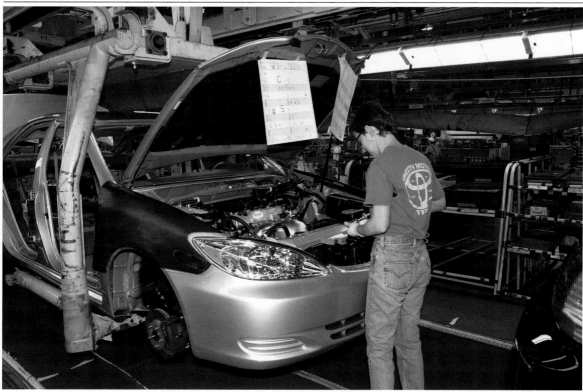

▲ Team members at Toyota's Georgetown, Kentucky, plant build about 2,000 vehicles each day.

A Toyota Georgetown, Kentucky, team member puts the finishing touches on an engine and prepares
▼ it to be installed into the vehicle in a process known as "Engine Marriage."

▲ At Toyota's Georgetown, Kentucky, plant Body Weld is the most automated area of the plant. Robots perform 97 percent of each body shell's 4,400 welds.

Visitors ride by giant coils of steel weighing up to 17 tons, which will be stamped into vehicle body
▼ parts at Toyota's Georgetown, Kentucky, plant.

A Toyota Georgetown, Kentucky, team member uses a *raku* seat—or floating chair—to move easily in and out of the vehicle.

A Toyota Georgetown, Kentucky, team member installs the main wiring harness on the Trim Line in Assembly.

Wild Turkey

1525 Tyrone Road
Lawrenceburg, KY 40342
(502) 839-4544
www.wildturkeybourbon.com

BOURBON

Wild Turkey Distillery sits on a hill next to the Kentucky River. Water from this naturally filtered limestone riverbed and corn from nearby farmers are the main ingredients in bourbon, a uniquely American whiskey. This tour shows almost all steps in crafting the bourbon named after founder Thomas McCarthy's private stock taken on a wild turkey hunt.

The first surprise is the metal-barred windows on the big, gray, square warehouses throughout the grounds. They provide vital air circulation to the rack houses where the bourbon ages. The tax-hungry government once required installation of the bars to prevent any barrels from leaving without proper fees being paid.

The initial step in producing bourbon is mixing corn, rye, and water. The mix is cooked and cooled, then malted barley is added. With special yeast added, this sour mash ferments in cypress-wood or stainless steel tanks. Watch the slow, gentle swirl of the thick yellow mash in the vats; carbon-dioxide bubbles rise to the surface as the yeast changes sugar to alcohol, called "distiller's beer." Stand next to the 40-foot-high copper still, where the alcohol is separated in a vaporization process.

Charred white-oak barrels then become the colorless whiskey's home. The tour guide explains that the burnt layers of wood inside the barrel give bourbon its distinctive flavor and color (whiskey must be aged in new, charred-oak barrels for two years to be legally called "bourbon"). Inside a cool warehouse amid racks of barrels on wood planks, you'll enjoy the sweet bourbon smell. Wild Turkey calls this the "angels' share" because one-third of each barrel's contents evaporates over the bourbon's eight years of aging. It's not until you walk through the quality control lab and the bottling area that the process seems any different from what it must have been 100 years ago.

Cost: Free

Freebies: Food made with Wild Turkey, such as a bourbon brownie; a barrel bung; lemonade; coffee; and recipes that use Wild Turkey; smells.

Video Shown: In 15-minute video, "a true Kentucky legend," master distiller Jimmy Russell, covers the history of bourbon to Wild Turkey distilling and its products.

Reservations Needed: No, except for groups of 20 or more people.

Days and Hours: Mon–Fri 9:00 AM, 10:30 AM, 12:30 PM, and 2:30 PM. Closed holidays.

Plan to Stay: 45 minutes for tour, plus time for snacks and visitors center. The visitors center is in a restored building with a small display of ceramic Wild Turkey decanters, historical mementos, a scale model of the bourbon production process, and a gift shop.

Minimum Age: No

Disabled Access: Visitors center is fully accessible. Remainder of the facility has gravel paths and flights of stairs to some areas.

Group Requirements: Advance notice requested for groups of 20 or more. No maximum size.

Special Information: Wear comfortable walking shoes. Tour runs all year, but not all areas are in production during certain weeks in July and August.

Gift Shop: Sells wide range of merchandise from T-shirts to barbecue sauce, so you can take a piece of Kentucky tradition home with you. Open Mon–Fri 8:30 AM–4:00 PM. Catalog available from (800) BUY-TRKY.

Directions: From Louisville, take I-64 East to Rt. 151 South to Rt. 127 South. Turn left on Rt. 44, which turns into U.S. 62 East. Bear right onto Tyrone Rd. (Rt. 1510) to distillery. From Lexington, take U.S. 60 West (take Business Route at split) to Versailles to U.S. 62 West to distillery. You're almost there when you see billboards announcing "Bird Sanctuary Ahead" and "Home of Wild Turkey."

Nearby Attractions: Beaver Lake and Taylorville Lake; Ripplewood Estate.

FEATURED TOUR

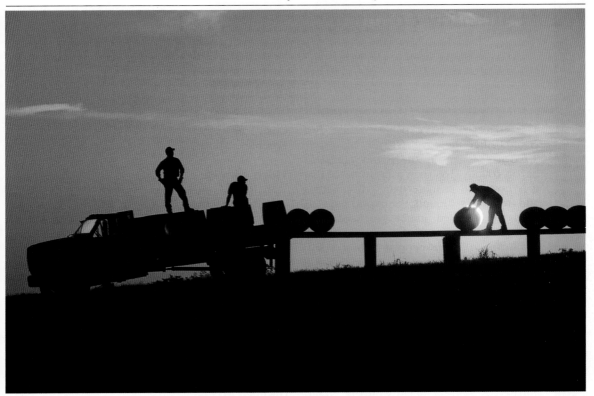

▲ Rolling barrels to the warehouse for aging at the Wild Turkey Distillery

Master distiller Jimmy Russell samples a batch of bourbon at the Wild Turkey Distillery in
▼ Lawrenceburg, Kentucky.

McIlhenny Company

Avery Island, LA 70513
(337) 365-8173 / (800) 634-9599
www.tabasco.com

TABASCO BRAND PEPPER SAUCE

This concentrated hot pepper sauce, first created after the Civil War on an exotic 2,200-acre island in the South Louisiana bayou country, has such a lively flavor that it is now sold in more than 110 countries and territories around the world and its labels are printed in 21 languages and dialects. McIlhenny Company grows the *Capsicum frutescens* peppers (tabasco peppers) in several countries to ensure a good harvest. But there is only one Tabasco sauce factory, and you'll recognize this modern redbrick building as soon as you open your car door and catch a whiff of the piquant pepper aroma.

A film explains that McIlhenny planted hot pepper seeds from Mexico or Central America. He created his sauce (brand-named Tabasco, a Mexican-Indian word) by mashing the peppers with Avery Island salt, aging the mash in wooden barrels, adding vinegar, and then straining the mixture.

Along a corridor in the modern factory, observe four lines of Tabasco sauce bottling from behind a long glass wall. The smell here isn't nearly as strong as it must be inside the packaging room. Some lines produce more than 300 bottles of Tabasco sauce a minute, helping the factory produce about 600,000 bottles a day.

After the bottles are spun around in the carousel and injected with the hot red pepper sauce, they journey naked down the assembly line. Machines automatically clothe the bottles with the familiar bright red octagonal caps, green foil neckbands, and diamond-shaped labels. The dressed bottles are then mechanically packed in boxes, ready to travel. Their final destination will be dining tables from Pennsylvania to Peking, where their red caps will be removed and they will "drop in" to spice up a meal.

Cost: Free

Freebies: Miniature Tabasco sauce bottle, recipes, and other McIlhenny products.

Video Shown: 11-minute overview of McIlhenny's history and operations, as well as Tabasco sauce origins and the full processing, including harvesting of peppers, mashing, aging, mixing with vinegar, and bottling.

Reservations Needed: No, except for groups over 20 people.

Days and Hours: Mon–Sun 9:00 AM–4:00 PM. Last tour 30 minutes before closing. May not see production Fri–Sun. Closed holidays and long weekends.

Plan to Stay: 25 minutes for video and tour, plus time for gift shop and grounds.

Minimum Age: None

Disabled Access: Yes

Group Requirements: Groups larger than 20 people should make advance reservations; 1 week's notice appreciated.

Special Information: Some production process details are in photos and captions above the viewing window.

Gift Shop: Tabasco Country Store sells a wide variety of Tabasco specialty foods and novelty items, from pepper earrings to lithographs, toys, cookware, ties, cookbooks, and spices. Open same hours as tour. Gift shop at Jungle Gardens entrance open until 5:30 PM (sells similar items). Catalog available at (800) 634-9599.

Directions: From New Orleans, take I-10 West to Exit 103A. Follow U.S. 90 through Lafayette toward New Iberia. Exit at LA 14 and turn left. At LA 329 junction, turn right. Stay on LA 329 approximately 6 miles. The road dead-ends at Avery Island, where the toll road has a nominal charge per vehicle. Signs will direct you to factory.

Nearby Attractions: Konriko tour (see page 169); Jungle Gardens and Bird City on Avery Island.

FEATURED TOUR

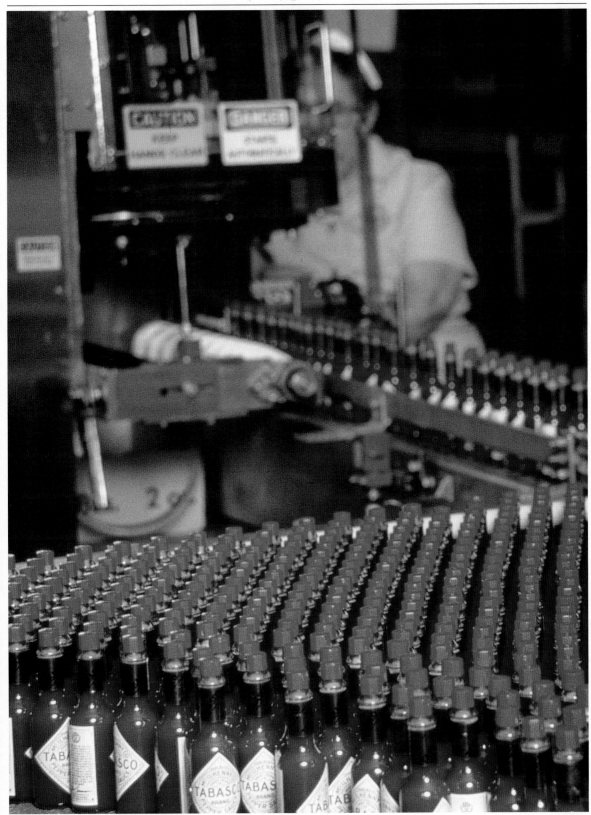

▲ The bottling line at McIlhenny Company's Tabasco Brand Pepper Sauce factory is a colorful sight, along with Jungle Gardens and Bird City on Avery Island.

Hallmark Visitors Center

Crown Center Complex
2501 McGee
Kansas City, MO 64141
(816) 274-5672
www.hallmarkvisitorscenter.com

Hallmark's slogan, "When You Care Enough to Send the Very Best," applies to its visitors center. You will walk through 14 exhibits that tell the story of the world's largest greeting-card company. See a 40-foot historical timeline and learn how Hallmark started when a man named Joyce C. Hall began selling picture postcards from his fourth-floor room at the Kansas City YMCA. The timeline has memorabilia from Hallmark's history intertwined with world events.

During the six-minute multimedia film presentation on the essence of creativity, listen and watch Hallmark artists explain how the creative process works. Did you know that Winston Churchill was an artist? One of his paintings hangs in the visitors center along with other originals by Norman Rockwell, Grandma Moses, and Saul Steinberg.

Another area is devoted to the craft and technology of card production. You can watch a technician make engraving dies—the metal plates that raise the three-dimensional designs on paper—or cutting dies, which work like steel cookie cutters to make unusually shaped cards. Two presses churn out the cards you might purchase 10 months from now. At the touch of a button, you can watch a machine turn ribbon into a miniature star bow and take one home with you.

View clips from Hallmark commercials and Hallmark Hall of Fame television dramas. Costumes, props, and a real Emmy award are on display. Hallmark employees' affection for company founder Hall shows in a display of Christmas trees that employees gave Hall from 1966 to 1982. Each tree's decorations reflect a theme of importance to the company during that year. To experience Hallmark's international appeal (cards sell in more than 100 countries), rub the sheep dog's nose on the handrail of one of the cards to hear birthday greetings in 12 languages. One of the newest exhibits features the Hallmark Keepsake Ornament collection. You can see some of the most popular Keepsake Ornaments, like the Starship Enterprise, the 1957 Corvette, Peanuts characters, and sports heroes.

Cost: Free

Freebies: Postcard and a bow

Videos Shown: Short videos on topics related to the exhibits are shown throughout the visitors center.

Reservations Needed: No, except for guided tours for groups of 10 or more.

Days and Hours: Mon–Fri 9:00 AM–5:00 PM and Sat 9:30 AM–4:30 PM. Closed Thanksgiving, Christmas Eve, Christmas, and New Year's. Also usually closed the first 2–3 weeks in January for yearly renovations.

Plan to Stay: About 1 hour, but can spend any amount of time for self-guided tour.

Minimum Age: None

Disabled Access: Yes. Call (816) 274-3613 for information.

Group Requirements: Escorted tours available for groups of 10 or more people. Groups should make reservations 2 to 4 weeks in advance. School/youth groups need 1 adult for every 7 children. Call (816) 274-3613.

Special Information: Hallmark Cards tour in Topeka, KS (see page 151). Some Hallmark Production Centers in other cities conduct tours by advance reservation; check with visitors center for information.

Gift Shop: Not in visitors center. The closest of the 47,000 independent retail outlets is in Crown Center.

Directions: Located in Crown Center Complex, about 1 mile south of downtown Kansas City. Take Grand Ave. to 25th St. and park in the Crown Center Parking Garage. Proceed to third level of Crown Center shops. The visitors center is located outside Halls department store.

Nearby Attractions: Ford Motor plant tour (call 816-459-1356); Kaleidoscope children's interactive exhibit (call 816-274-8301); *Arabia* Steamboat Museum; Toy and Miniature Museum.

FEATURED TOUR

▲ At the Hallmark Visitors Center in Kansas City, Missouri, push a button to watch robotic twists and turns transform 42 inches of ribbon into a souvenir bow for you to keep!

▼ Explore the world of creativity through a six-minute multimedia presentation. Hallmark artists and writers talk about their ideas and inspirations. See firsthand how the creative process works.

National Vitamin

7440 S. Industrial Road
Las Vegas, NV 89139
(702) 269-9600 / (888) 346-6848
www.nationalvitamin.com

VITAMINS

You may take vitamins daily, but you probably never imagined the sophisticated machines that manufacture tablets like vitamin C. Raw materials such as ginseng and echinacea are inspected by Quality Control, weighed and then taken to the blending room. There, a huge stainless steel V-shaped blender mixes precise amounts of these ingredients.

Once blended, some formulas are made into hard-shell capsules, while others become tablets. In the tablet manufacturing area, a tablet press forms dry powders into various shapes: round, oval or even dinosaur shape. The tablet press has an upper punch and a lower punch, and a die that forms the tablet's shape. The blended formula is loaded into each die cavity. The punches then apply up to five tons of pressure to form the tablets. The machine can produce up to 2,000 tablets per minute! It's so fast that, even looking at it directly, all you will see is a blur and the tablets leaving the machine. Fortunately a video monitor shows the process in slow motion. In the next room, watch as a large dryer-like machine coats tablets to keep them fresh or to disguise unpleasant tastes, then move to the Quality Control Lab, where chemists carefully test the final products and raw materials to meet strict quality standards of potency and purity.

In the next area, soft gel capsules like vitamin E take shape. Water, glycerin, and gelatin are heated to form a viscous, honey-like liquid that will make up the outside of the soft gels. The liquid is loaded into warm tanks, where it must remain heated until production begins. Next, these tanks are hooked up to the production machine, which forms and fills the golden capsules. The soft gels emerge on a conveyor, and then tumble inside long drying tubes along with special lint-free towels.

Next, a worker wheels trays of them into a drying tunnel in which humidity, air, and temperature are constantly regulated. The capsules dry there for 18 to 30 hours. Finally, workers inspect trays full of the yellow capsules and discard those that are deformed or leaking. The perfect capsules travel to the packing room, where the vitamins and supplements are loaded into bottles, capped, and labeled for shipment all around the world.

Cost: Free

Freebies: Choice of samples of vitamins, skin care products, or chewable vitamin C.

Videos Shown: 2-minute introductory video on nutrition and vitamins and video monitors throughout the tour.

Reservations Needed: No, except for groups over 30 people.

Days and Hours: Mon–Sun 6:00 AM–6:00 PM. Closed Easter, Thanksgiving, Christmas, and New Year's.

Plan to Stay: 25 minutes for self-guided tour and video, plus time for retail outlet.

Minimum Age: None

Disabled Access: Yes

Group Requirements: Guided tours available for groups of 15 or more. Groups of 30 or more should call a day in advance.

Retail Outlet: Sells vitamins, supplements, and botanicals, as well as health and body care products. At the smoothie bar you can add vitamins to a fresh fruit smoothie. Open same hours as tour.

Directions: From I-15 North, take the Las Vegas Blvd. Exit. Turn right on Las Vegas Blvd. After .5 miles, turn right on Warm Springs Rd. After .5 miles take a left on Industrial Rd. From I-15 South, exit at Blue Diamond Rd. West and go .25 miles. Take a right on Industrial Rd. The entrance is .75 miles on the right.

Nearby Attractions: Ron Lee's World of Clowns and Ethel M Chocolates tours (see pages 224 and 222); Shelby American Automobiles tour and museum (call 702-643-3000); casinos.

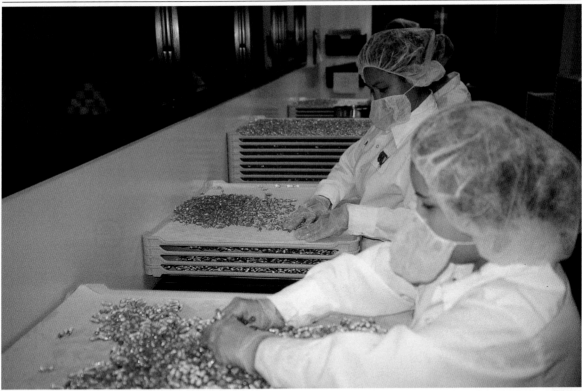

▲ All Soft Gel Capsules are hand inspected to insure complete quality control. Hand inspection is one of many quality control procedures prior to packaging.

A highly skilled operator sets controls on a Soft Gel encapsulation, at National Vitamin Company in Las Vegas, Nevada.
▼

Corning Museum of Glass

One Museum Way
Corning, NY 14830
(607) 937-5371 / (800) 732-6845
www.cmog.org

GLASS

Like a glass prism, a visit to the Corning Museum of Glass is multifaceted. The experience of the Glass Innovation Center, the Art and History Galleries, the Sculpture Gallery, the Steuben Factory, and the Hot Glass Show illuminates the history of glass, optical fiber communications, and glassmaking. The Museum's world-famous collection of more than 35,000 glass objects traces 35 centuries of human experience with glass, starting in ancient Egypt's 18th Dynasty, when the search for perfectly clear crystal began.

Learn how light transmits information through optical fibers in the Glass Innovation Center's interactive educational exhibits. The spherical mirror alters your perception. The float glass exhibit explains the production process of large panes of glass. An overhead monitor lets the audience look through the flameworker's lens as he melts glass rods over a single gas-flamed jet and forms tiny glass animals in an on-the-spot demonstration.

The real fascination is watching the Hot Glass Show. Walk along a frosted glass bridge and around to the Hot Glass Stage. In this intimate setting, with the Steuben Factory as a backdrop, you feel the heat from the furnace. Gaffers, whose cheeks as they blow into the long blowpipes resemble Louis Armstrong's when he's playing the trumpet, collect gobs of red-hot glass from a furnace containing molten glass. A narrator and master glassblower explain and demonstrate glassmaking before a walk downstairs offers a look into the working Steuben factory, the only place in the world where Steuben glass is made.

During this walk, look through the glass windows to see the engraving process that makes Steuben glass so unique and valuable. The engraver first coats the glass with protective shellac, then transfers an image onto its surface with India ink. To cut the design, the engraver presses the glass upward against as many as 50 different fine copper wheels on a rotating lathe. Intricate designs may take 300 hours to engrave.

Across the parking lot, at the Museum's Walk-in Workshop, you can make a glass flower, bead, picture frame, or magnet using a variety of glassworking techniques, for a nominal fee. Even the youngest visitors can sandblast a design on their own drinking glass.

Cost: Adults, $12; youth (6–17), $6; children and members, free; families (2 adults with dependent children), $36.

Freebies: No

Video Shown: 13-minute award-winning "Glass into Dreams" film and a variety throughout the galleries.

Reservations Needed: No, but recommended for groups larger than 20 people.

Days and Hours: Open Mon–Sun 9:00 AM–5:00 PM, July–Labor Day: Mon–Sun 9:00 AM–8:00 PM. Closed Thanksgiving, Christmas Eve, Christmas, and New Year's. Best time to see Steuben factory production is Mon–Fri 9:00 AM–5:00 PM. Hot Glass Shows all day, every day. Outdoor stage in summer.

Plan to Stay: 2 hours minimum

Minimum Age: None

Disabled Access: Yes

Group Requirements: Groups of 20 or more should call 2 weeks in advance for special group rates and reservations (call 607-974-2000). No maximum group size.

Special Information: No photography in Steuben factory visitor's gallery.

Gift Shop: Sells Steuben and other glass objects, glass-related books, souvenirs, and Corning tabletop and cookware products. Open same hours as Museum.

Directions: From New York City, take Rt. 17 West. Take Corning exit and follow signs. From Rochester, take I-390 South to I-86/Rt. 17 East. Follow above directions.

Nearby Attractions: Corning Historic Market Street shopping district; Finger Lakes Wine Country Visitor Center in CMoG Lobby; Babcock ladder tour (see page 233); Watkins Glen International Race Track; various wine trails; Rockwell Museum of Western Art; Benjamin Patterson Inn Museum; National Soaring Museum.

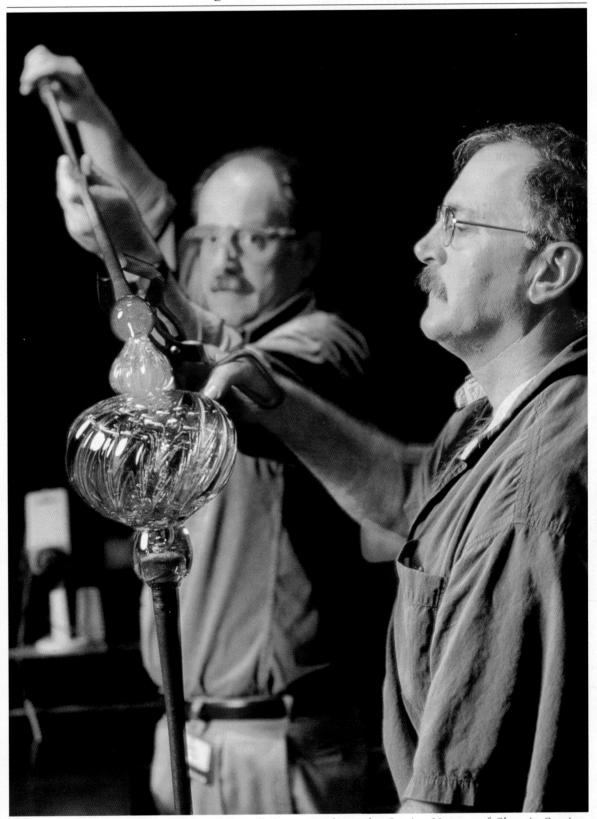

▲ Hot glassblowing is demonstrated live, all day, every day at the Corning Museum of Glass, in Corning, New York.

Rodgers Instruments

1300 N.E. 25th Avenue
Hillsboro, OR 97124
(503) 648-4181
www.rodgersinstruments.com

 RODGERS®
Rodgers Instruments LLC

ELECTRONIC AND ELECTRONIC-PIPE COMBINATION ORGANS

Next time you're in New York's Carnegie Hall or Philadelphia's Academy of Music, listen for beautiful music from an organ made by this leading builder of classic electronic and pipe organs. Rodgers prides itself on technical innovation in organ-building, whether by making the first transistorized organ amplifier (1958) or by introducing Parallel Digital Imaging Technology to create warmer, more authentic pipe-organ sounds. The technology and craft of organ-building resonate throughout the manufacturing area.

This guided tour shows all the steps involved in organ-making. Regardless of your interests—woodworking, electronics, or music—you'll find the process appealing. Don't expect huge machines or speeding assembly lines here; it takes weeks to make an organ. Instead you'll see skilled workers painstakingly laboring over each piece. Be sure to look for the Shoda machines in the cabinet shop area, where all the organ's wood parts begin their journey. The Shoda drills, saws, and shapes the wood according to a computerized program, while a vacuum seal holds the wood to the cutting table. This vacuum is so strong that a dollar bill placed on the worktable cannot be pulled across the surface!

Cut parts from such woods as Sitka spruce, American black walnut, oak, and mahogany are assembled in the case-up area. Here, sides, feet, key deck, back rails, and other support pieces are glued and clamped together, ensuring a dimensionally correct case. A "white sanding" process utilizes fine-grit sandpaper to give the wood a white flour-like surface. In the finishing department, instrument cases, benches, and pedalboard frames are stained, lightly sanded, and given a lacquer top coat. Notice that, despite all the sanding, the area is dust-free: air curtains outside the white-sanding room and finishing area prevent the dust from migrating.

It's often the multiple ranks of 61 pipes each that give organs their powerful presence. Look for pictures of one of the largest organs Rodgers ever designed and built—the 194-rank (11,000 pipe) organ at Houston's Second Baptist Church, which took one and a half years to build. Throughout the tour you'll see and hear the roles that traditional external pipes and internal electronics (now mostly computer surface-mount circuit boards) play in organ music. This contrast of technology and traditional craftsmanship makes the tour diverse: in one room an artisan hand-sands wood cases, while a computer technician next door tests circuit boards.

Cost: Free

Freebies: Demonstration CDs and literature

Video Shown: 12-minute video covering company history, organ construction, and sound technology, shown upon request.

Reservations Needed: Yes. No drop-in tours accepted.

Days and Hours: Tue and Thur 9:00 AM–12:00 PM. Closed for 1 week mid-August.

Plan to Stay: 45 minutes–1 hour

Minimum Age: No, but children must be able to wear safety glasses. Kids will enjoy the tour more if they're interested in music.

Disabled Access: Yes

Group Requirements: Groups must call 10 days in advance to make reservations. Maximum group size is 100 people.

Special Information: Photography in showroom only. Tours can be customized to your interests.

Gift Shop: No

Directions: From Portland, take I-5 South to Rt. 26 West. Get off at Cornelius Pass Rd. exit and turn right. Turn right onto Cornell Rd. Immediately after Hillsboro airport, turn right onto 25th Ave. Rodgers is on the right. Can also take the MAX rapid transit line from downtown Portland to the Hillsboro Fairgrounds exit. Rodgers is across the street, about .25 mile walk.

Nearby Attractions: Shute Park; Fairgrounds events; wine-tasting scenic route (Hillsboro to Salem); Hillsboro Blimp Factory at Hillsboro Airport Facility. Portland's attractions, including Oregon Zoo, Rose Test Gardens, and Japanese Gardens, are about 15 miles away.

FEATURED TOUR

▲ Rodgers Custom Touring 4-manual, features 244 keys made of Ivora and Rosewood. This organ is featured in concerts throughout the U.S. and Europe.

Rodgers Trillium 967, made in Hillsboro, Oregon. The T967 is the flagship of Rodgers' 3-manual
▼ instruments.

Herr's Snack Factory Tour

Visitors Center
Routes 1 and 272
Nottingham, PA 19362
(800) 63-SNACK
www.herrs.com

SNACK FOOD

Herr's snack food production has come a long way from when the company used a small, old-fashioned cooker in a barn. It now has an advanced and highly automated plant that makes tens of thousands of potato chips, corn chips, tortilla chips, popcorn batches, cheese curls, and pretzels every day. The comfortable, specially designed visitors center and café, creative video, and extensive guided tour provide a tasty education in how Herr's makes its products.

While watching the action through glass walls, you'll "ooh" and "aah" at the panoramic views. In the pretzel area, gaze at a 100-yard stretch of pretzel twists, in rows of 20 to 24 across, marching to massive ovens. In the corn chip, cheese curl, potato chip, and popcorn production sections, your vista overlooks the entire process. Follow the raw ingredients—either corn or potatoes—as they tumble in by the truckload at the beginning of the production line; travel along a conveyor belt through a series of machines that wash, slice, cook, or season them; then head out on bucket lifts to a sorting and bagging area. Other memorable images include machines and workers bagging and boxing together in almost symphonic unison, and the cavernous warehouse filled with snack-food boxes.

Except for the boxing of bags, machines do most of the work. Notice how only a few people oversee production in most areas. Smart machines can even sense discolored potato chips and use air jets to blow these rebels off the line. The guides salt and pepper the tour with interesting facts and figures about the company, including Herr's recycling efforts. But the best thing the guides do is grab samples of warm potato chips directly from the quickly moving conveyer belt. Bagged chips will never again taste the same!

Cost: Free

Freebies: Warm potato chips during the tour; small sample bag at end of tour.

Videos Shown: 10-minute video on company history, narrated by Herr family members; short videos throughout tour show unique view of snacks being made.

Reservations Needed: Yes, but can take walk-ins if space permits.

Days and Hours: Mon–Thur 9:00 AM–3:00 PM on the hour; Fri 9:00 AM, 10:00 AM, and 11:00 AM. Closed holidays.

Plan to Stay: 1.5 hours, including video, tour, gift shop, and café.

Minimum Age: None

Disabled Access: Yes

Group Requirements: With advance notice, can handle any size group, which will split into smaller ones for tour. Video shown in 140-seat auditorium.

Special Information: If you are interested in particular products, such as tortilla chips or cheese curls, call ahead for production schedule on day of your visit.

Gift Shop: Sells Herr's food products; logoed clothing items; Nottingham, PA, T-shirts; scale model of Herr's delivery truck; and Chipper the Chipmunk doll. Open Mon–Fri 8:00 AM–5:00 PM. Call for extended holiday hours. Catalog available from above number.

Directions: From Philadelphia, take I-95 South to Rt. 322 West exit. From Rt. 322, turn left onto Rt. 1 South. Turn left onto Rt. 272 South and right at light onto Herr Dr. Factory and Visitors Center at end of road. From Baltimore, take I-95 North to Exit 100. Take Rt. 272 North. Turn left at light onto Herr Dr.

Nearby Attractions: DaimlerChrysler and Hagley Museum tours (see pages 98 and 99), about 1 hour away; Longwood Gardens; Plumpton Park Zoo; Franklin Mint Museum; Brandywine River Museum; Lancaster County attractions about 30 miles away.

FEATURED TOUR

▲ See pretzels shaped and then baked golden brown at Herr's Snack Factory Tour, in Nottingham, Pennsylvania.

▼ Visitors enjoy fresh, warm Herr's potato chips right off the production line.

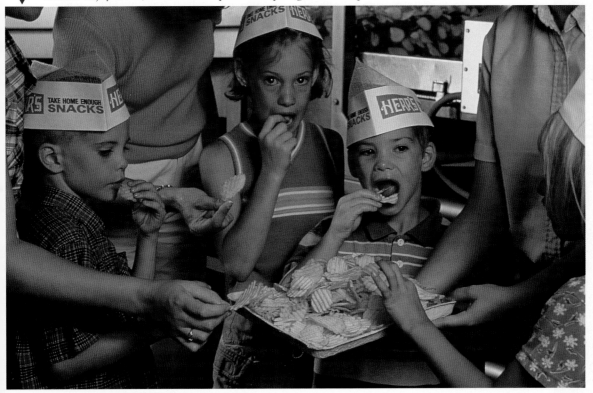

Martin Guitar

510 Sycamore Street
Nazareth, PA 18064
(610) 759-2837 / (800) 345-3103
www.martinguitar.com

GUITARS

Ever since C. F. Martin Sr. started making guitars in 1833, Martins have been widely recognized as one of the top U.S.-made products. The company has received highest accolades from the Buy America and Made in the USA foundations. Many popular musicians use Martins, including Paul McCartney, Willie Nelson, and Eric Clapton. The craftsmanship you'll see on this tour demonstrates why these famous musicians are among more than 800,000 satisfied Martin owners.

The guitar-making area resembles a large woodshop. Only recently have power tools and machines appeared, although most of the approximately 300 separate steps that go into making a Martin are done by hand. With so many things to see (including string-making), the guided tour moves quickly.

Stand beside workers as they diligently bend, trim, shape, cut, glue, fit, drill, finish, sand, stain, lacquer, buff, and inspect the different woods that will become Martins. Look for the station where a craftsman uses ordinary clothespins as clamps. These distinctly low-tech devices help secure for drying a glued, serrated strip of wood along the interior edge of the guitar's curvaceous sides. This lining provides additional surface area for attaching the front and back of the body.

Craftsmen use a variety of files, carving knives, and rasps to shape, finish, and attach the neck. Notice how the dovetail neck joint is meticulously trimmed and then checked to ensure a proper fit with the body. When you view a historic Martin or play a modern one in the museum after the tour, you'll really appreciate the three to six months of craftsmanship required to convert rough lumber into a Martin acoustic guitar—a true American classic.

Cost: Free. Group tours, nominal charge.

Freebies: Sound-hole cut-outs; product literature.

Videos Shown: Optional videos show production process, including interviews with C. F. (Chris) Martin IV, the sixth-generation family member who over-

sees the company. Request showing in Martin Museum.

Reservations Needed: No, except for groups.

Days and Hours: Mon–Fri 1:15 PM, best to arrive early. Closed holidays, week between Christmas and New Year's, and July 4th. Small lobby-area museum is open Mon–Fri 8:00 AM–5:00 PM.

Plan to Stay: 1.5–2 hours, including tour, video, gift shop, and museum.

Minimum Age: None, for families; 12, for groups.

Disabled Access: Yes

Group Requirements: Group tours must be arranged in advance. Will split larger groups into groups of 10.

Special Information: Photography permitted without flash. No video cameras.

Gift Shops: 1833 Shop sells Martin guitars, antique and used Martins on consignment, strings, supplies, books, clothing, and other memorabilia. Nearby in the old Martin factory (10 W. North St.) is Guitarmaker's Connection, which sells acoustic guitar tonewoods, kits, parts, instrument-making supplies, strings, and construction/repair books. Both open Mon–Fri 8:30 AM–5:00 PM. Combined catalog available from (800) 247-6931.

Directions: We suggest contacting Martin Guitar for directions from New York City and other points, and for their detailed map, "Navigating Nazareth." From Northeast Extension of Pennsylvania Tnpk., take Exit 33. Take Rt. 22 East to intersection with Rt. 191 North. In Nazareth, Rt. 191 turns left onto Broad St. Stay on Broad St. even though Rt. 191 turns right. Pass the Nazareth Boro Park, turn right onto Beil Ave., then right onto Sycamore St.

Nearby Attractions: Crayola FACTORY and Mack Trucks tour (see pages 284 and 290); Old Martin Homestead (call 610-759-9174); Allen Organ Company tour (call 610-966-2202); Lehigh Valley's attractions include Bushkill Falls, Dorney Park, and Wildwater Kingdom.

FEATURED TOUR

▲ Tight dovetailing calls for sure hand-craftsmanship at Martin Guitar in Nazareth, Pennsylvania.

▼ The bordered abalone pearl inlay on the D-50 Deluxe is unprecedented in its detail and elegance.

See additional photos, pages 1 and 289.

Zippo/Case Visitors Center

1932 Zippo Drive
Bradford, PA 16701
(814) 368-1932 / (888) 442-1932
www.zippo.com/about/zcvc

ZIPPO LIGHTERS AND CASE KNIVES

Located in the wooded hills of northwestern Pennsylvania, the Zippo/Case Visitors Center commands attention from the moment you enter the curving drive flanked by 14 custom made Zippo street lighters. Your eye is drawn first to an enormous three-bladed Case Canoe pocketknife topping the entrance of the building, and then upward to an imposing 40-foot Zippo lighter with a flickering neon flame.

The doors open directly into the Zippo/Case store. Straight across the store, two massive reproductions of chrome Zippo lighters beckon you into the museum, with its open ceiling and colorful exhibits. Take a few minutes to study the time line on the wall to your left, which contains photographs, video clips, and interesting factoids about Zippo, Case, Bradford, and the world. Next to the time line you'll see the famous Zippo lighter American flag, consisting of 3393 red, white, and blue Zippo lighters.

Begin your self-guided tour by watching the introductory video in the theater on your right. The maze of exhibits leads through an interactive station full of information about US and Canadian geography as shown on the surface of Zippo lighters. A WWII exhibit features a tableau of a military foxhole and a wall display of letters to George Blaisdell, the founder of Zippo, from commanders including Eisenhower and MacArthur. "Zippo in the Movies" highlights more than 1,000 documented appearances of Zippo lighters on the big screen. The largest exhibit is framed by a huge glass wall, where you can observe the Zippo Repair Clinic in operation. Zippo technicians repair approximately 1,000 lighters per day, follow the process of these repairs and you will truly appreciate Zippo's legendary guarantee: "It works, or we fix it free."

Continue through striking displays of rare historic Case knives, including a mesmerizing "knife in motion" hologram. The grand finale of the tour is *ZAC* ("Zippo And Case"), a 7-foot-high audio kinetic sculpture. Colorful, pool-size balls plop, ting, bang, and ring their way through a dynamic obstacle course, delighting adults and children alike.

Cost: Free

Freebies: No

Video Shown: 9-minute video on Zippo/Case history and products, and shorter clips at exhibits.

Reservations Needed: No, except for groups over 12 people.

Days and Hours: Visitors Center: Mon–Sat 9:00 AM–5:00 PM; June–December also Sun 12:00 PM–4:00 PM. Repair Center: Mon–Fri 9:00 AM–3:30 PM. Closed major holidays.

Plan to Stay: 1 hour for video, museum, and Repair Center, plus time for gift shop.

Minimum Age: None, for families; 5th grade, for groups.

Disabled Access: Yes

Group Requirements: Groups of 12 or more should call 1 week in advance (call 814-368-2711). Maximum group size is 65. Groups receive gold Zippo lighter lapel pin and collectors' guide.

Special Information: The 1947 Zippo Car "lives" at the Visitors Center when it's not traveling; its travel schedule is accessible via the website. Each year, members of the Case Collectors Club are offered exclusive limited-edition knives. Zippo/Case Swap Meet every other July.

Gift Shop: The Zippo/Case Store carries the full line of Zippo and Case products, including sunglasses and watches, as well as T-shirts, hats, and other items unavailable anywhere else. Open same hours as Visitors Center.

Directions: Take I-86 to U.S. 219 South, follow to Bradford. When U.S. 219 South ends, turn right. Proceed to intersection (4-way stop). Yield to right. After a quarter-mile, bear right at fork. Follow the signs to the Visitors Center.

Nearby Attractions: Northern Lights Candles Factory tour (call 800-836-8797); Willamette Industries Paper Factory tour (call 814-965-2521); Allegheny National Forest; Kinzua Bridge State Park; Knox Kane Railroad; Allegheny Arms and Armor Museum; Penn Brad Oil Museum.

FEATURED TOUR

▲ Zippo/Case Visitors Center, northern Pennsylvania's most visited museum, showcases two American icons, the Zippo lighter and the Case knife.

A revolving sculpture of Zippo lighters and Case knives and an extraordinary 7-by-11-foot flag
▼ comprised of 3,393 lighters showcase the museum entrance.

▲ Watch as Zippo repair technicians practice their craft, fulfilling the famous lifetime guarantee that "It works or we fix it free."

Your museum tour at Zippo/Case Visitors Center in Bradford, Pennsylvania, will include rare exhibits,
▼ prototypes, and the Zippo Repair Clinic.

▲ The 1947 Zippo Car is on display at the Visitors Center when it is not traveling throughout the U.S. This unique product mobile sports two jumbo lighters with lids that open to reveal crimson flames.

ZAC is a fascinating seven-foot audio kinetic ball machine full of motion, sound, and colors produced
▼ by its gears, chimes, chutes, and climbs.

Fenton Art Glass

420 Caroline Avenue
Williamstown, WV 26187
(304) 375-7772
www.fentongiftshop.com

GLASS

FENTON
Handcrafted Glass Artistry Since 1905

THE HISTORIC RIVER CITIES
OF OHIO AND WEST VIRGINIA

West Virginia
Wild and Wonderful

In western West Virginia, rich in mountains, sand, and natural gas, the ancient art of glassmaking is kept alive by a handful of artisans and factories. Fenton Art Glass began in 1905, when two Fenton brothers pooled $284 to start their business. Now in its fourth generation of family ownership and management, Fenton Art Glass continues this art in the U.S.A. The tour takes you from the extreme heat and speed of the glassmaking shops to the decorating area's exacting calm.

After a brief chemistry lesson (sand is glass's main ingredient), follow your guide onto the blow/press shop floor. Gatherers, handlers, and carriers dodge around you with gobs of red-hot glass, handles, and freshly blown or pressed pieces. Each worker, trained by apprenticeship, has a specific function in the team effort of creating each item. To produce a bowl, the "gatherer" rolls the long pole ("punty") inside the 2,200° furnace to gather a gob of glass, which is put into a bowl-shaped mold. The presser, one of the most experienced craftsmen in the shop, lowers a lever with exacting pressure, squeezing molten glass into a decorative bowl.

Downstairs, in an enclosed room, fresh-air-masked artisans paint crushed 22-karat gold onto glass items of all kinds. Elsewhere in the decorating area, artists paint designs on glass using crushed-glass pigments. When applying floral designs, an artist first paints the flowers' blossoms on a dozen pieces, returning later to add leaves and stems. You gain an appreciation for the steps involved in producing tomorrow's heirlooms.

Cost: Free

Freebies: Brochure on glassmaking

Video Shown: "Experience Fenton," 22-minute video in Museum Theater, covers production, how specific glass items are made, company history, and hand carving of cast-iron molds.

Reservations Needed: No, except for groups larger than 20 people.

Days and Hours: Mon–Fri 8:30 AM–9:30 AM and 11:00 AM–2:00 PM. Call for late-afternoon tour times, as factory work schedule changes. Closed holidays. No factory tours for 2 weeks starting end of June or beginning of July.

Plan to Stay: 2 hours, including tour, video, and museum, plus time for gift shop. Museum emphasizes first 75 years of Fenton Glass (1905–1980), and other Ohio Valley companies' glass. Museum has same hours as gift shop.

Minimum Age: 2. Supervise children carefully, since you get very close to the hot glass.

Disabled Access: Blowing/pressing area, gift shop, and museum are accessible. Stairs to decorating department.

Group Requirements: Groups of 20 or more need advance reservations.

Special Information: Wear closed-toe, thick-soled shoes. Glassblowing area is well ventilated but hot during summer. Watch where you walk.

Gift Shop and Factory Outlet: Sells Fenton's first-quality line at suggested retail, as well as retired, first-quality and preferred seconds at reduced prices. Also carries other fine gift and home décor items. Museum sells glassmaking history books. Annual February Gift Shop Sale and Summer Tent Sale. Open Mon–Sat 8:00 AM–5:00 PM, Sun 12:00 PM–5:00 PM. Additional hours April–December: Mon–Fri open until 8:00 PM. Closed New Year's, Easter, Thanksgiving, and Christmas. Catalog available from above number.

Directions: From I-77, take Exit 185; follow blue-and-white signs to gift shop. From Rt. 50, take I-77 North. Follow directions above.

Nearby Attractions: Lee Middleton Original Dolls factory tour (see page 262); Blennerhassett Island; Historic Marietta, Ohio, across Ohio River.

FEATURED TOUR

▲ A skilled glassworker attaches a handle to a pitcher at Fenton Art Glass in Williamstown, West Virginia.

▼ Every piece of handpainted Fenton glass is proudly signed by the artist.

Jelly Belly Center

10100 Jelly Belly Lane
Pleasant Prairie, WI 53158
(866) TOUR-JBC / (866) 868-7522
www.jellybelly.com

The original gourmet jelly bean.®

JELLY BEANS AND GUMMI CANDIES

Since Jelly Belly's Fairfield, California, factory tours (see page 4) have become so popular, the company expanded in 2001, opening a warehouse and distribution center in Pleasant Prairie to supplement the tours in California. Now you can hop on the Jelly Belly Express Train and ride around the new warehouse, stopping to learn about the Jelly Belly Candy Company's production process and sample flavors.

When you arrive, a 30-foot-tall, inflatable Jelly Belly bean with a candy corn hat greets you. Walk into the store and line up next to Jelly Belly Junction—a train station entry to the tour. Inside the warehouse, you will board the Jelly Belly Express, a colorful, four-car electric train with no tracks. Your tour guide drives the train, making commentary between stops.

First, watch the Welcome Video on a large-screen display, which details the company history. After you're on your way, you may be tempted to hop off the train for a moment or two once you see the boxes of candy stacked to the rafters. Be patient—sampling comes later! At the raw materials station, try to count how many sacks of ingredients it takes to produce a day's worth of candies.

Unlike tours of modern factories, you stop at the Candy Kitchen, which displays a mini-museum of reproduced equipment from the company's early days, including old candy machinery and candy kettles. The Panning Process shows off what makes Jelly Belly beans so special—machines add candy shells to intensely flavored centers; non–Jelly Belly beans have no flavoring in the center.

As you pass through Candy Alley, three-dimensional beans fly overhead. While viewing the Jelly Belly bean mosaics, you might recognize some of your favorite presidents, artistically rendered in lemon, cotton candy, and green apple flavors, among others. The dancing chorus line of animated Jelly Belly characters sends you along to the Shipping Department. Reward yourself after the tour with a trip to the tasting bar, where you can create your own Jelly Belly recipes by combining multiple bean flavors.

Cost: Free

Freebies: 3-ounce bag of jelly beans. Sample over 100 candies at tasting bar.

Videos Shown: Large screen videos of production and distribution processes shown during ride on Jelly Belly Express.

Reservations Needed: No

Days and Hours: Mon–Sun 9:00 AM–5:00 PM. Closed New Year's, Easter, Thanksgiving, and Christmas.

Plan to Stay: 40 minutes for train tour and sampling, plus time for retail area and snack bar.

Minimum Age: None

Disabled Access: Yes

Group Requirements: None

Special Information: No photography. Fairfield, CA, factory tour (see page 4).

Retail Store: Sells all Jelly Belly beans and Goelitz Confections, Belly Flops (discounted, irregular beans), gift baskets, jelly bean trinkets, hot dogs, ice cream, and desserts. Open same hours as center.

Directions: From Milwaukee, take I-94 (US 41) South to Exit 347. Turn left (east) onto SR 165 (Lakeview Pkwy). Turn left (north) on SR 31 (Green Bay Rd). In .25 miles, turn left (west) on Jelly Belly Ln. into the Jelly Belly Center. From Chicago, take I-94 (US 41) North into Wisconsin, to Exit 347. Stay on left side of ramp. Turn right (east) onto SR 165 (Lakeview Pkwy) and follow above directions.

Nearby Attractions: Great America Theme Park; McDonald's #1 Store Museum tour (see page 134); Chicago's attractions, including Chicago Mercantile Exchange, Chicago Board of Trade, Eli's Cheesecake World, and U.S. Post Office tours one hour away (see pages 126, 125, 128, and 136); Milwaukee's attractions, including Miller Brewery tour (see page 44), Milwaukee County Zoo, Boerner Botanical Gardens, and Milwaukee Art Museum, are about 45 minutes away.

FEATURED TOUR

▲ The Jelly Belly Express, an electric train, takes visitors down Candy Alley at the Jelly Belly Center in Pleasant Prairie, Wisconsin.

▼ A candy lover's haven, the large store sells hundreds of different candies and gifts made by the company.

Miller Brewing

Visitor Center
4251 West State Street
Milwaukee, WI 53208
(414) 931-BEER
www.millerbrewing.com

BEER

In 1855, German immigrant Fredrick Miller purchased the Plank Road Brewery. Surrounded by woods, the small brewing operation was no bigger than a Victorian house. Today, a replica of the Plank Road Brewery is just one of the historic highlights in Milwaukee's Miller Valley—the home of the nation's second largest brewer, Miller Brewing Company.

Walk outdoors and upstairs to Miller's packaging-center balcony. A blur of cans roars along conveyor belts that wind through wet machinery, packing up to 200,000 cases of beer daily.

The next stop is Miller's mammoth distribution center that covers the equivalent of five football fields. Typically, you can see half a million cases of beer.

In the brew house, Miller makes its beer, up to eight-and-a-half million barrels annually in Milwaukee alone. Climb 56 stairs to look down on a row of towering, shiny brew kettles where "wort," a grain extract, is boiled and combined with hops. Stroll through Miller's historic Caves, a restored portion of the original brewery where beer was stored before the invention of mechanical refrigeration.

Finish your tour at the Bavarian-style Miller Inn and sample a Miller beer or soft drink. Be sure also to take a few minutes to inspect the impressive collection of antique steins. In the summer, you can enjoy your beverage in an adjoining beer garden enlivened by music.

Cost: Free

Freebies: Beer (for those 21 years of age and older with proper ID), soda, peanuts, and postcards.

Video Shown: 15-minute video shows brewing process and overview of Miller's history.

Reservations Needed: No, but recommended for groups of 15 or more.

Days and Hours: Mon–Sat 10:30 AM–3:30 PM. Closed holidays and week between Christmas and New Year's Day.

Plan to Stay: 1 hour for video and tour, plus time for product sampling and gift shop.

Minimum Age: Under age 18 must be accompanied by adult.

Disabled Access: Plant tour: no. Visitor Center (includes video), Miller Inn, and Caves: yes.

Group Requirements: Groups of 15 or more people should call ahead for reservations. Maximum group size is 90. Limited reservations on Saturdays.

Special Information: Best time to see production is weekdays. Miller Brewing Company also gives tours and has a gift shop in Tumwater, WA (call 360-754-5217), and the Miller Marketplace and Brew Kettle Museum in Ft. Worth, TX (call 817-568-BEER).

Gift Shop: Girl in the Moon Brewery Shop sells clothing, caps, glassware, steins, mirrors, tap handles, and other Miller logoed items. Open Mon–Sat: summer 10:00 AM–5:30 PM; winter 10:00 AM–5:00 PM.

Directions: From Chicago, take I-94 West to 35th St. Turn right (north) on 35th St. Turn left (west) onto State St. Pass through "Miller Valley" (well marked) to last building on left, Miller Visitor Center and Gift Shop. From Madison, take I-94 East to Hwy 41 North to the State St. exit. Follow signs to right, down hill to traffic light. Turn left onto State St. Visitor Center is one block ahead on right.

Nearby Attractions: Quality Candy/Buddy Squirrel factory tour (see page 359); Miller Park (home of Milwaukee Brewers); Milwaukee County Zoo; Mitchell Park Horticulture ("The Domes"); Milwaukee County Museum; Milwaukee Art Museum; Boerner Botanical Gardens; Cedar Creek Winery. Miller Visitor Center front desk has information on and directions to many local attractions.

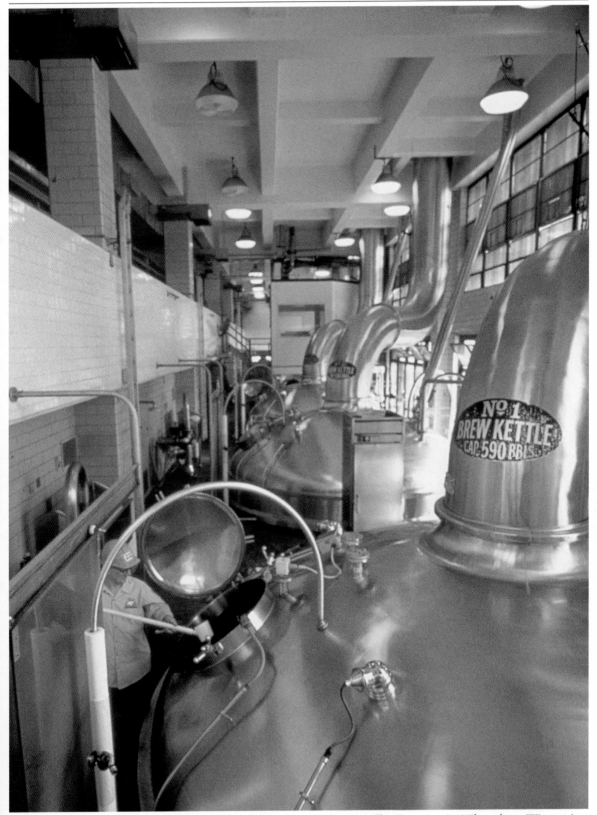

▲ Huge, gleaming brew kettles are one of the tour sights at Miller Brewing in Milwaukee, Wisconsin.

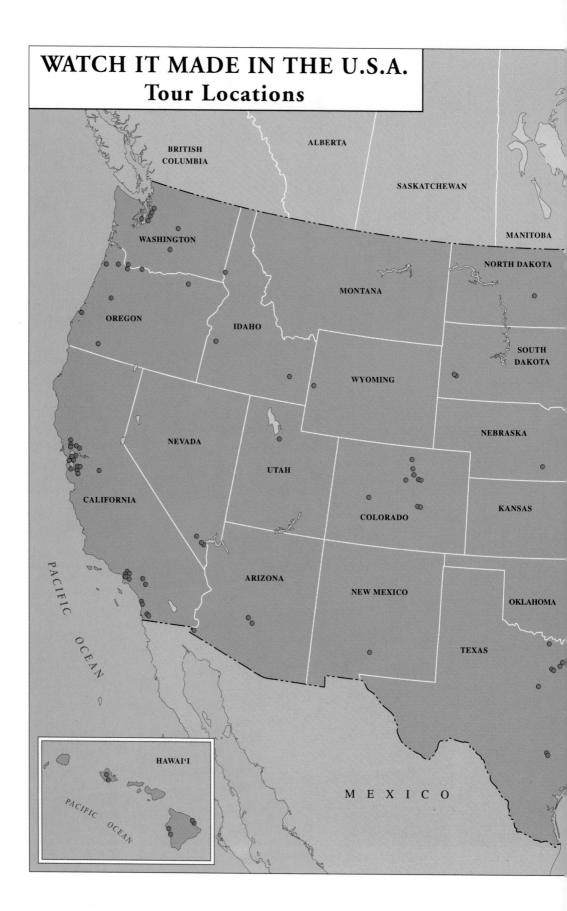

WATCH IT MADE IN THE U.S.A.
Tour Locations

BRITISH
COLUMBIA

ALBERTA

SASKATCHEWAN

MANITOBA

WASHINGTON

NORTH DAKOTA

MONTANA

OREGON

IDAHO

SOUTH
DAKOTA

WYOMING

NEBRASKA

NEVADA

UTAH

COLORADO

KANSAS

CALIFORNIA

ARIZONA

NEW MEXICO

OKLAHOMA

TEXAS

PACIFIC

OCEAN

MEXICO

HAWAI'I

PACIFIC

OCEAN

RUSSIA

ALASKA CANADA

CANADA

ONTARIO

QUÉBEC

NEW
BRUNSWICK

MAINE

MINNESOTA

WISCONSIN

MICHIGAN

NEW YORK

VT

NH

MA

CT RI

IOWA

PENNSYLVANIA

NJ

MD

DE

OHIO

ILLINOIS

INDIANA

WEST
VIRGINIA

MISSOURI

KENTUCKY

VIRGINIA

NORTH
CAROLINA

TENNESSEE

ARKANSAS

SOUTH
CAROLINA

GEORGIA

OCEAN

MISSISSIPPI

ALABAMA

LOUISIANA

FLORIDA

ATLANTIC

CAYMAN
ISLANDS

CUBA

HAITI

PUERTO
RICO

JAMAICA

DOMINICAN
REPUBLIC

U.S. VIRGIN
ISLANDS

Robinson Iron

1856 Robinson Road
Alexander City, AL 35010
(256) 329-8486
www.robinsoniron.com

Robinson Iron

ARCHITECTURAL IRONWORKS

Have you ever taken the New York City subway from Astor Place and admired the cast-iron kiosk entrance? If so, you've already seen Robinson Iron's handiwork. Perhaps you've sat on its benches, which line Pennsylvania Avenue in Washington, D.C., or daydreamed while watching water flow through the 12,000-pound Court Square Fountain in Montgomery. Robinson restored the fountain, as well as the intricate ironwork at Singapore's renowned Raffles Hotel. Although you cannot tour the foundry, where 2,500° molten iron flows like melted butter, you can watch skilled ironworkers turn the raw castings into ornate fountains, urns, lampposts, garden statuary, or perhaps customized railings for subway stations.

As you enter the shop, welding arcs hiss, grinding wheels squeal, and drills buzz, leaving no doubt that you're surrounded by heavy ironworking. Masked welders in the fabrication area wield plasma arc cutters, which produce a light as bright as a laser. A metallic, flinty odor fills your nose. When the sparks clear, you'll find the raw castings have become a 16-foot multi-tiered fountain for a municipal park, or a 400-pound deer, complete with antlers, for someone's backyard.

In the finishing area, workers spray-paint Charleston Green, Gloss White, or Black in a painting booth. An overhead crane lifts the mammoth ornaments into place, so workers can construct shipping crates around them. Before you end the tour, head outside down the path to the Pattern Shop, to see how the whole process starts. Pattern-makers follow blueprints from Robinson's designers to custom-carve, detail, and create a wooden master, which is then used to fashion a plastic or metal working pattern. The foundry uses the pattern to produce a hollow sand mold into which molten iron is poured. The raw casting it creates will go to the workers in the fabrication area, where you began. In the Atrium Showroom, finished pieces stand ready for your close inspection, admiration, and purchase.

Cost: Free

Freebies: No

Video Shown: Optional 15-minute video on company's history, by request only.

Reservations Needed: Yes. Call for reservation.

Days and Hours: Mon–Fri 8:00 AM–4:00 PM. Closed holidays. Production decreases during 4th of July week and Christmas week.

Plan to Stay: 45 minutes, plus time in showroom.

Minimum Age: None, although some areas are restricted for children under 5, who might stay in the Atrium Showroom to watch the fountain.

Disabled Access: Yes

Group Requirements: Groups of 8 or more people should call 1 day in advance.

Special Information: Plant can be quite noisy at times.

Showroom: The Atrium Showroom features a representative collection of ironworks from the company's catalog and its *Architectural Handbook* (both available for purchase in showroom or from above phone number or website), including small garden statuary, ornamental urns, and animal sculptures. Open same hours as tour.

Directions: From Birmingham, take Hwy. 280 East to Kelleton. Turn left on Business 280 (*not* Bypass 280). In 2 miles, where the road widens, watch on the right for Robinson Foundry. Take the first right after the foundry. Cross the railroad tracks. Robinson Iron is the brown metal building on your right. From Montgomery, take Hwy. 231 North to Wetumka. Turn right on Hwy. 9 North. Turn right on Hwy. 22 East. Turn left onto Hwy. 280 West. In a little over 1 mile, turn right on Robinson Rd. Bear right at the fork, and watch for Robinson Iron on your left.

Nearby Attractions: Russell Corp. clothing manufacturer tour (call 256-329-4000); Martin Lake; Kowaliga Marina; Horsebend National Military Park.

Mercedes-Benz

1 Mercedes Drive
Vance, AL 35490
(205) 507-2253
www.mbusi.com

Mercedes-Benz

Most Americans credit Henry Ford with the invention of the automobile. However, as you'll learn from the History Exhibit at the 24,000-square-foot Mercedes-Benz Visitor Center, the first automobile came to be known as the Mercedes-Benz (invented in 1886).

The Racing Exhibit portrays Mercedes' long and illustrious racing career through photographs of all the cars' famous drivers, historical racing footage, and a historical Mercedes-Benz racing vehicle. Many safety features were first tested in race cars and then incorporated into passenger cars.

Take a short bus ride to the M-Class plant, the company's first outside Europe. Walk into the huge, futuristic lobby with its high ceilings and large glass wall leading into the factory.

Sheet-metal panels for the M-Class, a sport-utility vehicle, come into the plant prestamped and subassembled on a just-in-time basis. The panels are welded together in the body shop. The vehicle leaves the body shop complete with four doors, tailgate, and hood, but it's only a colorless shell. Look through windows into the paint shop, where cars enter on the mezzanine level as raw steel precision-shaped bodies. In this clean room, workers wear astronaut-like suits and hair nets. The cars zigzag their way back and forth along the whole length of the paint shop, alternating between dip tanks and oven lines, and come out in front of you in glossy painted colors. The selectivity bank shuffles the cars around into assembly sequence as if it's playing checkers.

In assembly, notice that all the work is done without robotics—except for one robot that installs the windshield and back glass. One of the highlights is the "marriage" station on the final line, where the completed chassis is lifted up and team members bolt it to a completed body. You'll wish you had arranged for factory-direct delivery so you could drive your new M-Class vehicle right out of the Visitor Center.

Cost: Visitor Center: free; factory tour: ages 12–54, $5; seniors 55+, $4.

Freebies: No

Video Shown: 10-minute video overviews body, paint, and assembly. 1-hour video, "Big Auto Plant," shows entire manufacturing and development process.

Reservations Needed: Yes, for factory tour. No, for Visitor Center, except for groups of 10 or more people. Factory tours are limited in size, so call well in advance.

Days and Hours: Factory tour: Mon–Fri by appointment. Visitor Center: Mon–Fri 9:00 AM–5:00 PM, and 1st Sat of month 10:00 AM–5:00 PM. Both closed holidays. Factory closed July 4th week and week between Christmas and New Year's. Mercedes-Benz reserves the right to cancel the factory tour for production or safety reasons.

Plan to Stay: 1 hour each for factory tour and Visitor Center, plus time for Mercedes Boutique.

Minimum Age: 12 for tour; none for Visitor Center.

Disabled Access: Yes

Group Requirements: Groups over 10 people should call in advance at least 1 week for the Visitor Center and 1 month for the factory tour. Maximum group size is 25 people for factory tour.

Special Information: No photography in factory.

Gift Shop: Mercedes Boutique sells logoed key chains, caps, and T-shirts, coffee mugs showing the Visitor Center's silhouette, plus other Mercedes-Benz merchandise. Also carries lifestyle items such as hiking equipment and water bottles. Open same hours as Visitor Center. Closed holidays.

Directions: From Birmingham, take I-59/20 West to Exit 89. Turn left over the Interstate. Bear right onto Mercedes Dr. Visitor Center is first building on left.

Nearby Attractions: Tannehill State Park; Tuscaloosa's attractions, including Paul (Bear) Bryant Museum, Mound State Monument, and antebellum homes, about 17 miles away.

▲ A MBUSI Team Member carefully welds the body of an M-Class.

The Mercedes-Benz U.S. International plant in Vance, Alabama, is home to the Mercedes-Benz M-Class. ▼ A $600-million expansion doubles the size of the facility and its workforce.

Alaskan Brewing

5429 Shaune Drive
Juneau, AK 99801
(907) 780-5866
www.alaskanbeer.com

BEER

Small, family-like Alaskan Brewing Company brews Alaskan Amber (based on a Gold Rush–era recipe from the local extinct Douglas City Brewing Co.), Alaskan Pale, Alaskan E.S.B., Alaskan Stout, and seasonal beers. Since its start in 1986, Alaskan Brewing Company's beers have won awards for quality at annual beer festivals. To expand its production space, the brewery took over a golf driving range in the other half of this wooden building (to this day, some golf balls linger in the roof's insulation) and built two new additions.

The tour starts off right—with a glass of Alaskan Pale (its lighter, fruitier beer). Now that you're in the spirit, walk into the tour hallway. You can look through glass walls into the brewhouse at three 310-gallon kettles known as the mash tun, lauter tun, and brew kettle. If you're lucky, you'll see activity here—a worker transferring mixtures from kettle to kettle or shoveling "spent" (already used) barley. The majority of Alaskan beer is brewed in a new 100-barrel brewhouse, also visible from this area. In show-and-tell, the tour guide hands out malted barley (tastes like Grape Nuts) and hops (a bittering herb). Notice what used to be "Alaska's biggest six-pack," six 10-foot-high stainless steel fermentation tanks stacked in a row. Now there are 46 fermentation tanks, each 20-plus times the size of the small ones in the tank area.

Walk outdoors and upstairs to a landing. Through windows, peer inside at the bottling operation. In the hospitality room and gift shop, admire the national/international bottle collections on display. Find your home state's beer. If your local brewery is not represented, be sure to send Alaskan one for its extensive collection when you get home.

Cost: Free
Freebies: 5-oz. glasses of beer
Video Shown: No
Reservations Needed: No, but preferred for groups larger than 10 people.

Days and Hours: May through September: Mon–Sun 11:00 AM–4:30 PM, every 30 minutes; October through April: Thur–Sat, same time schedule. Closed July 4th, Thanksgiving, Christmas, and New Year's.
Plan to Stay: 30 minutes, plus time in gift shop.
Minimum Age: None. However, anyone under 21 years old must be accompanied by a parent or guardian. You must be 21 years old to sample beer.
Disabled Access: Yes
Group Requirements: Prefers 1 day's advance notice for groups larger than 10 people. Groups larger than 35 people will be divided into smaller groups.
Special Information: Best days to see bottling are Monday through Friday. If your timing is right, you can sample seasonal beers (usually made in the spring and fall) or one of the R&D brews called "Rough Draft."
Gift Shop: Sells T-shirts, sweatshirts, and baseball caps with beer label designs. Offers bottlecap fishing lures with the "Made in Alaska" bear design on a crown, and collectible pint glasses. Open same hours as tour. Merchandise is available on the website (www.alaskanbeer.com). Gift shop displays historical photographs and artifacts of Alaskan breweries from the 1800s to today.
Directions: From Juneau, take Egan Dr. to stoplight at the base of Vanderbilt Hill. Turn only way possible onto Vanderbilt Hill Rd. Turn right onto Anka Dr. Take second right onto Shaune Dr. The brewery is 1.5 blocks ahead on the left. You'll smell the strong scent of malt and hops as you approach on brewing days.
Nearby Attractions: Alaska Seafood Co. tour (call 907-780-5111); Mendenhall Glacier; DIPAC (salmon hatchery); Historic Downtown Juneau's attractions include the Capitol building and the Alaskan Bar & Hotel (features Alaskan's beer on tap); sport fishing.

Musk Ox Farm

Mile 50 Glenn Highway
Palmer, AK 99645
(907) 745-4151
www.muskoxfarm.org

MUSK OXEN

The name "musk ox" (the Eskimo word is *oomingmak*) is a misnomer—the animals neither have musk glands nor belong to the ox family. Rather, they are short, stocky beasts. Underneath the shaggy carpet of the musk ox's brown guard hair is a coat of fine, soft, warm hair called "qiviut." In the winter, qiviut protects the musk ox against wind and bitter Arctic temperatures. In spring, musk oxen shed their qiviut naturally. This "down," or underwool, is combed out of their coats, spun into yarn that is eight times warmer than sheep's wool, and knitted by Eskimo women into beautiful lacy stoles, scarves, and hats. The Musk Ox Farm is a nonprofit organization formed to breed and study musk oxen and to provide a native-run and -owned cottage knitting industry. It is the only herd of domesticated oxen in the world.

At the farm, you see extensive displays describing the history and background of the animals, and the special project of the Anchorage cooperative that sells the knitted qiviut items. Next you are shown where and how the furry beasts are combed. At a fenced-in walkway by the ox pens, the guide describes the animals' lives and habits, both in the wild and in captivity. In the wild, two bulls contest for dominance by banging their heads together. After circling around and challenging each other, they may back away as much as 50 feet and then run straight at one another, crashing their horns together in a sound that can be heard up to a mile away. You probably won't see any headbanging, but these curious creatures, who can weigh as much as 900 pounds, may approach and eat grass from your hand.

Stay as long as you like to observe these unique animals, or venture 50 miles away to the "Oomingmak" Co-operative in Anchorage. Here you'll see the lacy qiviut items that the Eskimo women made being washed, blocked (stretched on a pattern board to straighten the sides), and packaged at the front table of the small shop.

Cost: Adults, $8.50; seniors and students 13–18, $7; children 6–12, $5.50; children under 6 accompanied by an adult, free.

Freebies: No

Video Shown: No

Reservations Needed: No, except for groups larger than 12 people and for winter tours.

Days and Hours: Mother's Day through end of September: Mon–Sun 10:00 AM–6:00 PM. Tours run every 30 minutes. Open summer holidays. Winter tours by appointment only. Call ahead.

Plan to Stay: 30–45 minutes, plus time in gift shop.

Minimum Age: None

Disabled Access: Yes

Group Requirements: Groups of 12 or more people should call at least 1 day in advance. Groups larger than 50 people will be split into 2 or more staggered-time tours. Group rate is $6 per person.

Special Information: The animals are more active in the morning. Early groups on Monday, Wednesday, and Friday mornings can see the oxen being fed.

'Oomingmak' Musk Ox Producers' Co-operative in Anchorage: Watch the final blocking process of caps, scarves, and other knit items with each Eskimo village's signature knitting pattern. Call (907-272-9225).

Gift Shop: Sells qiviut items such as scarves, hats, and stoles. Also sells musk ox mementos such as stuffed animals, toys, mugs, and T-shirts. Open same hours as tour.

Directions: From Anchorage, take Glenn Hwy. North, through Palmer. About 2 miles past Palmer (at Mile 50), turn left onto Archie Rd. Follow signs to Musk Ox Farm, which is about .25 mile down the road on left.

Nearby Attractions: Reindeer Farm; Palmer Visitors Center; Iditarod Trail Headquarters and Dorothy Page Museum in Wasilla (about 11 miles away); Hatcher Pass; Independence Mine State Historical Park.

Cerreta's Candy

5345 West Glendale Avenue
Glendale, AZ 85301
(623) 930-1000
www.cerreta.com

CHOCOLATES, CANDY, AND CARAMEL POPCORN

Cerreta's Candy Company

Since 1968, this family-owned company has been producing chocolate candy that's sold at its retail store and in supermarkets throughout the western U.S.A. Because the entire factory is open, your nostrils fill with the sweet smell of cocoa and your ears hear the loud noises of mixers, enrobers, and conveyors turning chocolate into candy. Cerreta's makes four types of chocolate candy in this factory: mints, creams, caramels, and clusters. Throughout the factory, you will notice workers hand-pouring and hand-mixing ingredients into oversized copper kettles.

Since this is a self-guided tour, overhead monitors along the walkway help explain the candy-making process. Lean against the waist-high railing to see the action. The long, yellow, automatic molding machine makes French mints. A pale green, minty liquid fills one plastic tray, containing 32 molds, every six seconds. The trays are flipped over to allow the excess to flow out. Once the mint cools, chocolate centers are injected and cooled again before dollops of mint are added, sealing the chocolate inside. Notice the mile-long spiral conveyor in the glass-enclosed chilling room. After the mints travel around and around up the spiral, workers release the candies from their molds, much like removing ice cubes from plastic trays. The released candies travel down twin-lane conveyor belts to the specially designed wrapping machine, which swallows them up and spits them out wrapped at a rate of 1,000 candies per minute.

In the background, watch as a worker pours liquid caramel from a copper cauldron onto a long, refrigerated stainless-steel table. Once solidified, the caramel is cut into long ribbons. Some of the ribbons are fed into an automatic wrapping machine, which individually twist-wraps each caramel in clear cellophane. Unwrapped caramels and other centers, such as buttercreams and peanut brittle, travel to the enrobing machine. There, centers move along a wire conveyor belt and are drenched in chocolate. If they're making caramel popcorn, workers dig into the bowl to scoop and mix the coated popcorn to prevent sticking. It looks like so much fun, you'll want to put on a pair of rubber gloves and help them.

Cost: Free; chocolate pizza-making, $5.

Freebies: Sample of Cerreta's candy

Videos Shown: Videos on overhead monitors along walkway provide up-close view of the entire chocolate-making process.

Reservations Needed: No, except for groups of 30 or more people.

Days and Hours: Self-guided viewing: Mon–Sat 8:00 AM–6:00 PM. Guided tours: Mon–Thur 10:00 AM and 1:00 PM. Open-house chocolate pizza–making June through September: Mon–Thur 9:30 AM. Closed holidays. Even though there is limited production on Saturdays, you can view video monitors and see equipment.

Plan to Stay: 20 minutes for self-guided tour, plus time for retail store.

Minimum Age: None

Disabled Access: Yes

Group Requirements: Groups of 30 or more people should call 1 month in advance to arrange guided tours for special tour times.

Special Information: The tour is offered year-round; do call ahead, however, since limited production on Saturday and in summer. Hot in summer.

Retail Store: Sells entire selection of Cerreta's chocolates, caramels, and French mints. Open Mon–Sat 8:00 AM–6:00 PM. Closed holidays.

Directions: From I-10, take 59th Ave. North to Glendale Ave. Turn right, and Cerreta's will be on the right. You'll recognize the building by its upside-down copper cauldron–like awning.

Nearby Attractions: Ping Golf Equipment tour (see page 56); Saguaro Ranch Park.

Peanut Patch

4322 East County 13th Street
Yuma, AZ 85365
(928) 726-6292 / (800) USA-PNUT
www.thepeanutpatch.com

PEANUTS AND CANDY

The Peanut Patch has become a rich tradition in Southwest Arizona. A trip to or through Yuma would not be complete without stopping by for a visit to the George family, owners of the Peanut Patch. The Peanut Patch has come a long way from its humble beginnings as a local grower of peanuts. They no longer grow peanuts in Yuma, but they cook and sell peanuts of every description. You will get to see how a peanut plant grows, and watch the preparation of some peanut treats, such as peanut brittle and peanut butter.

Start off the tour with a peanut-growing lesson. You may be amazed to learn that peanuts, as legumes, grow underground; they are planted in March and are harvested in August. A single peanut plant remains from the hundreds that once grew on the farm. Pictures of successive growth stages of the peanut plant are also on display.

Walk through the kitchens of the store and watch peanut treats being made. One kitchen is devoted to making peanut brittle. Smell the butter, peanuts, and sugar as they simmer together in copper kettles. The hand-stirred mixture is poured onto old-fashioned marble slabs for cooling, and later it's broken into pieces of peanut brittle. In the second kitchen, watch employees hand-dip candies into rich chocolate. You can participate in the candy making and dip your own peanut clusters. Out in the store, look through a Plexiglas-enclosed area at the fudge bubbling in a stainless steel double boiler. By the end of your tour, you will have worked up quite an appetite from the sights and smells of all these peanut treats. Luckily, you get to taste the treats you just watched being made!

Cost: Free

Freebies: Fudge and peanut samples

Video Shown: No

Reservations Needed: No, except for groups larger than 10 people.

Days and Hours: October–November and January–April only: Tue and Fri, 10:00 AM. Closed Thanksgiving, Christmas, New Year's, and Easter.

Plan to Stay: 30 minutes, plus time for gift shop.

Minimum Age: None

Disabled Access: Yes

Group Requirements: Call at least 2 weeks in advance for reservations. Minimum group is 10 people. No maximum group size.

Gift Shop: Sells peanuts, other nuts, trail mixes, dried fruits, and candies. Offers unique Arizona specialties, such as cactus jellies and local farmers' products. Catalog available (call 800-USA-PNUT). Mon–Sat 9:00 AM–5:00 PM. Closed June 1–September 30, Thanksgiving, Christmas, New Year's, and Easter.

Directions: Take I-8 to Yuma. Take Ave. 3E exit. Go south to County 13th St. Turn left and travel 1.25 miles. The Peanut Patch will be on your left.

Nearby Attractions: Century House Museum; Yuma Crossing State Historic Park; Territorial Prison; Yuma River Tours.

Ping Golf Equipment

2201 West Desert Cove, Building 120
Phoenix, AZ 85029
(602) 687-5385
www.pinggolf.com

PING®

GOLF CLUBS

Long before Karsten Solheim began playing golf at the age of 43, he had an interest in golf clubs. Solheim, one of the golf industry's most recognizable figures, started perfecting golf clubs with the goal of making a fiendishly fickle game easier to play. The first putter he developed made a loud, shrill "ping" sound; hence, the eventual name for his clubs. When Julius Boros won the Phoenix Open in 1967 with a Ping putter, the popularity of Ping golf clubs increased. That same year Solheim left General Electric as a project engineer to start Karsten Manufacturing Corporation, the parent company of Ping Golf Equipment, in a small 20-by-40-foot building. Today the company employs about 1,000 workers, and the site covers most of a city block.

Your tour begins after you view the displays of the company's golf clubs, woods, irons, putters, and bags in the visitors center. The guide, usually a former golf professional, leads you past the original 1967 building. Currently the repair department, it initially served as Karsten's production area, machine shop, reception area, order desk, and shipping department.

Because of the size of the "campus," you walk in and out of buildings based on proximity rather than order of production. Since the iron and putter grinding area is so noisy, the guide explains the process only outside the building. The irons, cast by the off-site foundry, require grinding and tumbling for further shaping.

In the iron, putter, and wood assembly areas, shafts are cut to the correct length and installed into club heads, while clubs wait on shelves for grips. To attach a grip, two-way adhesive tape is wrapped around the shaft. A solvent poured onto the tape turns it into glue, and the grip is slid onto the shaft. The club's lie angle is adjusted for the height and swing habits of its future owner. In the stamping area, the clubs are stamped with individual serial numbers. The last part of your tour takes you to Karsten Engineering, a subsidiary that assists in designing clubs and other products. See milling machines and examine their handiwork at nearby display tables. After the tour, you'll want to play golf at one of the many golf courses in the Phoenix area.

Cost: Free
Freebies: Information sheets, brochures, personalized fitting recommendations.
Videos Shown: 3 videos on the history of Karsten and its subsidiaries.
Reservations Needed: Yes
Days and Hours: Tue and Thur 9:30 AM. Call for availability and reservations 3–4 months in advance.
Plan to Stay: 1.5 hours for tour, videos, and questions.
Minimum Age: 9
Disabled Access: Yes
Group Requirements: Cannot handle group tours larger than 10 people.
Special Information: No photography. Wear comfortable shoes for the half-mile of walking. Ping golf club owners and people interested in golf will enjoy the tour the most.
Gift Shop: No. Products sold through dealers and area golf courses.
Directions: From I-17, go east on Peoria Ave. Turn left onto 23rd Ave. Turn right on Desert Cove. Turn right on Karsten's Way and park in the lot on the left.
Nearby Attractions: Cerreta's Candy tour (see page 54); Metro Center Shopping Mall; Phoenix attractions include more than 100 golf courses.

Wal-Mart Visitors Center

105 North Main Street
Bentonville, AR 72712
(479) 273-1329
www.walmart.com

The Wal-Mart retail empire, with more than a million employees (called "associates") and billions of dollars in yearly revenues, began in the building that now houses the Visitors Center. From the outside, it's an exact replica of the first Walton's 5 & 10, opened by Sam and Helen Walton in 1950. The folksy center brings together the history, growth, philosophy, and present-day scope of the company. As you walk on the original checkerboard red and green linoleum tile floor, examining the displays and watching the videos, you're surrounded by a true American business success.

Merchandise from the 1950s and '60s sits in the front window. In the lobby is a cutout figure of Sam Walton (the store's first manager) next to a huge mural showing a typical 5 & 10 of the early '50s. Family portraits and other murals of the company's operations also hang throughout the center, along with early newspaper ads and memorabilia. The center has more than 40 separate displays. The most popular are the laser video programs on the history of the company and on the Walton family. One large exhibit is a timeline that traces the Wal-Mart story from its variety store roots to the present day. Mementos, photos, and products such as old Barbie dolls fill the display. At the push of a button is a narrated, illuminated photomap tracking the nationwide spread of Wal-Mart stores.

The Visitors Center holds many of Sam's prized possessions. The Presidential Medal of Freedom, the nation's highest civilian award, which Sam Walton received in 1992, is proudly displayed. So are his old red pickup truck and original office, complete with the apple crate used as a chair for guests. Other exhibits include Wal-Mart and Wall Street, Community Involvement, Satellite Communications, and Saving the Environment.

The Buy American exhibit features a changing display of the American-made products that Wal-Mart sells and the jobs created by this partnership of retailers and domestic manufacturers. The long-range goal of the Buy American program is to re-establish the competitive position of U.S.-made goods. You leave understanding more about the people and heritage behind what has been called "the retailing phenomenon of the century."

Cost: Free
Freebies: No
Videos Shown: Four 8-minute laser video programs on the company, the Walton family, the Medal of Freedom, and conversations between Sam and his brother.
Reservations Needed: No, however, recommended for groups of 10 or more people.
Days and Hours: Tue–Sat 9:00 AM–5:00 PM. Closed Thanksgiving, Christmas, and New Year's.
Plan to Stay: 30 minutes, plus time for videos.
Minimum Age: None, but recommends children be at least 10 to appreciate and enjoy the exhibits.
Disabled Access: Yes
Group Requirements: Groups of 10 or more people should call 2 days in advance.
Special Information: Exhibits change to reflect Wal-Mart developments. You may want to schedule your visit around Wal-Mart Stores, Inc.'s annual meeting (usually first week in June) in nearby Fayetteville. Tens of thousands attend the largest annual meeting in the U.S.A., which features live entertainment, enthused employees, and a real sense of the corporate culture.
Gift Counter: Sells Wal-Mart and Visitors Center logoed items, including mugs, key chains, and T-shirts. Open same hours as Visitors Center.
Directions: Take Hwy. 71 or Hwy. 71B to Hwy. 72. The Visitors Center is on the west side of the square in downtown Bentonville. Look for the big American flag and the building that says "Walton's 5 & 10."
Nearby Attractions: Terra Pottery Studios tour, 20 miles away, in Fayetteville (call 479-643-3185); University of Arkansas; Beaver Lake; Eureka Springs.

Alembic

3005 Wiljan Court
Santa Rosa, CA 95407
(707) 523-2611
www.alembic.com

ALEMBIC

Ron and Susan Wickersham started Alembic as a consulting firm that worked with the Grateful Dead, Jefferson Airplane, and Crosby Stills Nash & Young to improve the quality of live sound and recordings of live concerts. When Ron tried to craft a guitar with a higher bandwidth (and better sound quality), he ended up with low-output guitars. To make the sound louder, he designed the first active electric guitar amps to boost the signal—the birth of the modern-day electric guitar. While other companies focused on lead guitars, Alembic made instruments for bass guitarists and set the standard for bass design.

Inside the shop, see the complicated merging of electronics that create the electric guitar sound. Not many guitar companies make their own hardware, electronics, and pickups, and even fewer manufacture their own printed circuit boards like Alembic does. In the parts and subassemblies areas, watch as a worker assembles, winds, wires, tests, and casts the pickups for various instruments.

The CNC (Computer Numeric Controlled) machines drill the printed circuit boards and slot fingerboards for the frets while a worker buffs the brass parts so that they can be assembled to make a complete bridge. One of two giant glue presses clamps down on the necks to laminate them.

In the carving area, sawdust flies as workers sand contours into the wood before the necks are attached. After the guitar is assembled, it heads to finishing, where a worker wearing a space suit applies coats of spray to the instruments. The guitar sits for 24 hours between coats for the spray to cure before it is sanded and sprayed again—a high-gloss finish can require as many as 25 coats.

Finally, the guitar reaches set-up and inspection, where workers level the fingerboard, press in the frets, and add the strings and metal tuners. After the finishing touches are applied comes the most popular job:

plugging in and playing the guitars to check for buzzing and sound quality. One last person checks to make sure all the screws are in place, and the instrument gets approval to leave the factory.

Cost: Free

Freebies: Sample of exotic wood

Video Shown: No

Reservations Needed: Yes, call at least 1 day in advance.

Days and Hours: Wed 11:00 AM. Additional tour times can be scheduled Mon–Thur 10:00 AM–4:00 PM.

Plan to Stay: 1 hour

Minimum Age: None, but 1 adult required for every 2 children under 10.

Disabled Access: Yes

Group Requirements: None

Special Information: Tour is dusty and noisy. Dust masks and ear protection can be provided.

Showroom: Sells guitars and basses, strings, and guitar polish. Open Mon–Fri 10:00 AM–4:00 PM.

Directions: From San Francisco: Take 101 North over the Golden Gate Bridge. After about 45 minutes, take the Hearn Ave. exit. Turn left onto Santa Rosa Ave., left onto Hearn Ave., and go over the overpass. Take the first left onto Corby Ave. Corby makes a sharp right and becomes Bellevue. Take the first right onto Wiljan Ct. Alembic will be on your left. If you reach a stop sign, you've gone too far. From northern California: Take 101 South to the Hearn Ave. exit. Take the first left onto Corby Ave. and follow above directions.

Nearby Attractions: Luther Burbank Home and Gardens (call 707-524-5445); Martini & Prati Winery (call 707-823-2404). Calistoga attractions, including Old Faithful Geyser and the Petrified Forest, are about 30 minutes away. San Francisco attractions are about 1 hour away.

Basic Brown Bear Factory

444 DeHaro Street
San Francisco, CA 94107
(415) 626-0781
www.basicbrownbear.com

You'll enjoy playing teddy bear obstetrician on this tour. At this factory, discover how teddy bears are born and participate in their delivery. One of the few U.S. manufacturers of stuffed bears, Basic Brown Bear (BBB) lets you watch them handmake the cuddly creatures from start to finish.

In the cutting and sewing area, often the owner proudly explains her process. First, she draws each pattern on paper and makes a sample animal from the pattern. Workers use bandsaws to slice 24 layers of plush fabric into pattern pieces. Seamstresses sew together individual bear parts and outfits, stitching the sections inside out, then reaching inside to push out the bear legs, ears, and noses. Each seamstress can make about 35 baby bears or 10 grandparent bears a day, plus their clothes.

You learn that the first stuffed bears had shoe buttons for eyes. Now, grommets snap mushroom-shaped plastic eyes into place. A tour highlight is stuffing bears with polyester from a bright yellow machine used to fill life jackets during WWII. Now you can bring a bear to life by inflating it like a balloon. Wait on a line of yellow paw prints to push the filler's foot pedal. Out shoots a mixture of air and polyester. Another machine injects beans into bears. Once a bear is cuddly enough, its back is hand-sewn shut.

At the beauty parlor, workers smooth out bear seams with an electric wire brush. A pressurized-air "bear bath" or "bear shower" (depending on the critter's size) removes fur "fuzzies." Children (and adults) giggle when they too receive a "bear shower" or give a bear a "bath." Bears are dressed in their outfits, including company-made wire-rim glasses. Visitors leave with a special affection for the bears they brought to life.

Cost: Free tour. Prices for stuffing your own animal run from $12 to $300.

Freebies: No

Video Shown: 20-minute Emmy award–winning video, "The Teddy Bear Factory,"

with its catchy tune, tells how teddy bears are made.

Reservations Needed: No, except for groups of 8 or more people.

Days and Hours: Mon–Sun 10:00 AM–5:00 PM, on the hour. Last tour at 4:00 PM. Closed holidays.

Plan to Stay: 30 minutes, plus time for stuffing and showering your own bear, and the gift shop.

Minimum Age: 3

Disabled Access: Yes

Group Requirements: Groups of 8 or more people should call 2 weeks in advance. Maximum group size is 40.

Special Information: Can also stuff your own animals at BBB's other stores in The Cannery, near Fisherman's Wharf (call 888-900-2327), in Old Town San Diego (call 877-234-2327), and in the Mall of America in Bloomington, MN (call 800-396-2327).

Gift Shop: More than 30 styles of stuffed bears (and other animals) and bear clothes, all handmade by BBB, are sold exclusively at this location. Mon–Sun 10:00 AM–5:00 PM. Price list available from (800) 554-1910.

Directions: Westbound from the Bay Bridge, take 9th St./Civic Center exit and get into the immediate left-hand lane, which puts you onto 8th St. Stay on 8th St. until it ends at the traffic circle. Turn right onto Kansas St. Turn left onto Mariposa St. BBB is on the left-hand corner of Mariposa and DeHaro Sts. From the South Bay, take Hwy. 101 North. Take the Vermont St. exit and cross over Vermont St. onto Mariposa St. Stay on Mariposa St. until you reach DeHaro St. (about 4 blocks). BBB is on the left-hand corner.

Nearby Attractions: Scharffen Berger chocolate tour (see page 81); Anchor Brewery tour (across the street, call 415-863-8350); downtown San Francisco attractions are 10–20 minutes away, including Wells Fargo Bank Museum (call 415-396-2619).

See color photos, page 3.

Bradbury & Bradbury

940 Tyler, Studio 12
Benicia, CA 94510
(707) 746-1900
www.bradbury.com

VICTORIAN WALLPAPER

The beautiful Victorian wallpaper from the movies *Hook,* featuring Robin Williams and Julia Roberts, *The American President,* and *James and the Giant Peach* came from this Victorian wallpaper factory. These movie sets joined Walt Disney World and Euro-Disney, as well as countless bed and breakfasts and restored Victorian homes, in using Bradbury & Bradbury's handprinted wall and ceiling papers.

The smell of oil-based paint permeates the printing area, where long sheets of paper lay across six tables, each about 30 yards long and 1 yard wide. You'll watch as workers repeatedly bend over a table, place the patterned screen onto the specially coated paper, stroke the squeegee through the ink to create the printed design, and then switch on a small overhead fan to quicken the drying. To avoid smudges, the screen is put down only every other pattern length. After doing this for all six tables, the printer scampers back to fill in the missing patterns.

In the art department, you'll learn the strategy behind redesigning ornate nineteenth-century wall and ceiling papers. In a process analogous to the design of Lego blocks, the artists meticulously draw the patterns by hand on graph paper and also on a computer design system, striving to create modular patterns that can fit together in any size room. Since B&B is a small company, you can stand next to the printers and artists as they work to reproduce the past.

Cost: Free for individuals as well as school and nonprofit groups. $1 per person for bus tours.
Freebies: No
Video Shown: No

Reservations Needed: Yes, for groups of 10 or more.
Days and Hours: Mon–Fri 9:00 AM–5:00 PM. Closed holidays.
Plan to Stay: 30 minutes
Minimum Age: None
Disabled Access: The studio is all on one floor, but you must climb a few flights of stairs to reach it.
Group Requirements: Groups of 10 or more should call 1 day in advance. Maximum group is 44 people. Fee for bus tours.
Special Information: Be sure to ask if papers will be in production when you plan to visit. The paint smell may bother some visitors. To make an appointment to see the on-site showroom, call (707) 746-6262.
Gift Area: Nothing formal, but you can look through the samples, purchase a catalog, and place orders. Catalog and design service kit available. Bargain bin offers discontinued wallpaper and seconds at great discounts, sometimes $1 per roll. Open same hours as above.
Directions: The company recommends you call for specific directions since there are many forks in the road. From I-80, take I-780 to the exit for 5th St. (the last Benicia exit coming from the Bay Area). From 5th St., turn left onto Military East. Follow this road down, around, and under a bridge until it ends on Tyler. Make a right on Tyler. The company is located on the second floor of an old military building occupied by several arts-related companies.
Nearby Attractions: Zellique, Nourot, and Smyers glassblowers studio tours (call 707-745-5710 or 707-745-2614); Old State Capitol Building.

Buck Knives

1900 Weld Boulevard
El Cajon, CA 92020
(619) 449-1100 / (800) 326-2825
www.buckknives.com

KNIVES

First started in 1902 by Hoyt Buck, Buck Knives is a far cry from the five knives a day that Hoyt and his son Al handwrought in a 100-square-foot plant in 1947. Now run by the third and fourth generations, with a fifth-generation tour guide, the company flourishes in a 200,000-square-foot plant, producing well over 50,000 knives per week.

At the first of the 15 stations you visit on your tour, you see the fine blanking machines. Used for thinner blades such as Folding Hunter and pocketknives, the fine blanking machines, operating like large hydraulic cookie cutters, punch out parts from flat, uncoiled stainless steel. Further down the line, notice the fiery red sparks underneath the thick steel at the laser machine. The laser cuts hairline patterns outlining the circumference of blades as well as decorative elk and deer profiles inside the blades. Double disk grinders put the first edge on the blades and the hollow grinders create a concave finish, if needed. To harden, the blades travel through a 50-foot continuous furnace, which heats the steel to 1976°, then a deep freezer at 121° below zero, and then another oven to raise the temperature.

On the oval assembly line, affectionately called "The Dog Track," blades and handles are riveted together. Watch a worker hold a knife against a laminated leather stropping wheel to achieve maximum blade sharpness, known as Edge2X technology. The C.A.T.R.A. machine tests the sharpness of the blades by lowering paper down so the knife can slice through it. A worker loads knives onto a conveyer belt, which feeds into the Harper Buffer, which, much like a car wash, rotates and polishes the brass and handles. After this tour, you'll want to peel an apple or cut some nautical rope with a new, sharp Buck knife.

Cost: Free
Freebies: Logoed trinket

Video Shown: No

Reservations Needed: No, but recommended. Required for groups over 12 people.

Days and Hours: Mon–Thur 10:00 AM, 12:00 PM, 1:00 PM. Closed holidays and weeks around July 4th, Christmas, and New Year's.

Plan to Stay: 45 minutes, plus additional time in the company store.

Minimum Age: Children under 7 must be well supervised by an adult.

Disabled Access: Yes

Group Requirements: Groups over 12 people should call at least 2 weeks in advance. Maximum group size is 24 people, which will be split into 2 groups.

Special Information: Photography permitted only in designated locations. Very noisy, but headset blocks out noise so you can hear tour guide only. No open-toed shoes allowed.

Gift Shop: H.H. Buck and Son's Company Store sells Buck knives at a 20% discount, plus logoed T-shirts, mugs, etc. Open Mon–Thur 10:00 AM–3:00 PM. Closed holidays and weeks around July 4th and New Year's.

Directions: From San Diego, take I-5 North to I-8 East. Take Rt. 67 North. Turn left onto Bradley Rd. and right onto Cuyamaca Rd. Turn left onto Weld Blvd. Buck Knives is on the right. From Los Angeles, take I-5 South to Rt. 52 East until it ends. Turn left onto Mission Gorge Rd. and right onto Cuyamaca Rd. Turn right onto Weld Blvd. Buck Knives is on the right.

Nearby Attractions: Taylor Guitars tour (see page 84); Alpine Hunting Lodge; Qualcomm Stadium; Viejas Casino and Outlet Mall; San Diego's attractions about 30 minutes away include San Diego Zoo, San Diego Aerospace Museum, Natural History Museum in Balboa Park, and Sea World Adventure Park.

Callaway Golf

2180 Rutherford Road
Carlsbad, CA 92008
(760) 930-8687
www.callawaygolf.com

Callaway ®
G O L F

GOLF CLUBS, BALLS, AND PUTTERS

Callaway Golf Company designs and builds technologically advanced products to help golfers of all skill levels find more enjoyment from the game. The Carlsbad, California-based company revolutionized the industry with its Big Bertha line of drivers. The friendly, oversize clubs were named after a powerful World War I German cannon and helped position the company as the world's largest manufacturer of premium golf clubs. In recent years, the company has expanded its product line to include state-of-the-art golf ball manufacturing, as well as assembly of its best-selling Odyssey putter brand.

With some 25 golf club manufacturers in the area, Carlsbad is often called the Golf Club Capital of the United States. As the largest factory, Callaway Golf sprawls across more than 700,000 square feet of workspace in eight buildings, plus three greens at its private, 8.1-acre research facility where pros often stop by to test and tweak the latest products.

You can tour its 80,000-square-foot club assembly plant, which utilizes cellular or "lean" manufacturing to efficiently speed the latest steel, titanium, or carbon composite clubs through teams of cross-trained employees. You can see how each clubhead and shaft are assembled by hand, then weighed and adjusted using computer technology to ensure swingweight accuracy within tenths of a gram. Clubs are then detailed, inspected, packaged, and sent to the distribution center for worldwide shipping.

Down the street, the 225,000-square-foot golf ball manufacturing facility has state-of-the-art equipment that makes golf balls from core to cover. You can see automated machinery mix, mill, and compress rubber and tungsten for the core, then send the spheres down the line for subsequent layers of ionomer and urethane that will be crafted by machines and robots into the company's premium two- and three-piece golf balls. The company's most advanced ball technology, the HX, features a revolutionary new cover pattern that replaces traditional dimples with a network of pentagons and hexagons for improved aerodynamic efficiency.

Cost: Free

Freebies: Catalog, logo golf ball, and coupon for free soft drink and cookie.

Video Shown: No

Reservations Needed: Yes. Groups, see below.

Days and Hours: Club assembly tour: Mon–Fri 9:15 AM and 3:30 PM. Ball manufacturing tour: Mon–Fri 11:00 AM and 2:00 PM. Arrive 10 minutes early to sign nondisclosure waiver. Closed holidays and occasionally for plant maintenance.

Plan to Stay: 45–60 minutes for each tour.

Minimum Age: 6. Children must be able to wear safety goggles.

Disabled Access: Wheelchairs permitted. No crutches, canes, or walkers.

Group Requirements: Groups larger than 120 people should call 2 weeks in advance. Large groups are divided into groups of no more than 50 people.

Special Information: Comfortable, flat-heeled, closed-toe shoes are required for 1 mile of walking. No photography in plant.

Gift Shop: Employee store is part of tour, not open to the public. Sells shirts, golf balls, and other logoed items. Maps available showing nearby dealers who sell Callaway golf clubs.

Directions: From San Diego, take I-5 North. Take Palomar Airport Rd. exit. Turn right at end of exit. Turn left onto College Blvd. into industrial park. Take first right onto Aston St. At dead end, turn right onto Rutherford Rd. Follow to second to last building on right.

Nearby Attractions: LEGOLAND and Taylor Guitars tours (see pages 73 and 84); Nearby golf-club manufacturers occasionally give tours: Taylor Made (call 760-931-1991) and Acushnet (call 760-929-0377); Aviara golf course; Old Carlsbad; Carlsbad State Beach.

Fleetwood

5300 Via Ricardo
Riverside, CA 92509
(800) 326-8633
www.fleetwood.com

FLEETWOOD.

With its 32 different brands of RVs, Fleetwood is the largest manufacturer of recreational vehicles in the U.S.A. You can tour the plant that makes the Bounder, the number-one-selling motor home in North America, and the Southwind factory across the street. When introduced in 1985, with its jumping kangaroo logo, the Bounder revolutionized the motor-home industry with its patented basement and affordable price. Wearing a headset, you get to watch just about everything it takes to build an RV, except for the 12-mile road test.

The chassis yard is where production begins. Sitting in the sunny Southern California weather are five acres of Ford and Chevy chassis neatly arranged in long rows. These steel chassis are the foundation of Fleetwood's Power Platform. Once you're inside the plant, with its giant horseshoe-shaped assembly line, the Bounder seems to come together like a big puzzle. In fact, when the dash assembly is put over the engine, this marks what's referred to as the "zero point" for the modular construction of the RV.

Observing the Vacubond process used to build the walls, ceilings, and floors is most visitors' favorite part. All the pieces that make up the wall, including the fiberglass outside, the steel frame, and the vinyl interior wallpaper, are placed on a big table. As each layer goes down, glue is automatically sprayed along its surface. These walls-to-be are covered with what looks like plastic bags and locked down to the table. Vacuum hoses suck out all the air for one hour. This intense suction creates a perfect seal between the wall's layers. Fleetwood pioneered Vacubond construction for durability, plus thermal and sound insulation.

Construction of subparts seems to take place everywhere. You move in and out of the basement building, where the flooring layers come together, and see more carpentry at work in the cabinetry area. On another part of the line, a crane hoists the entire floor-and-basement assembly and sets it on the chassis. Workers scamper around to bolt the carriage together. Toward the back end of the horseshoe line, the Bounder enters the paint booths, and soon it moves to final finishing. Although the production takes about four days, RVs move at a pace that allows you to see the Bounder in all production stages.

Cost: Free

Freebies: Product brochures

Video Shown: 30-minute video on company history.

Reservations Needed: Preferred

Days and Hours: Tue, 10:00 AM. Closed holidays and between Christmas and New Year's. Tour times are subject to change; please call in advance.

Plan to Stay: 1–2 hours

Minimum Age: None, but children under 11 must be accompanied by an adult.

Disabled Access: Yes, but call ahead to make separate arrangements.

Group Requirements: No maximum group size, but should call 2 weeks ahead for space availability. Special times can be arranged for groups.

Special Information: May also see Flair, Southwind Storm, and Pace Arrow production during tour. No photography. Must wear closed-toe shoes. Tours at other Fleetwood RV plants throughout the U.S.A. available. Call (800) 444-4905 for information on other tours. Bounder tours also at Paxinos, PA.

Gift Counter: Sells T-shirts, hats, and other logoed items. Open Mon–Fri 8:00 AM–3:30 PM. Closed holidays.

Directions: From Los Angeles, take 60 Frwy. East. Exit at Market St. in Riverside. Turn left at exit onto Market St., right at Viacerro, which becomes Via Ricardo. Plant is on the left. Park in visitors' spaces at the appropriate plant.

Nearby Attractions: Graber Olive House tour (see page 68); Universal Studios, Paramount Pictures, and NBC Studios tours, approximately 60 miles west (see pages 85, 80, and 78); Lake Perris; Mission Inn; Disneyland, 45 miles west; Knott's Berry Farm, 40 miles west; Palm Springs.

Dreyer's & Edy's Grand Ice Cream

1250 Whipple Road
Union City, CA 94587
(510) 471-6622
www.dreyers.com
www.edys.com

Give 'em the good stuff.   Give 'em the good stuff.

ICE CREAM AND FROZEN YOGURT

William Dreyer and Joseph Edy started Dreyer's and Edy's Grand Ice Cream in 1928 on Grand Avenue in Oakland, California. Just one year later, they became famous by creating the world's first batch of Rocky Road ice cream. Now the company is the number-one premium ice-cream maker in the U.S.A. and the top exporter of premium ice cream to Japan. While your friendly guide sprinkles the tour with company trivia and industry facts, you'll learn, see, and taste how ice cream is made, from the cow to the cone.

After watching a video in the Double Scoop Depot, walk up marble fudge–colored stairs and take a walk down the Rocky Road to peer through glass windows overlooking the production floor. The assembly lines look like a maze of steel pipes and rapidly moving ice-cream containers. The base mix travels through the flavor vats, continuous flow freezer, and fruit feeders. Workers lift plastic bags of whatever ingredients are required for the flavor in production (perhaps strawberries for strawberry ice cream), pouring their contents into the feeder.

You first see the ice cream as it drops from the container-filler machines into round cartons. The windowed lids then twist down to cover the containers. At this point, the ice cream has the consistency of soft-serve. It moves through the inspection and shrink-wrap stations before resting in the hardening freezer for about seven hours at 40° below zero. This routine continues until workers produce up to 60,000 gallons per day, in some 20 flavors.

You'll shiver as you quickly pass through the gigantic warehouse and loading dock area, with wind chill temperatures 20°–30° below freezing. It's worth being cold for a few brisk moments to see the 1 million gallons of ice cream and frozen yogurt piled everywhere you look. At the end of the tour, you might run into John D. Harrison, the "Official Taster." The company insured his well-publicized taste buds for $1 million.

Cost: $2 per person

Freebies: Scoops of ice cream and frozen yogurt in your favorite flavors, and a bag of souvenir items that includes coupons, a factory poster, and a paper hat.

Video Shown: 11-minute video entitled "The Cool Facts" provides a close-up view of the ice-cream production process.

Reservations Needed: Yes. Prefers to consolidate individuals and families into a group tour.

Days and Hours: Mon–Fri 9:15 AM, 11:15 AM, and 2:00 PM. Closed holidays and week between Christmas and New Year's.

Plan to Stay: 1.5 hours including video, tour, and ice-cream tasting.

Minimum Age: 6

Disabled Access: Yes, except for 5 stairs into the freezer area.

Group Requirements: Maximum group size is 40 people, with reservations recommended approximately 2 months in advance.

Special Information: No photography. Freezer area can be refreshingly chilly, so warm-weather natives should bring a sweater. Wear flat-heeled shoes.

Gift Cabinet: The Double Scoop Depot has a gift cabinet with a small selection of logoed items, including T-shirts and book-covers. Open after tours.

Directions: Take I-880 to the Whipple Rd. exit. Make a right on Whipple Rd. The factory is about .7 mile ahead on the right.

Nearby Attractions: NUMMI auto plant tour (see page 79); C. F. Kennedy Community Center & Park; Town Estates Park; Oakland and San Francisco attractions about 30 minutes away.

▲ Visitors on the Dreyer's Grand Ice Cream tour visit the very chilly warehouse where almost 1 million gallons of ice cream are stored prior to delivery to supermarkets.

▼ Creamy ice cream fills cartons at Dreyer's & Edy's Grand Ice Cream in Union City, California.

Fortune Cookie Factory

261 12th Street
Oakland, CA 94607
(510) 832-5552

Did you ever wonder how the fortune got inside a fortune cookie? Ever want to write your own fortune? What you may think of as Chinese culinary secrets are revealed at the Fortune Cookie Factory, a 30-plus-year-old family business. Don't be disappointed, however, when the owner, a UC Berkeley–educated mechanical engineer, tells you that fortune cookies were not created in Asia. An ingenious Chinese restaurant owner in the U.S.A. invented them in the 1920s as an inexpensive and unique dessert.

Fortune cookies start as a mixture similar to pancake batter, made of whole-wheat flour, cane or beet sugar, water, and powdered whole eggs. Margarine, flavoring, and artificial coloring give the fortune cookies their golden color. A young Chinese worker concocts 100 pounds of batter in a vertical electric mixer, then races across the floor to pour it into one of the seven custom-made fortune-cookie machines. You will be mesmerized by the circular, methodical motion of this groaning machine. Batter flows through a spigot into individual 3-inch-diameter waffle irons. The individual plates clamp shut for their 4-minute circular journey through the 225° piano-shaped oven. Small, wafer-thin pancakes emerge, cooked on both sides and pressed to squeeze out all air pockets.

With great dexterity the worker seated in front of each oven removes each pancake, randomly grabs a fortune from her lap, places it on the pancake, folds the pancake in half like a taco, and bends it around a metal rod. For cooling, the cookies are placed points-down in a holding tray. Listen to the women chatter in Chinese while they hand-fold 15 to 16 fortune cookies per minute, or 50,000 per day.

Cost: $1 per person
Freebies: Sample bag of fortune cookies.
Video Shown: No
Reservations Needed: Not for viewing of the production process from the entrance of the production area. Yes for guided ex-

planation. Individuals need to latch onto guided group tours.

Days and Hours: Mon–Fri 10:00 AM–3:00 PM, but may want to call to check if English-speaking person is available. Closed major Chinese and some U.S. holidays.

Plan to Stay: 15 minutes for viewing, plus time for gift counter.

Minimum Age: 7, unless with family

Disabled Access: Yes

Group Requirements: Maximum group size is 25 people, which requires reservations 1 week in advance for guided tour.

Special Information: When the owner is there, he will gladly answer questions and tell you about his appearance on TV's *What's My Line?*, otherwise, look for a 1-page handout on the business and fortune cookie–making process.

Gift Counter: Small retail shop at front of factory sells bags of regular and flavored (e.g., strawberry, lime) fortune cookies, along with sassy and X-rated versions. You can also order customized fortune cookies (various sizes and messages, even with an engagement ring, if desired) and purchase bags of "misfortunes," which are broken fortune cookies. Price information available at above number. Open Mon–Fri 9:00 AM–4:30 PM.

Directions: From north of Oakland, take I-980 South and get off at the 11th/12th St. exit. Make a left onto 11th St. Turn left onto Alice and left onto 12th. Look for the factory storefront on the left side of 12th St. From south of Oakland, take I-880 North to Oak St. exit. Turn right at first intersection. Turn left on 12th. Storefront on left side.

Nearby Attractions: Golden Gate Fortune Cookies, in San Francisco's Chinatown, is a smaller business that has a viewing area near the retail counter (call 415-781-3956); Lotus Fortune Cookies, near San Francisco's city hall, uses an automated system to insert fortunes (call 415-552-0759); Oakland's Chinatown; Madison Park; Lake Merritt; Oakland Museum; San Francisco's attractions are across the Bay Bridge.

Frederick's of Hollywood Lingerie Museum

6608 Hollywood Boulevard
Hollywood, CA 90028
(323) 466-8506
www.fredericks.com

LINGERIE

Magical and mysterious and exciting things happen in Hollywood. So it doesn't surprise us that the sites and sounds of Hollywood range from the rich and famous to the theatrical. On Hollywood Boulevard alone, they span from Graumann's Chinese Theatre and Ripley's Believe It or Not to the Frederick's of Hollywood Lingerie Museum. Frederick's of Hollywood's stunning historic art deco building stands out on Hollywood Boulevard as a point of interest not to be missed.

Frederick's of Hollywood's flagship store opened in the building in 1946 when Frederick Mellinger brought the much-anticipated European fashions to American women, most notably black lingerie. In the 1950s, the company's designers introduced the Rising Star—the world's first pushup bra. In 1981, the company introduced the Thong panty. In 1998, Frederick's introduced its most recent bra innovation, the Liquid Lift, which uses fluid to create a natural feel and has since become one of Frederick's most popular bras.

To enter the Lingerie Museum you'll wind your way through current Frederick's of Hollywood fashions. Display cases along the walls show the changes in Frederick's lingerie and bra fashions over the years, and feature the Celebrity Lingerie Hall of Fame. Some of the historical highlights include black lace panties from Zsa Zsa Gabor, Judy Garland's nightgown, Lana Turner's slip, Ingrid Bergman's corset, and a girdle worn by Ethel Merman in *There's No Business like Show Business*. Two bras from Cher (one black, one white) and Madonna's black-and-gold bustier (with tassels, of course) worn during her "Who's That Girl?" tour bring the collection up to date. Not to leave men out, there are Tom Hanks' boxer shorts worn in the film *Forrest Gump*. You will leave surprised, bedazzled, and ready to shop.

Cost: Free

Freebies: No

Video Shown: No

Reservations Needed: No

Days and Hours: Mon–Fri 10:00 AM–9:00 PM, Sat 10:00 AM–7:00 PM, Sun 11:00 AM–6:00 PM.

Plan to Stay: 15 minutes, plus time in retail store.

Minimum Age: None, except discretion advised.

Disabled Access: Steps to get to museum area.

Group Requirements: None

Special Information: None

Gift Shop: Sells bras, teddies and panties, baby dolls and pajamas, corsets and hosiery. Open same hours as museum.

Directions: From Hwy. 101, take Vine St. exit. Go south and turn right onto Hollywood Blvd. Museum located at intersection with Whitley Ave.

Nearby Attractions: Graumann's Chinese Theatre (call 323-464-8111); Ripley's Believe It or Not; Guinness World of Records Museum (call 323-462-5991 or 323-463-6433).

Graber Olive House

315 East 4th Street
Ontario, CA 91764
(909) 983-1761 / (800) 996-5483
www.graberolives.com

Graber Olive House

OLIVES

Companies that mass-produce California olives tell you that the black, pitted variety found on pizzas and supermarket shelves are natural and tree-ripened. After visiting the Graber Olive House, you will know what these terms really mean. The C. C. Graber Co. is the oldest olive packer (1894) in the only U.S. state that produces olives.

A picker, who holds only a few olives in his hand at one time and drops them gently into a felt-bottomed bucket, carefully removes the cherry-red fruits from the tree. Mass-produced California "ripe" black olives are green when harvested, and then oxidized a uniform black to hide bruises. Graber olives turn a natural nut-like color in processing.

After viewing pictures of the olives and groves, you're led through the company's production area. In the grading room, smock-clad women face a conveyor belt and carefully pick "culls" (overripe, underripe, or imperfect) out of the olive procession before them. More than 1 million olives roll by the graders during an eight-hour shift. The perfect olives then move to the vat room where, using the Graber family recipe, they are stirred, soaked, and tended for about three weeks in round cement vats. After the careful curing process removes the olives' natural bitterness, they are ready to be canned.

The pampered olives undergo a thorough canning and sterilization process. Workers, using the "hand-pack filling machine," scoop olives into cans as they pass under a wheel. Paddles on the "Panama-paddle packer" rotate and push a small amount of water out of each can, forming a headspace for steam. The machine then hermetically seals each can. In the boiler room, carts filled with sealed cans of olives are rolled into a retort. The door is closed, and the olives are sterilized with 242° steam from the boiler (like that on an old train) for more than an hour. Finally, the cans are labeled with the Graber name familiar to gourmets around the world.

Cost: Free

Freebies: The "hospitality bowl" is filled with free olive samples.

Video Shown: 12-minute video on canning process.

Reservations Needed: No, except for groups of 10 or more people.

Days and Hours: Mon–Sat 9:30 AM–4:30 PM, Sun 10:00 AM–4:30 PM. Lunch break from 12:00 PM–1:30 PM. Tours are conducted all year, but grading, curing, and canning only take place in October and early November. Closed Christmas, Thanksgiving, New Year's, Easter, and July 4th.

Plan to Stay: 30 minutes for tour, plus time for museum and gift shop. Museum contains an original grading machine made by C. C. Graber and other items related to the olive business. Lawn area available for picnics.

Minimum Age: None

Disabled Access: Yes

Group Requirements: Groups larger than 10 people should call 1 week in advance. Large groups will be split into groups of 20.

Special Information: When the factory is not in production, tour goes through canning plant with a colorful explanation and photographs of the process.

Gift Shop: The Casa del Olivo Fancy Food and Gift Shop sells Graber olives, nuts, dates, fancy foods, gift baskets, candies, toys, cookbooks, and unusual pottery. La Casita sells kitchen supplies and works by local artists. Open Mon–Sat 9:00 AM–5:30 PM and Sun 9:30 AM–6:00 PM. Catalog is available at (800) 996-5483.

Directions: From Los Angeles and Palm Springs, take I-10 (San Bernardino Frwy.) to Ontario. Take the Euclid Ave. exit, then south to 4th St. Turn left onto 4th St. Graber Olive House will be on your left.

Nearby Attractions: Fleetwood Motor Homes factory tour (see page 63); San Antonio Winery tasting room (call 909-947-3995); Claremont Colleges; Griswald Center; Mission Inn.

Hershey's Visitors Center

120 South Sierra
Oakdale, CA 95361-9368
(209) 848-8126
www.hersheys.com

Hershey Foods Corporation

CHOCOLATE

"Wow, smell the chocolate!" will be your first words as you enter the Gift Shoppe. Hershey Foods Corporation, founded in 1894 by Milton S. Hershey in the small Pennsylvania town later named after him, is the country's largest candy maker; it makes approximately 33 million Kisses per day. Hershey's Oakdale plant makes fresh treats for the West Coast.

The video that is shown at the Gift Shoppe makes you feel as if you're in the factory. Listen to the history of Milton S. Hershey and how he started his successful chocolate factory. The video takes you through the process of where the raw ingredients come from right down to the finished chocolate bars. You will see the 10,000-pound vats called conch machines. The conch machines' granite rollers move back and forth on corrugated granite beds to create smooth chocolate paste from a mixture of cocoa butter, sugar, milk, and chocolate liquid.

You will see views of the high-speed computerized production lines that build well-known Hershey products such as the top-selling Reese's Peanut Butter Cups. After the brown paper cups land on a moving belt, they are lined with milk chocolate and then a layer of peanut butter. The top layer of chocolate is air-blown on and vibrated to ensure a smooth surface. In the wrapping and packaging area the peanut-butter cups move so quickly on a sophisticated "freeway" system that they deserve a speeding ticket. Even watch on the video each Hershey's Kiss, one of the most recognizable shapes in the world, receive its own silver evening gown and paper necklace.

Cost: Free
Freebies: Free candy bar for scheduled school groups only.
Videos Shown: 15-minute video, "The Cocoa Bean Story," about the production process; 22-minute video about Milton Hershey by Arts & Entertainment TV.

Reservations Needed: No, for Visitors Center. Yes, for prearranged school group factory tours.

Days and Hours: Mon–Sat 9:00 AM–5:00 PM, Thur until 7:00 PM. Closed holidays.

Plan to Stay: 30 minutes to watch tour video, plus time for Gift Shoppe.

Minimum Age: None

Disabled Access: Yes

Group Requirements: School groups only call (209) 848-5100, ext. 5625, at least 1 month in advance. No maximum group size. Pre-arranged scheduled school groups Tue, Thur, and Fri 8:30 AM–3:00 PM.

Special Information: See page 287 about the simulated factory tour at Hershey's Chocolate World in Hershey, PA.

Gift Shoppe: Sells Hershey's candy, T-shirts, and gifts, including teddy bears holding stuffed Kisses. Exhibits include a model 1915 wrapping machine. Open Mon–Sat 9:00 AM–5:00 PM, Thur until 7:00 PM. Closed holidays.

Directions: From San Francisco, take I-580 East to I-205 East. Take Hwy. 120 East to intersection of Hwys. 108 and 120. Go through intersection, travel 1 block, and turn left onto G St. Parking is on right. From Yosemite, take Hwy. 120 West. Continue on Hwy. 108/120 to Oakdale. Turn left onto Yosemite St. Turn left onto G St. Parking is on right. Phone recording has directions.

Nearby Attractions: Oakdale Cowboy Museum (call 209-847-7049); Oakdale Museum; Oakdale Brewing Company (call 209-845-BREW); Oakdale Cheese tour (call 209-848-3139); Delicato Vineyard tour (call 209-825-6212); Hershey's Visitors Center has list of additional nearby attractions and events.

Intel

Corporate Museum, Robert N. Noyce Building
2200 Mission College Boulevard
Santa Clara, CA 95052-8119
(408) 765-0503
www.intel.com/go/museum

intel. MUSEUM

COMPUTER CHIPS

Few U.S. companies embody the computer revolution like the Intel Corporation. The company recently expanded its museum to 10,000 square feet. It features five interactive areas—Intel History, Microprocessors, Applications Lab, Chip Design, and Chip Fabrication—where you'll learn how microprocessors (computer chips) are made, how they work, their effect on our lives, and their evolution. You'll also learn about Intel, the inventor of the microprocessor and the world's leading computer-chip manufacturer.

Located in Intel's headquarters at the heart of Silicon Valley, the museum looks futuristic and high tech with its display cases of silver-brushed steel and aluminum, glowing with a rainbow array of lights. Enter through the newest exhibit, Intel History. The evolution of the company is depicted through artifacts and stories sure to entertain, whether or not you have technical insight.

In the Applications Lab, notice a mannequin wearing a "bunny suit." (No, it doesn't have giant ears.) The workers who build computer chips wear this fully enclosed white suit, complete with air packs to filter their breathing. Computer-chip making requires factories thousands of times cleaner than hospital operating rooms. You can even try on pieces of the suit yourself in the Chip Fabrication area. Compare the modern "bunny suit" to the garments worn in the first Intel factory, displayed in the Microprocessors area's Then&Now section.

You cannot tour the factories where Intel actually makes its chips, so Intel brings the factory to you—the museum has monitors that show you the action occurring in the factories right at that moment! At the push of a button, you can hear what employees have to say about working in a chip-making factory.

The museum's exhibits appeal to all levels of technical knowledge and interest. Some are amusing, like the 10-foot-square talking microprocessor, and some are high tech, like the Chip Design area, where you can compare the dimensions of computer circuitry to the maze of a fingerprint, but all are informative and interesting.

Cost: Free

Freebies: No

Video Shown: Various video interviews with Intel engineers and scientists shown on kiosks.

Reservations Needed: No, except for scheduled guided group tours.

Days and Hours: Mon–Fri 9:00 AM–6:00 PM, Sat 10:00 AM–5:00 PM. Closed holidays.

Plan to Stay: About 1 hour, depending on your computer and engineering background and your desire to try the hands-on displays.

Minimum Age: None, but 12 is the recommended minimum. Displays have interactive components, enjoyed most by children interested in computers or science.

Disabled Access: Yes

Group Requirements: Maximum group size is 25 people, or 35 students. Minimum 8 people to be considered a group. Mon–Fri 10:00 AM–4:00 PM. Call (408) 765-0503 at least 1 month in advance to schedule a group tour.

Special Information: Dress appropriately—the museum is located in Intel's corporate headquarters. Bags and backpacks not permitted. No coat check. Various exhibits change regularly to highlight recent technical developments.

Intel Museum Store: Sells authentic Silicon Valley merchandise, including apparel, pens, gifts, computer devices, toys, and other items. Open same hours as museum.

Directions: Take Rt. 101 to the Montague Expwy. East. Turn left onto Mission College Blvd. The Robert N. Noyce Building is on left. Museum is to the left of the lobby and can be entered through a plaza directly in front of the building.

Nearby Attractions: Stanford Linear Accelerator Center tour (call 650-926-2204); Tech Museum of Innovation (call 408-294-8324); San Jose Children's Discovery Museum (call 408-298-5437); Great America Theme Park (call 408-988-1776).

▲ Children visiting the Intel Museum in Santa Clara, California, try on "bunny suit" outfits worn by workers in the ultra-clean computer chip factories.

Visitors at the Intel Museum use a hands-on exhibit to spell words using the "binary code" language
▼ of computers.

Jelly Belly Candy Co.

One Jelly Belly Lane
Fairfield, CA 94533
(707) 428-2838
www.jellybelly.com

JELLY BEANS, CHOCOLATES, AND GUMMI CANDIES

If you question whether former president Ronald Reagan's policies were good for the U.S. economy or for kids, then you should visit this factory that produces millions of jelly beans per day, or 14 billion beans annually. The publicity surrounding President Reagan's fondness for gourmet Jelly Belly jelly beans led to increased demand, round-the-clock shifts, a new factory, and amusing tours for children and adults. The company has been making candy since 1898, but it was the introduction of the Jelly Belly in 1976 that spurred its modern growth.

While you'll see how the company makes a variety of creative candies, such as its line of Pet Gummi candies, the highlight is watching how it makes the Jelly Belly beans in more than 40 flavors. At the tour's beginning, you'll stare at large mosaic portraits of famous faces and figures such as Ronald Reagan and the Statue of Liberty, each made of 14,000 jelly beans. Follow your tour guide along Jelly Belly Candy Trail, an elevated walkway inside the 215,000-square-foot factory. View the beans at different stages of their creation. Be prepared for intense aromas. Unlike standard jelly beans, Jelly Belly beans are flavored both in the center and in the shell. Machines pour the special bean-center mixture into cornstarch molds that hold 1,260 centers per tray. Guess the exotic flavors, like strawberry daiquiri or peanut butter, as the bean centers travel by in the distance.

After the centers harden overnight, mechanical arms flip the trays over, and the centers are placed into spinning, open stainless steel drums. Here, workers add four layers of flavored syrup and sugars to create the outer shells. Each bean is automatically checked for correct size and color before traveling through the bagging and boxing machines. You'll look down at a hopper filled with a colorful and flavorful sea of jelly beans. The correctly weighed amount of jelly beans drops into plastic packets below. However, workers hand-pack the Gummi candies, which are too sticky for machines.

Cost: Free

Freebies: 3-ounce bag of Jelly Belly beans with an official menu matching colors to flavors. Logoed paper hat to wear during the tour.

Videos Shown: Short videos show close-up view of candy making on weekends.

Reservations Needed: No

Days and Hours: Mon–Sun 9:00 AM–5:00 PM. No production on weekends, but see production video. Closed holidays and the last week in June through the first week of July.

Plan to Stay: 40 minutes, plus time for candy kitchen, café, and gift shop.

Minimum Age: None, with 1 adult for every 6 children.

Disabled Access: Yes

Group Requirements: None

Special Information: No photography. Jelly Belly Center in Wisconsin also gives tours (see page 356). In exhibition candy kitchen, view candy makers hand-dipping chocolates and making toffee and caramel apples.

Retail Store: Sells more flavors of jelly beans than you can imagine (not only exotic fruit tastes, but also unusual flavors like toasted marshmallow, buttered popcorn, and jalapeño). Look for 2-pound bags of Belly Flops, factory seconds. Open Mon–Sun 9:00 AM–5:00 PM. Jelly Belly Café serves Jelly Belly–shaped pizzas, hamburgers, and buns. Ice cream counter.

Directions: From the San Francisco/Oakland area, take I-80 East to Hwy. 12 East. Turn right onto Beck Ave., right onto Courage Dr., right onto North Watney Way, and right onto Jelly Belly Ln. From Sacramento, take Abernathy exit left to Hwy. 12 East, then follow the above directions.

Nearby Attractions: In the same industrial park, Anheuser-Busch (Budweiser) Brewery tour (call 707-429-7595), Thompson Candy self-guided tour (call 707-435-1140), and VG Buck Olive Oil tasting (call 800-865-4836); Marine World Africa U.S.A.; Seguin Moreau barrel making tour (see page 82), Napa Valley wineries, and Culinary Institute of America located 20 minutes away.

See color photos, page 5.

LEGOLAND

One LEGOLAND Drive
Carlsbad, CA 92008
(760) 918-5346
www.legoland.com

LEGO BRICKS, LEGO MODELS, THEME PARK

Thirty million LEGO bricks were used to create the 5,000 LEGOLAND models decorating the park. And they're not the simple constructions you may have built as a child. Miniland includes an incredibly accurate four-foot-tall replica of the White House, complete with tiny LEGO visitors. Near-life-size LEGO lions, giraffes, and elephants abound. Head over to the factory tour to see brick making, then to the model shop to watch model assembly.

At the Factory Tour, see animated miniaturized versions of the machines that mold, paint, and package LEGO bricks. In the first room, watch as the injection mold machine molds a brick. In another, see "partially assembled" pieces created, like little wheels being attached to little axles for LEGO cars.

In the Model Shop, watch the video in the breezeway and peer through the glass to see the model makers at work. You may see one of them sketching a building—like New York's Chrysler Building—or creating an architectural drawing on LEGO graph paper of a 1:20 scale model.

The next step in creating a LEGO model is the prototype. The prototype may be a smaller version or even just one section of the model; if the model is symmetrical, the model makers may build just half of it. For a LEGO Donny Osmond, half the head was created as a prototype and then a mirror was held up to see the complete Donny. A prototype's bricks are not glued together, making changes easier. Look for model prototypes displayed behind the glass at the Model Shop, and the finished models throughout the park.

Afterward, see the gluing of the model. Tubes with brushes on the ends hang from what look like IV bags suspended from the ceiling. The glue runs from the bag into the brush as the model makers brush the glue onto every LEGO brick, assembling the final model. Pipes suck glue fumes out of the air, protecting the model makers. Once the bricks are glued together, the model is coated with UV protectant so it can withstand the California sun.

Cost: Included in admission charge to the LEGOLAND Park.

Freebies: No

Video Shown: 10-minute video on model-making process at Model Shop and 5-minute video on packaging and shipping at Factory Tour.

Reservations Needed: No

Days and Hours: Hours change frequently. Please check the website.

Plan to Stay: All day at LEGOLAND. 15 minutes for Model Shop tour and video, 15 minutes for Factory Tour video and tour, plus time for gift shop.

Minimum Age: None, but is designed for families with children ages 3 to 12.

Disabled Access: Yes

Group Requirements: School groups must make reservations 3 weeks in advance (call 760-918-KIDS). Groups may get discount if they call in advance, depending on size.

Special Information: Youth Group programs include day camps. LEGO is a contraction of the Danish words *leg godt,* meaning "play well." In Latin it means "I put together" or "I assemble."

Gift Shop: Seasonally sells make 'n' take models made at the model shop. Make your own LEGO creations and purchase what you make. Open same hours as LEGOLAND.

Directions: From I-5, take Cannon Rd. exit in Carlsbad. Go east, following signs to LEGOLAND Dr.

Nearby Attractions: LEGOLAND's 40 LEGO-themed attractions, rides and shows; Callaway Golf and Taylor Guitars tours (see pages 62 and 84).

Los Angeles Times

202 West 1st Street
Los Angeles, CA 90012
(213) 237-5757
www.latimes.com

Los Angeles Times

If you ever wondered how that story in your newspaper got there, you'll enjoy touring the *Los Angeles Times*. The sound of clattering typewriters has given way to the relative quiet of computers in the newsroom. This tour of one of the world's great newspapers begins with the history of the *Times* and how it has grown along with the Southern California region. Then, you'll visit the newsroom, where a vast expanse of reporters work busily on late-breaking stories and rush to meet deadlines.

Discover that the Food Department has an ultra-modern, full working kitchen, where staff members carefully taste-test dishes before the recipes appear in the paper. See how the Editorial Department works, learn about the paper's different editions, and walk by the library (known as the "morgue") and photography areas, containing more than 4.5 million negatives. Photography buffs will enjoy the magnificent display of old cameras used by *Times* photographers. Huge black cameras with giant flashbulbs recall a time before television, when newspapers were almost our only eyes on the world. In the composing room, every page of the paper is carefully laid out with stories and ads before being printed.

The *Times* printing plant, two miles away, is open by reservation. You'll see the state-of-the-art pressroom, which extends nearly the length of two football fields, and the newsprint storage area, where robot-like automated vehicles carry 2,500-pound rolls of newsprint. While you'll see very few people, you will hear and see the beeping and flashing robots as they glide around. Visit plate making, where newspaper pages are converted from photographic negatives to aluminum printing plates, and observe the distribution system that takes newspapers from the press to the delivery truck. It's exciting to watch the newspaper-printing process in this massive, super-automated plant.

Cost: Free

Freebies: *Times* pencil, plus reporter's notepad for those 18 or under.

Video Shown: No

Reservations Needed: Yes, call 1 week in advance. Printing plant tour: individuals latch onto group tours.

Days and Hours: Editorial tour: Tue and Thur 1:30 PM. Printing plant tour: see group information below. Closed holidays.

Plan to Stay: 45 minutes to 1 hour for either tour.

Minimum Age: 10, or 5th grade

Disabled Access: Yes

Group Requirements: Groups larger than 10 people need to call 1 month in advance. Group tours are by reservation Mon–Fri 9:30 AM, 11:00 AM, and 1:30 PM for either plant. Call (213) 237-5757 to schedule. Maximum group size is 20 people.

Special Information: The *Times'* Globe Lobby contains circa-1935 murals, a rotating globe of the world, and a historical display.

Gift Counter: Sells logoed pens, jackets, mugs, and shoulder bags. Open Mon–Fri 8:00 AM–4:00 PM.

Directions: Editorial Plant: From Frwy. 101 South heading toward downtown L.A. (past Frwy. 110), take Broadway exit. Turn right onto Spring St. Pass the *Times* entrance at the corner of 1st and Spring Sts. and park in the *Times* garage at 213 S. Spring St. From Frwy. 10 East, exit onto one-way Spring St. Follow directions above. Olympic Printing Plant: directions provided with reservations.

Nearby Attractions: Paramount Pictures, Universal Studios, and Warner Bros. Studios, tours (see pages 80, 85, and 86) are 7–15 miles away; NBC Studios tour (see page 78), about 30 minutes away; Museum of Contemporary Art; The Music Center; Little Tokyo; Olvera Street.

Marin French Cheese

7500 Red Hill Road
Petaluma, CA 94952
(707) 762-6001 / (800) 292-6001
www.marinfrenchcheese.com

CHEESE

Thousands of miles away from France, this fifth-generation company has been making Camembert, Brie, and other soft-ripened French cheeses under the Rouge et Noir label since 1900. The Thompson family started at their ranch location in 1865, when they hand-dug the original cellar, which is still in use today. Until the 1950s they made their own wooden boxes for the individual cheeses.

While you wait in the cool cellar for your tour you can look at some of this old equipment, including a 1906 box-making machine. Follow your tour guide down the hall to look through windows into each of the small cheese-making rooms.

In the Make Room, the white, chunky, cottage cheese–like curds are poured from buckets into rows of metal molds that resemble empty baked-bean cans. As the molds are filled with four inches of curd, white liquid whey pours out. The whey continues to drain out until the curd is only one inch thick. The cheese stays in the molds for approximately 18 hours.

Across the hall in the Salt Room, the cheese, now removed from the molds, soaks in salt brine. The Brie wheels soak the longest. Although you cannot go down to the aging cellars, the tour guide explains that the Camembert and Brie sit in the cellar for about 11 days so the edible mold can develop on the outside of the cheese.

Next, walk upstairs to watch women seated at a table hand-packing the cheese. In the adjacent tasting area are historical photographs of the company's earlier cheese-making methods, awards its cheeses have won, and a display of all its products. On a red-and-white-checked tablecloth, cheeses for tasting sit invitingly on red-and-black logoed porcelain plates covered by glass cheese domes. After you sample the cheeses, you'll be ready for your own wine-and-cheese picnic.

Cost: Free

Freebies: Crackers and cheese samples in the tasting area and sales room; recipe brochure.

Video Shown: No (possible in future)

Reservations Needed: Yes

Days and Hours: Production times vary; call ahead. Tours generally on the hour Mon–Sun 10:00 AM–4:00 PM. Best time to see production is 1:00 PM, when the curds are poured. No production on weekends.

Plan to Stay: 20 minutes for tour, plus time in sales room and on 5-acre grounds, which include duck pond and picnic tables.

Minimum Age: None

Disabled Access: Yes

Group Requirements: Groups over 10 people should call 5 days in advance. No maximum group size.

Special Information: Can rent barbecue area for weddings and parties.

Sales Room: Sells all the Rouge et Noir cheeses (including flavored Bries), wine, bread, sandwiches, and other picnic supplies. Offers gift assortment packs and logoed aprons, wineglasses, T-shirts, and caps. Open Mon–Sun 9:00 AM–5:00 PM.

Directions: From San Francisco, take Hwy. 101 North to Novato. Turn left onto San Marin Dr., right onto Novato Blvd., and left onto Petaluma–Pt. Reyes Rd. You can't miss the giant cheese-wheel sign .25 miles ahead on right. From Santa Rosa, take Hwy. 101 South to Petaluma. Turn right onto E. Washington St., left onto Payran St., and right onto D St. Continue about 9 miles past the town. Marin French Cheese will be on your right.

Nearby Attractions: Sonoma Cheese self-guided tour (call 800-535-2855); Pt. Reyes National Seashore; Bodega Bay; Petaluma Adobe State Historic Park; Petaluma Historical Library; The Great Petaluma Mill.

Mrs. Grossman's

3810 Cypress Drive
Petaluma, CA 94954
(707) 763-1700 / (800) 429-4549
www.mrsgrossmans.com

STICKERS

Mrs. Grossman is Andrea Grossman—a name legendary among sticker collectors and scrapbookers. She is president and founder of Mrs. Grossman's Paper Company, the oldest and largest decorative sticker manufacturer in the U.S. Started in 1975 as a stationery line, Mrs. Grossman introduced Stickers by the Yard in 1979 after satisfying a customer's request for a simple red heart sticker for Valentine's Day. Now the company has a heart as a logo and a motto—its mission statement focuses on treating employees, vendors, and customers respectfully, caringly, and honestly.

When you walk into the recently expanded 110,000-square-foot striking glass plant overlooking a bird sanctuary, you will feel like you have walked into someone's life. In the lobby, the soft-red furniture will welcome you. Walk up the glass stairs under the magical neon Mrs. Grossman's sign. Along the walls all around you is a sticker museum showing the sticker designs from the company's beginning—you may find yourself remembering some of the retired stickers such as the camel and the kangaroo.

After watching a video and perhaps winning some prizes during a question-and-answer session, venture into the factory. This is such a friendly place—wave to the employees and they will wave back. In the printing department, your tour guide may quiz you on how many hours it takes to make 400,000 stickers (10 hours—four to set up, four for printing, and two for cleaning and maintenance). Amazingly, six massive 10-color presses pour out 360,000 stickers an hour. You may notice an ammonia smell—ammonia helps the ink dry faster.

A tour highlight is the high-tech, 20-foottall, computer-driven LaserWeb that resembles a space ship with flashing lights, countless control panels, and four monitors. A camera inside the machine allows you to watch as the laser passes over a copper template, shooting a design onto a sticker. Watch on a giant video screen as a 10,000°F laser causes paper molecules to explode, creating intricate, fanciful details such as

lace for scrapbooks and heritage albums. Follow your guide into the warehouse where rolls of stickers are stacked 40 feet high, storing 3,000 miles of stickers. At the end of the tour, you can make a hands-on card or scrapbook project. You leave with a feeling that loving kindness prevails—you may even want to work here.

Cost: Free

Freebies: Stickers

Video Shown: 20-minute award-winning video narrated by the company's favorite dog, Angus, an Australian shepherd. Covers the life of a 20-cent sticker from concept to design, prepress to printing, and sales to shipping.

Reservations Needed: Yes

Days and Hours: Mon–Fri 9:30 AM, 11:00 AM, 1:30 PM, and 3:30 PM. Closed holidays.

Plan to Stay: 1.5 hours, plus additional time in the 2,000-square-foot retail store and to enjoy the walking path around bird sanctuary with geese, pelicans, ducks, and swans.

Minimum Age: None

Disabled Access: Yes

Group Requirements: Large groups will be split.

Special Information: Monthly special events and evening sticker art classes available. Mrs. Grossman is often on the premises, as are the 5 dogs she and her son, Jason, own.

Gift Shop: Sells all 650 of the company's current designs, sticker kits and collections, and scrapbooking supplies. Open Mon–Fri 9:00 AM–5:30 PM. Closed some holidays.

Directions: From San Francisco, take Hwy. 101 North. Turn left onto Lakeville Hwy. (Hwy. 116 East). Turn right onto South McDowell St. Turn right into parking lot.

Nearby Attractions: Marin French Cheese tour (see page 75); Petaluma Adobe State Historic Park; Shollenberger Park; Napa Valley wineries; San Francisco's attractions including Basic Brown Bear tour (see page 59), Golden Gate Bridge, and Fisherman's Wharf are about 1 hour away.

▲ In Petaluma, California, Mrs. Grossman's company store sells 650 different stickers.

The LaserWeb is the only laser-cutting system in the world that can produce Mrs. Grossman's Paper
▼ Whispers stickers.

NBC Studios

3000 West Alameda Avenue
Burbank, CA 91523
(818) 840-3537
www.nbc.com

NBC is the only major television network that provides tours to the public. Your tour guide will take you through the life of a television broadcast, from its conception to the building of the set, from the studio taping to your television at home. Visit the actual facilities as shows are taping in the studio next to you. Walk the halls of the stars and keep your eyes peeled for Jay Leno.

Begin your tour in the carpenter shop. Here, carpenters and artists work side by side to build and put the finishing touches on sets for NBC shows and events. Though sometimes huge, the sets are made with lightweight plywood and fiberglass brick so they don't become too heavy. The sets have to be fit together inside the studio due to the size limitations of studio doors.

Walk down the main hallway, cluttered with the sets for *Days of Our Lives*. Learn how this daily one-hour show is really a 24-hour-a-day operation. Sets are ever-changing. The show is taped year-round, unlike seasonal shows, which can run repeats in the summer. Peek into the studio if the door is open.

Follow your guide through the midway, where the stars park their cars. Check to see what Leno drove to work that day—he owns around 30 vintage cars and even more motorcycles, including a Stanley Steamer, a classic Duesenberg, and a WWI-era motorcycle.

If the *Tonight Show* is not in session, go into Studio 3. Sit in the audience chairs and watch the bustle of setup onstage. The show is taped live with only about one and a half hours for editing before it is broadcast on the East Coast.

On the special-effects set, learn how the blue Chroma Key screen works, while a volunteer plays weatherman or flies like Superman. Your tour ends in the guest relations patio, which you may recognize as the Salem Place Mall from *Days of Our Lives*.

Cost: Adults $7.50; seniors (60 and over) $6.75; children (5–12) $4; under 5, free.

Freebies: No

Videos Shown: 6.5-minute video on the history of NBC and the tour, plus a behind-the-scenes look at production; 1-minute video on wardrobe and make-up techniques.

Reservations Needed: No, but tickets sold on first-come, first-served basis. Yes, for groups of 15 or more people.

Days and Hours: Mon–Fri 9:00 AM–3:00 PM. July and August also Sat 10:00 AM–2:00 PM. Tours every half-hour. Closed some holidays.

Plan to Stay: 70 minutes, plus time for the gift shop.

Minimum Age: None

Disabled Access: Yes

Group Requirements: Groups of 15 or more people should call NBC Group Services, at (818) 840-3551, at least 2 weeks in advance. Groups over 15 people will be split. Group reservations when available. Reservations difficult between Christmas and New Year's.

Special Information: No photography. Tours will not go into studios during production. Tours before 1:30 will likely include the *Tonight Show* studio. Free audience show tickets available daily at NBC's ticket counter on first-come, first-served basis. Send ticket requests to NBC Tickets at above address or call above number for more information. NBC Studios in New York City (see page 237) also gives tours.

Gift Shop: NBC Peacock Shop sells merchandise from NBC shows along with logoed souvenir items. Open same hours as tour.

Directions: From the south, take Frwy. 405 North to 101 East (to L.A.). From the left lane, merge into Ventura Frwy. 134 East. Exit Buena Vista offramp. Turn left on Riverside Dr. Turn right on Bob Hope Dr. and follow signs to NBC Studios tour. From the east, take Frwy. 10 West to Frwy. 5 North. Exit Alameda Ave. West. Studio is 2 miles ahead, near St. Joseph's Hospital.

Nearby Attractions: Universal Studios, Paramount Pictures, and Warner Bros. tours (see pages 85, 80, and 86); Gene Autry Western Heritage Museum.

New United Motor Manufacturing Inc.

45500 Fremont Boulevard
Fremont, CA 94538
(510) 498-5765 / (510) 770-4008
www.nummi.com

TOYOTA AND GM CARS AND TOYOTA PICKUP TRUCKS

Automobile factory tours always offer a special excitement. Because the General Motors/Toyota joint venture (nicknamed "NUMMI") uses this refurbished GM plant, it's a showcase of Japanese manufacturing techniques within the context of U.S. union-management relations. As your electric tram motors more than 1 mile over the factory floor, watch workers (called "team members"), giant machines, and robots build the Pontiac Vibe, Toyota Corolla, and Toyota Tacoma pickup truck.

Because of the plant's layout, your narrated trip does not follow the exact sequence of building cars and trucks. However, you will see most of the steps in the manufacturing process. Each of the plant's work areas—whether for stamping, body and welding, assembling, or inspecting—manufactures cars and trucks at a measured pace along the plant's 1.2 miles of assembly line. For example, as an engine is hydraulically lifted into the car engine compartment overhead, team members scramble to bolt the engine into place within 67 seconds, the scheduled time each unit spends at each workstation in the car-assembly area.

A cacophony fills the air: drilling, crunching, hissing, and buzzing. Since the plant has the largest metal parts–stamping facility on the West Coast, a constant thumping reverberates through part of the plant. Suddenly you may hear music playing. A team member on the assembly line has spotted a quality problem and pulled the Andon Cord. If the problem can't be resolved quickly, production stops on that section of the line, and the music keeps playing until the problem is fixed. (Each area has its own tune.) This cord empowers all team members to guarantee quality in the manufacturing process, what the Japanese call *Jidoka*. Even if you're not interested in the details of the Toyota production system, you'll marvel at the movements and flying sparks generated by more than 100 computerized welding robots.

Cost: Free

Freebies: Currently no souvenirs

Video Shown: No, but captioned pictures in the tour waiting room explain the different manufacturing steps.

Reservations Needed: Yes. Individuals and families must join a scheduled group tour.

Days and Hours: Tue–Fri 9:30 AM and 11:30 AM. Tour content and schedule may change due to production requirements and model change activities. Call for tour times. Closed holidays and week between Christmas and New Year's.

Plan to Stay: Approximately 2 hours, including introductory talk, tour, and wrap-up Q&A session.

Minimum Age: 10. Tours for children ages 10 to 18 require 1 adult for every 10 children.

Disabled Access: Yes, but not all parts of tour are wheelchair accessible. Call for special accommodations.

Group Requirements: Maximum group size is 48 people. Tours need to be scheduled 3–4 months in advance for larger groups.

Special Information: No photography. Because tour is by electric tram, there's not much walking.

Gift Shop: No

Directions: From I-880 North, use the Fremont Blvd. exit just past Mission Blvd. Turn right at first light and take immediate right. Visitor parking on left after three stop signs. If traveling south on I-880, use the second Fremont Blvd. exit, just past Auto Mall Pkwy. (Do not take the earlier Alvarado Niles/Fremont Blvd. exit). Plant is visible from freeway. Upon exiting, stay left to loop back over freeway. Turn right at first light. Follow above directions. Ask for map when making reservations.

Nearby Attractions: Dreyer's & Edy's Grand Ice Cream factory tour (see page 64); Intel Museum (see page 70); Great America Theme Park; Mission Peak Regional Park.

Paramount Pictures

5555 Melrose Avenue
Hollywood, CA 90038
(323) 956-1777
www.paramount.com

A Paramount Communications Company

MOVIES AND TELEVISION SHOWS

Paramount Pictures, founded in 1912, shows the true TV and movie fan current moviemaking techniques while retaining its nostalgic charm. The only major studio still located in Hollywood, Paramount provides an exciting behind-the-scenes look at movie and television production. Tours of this original, classic studio are never exactly alike, since old sets are taken down and new projects begin every day.

Your tour guide will point out a number of famous Paramount landmarks along this two-hour walking tour. You will see sets not only for such television shows as *I Love Lucy, Happy Days,* and *Cheers,* but also for some of Paramount's best-known movies, such as *The Godfather, Star Trek,* and *The Hunt for Red October.* Stroll by the famous Wardrobe Department, as well as a display of Oscars and Emmys on loan from stars who have awards to spare.

As you peer through the old Bronson Gate, the arched gateway entrance synonymous with Paramount Pictures, and gaze upon the famous Hollywood sign in the hills, you'll hear the story about this passage being the magic gateway to the Silver Screen for aspiring stars. Carefully study the roof architecture of some of the soundstages to identify the three film production companies located here before Paramount took over the site in 1928.

Notice the B tank, a body of water used for shooting miniatures and special effects, such as the parting of the Red Sea in the 1956 filming of *The Ten Commandments.* The 100,000-gallon-capacity water tower still marks the borderline dividing Paramount and RKO Studios, which was acquired by Paramount. Stroll through Production Park, not only the company's business hub, but also one of the most photographed areas in Hollywood. On screen, its buildings double as college campuses, foreign embassies,

police precincts, hospitals, and more. At any point on the tour, you may suddenly see your favorite performer.

Cost: Free to be member of studio audience.

Freebies: Tickets to the TV shows filmed at Paramount.

Video Shown: No

Reservations Needed: Yes, call 1 week in advance.

Days and Hours: *Studio tours have been discontinued, perhaps permanently. From late July–March can be member of studio audience.*

Plan to Stay: 2 hours

Minimum Age: To watch most of the TV shows, 18.

Disabled Access: Yes

Group Requirements: Groups should call at least 1 week in advance to check the shooting schedule, make tour reservations, and arrange for group discount. Maximum group size is 100 people.

Special Information: No photography. Even with reservation, admission not guaranteed so best to arrive early when gates open.

Gift Shop: No

Directions: From Los Angeles, take 101 Frwy. North to Melrose Ave. exit. Turn left onto Melrose Ave. Parking information provided with reservation. From San Fernando Valley, take 101 Frwy. South to Gower St. exit. Make a right onto Gower St., go down hill. Turn left onto Melrose.

Nearby Attractions: Universal Studios, NBC Studios, and Warner Bros. tours (see pages 85, 78, and 86); Frederick's of Hollywood Lingerie Museum (see page 67); Mann's Chinese Theatre, with famous people's footprints in the forecourt; Downtown Hollywood's famous streets, including Hollywood Blvd., the Sunset Strip.

Scharffen Berger

914 Heinz Avenue
Berkeley, CA 94710
(510) 981-4050 / (510) 981-4066
www.scharffenberger.com

If you're looking for supersweet American-style chocolate, this isn't the place—John Scharffenberger and Robert Steinberg founded Scharffen Berger Chocolate Maker in 1996 to celebrate a richer, older tradition of chocolate making. With vintage machinery and gentle hands, workers coax a blend of cocoa beans from small plantations near the equator into dense dark chocolate used for both baking and snacking.

Enter this refurbished 1906 vintage brick warehouse. Your tour guide tells the history of chocolate and the company (the only American chocolate-making company founded in the last 50 years), punctuated with samples of chocolate in every stage from cocoa bean to finished product. The pure, sugarless chocolate dissolves on your tongue with such an intense flavor that you might have a hard time finishing. Don't miss the cacao nibs: little, nutty nuggets of roasted and crushed cocoa bean.

Next, follow your tour guide into the bean room, where burlap bags of beans stay isolated to prevent flavor pollution. The 1920 German Bauermeister, a cleaning machine that resembles a clunky piece of modern art, sucks up the beans, rattles them around, and then shoots the cleaned beans through a brush into a bin. The debris falls into burlap sacks (it will be resold as chicken feed later).

The cleaned beans roast for one hour at 280° before going into the winnower, where the nibs pour out from side holes into bins. Workers sift out the small nibs by hand: they will become Nibby Bars. Walk up the portable staircase to look down at the large nibs grinding inside the melanger. Two granite rollers spin in opposite directions on a rotating granite plate, crushing the nibs into chocolate liquor. Sugar, vanilla, soy lecithin, and cocoa butter complete the recipe. Scharffen Berger recipes vary; each country's beans have subtle, but distinct, flavors.

In the main tempering machine, the chocolate heats, cools, heats, and cools to become shiny with a good snap. Next, it shoots up a pipe, drops into molds, and travels through the cooling tunnel on its way to the assembly line. Workers hand-wrap the finished chocolates and send the slightly imperfect ones back to be re-melted. This chocolate is intense—you will leave your tour still euphoric from the samples you ate an hour earlier.

Cost: Free

Freebies: Chocolate samples

Video Shown: No

Reservations Needed: Yes. Individuals or small groups may reserve on website or call at least 2 weeks in advance. Groups larger than 15, see group requirements.

Days and Hours: Mon–Sat 10:30 AM and 2:30 PM.

Plan to Stay: 1 hour for tour and sampling, plus time in gift shop.

Minimum Age: 8

Disabled Access: Yes

Group Requirements: Groups of 15 or more can email tours@scharffen-berger.com or call (510) 981-4066 for 1:00 PM only. Groups cannot make reservations through the website. $30 group tour fee, payable at time of reservation, redeemable in gift shop. Maximum group size is 25.

Special Information: No open-toed shoes.

Gift Shop: Sells Nibby Bar, Mocha, Bittersweet, and Semisweet chocolate, cocoa powder, chocolate sauce, T-shirts, hats, books, fondue pots, and cooking utensils. Open Tue–Sat 10:00 AM–5:00 PM.

Directions: From San Francisco, take I-80 East. Take Ashby Ave. exit and keep left. Turn left onto Ashby Ave., left onto 7th St. and right onto Heinz Ave. Scharffen Berger will be on right.

Nearby Attractions: University of California at Berkeley Botanical Garden; Hooper's Chocolate factory tour (call 510-653-3703). San Francisco attractions, including Basic Brown Bear Factory (see page 2), Ghirardelli Square, Golden Gate Park, and Fisherman's Wharf are about 40 minutes away. Dreyer's & Edy's and Jelly Belly tours (see pages 64 and 4) 30 minutes to 40 minutes away; Intel Museum (see page 70) 1 hour away.

Seguin Moreau

151 Camino Dorado
Napa, CA 94558
(707) 252-3408
www.seguinmoreau.com

WINE BARRELS

While everyone knows that Napa Valley wineries offer tours, you may not know that in South Napa you can watch the ancient art of barrel making. Of 22 cooperages in the U.S. (most make whiskey barrels), only three are in Napa Valley. Seguin Moreau's Napa cooperage is a division of Seguin Moreau, France's oldest cooperage, established in the late 1800s.

As soon as your guide opens the doors to this cooperage built in 1994, you'll smell a pleasant vanilla aroma from the toasting barrels. You stroll along an open-air walkway just a few feet from the action. Brown overhead signs clearly mark all 12 of the production stations. Diagrams along the walkway show you which steps are performed in each of the two large, high-ceilinged rooms. With all the small fires in the first room, you wonder if some ancient witchcraft is brewing. Flames, water, and banging hammers are the key tools for shaping barrels. No glue is used. More modern woodworking machinery is used in the second room to finish the barrels.

American white oak, split from 90-year-old trees, seasons outdoors for two to three years to reduce moisture and tannins. Then the wood is ready to be cut into 37.5-inch-long staves and arranged in pairs—one wide, one narrow. With great skill, a master cooper "raises a barrel" by vertically arranging 27 to 30 of these alternating-width staves into a "rosette." He lines up the tops of the staves against the inside of a metal hoop, with the bottoms flaring out to form a teepee. If done correctly, the barrel could stand alone without the metal hoop; otherwise, the staves will fall into a tangled pile. To hold them tightly, metal hoops are pounded into place by the cooper circling the barrel in what's known as the "barrel-maker's dance." The staves are bent into the barrel shape with the help of moisture, heat, and an electric winch. The bending process takes approximately 20 minutes.

The barrels then move to the fires, where they are toasted for approximately one hour along a row of 12 small campfires. The coopers turn them over regularly so the insides toast evenly. The toasting releases natural flavors that enhance the taste of the wine that will eventually be put in the barrel. Barrelheads, assembled with wooden dowels and river reed, are toasted in a large oven. A cooper wedges the head into place with a shoehorn-like tool. At station 12 in the second room, the barrel rolls under the sanding belt. Each barrel takes 17 coopers about four hours to make.

Cost: Free

Freebies: Great toasting wood smells!

Video Shown: 10-minute video covers company history, where wood comes from, and barrel-making process at Seguin Moreau's French facility.

Reservations Needed: Recommended

Days and Hours: Mon–Fri 9:00 AM, 11:30 AM, and 1:30 PM. Closed week of July 4th and week between Christmas and New Year's.

Plan to Stay: 40 minutes for tour and video.

Minimum Age: None

Disabled Access: Yes

Group Requirements: Groups over 50 people will be split.

Special Information: No video cameras. Due to the flames, cooperage is very hot in the summer.

Gift Area: Sells logoed polos, mugs, and other items. Open Mon–Fri 8:00 AM–5:00 PM.

Directions: From Oakland/San Francisco, take I-80 East to Napa turnoff (Hwy. 37 West). Take Hwy. 29 North. After the Napa Airport on left, you'll pass Seguin Moreau on your right. Turn right onto Hwy. 12 East. Turn left at traffic light onto N. Kelly Rd. and left onto Camino Dorado. Seguin Moreau will be on your right.

Nearby Attractions: Hakusan Sake self-guided tour (call 800-564-6261); Carneros area winery tours include Domain Carneros Sparkling Wine (call 707-257-0101) and Artesa Vineyards & Winery (call 707-224-1668). For general information about Napa Valley winery tours, call (707) 226-7459.

Sunset

80 Willow Road
Menlo Park, CA 94025
(650) 321-3600
www.sunset.com

Sunset

Sunset magazine was founded in 1898 by Southern Pacific Railroad Company as a promotional tool to encourage westward travel, and was named after the Southern Pacific's Sunset Limited train route. The magazine evolved into a gardening, travel, food, and home-improvement magazine for the West. The company now publishes seven monthly regional editions of *Sunset* magazine for 13 Western states. Each edition focuses on that region's needs and interests, particularly in travel and gardening. In 1931 Sunset published its first cookbook. You can take a self-guided walk through its display gardens.

Sunset's adobe-style home was designed by renowned architect Cliff May and opened in 1952. Enter the light, airy main lobby through the thick, hand-carved, 10-foot-tall front doors. Notice some of the interesting interior architectural features, such as the desert-tile lobby floor and the adobe brick walls—each brick is two feet deep and weighs 30 pounds!

Outside, stroll through the formal gardens created by landscape designer Thomas Church. This "Walk through the West" features native plants from Southern California to Washington, plus Hawaii. You'll first walk past the Old Man live oak, growing increasingly lopsided as it chases the sun.

Walk along the curved walkway to the Southwest Desert and Southern California section, which features cacti, succulents, and certain perennials that will grow under extreme drought conditions. Notice the large Southern yucca, which is probably 150 years old. Further along the walkway is the Central California area. The lawn here is sometimes mowed into a putting green in the summer. Notice how the sun shines through the "Monterey Peninsula."

Huge coast redwoods reign over the garden's Northern California section. Look up at the magnolia blossom trees. Four Chardonnay and four Cabernet grapevines represent the Sonoma and Napa Valleys.

Wet winters and cold temperatures characterize the climate for the Northwest. Here you'll see dogwood, firs, and many types of rhododendron, including azaleas.

After the peaceful, perfectly manicured formal gardens, you visit the organic test garden used for editorial projects. This 3,200-square-foot garden is divided into four test plots. Ever changing, the beds may contain 30 varieties of gourmet lettuce, or hyacinth and tulips in the spring. Next time you browse through *Sunset*'s brightly colored garden photographs, you'll know where they were taken.

Cost: Free

Freebies: Walking tour map, which includes company history.

Video Shown: No

Reservations Needed: No, except for groups larger than 10 people.

Days and Hours: Mon–Fri 9:00 AM–4:30 PM. Closed holidays.

Plan to Stay: 20 minutes

Minimum Age: None, however, children should be interested in horticulture.

Disabled Access: Yes

Group Requirements: None

Special Information: No professional photography allowed. Best times to tour are spring (when the gardens are in full bloom) and Christmas (when crafts projects are displayed in lobby).

Gift Shop: No, however, Sunset books are displayed and can be ordered in lobby or by calling (800) 526-5111. Also sells magazines in lobby. Subscribe to *Sunset* magazine by calling (800) 777-0117.

Directions: From San Francisco, take Hwy. 101 South to Willow Rd./Menlo Park West exit. Follow Willow Rd. for approximately 1 mile. Sunset is on your left.

Nearby Attractions: Intel Museum (see page 70); Filoli Estate; Allied Arts Guild; Stanford Linear Accelerator Center tour (call 650-926-2204).

Taylor Guitars

1980 Gillespie Way
El Cajon, CA 92020
(619) 258-1207
www.taylorguitars.com

Kurt Listug and Bob Taylor started Taylor Guitars in 1974 in a dank, dusty warehouse where they turned out a couple of guitars each week and barely covered their costs. Gradually, Taylor's craftsmanship and Listug's sales skills attracted musicians like Neil Young and Bonnie Raitt. Sales to such well-known artists helped raise the public's awareness of the company. Today, Taylor Guitars creates 39,000 acoustic guitars per year and grosses over $40 million from production in its 143,000-square-foot facility. Listug and Taylor never gave up creative control, and the company continues to heighten industry standards with a combination of luck, intuition, and innovation.

On the tour, learn that Taylor accidentally revolutionized the neck attachment process because he did not know how to make a traditional dovetail to fasten the neck to the body. Instead of using glue, which impedes the transference of resonance and creates a deadening effect, he planed the surface of the body flat and bolted on the guitar neck, resulting in greater stability and a more articulate tone.

At the CNC (Computer Numeric Controlled) stations, peer through the bulletproof plastic on both ends of the milling machines, where precision equipment produces necks and bracing materials to rigid specifications. To form curves and shapes, a vacuum holds blocks of tonewoods in place while the shaping tool glides vertically and the bed slides horizontally.

Computer-guided laser cutters work out the shapes of the top, back, and sides. The laser burnishes and heat-seals the edge of the wood—no saw blade lifts the grain and leaves a rough edge. Diamond-tipped cutting tools adjust the depth and width of the sound holes and decorative rosette for the tops. In the body department, a Multicam milling machine prepares the top, sides, and back for attachment to one another, perfectly fitting the pieces of wood together. Workers then check the glue joints with an ultraviolet light that illuminates any spilled glue.

The repair department provides some of the most unusual sights. Taylor veterans rescue forlorn guitars—run over by cars or dropped at airports—that bereaved owners send in, hoping to salvage at least part of a beloved instrument.

In the finish and final assembly area, preassigned necks and bodies meet according to the numerical tracking system, and each guitar bakes in ultraviolet light for three 23-second exposures to cure the finish, similar to the process used to finish airplanes. Try not to stare at the gleaming rows of finished Taylor Guitars like a child in a candy shop.

Cost: Free

Freebies: Logoed sound hole coasters cut from Taylor Guitar tops, catalogs, *Wood & Steel* publication, videos.

Video Shown: 40-minute video, "Taylor on Guitars: New Neck Designs," shown in lobby.

Reservations Needed: No, except groups larger than 10.

Days and Hours: Mon–Fri 1:00 PM. Closed major and company holidays. Closed 2 weeks around Christmas and New Year's.

Plan to Stay: 1.5 hours

Minimum Age: None, but children should have an interest in guitars.

Disabled Access: Yes.

Group Requirements: Groups larger than 10 people should call 10 days in advance. Groups larger than 15 people will be split into smaller groups.

Special Information: Check website for Taylor performances and workshops held nationally.

Gift Counter: Sells Taylorware clothing and guitar straps. Taylor Guitars available from more than 800 dealers. Open Mon–Fri 8:00 AM–4:30 PM.

Directions: From San Diego, take I-8 East to El Cajon. Take Hwy. 67 North. Exit at Bradley St. Turn left (west) onto Bradley St. and right onto Cuyamaca St. Take left onto Gillespie Way. Taylor Guitars will be on the left.

Nearby Attractions: Callaway Golf and LEGOLAND tours (see pages 62 and 73); San Diego's attractions include San Diego Zoo, Wild Animal Park, and Sea World.

Universal Studios Hollywood

100 Universal City Plaza
Universal City, CA 91608
(818) 622-3801
www.universalstudioshollywood.com

MOVIES AND TELEVISION SHOWS

Film pioneer Carl Laemmle established Universal Studios in 1915 on a former chicken ranch. In the early days of silent pictures, visitors ate box lunches provided by the studio and sat in bleacher seats watching films being made. With the advent of "talking pictures," the tours stopped.

Largely as an effort to boost the lunchtime business at the Studio Commissary, Universal reopened its doors to the public in 1964. Millions of dollars and visitors later, Universal Studios Hollywood has developed its famed 420-acre studio lot into a first-rate theme park. Attractions provide a fun family experience through which to learn the secrets of motion picture and television production.

Universal Studios Hollywood really is a trip into what it feels like to be in a movie. It's not about what it's like to be an actor in a film, but rather what it's like to be a character in a Hollywood adventure story. While Charlton Heston or Ava Gardner did their *Earthquake!* scenes in hundreds of boring pieces, the tour puts the pieces together and plays them at full speed.

You can enjoy the Backlot tram tour, which visits famous production sets of the world's largest movie studio. This tram ride takes you past renowned sets from *Jurassic Park, The Grinch Who Stole Christmas, Apollo 13, End of Days, Animal House,* and *Back to the Future,* among many others. Television sets you'll recognize include those from *Murder, She Wrote; Dr. Quinn, Medicine Woman; Leave It to Beaver; McHale's Navy;* and *Sliders.*

The World of Cinemagic provides insights into special effects used in *Back to the Future* and *Psycho.* Several audience members can participate in the demonstrations. One show teaches how sounds and voices are dubbed into an already-shot film through Foley and ADR (automated dubbing replacement technique).

Cost: Backlot tram tour price is included in the general admission charge for Universal Studios.

Freebies: No

Video Shown: Many attractions include videos.

Reservations Needed: No, except for groups of 20 or more people.

Days and Hours: Mon–Fri 10:00 AM–6:00 PM, Sat–Sun 9:00 AM–7:00 PM. Open 8:00 AM–10:00 PM during peak days and in the summer. Box office opens 30 minutes before park. Closed Thanksgiving and Christmas.

Plan to Stay: All day at Universal Studios. The Backlot tour lasts 45 minutes.

Minimum Age: None

Disabled Access: Yes

Group Requirements: Groups of 20 or more people should call Group Sales (818-622-3771) 3–4 days in advance or write Universal Studios (at the above address) to reserve tickets. Groups receive 10 percent discount off box-office prices.

Special Information: A booth at the studio offers free tickets to TV show productions; however, some of these shows are not filmed at Universal. In addition to the Backlot tram tour, other Universal Studios' movie-related attractions include "Terminator 2: 3D," "Nickelodeon Blast Zone," "Animal Planet Live!," "Jurassic Park—The Ride," "Waterworld—A Live Sea War Spectacular," "Back to the Future—The Ride," "The E.T. Adventure," "Backdraft," and "The Wild, Wild, Wild West Stunt Show"; a new attraction is added each year.

Gift Shop: Many gift shops sell posters, videos, clothes, jewelry, mugs, and toys, with logos.

Directions: Located between Hollywood and the San Fernando Valley just off the Hollywood (101) Frwy., Universal Studios is accessible from either the Universal Center Dr. or Lankershim Blvd. exits. Follow "Universal Studios" signs and marquee to park.

Nearby Attractions: Paramount Pictures, NBC Studios, and Warner Bros. Studios tours (see pages 80, 78, and 86); Audiences Unlimited offers free tickets for taped TV shows (call 818-506-0067); Universal CityWalk.

Warner Bros. Studios

4000 Warner Boulevard
Burbank, CA 91522
(818) 954-1744
www.wbstudiotour.com

MOVIES AND TELEVISION SHOWS

By some estimates, entertainment is the United States's second-largest export and pumps $50 billion into the U.S. economy. Begun in 1918, when films were silent, today Warner Bros. displays the latest technological advances in filmmaking.

The Warner Bros. tour is different from any other studio tour in California. Here, you will take an exclusive VIP tour designed for small groups seriously interested in the inner workings of a major studio. Because this is a VIP tour, production schedules are checked every morning to ensure that visitors see the most action possible. Some of the biggest stars, both human and animated, have worked at Warner Bros.—since this is a busy studio, don't be surprised if you see one of them walk by!

You will travel by electric cart to a variety of television and movie sets. Since these sets change with each new film, you may find yourself under a blazing sun in the Sahara, in romantic moonlight on Paris's Left Bank, or on an exotic, narrow avenue in crowded old Shanghai, all while actual movies or TV shows are being filmed.

Your guide may take you into the extensive Prop Shop and explain, "No, it's not a garage sale or fire sale, it's the Prop Shop." Or you may visit the impressive Wardrobe Department (with one of the world's largest costume collections) or the Mill (where sets are created). You may explore exterior sets like Laramie Street, used in a number of Warner Bros. westerns, and French Street, where many scenes from *Casablanca* were filmed. Discover that these exterior sets are basically shells with open backs. At the Sound Facilities, you may catch a symphony orchestra recording a movie's theme song, actors redoing dialogue that couldn't be properly recorded on the set, or technicians creating sound effects.

Opened in 1996, the Warner Bros. Museum features costumes, props, animation cels, and film clips. See the black-and-white hats from *My Fair Lady,* original correspondence about Humphrey Bogart, and candid shots of Errol Flynn. Stand between Bugs Bunny and Daffy Duck in a human-scale animation cel to see how you would look in cartoons.

Cost: $32 per person ($4 AAA discount)

Freebies: A VIP tour brochure

Video Shown: 10-minute video shows highlights from Warner Bros. films since the first talking film, *The Jazz Singer,* in 1927.

Reservations Needed: No, but recommended

Days and Hours: Mon–Fri 9:00 AM–3:30 PM, every half hour. Tour schedule can vary. During summer, some holiday tours can be specially arranged.

Plan to Stay: 2.25 hours for video, museum, and tour, plus time for gift shop.

Minimum Age: 8

Disabled Access: Yes

Group Requirements: Electric cart capacity is 12 people. Groups larger than 12 take walking tour of 110-acre lot. Call in advance for reservations. $7 discount per person for groups larger than 20 people.

Special Information: Wear comfortable walking shoes. Limited photography.

Gift Shop: Sells T-shirts, pins, and hats with W.B. logo. Open Mon–Fri 9:30 AM–4:00 PM.

Directions: From San Fernando Valley, take 101/134 Frwy. (Ventura Frwy.) East to Pass Ave. exit. Turn right onto Pass Ave. Turn left onto Riverside Dr. Turn right onto Hollywood Way; the Hollywood Way gate (Gate 4) is 1 block down the street. From Hollywood, take 101 Frwy. (Hollywood Frwy.) North. Take the Barham Blvd. exit. Turn right onto Barham Blvd., and when you cross the Los Angeles River, Barham becomes Olive Ave. The studio is on your right. Stay on Olive Ave. as it curves around the studio, until you reach Hollywood Way. Turn right into the studio and park at VIP tour center.

Nearby Attractions: NBC Studios, Paramount Pictures, and Universal Studios tours (see pages 78, 80, and 85).

Celestial Seasonings

4600 Sleepytime Drive
Boulder, CO 80301-3292
(303) 581-1202
www.celestialseasonings.com

TEAS

At the corner of Sleepytime Drive and Zinger Street, named after its two best-selling teas, lies the home of Celestial Seasonings. Since it began in 1969 with Mo's 36, president Mo Siegel's own herbal tea blend, Celestial Seasonings has become the largest U.S. herbal tea manufacturer—1.3 billion tea bags per year. This tour offers much more than a standard factory-floor tour. You also learn about the company's marketing approach and get your sinuses cleared while visiting the Peppermint Room.

After an enthusiastic introduction by your guide in the welcoming area (be sure to hug the cuddly, six-foot Sleepytime Bear), you may participate in a consumer test. Next to the lobby is a gallery showing the original paintings for the tea box designs.

The storage and production areas are a maze of pallets stacked with burlap bags of herbs. In a mini botany lesson, learn that black tea comes from the *Camelia sinensis* tea plant, and herbal "tea" from a variety of plants and herbs. To prevent its absorbing other flavors, the black teas are isolated in their own rooms, in wooden crates stenciled with their country of origin. As the tour guide raises the metal door allowing you to enter the world of mint, you will be bombarded with intense peppermint and spearmint aromas.

On the main production floor, rock and roll music plays over the roar of the machines. Here you'll see how tea gets into those little bags and brightly printed boxes. Package-forming machines simultaneously fold recycled cardboard and insert liners. Look for the big machines in the center of the production floor with wheels of porous, coffee filter–like paper and a hopper on top. As the continuous stream of tea drops between the merging top and bottom paper layers, the paper is heat-sealed to form the bags. Groups of 24 bags are then inserted into boxes. When the open boxes roll past you on the conveyor belt, take a peek in at your freshly formed favorite flavors.

Cost: Free

Freebies: Samples of any or all iced or hot flavors at the tea bar.

Video Shown: In art gallery, 7-minute video on company history and manufacturing process.

Reservations Needed: No, except for groups of 8 or more people.

Days and Hours: Hourly tours Mon–Sat 10:00 AM–3:00 PM and Sun 11:00 AM–3:00 PM. Closed holidays.

Plan to Stay: 45 minutes for tour, plus time in Tea Shop & Emporium, Celestial Café, herb garden, and tea sampling.

Minimum Age: 5, for factory floor.

Disabled Access: Yes

Group Requirements: Groups of 8 or more people should call (303-581-1317) 1 month in advance for reservations. Groups larger than 20 will be divided into smaller groups.

Special Information: No photography. Flat shoes recommended. For busy summer tour season, arrive well in advance of desired tour time. Breakfast and lunch available at the Celestial Café.

Gift Shop: Tea Shop & Emporium sells all Celestial Seasonings teas and many logoed items, including mugs and magnets with tea-box designs, and Sleepytime Bear T-shirts, hats, and aprons. Bargain boxes of teas. Open Mon–Fri 9:00 AM–6:00 PM, Sat 9:00 AM–5:00 PM, Sun 11:00 AM–4:00 PM. Closed holidays.

Directions: From Denver, take I-25 North to U.S. 36 West. Take Hwy. 157 (Foothills Pkwy.) North, which becomes Hwy. 119 heading northeast. Turn right onto Jay Rd. Turn left onto Spine Rd., then turn left onto Sleepytime Dr. From Boulder, travel northeast on Hwy. 119 (Longmont Diagonal) and follow directions above.

Nearby Attractions: Leanin' Tree Museum of Western Art; Boulder's attractions, including Pearl Street outdoor mall and hiking in the Rockies, are about 15 minutes away.

Compromise and Smuggler Mines

0100 Smuggler Mountain Road
Aspen, CO 81611
(970) 925-2049

SILVER

You know you're in for an adventure as you ride up Aspen Mountain's Little Nell ski run in a white Suburban. Before you enter the cabin just outside the entrance to Compromise Mine, take in the panoramic view of Aspen. In the cabin, you don a hard hat and adjust its size to fit your head using a knob in the back. The tour guide, one of the owners of the mine, points out your location on the wall map.

Outside, board an 18-gauge tour car and ride 2,000 feet underground behind an electric mine locomotive. Chug along skinny tracks into the dark, narrow, cold tunnel. The pitch-blackness is sporadically punctuated by candles burning. The four-foot-wide, seven-foot-tall tunnel gives way to larger cave-like openings. These open stopes, or underground chambers, were created by the removal of ore. One of the stopes is more than 1,200 feet deep. Disembark at station #8. Look down a ladder that goes down 100 feet. A series of ladders go down 800 feet. With a constant underground temperature of 55°, your breath makes white, puffy clouds.

On the tour you learn that the Compromise Mine is one of the largest and richest silver mines in the Aspen Mining District. In the early 1880s, immense bodies of high-grade ore were discovered in the area mines. Often veins that contain silver continued between mines. Legal battles ensued over ownership. David M. Hyman tried to prove he owned a continuous vein, while Jerome B. Wheeler argued it was not continuous. In the end a compromise was reached, thus the name Compromise Mine. The mine remained productive until 1893, when the demonetization of silver caused Aspen's mining industry to collapse. Subsequent intermittent mining ceased in the 1930s. Since 1986, Aspen Mountain Mining Corporation rehabilitates tunnels and drives new workings in search of silver ore deposits in Compromise Mine.

Since the grandfather of one of the current owners actually mined Smuggler Mine, the main focus is the preservation of Aspen history. A walking tour of Smuggler Mine covers two levels of the mine. Climb up stairs to the second level, which overlooks the first. Walk 1,200 feet into the mine. Smuggler Mine, on the National Historic Register, is steeped in history. It is one of Aspen's most famous silver mines and one of the few still open today. The world's largest nugget of silver, removed from the seventh level, weighed 1,840 pounds. As you take your next chairlift up Aspen Mountain, you now have a new appreciation of life underground.

Cost: Compromise: Adults, $30; children under 12, $20. Smuggler: Adults, $20; children under 12, $15.

Freebies: Ore samples

Video Shown: No

Reservations Needed: Yes, 1 week in advance.

Days and Hours: Compromise: July and August Sat 9:00 AM, 11:00 AM, 1:00 PM, and 3:00 PM. Smuggler: Year-round, by reservation

Plan to Stay: Compromise: 2 hours. Smuggler: 1.5 hours.

Minimum Age: 5

Disabled Access: Compromise: Need to be able to ride in Suburban and rail car.

Group Requirements: Smuggler: 4-person minimum.

Special Information: Wear warm clothing, as mine temperature is 55° year-round. Dark, wet, slippery ground.

Gift Area: Sells T-shirts and hats.

Directions: Compromise: Downtown Aspen pickup. Smuggler: From Aspen, take Hwy. 82 toward Independence Pass. After small bridge, take third left. Park Ave. runs into Park Circle, which runs into Smuggler Mountain Rd. Mine gate after one hairpin turn.

Nearby Attractions: Aspen and Snowmass Mountains; summer Aspen Music Festival; Snowmass Ranch; Maroon Lake scenic trail; Ashcroft ghost town.

Coors

13th and Ford Streets
Golden, CO 80401
(303) 277-BEER
www.coors.com

Coors.

The world's largest single-site brewery sits at the base of the Colorado Rockies between two "tabletop" mountains. In addition to the distinctly nonindustrial setting, the brewery tour has other memorable sights. The "Coors Copper Kitchen" brewhouse observation area is bordered on two sides by 50 handmade copper kettles, each the size of an above-ground swimming pool. Each kettle's sides are white ceramic tile, while its top is a dome of shiny copper with a long, narrow, copper neck. The kettles have assigned roles in the brewing process, which your guide will gladly explain.

Founded in 1873, Coors claims it is the only brewer in the U.S.A. to do most of its malting on-site. Before barley can be used in the brewing process, its starch must be converted into malt. The barley steeps in two-story-deep stainless-steel tanks, which prepares it for growth. Next, the barley is spread out on long screens called "germination beds." After the seeds sprout, the barley is roasted for 14 hours in immense kilns, then aged and milled.

The stillness of the malting process contrasts with the speedy aluminum-can packaging machine area. Thousands of cans converge here every minute and then roll by in 6-, 12-, and 24-pack cartons.

Cost: Free

Freebies: 3 beer samples in Coors' hospitality lounge for visitors age 21 or older, with picture ID. Serves most Coors brands and assorted soft drinks.

Videos Shown: Peter Coors' welcome message, shown at tour entrance area. Another video shows can and bottle manufacturing, filling, packaging, shipping, and distributing.

Reservations Needed: No, except for groups of 20 or more people.

Days and Hours: Mon–Sat 10:00 AM–4:00 PM. Closed holidays. Call for schedule around holidays.

Plan to Stay: 40 minutes for brewery tour, plus time for beer sampling, gift shop, and shuttle-bus tour from Coors parking lot through Historic Golden. Coors grounds also have interesting features, including a 16-foot-high, 13-foot-wide original copper brew kettle used in the 1880s. (It stands at the main entrance.) Veterans' memorial salutes the "Defenders of Freedom."

Minimum Age: Under 18 must be accompanied by adult.

Disabled Access: Yes, an alternative route is available.

Group Requirements: Groups of more than 20 people should make reservations 1 week in advance (call 303-277-2552).

Special Information: For special-needs tours call 303-277-2552. Tours also offered at Coors' Memphis, TN, brewery (call 901-368-BEER).

Gift Shop: Coors & Co. sells a wide range of logoed clothes and beer souvenirs, including mugs, glasses, barstools, and tap handles. Look for the popular blinking bottle-cap buttons. Open Mon–Sat 10:00 AM–5:00 PM. Closed holidays.

Directions: From Denver, take I-70 West to Hwy. 58 West to Golden. Exit at Washington Ave. and turn left on Washington, then left onto 13th St. to Ford St. for visitors' parking. You're in Golden when you see the archway over the main street ("Howdy, Folks! WELCOME TO GOLDEN—Where the West Lives!") and smell the malted barley. Parking-lot shuttle takes you on a brief tour around Golden and then to brewery.

Nearby Attractions: Colorado Railroad Museum; Foothills Art Center; Buffalo Bill Memorial Museum and Grave; Rocky Mountain Quilt Museum; Golden Pioneer Museum; Heritage Square Village.

See color photos, page 7.

Hammond's Candies Since 1920

4969 Colorado Boulevard
Denver, CO 80216
(888) CANDY-99
www.hammondscandies.com

CANDY

Ever wonder how candy canes or other hard candies get their stripes? At Hammond's you'll see how hard candy has been made by hand since the 1920s. First, step into the packing room, where workers pack lollipops or candy canes.

Next, through a wall of windows in the kitchen, you'll see large copper kettles. Inside, 50 pounds of sugar, water, and corn syrup heats to over 300°. Two men lift and carry a huge kettle and pour the bubbling, amber-colored liquid onto a metal table. Next you may see the candy maker adding different colors to areas of this sheet of candy: for a candy cane, he scoops out some red paste with a spatula and mixes it into one section, then adds green in another corner. Another section remains clear. Finally, the "scrap"—the crushed beginnings and ends of other candy—is melted into another section: this will become the candy canes' center.

Once the sheet has cooled, the candy maker cuts the color sections with giant scissors—these will become the candy canes' stripes. A clear section is placed on a taffy-puller-like machine. As the machine pulls, it adds air, turning the candy white. Next the red, white, and green sections are laid out on a heated table in a long, flat "blanket."

The cooks then place the center piece on the puller, to add air (so it will melt faster in your mouth) and flavoring, like cherry. Next this centerpiece, which is shaped like a big duffel bag, is placed on the blanket of stripes, and the blanket is wrapped around it. The candy makers put this roll on a heated canvas mat. The mat is on a machine that rotates the bundle. When the bundle is hot enough, a cook takes one end in his hands and pulls it to the width of a candy cane. As the cook pulls, the machine rolls the bundle. This motion creates the twist in the candy cane stripes. As the cook cuts the strip into pieces, a worker takes each piece from him and puts a crook in it. Other workers place the canes on trays to cool, and then they roll the finished candy canes into the packaging room.

Cost: Free

Freebies: Candy samples

Video Shown: 10-minute segment about the tour, from a Food Network program.

Reservations Needed: No, except for groups over 10 people or special needs groups..

Days and Hours: Mon–Fri 9:00 AM–2:30 PM, every 30 minutes. Closed Easter, Memorial Day, July 4th, Labor Day, Thanksgiving, Christmas, and New Year's.

Plan to Stay: 30 minutes for tour and video, plus time for gift shop.

Minimum Age: None

Disabled Access: Yes, call a day ahead for reservations.

Group Requirements: Groups of 10 or more people should call in advance.

Special Information: Must wear hairnets. Very small children may wear a hat. Strollers do not fit in factory. Tour can be hot in the summer in the cooking area. Candy Cane Festival held in December. Call for dates.

Gift Shop: Sells factory seconds, a range of handmade candies, Christmas decorations, books on candy making, and T-shirts. Mon–Fri 9:00 AM–4:00 PM.

Directions: From I-70, take Colorado Blvd. exit. Go north on Colorado Blvd. and turn left onto 48th Ave. Take an immediate right onto the frontage road. The factory is one block down on the left side of the street.

Nearby Attractions: U.S. Mint tour (see page 94); Denver Zoo; Denver Museum of Natural History; Denver Museum of Miniature Dolls & Toys; City Park and Botanical Garden.

See color photos, page 9.

Michael Ricker Pewter

2050 Big Thompson Avenue
Highway 34 East
Estes Park, CO 80517
(970) 586-2030 / (800) 373-9837
www.ricker.com

PEWTER SCULPTURES

MICHAEL
RICKER
PEWTER

What do former president Gerald Ford, golf great Arnold Palmer, and basketball star Magic Johnson have in common? All have been featured in pewter sculptures by Michael Ricker. Ricker has not only created sculptures of people but also designed elaborate chess sets, animals, and even corporate gifts (including a trash can for a waste-management company!).

Notice his grand pewter projects, such as *America's Moments 1950's Drive-In* and *Park City*. Your tour guide will point out the incredible details, from squirrels in the trees to a working carousel. The size is also astounding: *Park City,* the world's largest pewter sculpture, covers about 300 square feet. Ricker likes to think of them as three-dimensional history books, capturing a sense of American life in an earlier era.

Your video tour takes you inside the casting studio. The process begins when liquid rubber is poured around an original Michael Ricker wax sculpture to form a mold. The mold is cast repeatedly using a pewter alloy brought to liquid form at 500°. These multiple castings are then used to form vulcanized rubber molds which, when spun in a centrifugal casting machine, will create up to 20 castings with each pour of molten pewter. Upon cooling, these castings are forced from the mold and separated. An artisan removes flashing (the jagged edges) and applies graphite patina and clear sealer. Some designs require welding, sanding, and adornment before being mounted on bases, packed, and shipped to galleries across the country.

Most of the sculptures are produced in limited editions, and many of the editions are sold out before production even begins. Michael Ricker tends to be a night owl and does most of his artistic work late into the night. However, he is often in the gift shop in the afternoons, meeting customers.

Cost: Free

Freebies: Small pewter snowflakes

Video Shown: 5-minute video about Michael and his commissioned pieces.

Reservations Needed: Yes, preferred.

Days and Hours: Museum: Summer (Memorial Day through Labor Day): Mon–Thur 9:00 AM–8:00 PM, Fri and Sat 9:00 AM–6:00 PM, Sun 10:00 AM–6:00 PM. Winter: Mon–Sun 11:00 AM–5:00 PM. Closed Thanksgiving, Christmas, and New Year's.

Plan to Stay: 30 minutes for guided tour of the museum and video tour, plus time in gallery.

Minimum Age: None

Disabled Access: Yes

Group Requirements: Groups over 10 people will be split into smaller groups.

Special Information: A kiosk keeps a database of other galleries, the active market for Ricker sculptures. Many collectors also belong to the Michael Ricker Collector's Society, which publishes a quarterly magazine featuring Michael's newest sculptures and the latest secondary market reports.

Gallery: Carries a large assortment of Ricker's work, from large, rare figures to small gift pieces. Open same days and hours as museum.

Directions: Take I-25 to Hwy. 34 West. Travel through Loveland and up Big Thompson Canyon into Estes Park. Michael Ricker Pewter is the gray building on left after the mouth of the canyon.

Nearby Attractions: Celestial Seasonings tea tour (see page 87); the Stanley Hotel; Rocky Mountain National Park; Estes Park. Denver's attractions, including Hammond's Candies and U.S. Mint tours, are about 2 hours away (see pages 90 and 94).

Simpich

2413 West Colorado Avenue
Colorado Springs, CO 80904
(719) 636-3272 / (800) 881-3879
www.simpich.com

Simpich Character Dolls

DOLLS

The Simpich Dolls story begins like a fairy tale: Once upon a time (that's 1952), two newlyweds on a limited budget made dolls for family Christmas gifts. Today, although they no longer work out of their home, Bob and Jan Simpich still design all Simpich character dolls themselves. Bob specializes in elves, Santas, and historic figures, while Jan prefers cloud babies, angels, and children's storybook figures.

Ideas for character dolls come from everywhere—history, religion, and even their own children and grandchildren. Bob and Jan create the originals out of a claylike, plastic Super Sculpey, which is oven-baked and sent to the casting department for an original, or "mother," mold. It may take several tries to create the perfect mother mold that captures all the facial feature details.

The "factory" thrives behind a Tudor facade and above its retail doll shop in the Old Colorado Historic District. The self-guided tour of this "Santa's workshop" takes you through the painting, sewing, and finishing steps. Astonishing attention to detail is required to paint the cheeks, mouths, eyes, and beards of these intricate miniature heads. Racks of dangling painted heads wait to join their bodies. Labeled racks, including Santas, angels, and elves, fill a long wall in the sewing room. Home workers handle many intermediary steps, such as base-wrapping each body's wire skeleton with raw cotton batting, piece-sewing petticoats and other outfit parts, and partial assembly.

The pieces magically come together in the sewing and finishing rooms. As many as a dozen outfit parts are hand-sewn onto each doll, and some even get individually designed bouquets and hats to match their costumes. In the finishing room, dolls are attached to bases and receive final accessories. You will leave with affection for the dolls and an appreciation of the four-month process from mother mold to completed doll.

Cost: Free
Freebies: Catalog and newsletter
Video Shown: 15-minute video on David Simpich marionettes.
Reservations Needed: Only for guided group tour.
Days and Hours: Mon–Sat 10:00 AM–5:00 PM. You'll see the most production Mon–Fri. Closed holidays and Christmas through the week following New Year's.
Plan to Stay: 20–30 minutes for self-guided tour, plus time in retail store.
Minimum Age: None
Disabled Access: Doll shop, finishing, and originals are on street level. Workshop is upstairs.
Group Requirements: Groups larger than 20 people will be divided into smaller groups. Call 1 day in advance to arrange for a tour guide.
Special Information: Casting department is not on the tour.
Retail Store: Doll shop sells all Simpich character dolls, including storybook, historical, and Christmas dolls, in creative displays. Look for the glass case showing a small selection of Simpich dolls created since 1952 and newspaper articles documenting the company's growth. Open Mon–Sat 10:00 AM–5:00 PM. Closed holidays and the week following New Year's. Simpich catalog and information about the David Simpich marionettes available at above number.
Directions: From Denver, take I-25 South to Garden of the Gods exit. Turn right onto Garden of the Gods Rd. Turn left onto 30th St. Turn left onto Colorado Ave. Simpich is on your right at 24th St.
Nearby Attractions: Van Briggle Art Pottery tour (see page 95); Patsy's Candies tour (call 719-633-6777); Old Colorado Historic District shops and restaurants; Michael Garman Gallery; The Broadmoor; Cave of the Winds; Pike's Peak; Garden of the Gods.

Stephany's Chocolates

6770 West 52nd Avenue
Arvada, CO 80002
(800) 888-1522
www.stephanys-chocolates.com

Stephany's® Chocolates OF COLORADO

CHOCOLATES AND TOFFEE

Colorado's high altitude and low humidity are important ingredients in Stephany's award-winning Colorado Almond Toffee. Of course, butter, almonds, and sugar help, too. On this candy-maker tour, you will be allured by sweet smells, warmed by the care given to each chocolate, and tempted to stick your fingers into the chocolate or toffee bowls for tastes. This is truly chocolate-lovers' heaven.

A rich toffee smell permeates the toffee area. Melted with sugar and almonds, 68-pound blocks of butter swirl around a copper fire kettle. Two workers grab the fire kettle and pour the luscious mixture onto a cooling table. One worker uses a trowel to spread the toffee to the uniform thickness marked by metal strips at the edge of the table. The worker rolls a bladed metal rolling pin over the length and width of the table, cutting the slab into small sections. The toffee solidifies quickly. Workers then break it into individual bars, which await a chocolate shower and a chopped-almond bath.

You smell the peppermint long before you reach the Denver Mint room. Here, chocolate and mint layers are poured and spread onto a wooden former bowling lane, now a table covered with brown paper. A worker pushes a bladed rolling pin to cut one-inch squares. A roller on tracks moves beneath the brown paper to break the mints apart. From one end of the table, a worker pulls out the brown paper, and the mints fall like dominoes onto a holding tray.

Walk between the two candy enrobing machines. Notice that each and every nut or filling is individually placed by hand on the conveyor belt. After each piece receives a chocolate coating, a thin chocolate stream flows through a stringer to put a design on top. Then it's off through the refrigerated tunnel for cooling. In the chilly packing room, workers grab different chocolates from the shelves and place them into brown paper-cup liners and gift boxes. A few strokes with the badger brush shines the chocolates and readies the gift box for shrink-wrapping or ribbons and holiday ornaments.

Cost: Free

Freebies: Taste of raspberry cream and small piece of toffee. Also, a paper hat to wear on the tour.

Video Shown: No

Reservations Needed: Yes. Families and individuals need to join scheduled group tours.

Days and Hours: Mon–Thur at 9:30 AM, 10:30 AM, 11:30 AM, and 1:00 PM. Closed holidays.

Plan to Stay: 45 minutes for tour, plus time in retail store.

Minimum Age: 9, although exceptions made when with parents.

Disabled Access: Yes. While there are several steps at main entrance, the tour is on one level.

Group Requirements: Minimum group is 6 people. Groups larger than 15 people are split into smaller groups. Call at least 3 days in advance.

Special Information: Wear rubber-soled shoes—the floor can be slippery.

Retail Store: Sells various-size boxes and gift baskets of Colorado Almond Toffee, Denver Mints, and assorted chocolates; also, individual candies, discounted seconds, and solid chocolate sculptures such as dinosaurs, Ferraris, and teddy bears. Open Mon–Fri 9:00 AM–5:00 PM. Catalog available at above number. Other Stephany's retail stores throughout Colorado.

Directions: From Denver Airport, take I-70 West to Wadsworth Ave. North to 52nd Ave. Turn right and proceed 3 blocks. Stephany's Chocolates is on the right.

Nearby Attractions: U.S. Mint and Hammond's Candies tours (see pages 94 and 8); Mile High Stadium, Coors Field, and other Denver attractions, including Denver Art Museum, Confluence Park, and Larimer Square, about 20 minutes away.

U.S. Mint

320 West Colfax Avenue
Denver, CO 80204
www.usmint.gov

COINS

The Denver U.S. Mint produces more than 10 billion coins per year. From a glass-enclosed observation area you'll see many of the production steps. The Mint starts with pre-shaped blanks for pennies and 8,000-pound metal coils for other coins. These coils first pass through presses that punch out blanks, which are slightly larger than the finished coins. Blanks are very hard, so they are softened in a 1,400° annealing furnace.

In the coin press room, shiny blanks are converted into their familiar identities. Watch workers dump crates of blanks into the top of the machine. The coin presses are sheltered in blue huts for noise abatement. The large blue Bliss press can produce about 800 coins per minute. Its smaller, longer counterpart, the Schuler press, can produce more than 800 coins per minute, with each die stamp lasting about 1 million strikes.

In the counting and bagging area, the enormousness of the production process becomes clear. Overhead hoists dump gondolas filled with shimmering coins into vibrating hoppers on top of the counting machines. Workers standing in front of the machines use hand-held sewing machines to seal each bag once it is filled with the proper number of coins. As the tour ends, you walk through richly decorated, marble-floored hallways of the original mint building, complete with nine grand turn-of-the-20th-century chandeliers. You will also see a sentry box by the stairs, the foremost means of dissuading robbers in the 1930s.

Cost: Free
Freebies: No

Video Shown: No
Reservations Needed: See website.
Days and Hours: *For security reasons, public tours have been discontinued until further notice. Please check their website as it is kept very current regarding changes in policy.*
Plan to Stay: 30 minutes for exhibits and tour, plus time for numismatic sales room.
Minimum Age: Children under 14 must be accompanied by an adult.
Disabled Access: Yes
Group Requirements: None
Special Information: No photography in building. Expect lines to enter the building during summer, so arrive early in the day to ensure a tour. Tours available at U.S. Mint in Philadelphia, PA (see page 298).
Sales Room: Sells proof and commemorative sets, medals produced by U.S. Mint, and other numismatic items. Store is on Delaware Street, just south of Colfax. Open same hours as tour. Closed government holidays. Catalog information at (202) 283-2646 or (800) USA-MINT.
Directions: Located in downtown Denver, between Delaware and Cherokee Sts. From I-25, take exit for downtown Denver and follow signs to Denver Mint. Look for the building with Italian Renaissance architecture. Park on the street or in a downtown lot.
Nearby Attractions: Stephany's Chocolates and Hammond's Candies tours (see pages 93 and 8); downtown Denver attractions, including the Denver Art Museum, Colorado History Museum, and State Capitol.

Van Briggle

600 South 21st Street
Colorado Springs, CO 80904
(719) 633-7729
www.vanbriggle.com

Van Briggle ART POTTERY

POTTERY

The original designs for Van Briggle Art Pottery date back to 1899. Van Briggle's *Despondency,* a vase with a figure of a despondent man molded around the rim, was first exhibited in Paris in 1900, where it won first place. A reproduction can be viewed in the Van Briggle masterpiece reproduction area. In addition to winning many awards, Artus Van Briggle reproduced a creamy, dull glaze known as "dead" matte glaze, which had been used by 14th-century Chinese. A tour of the company gives you a sense of the man and of his wife's continuation of his legacy, and an understanding of the process of making art pottery.

At the beginning of the guided portion of your tour, a potter demonstrates throwing pottery on an original early-1900s Van Briggle kick wheel. Next you move into the casting department, where rows of white chalky plaster molds are used to duplicate sculptured and wheel-thrown pieces. Liquid clay, or "slip," is poured into these molds. As the slip conforms to the exact design of the mold, the mold absorbs moisture from the slip. The longer the slip stays in the mold, the thicker the piece becomes. Excess slip is poured from the mold, leaving a hollow clay piece that is removed by hand.

The balance of your tour is self-guided, allowing you to spend as much time as you want viewing different processes and reviewing the explanatory displays, tape, and historical photographs. In the etching department, watch workers use damp sponges, carving instruments, and small turntables to smooth and refine the patterns of the unfired clay pieces called "greenware." Pottery stacked on shelves awaits one of the two kiln firings required to finish a piece. Between the first (or "bisque") firing and the second, glaze is applied to add color. In front of the kilns, displays show the piece's progression from a mold to the finished work.

Follow the curved shape of the building, past one of the largest wheel-thrown vases, to the historical photographs of Artus Van Briggle and early studios. Additional photographs show the transformation of the 1899 Colorado Midland Railroad roundhouse, where trains once chugged under the building's archways, to the current home of Van Briggle Art Pottery.

Cost: Free
Freebies: No
Video Shown: No
Reservations Needed: No, except for groups larger than 20 people.
Days and Hours: Mon–Sat 8:30 AM–4:30 PM. Limited production on Saturday. Closed Thanksgiving, Christmas, and New Year's.
Plan to Stay: 20 minutes for partially self-guided tour, plus time in showroom.
Minimum Age: None
Disabled Access: Yes
Group Requirements: Groups larger than 20 people should call 1 day in advance.
Showroom: Sells art nouveau decorative pottery and lamps. Also sells Van Briggle pottery collectors' books. Open Mon–Sat 8:30 AM–5:00 PM. Catalog available from (800) 847-6341.
Directions: From Denver, take I-25 South to Exit 141. Follow U.S. 24 West to 21st St. You're there when you see the curved shape and large tan bricks of this former railroad roundhouse, now on the National Registry of Historic Places. From Pueblo, take I-25 North to Exit 141. Follow the directions above.
Nearby Attractions: Simpich Character Dolls tour (see page 92); Patsy's Candies tour (call 719-633-6777); Pioneer's Museum; Ghost Town; The Broadmoor; Cave of the Winds; Pike's Peak; Garden of the Gods; Old Colorado City.

New England Carousel Museum

95 Riverside Avenue, Rt. 72 West
Bristol, CT 06010
(860) 585-5411
www.thecarouselmuseum.com

CAROUSELS

Walk into the rustic, Victorian building and find a magical carousel land, filled with horses and other carousel essentials in every stage of restoration and production. Inside the 33,000-square-foot renovated hosiery factory, the pieces range from horses, menagerie figures, and carousel pieces from the early 1800s to contemporary pieces by Juan Andreu, the museum's master carver. Andreu's creations include a UConn Husky carousel dog and a full-size dolphin. Few antique menagerie pieces, such as lions, tigers, swans, and frogs, have survived the popularity of the horse, so they usually have tremendous value today.

In the carving shop, antique horses become time capsules once their hollow bellies are opened for restoration. Onlookers have seen beehives, ride tickets, personal letters, and even Irish Sweepstakes tickets. Some horses have been restored to their former glory, while others appear only in primer coat or bare wood.

Try to tell the difference between Coney Island, Philadelphia, and Country Fair carving styles. Coney Island horses probably look the most familiar with their glitzy gold and jeweled exteriors, but Philadelphia horses are so realistically carved that you might be tempted to feed them an apple or two. Most of the Country Fair horses represent the portable carousel era and were often smaller and less detailed since they had to travel.

Exhibits of private collections recount the history of the carousel and its carvers. The band organ—originally considered an annoying idea because it blasted its theme song with no volume control—ended up the defining attractor of ride-goers. Trim pieces, like chariots, were introduced to accommodate the fashionable wide skirts of the 1800s, and the mirrors, lights, and paintings on rounding boards and valences were designed to hide the ride's mechanism.

The next time you go to a fair or amusement park, find yourself expertly identifying standers (three legs down, one up), prancers (back legs down, front legs up), and jumpers (four legs up) as they move up and down. If you really want to impress everyone around you, explain the reason American rounding boards do not spell out a message while they twirl like the British carousels do—the American mechanism spins the carousel the other way to sidestep the British patent.

Cost: Adults, $4; seniors, $3.50; children 4–14, $2.50; children under 4, free.

Freebies: Brochures

Video Shown: 40-minute video on history of carousel.

Reservations Needed: No, except for bus groups.

Days and Hours: Mon–Sat 10:00 AM–5:00 PM, Sun 12:00 PM–5:00 PM. December 1–March 31: closed Mon–Wed. Closed Easter, Christmas, New Year's.

Plan to Stay: 1.5 hours for tour, video, and gift shop.

Minimum Age: None

Disabled Access: Yes

Group Requirements: Bus tours or groups of 30 or more people call 1 week in advance to get 10% discount.

Special Information: No tripods without permission in writing. Personal photos only. Meeting rooms available by calling main number. Museum of Fire History and working artists studio on second floor. Children under 6 will enjoy a ride on the Tots Carousel and the Carousel Classroom, where they can cut out and color their own carousel crafts.

Gift Shop: Brass Ring sells jewelry, music boxes, wind chimes, brass rings, clothing, miniature ceramic carousels, and carousel novelty items.

Directions: From Rt. 84 East take Rt. 229 West St., Exit 31, to Bristol and follow Rt. 72 West to museum. From Rt. 84 West, take Exit 33 to Rt. 72 West (Bristol-Plainville). At end of expwy., take right onto Rt. 72 West.

Nearby Attractions: ESPN tour (call 860-766-2000); Bushnell Park Carousel; American Clock and Watch Museum; American Lock Museum; Lake Compound's Festival Park.

White Flower Farm

Route 63
Litchfield, CT 06759
(860) 567-8789
www.whiteflowerfarm.com

White Flower Farm
PLANTSMEN SINCE 1950

MAIL-ORDER NURSERY

American industry is more than just big factories, labs, and technology. In 1939, William Harris and his wife, Jane Grant, two successful writers from New York, converted a barn in Litchfield, Connecticut, into what would sprout into one of America's best-known mail-order nurseries. Their gardening avocation evolved into an obsession and then a local nursery. Their focus changed in 1950, when the first issue of *The White Flower Farm Garden Book* was mailed to a list of nursery (now called garden center) visitors. Today, gardeners from every state have ordered from this exquisitely written and photographed catalog.

On this self-guided tour of the retail garden center grounds (not of the mail-order business), you learn more about the company's products and history, plus enjoy walking around the beautiful settings. Depending on the season of your visit, you will see examples everywhere of what appears in the various catalogs. In the Display Gardens, for instance, you find a broad sampling of the colorful perennials that have made White Flower Farm famous. In early spring you enjoy the bulbs and by the fall its asters and mums. Throughout the grounds, most plants are labeled with both their common and botanical names.

Other tour favorites range from the rose arbor, dwarf conifer border, and shrub gardens, to the greenhouse with the stunning Blackmore & Langdon tuberous begonias. The rose arbor, at peak by early summer, serves as a showcase for disease-resistant varieties that the company has offered since the early 1990s. The shrub garden is filled with the flowing shrubs that have graced past editions of the *Garden Book*.

Company historical sites also include the barn that the company founders purchased and first turned into their country residence. Notice the all-white perennial border around part of the' house, now called the Moon Garden because the white flowers gleam even by moonlight. White.Flower Farm takes its name from this border garden.

Cost: Free, possible fee in future.
Freebies: Current catalogs
Video Shown: No
Reservations Needed: Reservations required for groups over 20 people.
Days and Hours: April–September: Mon–Sun 9:00 AM–5:30 PM. October–December: Mon–Sun 10:00 AM–5:00 PM. Closed January, February, March, Christmas, Thanksgiving, and July 4th.
Plan to Stay: At least 1 hour, if you want to go through all areas of the grounds and gardens, plus additional time for the retail store.
Minimum Age: None
Disabled Access: Most of the grounds are not wheelchair-accessible because of steps and stone walkways in parts.
Group Requirements: Reservations required for groups over 20 people and bus tours.
Special Information: Pick up self-guided tour map in the retail store or at the Visitor Information Center (when open).
Gift Shop: The Store at White Flower Farm sells a broad range of indoor and outdoor plants, plus gardening tools, books, pots, and gifts. The store does not duplicate all the catalog offerings. Depending on the growing season, varieties, sizes, and prices vary. Not an outlet store for catalog, although will have some specials at end of growing season for certain plants. Open same schedule as above. Catalog available at (800) 503-9624.
Directions: From I-84, take exit for Rt. 8 North, then eventually turn onto Hwy. 118 West. Turn left onto Rt. 63 South. Located 3.5 miles south of Litchfield Center.
Nearby Attractions: Litchfield Historical Society Museum; Topsmead State Forest; Housatonic Meadows State Park; Hartford's attractions about 1 hour away.

DaimlerChrysler

550 South College Avenue
Newark, DE 19713
(302) 453-5113
www.4adodge.com/durango

Every Dodge Durango you see on the street comes from the Newark Assembly Plant. Originally constructed in 1951 as a tank factory for the Korean War, the first cars rolled off the assembly line in 1957. Forty years later, Chrysler redesigned the plant to make the Dodge Durango and now produces 874 trucks there each day.

Inside the 3.4 million-square-foot factory, truck bodies, innards, doors, and seats travel on separate conveyor belts and carriages on the factory floor and overhead, miraculously meeting their matching parts at the right time. While shells move like bumper cars on a metal grid above, workers and robots build the bodies several feet below. Once the outside and inside meet, six robots with super-efficient elbows and wrists attack the frame with 80 welds, and then conveyor belts send the truck to the separate paint shop building, visible only in the video. Sixteen hours later, the truck comes back from the paint shop, still riding the same pedestal carriage on the belt.

When the truck returns to the line, tires roll off hydraulic balls to ease the strain for workers, and the nut runner tightens all six bolts to a preset torque before the truck lands on its own wheels for the first time on the flat-top conveyor. Workers place pads beneath each 75-pound door, attach a mechanical suction device, and press a button to evacuate the air and remove the door.

Seats travel overhead from the back of the plant to join their destined trucks. The "Power and Free" opens its orange arms like a clamshell to release the truck body, and a worker grabs seats with a mechanical swivel arm and pushes them into place through the back door. At the end of the line, the doors match back up with their original trucks.

Inspectors caress each truck for bumps or scrapes and check the lights, radio, and seatbelts. No truck can leave the plant before it passes the roll test, which includes testing everything from transmission shifts to the thermometer in the air conditioner.

Throughout the factory, morale boosters encourage a conscientious workforce with stickers that read "Plan, Do, Check, Act" and "Overprocessing=Waste." In the late 1970s, Chrysler CEO Lee Iacocca accepted government funding and pledged to make his factories higher quality and more efficient by listening to employee suggestions and rearranging the management structure. Today, employees at the Newark Assembly Plant send suggestions by computer to lessen physical strain and increase product quality, and corporate headquarters implements about 90 percent of the ideas.

Cost: Free
Freebies: Safety goggles
Video Shown: 6-minute video on painting process.
Reservations Needed: Yes
Days and Hours: September 1–May 31 only: Tue and Thur 9:30 AM and 6:00 PM. Tours can be difficult to reserve due to production shutdowns.
Plan to Stay: 1.5 hours
Minimum Age: 14
Disabled Access: Call ahead to make special arrangements.
Group Requirements: School groups call 1 week in advance.
Special Information: No dresses, soft sneakers, or open-toed shoes.
Gift Shop: No
Directions: From Baltimore, take I-95 North toward New York. Take Rt. 896, Exit 1, toward Newark/Middletown. Keep left at fork in ramp. Turn left onto Rt. 896 South. Rt. 896 turns into South College Ave. From Philadelphia, take I-676 East to I-95 South. Take Rt. 896 North, Exit 1B, toward Newark and turn left onto South College Ave./Rt. 896 South.
Nearby Attractions: Hagley Museum tour (see page 99); Winterthur Museum and Longwood Gardens are about 30 minutes away.

Hagley Museum

Route 141
Wilmington, DE 19807
(302) 658-2400
www.hagley.org

DUPONT BLACK POWDER

A mix of breathtaking landscaping and industrial ruins, a visit to Hagley's 235-acre museum shows every facet of life in an industrial river community. The largest powder yard in America, the DuPont community spreads two miles down the Brandywine River. Eleuthère Irénée du Pont came to America from France in 1800. He chose the banks of the Brandywine River as the site for his black powder mills because of the natural water-energy, the available timber and granite, and the ease of river transportation for the black powder ingredients.

Of the original 200 buildings, 45 remain as functioning relics of the DuPont black powder reign. In the powder yard, waterwheels and water turbines channel water to operate machinery. Pairs of roll mills with a waterwheel between them produce enough energy to spin two eight-ton iron wheels inside a massive wooden bowl, used for mixing black powder ingredients. Now a scenic, botanical masterpiece, the powder yard used to be smelly, noisy, dirty, and dangerous, with 288 unplanned explosions and 228 deaths during the 19th century. The architecture reflects the risks—building walls are three-foot-thick stone with "flyaway" roofs angled toward the river.

Eleutherian Mills, the first du Pont family home, sits atop a hill overlooking the factory and workers' community. Tour the Georgian-style home where five generations of du Ponts lived, and visit the first company office next door. Auto lovers should also check out the 1928 DuPont Motors car in the barn.

At the 1875 Machine Shop, ask volunteers to demonstrate and explain how leather belts transfer from one pulley to another, animating heavy drilling equipment. The shuttle bus will stop at the Engine House where the red and green wheel turns under steam power, whistling as it works. On Blacksmith Hill, volunteers in period dress relate life in the late 19th century in the Gibbons House, where powder yard foremen and their families once lived.

Cost: Self-guided tour: Adults, $9.75; students and senior citizens, $7.50; children 6–14, $3.50; children under 6, free; household, $26.50. Call for group rates.

Freebies: Brochures and Hagley Visitor's Guide.

Video Shown: 5-minute orientation video on company history.

Reservations Needed: No, for self-guided tours. Yes, for group tours.

Days and Hours: Mon–Sun 9:30 AM–4:30 PM. Mon–Fri, guided group tour only at 1:30 PM. Tickets on sale at 1:00 PM. School tours: mid-September through mid-June. Closed Thanksgiving and Christmas.

Plan to Stay: 4 hours for self-guided tour and gift shop. Guided tours vary.

Minimum Age: None

Disabled Access: Yes, but all areas may not be accessible. Call ahead to check.

Group Requirements: Groups of 15 or more people must make reservations at least 2 weeks in advance for guided tour. Guided tours can be conducted for groups under 15 people if visitors pay for 15. Maximum group size is 70 people.

Special Information: Wear comfortable walking shoes. No photography of furniture. Offers variety of specialized tours to groups. Call or visit website.

Gift Shop: Sells books, miniature working cannons, cards, T-shirts, stuffed animals, thimbles, and prints.

Directions: From the south, take I-95 North to the Newport Exit. Follow Rt. 141 North for 7 miles. Pass Rt. 100 and look for Hagley on the left. From the north, take I-95 South to I-495 South. Take Rt. 141 North and follow above directions.

Nearby Attractions: DaimlerChrysler and Herr's tours (see pages 98 and 32); Winterthur Museum; Longwood Gardens; Natural History Museum; Delaware Art Museum.

Bureau of Engraving and Printing

14th and C Streets, S.W.
Washington, D.C. 20228
(202) 874-3188 / (202) 874-2330
www.moneyfactory.com

MONEY

After entering the mammoth gray federal building that houses this bureau, you'll be showered with a wealth of information in display cases and videos about our nation's paper currency and other items, such as U.S. postage stamps. From a narrow, glass-walled, overhead walkway, the guided tour allows you to watch several steps in paper currency production. In the first step, not included on the tour, engravers hand-cut the currency design into soft steel. This engraving, used to create the master die and plate, begins the unique intaglio printing process that deters counterfeiting.

The printing itself is mesmerizing. Sheets of money, each with 32 bills in a four-by-eight pattern, rhythmically spin off the press at 8,000 sheets per hour. Stacks of money, called "skids," are everywhere. You'll wonder how the workers appear to treat their jobs with such detached calm. After inspections, overprinting of the serial number and Treasury seal, and cutting, the final product is a "brick" of 4,000 notes sent to the Federal Reserve Districts for local distribution.

The Bureau has been producing U.S. postage stamps since 1894. Here you will see the web-fed process of making U.S. postage stamps.

Cost: Free

Freebies: Unfortunately, no money! Informational brochures from the gallery and the visitors center.

Videos Shown: A short video, "The Buck Starts Here," explains the history of paper currency in the U.S. While you wait in line, a 20-minute overhead video quiz challenges your trivia knowledge of currency and stamps.

Reservations Needed: No

Days and Hours: During peak season (April–September): Mon–Fri 9:00 AM–2:00 PM. June–August: evening tours also, Mon–Fri 5:00 PM–7:00 PM. Tours every 10 minutes. Tickets marked with a designated time must be obtained at the booth on Raoul Wallenberg Pl. (formerly 15th St.). Tickets may be gone by 11:00 AM, so get in line early (booth opens at 8:00 AM). Booth opens at 3:30 PM for evening tours. During non-peak season (October–March): Mon–Fri 9:00 AM–2:00 PM. Line forms on the 14th St. side of the building for the tour. Congressional VIP tours Mon–Fri. 8:15 AM and 8:45 AM only. Ask your congressperson about tickets for this tour. Closed federal holidays and week between Christmas and New Year's.

Plan to Stay: 45 minutes, including displays, videos, and tour, plus time for the visitors center gift shop, and waiting time.

Minimum Age: None

Disabled Access: Yes. Upon request, accommodations for the hearing-, sight-, and physically impaired.

Group Requirements: Maximum group size is 60 people.

Special Information: Upon request, group tours in French, German, Japanese, Spanish, and Hebrew. Security is very tight. No backpacks allowed in tour. Thorough search performed on everyone entering the building.

Gift Shop: Sells a variety of items relating to paper money, including uncut sheets of new money and bags of shredded currency. There are videos on engraving, stamp production, and the identification of mutilated currency. Open Mon–Fri 8:30 AM–3:30 PM. Located on the opposite side of the building from the tour entrance.

Directions: Located immediately southwest of the Washington Monument grounds and west of Jefferson Memorial. Parking is nearly impossible to find in this area. Take the Metro (subway) blue line/orange line to the Smithsonian stop and walk out the Independence Ave. exit. Turn left on 14th St. or Raoul Wallenberg Pl., depending on where you need to obtain tickets.

Nearby Attractions: United States Holocaust Memorial Museum; Washington Monument; Jefferson Memorial; Smithsonian Institute.

Correct Craft

6100 South Orange Avenue
Orlando, FL 32809
(407) 855-4141 / (800) 346-2092
www.correctcraft.com

**SKI NAUTIQUES
WATER-SKI BOATS**

After seeing the water-ski extravaganza at nearby Sea World in Orlando, you may wonder how Ski Nautiques, its official ski towboats, are made. A tour of Ski Nautique manufacturer Correct Craft shows you in one hour the two-week process of building the premier inboard water-ski towboat. Correct Craft, started in 1925 by W. C. Meloon, is now a third-generation family business.

A short van ride from the corporate offices brings you to the open-air factory. Starting with a mold, fiberglass boats are actually built from the outside in. To create the shiny, colorful stripes of the hull's exterior, the interior surface of the mold is sprayed in sections with gelcoat. Then workers wearing floor-length aprons and safety gear use spray guns resembling oversized dentist-drill arms to apply the initial "skin coat" of fiberglass. A mixture of fiberglass and epoxy resin shoots out of the gun, looking like cotton candy when it hits the mold. Next, the entire inside of the mold is coated with cloth-like fiberglass sheets to form a solid unit. Workers use hand-rollers to smooth the hull's surface and inhibit the development of air pockets.

In another area, you can touch a smooth hull or deck just hoisted out of its mold. To reduce vibration and noise, ISODAMP CN (used by the Navy) is put on the inside of the hull's walls and the floor. In the engine area, a carousel-like crane swings around to lower an engine onto its frame. After the engine is bolted into place, workers install the dashboard, carpeting, interior trim, and seating. Each boat is tested under actual running conditions for at least 30 minutes in a nearby lake before decorative decals and graphics are applied. The water-skiers who go on this tour will immediately want to take one of the boats out for a pull.

Cost: Free

Freebies: Stickers

Video Shown: Upon request, a detailed 15-minute video on company history and production process is shown in the waiting area.

Reservations Needed: Yes, call 1 week in advance.

Days and Hours: Mon–Fri 2:00 PM. Closed 2 weeks around Christmas and 2 weeks in July. Closed federal holidays.

Plan to Stay: 1 hour

Minimum Age: 10

Disabled Access: Yes

Group Requirements: Groups should call ahead. Large groups will be split into groups of 10–15 people.

Special Information: Even though it's an open-air facility, you'll get a strong resin smell in the area where the fiberglass is applied. Watch out for forklifts moving through the maze of hulls and decks in various stages of production. Look for a 1934 wooden replica of a Correct Craft displayed in the waiting area. Future plans to move to new facility.

Gift Area: Fashion Nautique carries a wide array of Correct Craft clothing and accessories. Open Mon–Fri 8:00 AM–5:00 PM.

Directions: From I-4 West, turn left onto Michigan, right onto Orange Ave. Company offices are on right. From I-4 East, take Kaley exit, head east, then turn right onto Orange.

Nearby Attractions: Magic of Disney Animation Studios and Nickelodeon Studios tours (see pages 106 and 108); Regal Marine tour (call 800-US-REGAL); Sea World; Wet 'n' Wild. In Sarasota, on Florida's west coast, Wellcraft boat manufacturer gives tours (call 941-753-7811).

E-One

1601 S.W. 37th Avenue
Ocala, FL 34474
(352) 861-3521
www.e-one.com

FIRE TRUCKS

Whether you've wanted to be a firefighter since childhood or you've just watched the trucks careen around street corners, this will give you a new appreciation for fire trucks. Emergency One has become one of the world's leading manufacturers of emergency vehicles, building fire trucks, airport crash fire rescue vehicles, and ambulances.

E-One makes custom fire trucks according to the customer's requirements, such as community water sources and building heights. Two- to four-person teams work on the trucks in various stages of production. As you proceed through the factory-floor tour, notice the different fire truck varieties (aerial and pumper), and the many cab, body, and chassis designs.

In the body plant, power shears resemble guillotines as they chop diamond-patterned aluminum sheets. See sparks fly as a face-shielded worker welds the body frame together. Once the body is structurally sound, sanders and grinders transform it into a bright, shiny fire engine. In the paint shop you'll notice that there is no one official "fire-engine red." (Be sure to ask your tour guide why fire engines are red and for additional anecdotes.)

In the assembly area, two rows of black chassis patiently await their bodies and other accessories, such as pumps and electrical wiring. At the end of the line, a crane lowers a freshly painted custom cab onto its chassis. Check the shipper ID label on the dashboard window or cab—some fire-fighting vehicles are headed for Small Town, U.S.A., others to some exotic South Pacific island. In the final rigging area, you'll want to climb up into a fire-engine cab, sit in the thickly padded seats, touch the sophisticated control panel, and turn the steering wheel, pretending you're a firefighter.

Cost: Adults, $6; seniors, $4; children 6–12, free. Firefighters and their immediate families, free.

Freebies: Logoed hat

Video Shown: No

Reservations Needed: No, except for groups larger than 10 people.

Days and Hours: Mon–Fri 9:00 AM, 11:00 AM, and 1:00 PM. Closed holidays and week between Christmas and New Year's.

Plan to Stay: 1 hour, plus time for the gift shop.

Minimum Age: 6. Children under 6 receive a 20-minute abbreviated tour of the vehicle delivery center.

Disabled Access: Yes, call ahead.

Group requirements: Group size limited to 25 people per tour guide. Call at least 1 week in advance.

Special Information: See more production before 2:00 PM. Since tours are handled on a drop-in basis, you may have to wait until the guide returns to begin your tour. If there are 5 or fewer people on the tour, you'll ride around in a golf cart. Otherwise, you'll walk the tour route, so wear comfortable, closed-toe shoes. Occasionally, you may hear the sound of a fire-truck siren. Don't worry, it's just a test.

Gift Shop: The Fire Locker Shop sells T-shirts, clothes, hats, mugs, bags, Christmas ornaments, and scale models of fire trucks, all with the E-One logo. Open Mon–Fri 8:00 AM–5:00 PM. Catalog available from (800) 788-3726, (352) 237-1122, or www.firelocker.com.

Directions: From the Florida Tnpk., take I-75 North to Exit 69 (the second Ocala exit). You can see the plant on the right from I-75. Go right at exit. Turn right at S.W. 33rd Ave., then right at S.W. 7th. Follow service road that cuts back to left. The Welcome Center is the first building on the left.

Nearby Attractions: Silver Springs attractions; Wild Waters; Don Garlits' Drag Racing Museum.

Gonzalez y Martínez

2103 East 7th Avenue
Tampa, FL 33605
(813) 248-8210 / (888) 805-5897
www.gonzalezymartinez.com

CIGARS

Even though we don't write about tobacco tours in this book, we include this more as a history lesson than as a factory tour; cigar making is the industrial history of Tampa. In 1885 Don Vicente Martínez Ybor, a Cuban cigar factory owner, fled Cuba's political unrest to establish his cigar empire in a section of Tampa. Referred to first as "Mr. Ybor's City," later as Ybor City, this district, at its peak, had 200 cigar factories with 12,000 *tabaqueros* (cigar makers). Only a handful of master *tabaqueros* still hand-roll cigars in Tampa.

The Gonzalez y Martínez family tradition of cigar making was born shortly after the turn of the 20th century, after their recent arrival from Cuba and the marriage of Marcelíno Gonzalez to Francísco "Don Pancho" Martínez's daughter. Four generations later, Richard Gonzmart, Don Pancho's great-grandson, continues the family tradition.

You enter this cigar factory and store through a separate entrance of the famous Columbia Restaurant, recognizable by its colorful fruit-bouquet Spanish tile. Opened in 1905 and now in its fourth and fifth generations of family ownership and operation, the Columbia Restaurant is the oldest restaurant in Florida and the largest Spanish restaurant in the world.

Inside, the *tabaquero* sits at a dark brown wooden desk, surrounded on three sides by cases displaying cigars and a packing area behind him. The *tabaquero* classifies and separates the best leaves for filler, binder, and wrapper. From a pile on his desk, he selects several brown, almost-brittle, paper-thin, whole tobacco leaves. Next, he deveins these wrapper leaves. With a small water spray bottle, he moisturizes the leaves to obtain flexibility and restore silkiness. Stretching the wrapper leaves for rolling, he tightly rolls them around scraps of dried tobacco leaves, "filler," and twists the ends shut. After he chops off the excess with a blade, he carefully stacks each cigar on top of the desk, getting them ready for storage in their walk-in humidor.

Today Ybor City is being revived. Restored red-arched brick buildings with second-floor latticework balconies line the cobblestoned streets of 7th Avenue, the main thoroughfare. Nevertheless, traces of its cigar-making history remain.

Cost: Free
Freebies: No
Video Shown: No
Reservations Needed: No
Days and Hours: Mon–Sat 10:00 AM–6:00 PM.
Plan to Stay: 10 minutes, plus additional time in the store and Columbia Restaurant.
Minimum Age: None
Disabled Access: Yes
Group Requirements: None
Special Information: Can make personalized cigar labels for special corporate or personal occasions such as births, anniversaries, and wedding announcements.
Retail Store: Sells cigars ranging from Don Casimiro Collection, handmade in Tampa, to Private Batch Bourbon Cigars and cigar-related paraphernalia. Open Mon–Sat 10:00 AM–6:00 PM.
Directions: From I-275, take I-4 East. Take Exit 1. Turn right off ramp. Turn left onto 21st St. Will be on left at corner of 7th Ave.
Nearby Attractions: Ybor City State Museum provides cigar-making demonstrations on weekends. Exhibits tell about immigrants' lives and Ybor's history. Down the street, visit tiny restored "casitas," cigar workers' shotgun-style houses (call 813-247-6323); Ybor City State Museum provides map for Heritage and Factory walking tour of Ybor City; Tampa Rico Cigar Company tours (call 813-247-6738); Ybor City Brewing Company tours (call 813-242-9222); Busch Gardens; Adventure Island; Museum of Science and Industry.

Hoffman's

5190 Lake Worth Road
Greenacres City, FL 33463
(561) 967-2213 / (888) 281-8800
www.hoffmans.com

hoffman's *Chocolate Shoppes*

CHOCOLATES

Begun in 1975, when Paul Hoffman and Theresa Hoffman Daly paid $1,400 at an auction for an existing candy shop, this family-operated company now makes 200,000 pounds of candy per year. In this Tudor-style chocoholics' heaven, viewing windows at the right side of the store overlook the kitchen.

Directly in front of the observation window, the enrobing machine coats candy centers with an avalanche of chocolate. You may be lucky enough to watch peanut brittle or "jitterbugs" being made. Two workers pour a 300° mixture of butter, sugar, and almonds from a copper kettle onto a marble slab. They spread the mixture with metal spatulas, cut it in half with a pizza cutter, and flip it over. Then, with a comb-like spatula, they spread out the edges to "stretch" the peanut brittle.

Further back in the kitchen, buttercream centers proceed on a wire belt to another enrober. A worker waits for the chocolates to emerge, then hand-marks the type of center (for example, "R" for raspberry). After watching these candies being made, you'll be ready to sample some, especially the famous chocolate-covered pretzels.

You can walk off these extra calories in Hoffman's three-quarter-acre botanical gardens. Stroll among exotic and rare plants, a rainforest area, a miniature cacao plantation, and a fruit-salad section with pineapple, banana, and orange trees.

Every holiday season the garden is transformed into Hoffman's Holiday Wonderland, sparkling with more than 100,000 lights. It includes a giant gingerbread house, animated carolers, a custom-made menorah, a 15-foot Christmas tree, a life-size nativity scene, and Santa's North Pole Village.

Another garden highlight is the Candyland Railroad, a G-scale model community with more than 500 feet of track. Railcars make stops at Coconut Cream Cottage, Rocky Candy Mine, and Pecan Truffle Pond. The formal garden features topiaries shaped like a golfer, unicorn, and reindeer.

Cost: Free

Freebies: Sample chocolates

Video Shown: 13-minute video about chocolate-making, the botanical gardens, and Candyland Railroad.

Reservations Needed: No, except for groups larger than 15 people.

Days and Hours: Mon–Fri 9:00 AM–3:30 PM. Closed Thanksgiving, Christmas, New Year's, and Easter.

Plan to Stay: 25 minutes for self-guided viewing through observation window and video, plus time for gardens, trains, and Chocolate Shoppe.

Minimum Age: None

Disabled Access: Yes

Group Requirements: Groups larger than 15 people should call 1 week in advance to arrange a video presentation. Groups over 40 people will be split into smaller groups. No maximum group size.

Special Information: Best time to see production is from August 15 to Easter. During summer, call ahead for production schedule.

Retail Store: Chocolate Shoppe sells Hoffman's 80 varieties of chocolates. Open Mon–Sat 9:00 AM–8:00 PM, Sun 9:00 AM–6:00 PM, and from Thanksgiving to December 31, daily 9:00 AM–10:00 PM. Closed Thanksgiving, Christmas, New Year's, and Easter. Catalog available from (888) 281-8800.

Directions: From I-95, exit at 6th Ave. South in Lake Worth. Head west approximately 2 miles to Military Trail. Turn right onto Military Trail. Turn left onto Lake Worth Rd. Hoffman's is down the road on left. From Florida Tnpk., take Exit 93 (Lake Worth Rd.). Turn left and travel about 3 miles. Hoffman's is on right.

Nearby Attractions: Palm Beach and Knollwood Orange Grove tours (see pages 109 and 105); International Museum of Cartoons; Kravis Center; Lion Country Safari; Palm Beach Community College Museum of Art; Morikami Museum and Japanese Gardens; Lake Worth Beach.

Knollwood Groves

8053 Lawrence Road
Boynton Beach, FL 33436
(561) 734-4800 / (800) 222-9696
www.knollwoodgroves.com

Knollwood Groves

CITRUS FRUIT

If citrus fruits are what you crave, and you want some time away from the beaches and malls, Knollwood Groves offers a relaxing experience. It's one of Palm Beach County's oldest citrus groves, first farmed with grapefruit trees in 1930 by partners in the famous *Amos and Andy* radio show. Your tour on the tram (the Orange Blossom Special) meanders through the grove's 30 acres.

You'll learn more than just the citrus-farming business, as the narrator talks about Florida history, native American Indians, and alligator handling. After you pass the turtle and alligator pond, perhaps with snowy white egrets within view, you'll spend most of the time viewing the variety of trees. The grove has 20 kinds of citrus trees, which are pruned to between six and ten feet to allow easy picking, along with larger water oak, banyan, avocado, fig, cypress, sapodilla (source of chewing gum), and Florida cherry trees. The gumbo-limbo tree is a favorite, as its bark color and texture has led locals to rename it the "sunburned tourist tree." The area where the trees are densest, which is particularly cool on hot days, is called a jungle "hammock" by the Indians—a higher ground of trees that forms a natural roof overhead.

The sites on the covered-tram ride include some eclectic places that give the tour a very homegrown, natural feel. You stop briefly to explore an authentically re-created Hallpatee Seminole Indian village, with a live-alligator pit nearby. When Martin Two-Feather leads his longer tour, he provides extra doses of Florida Indian history and demonstrates alligator handling. Plus, you can't miss waving to the three wild boars. At the end of the peaceful, tractor-pulled tram ride, you enter the busy processing area, where the fruit is automatically washed and sorted, and then hand-packed.

Cost: Standard tour, $1; alligator-handling tour, $4–$6; children under 3, free.
Freebies: Fresh juice and fruit samples
Video Shown: 1-hour educational videos on citrus industry play continually in store.

Reservations Needed: No, except for groups over 20 people.
Days and Hours: November–May: Mon–Sun 10:00 AM–4:00 PM (tours on the hour). April–October (off-season, call for exact dates): Mon–Sat, usually 12:00 PM and 2:00 PM. Closed holidays. Special alligator-handling tour with Martin Two-Feather: Sat 2:00 PM and during weeks around Christmas and Easter, Mon–Sun 2:00 PM.
Plan to Stay: 30 minutes for standard tour, plus time for gift shop and fruit store, snack bar, picnic area, and many porch swings for relaxing. Longer tour with Martin Two-Feather, which features demonstrations at the Indian village and alligator handling, lasts about 1.5 hours.
Minimum Age: None
Disabled Access: Advance notice appreciated for lifting wheelchairs into tram.
Group requirements: Minimum group size is 20 people, with 2 days' advance notice. Special tour times can be arranged for motor coach tours. School-group tours in morning.
Special Information: Can watch juicing machines at small building near restrooms.
Gift Shop and Fruit Store: Sells variety of fresh fruit, vegetables, and juices, orange jams and jellies, citrus candy, local gourmet products, fudge, and Native American crafts. Snack bar with sandwiches. Dean's pie stand sells corkscrew, spiral-cut, open-face apple pie. Since 1973, Dean has been making these 3-pound apple pies, each requiring 4.5 hours to make. Mail-order department in gift shop for shipping fruit and gift baskets. Open same days as tours, 8:30 AM–5:30 PM. Catalog available at above number.
Directions: Take I-95 to Gateway exit. Head west on Gateway Blvd. to Lawrence Rd. Turn right; company is ahead on left.
Nearby Attractions: Palm Beach Groves and Hoffman's Chocolate tours (see pages 109 and 104); Loxahatchee Game Preserve; Lion Country Safari; and the beach.

The Magic of Disney Animation

Disney-MGM Studios
Walt Disney World Resort
Lake Buena Vista, FL 32830-0040
(407) 824-4321
www.disneyworld.com

The Walt Disney Company, with its giant theme parks, real estate holdings, and Oscar-winning movies, started as an animation studio in 1923. Whether you wonder how cartoon characters (like the ubiquitous Mickey Mouse) are drawn or what the newest Disney animated film will be, the answer is found on the Magic of Disney Animation tour at Disney-MGM Studios. The lobby displays of Walt Disney Studios' Oscars and of animation cels from current movies, the entertaining videos throughout the tour, and the busy animators all combine to bring this creative art to life.

You get to meet and talk with an animator. Then, through glass walls surrounding the animation studio, you can see part of the large production staff used to make animated shorts and movies. Animators have assigned roles, much like the characters they draw. Some animators sketch the character only at its furthest points of movement, while other artists add the in-between positions, redraw the series to refine the detail, or create special effects and the "sets" on which the animated characters perform.

Although computers now play a major role in the process, the Disney family remains committed to the art of hand-drawn animation. The animators, whose cubicles display interesting collections of personal knick-knacks and posters, sketch a few lines and flip back to other drawings on their light boards to see if the current etching follows sequence, often erasing and resketching. Other parts of the tour show you what's involved in transferring the paper drawings to plastic cels, in mixing the paints and inking the cels to create the colors needed for every character and scene, and in photographing the cels to create the illusion of life.

Cost: Included in admission charge to the theme park at Walt Disney World Resort.

Freebies: No

Videos Shown: During various stages of the tour, you watch entertaining and informative videos. See an introductory video with Robin Williams, a collection of Disney cartoons, and a video that shows what it's like to be an animator and presents clips from classic Disney animated films.

Reservations Needed: No

Days and Hours: Mon–Sun 9:00 AM–7:00 PM. Most activity Mon–Fri. Hours change depending on theme park hours and season. Open 365 days a year.

Plan to Stay: All day at Disney-MGM Studios. The Magic of Disney Animation tour lasts 35 minutes, plus the wait time before the tour.

Minimum Age: None

Disabled Access: Yes

Group Requirements: Groups larger than 10 people can call (407) 824-6750 in advance to order tickets to the theme park.

Special Information: Take this tour in the morning to avoid the longest lines, and try to go during the workweek. Tour is available on weekends and holidays, and you'll sometimes see an animator hard at work on a project. Other animation tours for student groups available through Youth Education Series. Call (800) 833-9806 for more information.

Gift Shop: The Animation Gallery sells figurines and cels of your favorite animation characters, along with books, videos, and other Disney cartoon character items. Open same hours as theme park.

Directions: From Orlando, take Exit 26 off I-4 and follow the signs. From Kissimmee, stay on U.S. 192 and enter at the main Disney entrance.

Nearby Attractions: All attractions and shows at Disney-MGM Studios. The Studios Backlot tour teaches you about moviemaking and television production, and provides glimpses of current Disney projects in production.

New Piper Aircraft

2926 Piper Drive
Vero Beach, FL 32960
(561) 567-4361
www.newpiper.com

The Piper name has been synonymous with small aircraft since the introduction of the Piper Cub in the late 1930s by a former Pennsylvania oilman, William T. Piper. After producing thousands of bright yellow Cubs for pilot training during World War II, Piper moved its base from central Pennsylvania to a sprawling facility in Florida where it has developed more than 100 single- and twin-engine models and built more than 150,000 planes. In the summer of 1995, New Piper Aircraft Inc. became a reality when President/CEO Charles Suma and a nucleus of employees took over the assets of the Piper Aircraft Corporation. Retired company workers conduct informative, in-depth tours of New Piper's 1.2 million-square-foot plant, where you will learn all about the planes in which many pilots are first taught how to fly.

Your tour begins in Building 1, appropriately where the manufacturing process itself begins with the making of the custom tools and dies used to manufacture various parts of the finished aircraft. Next, watch as workers put 4,000-pound rolls of raw aluminum through giant shearing machines to cut the metal to a workable size. As you move along, you'll see this metal transform into the skin and bones of an airplane.

Parts like wing flaps, landing gear, and hydraulic lines fill in the skeletal airframe; discover how they are made in the subassembly areas, fastened in place, and calibrated. Watch computer-controlled milling and routing machines robotically cut, drill, bore, and shave these parts into shape while spewing tiny shards of metal. Get a glimpse at nearly-completed aircraft ready for its first test flight before heading to the most exciting part of the tour: the mating of the wings and fuselage. An overhead crane sets the fuselage down over the single, continuous wing piece as it is held steady by a jig. With this step, the elaborate birth of an airplane seems complete, and your imagination can take flight.

Cost: Free

Freebies: Brochures on Piper aircraft

Video Shown: 5–10-minute video on company history and safety

Reservations Needed: Yes

Days and Hours: Tue and Fri at 10:00 AM and 2:00 PM. Closed Memorial Day, July 4th, Labor Day, and weeks of Thanksgiving and Christmas.

Minimum Age: 5

Plan to Stay: 1–2 hours

Disabled Access: Yes

Group requirements: Groups should call 1 week in advance. No maximum group size.

Special Information: Piper Aviation Museum in Lock Haven, PA, covers some of the history of the original Piper Company. Call (570) 748-8283.

Gift Shop: Piper Pilot Shop sells a variety of logoed merchandise, including miniature airplane models, clothing, and luggage. Open Tue–Fri 9:00 AM–5:00 PM. Online ordering is available through the Pilot Shop website (www.newpiper.com).

Directions: From I-95 South, take Exit 68 (Vero Beach exit). Turn left onto Rt. 60. Turn left on 34th Ave. Turn right on Aviation Blvd. Turn right onto Piper Dr. and pass 2 parking lots on right. Make a right just before the white stone company sign.

Nearby Attractions: Kennedy Space Center in Cape Canaveral is 50 miles away.

Nickelodeon Studios

Universal Studios
1000 Universal Studios Plaza
Orlando, FL 32819
(407) 363-8000
www.universalorlando.com

TELEVISION SHOWS

On this tour you'll learn about sophisticated television technology. You may also taste Gak or get green-slimed with edible green goo. Sound contradictory? It won't, once you visit the world's first television network designed especially for kids. Nickelodeon's production complex at the Universal Studios theme park at the Universal Orlando resort is a combined state-of-the-art television studio and backstage tour facility. On days that shows are taped, your kids can sometimes join the live studio audience.

Look down through glass windows at the cobweb of lighting-grid hoists that hover over the ultramodern sound stages. Each stage is big enough to park a 747 jet in. See the sets for Nick shows. You'll appreciate the magic of television when you notice the difference between how sets look in person, compared to on television. Glass walls also expose the audio and video working control rooms. The 50 monitors in the video control room resemble a giant jigsaw puzzle, with the director picking the best shots for the program.

You'll also see the wardrobe room, the hair/makeup room, and the open-walled "kitchen" where they "cook" green slime, Gak, and other recipes unique to Nick programs (there's actually a Gak-meister who concocts messes). After viewing the behind-the-scenes stuff, kids and their families can engage in some favorite Nick games and help create new ones. In the Nickelodeon Game Lab, you feel like you're on a real game show, as you participate in *Double Dare* stunts—with luck, you may get green-slimed! You leave with a new pop-culture vocabulary and an appreciation for what's involved in producing kids' TV.

Cost: Included in the general admission charge for Universal Studios.

Freebies: Sometimes

Videos Shown: Throughout the tour, brief videos describe the production process. The videos add to the tour, especially if shows are not in rehearsal during your visit.

Reservations Needed: No

Days and Hours: Mon–Sun 10:00 AM–5:00 PM. Universal Studios open later during peak days and in summer. Last tour 1 hour before Universal Studios closes. Open 365 days a year.

Plan to Stay: All day at Universal Studios. Nickelodeon tour is 40 minutes, plus any wait in line before the tour.

Minimum Age: None

Disabled Access: Yes

Group Requirements: For group ticket information to Universal Studios, call (407) 363-8210.

Special Information: Tour lines are shorter in the morning. As you wait in line, kids will be entertained by Sega video games and the Green Slime Geyser, a 17-foot-high green fountain made of pipes, tubes, and other odd-looking machines, that rumbles, hisses, and periodically erupts slime. It's a landmark at the Nick studio entrance. Call (407) 363-8586 2 or more weeks in advance to find out what shows will be in production or whether a live audience is needed. Families should check with Guest Services lobby on day of visit.

Gift Shop: A cart on the corner sells Nick T-shirts and sweatshirts, Ren & Stimpy dolls, and other Nick paraphernalia.

Directions: Take I-4 to Exit 29 or Exit 30B. Follow the signs for Universal Orlando.

Nearby Attractions: More than 40 rides, shows, and attractions at Universal Studios, including "Men in Black Alien Attack," "E.T. Adventure," "King Kong Kongfrontation," and "Back to the Future...The Ride."

Palm Beach Groves

7149 Lawrence Road
Boynton Beach, FL 33436
(561) 965-6699 / (800) 327-3208
www.pbgroves.com

CITRUS FRUIT

PALM BEACH GROVES
A^{nd} MARKETPLACE

More citrus fruit grows in Florida than almost anyplace else in the world. Unfortunately, none of the large commercial groves and processing plants offers public tours. However, at Palm Beach Groves you can tour a small working grove, visit the processing and packing area, wander through tropical gardens, and go home with plenty of fresh fruit and juice from the abundantly stocked retail store.

You'll see and learn about a wide variety of citrus fruits during your ride through the grove in a tractor-pulled covered cart. Each type of orange, such as navel, temple, and honeybell (a hybrid between grapefruit and tangerine), has a 4- to 15-week season. Surrounded by orange trees, you'll enjoy the peaceful, fragrant journey—a real contrast to the noisy South Florida malls. After the tram ride, walk through the areas where the fruit is washed, sorted, and packed, the intermediate steps between the tree and your table. Nearby you can look through glass windows at machines that squeeze oranges and grapefruits for juice.

On the washing line the oranges wiggle and roll around through a shallow water-bath and rinse, then travel to the sponge and hot-air dryers. Notice the simple but effective method of mechanically sorting the oranges by size. The grading machine resembles a pinball machine. The fruit rolls down a ramp, leaning against an opening that gradually increases in size. The smaller fruits fall through the narrowest opening at the beginning and the biggest, most expensive ones fit through the largest opening toward the end. The oranges drop into hammocks, which cushion their fall into wooden crates. Try to guess which orange will fall into which size crate.

Cost: Free
Freebies: Tastes of citrus fruits; samples of juice and other foods.

Video Shown: No
Reservations Needed: No
Days and Hours: Mid-October (call for date)–April only: Mon–Sun 10:00 AM–4:00 PM on the hour for orange grove tours. Tour of the packing and processing area is self-guided. Call ahead to see when they will be packing and processing the fruit (busiest November–March).
Plan to Stay: 20 minutes for tour, plus time for Marketplace, gift shops, and gardens.
Minimum Age: None
Disabled Access: Yes; a few steps up to tram.
Group Requirements: Can handle any size group. Suggest 1 day's advance notice.
Special Information: A small nature walk through the grove's tropical gardens features colorful wandering peacocks and a unique sausage tree. Make sure you try some of the seasonal oranges, such as the juicy honeybells (available only in January).
Marketplace and Gift Shop: Marketplace sells a wide selection of fresh citrus fruit, Florida-made products such as jellies and gourmet sauces, homemade fudge, and fresh soups and sandwiches. Also sells native foliage and plants. For special deals, go to the Juice Fruit Room, where you pack your own fruit that's irregularly shaped or sized, or slightly overripe. Gift shop sells Florida-related items such as citrus perfumes, shells, and T-shirts. Visit or call mail-order department for shipments of fresh fruit and gift baskets. Open mid-October–April, Mon–Sun 9:00 AM–5:30 PM. Summer, Mon–Sat 9:00 AM–5:30 PM, Sun 11:00 AM–5:30 PM. Catalog available from 800 number above.
Directions: Take I-95 to Hypoluxo Rd. exit, then go west to Lawrence Rd. Turn left and go about .25 miles. Look for signs on right.
Nearby Attractions: Hoffman's chocolate and Knollwood Groves tours (see pages 104 and 105); Loxahatchee Game Preserve; Lion Country Safari; the beach.

Whetstone Chocolates

Two Coke Road
St. Augustine, FL 32086
(904) 825-1700
www.whetstonechocolates.com

CHOCOLATES

The small ice cream and candy shop founded by Henry and Esther Whetstone in 1967 is now a 94,500-square-foot facility that produces 500 to 1,800 chocolates per minute. This self-guided tour provides a view of the major steps in making Whetstone's specialty chocolates. Although much of the production is now automated, many areas of production still use a hands-on approach.

Start with a 15-minute video about the history of chocolate, its harvesting and journey from bean to finished product, including a complete tour of the plant when all chocolate is in production. Afterwards, meet and activate a robot used on the factory line and see a kettle full of 500 pounds of melting chocolate.

In the molding room, the chocolate begins its 35-minute journey from liquid to finished product. Approximately 400 molds, each containing as many as 24 cavities, wait patiently to be filled with chocolate from a 10,000-pound melter. The melter maintains the chocolate at a temperature of 115°. The chocolate is pumped from the melter into a tempering machine, which cools it to 85° by moving it through a series of cooling chambers, giving the chocolate a shiny appearance. The tempered chocolate is then sent through heated pipes to the depositors, which funnel it into the molds. If the product requires a filling (such as a nut, caramel, or fruit piece), the molds are sent to another filling station. After filling, more chocolate is added to finish the piece.

As you walk along the factory's elevated, glass-enclosed walkway, signs above the machines give a brief description of the processes below. The chocolates move into the packing room, where stacks of boxes await filling. Here, the pieces are inspected for flaws (unacceptable chocolates are recycled) and then hand-packed. Some varieties of Whetstone chocolates are individually adorned with brightly colored foil wrap by a wrapping machine before being packaged.

Watch Whetstone's famous chocolate seashells go from liquid chocolate to scalloped, molded shells. Also see how they make the chocolate orange, which breaks into 18 slices when whacked. At the enrobing machine, nuts, toffee crunch, caramels, and caramel pecan monkeys ride along a conveyor belt and pass under a chocolate waterfall. Whetstone continually researches and tests new flavors and shapes of chocolate.

Cost: Free

Freebies: Chocolate seashell sample

Video Shown: 15-minute video in theater shows the history and technology of chocolate making.

Reservations Needed: No, except for groups larger than 15 people.

Days and Hours: Mon–Sat 10:00 AM–5:00 PM. Best time to view production is Mon–Fri 10:00 AM–2:00 PM. Limited production on Saturdays. Closed Thanksgiving and Christmas. Since factory production schedules frequently change, call (904) 825-1700, ext. 25.

Plan to Stay: 30 minutes for self-guided tour and video, plus time for the Factory Outlet Store.

Minimum Age: None

Disabled Access: Yes

Group Requirements: Groups larger than 15 people can request a special guided tour by calling (904) 825-1700, ext. 24, in advance. Large groups will be split into groups of 25 people. Bus groups welcome.

Outlet Store: The Factory Outlet Store sells entire selection of Whetstone chocolates and candies (such as assorted chocolates, caramel pecan monkeys, sea shells, chocolate oranges, and Scenes of St. Augustine candy bars) and gift items. Call (800) 849-7933 or visit above website to order.

Directions: From I-95, take SR 207 North to SR 312 East. Whetstone is located at the intersection of SR 312 and Coke Rd.

Nearby Attractions: San Sebastian winery tours (call 904-826-1594); St. Augustine's Historic District includes the Nation's Oldest House; Castillo de San Marco Spanish fort; Spanish Quarter Museum; Lighthouse Museum and Lighthouse; coastal beaches.

▲ Workers packaging foil-wrapped oranges at Whetstone Chocolates Factory in St. Augustine, Florida.

▼ The finished product: Whetstone Chocolates Foil Oranges.

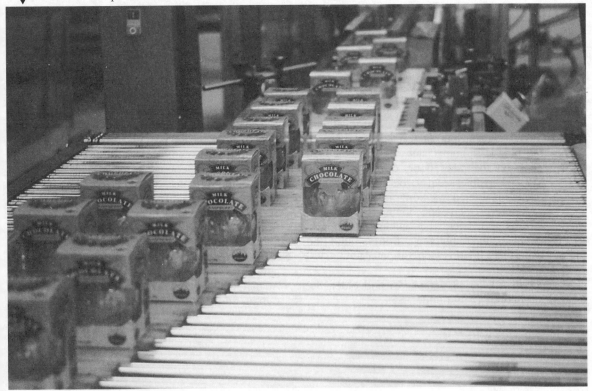

CNN

One CNN Center
Atlanta, GA 30348-5366
(404) 827-2300
www.cnn.com/studiotour

CNN Center's naturally lit atrium greets you at the global headquarters of Turner Broadcasting System. Your tour of the world's news leader begins as you ride one of the world's largest free-span escalators (eight stories) to an area exhibiting CNN's growth paralleling world events from the past 20 years. Next, step inside a re-creation of CNN's main control room where you can see and hear behind-the-scenes elements of the network live.

Follow your tour guide into the CNN Special Efx Studio. Examine the Tele-PromTer. It is like those used in newsrooms around the world. Watch your guide on a monitor point to various graphics just as your favorite newscaster points to a weather map. You may be surprised to discover they are actually pointing to a blank blue wall. This high-tech Chroma Key system allows maps and other graphics to be superimposed onto the blank wall by the camera. But beware, if the newscasters are also wearing blue, they'll disappear!

Peer through glass walls high above the main newsroom floor and observe the researching, gathering, and reporting of news. The tour guide explains how producers, writers, and anchors work together on the complex news-gathering process, which continues 24 hours a day, seven days a week. It takes two to three hours to put together a news segment, but late-breaking stories can be broadcast immediately. Everywhere you look on the news floor, dozens of neatly dressed people seem to be staring intently, either up at the news monitors, ahead at their computer screens, or down at their keyboards and notes while talking on phones. Satellites feed the news from around the world into hundreds of computer terminals.

Cost: Adults, $8; seniors 65 and older, $6; children 12 and under, $5.

Freebies: CNN Studio Tour pins

Video Shown: Short video in the tour finale area showcases Turner Broadcasting networks, such as TBS, TNT, and the Cartoon Network.

Reservations Needed: No, but advance reservations recommended. Same-day reservations not available.

Days and Hours: Mon–Sun 9:00 AM–5:00 PM, except Thanksgiving, Christmas, and Easter. Each day's tour tickets go on sale at 8:30 am.

Plan to Stay: 45 minutes including video and tour, plus time for the Turner Store.

Minimum Age: 6

Disabled Access: Yes, with 1 day's notice.

Group Requirements: Groups of 20 or more people must call 24 hours in advance for reservations and group discounts.

Special Information: No photography.

Gift Shop: The Turner Store, on the retail level of CNN Plaza, sells logoed merchandise including CNN, TBS, TNT, the Cartoon Network, and Sport South Network. Open Mon–Sun 9:30 AM–7:00 PM. Closed Thanksgiving, Christmas, and Easter. Call (404) 827-2100.

Directions: By train, take MARTA to Stop W1, "Omni, World Congress Center, Georgia Dome." By car, take I-75/85 North to Exit 96 (International Blvd.). Follow signs to the Georgia World Congress Center. From I-75/85 South, take Exit 99 (Williams St./Downtown). Again, follow signs to the Georgia World Congress Center. CNN Center is on the corner of Centennial Olympic Park Dr. and Marietta St. in downtown Atlanta, across the street from the Georgia World Congress Center and next door to the Omni.

Nearby Attractions: Downtown Atlanta's attractions, including World of Coca-Cola Atlanta (see page 114), World Congress Center, and Underground Atlanta.

Lane Packing

Highway 96 East & 50 Lane Road
Fort Valley, GA 31030
(478) 825-3592 / (800) 277-3224
www.lanepacking.com

PEACHES

Did you know that there are over 40 varieties of peaches grown in the state of Georgia, and that more than 30 are grown at Lane Packing Company? Junegold, Southern Pearl, Rubyprince, Lane Luck—you'll find these varieties and many more, with equally pretty-sounding names, at this peach packing operation. A fourth-generation family business that farms approximately 3,000 acres of peaches and 1,500 acres of pecans, it houses one of the most modern peach processing facilities on the East Coast.

From a 59-inch platform overlooking this operation, with the aid of informational signs describing each process, see firsthand how fresh-from-the field peaches make their journey through the processing facility. During your self-guided tour, hear the children around you giggle with happiness as the automatic dumping system releases approximately 1,000 pounds of peaches per minute into a large bath of flowing, 36° water. Gently bobbing up and down, they take a relaxing ride to their next stop: the grading area. Here, standing on both sides of several conveyor belts, white-gloved workers inspect, by touch and sight, the slowly moving peaches. Deemed too soft or as having other physical defects, some of the peaches depart from the others on the number two line, where they are re-graded, packed, and sold at a reduced price.

Meanwhile, proudly standing in single file on a conveyor belt, each of the peach elite is electronically weighed and labeled with a PLU sticker, after having been washed and waxed. They then proceed to one of 12 filling stations according to their size. At each station, 25 pounds at a time slide down a chute into a half-bushel box waiting below. After packaging, they are loaded into a refrigerated truck and await departure for their next destination.

In most cases, this next destination is a home where the customers enjoy the peaches in their simplest form. However, after your tour, explore the variety of peach products at the Peachtree Café, Roadside Market, and Just Peachy Gift Shop: peach ice cream, amaretto and peach syrup, peach butter, and peach tea... Discover there's no end to the delights of peaches, and see them all at Lane Packing Company.

Cost: Free
Freebies: Samples of peaches and peach products
Video Shown: Video that describes the peach-packing process is shown in the retail area.
Reservations Needed: No, but recommended for groups of 20 or more people.
Days and Hours: Mid-May–mid-August: Mon–Sun, 8:00 AM–8:00 pm, depending upon the availability of peaches.
Plan to Stay: 20 minutes for the tour, plus additional time for eating at the café and browsing the gift shop and market.
Minimum Age: None
Disabled Access: Yes
Group Requirements: Groups of 20 or more people should call in advance, but not necessary. You can request to have a tour guide.
Gift Shop, Roadside Market, and Café: The Just Peachy Gift Shop sells peach-themed jewelry, shirts, toys, dishes, and baskets. Roadside Market offers fresh farm produce, as well as peach and vidalia onion products. Peachtree Café serves a variety of food, including barbecue sandwiches, a daily fresh fruit bar, peach and blackberry cobbler, and peach ice cream. Open year-round, Mon–Sat 9:00 AM–5:30 PM, Sun 12:00 PM–5:30 PM.
Directions: From I-75 take Exit 142 GA Hwy. 96 West approximately 5 miles. Lane Packing Company is on the right.
Nearby Attractions: Andersonville National Cemetery and Historical Site; Georgia Music Hall of Fame; Georgia National Fairgrounds and Agricenter; Georgia Sports Hall of Fame; Hay House, The Palace of the South; Massee Lane Gardens; Museum of Aviation.

World of Coca-Cola Atlanta

55 Martin Luther King Jr. Drive S.W.
Atlanta, GA 30303-3505
(404) 676-5151
www.woccatlanta.com

SODA

A mammoth neon logo and colorful flags from more than 200 Coca-Cola-enjoying nations welcome you to this Coca-Cola attraction. At this three-story, multimedia celebration of Coke, you will learn about the savvy marketing that catapulted what originally started as a headache remedy into the world's number-one soft drink. In fact, if all the Coca-Cola ever produced were placed in eight-ounce bottles and laid end to end, the line would stretch to the moon and back 1,323 times. (This and other impressive facts are continuously flashed on an electronic billboard.)

View the "Bottling Fantasy," a whimsical sculpture that turns the bottling process into art. Then take a nostalgic journey through 100-plus years of history, past display cases showing early bottling equipment and advertisements, billboards, and trinkets featuring 1920s vaudeville stars. For more interactive time travel, step into giant Coca-Cola cans called "Take 5 Units" and touch the video screens inside. Five-year sips of world events and lifestyles from 1886 to the present are combined with Coca-Cola history. Sit in a replica 1930s soda fountain, while a soda jerk flicks the fountain handle one way for fizz and the other way for flavored syrup.

The Coca-Cola Great Radio Hits kiosk blares with music stars singing Coke radio jingles from the 1960s to the present. (Even the Moody Blues sang "Things Go Better with Coke"!) View Coke's classic television commercials.

In Club Coca-Cola, aerial liquid jets deliver your free soft drink. Once you place your cup under the fountain, an infrared sensor triggers overhead spotlights that illuminate your cup. The glass tubing and neon around you begin to pulsate, and soda arches 20 feet from a hidden high-pressure nozzle, scoring a hole-in-one into your cup. After leaving this futuristic soda fountain, be sure to watch the international Coca-Cola commercials and sample exotic flavors (like Fanta Peach from Botswana).

Cost: Adults, $6; seniors 55+, $4; children 6–11, $3; under 6 (with adult), free.

Freebies: Large variety of Coca-Cola products, plus 20 exotic flavors not available in the U.S.A.

Videos Shown: Optional 10-minute presentation called "Every Day of Your Life," shown in large-screen, high-definition cinema. Other videos shown throughout the exhibits. Videos closed-captioned for the hearing impaired.

Reservations Needed: No. Recommended for groups over 20 people.

Days and Hours: Mon–Sat 9:00 AM–5:00 PM, Sun 12:00 PM–6:00 PM. Expect long waits during holidays and Atlanta-area events. Closed Easter, Thanksgiving, and Christmas and at 3:00 PM Christmas Eve and New Year's Eve.

Plan to Stay: 1.5 hours for displays, plus time for gift shop and waiting.

Minimum Age: None

Disabled Access: Yes

Group Requirements: Groups larger than 20 people can make reservations in advance to receive express entry and discounted admission. Call (404) 676-6074 Mon–Fri 9:00 AM–5:00 PM.

Special Information: Foreign language brochures available. Arrive earlier in day to avoid longest wait. Coca-Cola fans will also want to visit Coca-Cola Bottling in Kokomo, IN (see page 140).

Retail Store: Everything Coca-Cola features logoed clothing, gifts, and collectibles. Open same hours as attraction.

Directions: From I-75/85 North, take Exit 246 (Central Ave. exit). Follow Central Ave. as it goes over expressway to Martin Luther King Jr. Dr. Museum is at intersection. From I-75/85 South, take Exit 248A (State Capitol/MLK Dr.). Go straight on Martin Luther King Jr. Dr. 3 blocks to intersection with Central Ave.

Nearby Attractions: Downtown Atlanta's attractions, including CNN tour (see page 112); Underground Atlanta; State Capitol; Georgia World Congress Center; Atlanta Heritage Row (history museum).

Big Island Candies

585 Hinano Street
Hilo, HI 96720
(808) 935-8890 / (800) 935-5510
www.bigislandcandies.com

CANDIES
BIG ISLAND

CHOCOLATE-COVERED MACADAMIA NUTS AND COOKIES

You may be surprised at how far Big Island Candies will go in order to keep its customers entertained. Priding itself on its uniqueness, the company tries dipping almost anything in chocolate, and some of its successful (albeit unusual) experiments have produced chocolate-covered animal crackers, fortune cookies, and even *ika* (cuttlefish). Its more conventional products include original and chocolate-dipped shortbread and local favorites such as macadamia ("mac") nuts. Big Island Candies has been producing high-quality chocolates since 1977, when owner Allan Ikawa sold everything, including his boat and his house, to open the company.

On a self-guided tour, you may be tempted to dive through the factory's big glass windows into one of the cylindrical white melters that melt up to 1,000 pounds of chocolate into liquid form. The stainless-steel melters also temper the chocolate, thus ensuring that it will have a glossy finish. As you move to the next window, smell the shortbread cookies baking in the factory's six ovens. Big Island Candies is one of the few facilities of this size that still do hand-dipping, making chocolates the old-fashioned way. Dippers clad in red shirts and black aprons walk over to the melters to fill their bowls with the sweet brown liquid.

Returning to their station, the dippers pour mac nuts into the chocolate-filled bowl. Skillfully grabbing a nut (or a cuttlefish, cookie, or animal cracker) with one hand, they smother it with more chocolate with the other hand and pop it into the cavity of a candy tray that stands on a scale in front of them. The scale ensures that each tray of candy has the proper weight. You may be amazed by the swiftness with which some of the dippers cover items with chocolate, deftly filling their trays at top speed and with incredible dexterity.

Knowing that many visitors come to Big Island Candies in search of *omiyage* (gifts bought for friends and family, following an Asian tradition), the company creates distinctive packaging for its candies. You leave Big Island Candies knowing that the gourmet candies and chocolates inside those beautiful boxes are made with skill and care.

Cost: Free

Freebies: Chocolate, cookie, and Kona coffee samples.

Video Shown: No

Reservations Needed: No, except for groups larger than 25 people.

Days and Hours: Daily 8:30 AM–5:00 PM, with the best time to see production Mon–Fri before 3:30 PM. Limited production on weekends and holidays.

Plan to Stay: 30 minutes for the self-guided tour, plus time in gift shop.

Minimum Age: None

Disabled Access: Yes

Group Requirements: Groups of over 25 people should call at least 1 day in advance.

Special Information: Japanese-speaking sales representatives are available.

Gift Shop: Sells all of the company's products, including chocolate-covered mac nuts, rocky road (mac nuts, marshmallows, and chocolate), crunchies (mac nuts, potato chips, and chocolate), crunch (mac nuts, crisp rice, and chocolate), and chocolate-dipped shortbread cookies, fortune cookies, animal crackers, and *ika*. Open Mon–Sun 8:30 AM–5:00 PM. Open every day of the year. Gift guide available from above number.

Directions: From Hilo airport, go through one traffic signal and take third right onto Hinano St. Big Island Candies will be on the corner. From Hamakua coast, stay on Kamehameha Ave. Turn right onto Kanoelehua Ave, right onto Kekuanaoa St., and right onto Hinano St. Big Island Candies will be on right.

Nearby Attractions: Mauna Loa Macadamia Nuts, Holualoa Kona Coffee, and Ueshima Coffee tours (see pages 119, 117, and 120); Hilo Bay; Hawaii Volcanoes National Park (with its live volcano).

Dole Pineapple Plantation

64-1550 Kamehameha Highway
Wahiawa, HI 96786
(808) 621-8408
www.dole-plantation.com

PINEAPPLE

When you think of Hawaiian products, pineapple is likely at the top of your list, with Dole the most well-known brand name. Founded in Hawaii in 1851, Dole Food Company, Inc., is the largest producer and marketer of fresh fruits and vegetables in the world. Dole has offered different types of visitor experiences on Oahu, including tours of its canning operation that closed in 1993 (converted into retail and office complex). The Dole Plantation, located on Oahu's North Shore on the same site the company first used to grow pineapples, offers a retail, historical, agricultural, and gastronomical experience.

When you first drive up, you see a splendid re-creation of a plantation mansion. The roof is tall and peaked, sheathed in materials that show the tin roofs of old-time plantation building. Surrounding the center of the building is a traditional cooling verandah, ringed by tall trees and lush landscaping. Off to the right in front is the Pineapple Garden Maze, a fun challenge listed in the *Guinness Book of World Records* as the world's largest maze.

Inside the building, high ceilings with a rough-hewn finish attempt to give the appearance of a traditional pineapple warehouse. Special areas sell a variety of goods, foods, and snacks, designed to represent a traditional marketplace, a country store, and a series of building facades reminiscent of old Haleiwa Town. Look on the walls for displays chronicling the history of pineapple and for the dozens of oversized pineapple cans sporting authentic Hawaiian pineapple labels. Spend time learning from Dole's experts how to choose and slice pineapples.

Roam the grounds outside to learn more about pineapples. A special garden showcases varieties of pineapple plants from around the world. Exhibits cover the history and origins of the pineapple, Jim Dole's contributions to the industry, and more on how pineapples are grown and processed. After walking through these areas, and conquering the nearly two-mile path of the Garden

Maze, you'll enjoy the frosty Dole Whip back in the Plantation.

Cost: Plantation and display gardens: free. Maze: adults, $5; children 4–12, $3.

Freebies: Pineapple chunks after cutting demonstration. Paper sun visor at Maze.

Video Shown: 20-minute continuous loop video on pineapple processing.

Reservations Needed: No, except for groups over 25.

Days and Hours: Daily 9:30 AM–5:30 PM (9:00 AM–6:00 PM during busy season). Maze closes at 5:00 PM. Closed Christmas. Pineapple cutting demonstration every hour on the hour, often followed by tour of the gardens.

Plan to Stay: 1 hour, plus time for the Maze.

Minimum Age: None

Disabled Access: Yes

Group Requirements: Groups over 25 people, $4 each. Call 1 week in advance.

Special Information: They are considering the addition of train tours through the pineapple fields. On Maui you can go on a working plantation tour unaffiliated with Dole (call 808-669-8088).

Gift Shop: The Dole Plantation is mostly a large themed retail store dedicated to everything pineapple, with hundreds of pineapple-related and Dole brand products, including pineapple candy, chocolates, cakes, cookies, and Waialua brand coffee. You can also purchase fresh pineapples to ship anywhere. Plus, it sells a variety of other goods, from local handicrafts to jewelry from Maui Divers. Outside along the lanai are tables for eating your pineapple snacks.

Directions: From Waikiki, take H1 West to H2 North. Continue to Kamehameha Hwy. 99. Located just North of Wahiawa.

Nearby Attractions: Wahiawa Recreation Area & Botanical Gardens; Honolulu attractions, including Maui Divers tour (see page 118) about 40 minutes away; Pearl Harbor 30 minutes away.

Holualoa Kona Coffee

77-6261 Mamalahoa Highway
Holualoa, HI 96725
(808) 322-9937 / (800) 334-0348
www.konalea.com

KONA COFFEE

When you sit down to drink your morning coffee, do you know whether you're drinking peaberry, extra fancy, or triple X? Did you know that it takes 100 pounds of picked coffee to produce just 15 pounds of roasted coffee? Become an informed coffee consumer and watch coffee being processed and roasted at Holualoa Kona Coffee Company, located in the heart of Kona coffee country, a 50- to 60-mile region on the western side of the Big Island. Hawaii is the only state in the U.S.A. that produces coffee, and only coffee grown in this region may carry the Kona label.

At Holualoa, your guide describes the life of the coffee bean from the moment it's picked from the tree as a red "cherry," until it's dried to become the beige bean called "parchment." Then you see the hulling process, where parchment beans are dumped into a tall, thin elevator. The elevator pours the parchment into the huller, which removes the parchment skin from the beans to reveal green coffee beans, which are then dropped by another elevator into the grader. The grader comprises a series of screens with different-size holes stacked one atop another. The screens shake, causing the coffee beans to fall through the appropriately sized holes. The largest (and best) beans, including grades like peaberry, extra fancy, and fancy, are separated from the smaller, lower grades such as number one, prime, and triple X. Peaberry, the most valuable bean, has a distinct flavor and shape. A gravity table further separates the coffee, this time by density.

In the next building you'll watch the coffee whirling around in the 40-pound roaster, which resembles a large oven. During roasting, air from a blower tosses the coffee beans around to prevent burning. The person who does the roasting explains how to take care of your coffee and how to distinguish good beans from low-quality ones. You'll learn that medium-roast coffee has more caffeine than dark roast because the longer coffee is roasted, the more caffeine is roasted out. By the end of this tour, you'll have a good understanding of what it takes to get the coffee from the tree to your cup.

Cost: Free

Freebies: Cup of fresh-brewed coffee

Video Shown: No

Reservations Needed: No, except for groups larger than 10 people.

Days and Hours: Mon–Fri 8:00 AM–4:00 PM, with the best time to see production from 9:00 AM–2:00 PM. Closed holidays and the Friday before Easter.

Plan to Stay: 30 minutes, plus time in gift area and working farm.

Minimum Age: None

Disabled Access: Yes

Group Requirements: Groups of over 10 people should call 1 day in advance. Groups of over 30 people will be divided into smaller groups.

Gift Area: Holualoa T-shirts and coffee are sold in the packaging room, where the tour ends. Open Mon–Fri 7:30 AM–4:00 PM. Brochure available from above number.

Directions: From Keahole Airport, take Hwy. 11 South. Turn left at the sign for Holualoa. Go all the way to the top of the mountain and turn right onto Mamalahoa Hwy. Turn left at the sign for Holualoa Kona Coffee. From the south, take Hwy. 11 North. Turn right at sign for Holualoa/Keauhou. Turn left onto Mamalahoa Hwy. Turn right at sign for Holualoa Kona Coffee, just past the mile 2 marker.

Nearby Attractions: Big Island Candies, Mauna Loa Macadamia Nuts, and Ueshima Coffee tours (see pages 115, 119, and 120); Kona Coffee Country driving tour map available from Kona-Kohala Chamber of Commerce (call 808-329-1758); November Kona Coffee Cultural Festival; Punulau'u (southernmost bakery in U.S.A.) viewing windows (call 808-929-7343); Kailua-Kona, a resort town.

Maui Divers of Hawaii

The Maui Divers Jewelry Design Center
1520 Liona Street
Honolulu, HI 96814
(808) 943-8383
www.mauidivers.com
www.mauidiverstour.com

MAUI DIVERS
OF HAWAII

Black coral is the official Hawaii State Gemstone, and this tour shows you why. Since its days of filling scuba tanks, back in 1958, Maui Divers has become the world's largest precious coral jewelry manufacturer. The company's founders initially experimented, making jewelry with rare black coral from the deep waters off Lahaina, branched out into pink and gold coral, then moved the company to Oahu. The video and tour show how they make their unique jewelry, which combines coral with gold, diamonds, pearls, rubies, or other precious gems.

You can watch most of the detailed process through glass windows that put you close to the deeply focused, blue-smocked workers. You see the design, waxing, casting, polishing, lapidary, and assembly areas. Designers make sketches for the goldsmiths, who then turn the drawings into three-dimensional jewelry carved from gold. The lost-wax casting process involves wax patterns of the jewelry being assembled into what looks like a small tree. Plaster molds are formed around this tree and heated in an oven to melt away the wax patterns, hence the name "lost wax." Gold is poured into the plaster molds. Once shattered, the molds reveal an exact gold replica of the wax tree. Gold rings and pendants are cut from the tree, then sanded and polished.

Notice the vacuum hoods under many of the machines in the finishing areas. These draw the gold mist into a central water bath, which is then refined. This process recovers over $500,000 in gold per year.

The tour guide escorts you through other areas, where skillful workers carefully cut, solder, polish, and inspect the gold pieces, or set precious gems into them. Notice the "Million Dollar Wall" in the coordinating area. Here, diamonds, pearls (some from the South Seas), emeralds, and sapphires are sorted and sized.

Cost: Free

Freebies: No

Video Shown: 9-minute video on deep-sea coral mining, company history, and jewelry production. Available in major foreign languages.

Reservations Needed: No, except for groups larger than 50 people.

Days and Hours: Mon–Sun 8:30 AM–5:00 PM. Usually no production Sat, Sun, and holidays, although visitors will still see video and manufacturing area and display cases on production steps.

Plan to Stay: 30 minutes for video and tour, plus time for showroom and gift store.

Minimum Age: None

Disabled Access: Yes

Group Requirements: 2 hours advance notice requested for groups larger than 50 people. No maximum group size. Translators and light refreshments for groups on request.

Special Information: No photography

Showroom: Tour ends with store selling the world's largest selection of original fine coral jewelry designs, including black, red, and pink coral rings, earrings, cufflinks, and pendants in 14-karat gold settings; pearl and South Sea pearl earrings and necklaces; and gold dolphins, pineapples, and whales. Open same hours as tour. Second-floor stores have costume jewelry, local art, gift items, and a selection of designer line items. With escort, can visit both stores without touring.

Directions: Free shuttle bus available from many hotels. Within walking distance of Ala Moana Shopping Center. If driving, take Ala Wai Blvd. Turn right onto Kalakaua Ave. Turn left at Beretania St., left at Keeaumoku St., and left at Liona St. Maui Divers is on your left. Take elevator up to lobby entrance.

Nearby Attractions: Dole Pineapple Plantation (see page 116); Waikiki Beach; Ala Moana Shopping Center; Academy of Art Museum; Capitol Building; Iolani Palace.

Mauna Loa

Macadamia Road, Volcano Highway
Hilo, HI 96720
(808) 966-8618 / (888) MAUNA-LOA
www.maunaloa.com

MACADAMIA NUTS AND CANDY

Few factory tours offer the sweet smells of roasting nuts and melting chocolate along with a nature trail to walk off the free samples and goodies available at the gift store. Although almost all the macadamia nuts (or "mac nuts") sold worldwide are produced in Hawaii, the nut is actually native to Australia and wasn't grown in Hawaii until 1921. When Mauna Loa began marketing mac nuts under the Mauna Loa brand in 1976, their popularity mushroomed. This tour of the world's largest mac nut company provides a look through gallery windows at mac nut processing and packaging and at chocolate production.

Fresh from the 40-foot-high macadamia tree, the mac nut kernel sits inside a leathery brown, extremely hard shell. After shelling (burnt shells and husks fuel the entire plant), the nuts enter the main processing factory. Electric eyes automatically grade and sort the nuts, allowing only light, uniformly colored specimens to continue along to the roaster. Blue-hatted workers stand over the conveyor belt, also searching the stream of nuts for rejects.

The nuts are dry-roasted in large rectangular ovens, traveling slowly through the ovens on conveyor belts for 15 minutes. When roasting ends, the nuts are sorted again, and some are salted, candy-glazed, or made into mac nut brittle. Watch the packaging machine shoot them into fast-moving open metal tins, which then move down the line for vacuum-sealing.

Walk across the parking lot and up a staircase outside the building to look in the exterior windows into the factory. Inside, the smell of chocolate replaces the aroma of mac nuts in the candy factory, where chocolate waits in big steel melters. The nuts drop onto chocolate pads, then travel through the enrobing machine that covers them in a wave of chocolate. Rows of white-gloved, blue-smocked workers neatly hand-pack the chocolates in boxes after they leave the long cooling tunnels.

Cost: Free

Freebies: Samples of nuts and candy.

Video Shown: 7-minute video on mac nut farming, harvesting, and production. Shows continuously on the lanai near the gift store. Available in Japanese.

Reservations Needed: No, for self-guided tours. Yes, for guided tours.

Days and Hours: Self-guided tour and video: Mon–Sun 8:30 AM–5:00 PM. Guided tour: production times vary; call in advance.

Plan to Stay: 15 minutes for self-guided tour, plus time for video, nature walk, and gift store.

Minimum Age: None

Disabled Access: Yes, for candy factory; 20 stairs in the mac nut processing factory.

Group Requirements: Groups larger than 50 people should call 5 days ahead to schedule guided tour. No maximum group size.

Special Information: September–February is busiest production schedule.

Gift Shop: Sells all Mauna Loa mac nuts and candies, mac nut ice cream, mac nut popcorn, and logoed items including shirts and hats. Open Mon–Sun 8:30 AM–5:00 PM. Catalog available from (888) MAUNA-LOA.

Directions: Located between Hilo and Keaau. Take Hwy. 11 to Macadamia Rd. Turn left if coming from Hilo and right if coming from Hawaii Volcanoes National Park. Drive through the Keaau Orchards to the yellow-and-blue Mauna Loa Macadamia Nut Visitor Center on left.

Nearby Attractions: Big Island Candies, Holualoa Kona Coffee, and Ueshima Coffee tours (see pages 115, 117, and 120); Kailua Candy Co. (call 800-622-2462); Hawaii Volcanoes National Park; Mauna Loa Village and open market about 2.5 hours away.

Ueshima Coffee

82-5810 Napoopoo Road
Captain Cook, HI 96704
(808) 328-5662 / (888) 882-5662
www.ucc-hawaii.com

UESHIMA
COFFEE
COMPANY

While you likely know that you can spend a few days in Napa Valley in California touring wineries, very few people know that they can do the same with coffee-growing farms and roasting facilities in the Kona region of the Big Island of Hawaii. On the western side of the island, Kona's rich volcanic soil and moderate climate nurture the production of this world-famous coffee.

At the Ueshima Espresso Bar & Roastery store, peer through big glass windows to witness the roasting, grinding, and packaging of the coffee. A side room includes panels and displays about the farming and milling of coffee. The store is part of a coffee mill originally built to process pineapple, a crop that never became a commercial success in Kona.

The company claims that this is the only facility on the west side of the island where you can observe the entire process, from roasting to packaging. Coffee roasting begins with the raw green beans that the state of Hawaii has certified as "Kona" in both origin and quality. About 135 pounds of beans, already sorted by size and grade, are fed into the roaster that aromatically spins around and around.

To preserve the balance, flavor, and unique acidity of this exquisite coffee, the company cooks the certified Kona to a "city" roast that maximizes the body for which Kona is known. To ensure the coffee reaches this optimal roast each time, look for the color meter they use with each roasting.

If the coffee is ground here, they use the "crackulator," a specially designed grinding machine. It looks like a big steel tub connected to vacuum tubes. The crackulator reduces the amount of heat in the grinding process compared to a normal grinder, thus preserving the quality of the coffee. A vacuum process removes more of the chaff or "silver skin" found on the roasted coffee bean. Through other windows you see the conventional grinders, flavoring equipment, and row of packaging machines filling bags

of this coffee lovers' delight, for your brewing pleasure.

Cost: Free, unless combined with a tour to roast your own coffee.

Freebies: Fresh-brewed coffee, macadamia nuts, and chocolate-covered Kona beans.

Video Shown: Short videos in adjoining room that also has displays on coffee farming and history of the company and mill.

Reservations Needed: No, except for groups over 20 people and for personal roasting tour.

Days and Hours: Mon–Sun 9:00 AM–5:00 PM. Closed Thanksgiving and Christmas.

Plan to Stay: 15 minutes for tour, plus time in gift shop.

Minimum Age: None

Disabled Access: Yes.

Group Requirements: Prefers if groups over 20 people call ahead.

Special Information: Farm tours available Mon–Sun 9:00 AM–4:00 PM. Private roasting tours available that allow you to roast your own coffee and put it into bags with your picture on it for $30 per person. Japanese translators available most days.

Gift Shop: 100 percent pure Kona coffee (both ground and whole bean), including Kona Peaberry. This special type of coffee bean is usually found only at the tip or upper part of each coffee branch and makes up less than 5 percent of Kona's total coffee production. Also sells shirts, local island souvenirs, chocolate-covered coffee bean and mac nut candies, and cold drinks.

Directions: From Hwy. 11 South, turn right down Napoopoo Rd. Store is on the right.

Nearby Attractions: Holualoa Kona Coffee, Big Island Candies, Mauna Loa Macadamia Nuts tours (see pages 117, 115, and 119); Kona Coffee Country driving tour map available from Kona-Kohala Chamber of Commerce (call 808-329-1758); November Kona Coffee Cultural Festival; Kailua-Kona, a resort town.

Idaho Potato Expo

130 Northwest Main
Blackfoot, ID 83221
(208) 785-2517
www.ida.net/users/potatoexpo

POTATOES

You may hear the whistle of an enormous train passing by as you enter the 1912 railroad depot that houses the Idaho Potato Expo. Your first questions when visiting the potato state may be "What does a potato field look like? Did we pass one on the way here?" The answer is found on a huge photograph of a potato field displayed by the entrance. Hungry? Snack on a free baked potato in the gift shop, or take home a small sack of spuds to enjoy later. Then proceed to the next room to watch a video on how the potato gets from the field to the grocery store. All this may make you wonder what you would look like as a potato. To find out, just stick your head through one of the holes by the museum entrance and have your photo taken as Farmer Potato in overalls, or as Mrs. Potato.

The museum displays tell the history of the potato, from a Native American hookah pipe smoked to worship the potato god, to photos and placards detailing potato farming through the centuries. Step into the mock potato cellar that feels and smells like the real thing: wooden potato barrels and a starchy odor surround you.

A commentator once said Marilyn Monroe's figure would look good even in a potato sack. You'll probably agree when you gaze at the photograph of Marilyn donning a burlap sack from a local market. Her agent set up the photo shoot as a publicity stunt, and you can take it home as a poster from the gift shop. Finally, check out the world's largest potato chip, over two feet in diameter on one side. Now that you've read about, seen, and smelled potatoes, head to the picnic tables outside and enjoy eating them.

Cost: Adults, $3; children over 8, $1; families, $8; seniors and AAA members, $2.50.

Freebies: Choice of a baked potato with butter or sour cream, or a little sack of potatoes.

Videos Shown: 10-minute videos showing how potatoes get from the ground to the grocery: one is "fun" and geared for kids, the other more serious, for adults.

Reservations Needed: No, except for groups of 15 or more people.

Days and Hours: May 15–September 15 only: Mon–Sat 10:00 AM–5:00 PM, Sun 12:00 PM–5:00 PM. Closed July 4th, Labor Day, and Memorial Day.

Plan to Stay: 30 minutes for museum and video, plus time for gift shop.

Minimum Age: None

Disabled Access: Yes

Group Requirements: Groups of 15 or more should call in advance. Group discount is $2 per person for 15 or more people.

Special Information: There is a park and a picnic area on the grounds.

Spud Seller Gift Shop: Sells potato cookbooks, potato fudge, potato lotion, potato chip cookies, and potato gift boxes, as well as T-shirts, hats, and postcards. Open May 15–September 15: Mon–Sat 10:00 AM–5:00 PM, Sun 12:00 PM–5:00 PM.

Directions: From Idaho Falls, take I-15 South to the second Blackfoot exit. After exit, go straight. Turn left onto Northwest Main. The Expo is 1.5 blocks down, on the right. Look for the old railroad depot. From Pocatello, take I-15 North to the second Blackfoot exit. Follow directions above.

Nearby Attractions: Bingham County Historical Museum (history of the Blackfoot area); Fort Hall Indian Museum; Craters of the Moon National Monument; and Sun Valley, Yellowstone, and Grand Teton national parks are all less than 1.5 hours away.

Potlatch

805 Mill Road
Lewiston, ID 83501
(208) 799-1429 / (208) 799-0123
www.potlatchcorp.com

Potlatch

Potlatch's Lewiston complex is an integrated sawmill, pulp and paper mill, and tissue mill. The tour lets you see the transformation of wood into lumber, paperboard, and tissue products, all at one site. Wood waste from the lumber mill is used by the pulp mill and is also converted into energy for the entire complex.

The sawmill produces approximately 160 million board feet of lumber annually, enough to build about 10,000 average-size homes. The mill's saws are computer-assisted and use laser scanners to determine the best combination of cuts. The buzz of saws and the clatter of chains and conveyors moving the logs through the process of debarking, squaring, edging, and trimming make the mill a very noisy place.

Large piles of wood chips and sawdust wait near the digesters that cook them into pulp. The digesters (not on the tour) break down the natural glue, called lignin, that holds the wood fibers together. The pulp goes to the fiber line, which removes additional lignin and purifies and whitens the pulp. The seemingly endless paper machines produce the paperboard used in milk and juice cartons, paper cups, and other food packages. The extruders laminate polyethylene to the paperboard to make liquid-tight containers.

The tissue machines produce paper towels, toilet paper, napkins, and facial tissue (at a rate of one mile per minute), which is sold under store labels by major supermarket chains. The mixture of pulp and water is formed on a screen that drains water from the sheet. Additional water is squeezed from the sheet before it circulates around a large, steam-heated "Yankee" dryer. A thin blade then peels the dried tissue sheet from the Yankee, and the tissue sheet is wound onto what looks like the world's largest paper-towel roll. For some products, such as bathroom and facial tissue, parent rolls are combined to make multiple-ply tissues. It's no surprise that Potlatch manufactures enough single rolls of toilet paper each year to supply the equivalent of at least one roll to every American.

Your tour ends in the calm of the greenhouse. Row upon row of young pine, fir, and cedar seedlings, each under one foot tall, illustrate how much wood is used in the production of lumber and paper products. The greenhouse produces more than 3.5 million seedlings per year for reforesting the company's lands.

Cost: Free

Freebies: Pencils and brochure about the company and its product manufacturing.

Video Shown: 5-minute video overviews tour safety precautions.

Reservations Needed: Yes

Days and Hours: Production times vary. Call in advance. Closed holidays and during weeklong maintenance shutdowns.

Plan to Stay: 3 hours

Minimum Age: Under 10 must be accompanied by adult.

Disabled Access: Stairs throughout tour route. Can do drive-through tour if prior arrangements are made.

Group Requirements: Groups larger than 15 people should make reservations at least 1 week in advance.

Special Information: No flash photography. Some areas are very noisy and can be hot during the summer. Wear comfortable shoes for at least 1 mile of walking. Certain areas may not be open due to construction.

Gift Shop: No

Directions: In Lewiston, follow Main St. East to Mill Rd. You will see signs for Potlatch. Enter complex at the main gate. Guard will direct you to parking.

Nearby Attractions: Luna House Museum; Nez Perce National Historical Park; Hell's Canyon Recreational Area; Lewis and Clark Trail sites.

Swiss Village Cheese Factory

4912 Franklin
Nampa, ID 83687
(208) 463-6620

If you've never heard a cheese curd squeak, head to the Swiss Village Cheese Factory to munch on a curd and listen to Rosebelle, the cheeky mechanical cow head, spurt pertinent tidbits—like 35,000 cows produce milk daily for Swiss Village Cheese.

From the exterior, the factory looks like a chalet in a field, but the view inside is all about cheese. Two huge double-paned windows on the first floor and six on the second floor watch over the cheese-making room. Go to the second floor for the best view. Thousands of gallons of milk arrive at the factory every day. They are pasteurized and cooled to the correct temperature to form curds. Stainless steel pipes pump the curds up into long, stainless steel tubs called cheddaring tables. Water and whey drain from the milk and cheese, which workers and machines keep stirring and milling, using rakes resembling large pitchforks, to catch clumps so they cannot form a block.

Before the water and whey drain magically through a screen beneath the cheddaring table, see the water, whey, and curds form a soupy, lumpy substance, unrecognizable as cheese.

As the cheese begins to take shape, three workers constantly stir with the rakes, adding spices or salt to make cheddar, hot pepper, colby jack, provolone, muenster, and mozzarella.

From the pipe under the tubs, a vat pump sends the cheese across the factory into 40-pound, stainless steel blocks, already lined with gauze. Workers load up to 32 blocks of cheese onto a cart, where a large steel cylinder with built-in air pressure weights down the cheese, condensing it.

The whole process takes around four hours, but aging can take anywhere from 30 days for mild cheese to 60-plus for medium or sharp. The cheese curd samples on the first floor squeak because they are so new. Hint: to get back the squeak in your cheese curds after a few days, place the curd inside a plastic bag and heat in a pan of water for five minutes.

Cost: Free
Freebies: Cheese samples
Video Shown: 8-minute video on cheese-making process
Reservations Needed: No, for self-guided tours. Yes, for guided tours.
Days and Hours: Mon–Sat 8:00 AM–7:00 PM, Sun 10:00 AM–5:00 PM. Call ahead for best production times.
Plan to Stay: 25 minutes for tour, video, and retail store, plus time in café.
Minimum Age: None, but children over 5 will most enjoy tour.
Disabled Access: First floor viewing level is accessible.
Group Requirements: Groups over 15 should call 1–2 weeks in advance. Groups receive pencils, balloons, and hats for kids.
Gift Shop: Sells Idaho souvenirs and dairy products. Open same hours as tour.
Directions: From Boise, take I-184 West and exit onto I-84 West. Take the Garrity Rd. exit and turn right onto Garrity Rd. Merge onto Franklin Rd. after 1 mile.
Nearby Attractions: Potlatch tour (see page 122); Meridian Springs. Boise's attractions, including the Boise Art Museum and Kathryn Albertson Park, are 20 minutes away.

Caterpillar

100 N.E. Adams Street
Peoria, IL 61629
(309) 675-4578
www.caterpillar.com

BULLDOZER

Although this tour has become very difficult for the general public to go on, we decided to include it in the book because the company's construction equipment represents some of the finest American-engineered and made products. The company is the world's largest manufacturer of construction and mining equipment, natural gas engines and industrial gas turbines, and diesel engines. Caterpillar is one of a few American companies that leads its industry worldwide while principally making its products in the U.S.A.

The tours to prospects, end users, and dealers have become a major selling tool for the company and are customized to the interests of the visitors. You see most of the main assembly steps from start to finish, with the subassembly stations off to the side in this massive facility (6.5 acres under one roof).

Each part of the process seems closely choreographed. The Cat slowly paws down the main assembly line, starting with the frame rails. Air pallets move the heavy frame from position to position. The tractor-to-be seems to move like a hovercraft down the line. Overhead hoists and cranes lower the pieces into place. Workers bolt down the cab, transmission, engine, and other parts. Midway through, the bulldozer goes through quality control computer tests, then on to the paint booth. The sounds of hammer and bolt guns fill the air and hydraulic lines hang from above.

Near the end, you see them start up the king of tractors, with the worker riding on what looks like a giant elephant in a parade, and watch them even apply the decals. Look for the heavily customized versions, usually modified for the project or part of the world the Cat will travel to from the factory. In the display room, you can sit on some of the models and even honk the horn. Visitors leave with the fascination they had as children watching this monster-sized earth-moving equipment build roads and buildings, having now learned what it takes to make these giant yellow machines themselves.

Cost: Free

Freebies: Limited to customers

Video: 10-minute video welcomes visitors to the factory and supporting facilities.

Reservations Needed: Yes. Limited space for non-customer tours. Must make reservations 3–6 weeks in advance. Subject to availability.

Days and Hours: Mon–Fri by appointment only. Closed major holidays, last two full weeks of July, week between Christmas and New Year's.

Plan to Stay: 1.5 hours

Minimum Age: 12

Disabled Access: Explain special needs when making reservations.

Group Requirements: See Reservations Needed above. Company will want to know background of people in group.

Special Information: No cameras. Very serious about no shorts or open-toed shoes. You walk on factory floor, so wear comfortable shoes. Customers are able to go on more specialized tours of the foundry and other plants.

Gift Shop: Cat Merchandise Center in downtown Peoria. Sells wide range of logoed Caterpillar items. Open Mon–Fri 10:00 AM–6:00 PM, Sat 10:00 AM–2:00 PM. Call (309) 676-7990 for holiday hours.

Directions: Tour begins at World Headquarters in downtown Peoria. Directions given out when reservations made.

Nearby Attractions: Wildlife Prairie Park; Glen Oak Zoo; McGlothin Farm; Tower Park Observatory; African American Hall of Fame; Lakeview Museum; Peoria Mineral Springs.

Chicago Board of Trade

141 West Jackson Boulevard
Chicago, IL 60604
(312) 435-3590 / (312) 435-3625
www.cbot.com

◎ **Chicago Board of Trade**

**GRAIN AND FINANCIAL
FUTURES AND OPTIONS**

Major futures markets at work combine Super Bowl competitiveness, Rose Bowl Parade colors, and Mardi Gras pandemonium. From large, glass-walled observation galleries above the Chicago Board of Trade (CBOT) trading floors, you'll see throngs of traders feverishly shouting, waving their arms, using hand signals, and throwing pieces of paper.

A 60,000-square-foot addition, completed in 1997, gives the CBOT the world's largest contiguous trading hall at 92,000 square feet. The trading floor is bigger than the combined playing fields of the Chicago Cubs and the White Sox. The trading hall has 876 booths located among and around its eight trading pits.

In the various pits, traders use a variation of the centuries-old auction system—appropriately called the "open outcry method"—for buying and selling. With all the skill of a third-base coach, they also use hand signals to cut through the noise. The sea of colors comes from ID badges and lightweight jackets worn by floor personnel. At the tops of the side and far walls are boards with numbers that show futures prices.

Adjacent to the agricultural gallery, a mini-museum houses artifacts and photos tracing the early days of commodity trading. Look at century-old grain measuring and grinding devices. View a visual history of the exchange, including photographs, drawings, documents, and architecture from its beginnings (opened in 1848) to the present day. After examining the mechanics of floor trading and the mini-museum, you'll be even more interested in the financial section of your newspaper.

Cost: Free
Freebies: English and foreign-language brochure and a card illustrating hand signals.
Video Shown: Award-winning film "A Window on Futures."

Reservations Needed: Yes. *While Visitor Gallery used to be open to general public, now only open to groups sponsored by CBOT member or CBDT management, or industry or education groups.*
Days and Hours: Mon–Fri with educational presentations and video at 9:00 AM, then every half-hour until 12:30 PM. Closed national holidays.
Plan to Stay: 30 minutes each, plus time for videos and displays.
Minimum Age: 16
Disabled Access: Yes
Group Requirements: Require reservations at least 2 weeks in advance for groups of 10 or more, with customized presentations available. Minimum age for groups is 16 years old.
Special Information: In addition to presentations in English, audio and video explanations are available in 12 languages: Japanese, Chinese, Korean, French, German, Spanish, Portuguese, Italian, Russian, Greek, Danish, and Polish.
Gift Shop: Gift counter sells logoed items, including pens, caps, T-shirts, mugs, golf tees, and teddy bears. CBOT catalog available at number above.
Directions: The landmark art deco CBOT building, topped by a 31-foot statue of Ceres (Roman goddess of grain and harvest), is at the intersection of LaSalle and Jackson.
Nearby Attractions: Chicago Mercantile Exchange, Eli's Cheesecake World, and U.S. Post Office tours (see pages 126, 128, and 136); *Chicago Tribune* tour under construction (see page 127); Chicago Stock Exchange Visitors Gallery (call 312-663-2222); Chicago Board Option Exchange Observation Gallery (call 312-786-5600); Federal Reserve Bank Visitors Center and tour (call 312-322-5111); Quaker Oats Lobby Exhibit (call 312-222-6887).

Chicago Mercantile Exchange

30 South Wacker Drive
Chicago, IL 60606
(312) 930-8249
www.cme.com

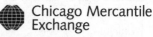 Chicago Mercantile
Exchange
ENGINEERING MARKET FAITH™

AGRICULTURAL AND FINANCIAL FUTURES

Opened in 1898 as the Chicago Butter and Egg Board, Chicago Mercantile Exchange Inc. (CME) now has $1.6 trillion daily in underlying value of trading in items ranging from pork bellies to currency. The fourth-floor visitor gallery overlooks the livestock and equity index futures trading floor. Through gaps in the glass walls, you can hear traders shout bids and offers in the pit. Look over the shoulders of clerks at their trading desks, which line the outer perimeter of the pit. Watch as they take phone orders, review charts, or hand-signal desired deals. Clerks and runners dressed in gold coats constantly signal prices. In the middle of the pit, traders wearing multicolored jackets may shout such price and quantity combinations as 20 on 10.

The goal is to be seen and heard. There may be as many as 4,000 traders on the floor at any one time. And as a trader, you want your bid to garner attention. In order to stand out from this colorful sea of people, an independent trader may wear an American flag jacket, or one with hogs, pigs, or cattle on it.

Exchange representatives answer questions and explain what the different hand signals mean. The representative explains how an order gets placed, beginning with the CME member taking a telephone order and writing it on an order slip. Learn that financial futures are a form of risk management. A bright LED price board wall display flashes real-time trades as reported by light-blue-jacketed exchange staff.

A second gallery overlooking the upper trading floor, not necessarily open to the public, handles currency futures and interest rate futures. The design of the pits is different; each product trades in its own pit. A huge flag of the country whose currency trades hang above each pit. CME trades futures and options on futures on 13 foreign currencies. The right side of the gallery faces the Eurodollar pit, home of one of "the world's most actively traded futures contracts." Here traders take positions in contracts trading up to 10 years in the future. You leave with a better understanding of financial markets, the trading process, and how business can do business more efficiently.

Cost: Free

Freebies: Map of trading floor or brief description of products traded

Videos Shown: Interactive videos explain the trading process and Merc history.

Reservations Needed: *For security reasons, visitors gallery is closed to the public until further notice. Will host prearranged visits for groups of 10 or more people.*

Days and Hours: Mon–Fri 8:30 AM–3:15 PM with presentations at 9:00 AM, 10:00 AM, and 11:00 AM. Closed financial holidays. Note: day before holidays trading floors close at 12:00 PM.

Plan to Stay: 30 minutes each, plus time for videos and displays.

Minimum Age: None, except for 7th grade for groups.

Disabled Access: Yes

Group Requirements: Reservations required at least 2 weeks in advance for groups of 10 or more. Maximum is 75 people. Access registration form on website.

Special Information: No photography. No cell phone use allowed in gallery.

Gift Shop: Sells logoed items, including pens, caps, T-shirts, mugs, Beanie Babies, office accessories, and sports bags. Open Mon–Fri 8:45 AM–3:15 PM.

Directions: Located at Wacker and Monroe, 1 block from Sears Tower. Take Brown and Purple L Line to Loop Washington and Wells stop. Walk west 2 blocks.

Nearby Attractions: Chicago Board of Trade Visitors Gallery, Eli's Cheesecake World, and U.S. Post Office tour (see pages 125, 128, and 136); *Chicago Tribune* tour under construction (see page 127); Chicago Stock Exchange Visitors Gallery will reopen (call 312-663-2222); Federal Reserve Bank Visitors Center and tour (call 312-322-5111); Quaker Oats Lobby Exhibit (call 312-222-6885); Sears Tower.

Chicago Tribune

Freedom Center
777 West Chicago Avenue
Chicago, IL 60610
(312) 222-2116
www.chicagotribune.com

Chicago Tribune

The *Tribune* printed 400 copies of its first issue on June 10, 1847. It now prints that many papers in less than one second on 10 massive offset presses that produce up to 70,000 newspapers per hour and more than 1 million every Sunday. This tour gives you a firsthand look at how the *Tribune* is printed, inserted, bundled, and delivered by one of the world's largest and most technologically advanced newspaper printing facilities.

In the mammoth newsprint warehouse area, about the size of two football fields, the amount of paper used to print this popular newspaper seems overwhelming. Newspaper rolls are the size of small cows. The *Tribune* uses 5,000 one-ton paper rolls every week. Fortunately, the newsprint produced by the *Tribune*'s major supplier is made from 60 percent recycled paper. Train tracks run alongside the warehouse to accommodate the 18 railroad cars full of paper it receives five days per week.

Tower presses move so fast that the newspaper looks like a gray checkerboard blanket rolling up and down along the plates and cylindrical drums. Each press is a series of 10 units. The *Tribune* is proud of its increased color-printing capacity, which is the tenth unit. The color tower units contain four vertically stacked printing machines, one each for blue, red, yellow, and black ink. Each press also cuts and folds the paper into sections.

In the busy packaging area, advertising sections are automatically bundled for insertion into the completed paper. Machines stack the papers, bundle them together with a brown paper wrap stamped with an ink code, and send them on their way in bright yellow carts.

Cost: Free

Freebies: Special section of famous *Tribune* front pages, ranging from the Bulls' first NBA title to Abraham Lincoln's election as president, and a button.

Video Shown: 9-minute video reviews the *Tribune*'s history and the process of writing, printing, and selling the newspaper.

Reservations Needed: Yes

Days and Hours: *Building under construction at press time. Future of tours uncertain.*

Plan to Stay: 1 hour

Minimum Age: 10

Disabled Access: Yes. One attendant needed for each individual using a wheelchair.

Group Requirements: Maximum group size is 50 people, with 1 adult required for every 10 children. Make reservations as far ahead of tour date as possible.

Special Information: Cannot always predict whether presses will be running during your visit. Most local newspapers give tours; contact your local paper for tour information.

Gift Shop: Not in Freedom Center. Store in the *Tribune* Tower at 435 N. Michigan Ave. sells *Chicago Tribune* merchandise (books, clothing, etc.). Open Mon–Fri 8:00 AM–6:00 PM, Sat 10:00 AM–4:00 PM. Call (312) 222-3080.

Directions: From I-90/94, take the Ohio St. exit. Turn left onto Orleans St. and left onto Chicago Ave. The guard in the security booth will direct you to visitors' parking.

Nearby Attractions: Chicago Board of Trade, Chicago Mercantile Exchange, and U.S. Post Office tour (see pages 125, 126, and 136). Chicago's attractions include Sears Tower, Shedd Aquarium, Adler Planetarium, Lincoln Park Zoo, and the Museum of Science and Industry.

Eli's Cheesecake World

6701 West Forest Preserve Drive
Chicago, IL 60634
(773) 736-3417 / (800) 999-8300
www.elicheesecake.com

CHEESECAKE

After its public debut at the Taste of Chicago in 1980, Eli's Cheesecake has become a sweet symbol of success for the Windy City. Eli Schulman, a guy from the "West Side of Chicago," created a special dessert for his restaurant, Eli's The Place for Steak. His son Marc continues Eli's level of dedication and commitment to making the best quality cheesecake.

Before starting your tour, notice the mural highlighting Eli's Cheesecake's history. In the back of this bright, atriumed café, look through the glass window into the research and development department. This 62,000-square-foot bakery, built in 1996, uses more than 4 million pounds of cream cheese, 500,000 pounds of eggs, 250,000 pounds of butter, and 13,000 pounds of Bourbon vanilla annually.

After donning your hairnet, walk through the double doors. Racks filled with all-butter cookie crusts baked twice the previous night await today's production. In the mixing area, a crane system lifts up and tilts the mixing bowl, which contains 500 pounds of batter for each batch of cheesecake. A big spatula with a black plastic paddle fills each crust. 18,000 cheesecakes march along the conveyor through the 70-foot tunnel oven. Stand on the royal blue nonskid path observing rows 10 cheesecakes wide emerge.

After baking, the cheesecakes take a leisurely two-hour journey spiraling up and back down a two-story cylindrical cooling tower. This densely coiled spiral cooler slowly cools more than 2,000 cheesecakes at one time. Cheesecakes travel single-file down the conveyor belt and are depanned individually by hand.

In the blast freezer, cakes freeze solid in eight to ten hours. More than 30 trained pastry chefs and cake decorators hand-decorate some two-thirds of Eli's cheesecakes. Decorating a cheesecake involves great teamwork, taking up to three different steps. After decorating, cheesecakes are sliced, packaged, and shipped.

Cost: Adults, $3; children under 12, $2 (costs go to Eli's Charitable Fund to support the community).

Freebies: Cheesecake slice

Video Shown: Slide show on Eli's history and the baking process.

Reservations Needed: No, for the 12:00 PM "Sneak Peek" tour. Yes, for groups over 10 people and for "quiet tours" (no production) on weekends.

Days and Hours: Mon–Fri 12:00 PM. Tour packages available for groups of 10 or more 10:00 AM–3:00 PM. Call ahead to confirm the bakery is in production, otherwise Eli's offers a modified tour.

Plan to Stay: 25 minutes for tour, plus additional time in the retail store.

Minimum Age: 3

Disabled Access: Modified tour available.

Group Requirements: Groups over 10 people should schedule at least 2 weeks in advance, with contract and payment. Enjoy tour packages such as "Lunch & Munch," "The Ultimate Eli's Experience" (participate in "Quality Star" taste test and decorate your own cheesecake), and "Sail and Dine" (includes sightseeing cruise plus lunch at Eli's The Place for Steak). Group discount in café. Maximum group size is 45.

Special Information: No photography or strollers. Must wear rubber-soled, low-heeled shoes, otherwise receive modified tour. September Cheesecake Festival.

Retail Store: Café sells many of Eli's 100 cheesecake varieties and logoed merchandise including hats, T-shirts, and polo shirts. Selection ranges from Original Plain (for the "cheesecake purist") to award-winning White Chocolate Macadamia, plus holiday specials like Egg Nog. Open Mon–Fri 7:00 AM–6:00 PM, Sat 9:00 AM–5:00 PM, Sun 11:00 AM–5:00 PM. From website, can order Eli's C-Cake, picking from some 600 combinations of decorations and toppings.

Directions: From I-90/94 West, take Montrose St. Turn left. At light, turn left just before factory onto Forest Preserve Dr. Turn right into parking lot.

Nearby Attractions: Chicago Board of Trade and Chicago Mercantile Exchange tours (see page 125 and 126); Eli's The Place for Steak; Chicago's attractions include Sears Tower, Shedd Aquarium, and Lincoln Park Zoo.

▲ The late Eli Schulman, founder of Eli's Cheesecakes in Chicago, Illinois, shows off the dessert that made him famous.

Eli's cheesecakes enter a huge 70-foot-long tunnel oven, which can hold 3,000 cakes at a time!

▼

Great American Popcorn Company/ Rocky Mountain Chocolate Factory

205 / 311 South Main Street
Galena, IL 61036
(877) 777-KORN / (800) 235-8160
www.greatpopcorn.com
www.rockymtchoc.com

POPCORN AND CHOCOLATE

Although separate stores, the Great American Popcorn Company and the Galena Rocky Mountain Chocolate Factory franchise share a common family and a delicious motto: Try anything to see if it tastes good. Charles and Ann Henle bought the Rocky Mountain franchise in 1990. About 70 percent of their handmade candy comes from the Durango, Colorado, factory. David Lewis and Catherine Henle-Lewis had been involved in her parents' business, Rocky Mountain Chocolate, for nearly 12 years before opening the Great American Popcorn Company next door in 1994.

Dave and Catherine hear the words, "I didn't know you could do this with popcorn!" all the time. They create new popcorn flavors by imagination or customer request, swirling in experiments at whim alongside their steady production of sweet Vanilla Caramel and Amaretto & Almonds, cheesy Bacon & Cheddar and Sour Cream & Chives, and spicy Blazing Saddles and Hellfire & Damnation.

At the start of the tour, hear the science behind corn popping before corn kernels stream into the middle vat of a five-foot-tall popper. Special mushroom corn makes a ball shape when popped and does not break into pieces like butterfly corn. Two heads shoot out the corn, which goes into giant bulk bags. To make caramel corn, brown sugar, corn syrup, and butter heat together in a "coater cooker," a 10-gallon automatic round drum. Then the popcorn tumbles in the mixture, giving each piece a rich coating. Popcorn rarely makes it from the cooling trays to storage bags; the warmth and aroma entices customers to buy on the spot.

Next door at Rocky Mountain, Truffles, the signature Rocky Mountain bear, sits four feet tall in a rocking chair out front to greet visitors. His sign says: "I will work for chocolate." Store workers break 10-pound blocks of milk and dark chocolate into pieces and melt them down in the large tempering kettles. Looking like witches with a brew cauldron, they mix in and cook the sugar, corn syrup, evaporated milk, and butter with a wooden paddle until the fudge reaches 231°. The fudge ripples over a 700-pound granite slab and mixes with chocolate liqueur before workers form it into fudge loaves. Taster spoons, loaded with warm, gooey fudge and given out several times during production, are the highlight of the tour.

Cost: Free
Freebies: Popcorn, fudge, chocolate bark
Video Shown: No
Reservations Needed: No, except for groups larger than 15.
Days and Hours: Daily 9:30 AM–5:30 PM. June 1–November 1: extended hours Fri and Sat 9:30 AM–9:00 PM.
Plan to Stay: 20–25 minutes for each tour.
Minimum Age: None
Disabled Access: Yes
Group Requirements: Groups of 15 or more will be split between the 2 stores. Call at least 1 day in advance.
Special Information: No video or photography of specific items, but can take pictures with store owners. No smoking. Customers can call ahead to request production of specific items.
Retail Stores: Sell all Rocky Mountain candies and gift items, hundreds of popcorn flavors by bag or tin, gift baskets, ice cream, figurines, and stuffed animals.
Directions: From Chicago, take Rt. 20 West to Joe Davis County. Rt. 20 turns into Main St. Go through floodgates. Great American Popcorn and Rocky Mountain are on the same block.
Nearby Attractions: Ulysses S. Grant's home; Galena Water Park; Stillman Bed and Breakfast tea room; historic mansions of Galena.

Haeger Potteries

7 Maiden Lane
East Dundee, IL 60118
(847) 426-3033 / (847) 426-3441
www.haegerpotteries.com

ARTWORK POTTERY

Founded by David Haeger in 1871, Haeger Potteries today is directed by Alexandra Haeger Estes—the fourth generation of the Haeger family to be involved with the company. Started as a brickyard that helped rebuild Chicago after its Great Fire, Haeger Potteries is now one of the world's largest art pottery factories. While you can no longer tour the factory, you can watch the pottery production video and visit the Haeger Museum.

After an introductory talk about the production process, your video tour begins. Watch the automatic casting machines fill plaster molds with slip—liquid clay. Notice the hanging trolley system that slowly travels its four-mile course with dried pottery (greenware) perched on wooden shelves that look like birdcage swings.

Workers carefully pry the molds open, then give each artwork a hand sponge bath before drying. The block-long kiln and the round kiln are located in the Great Kiln room, where you'll almost feel the heat. The brown brick kilns are 220° at the entrance and 2,000° in the center. Workers neatly stack the greenware pieces—close to each other but not touching—onto railcars headed for a 12-hour trip through the kiln.

After its first kiln baking, the bisque is hand-dipped into a water-based glaze. The glaze, absorbed into the dry, porous bisque, dries almost immediately. A worker then takes the piece from a lazy-Susan table and showers it with glaze in a spray booth. These alternative glazing methods give the pottery its vibrant colors when it's fired again in the kiln.

The Haeger museum includes a vase determined by the *Guinness Book of World Records* to be one of the world's largest. Made in 1976 by Haeger's master potter, it took three months and 650 pounds of clay to complete. Among other Haeger items, the display cases show discontinued ceramic animal designs, a Harley-Davidson hog bank, a sculptured bust of Carl Sandburg, and a large Hummel figure (Hummel and Haeger exchanged artworks on Haeger's 100th anniversary). Explore the 25,000-square-foot, seven-showroom outlet store that sells most of Haeger's 800 different items.

Cost: Free
Freebies: No
Videos Shown: 20-minute video on manufacturing process; 15-minute video on company history.
Reservations Needed: No
Days and Hours: Mon, Thur, Fri 10:00 AM–6:00 PM, Sat, Sun, and most holidays 11:00 AM–5:00 PM.
Plan to Stay: 35 minutes for video tour, plus time for museum and outlet store.
Minimum Age: 4, when accompanied by responsible adult; 5, for school groups.
Disabled Access: Outlet store and museum are accessible.
Group Requirements: None
Outlet Store: Sells pottery lamps, vases, bowls, sculptures, the best-selling *Rendezvous* (lovers back-to-back), dried and silk floral arrangements, housewares, factory seconds, overruns, and one-of-a-kind and discontinued pieces. Open Mon, Thur, and Fri 10:00 AM–6:00 PM. Open Sat, Sun, and most holidays 11:00 AM–5:00 PM.
Directions: From Chicago, take I-90 West to Rt. 25 North. Turn left onto Rt. 72. Turn left onto Van Buren St. Haeger Potteries is on your right.
Nearby Attractions: Spring Hill Mall; Santa's Village Theme Park and Racing Rapids Action Park; Fox River Recreational Trail; the Milk Pail Village; Chicago's attractions include Chicago Mercantile Exchange, Chicago Board of Trade, McDonald's Museum, and U.S. Post Office tours (see pages 126, 125, 134, and 136) 45 minutes away.

John Deere

Harvester Works
1100 13th Avenue
East Moline, IL 61244
(800) 765-9588 / (877) 201-3924
www.johndeere.com

HARVESTERS

JOHN DEERE

The harvester, or "combine" as it's called in the trade, is one of the machines that revolutionized farming and made possible America's tremendous production of grain and corn. For example, a combine with a claw-like "header" attachment can harvest as many as 12 corn rows at a time, picking and shelling the ears along the way. At John Deere, the world's largest producer of agricultural equipment, you'll see many steps involved in making its Maximizer combines.

The techniques definitely differ from those used by pioneer blacksmith John Deere when he started the company in 1837. Along with the hissing and thumping machines heard at most factories, you'll also see robots welding, lasers cutting steel, and electrical charges applying paint in this 260-acre, world-class manufacturing plant. Considering this factory's size, don't be surprised to see workers scurrying around on bicycles. Your John Deere–retiree tour guide will hand you a piece of metal. Feel the smooth cut on it, made by the combination laser-and-punch machine. Sparks fly as hooded welders apply their skills on smaller pieces, while robotic arms on the automated welding systems seal frames and grain-tank cells.

Watch a combine body slowly emerge and then hover on its hoist after being dipped into an electrically charged bath of green paint. The electric charge bonds the paint to all exposed surfaces on the submerged combine, even in joints and hidden crevices. After seeing several subassembly stations, you'll watch combines come to life on the main production line. Assemblers carefully position completed parts, such as the power shaft, cab, feeder house, and engine. You will sense the pride of the worker who smoothly applies the finishing touch: the John Deere decal.

Cost: Free
Freebies: Brochure with description and pictures of the manufacturing process.
Video Shown: No
Reservations Needed: Yes, ask for map.

Days and Hours: Mon–Fri 8:00 AM, 10:00 AM, and 12:30 PM. Closed major holidays, week between Christmas and New Year's, and 2 weeks in the summer (usually end of July and beginning of August). Tours subject to change. Please call above numbers for tour availability.
Plan to Stay: 1.5 hours
Minimum Age: 12
Disabled Access: Yes. You ride through the factory in a tram pulled by a small John Deere tractor.
Group Requirements: Make reservations at least 1 month in advance. Maximum size is 80 people.
Special Information: No video cameras or sandals allowed. Closed-toe shoes required. John Deere tractor plant in Waterloo, IA (see page 148). Visit John Deere Pavilion in Moline, IL (see page 133).
Gift Shop: Adjacent to the new John Deere Pavilion at the John Deere Commons. Sells a variety of John Deere memorabilia, replica toys, and logoed clothing.
Directions: When you make reservations, ask the Guest Services Department for a map, since many area highways have multiple designations—almost guaranteeing confusion. From Chicago, take I-88 to the exit for Hwy. 5. Turn right at 70th St., which becomes 7th St. Turn right on 13th Ave. Look for the big green John Deere Maximizer combine parked on the factory's front lawn. From Iowa, take I-80 to I-74 East. Get off at the John Deere Rd. East exit. Turn left at 70th St. and follow the above directions.
Nearby Attractions: John Deere Pavilion features interactive displays about agriculture, plus modern and vintage farm equipment (see page 133); Deere & Co. Administration Center displays current and historical John Deere products, Girard Mural (includes more than 2,000 farming-related historical items dated 1837 to 1918), and video tour of this architecturally famous world headquarters; Collectors Center displays antique tractors; John Deere Historic Site.

John Deere Pavilion

1400 River Drive
Moline, IL 61265
(309) 765-1000 / (800) 765-9588
www.johndeerepavilion.com

John Deere
PAVILION

AGRICULTURAL EQUIPMENT

Deere & Company's visitor center, the John Deere Pavilion, celebrates the past, present, and future of agriculture, as well as the history of the company. The 14,000-square-foot Pavilion is like one you'd see at a fairground, except the walls are made almost entirely of glass. Inside, stop at reception to request your own personal tour guide, likely a Deere retiree, who will happily customize your visit any way you like.

If you've never been on a farm, this is your chance to climb aboard a brand-new, shiny green tractor, combine, or cotton picker that sits on the Pavilion floor. How has equipment like the tractor changed over the years, since Deere made the 1918 Waterloo Boy model? To find out, compare the new machines to their antique counterparts, also on display at the Pavilion (but don't climb on the antiques—they're too fragile). To see a tractor or combine in action, take a virtual tour at one of the touch-screen displays. "Tour" the combine factory and watch employees assemble this boxy piece of machinery, then see the machine harvest wheat, soy, and corn. At another station the "tour" shows workers assembling tractors. Notice all the different attachments—each attachment performs a different task on the field.

"Cornucopia" is a touch-screen exhibit that takes you from the beginning of a product's life until it gets to market. Learn the life story of apples, pork, or cotton. Another interactive exhibit called "The Past" walks you through the history of agriculture, while "The Future" educates guests about how the world will feed its booming population, which may double in the next 40 years. Like many guests, you may find yourself returning to the Pavilion again and again simply to reminisce and share experiences of life on the farm.

Cost: Free
Freebies: No
Video Shown: 10-minute film, "The Bounty,"

about the challenges of farming from the planting season to the harvest.

Reservations Needed: No
Days and Hours: January–March: Mon–Fri 9:00 AM–5:00 PM, Sat 10:00 AM–5:00 PM, Sun 12:00 PM–4:00 PM. April–December: Mon–Fri 9:00 AM–6:00 PM, Sat 10:00 AM–5:00 PM, Sun 12:00 PM–4:00 PM. Closed Easter, Thanksgiving, Christmas, and New Year's.

Plan to Stay: 1 hour for tour and "The Bounty," plus time for store.
Minimum Age: None
Disabled Access: Yes
Group Requirements: Groups of 30 or more should call in advance if possible.
Special Information: No videotaping of "The Bounty." Visit John Deere factory tours in East Moline, IL (see page 132) and Waterloo, IA (see page 148).
Gift Shop: John Deere Store sells a variety of items emblazoned with the company logo, from baseball caps and towels to fishing lures and mailboxes. January–February: Mon–Sat 10:00 AM–5:00 PM, Sun 12:00 PM–4:00 PM. March–December: Mon–Fri 10:00 AM–6:00 PM, Sat 10:00 AM–5:00 PM, Sun 12:00 PM–4:00 PM.
Directions: From the east, take I-74 West into Moline. Take the 7th Ave. exit (last Illinois exit). Turn left on 7th Ave. Go 4 blocks and turn right on 15th St. Go 4 blocks. From the west, take I-80 to I-74 East. Follow I-74 East across the Mississippi River to Illinois. Take the River Dr. exit (the first exit). Turn left on River Dr. and go 4.5 blocks. John Deere Pavilion is on the corner of River Dr. and 15th St.
Nearby Attractions: John Deere Harvester Works tour (see page 132); Moline Tractor & Plow Co. half-block away on John Deere Commons (call 800-240-5265); Mississippi River; Historic Deere family homes; Deere & Company Administrative Center; Tournament Players Club at Deere Run.

See color photos, page 11.

McDonald's #1 Store Museum

400 North Lee Street
Des Plaines, IL 60016
(847) 297-5022
www.mcdonalds.com

FAST FOOD

If you're a hungry traveler, the sign advertising 15-cent hamburgers may beckon you like a desert mirage. But after parking next to a vintage Chevrolet Bel Air coupe and walking up to this retro-restaurant's counter you'll realize that what you've discovered is not the cheapest burger this side of 1960, but the McDonald's Museum.

The museum is a restoration of the first McDonald's corporation franchise that opened on this site in 1955. Clean-cut mannequins tend the restaurant, serving up a simple menu: burgers, cheeseburgers, fries, shakes, milk, coffee, and soda. Most of the compact, clean operation is open to the customers' view. Outside on the original sign, Speedee, a winking little logo-man with a hamburger head, advertises "speedee" service and 15-cent burgers.

Red-and-white restaurants like this launched the McDonald's empire, which now includes more than 25,000 restaurants in more than 100 countries. In 1954 milkshake multimixer salesman Ray Kroc, intrigued by an order for eight machines, flew out to California to observe the restaurant operation of brothers Dick and Maurice McDonald. While his original intent was to sell them more multimixers, Ray Kroc saw his future in franchising McDonald's restaurants. Kroc left California as the brothers' franchise agent and opened his first franchise in Des Plaines, Illinois, on April 15, 1955.

Right away, you'll notice the quintessential seating and drive-thru are missing, just as they were from the original operating restaurant. During winter months, a removable Plexiglas "winter front" was added to the front of the building so customers would not have to stand in the cold at the service window.

While visitors are not allowed to enter the kitchen area, most of it is visible from the outside. In the customer service and food preparation areas, you'll see the authentic equipment used in those days. Hamburgers and cheeseburgers were grilled; fresh potatoes were washed, sliced, blanched, and fried; milkshakes were whipped up, of course, on multimixers. Although these techniques may not strike you as antiquated, the prices will. The most expensive item on the menu was a 20-cent milkshake. Downstairs, in the small exhibit area, you will see historic photos, the daily sales log from April of 1955, and a short video.

Cost: Free
Freebies: Postcard of museum
Video Shown: 3-minute video on company history.
Reservations Needed: No
Days and Hours: Memorial Day–Labor Day: Thur–Sat 10:30 PM–2:30 PM, but call to confirm since entire schedule changes every year. Closed balance of the year.
Plan to Stay: 20 minutes
Minimum Age: None
Disabled Access: Restricted to upper floor
Group Requirements: None
Special Information: The oldest operating red-and-white McDonald's restaurant is in Downey, CA. The restaurant has a small gift shop and historic exhibit area. Call (562) 622-9248.
Gift Shop: No, but if you're hungry, a real McDonald's is across the street.
Directions: Located in vicinity of O'Hare Airport. From the south, take I-294 (Tri-State Tollway) North to Dempster West exit. Go west on Dempster (U.S. 14) to Lee St. Turn right onto Lee and go about 2 blocks. Just before Lee converges with Rand Rd., you'll see the museum on your left. From the north, take I-294 to Golf Rd. West exit. Go west on Golf Rd. (Rt. 58) to Mannheim Rd./River Rd. (U.S. 45). Turn left on U.S. 45 and proceed south. Just after you cross Rand Rd., you'll see the museum on your right.
Nearby Attractions: Botanical Gardens; Des Plaines Historical Museum; Woodfield mall, about 20 minutes away; Chicago's attractions, including the Sears Tower, are about 30 minutes away.

Mitsubishi Motor Manufacturing

100 North Mitsubishi Motorway
Normal, IL 61761-8099
(309) 888-8000
www.mitsubishicars.com

CARS

MITSUBISHI
MOTOR MANUFACTURING

Mitsubishi Motors began producing cars at its only North American automobile manufacturing facility in 1988, originally in a joint venture with Chrysler Corporation under the name Diamond-Star Motors. The company name was changed in 1995 to Mitsubishi Motor Manufacturing of America. The plant, which occupies more than 2.5 million square feet—the equivalent of approximately 52 football fields—was designed for assembly of several different models intermixed on the same production line. With more than 3,100 employees, the factory produces such popular models as the Mitsubishi Eclipse and Eclipse Spyder convertible, Mitsubishi Galant, Chrysler Sebring coupe, and Dodge Stratus coupe. Construction is under way for the future production of a new mini–sport-utility vehicle.

The catwalk tour shows you some of the advanced robotics and just-in-time inventory management that have made the facility one of the most technologically advanced auto assembly plants in the world.

The plant is made up of five shops: Stamping, Body, Plastics, Paint, and Trim & Final. Out of your view, the automobile body parts are stamped on seven massive presses and the bumper fascias are formed in one of nine injection-molding machines—operations not always found within assembly facilities. However, you can't miss the automated guided vehicles (AGVs) that transport parts and equipment between the Stamping and Body Shops. Without any apparent human intervention, the AGVs follow locator plates and wires in the floor to deliver racks to waiting workers.

The plant has more than 700 robots to perform monotonous, cumbersome, and more dangerous tasks. The Body Shop is 90 percent automated, with robots installing doors, hoods, and tailgates according to a highly synchronized order. With colorful sparks flying, the robots, which look and move like metallic and wire-filled praying mantises, precisely fit and weld the vehicle bodies together.

If you find all the noise, sparks, and technology unnerving, just listen to classical music (Beethoven and Mozart) playing throughout the Body Shop. It signifies the start and end of robotic functions. More robots assist workers on the Trim & Final assembly line, installing seats, tires, batteries, windshields, instrument panels, and all fluids except gasoline.

Cost: Free

Freebies: Brochure

Video Shown: 15-minute video provides background on factory and shows all stages of production, including those not seen on the catwalk tour.

Reservations Needed: Yes. Reservations only made up to 3 months in advance.

Days and Hours: 2 tours offered on Friday only. Subject to change due to production schedule changes. Closed holidays and weekends. No tours during model changeover period. Some extended shutdown periods.

Plan to Stay: 1.25 hours for video, discussion, and tour.

Minimum Age: 10

Disabled Access: Yes

Group Requirements: Maximum group size is 50.

Special Information: No photography. More than a half-mile of walking.

Gift Shop: No

Directions: From Rockford or Chicago, once on I-55/74, follow I-74 West toward Peoria (Exit 163). Off I-74, exit at Mitsubishi Motorway (Exit 125). The facility will be on your left. Follow the signs to the visitor parking north of flagpoles. From Decatur, St. Louis, or Champaign, once on I-55/74 take Rt. 9 (Exit 160B). Turn right on Mitsubishi Motorway. Factory will be on your right. Follow signs for visitor parking north of flagpoles.

Nearby Attractions: Beer Nuts Factory Outlet, with video of Beer Nuts being made (call 309-827-8580); Bloomington's other attractions, including Prairie Aviation Museum, Illinois State University Planetarium about 20 minutes away.

U.S. Post Office

433 West Harrison Street
Chicago, IL 60607
(312) 983-7550
www.usps.com

UNITED STATES
POSTAL SERVICE

MAIL

There are few things we take more for granted than the delivery of our mail. This is one of the newest, most technologically advanced mail-distribution centers in the world. It replaces the post office building next door that was once the world's largest post office. After the tour you'll no longer wonder what happens to your letter between the time you drop it in the mailbox and the time it's delivered. You'll discover the steps involved in processing the mail, from initial cancellation of postage stamps to final sorting by carrier route.

Automation plays a big role. In the old, massive, warehouse-like building, the post office simultaneously used different generations of technology, so the tour presented a living museum on the evolution of automation equipment. Mail sorting in the new building relies on high-tech equipment that moves at lightning speed, using bar code technology and optical character readers (OCRs) to sort the mail. The OCR scans the address and sprays a bar code on the bottom of each letter at a rate of 11 pieces of mail per second. The OCR does a rough sort by region, with other machines reading the bar codes to sort by delivery route. The mail moves so quickly through these machines that it looks like one continuous stream of paper. The mail races through the bar code readers and parks itself in the proper zip code slot.

Machines in other areas cancel the stamps, weed out oversized pieces, or handle bundles and large flat pieces. Computers then automatically direct the sorted mail to the proper transportation route. The next time you open your mail, you'll appreciate what that envelope has been through.

Cost: Free
Freebies: No
Video Shown: No
Reservations Needed: Yes
Days and Hours: Mon–Fri 10:30 AM and 12:30 PM. Closed national holidays.
Plan to Stay: 1–2 hours depending on what areas you visit.
Minimum Age: 10
Disabled Access: Yes
Group requirements: Can handle groups of up to 100 people with at least 1 week's advance notice. Lunch available in cafeteria with advance notice.
Special Information: Substantial walking involved. Guides can individualize tour to special interests, which is why tour length varies. Many post offices like to give tours, so contact your local P.O. for information.
Gift Shop: Philatelic store in building lobby. Sells a large collection of commemorative stamps and books. Open Mon–Sun 24 hours per day.
Directions: From I-90/94, take the exit for Congress Pkwy. East. Take the Canal St. exit and turn left. Post office is located on corner of Harrison and Canal. Customer parking lot on Harrison. From I-290, take the Canal St. exit. Free customer parking on Harrison side of building entrance ramp next to river.
Nearby Attractions: Chicago's attractions include Chicago Mercantile Exchange, Chicago Board of Trade, and Eli's Cheesecake World (see pages 125, 124, and 128), Sears Tower, Shedd Aquarium, Adler Planetarium, Lincoln Park Zoo, Art Institute, and the Museum of Science and Industry.

Amish Heritage Furniture

52886-A State Road 13
Middlebury, IN 46540
(574) 825-1185 / (800) 870-2524
www.ahfurniture.com

Company founder R. Gene Beachy's great-grandfather was an Amish farmer in northern Indiana who built furniture in his spare time. Out of respect for this elder, the tour begins in front of an elegant, popular piece of furniture the company calls "Grandpa's Secretary," a desk-and-cabinet reproduction that dates back to 1892. While the company's construction methods make use of electric saws, planers, drills, and sanders, reminding you of a modern woodshop, you'll also see carpentry techniques that would make great-grandfather proud.

The company's workforce is almost entirely Amish. The scarcity of farming jobs has led the Amish to work in factories such as this one. If your only experience with the Amish is watching them in horse-drawn buggies, you may be surprised to see men and women skillfully handling power tools. Except for the sneakers, the men wear the typical Amish plain pants and hats, and the women wear solid-colored dresses and bonnets—very different than the T-shirt and jeans worn by many American factory workers.

The furniture's solid-lumber construction begins with piles of pine, oak, or cherry boards cut to the required length in the mill area. To make the wood panels used to build the furniture, the boards interlock by tongue-and-groove cutouts and are placed on what looks like a steamboat's paddle wheel. Glue is placed between each pair of boards and the pressure applied produces an almost seamless wood panel.

Each piece is then individually bench-built, so you can watch a craftsperson use panels or wood spindles to construct a desk, table, chair, or dresser. Workers sand the wood, spray stains, and hand-rub oil finishes. Hovered over a dresser, for example, you may see a worker hammering nails, fitting a mortise-and-tenon joint, or showing their pride in the furniture's quality by signing and dating the piece.

Cost: Free

Freebies: No

Video Shown: 10-minute video on furniture-making runs in showroom area.

Reservations Needed: Yes, for guided tour. No, to watch production from observation window in back of showroom.

Days and Hours: Mon–Fri 1:30 PM and 3:00 PM for guided tour. Can watch production through window Mon–Fri 9:15 AM–12:00 PM and 12:30 PM–4:00 PM. Closed holidays.

Plan to Stay: 20 minutes for tour, plus time for showroom.

Minimum Age: 6, for guided factory floor tour; none, to observe from window.

Disabled Access: Yes

Group Requirements: No maximum size. Larger groups will be split into 12 people per tour. Prefers 2 days' advance notice.

Special Information: No photography, since the Amish do not want photographs taken of themselves. Audio-cassette driving tour for area furniture-makers (for information contact Elkhart Convention and Visitors Bureau, 800-262-8161).

Showroom: Sells all furniture made at factory, including dining-room tables, chairs, desks, dressers, and bed frames. Occasional discounts available. Open Mon–Fri 9:00 AM–5:00 PM, Sat 10:00 AM–5:00 PM. Closed holidays.

Directions: From I-80/90 (Indiana Toll Rd.), take Exit 107. Turn right onto SR 13 South. Company is ahead on left.

Nearby Attractions: RV tours, including Coachmen, Jayco, and Holiday Rambler (see pages 139, 142, and 141); Walter Piano's tour (see page 147); Deutsch Kase Haus cheese factory, with observation windows in back of gift shop (call 219-825-9511 about production schedule); Shipshewana Flea Market and Auction, the Midwest's most popular outdoor flea market; Swartzendruber Hardwood Creations, located in the restored Old Bag Factory in Goshen, has an observation deck (call 219-534-2502).

Berne Furniture

150 Berne Street
Berne, IN 46711
(219) 589-2173
www.berne.com

Step into an Old World oasis in the middle of Indiana. Settled by Mennonite immigrants from Canton Bern in Switzerland, Berne, Indiana, is known for its Amish village, quaint Swiss chalets, flower boxes, and congenial atmosphere. In the midst of it all, you'll find Berne Furniture, established in 1925 by Swiss settlers. Today Berne Furniture is still highly dedicated to the quality and excellence of Swiss custom upholstery.

Wood from nearby lumber mills is brought directly to Berne Furniture. Inhale the fresh smell of cut wood and brace yourself against the whir of the saw blades. Watch a craftsman guide a wood block against the jigsaw to achieve the perfect curve for a chair back. After the pieces are cut, holes are bored into the wood so the pieces can be connected, without nails, by inserting dowels.

After the frame is complete, steel springs are attached by hand. The worker tacks down the rows of springs along the seat of the frame, a mass of coils bobbing and swaying slightly like an exhibit of modern art. Each spring is then hand-tied with twine in eight directions for stability, so the base looks like a spider's web. Each end of the twine has to be nailed to the base. Hold your breath as the craftsman holds the nails in his mouth! With a magnetic hammer he grabs a nail from his mouth and swiftly pounds it into the frame.

In the cutting room, 1,000 different fabrics of every color and texture line the wall. Cutting tables 13 yards long fill the room, making it look like a giant banquet hall. Cutters use heavy cardboard patterns to determine the piece shapes. Each cutter pays special attention so that the design on the fabric will match from one piece to another. They cut meticulously straight edges with heavy, 13-inch-long shears.

You will be surrounded by the whirring and clicking of 30 sewing machines as you walk right through the middle of the sewing room. On your right, seamstresses nimbly maneuver fabric for cushions and throw pillows. On your left, they work on the pieces that will upholster the arms, backs, and bases. Not quite like your grandmother's sewing machine, these computerized electronic machines help the seamstresses be efficient and precise.

The upholsterers wrestle the fabric into exactly the right position before tacking it to the frame with an air-powered staple gun. When the master upholsterer is finished, another person will apply a hand-tailored skirt or artfully carved legs. Finally, all the loose threads are cut, stray padding is brushed away, and the Berne label is applied to every cushion.

Cost: Free

Freebies: Brochure detailing the company's history, products, and process.

Video Shown: No

Reservations Needed: Yes, 1 day in advance.

Days and Hours: Mon–Thur 9:30 AM, 10:30 AM, and 12:30 PM. Closed holidays and July 4th week and between Christmas and New Year's.

Plan to Stay: 1 hour

Minimum Age: 12, although younger children may attend if well supervised.

Disabled Access: Yes

Group Requirements: Maximum group size 25–30 people. Larger groups can be split.

Special Information: Visitors are required to wear safety glasses.

Gift Shop: No. Will provide directions to local dealers.

Directions: From Fort Wayne, take Hwy. 27 South to Rt. 218 East (Main St.). Turn left on Behring St. Berne Furniture is on the corner of Berne and Behring Sts.

Nearby Attractions: Hitzer Stove Factory tour (call 219-589-8536); Swiss Heritage Village; Amishville USA; July Swiss Days Festival.

Coachmen

423 North Main Street
Middlebury, IN 46540
(888) 422-2582
www.coachmenrv.com

RECREATIONAL VEHICLES

The RV industry has many start-up stories as colorful as Bill Gates' at Microsoft and Steven Jobs' at Apple Computer. The Corson brothers (Tom, Keith, and Claude) founded the company back in 1964, naming it after an inn Tom spotted along the Ohio Turnpike. From a meager start in capital, Coachmen now has record sales growth and revenues exceeding $500 million.

At this sprawling industrial complex, you'll get picked up for your tour at the Coachmen Caravan Visitors Center in a modern bus or a new motor home like those coming off the line. On the way to the tour site, the guide (who is also a sales representative) points out the buildings where the cabinets are made, and where the floors, walls, and ceilings are formed and laminated in the vacubond process. Across from the chassis prep/frame shop/body shop building sits what looks like a football field's worth of Ford and Chevy chassis.

Walking through the travel trailer and fifth-wheel building you can see these RVs come to life. At each station along the line, a different feature is added, whether it is the flooring, walls, or the familiar Coachmen Dalmatian logo. Saws buzz, overhead cranes lift front and rear fiberglass RV cabs and walls, and workers nimbly insert wiring and plumbing.

The Class A motor home tours usually occur after production ends at that plant for the day. Therefore, it offers a quieter industrial experience that gives you time to explore the RV innards. At different points along the inverted L–shaped assembly line, these big, bus-size motor homes sit in various stages of their evolution. At one point the RV just has its floors, then the next RV also has its side walls, and the next has its appliances, and so on. Near the end of the line is a big "rain booth" that exposes the finished RV to storm conditions for up to one hour, revealing any leaks.

Cost: Free

Freebies: A small item at Visitors Center.

Video Shown: No, but can request video in Visitors Center.

Reservations Needed: Yes, call one week in advance.

Days and Hours: Travel trailers and fifth-wheels: Mon, Wed, Fri 3:00 PM. Class A motor homes: Tue and Thur 3:00 PM. Schedule may change; call in advance.

Plan to Stay: 1 hour for tour, plus time for gift area in Visitors Center.

Minimum Age: None

Disabled Access: No

Group Requirements: None

Special Information: Travel trailer and fifth-wheel tours available at the Fitzgerald, GA, plant (call 229-423-5471).

Gift Area: Coachmen Caravan Visitors Center sells Dalmatian-logoed items including T-shirts, jackets, key chains, and Dalmatian beanies. Open Mon–Fri 8:00 AM–5:00 PM. Closed holidays. Price list available at above number.

Directions: From I-80/90 (Indiana Toll Rd.), take Exit 107. Turn right onto SR 13 South, which becomes Middlebury's Main St. At the north end of Middlebury, you'll see a friendly billboard at entrance to company complex. Tour begins at Caravan Visitors Center.

Nearby Attractions: RV tours, including Jayco and Holiday Rambler (see pages 142 and 141); Elkhart County is the RV manufacturing capital of the world. Local Convention & Visitors Bureau lists companies that give tours (call 800-262-8161). RV/MH Heritage Foundation Museum (call 574-293-2344); Amish Heritage Furniture tour (see page 137); Deutsch Kase Haus cheese factory, with observation windows in back of retail store.

Coca-Cola Bottling

2305 North Davis Road
Kokomo, IN 46901
(765) 457-4421 / (800) 382-8888 (within Indiana)
www.coca-cola.com

SODA

When pharmacist Dr. John Pemberton invented Coca-Cola in 1886, he could not have imagined that it would be manufactured by thousands of bottling plants throughout the world. Very few of these Coca-Cola bottling plants are independently owned, and even fewer give tours open to the general public. The Severns family purchased the Coca-Cola franchise for the Kokomo area in 1936 and is very proud of what it gives to the community, including welcoming tour visitors. With the third generation of Severns active in the business, a sense of the family's influence pervades the company.

Standing next to the bottling line you may see different sizes ranging from 8-ounce to 2-liter Classic Coke plastic bottles being filled (aluminum cans are not filled at this factory). Try to follow one bottle's journey through the filler and capper machines. Pre-labeled bottles are rinsed and move single-file along a conveyer belt to the circular filling machine. The bottles ride up and down like a merry-go-round. At the top of its ride, each bottle is automatically attached to a filler head. Hear rhythmic bursts of carbon dioxide gas shoot into each bottle, giving the soda its fizz. The 2-liter bottles are gravity-filled with syrup and water at the rate of 98 bottles per minute, with 20-ounce bottles speeding up to 230 per minute.

At the capping machine, red plastic caps slide down a chute and screw onto each spinning bottle. This happens in less than one second, to prevent any bubbles from escaping. Then the bottles march single file to the packaging area. The packing machine grabs eight 2-liter bottles and drops them into red plastic logoed trays. These cases waddle up the conveyor belt and overhead to the warehouse.

In the syrup room, white 5,000-gallon tanks contain liquid sugar, corn syrup, or the top-secret-recipe Classic Coke syrup. Silver tanks hold syrup for individually mixed drinks, such as Sprite. Your guide explains that one gallon of syrup concentrate yields 178 cases of soda—enough soda for a person's lifetime.

Cost: Free

Freebies: Refreshment during tour and logoed souvenir.

Video Shown: No

Reservations Needed: Yes

Days and Hours: Tue and Thur 10:15 AM and 1:15 PM. Other times possible. Closed holidays.

Plan to Stay: 45 minutes

Minimum Age: None

Disabled Access: Yes, but not all areas are wheelchair accessible.

Group Requirements: Groups over 10 people should call 2 weeks in advance. Call further in advance for June, September, and October tours.

Special Information: Chlorine smell in water treatment room. If plant is making artificially sweetened drinks such as Diet Coke or Diet Sprite, you can taste the NutraSweet in the air, even though you can't see it. Watch for puddles of soapy water used to lubricate the machines. Coca-Cola fans will also want to visit World of Coca-Cola Atlanta in Atlanta, GA (see page 114).

Gift Counter: Small lobby area sells logoed Coca-Cola hats, bags, T-shirts, and Christmas ornaments. Open Mon–Fri 8:00 AM–5:00 PM. Closed holidays.

Directions: From Indianapolis, take U.S. 31 North through Kokomo. Turn left onto Morgan St. Turn right onto Davis Rd. The plant will be on your left. From Ft. Wayne, take U.S. 24 West to U.S. 31 South. Turn right onto Morgan St. Turn right onto Davis Rd. The plant will be on your left.

Nearby Attractions: Kokomo Opalescent Glass tour (see page 144); Seiberling Mansion; Elwood Haynes Museum (invented first successful gasoline-powered car); Circus Hall of Fame located about 20 miles away in Peru.

Holiday Rambler

606 Nelson's Parkway
Wakarusa, IN 46573
(574) 862-7211 / (800) 650-7337
www.holidayrambler.com

HR HOLIDAY RAMBLER

RECREATIONAL VEHICLES

Holiday Rambler began in 1953, when Richard Klingler and his father built a boxy little 13-foot trailer in their garage. It might not have been much to look at, but it had all the necessary furnishings for a family getaway: bunk beds, dinette, hot plate, ice-box, and heater. Klingler and the company he founded, however, were not satisfied with bare necessities. Today, 50 years later, Holiday Rambler, now a division of Monaco Coach Corporation, continues its trademark style and technological innovations, such as Alumaframe construction and exclusive kitchen suite slide-outs.

After your guide tells you about the company's history and the production of premium recreational vehicles, you'll visit the factory floor to watch the construction of motorized and towable RVs. More than 800 employees work on the RVs as they move down the line. HR is especially proud of its Alumaframe construction; all Holiday Ramblers are built with this durable, light-weight frame. Workers carefully interlock C-channel aluminum studs at the joints, then double-weld each joint together.

Notice how employees fit two layers of insulation and a moisture barrier into the frame before adding aluminum skin on the outside and paneling on the inside. Equal care is taken with the roof. Workers busily rivet and seal the roof together and onto the frame to prevent leakage.

All cabinets are made on the premises. Peek inside at the wooden cabinets and interiors—you'll be reminded more of a luxury hotel than wilderness. Enjoying the great outdoors does not have to include "roughing it"!

Cost: Free
Freebies: Holiday Rambler pen and product literature.
Video Shown: No

Reservations Needed: No
Days and Hours: Mon–Fri 10:00 AM and 2:00 PM.; arrive 15 minutes in advance. Closed holidays.
Plan to Stay: 2 hours
Minimum Age: 2
Disabled Access: Yes, please make arrangements in advance.
Group Requirements: None
Special Information: No photography or open-toed shoes. Information available about the Holiday Rambler RV Club, the oldest company-sponsored enthusiast organization in the industry. Towable manufacturing facility in Elkhart, IN, gives Holiday Rambler Towables tours Mon–Fri 10:00 AM and 2:00 PM. Call above number. Coburg, Oregon facility gives tours of Navigator, Ambassador, and Admiral production Mon–Fri 10:00 AM and 2:00 PM. Call (800) 634-0855.
Gift Shop: No
Directions: From the west, take Tollroad 80/90 East to the first South Bend exit. Take Hwy. 20 Bypass East to SR 19 South, then go south 7 miles to Wakarusa. Turn right at second traffic light onto Nelsons Pkwy. Holiday Rambler will be on the left. From the east, take Tollroad 80/90 West to Elkhart exit. Take SR 19 South. Proceed as above. Holiday Rambler will be on the right.
Nearby Attractions: RV tours, including Coachmen and Jayco (see pages 139 and 142). Elkhart County is the RV manufacturing capital of the world. Local Convention & Visitors Bureau lists companies that give tours (call 800-262-8161). The RV/MH Heritage Foundation (call 574-293-2344) features museum, library, exhibition hall, and Hall of Fame dedicated to recreational vehicle and manufactured housing industries.

Jayco

58075 State Road 13 South
Middlebury, IN 46540
(574) 825-5861
www.jayco.com

RECREATIONAL VEHICLES

Since the mid-1960s, when Jayco founder Lloyd Bontrager first built his pop-up camper prototypes in a converted chicken coop, family members and friends have been an integral part of Jayco's success. Watching the construction of Travel Trailers and Fifth Wheels, the RVs that fit into the back of a pickup truck, you still sense that family feeling, even though Jayco is now one of the five largest RV manufacturers in the country. About 70 percent of Jayco's 1,100 workers are Amish or Mennonite, and their dedication to quality is evident as you travel through the factory.

Every Jayco trailer begins with a tubular steel frame built by a firm that specializes in RV frames. Workers lay tongue-and-groove plywood floor, insulate with fiberglass, and use Polyflex fabric on the bottom. Following these steps, you'll see the entire trailer flipped upside-down, like an immense turtle on its back. Workers attach axles and wheels to the underbelly and install a fresh-water tank. The unit is turned back over and placed on dollies that run down a track to various workstations in the plant.

Next, they lay the carpeting and linoleum. Workers then attach white-pine sidewalls, which have the interior paneling fastened with glue and brand nails. Look up and you'll see the cabinet shops above the plant floor. Wood from the mill room is assembled into cabinets. Each production line, for the Jay Flight, Qwest, Eagle, and top-of-the-line Designer Travel Trailer and Fifth Wheels, has its own cabinet shop. Carpenters slide the finished cabinets down a ramp to the production area.

Toward the end of the RV's construction, workers attach the roof. They screw on tapered trusses or two-by-fours for the rafters, then stretch a rubber or aluminum roof over them. The area resounds with noises of drills, routers, and sanders. The RV's "skin" of .024-gauge aluminum or fiberglass is then secured onto the units. Once the RV's body is complete, appliances, drawer and cabinet fronts, windows and custom-made upholstery are added. Afterwards, at your leisure, you can view completed trailers displayed in a campground setting.

Cost: Free

Freebies: Product brochures. A follow-up letter includes a Jayco key chain.

Video Shown: 15-minute video on the company's history and production methods.

Reservations Needed: No, except for groups larger than 10 people.

Days and Hours: Mon–Fri 1:30 PM; June–August also 9:30 AM. Display area and Visitors' Center open Mon–Fri 8:00 AM–5:00 PM. Closed holidays. No production July 4th week, and week between Christmas and New Year's.

Plan to Stay: 1.5 hours for video and tour, plus time for gift area, display area, and Visitors' Center.

Minimum Age: None

Disabled Access: Yes, although must be careful of tools and wires on factory tour. Non-motorized wheelchairs only.

Group Requirements: Groups larger than 10 people need to make reservations 10 days in advance. Maximum group size is 50.

Special Information: No photography or video cameras allowed. Upon request, tours available of the mini–motor home and fold-down production buildings. Visitors' Center displays Jayco memorabilia, including brochures from 1968.

Gift Area: Sells logoed items, including mugs, clothing, and license plates. Open same hours as Visitors' Center. Closed holidays.

Directions: From I-80/90 (Indiana Toll Rd.), take Exit 107 for SR 13 South to Middlebury. Located on right, just south of the intersection with U.S. Rt. 20.

Nearby Attractions: Holiday Rambler and Coachmen tours (see pages 141 and 139). Elkhart County is the RV manufacturing capital of the world. For a list of tours, call (800) 262-8161. The RV/MH Heritage Foundation (call 574-293-2344) features museum, library, exhibition hall, and Hall of Fame dedicated to recreational vehicle and manufactured housing industries.

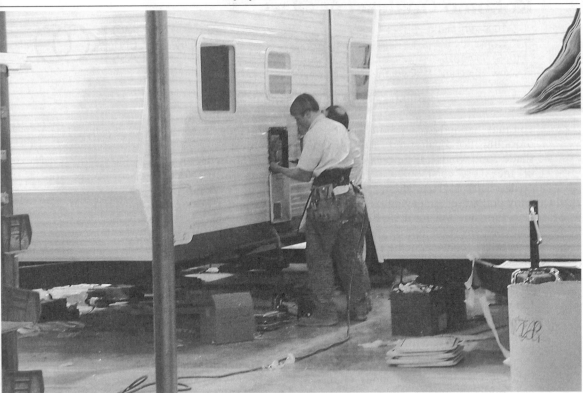

▲ Watch the construction of the Jayco Travel Trailers and Fifth Wheels.

▼ When you visit Jayco in Middlebury, Indiana, you'll see a predominately Amish and Mennonite workforce.

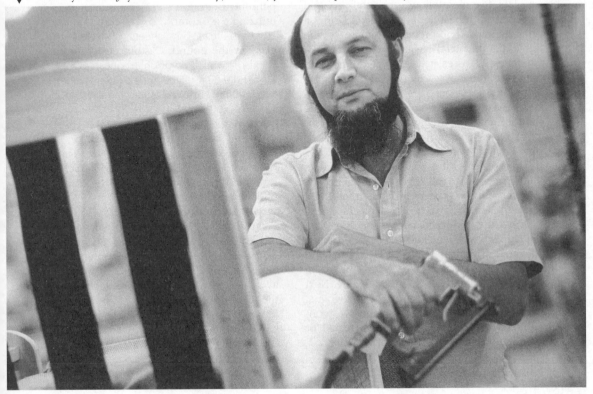

Kokomo Opalescent Glass

1310 South Market Street
Kokomo, IN 46902
(765) 457-1829
www.kog.com / www.theopshop.com

OPALESCENT AND CATHEDRAL GLASS

Spiritual stained-glass church windows, drooping floral-patterned Tiffany lampshades, and whimsical suncatchers are some of the most common uses of Kokomo opalescent glass. Founded in 1888, the company prides itself on having created its sheet glass the same way for more than 100 years. The company, now run by the great-grandsons of the founders, is the oldest maker of opalescent glass in the world. It originated the cat's-paw texture for Tiffany & Co.

As soon as you walk into the factory, you feel the heat wafting from the 2,600° circular furnace. Each of the 12 fiery-orange glowing portholes of the furnace contains a cherry clay pot that holds 1,000 pounds of molten glass.

Once the table man rings a bell, each ladler scoops up to 70 pounds of molten glass out of the furnace and skips along the concrete floor, bouncing the ladle to keep the glass from hardening. Their stride resembles a Native American ceremonial dance. Since up to five colors can be cast per sheet of glass, five men follow each other in rapid succession, repeating this dance. Using a long-handled two-pronged pitchfork, the table man blends the glass, swirls it around, stretches it, tosses it like pizza dough, and almost effortlessly eases this 50-pound glob of molten glass onto the rollers. The rollers swallow up the glass and flatten it, with the bottom roller controlling the texture.

The one-eighth-inch-thick glass sheet travels through the 140-foot-long annealer for its one-hour cooling. As the glass hardens, its colors and patterns reveal themselves. Using T-squares and glass cutters, workers trim off the excess glass to create 32-by-80-inch sheets. Room 4, the stockroom, houses sheets of glass in narrow, wooden, two-tiered racks. Since Kokomo makes approximately 540 colors and color combinations of sheet glass, this room contains a paintbox of color and texture. Next time you go to your church or synagogue, you'll admire the stained-glass windows, wondering whether they were newly created or restored with Kokomo Opalescent Glass.

Cost: Free

Freebies: No

Video Shown: No

Reservations Needed: No, except for groups over 6 people.

Days and Hours: Wed and Fri 10:00 AM. Closed holidays. No tours in December. Call first, since company shuts down occasionally for repairs.

Plan to Stay: 1 hour, plus time in Op Shop.

Minimum Age: None, but must be extremely careful since you are near people carrying hot molten glass, and broken glass is on floor.

Disabled Access: Yes, but please call in advance.

Group Requirements: Groups larger than 6 people should call 2 weeks in advance.

Special Information: The extreme heat, especially in summer, can cause heat exhaustion for older visitors. No open-toed or open-heeled shoes. No photography.

Gift Shop: Op Shop sells paperweights, perfume bottles, vases, and suncatchers utilizing Kokomo opalescent glass. Hobbyists can buy sheets of rolled art glass by the pound. Custom design work is also available upon request. Open Mon–Fri 9:00 AM–5:00 PM. May–September: Sat 9:00 AM–1:00 PM. October–April: Sat 9:00 AM–5:00 PM.

Directions: From Indianapolis, take Hwy. 31 North. Turn left onto Markland Ave. in Kokomo. Turn left onto Home Ave. Turn right onto State St. Cross railroad tracks. Kokomo Opalescent Glass is at the corner of State and Market Sts.

Nearby Attractions: Coca-Cola Bottling Plant tour (see page 140); other glass-related attractions, including Seiberling Mansion, utilize Kokomo glass; Greentown Glass Museum; several companies 30 miles away in Elwood give tours, including the House of Glass (call 765-552-6841); Elwood Haynes Museum (invented first successful gasoline-powered car).

Perfection Bakeries

350 Pearl Street
Fort Wayne, IN 46802
(219) 422-5631 (ext. 289) / (800) 347-7373 (ext. 289)
www.auntmillies.com

BREAD

Food manufacturing is highly automated in big bakeries with lopsided ratios of workers-to-units-produced. Perfection Bakeries has about 30 production people who make 180,000 loaves per day of such well-known breads as Sunbeam, Aunt Millie's, Country Hearth, and Holsum. This tour shows you high-speed bread-making at its most mechanized, with techniques very different from those used in 1901, when the company started baking wafers.

As you would do at home, Perfection combines ingredients in the mixer, bakes dough in the oven, and slices the bread before eating. But there the comparison ends, since Perfection's process is much bigger, faster, and more intensely aromatic. About every 10 minutes, a trough filled with 2,000 pounds of dough rises above a "J" divider and drops a mushy blob of dough into a machine, which separates it into softball-size portions. A "rounder" machine then rounds and flours the dough before it heads for the "proofer."

Once the dough comes out of the overhead proofer, it moves through a "sheeter," which rolls it flat to remove gases and air bubbles. Then it falls into pans on five-across trays. Even the ovens seem to be in constant motion, welcoming and expelling loaves after an 18-minute baking. The depanners magically lift the hot bread from the pans using small suction cups. The baked loaves cool on a one-mile overhead conveyor-belt cooling system. While cooling, the bread is inspected for foreign objects; occasionally you'll see a loaf almost mysteriously flying off the line.

Slicing and packaging must be done quickly, while the bread is still warm; otherwise, the slices lose moisture that keeps the loaf fresh. The tour guide explains some nuances of slicing bread, such as why pumpernickel is sliced thinnest. The bagging process is like inflating a balloon, except that the loaf follows the air into a bag that is then automatically tied. After watching state-of-the-art mass bread production, you'll never again take for granted that bread in your local supermarket.

Cost: Free

Freebies: Samples of warm bread with jam and margarine; gift bag of promotional items.

Video Shown: 12-minute video on bread production.

Reservations Needed: Yes. *Due to downsizing, tours indefinitely suspended.*

Days and Hours: Tue and Wed at 9:00 AM and 10:00 AM. Closed holidays.

Plan to Stay: 1 hour for talk on nutrition and company history, video, tour, and sampling.

Minimum Age: 10

Disabled Access: Yes

Group Requirements: Book 2 weeks in advance.

Special Information: No photography. Warm during summer tours.

Thrift Store: Located on the west side of building. Sells 2-day-old breads at discount. Open Mon–Fri 9:00 AM–5:30 PM and Sat 8:30 AM–4:00 PM. Closed holidays.

Directions: Atop the bakery is a unique billboard of bread slices continuously spilling from a bag of Sunbeam bread. More than 750 million slices have "fallen" from the yellow wrapper. Find this billboard and bakery from I-69 by taking Exit 102 to the east (Hwy. 24 W). This becomes Jefferson Blvd. Follow Jefferson Blvd. into the city. Turn left (north) onto Ewing St., right onto Main St., and immediate left into the Light & Breuning parking lot.

Nearby Attractions: Sechler's pickles tour (see page 146); Fort Wayne Newspapers (call 219-461-8274); Botanical Gardens; Science Central.

Sechler's

5686 State Route 1
St. Joe, IN 46785
(219) 337-5461 / (800) 332-5461
www.sechlerspickles.com

PICKLES

Like all pickles, Sechler's start out as cucumbers, salt, and water. Now in its third generation, Sechler's started making pickles in 1921. The first packing was done in the basement of Ralph Sechler's home, now the plant's office.

Trucks full of fresh cucumbers are unloaded into zigzagging grading machines. From a 20-foot elevation, the cucumbers fall into slats; smaller cukes roll through the first slats, and larger ones fall through slats at the end. Once sorted into seven sizes, the cukes are weighed in 20-bushel (1,000-pound) boxes. Farmers are paid by the number of pounds of each size cucumber; midgets (or "gherkins") are the most expensive.

In the tank yard, 120 ten-foot-high wooden pickle vats stand in neat rows. Each holds up to 750 bushels (or 37,000 pounds) of pickles. The cucumbers are placed in these tanks by size, salt brine is added, and the tanks are closed with wooden lids. The pickles are usually in these tanks for at least 10 weeks, but may stay as long as one-and-a-half years, depending on demand and the cycle relative to next year's crop.

In the processing room, pickles cook in 110° to 140° water for 24 hours to remove some of the salt. Cutting machines slice, dice, chip, grind, and chop the inspected pickles into numerous shapes and sizes. The pickles marinate for one to two days in dill brine, or seven to ten days in vinegar and spices for sweet flavoring. Smells of hot peppers, raisins, or oranges fill the air, depending on the variety in production.

Workers stand at a stainless-steel table hand-packing spears and peppers. Machines pack whole pickles, relishes, and hamburger chips. Jars move along the conveyor belt single-file, filling with pickles. The excess pickles roll into a cylinder below and recirculate back to the top of the machine. Down the line, the "juicer" overflows the jars with juice or brine. As the cap is put on, a burst of steam shoots across it, cooling, condensing, and pulling down the center of the lid

to form a pressure seal. The "dud" detector measures the jar's resulting vacuum level by measuring the recess in the lid. If the center isn't pulled down enough, the machine rejects the jar and sends it back through the line.

Cost: Free

Freebies: Paper hat and samples of all varieties in the showroom.

Video Shown: Sechler's 75th anniversary video, with historic and product footage. Request to see video in showroom.

Reservations Needed: No, except for groups over 6 people.

Days and Hours: Tours only April 1–October 31: Mon–Fri 9:00 AM–11:00 AM and 12:30 PM–2:00 PM, every half-hour. Closed holidays.

Plan to Stay: 30 minutes for tour and tasting, plus time in showroom.

Minimum Age: None

Disabled Access: Yes

Group Requirements: Groups larger than 6 people should call 2 days in advance. No maximum group size.

Special Information: Wear comfortable shoes. Be alert for wet floors and forklift.

Showroom: Sells over 30 varieties of pickles, such as orange-flavored spears and candied raisin crispies. Display cases show company history. Open year-round Mon–Fri 8:30 AM–4:30 PM, Sat 8:30 AM–12:00 PM. Closed major holidays. Mail-order form available from (800) 332-5461.

Directions: From Fort Wayne, take I-69 North to Dupont exit. Turn right on Dupont. Go straight through traffic light onto SR 1 North. Sechler's is 20 miles ahead (through farm country) on your left. From Auburn, take SR 8 East. Turn right onto SR 1 South. Sechler's is on your right.

Nearby Attractions: Auburn Cord-Duesenberg Museum; National Automotive and Truck Museum; Fort Wayne's attractions, including Perfection Bakeries (see page 145), are 20 miles away.

Walter Piano

25416 County Road 6
Elkhart, IN 46514
(574) 266-0615 / (574) 674-0467
www.walterpiano.com

PIANOS

Elkhart, Indiana, is probably the musical instrument manufacturing capital of the U.S.A., with major saxophone, clarinet, flute, and other companies located in this area. The most accessible general-public tours are at Walter Piano, one of the only six piano manufacturers left in the U.S. Walter Piano, a family-owned company which started making high-end consoles and upright pianos in 1970, is as much cabinetmaker as piano-maker.

It takes four to five weeks to make one complete piano. You'll first feel like you've walked into a large cabinet shop. Workers hand-sand, saw, and drill cherry, oak, or mahogany cabinet parts. The cabinet parts for four pianos travel together on each cart. In spray booths, workers spray various stains, sealers, and lacquers.

In another area, a worker attaches the cast-iron piano plate to a wooden sound-board/frame assembly. More than 400 bridge pins are hammered by hand at an angle into the treble and bass bridge. With an air hammer, the worker punches in about 250 shiny nickel-plated tuning pins, then slides the frame assembly over to the next station. Pulling wire from coils overhead, the stringer hand-threads the wire through the hole in each tuning pin, snips it, and wraps the wire around the pin three times with a special tool. The stringer weaves the wire around the bridge pins and back through and around the next tuning pin for all 250 pins. It takes an experienced stringer one hour to do it all, while a new stringer takes eight hours.

After the cabinet and strung back are mated, soundboards travel through the factory to receive actions, hammers, and keys. (Since actions and keys are no longer made in the U.S., they are the only non-U.S.-made parts.) Pianos are tuned, weighted, and adjusted at each stage before final tuning and regulation.

The company also makes grand pianos, so you may be lucky enough to catch them bending the rim for one. This may be the only time you'll see a grand piano standing vertically, 6 feet tall. Strips of veneer, 16 feet long, are first glued together. A small crane raises the center of the glued strips, allowing the veneer to droop around the inside rim bending form, called an "inner cull." The outer cull is then lowered, and workers clamp the two culls together to compress and mold the layers of veneer.

Cost: Free

Freebies: Felt-covered piano hammers

Video Shown: No

Reservations Needed: Yes

Days and Hours: Mon 1:00 PM, unless special arrangements made. Closed holidays, first 2 full weeks of July, and week between Christmas and New Year's.

Plan to Stay: 45 minutes for tour plus time in the showroom.

Minimum Age: None

Disabled Access: Yes

Group Requirements: Minimum group size is 12 people; maximum group size is 30. Groups of 20 or more can be accommodated with additional tour times. Call at least 2 days in advance.

Special Information: While there are strong lacquer fumes in the finishing room, it is possible to bypass this room. No photography.

Showroom: Wide variety of console and grand pianos made by Walter Piano as well as other manufacturers. Also sells grandfather clocks. Open Mon–Fri 10:00 AM–5:00 PM (Mon and Thur until 7:00 PM), Sat 9:00 AM–1:00 PM.

Directions: From I-80/90, take Elkhart Exit 92. Turn left onto Cassopolis St. At second traffic light, turn left onto CR 6. Walter Piano is about 1 mile ahead on your right.

Nearby Attractions: Other musical instrument manufacturers give tours on a limited basis. Contact the Elkhart Convention and Visitors Bureau for a list (call 800-250-4827); Amish Heritage Furniture, Jayco RV, and Coachmen RV tours in Middlebury (see pages 137, 142, and 139); Amish Acres.

John Deere

Waterloo Works
3500 East Donald Street
Waterloo, IA 50701
(319) 292-7697 / (if no answer, call 319-292-7668)
www.deere.com

TRACTORS

JOHN DEERE

Deere began building tractors in downtown Waterloo in 1918 and moved to the current location in 1981. Many of the old two-cylinder John Deere tractors, manufactured from 1918 to 1960 and affectionately known as "Johnny Poppers," are still in active use. The tour shows you manufacturing techniques to make their highly-rated tractors.

A company retiree leads your tour through the tractor assembly building (48 acres under one roof). The air is filled with the scent of machine oil and the sound of presses and conveyors. Tractor-building requires many subassembly steps, such as constructing the cab, before the main assembly lines put it all together. A computer system guides the tractors through assembly, keeping tabs on parts drawn from some 40,000 storage bins. Hydraulic presses, with a force of nearly 2,000 tons, form pre-sized sheet steel blanks into tractor frames, fenders, and other parts. Lasers cut out plates for the sides of fuel tanks. Robotic welders join parts with impressive consistency and rainbows of sparks.

An overhead conveyor carries completed parts on a two-mile journey through paint operations. Three chassis lines and three final assembly lines move at a measured pace. In about two hours the tractor frames become complete machines. Notice how carefully the cab and other parts are lowered from an overhead conveyor hoist and mounted on the tractor frame. Near the end of the line, after fluids are added, workers test wheel-less tractors for such features as engine start-up, speed and power levels, and brake and park/lock security.

Unlike row-crop tractors, the heavy-duty four-wheel-drive tractors are assembled using a modular, team concept. The production area is arranged in process groups called "cells," with each cell's operators responsible for assembling a related family of parts. Once a cell's work is completed and checked, the tractor moves to the next cell.

Cost: Free

Freebies: Brochure on tractor production

Video Shown: 18-minute video overviews the entire John Deere Waterloo Works.

Reservations Needed: Preferred for individuals and families. Required for groups larger than 10 people.

Days and Hours: Mon–Fri 8:00 AM, 10:00 AM, and 1:00 PM. Closed major holidays and week between Christmas and New Year's. Summer shutdown last week of July–first week of August. (Call about more extended summer shutdown.)

Plan to Stay: 2.5 hours

Minimum Age: 13

Disabled Access: Yes

Group Requirements: Groups larger than 20 people should make reservations 10 days in advance.

Special Information: No video cameras. For information on John Deere factory tours nationwide (including Davenport, Dubuque, Des Moines, and Ottumwa, IA), call Visitors' Services at Corporate Headquarters in Moline, IL (800-765-9588). East Moline, IL, plant produces harvesters (see page 132). John Deere Pavilion in Moline, IL, displays history of agriculture exhibits (see page 10).

Gift Shop: Sells wide variety of logoed items, including T-shirts, hats, and belt buckles. Open to tour visitors. Call (319) 292-7564 about other hours.

Directions: From Dubuque, take Hwy. 20 West to Exit 68 North in Waterloo. Follow exit road north. Turn left onto Gilbertville Rd. Turn right onto North Elk Run Rd. Turn left onto East Donald St. From Des Moines, take I-80 East to Hwy. 63 North. Exit at Hwy. 20 East to Waterloo Exit 68 North. Follow the directions above.

Nearby Attractions: Other John Deere tours in Waterloo available at the Foundry, Component, and Engine Works (call 319-292-7697 for information); Wonder Bread bakery tour (call 319-234-4447); Groute Museum of History and Science; Waterloo Recreation and Arts Center; George Wyth Memorial Park.

Krauss Furniture Shop

2783 Highway 6 Trail
South Amana, IA 52334
(319) 622-3223
www.kraussfurniture.com

FURNITURE

Krauss Furniture is located in Iowa's Amana Colonies, which were founded in 1855 by German immigrants escaping religious persecution. The Amana Colonies offer an abundance of family activities, including many craftwork tours. The moment you walk in the door at Krauss, the smell of walnut, cherry, and oak woods mixed with the odor of fresh varnish will tell you this is a furniture factory. As you saunter between the yellow lines on this self-guided tour, you watch as many as 15 craftsmen building custom-made tables, chairs, cupboards, bedroom sets, rockers, and clock cabinets. Krauss completes up to 1,000 pieces per year.

You'll see many different types of woodworking tools, some brand new and others over 80 years old. In the cutting area, workers dry, machine, glue, and rough-sand all the lumber used. A lathe-worker, covered head-to-toe with sawdust and chips, turns spindles to make the furniture legs. Planers reduce the boards to equal thickness. They are then glued into panels, rough-sanded, and cut into rough lengths.

Krauss does not use an assembly line to make furniture. Each craftsman has his own workbench and builds the furniture, one piece at a time, from start to finish. The method is the old-time hand-fitted, dovetailed or mortise-and-tenon joinery. Woodworker hobbyists will covet these craftsmen's tools, time, and skill in building furniture. In the finishing area, the workers sand and finish the pieces. The finish, Krauss Furniture's pride, is painstakingly sprayed and brushed on (as many as seven coats) and sanded off until it is completely smooth. When the oil is finally applied for a hand-rubbed finish, workers show the same affection as parents brushing their children's hair.

Cost: Free

Freebies: Product brochure

Video Shown: No

Reservations Needed: No, except for motorcoach tours.

Days and Hours: Mon–Fri 8:00 AM–4:00 PM. Sat 9:00 AM–4:00 PM. Not always in full production on Saturday, so call ahead. Closed major holidays.

Plan to Stay: 15 minutes for the self-guided tour, plus time for the showroom.

Minimum Age: None

Disabled Access: Yes

Group Requirements: Bus tour groups can get guided tour. Call 1 week in advance.

Special Information: Sawdusty setting.

Showroom: Sells all Krauss wood pieces, from large furniture to smaller gift items. Most smaller wooden items, such as magazine racks and picture frames, are made by local retired people. Picture albums show custom-designed furniture that can be built to order. Open Mon–Fri 8:00 AM–5:00 PM, Sat 9:00 AM–5:00 PM, and May through December also Sun 1:00 PM–4:00 PM. Catalog available.

Directions: From I-80, take Exit 225 for Hwy. 151 North. At the T-intersection with Hwy. 6 Trail, go left 2 miles. Krauss Furniture is on the north side of Hwy. 6 Trail (large clock outside building). From Hwy. 6 Trail West, Krauss is about 1 mile east of South Amana.

Nearby Attractions: The Amana Colonies have a number of attractions and a world-renowned tradition of craftsmanship. Some other local businesses that offer tours or work-area viewings include Amana Woolen Mill (call 319-622-3432), Schanz Furniture and Refinishing (call 319-622-3529), Amana Furniture and Clock Shop (call 319-622-3291), Ehrle Brothers Winery (call 319-622-3241), and Village Winery (call 319-622-3448).

Winnebago Industries

1316 South 4th Street
Forest City, IA 50436
(641) 585-6936
www.winnebagoind.com

MOTOR HOMES

Winnebago Industries was born in 1958, when a group of local businesses, worried about Iowa's depressed farm economy, persuaded Modernistic Industries of California to build a travel-trailer factory in Forest City. Local businessmen soon bought the factory and, in 1960, named it Winnebago Industries, after the county in which it was located. Since 1966, when the company started making motor homes, the name Winnebago has become synonymous with "motor home."

You will not doubt Winnebago's self-proclaimed position as an industry leader after touring the world's largest RV production plant. The company prides itself on its interlocking joint construction and on the fact that it produces the majority of parts in-house, including fabric covers for its seats and sofas. The 200-acre factory includes the main assembly areas (which you'll see on the tour), metal stamping division, plastics facility, sawmill and cabinet shop, and sewing and design departments.

In the chassis prep building (not on tour), parts of the all-steel frame are stamped out on the "Dinosaur." Sparks fly as workers weld floor joints and storage compartments to the chassis. The completed RV (including windshield) will be set into this steel frame. The front end drops from a mezzanine onto the chassis and is aligned by laser beams.

The motor-home production lines are in a building employees affectionately call "Big Bertha." From your vantage point on the catwalk, you'll see the developing motor homes creep down three 1,032-foot-long assembly lines at 21 inches per minute. First, workers install a heat-resistant laminated floor. Next, they install the bathroom fixtures, then screw the Thermo-Panel sidewalls (made of block foam embedded with an aluminum frame and steel supports, interior paneling, and an exterior fiberglass skin) onto steel outriggers extending from the floor of the motor home. Further down the line, cabinets are installed.

Finally, the entire unit receives a one-piece, fiberglass-covered, laminated roof. The motor home is then driven to the company's stitchcraft building to receive its furniture and window coverings. The completed motor home is rigorously inspected in the test chambers, where it experiences severe "rainstorms." Select units also travel through a test track of road hazards.

Cost: Free

Freebies: Winnebago Industries product brochures

Video Shown: 22-minute "Winnebago Industries Factory Tour" video takes you through a detailed view of the world's largest motor-home factory. When no factory tours, visitors can watch this video as well as informative videos on individual Winnebago, Itasca, Rialta, and Ultimate motor homes.

Reservations Needed: No, except for groups larger than 6 people.

Days and Hours: April–October: Mon–Fri 9:00 AM and 1:00 PM; November–mid-December: Mon–Fri 1:00 PM. No tours mid-December–March 31. Closed holidays and 1 week in July.

Plan to Stay: 1.5 hours for video and tour, plus time for Visitors Center motor-home exhibits and wall displays.

Minimum Age: No, but small children must be accompanied by an adult.

Disabled Access: Yes, for Visitors Center. Factory tour includes 3 staircases.

Group Requirements: Groups larger than 6 people should make reservations 2 weeks in advance.

Special Information: Photography allowed in Visitors Center but not in plant.

Gift Shop: Winnebago-Itasca Travelers Club gift shop sells logoed items, including jackets, shirts, and caps. Open 8:30 AM–4:00 PM year-round. Closed holidays.

Directions: From I-35, exit at Hwy. 9 West. At junction of Hwy. 9 and Hwy. 69, take Hwy. 69 South. Turn right on B14 and immediately turn right on 4th St. in Forest City. Visitors Center is on right.

Nearby Attractions: Pammel RV Park; Pilot Knob State Park; Mansion Museum; Waldorf College; Heritage Park.

See color photos, page 13.

Hallmark Cards

240 South East Madison Street
Topeka, KS 66607
(785) 233-3241
www.hallmark.com

Birthdays, graduations, weddings, and holidays all have one thing in common—they are perfect occasions to send a Hallmark card. Travel into the world of Hallmark and find out exactly what it takes to make a card at their 716,000-square-foot, two-story manufacturing plant in Topeka, Kansas. As you walk into the receptionist area, look to your right to see a wooden mural by former Hallmark artist Robert Sneeburg. After receiving safety instructions (stay between the marked lines), prepare to enter an enormous factory floor and experience why Hallmark can say, "When you care enough to send the very best."

Your tour guide, who works on the manufacturing floor, begins the tour at the foil department. Hallmark's reputation for intricate detail is evident as you watch gold, silver, and other color foils being applied to create captions, art design, and lettering on cards. In contrast, your next stop at the large die-cut area proves that Hallmark is an enormous operation. Massive machines standing taller and wider than a conversion van cut cards out of litho sheets and send them down a conveyer belt to be stacked.

Next, walk past the clang-clunk of the die-cut machines to the screen-print operation. Screen-printing applies ink to large sheets of stock. Each sheet that comes out travels along a 30-foot round conveyer to allow the ink to dry. See the end of the manufacturing process as you walk through folding, quality control, and packaging.

Your last stop on the first floor is envelope production. It's the nosiest and one of the busiest rooms in the factory, where envelope machines produce over 3 billion envelopes per year for all of Hallmark. Watch five-foot-high paper stock disappear into the machines and emerge as a completed envelope only a little larger than your hand.

The second floor is devoted to more detailing and packaging. Enter the Christmas card box-set area. From February to October, this area die-cuts, folds, and packages all the Christmas card sets you see in stores. Next, walk through the handwork area where employees perform miscellaneous packaging/repackaging and hand-finishing touches. Then walk into the "flitter" department, where they add that extra sparkle to many Hallmark cards. You can guess what their specialty is—glitter!

Cost: Free

Freebies: Hallmark pencil

Video Shown: No

Reservations Needed: Yes, all groups must give notice at least 1 week in advance.

Days and Hours: Mon–Fri 8:30 AM–10:00 AM, 12:30 PM–2:00 PM.

Plan to Stay: 1 hour

Minimum Age: 12

Disabled Access: Yes

Group Requirements: Groups of 10 or more should call at least 2 weeks in advance. Maximum group size is 45.

Special Information: No cameras allowed. No cell phones used in plant during tour. Hallmark Visitor Center in Kansas City, MO (see pages 20–21).

Gift Shop: No

Directions: From I-70 East, take Exit 183 for downtown and Salina. Get off at 4th St. exit onto Madison St. Turn left at stop light into Hallmark parking lot. From I-70 West, take 3rd St. exit. Continue through intersection to stoplight. Turn left at light onto 4th St. Hallmark parking lot will be on your left.

Nearby Attractions: State Capitol Building; Governor's Mansion; Kansas Museum of History; *Topeka Capital-Journal;* Air Museum (Forbes Field); Gage Park and Zoo.

Reuter

1220 Timberedge Road
Lawrence, KS 66049
(785) 843-2622
www.reuterorgan.com

Reuter
Preferred Pipe Organs

PIPE ORGANS

Since 1917 Reuter Organ Company has produced custom-built organs for churches, universities, and homes. Housed in a 75,000-square-foot building, 50 craftsmen build six to twelve pipe organs per year. Construction of each organ takes two to four months, so you'll see several in progress during your tour.

No two organs are identical. Each organ's size depends on its site, so engineers draw individualized musical and architectural plans. Musical plans incorporate pipe scales and other aspects relating to acoustics. Architectural plans specify arrangement of the parts and perhaps a rendering of the finished and installed organ.

In the pipe department, workers cut sheets of zinc, copper, and spotted metal (a tin-lead alloy) to each pipe's size and shape. Metal is rolled on mandrels to form the pipes, then pipes are hand-soldered or tig-welded. Pipes range from 32 feet tall to the size of a pencil. The number of pipes in each organ varies from a few hundred to over 6,000. Pipes are arranged in ranks, a rank having 61 pipes. Each rank is analogous to an orchestral instrument. "Voicers" essentially "teach" these new organ pipes to "sing," then refine their sound so each rank's pipes sound like one voice.

As you tour this factory building, notice the skilled woodworkers and metalsmiths meticulously hand-fashioning organ parts. As you smell the raw wood and feel the sheepskin leather, appreciate the handwork that goes into each organ. The wood used for the console, organist's bench, and decorative case matches the purchaser's décor.

Everything comes together in the assembly room. Here, workers assemble the wind chest and build the framework that supports the organ. They test the organ musically, in the same arrangement as its final destination. Now you hear the full "color of sounds" that the different organ ranks create. Once you see the fully assembled cre-

ation, you'll understand why the pipe organ is known as the King of Instruments.

Cost: Free
Freebies: Brochures
Video Shown: No
Reservations Needed: Preferred for individuals. Required for groups (see below).
Days and Hours: Mon–Fri 10:00 AM–2:00 PM, break from 12:00 PM–1:00 PM. Closed holidays and Christmas through New Year's.
Plan to Stay: 1 hour
Minimum Age: No, for families; age 12, for groups.
Disabled Access: Yes
Group Requirements: Groups larger than 15 people will be divided into smaller groups, each with its own guide. Call 2 weeks in advance for reservations. Maximum group size is 25–30 people.
Special Information: Recommends walking shoes. Finished organs are not tested on every tour because an organ is completed every 1–2 months. Call ahead to arrange your tour accordingly.
Gift Shop: No
Directions: From Kansas City, take I-70 West to West Lawrence exit. Turn right at first light on Princeton. Turn right again at stop sign on North Iowa St. Proceed north on North Iowa St. about 1.5 miles. Round the corner at Lakeview Rd. and turn right onto Timberedge Rd. Enter the Reuter building on the west side. From Topeka, take I-70 East to West Lawrence exit and follow above directions.
Nearby Attractions: Historic downtown Lawrence; Riverfront Mall; Kansas University; Haskell Indian Nations University; Hallmark Cards tour (see page 151) in Topeka, about 40 minutes away; attractions in Kansas City, MO, including the Hallmark Visitors Center (see page 20), are about 45 minutes away.

American Printing House for the Blind

1839 Frankfort Avenue
Louisville, KY 40206
(502) 895-2405
www.aph.org

BRAILLE AND LARGE-TYPE PUBLICATIONS, AUDIO BOOKS, AND EDUCATIONAL AIDS

American Printing House for the Blind (APH) is the world's oldest (founded in 1858) and largest nonprofit company devoted to making products for visually impaired people. The company likes to say that the tour through this multimedia company teaches visitors about a "world they never saw before."

Your journey begins in the display room surrounded by the range of APH products, including a *Reader's Digest* in Braille. Turning a print book into Braille is not a simple process in which workers magically scan in a print page and out pops a perfect Braille version. It begins with computers and software that help workers with the first step in translating the written text into Braille.

Proofing this computer-generated output is the key to the Braille publications' accuracy. A blind person reads an entire book aloud from the Braille proof pages, while a sighted person follows along in the print copy, marking errors and corrections. The corrections are made on the computer disk, and the disk output is sent straight to a machine that punches the raised dots of the Braille alphabet onto printing plates. You can see the modified rotary and clamshell presses as they spin out Braille pages from these plates.

APH has 10 recording studios for turning print books into talking versions. Peek in at the professional narrator and technicians at work. In the audiotape duplication areas, 40 duplicators spin simultaneously to make copies from the master. Either before or after your tour, visit the interactive museum that chronicles the international history of the education of blind people.

Cost: Free

Freebies: A Braille copy of the special edition of *My Weekly Reader,* a grade school-age magazine in Braille and print, and a Braille alphabet card.

Videos Shown: 3 brief videos on history of Braille, the process of printing a Braille book, and how a talking book is made.

Reservations Needed: No, except for groups of 10 or more people.

Days and Hours: Plant tour: Mon–Thur 10:00 AM and 2:00 PM. Museum: Mon–Fri 8:30 AM–4:30 PM. Closed holidays.

Plan to Stay: 1 hour, plus time for museum and gift counter.

Minimum Age: No required minimum for museum or plant tour for small groups, but recommend 2nd grade and up. Approximately 10 percent of the 300-person workforce is disabled.

Disabled Access: Yes

Group Requirements: Groups over 10 people can receive guided tour of the plant and/or museum by calling a minimum of 1 week in advance. Maximum size is usually about 45 people (one busload). Minimum age for school groups for plant tour is 4th grade. School groups of 1st- to 3rd-graders will have hands-on museum tour and partial plant tour.

Special Information: No photography in plant. National Braille Press in Boston, MA, also offers public tours (see page 188).

Gift Counter: Sells T-shirts with Braille alphabet, Braille key chains, and note and holiday cards. Usually open just during tour hours, but you can purchase items online at above website. Catalog available for all APH products by calling (800) 223-1839.

Directions: From I-64 East, take Exit 7, Story Ave. Then immediately turn left at Spring St. Turn left at Mellwood Ave. After you go under highway, turn right on Frankfort Ave. APH is at top of hill on left. From I-64 West, take Exit 7 for Mellwood Ave. Turn right onto Frankfort Ave. and follow directions above. Company can fax you directions from different locations.

Nearby Attractions: Louisville area attractions, including Colonel Harland Sanders Museum, Ford, Louisville Stoneware, and Hillerich & Bradsby (Louisville Slugger) tours (see pages 156, 158, 160, and 159).

Churchill Weavers

100 Churchill Drive
Lorraine Court
Berea, KY 40403
(859) 986-3127
www.churchill-weavers.com

CHURCHILL WEAVERS

BLANKETS, THROWS, AND SCARVES

It takes hard work and heritage to hand-weave a beautiful Churchill Weavers blanket or throw. Churchill Weavers, nestled in a small college town where Kentucky's Bluegrass meets its Cumberland Mountains, encompasses history, pride, and craftsmanship. MIT graduate and industrial engineer Carroll Churchill and his wife, Eleanor, an English schoolteacher, returned from missionary work in India to found Churchill Weavers in 1922. Eleanor chose Lila and Richard Belando to continue the Churchill legacy. In 1996 Crown Crafts, a leader in home fashion textiles, acquired Churchill Weavers. Today Lila and Richard still carry on the leadership of this unique company.

Your self-guided tour includes the historic loomhouse, residence to almost 50 looms. Notice that the weathered brown of the looms matches the building's ceilings, walls, and wooden plank floors. In the loomhouse is the waterwheel-like "warper." Threads are wrapped around it according to a written pattern, then wound onto a warp drum that fits into the back of a loom.

The highlight of the tour is watching wooden looms in action, as weavers create baby blankets, throws, table linens, scarves, and fabrics for other products. Watch an agile weaver alternate between pulling the beater forward with her left hand and "throwing" the shuttle with her right. At the same time, as if playing an organ, she steps on foot pedals to create a pattern. The rhythm of the weavers at their looms sounds like the hoofbeats of galloping horses. The rhythm breaks only when a weaver stops to replace a yarn-filled bobbin in the shuttle, then it begins again.

Menders check newly woven cloth on light boards and repair flaws. From warping to weaving to tying the fringes, you will observe this timeless, hands-on process of "constructing" fabrics. These beautiful "high-touch" items, made by loving hands, help balance the high-tech, fast-paced world in which we live.

Cost: Free

Freebies: No

Video Shown: 4-minute optional video in gift shop shows the company's history and its weaving process.

Reservations Needed: No, for self-guided tour. Yes, if groups want tour guide.

Days and Hours: Mon–Thur 9:00 AM–12:00 PM, 12:30 PM–4:00 PM. Call about Fri hours. Loomhouse hours vary seasonally. Closed Christmas and New Year's.

Plan to Stay: 20 minutes for tour, plus time for video and gift shop.

Minimum Age: None

Disabled Access: Yes

Group Requirements: Maximum group is 40 people. Tour guide can be arranged if booked 3–4 days in advance.

Special Information: Due to the intense concentration required by the weaving process, please do not disturb the weavers at work.

Retail Store: Sells baby blankets, scarves, stoles, throws, and decorative pillows made by Churchill Weavers, and pottery, candles, baskets, and woodcrafts from all over the U.S.A. The outlet room sells woven seconds and overruns by Churchill craftspeople. Open Mon–Sat 9:00 AM–6:00 PM, Sun 12:00 PM–6:00 PM. Catalog available from the above number.

Directions: From Lexington, take I-75 South to Exit 77. Follow Walnut Meadow Rd. to second traffic light. Turn left onto Rt. 25 North and pass Berea Hospital. Bear right onto Hwy. 1016. Follow the signs to Churchill Weavers. From the south, take I-75 North to Exit 76. Stay on Rt. 25 North through town, past Berea Hospital. Continue with above directions.

Nearby Attractions: Berea is the folk arts and crafts capital of Kentucky. You can purchase the works of local craftspeople while observing them in their studios scattered throughout the town. At Berea College you can watch students produce a variety of crafts.

▲ Cones of yarn are carefully and methodically turned into warps on one of two pre–World War II warpers.

Just as it has been for the past 80 years, a weaver works on a handmade fly shuttle loom, built by the craftspeople at Churchill Weavers in Berea, Kentucky.

▼

Colonel Harland Sanders Museum

KFC Headquarters
1441 Gardiner Lane
Louisville, KY 40213
(502) 874-8300
www.kfc.com

FAST FOOD

In Japan, Colonel Sanders is Ohji-san, or "Grandfather," and his statue stands near every one of the restaurants he inspired. A life-size statue honors the man who above all else demonstrated that the little guy can succeed in America.

Harland Sanders, born in 1890, held many jobs to support his family—streetcar conductor, cook, justice of the peace, and automobile mechanic.

Some of the rare photos show Sanders' Court Restaurant. About 1930, Sanders began cooking chicken for customers at his auto service station (later a restaurant) along busy U.S. 25. At Sanders' Court he perfected his famous secret blend of 11 herbs and spices, and developed the innovation of frying chicken in a pressure cooker. The original cooker made such a difference. In 1935 Governor Ruby Laffoon made Sanders an honorary Kentucky colonel for his contribution to the state's cuisine.

Unfortunately, a highway bypass closed the restaurant in the early 1950s. After paying his bills, Sanders had nothing to live on except his Social Security check. With his wife, Claudia, he hit the road, making samples of his chicken and offering franchise deals to restaurant owners. The idea was so successful that, in 1964, he sold his interest in Kentucky Fried Chicken and became the company's spokesman, wearing his now-famous white suit.

The Colonel traveled extensively around the world, met many dignitaries and celebrities, and gave millions of dollars to charities. The Colonel's favorite award was a wire chicken presented to him by the National Restaurant Association. KFC is the world's most popular chicken restaurant chain—10,800-plus restaurants in 91 countries. You'll forever associate KFC with the 66-year-old man who began an empire with a $105 Social Security check.

Cost: Free

Freebies: No

Video Shown: No

Reservations Needed: No, except for groups larger than 15 people.

Days and Hours: Mon–Thur 8:30 AM–4:30 PM, Fri 8:30 AM–12:30 PM. Closed standard holidays. *Only can see small portion of Sanders' office. Visit Corbin, KY, to see more. See special information below.*

Plan to Stay: 10 minutes

Minimum Age: 8

Disabled Access: Yes

Group Requirements: Groups of 15 people or more should call at least 2 weeks in advance. Maximum group size is 35.

Special Information: In the lobby of the KFC corporate headquarters, so dress appropriately. The café and motel in Corbin, KY, where the Colonel concocted his secret recipe, has been restored to its mid-1940s glory (call 606-528-2163).

Gift Shop: No, but the closest KFC is on Bardstown Rd.

Directions: Take I-264 to Newburg Rd. exit. Go south and turn right onto Bishop Ln. Turn right onto Gardiner Rd. Museum is in KFC corporate headquarters, which has an antebellum plantation facade.

Nearby Attractions: Ford, American Printing House for the Blind, and Louisville Stoneware tours, and Hillerich & Bradsby (Louisville Slugger) Museum (see pages 158, 153, 160, and 159); Hadley Pottery tour (call 502-584-2171); Louisville's attractions include J. B. Speed Art Museum, Churchill Downs/Kentucky Derby Museum, and Kentucky Art and Craft Center.

Corvette

Corvette Drive
Bowling Green, KY 42101
(270) 745-8419
www.chevrolet.com/corvette

Since it was first built in 1953, General Motors' Corvette has become an American automotive icon, representing muscle, fantasy, and youth. The television series *Route 66*, about two bachelors who traveled American highways in their 'Vette, increased the car's popularity. In 1981 GM moved Corvette assembly to a Bowling Green complex the size of 22 football fields.

Led by a guide who points out the car's special features, you'll walk on the plant floor to witness the major steps in the sports car's production. See the frame and body take shape; the engine and drive train go together, the windshields attached, and the joining of the chassis and body.

Computerized robots weld the steel frame together before the Corvette receives its signature fiberglass body panels. Once the panels are painted, they return to the main assembly floor, where workers install them along with other parts such as seats, wheels, and removable roof. While the car's body is being assembled in the trim area, the engine and drive train are assembled in another area. When the two come together it's called "body marriage," with workers scampering underneath the car to connect the chassis and body.

Almost everywhere you look, Corvettes in some stage of assembly move past on a multilevel network of conveyors that cover about six miles. A worker sits in the car and starts the engine. Like a baby's first cry, the engine makes its initial roar. It may take a couple of seconds for the car to start but, once running, it idles for some time while workers make various checks throughout the car. Only when the car is fully built do all four wheels touch the ground for the first time. Even if you didn't arrive as a diehard Corvette enthusiast, you'll leave as one.

Cost: Free
Freebies: No

Video Shown: 6-minute video on plant safety regulations, plus steps not on the tour, such as body painting.

Reservations Needed: No, except for groups of 10 people or more.

Days and Hours: Mon–Fri 9:00 AM and 1:00 PM. Closed holidays, week between Christmas and New Year's, 2 weeks in summer (usually starting early July), and for model changes and production shutdowns. Always call ahead.

Plan to Stay: 1.5 hours for tour and video, plus time in gift shop.

Minimum Age: None, but children under 6 may be intimidated by the noise. School groups minimum 4th grade.

Disabled Access: Yes

Group Requirements: For groups larger than 10 people, call (270) 745-8287 for reservations 1 week in advance. Maximum group size is 50 people, and other times can be scheduled.

Special Information: No photography on tour. 1 mile of walking. No open-toed shoes.

Gift Shops: Sell Corvette memorabilia including T-shirts, hats, and key chains. Open during tour hours.

Directions: From I-65 take Exit 28. For plant, turn right at Corvette Dr., then right after entering the gate. Follow signs to tour parking. For museum, turn left at Corvette Dr.

Nearby Attractions: National Corvette Museum across the street from the plant houses more than 50 Corvette models and one-of-a-kind concept cars representing the history of Corvette. Also displays thousands of Corvette-related photos, movies and videos, advertisements, scale models, and rare memorabilia. Call (270) 781-7973 or go to www.corvettemuseum.com. Other attractions include Beech Bend Raceway Park and Mammoth Cave National Park.

Ford

Fern Valley Road at Grade Lane
Louisville, KY 40213
(502) 364-3551
www.fordvehicles.com

**SPORT-UTILITY VEHICLES
AND PICKUP TRUCKS**

Since 1913 Ford has had operations in Louisville, which now includes both the Louisville Assembly Plant and its massive heavy-truck plant. Ford made 12 Model Ts a day back in 1913. Now the home of the popular Explorer, Ranger, and Mercury Mountaineer, this plant has substantially quickened its pace to 87 vehicles per hour (the auto industry norm is 60, making this plant possibly the fastest in the world). You get to see almost all the production steps, although not in the order of assembly, as all the vehicles are built on one long line.

The body area is always one of the most exciting places to visit at an automobile plant. It's the scene most often shown of car factories on TV: skeleton car bodies and robots marching together in perfect unison, with colorful sparks flying. Here you can watch the real thing. With the help of more than 140 robots, the stamped sheet metal that comes from other Ford plants is precision-fitted and welded to exact specifications. The robots help transfer parts, spot-weld, and apply sealer. The body then heads to the paint area, which is usually not on the tour.

In the trim area most of the vehicles' insides are added, filling up the painted shell. It's truly an industrial symphony of sounds from the machines and tools that buzz, crunch, and hiss. With robots' assistance, workers bend, twist, and reach to install various interior and exterior parts, such as wiring, door glass, windshields, door handles, instrument panels, and horns.

The chassis is built in another area. Notice how the frame is actually upside down when workers install the fuel and brake lines, body mounts, and wiring. The frame is then flipped over before the bumpers are added, along with the engine, transmission, and driveshaft. Another favorite site is the "body drop." The body, hanging from a part of the 20-plus miles of conveyors in the fac-

tory, is lowered and secured to the frame. After more parts are added, including the all-important tires and seats, the vehicle is started and heads off for final inspection. The inspectors act like the pickiest buyers, checking even the tiniest mechanical and visual details.

Cost: Free

Freebies: Brochures about the history of Ford in Louisville and the assembly process.

Video Shown: 10-minute video of material similar to that covered in the brochure.

Reservations Needed: Yes

Days and Hours: Mon at 9:30 AM (moved to Tue if Mon is holiday), although special tours occasionally arranged.

Plan to Stay: 2 hours for talk, video, and tour.

Minimum Age: None, but young children could be intimidated by the noises.

Disabled Access: Yes

Group Requirements: The total number of visitors is limited to 150 each session. Groups need to schedule months in advance to ensure space availability.

Special Information: Will walk approximately 1.5 miles during tour. Ford's St. Louis Assembly Plant offers limited tours of Explorer production (call 314-731-6365).

Gift Shop: No

Directions: From I-65, exit at Fern Valley Rd. Plant is visible from exit regardless of which direction you travel. Drive to plant entrance and park in administrative lot.

Nearby Attractions: UPS Louisville air tour (call 502-359-8252); Louisville's attractions, including Louisville Stoneware and American Printing House for the Blind tours and Louisville Slugger and Colonel Harland Sanders (KFC) Museums (see pages 160, 153, 159, and 156), and Churchill Downs/Kentucky Derby Museum, are about 30 minutes away.

Hillerich & Bradsby

Louisville Slugger Museum
800 West Main Street
Louisville, KY 40202
(502) 588-7228
www.sluggermuseum.org

Louisville Slugger®

The Louisville Slugger bat, created by Bud Hillerich in 1884, has been called "one of the greatest original American products ever made." In 1996 Hillerich & Bradsby moved their plant from Jeffersonville, Indiana, to their signature product's namesake town, Louisville, Kentucky. They also opened the Louisville Slugger Museum, a tribute to baseball's greatest hits and hitters. You'll see actual bats swung by such legendary sluggers as Ty Cobb, Lou Gehrig, and Joe DiMaggio, plus the bat Babe Ruth used during his 1927 record-setting 60-home-run season. Listen to Hall of Fame broadcasters call baseball's greatest moments. Take the field in a replica of Camden Yard. Choose a famous pitcher to throw the ball in your direction at 90 miles per hour.

After walking through the museum and a replica of a Northern white ash forest, take a guided tour of the plant. With the ever-present smell of wood in the air, H&B uses three techniques to turn the Northern white ash billets into bats. Most of the bats are made on automatic lathes that carve out the most popular models, about one every 15 seconds.

It takes about 40 seconds to make a bat on the tracer lathes. Workers use a metal pattern of the exact bat shape and guide the machine to trace this pattern, a process similar to copying a key at the hardware store. Only about five percent of their professional bats are hand-turned, a technique used only for unusual models.

With sizzle and smoke, the famous oval trademark, bat model number, and the player's autograph are seared into the "flat of the grain." Behind the branders are large cabinets holding more than 8,500 professional baseball players' autograph brands. The bats go through more production steps, but it's the thrill of watching the branding that you'll remember the best. You'll leave the museum and tour having witnessed a part of true Americana.

Cost: Adults, $6; seniors 60+, $5; children 6–12, $3.50; children 5 and under, free.

Freebies: 16-inch miniature wood bat

Video Shown: 13-minute film, "Heart of the Game," relives some of the greatest hits in baseball.

Reservations Needed: No, except for groups larger than 20 people.

Days and Hours: Mon–Sat 9:00 AM–5:00 PM April 1–November 30; also open Sun 12:00 PM–5:00 PM, but no bat production. Last factory tour is at 4:00 PM. Closed holidays. Call regarding schedule for week between Christmas and New Year's.

Plan to Stay: 1.5 hours for tour and museum, plus time for gift shop.

Minimum Age: Discourages children under age 5.

Disabled Access: Yes

Group Requirements: Reservations needed for groups over 20 people. At least 1-month advance notice suggested for summer tours. Call (502) 588-7227.

Special Information: No photography in plant.

Gift Shop: Sells Louisville Slugger, Power-Bilt, and Louisville Hockey logoed items, including T-shirts, hats, towels, gym bags, and pen bats. Catalog available. Open same hours as tour.

Directions: From Indianapolis, take I-65 South to I-64 West. Exit on 3rd St. Turn right onto River Rd. Turn left onto 8th St. You can't miss the Louisville Slugger Museum—just look for the world's tallest bat. From Cincinnati, take I-71 South to I-64 West and follow above directions.

Nearby Attractions: Colonel Harland Sanders (KFC) Museum, Ford, Louisville Stoneware, and American Printing House for the Blind tours (see pages 156, 158, 160, and 153); Louisville Science Center (across the street from the Louisville Slugger Museum); Kentucky Derby Museum; Churchill Downs.

Louisville Stoneware

731 Brent Street
Louisville, KY 40204
(502) 582-1900
www.louisvillestoneware.com

LOUISVILLE
STONEWARE

POTTERY

Raw clay, mined from western Indiana, forms a small hill against the back wall of the clay-making room. Since 1905 this has been the main ingredient for the artistic, durable, authentic American pottery made by Louisville Stoneware. The guided tour includes the clay-making room, where clay dirt is vigorously mixed with water to make a clay "soup." Under high pressure, a press pushes liquid clay through filters with water dripping out the bottom. In the pug mill, the resulting firm cakes of fine clay are chopped into stiff or soft mud or turned into liquid slip clay. In a process called "slip casting," this fluid slip is poured into angular plaster molds to form items such as bird feeders and birdhouses.

The guided tour shows you the "jiggering," handle-pulling, glazing, hand-painting, and kiln-loading. Jiggering, another process of romancing the clay, is used for more concentric shapes. Leaning over a spinning pottery wheel, a potter places clay onto a concave plaster mold (shaped like the inside of a bowl) and then lowers the jigger handle to form the plate or bowl. The potter uses a water-drenched sponge to smooth the clay's surface. Each plate hardens on its individual plaster mold. Throughout the factory, you will see earthenware drying on 6- to 10-foot-high storage conveyors, whose shelves can be rotated or advanced when full.

You can stand next to the artists as they hand-paint traditional patterns directly onto the dried clay piece. At first appearing pastel, the final underglaze colors reveal themselves only after a white translucent glaze is applied and the piece is fired at a high temperature. You'll feel the heat emerging from the three kilns, which hold 1,000 pieces each. The whole firing process takes almost a full day—10 hours to reach 2,350°, and then 12 hours to cool.

Cost: Free
Freebies: No

Video Shown: No
Reservations Needed: No, except for groups larger than 8 people.
Days and Hours: Mon–Fri 10:30 AM, 12:00 PM, and 1:30 PM. Also 2:30 PM in summer. Closed holidays.
Plan to Stay: 15–25 minutes for the tour and video, depending on whether you see the clay-making process, plus time for outlet store.
Minimum Age: None
Disabled Access: Yes
Group Requirements: Groups larger than 8 people should call 1 day in advance for desired time. Large groups will be split.
Special Information: Since there are 3 firing kilns, the factory can be hot.
Gift Shop: Visitors center sells colorful dinnerware, giftware, bakeware, birdhouses, flowerpots, and spiritual items. Ask about personalized services and bridal registry. Bring the kids to Paint Your Own in the pottery studio. Sells factory seconds up to 40 percent off regular prices. Annual tent sale in July sells seconds at additional savings. Open Mon–Sat 9:00 AM–6:00 PM. April–December, also open Sun 12:00 PM–5:00 PM. Catalog available from (800) 626-1800.
Directions: From Lexington, take Rt. 64 West to 3rd St. South (one way). Turn left onto Broadway, then right onto Brent St. Located 2.5 blocks ahead on left. From the Louisville area, take Rt. 65 North to Broadway exit. Turn right onto Broadway, then right onto Brent St.
Nearby Attractions: Louisville Slugger, Colonel Harland Sanders (KFC) Museums, Ford, and American Printing House for the Blind tours (see pages 159, 156, 158, and 153); Hadley Pottery tour (call 502-584-2171); Speed Art Museum; Churchill Downs/Kentucky Derby Museum; Kentucky Art and Craft Center.

Maker's Mark

3350 Burks Spring Road
Loretto, KY 40037
(270) 865-2099
www.makersmark.com

Maker's (S̲IV) Mark®

BOURBON

An illustration of the Maker's Mark distillery appears on its bottles; the label invites you to visit "any time you're in the neighborhood," so you know the place must be special. Just as Bill Samuels Sr. wanted to create his own distinctive bourbon by using gentle winter wheat instead of rye, he wanted to restore a historic distillery complex into the home of Maker's Mark.

Your tour of this National Historic Landmark distillery begins near the stone-walled creek that runs through the peaceful, landscaped grounds, where you'll hear a brief history of the distillery. Its black buildings feature bright red shutters with a Maker's Mark bottle cutout. Unlike larger distilleries' 600-barrel-per-day production, Maker's Mark crafts about 40 per day.

In the still house you'll smell corn, wheat, and malted barley cooking. The bubbling yellow mash ferments in century-old cypress vats. Vaporization of the mash in the shiny copper still separates out the whiskey, which is placed in charred oak casks for aging. When you enter the aging warehouse's ground floor, the aromas alone tell you what's in the barrels. Barrels reach maturity only after completing a rotation system in which the newest barrels are placed on the warehouse's hot upper floors and are gradually moved to the cooler lower levels.

Only in the bottling house does the production pace quicken. Near the end of the line, two women dip each bottle's glass neck into red sealing wax and then twist the bottle out to allow the excess to drip off and run down the neck. Notice each worker's distinctive dipping and twisting technique.

Cost: Free

Freebies: Iced tea and lemonade; bottle labels; great smells.

Video Shown: No

Reservations Needed: No, except for groups larger than 25 people.

Days and Hours: Mon–Sat 10:30 AM, 11:30 AM, 12:30 PM, 1:30 PM, 2:30 PM, and 3:30 PM, Sun 1:30 PM, 2:30 PM, and 3:30 PM. No production from mid-August to mid-September, but tour still runs. Limited weekend production. Closed Thanksgiving, Christmas Eve, Christmas, New Year's, and Easter Sunday.

Plan to Stay: 40 minutes for the tour, plus time for visitors center, Quart House, and Gift Gallery. Once a pre–Civil War distiller's home, the visitor's center has pieces from the Samuels' collection of early-1800s furniture and other historical and crafts items. The Quart House, oldest standing in America, is a restored pre-Prohibition retail package store.

Minimum Age: Recommends that children under 10 be accompanied by an adult.

Disabled Access: Yes. Paved walking paths between buildings.

Group Requirements: Requests at least 2 weeks' notice for groups of 25 people or more. Maximum group size is 50, but can handle larger groups in special situations.

Special Information: Wax dipping of bottles does not occur every day, but visitors can purchase souvenir bottles to dip in signature wax.

Gift Shop: The Gift Gallery in the visitor center sells logoed and craft items, including shirts, sweaters, jackets, key chains, and shot glasses. Also, gourmet sauces and candies made with Maker's Mark. Open Mon–Sat 10:00 AM–4:30 PM, Sun 1:00 PM–4:30 PM. Call number above for mail-order product list.

Directions: From Bardstown, take KY 49 South and follow signs to distillery. You're there when you see the sign that says, "You've Just Found the Home of Maker's Mark."

Nearby Bourbon-Related Attractions: Heaven Hill Distillery tour (call 502-348-3921); Oscar Getz Museum of Whiskey History (call 502-348-2999); Jim Beam's American Outpost (call 502-543-9877); Annual Bardstown September Bourbon Festival.

Old Kentucky Candies

450 Southland Drive
Lexington, KY 40503
(800) 786-0579
www.oldkycandy.com

CHOCOLATES

Bourbon Chocolates, Bourbon Cherries, Chocolate Thoroughbreds, and Kentucky Derby Mints—the names alone are enough to attract you to this candy-factory tour. Combine the tour with plentiful free samples before, after, and even right off the assembly line, and you have the makings of a tasty experience.

The chocolate in these famous Kentucky candies starts as 10-pound bars of Guittard chocolate. In the molding area, melted chocolate sits in a mixer while a rotating blade slowly turns it into a creamy paste. While the tour guide is pointing to overhead photographs and explaining how cocoa beans are harvested and the chocolate is made, you'll be tempted to sneak your finger into the mixer for a taste. Nearby are stacks of Old Kentucky's popular molds, including a 75-pound Easter bunny, dentures, and a horse's behind.

As you stroll through the candy "kitchen," you often see 8-by-3-foot slabs of fudge and candy centers cooling before they are cut with a ridged rolling pin. In the production room, glass jars of maraschino cherries may be marinating in 101-proof Jim Beam bourbon. Stand next to the conveyor belt while the candies receive a bottom chocolate base, then go through a "chocolate car wash" that coats them in chocolate. Looped chains drop down to caress the tops of the candies, creating a swirl design. After the candies exit the cooling tunnel, workers carefully hand-pack the chocolates—a job that must require great willpower to prevent nibbling.

Cost: Free
Freebies: Plentiful candy samples, including a candy directly off the assembly line.
Video Shown: No
Reservations Needed: Yes. Individuals and families may have to join a group tour.
Days and Hours: Mon–Thur 10:00 AM–3:00 PM. Closed holidays.

Plan to Stay: 20 minutes for tour, plus time for gift shop.
Minimum Age: None
Disabled Access: Yes
Group Requirements: 1 day's advance notice for groups. No maximum size. Large groups split into groups of 25 people.
Special Information: If interested in seeing specific candies made, ask when you book the tour.
Retail Store: Sells all of the company's different kinds and shapes of candies. Look for gift baskets shaped like horse heads, horseshoes, and Kentucky maps. Glass showcases filled with truffles sit next to canisters of various free samples. On the store's front table, notice the upside-down mushroom-shaped jar filled with cherries aging in bourbon. (Unfortunately, once the cherries are aged, Kentucky liquor laws do not allow the sale of this cherry-flavored bourbon.) Open Mon–Fri 9:00 AM–6:00 PM, Sat 9:30 AM–5:30 PM, Sun 1:00 PM–5:00 PM. Catalog available from above number.
Directions: From Cincinnati, take I-75 South to Exit 115 for Newtown Pike. Go west on Circle 4 (New Circle Rd.). Take exit for Harrodsburg Rd. toward Lexington. Turn right onto Lane Allen Rd., which becomes Rosemont Garden. Turn right onto Southland Dr. Old Kentucky is on the right. Factory is in the back of its retail store, in a shopping center. From Louisville, take Rt. 60 East to New Circle Rd. exit. Make immediate left onto Nicholasville Rd. Turn left onto Southland Dr. and go past railroad overpass. Old Kentucky is on the left.
Nearby Attractions: Rebecca-Ruth Candies, Toyota, and Three Chimneys horse farm tours (see pages 163, 165, and 164); Kentucky Horse Park; Boonesborough State Park; Fort Harrod State Park.

Rebecca-Ruth Candies

112 East 2nd Street
Frankfort, KY 40601
(502) 223-7475 / (800) 444-3766
www.rebeccaruth.com

CHOCOLATES AND BOURBON BALLS

Kentucky's famous 100-proof bourbon whiskeys—and a lot of local pride—are key ingredients in this family-owned company's world-renowned chocolates. These chocolates are as rich as the history surrounding the Rebecca-Ruth name itself. Founded in 1919 by two uncommonly courageous schoolteachers, Rebecca Gooch and Ruth Booe, the company's popularity grew as a result of the women's highly acclaimed chocolates and was aided by their creative sales techniques—which included loudly plugging their products on street corners. Ruth Booe originated the "Bourbon Ball." Made with real Kentucky bourbon and crowned with a Southern pecan, this confection has become the treat of the South.

The brightly striped awning shading this small, house-like store and factory creates an unpretentious atmosphere. The 10 to 15 employees (some of whom have been here for over 30 years) make about 100,000 pounds of confections a year.

In the cream-candy room are articles about Rebecca-Ruth from national magazines such as *Southern Living* and *Gourmet*. Workers pull candy cream on a hook by hand and then use a taffy-pull machine. When it's "just right," the rope of candy is cut into pieces and left to sit. It becomes very creamy, rich, and flaky. Pecan brittle and pecan butter are also made in this room.

In the kitchen, the cast-iron candy furnace and copper kettles emit the sweet scent of hand-stirred, melting sugars. In the production area, large mixers prepare rich fillings for their assembly-line journey down the enrobing line. First the candy dough is extruded onto a belt, and then it goes through a "chocolate waterfall." Two workers personally apply the finishing touches: a luscious southern pecan, sprinkles, or a swirled flourish on top.

A tour highlight is seeing "Edna's table." For close to 70 years, Edna Robbins handmade delicacies on the same marble table used by Rebecca and Ruth. (Ruth bought "Edna's table" for $10 in 1917.)

Cost: Free

Freebies: Samples of the original Bourbon Balls and other chocolates (children receive nonalcoholic samples only).

Video Shown: 8-minute video on candy production.

Reservations Needed: No, except for bus groups.

Days and Hours: January–October: Mon–Sat 9:00 AM–4:30 PM. Closed holidays.

Plan to Stay: 10–15 minutes, plus time in retail store.

Minimum Age: Young children should be accompanied by an adult.

Disabled Access: No

Group Requirements: Bus operators should call (800) 444-3766 to make reservations or obtain additional information.

Special Information: Video cameras not allowed. Production more likely in mornings, before candy holidays, and in September and October.

Retail Store: Sells a wide variety of liquor-cream chocolates (including Bourbon Balls, Kentucky Irish Coffees, and Kentucky Mint Juleps), and liquor-free chocolates, including nut clusters, butter creams, and Kentucky Creamed Pull Candy. Open year-round Mon–Sat 8:00 AM–5:30 PM, Sun 12:00 PM–5:00 PM. Closed Christmas, New Year's, and July 4th. Catalog available from 800 number above.

Directions: From Lexington, take I-64 West to Frankfort Exit 58, then take U.S. 60 West. Turn left onto Second St. Rebecca Ruth is on left. From Louisville, take I-64 East to Frankfort Exit 53. Take Rt. 127 North to U.S. 60 East, which becomes Second St. Stay on Second St. Cross over Capital Ave. Rebecca-Ruth is on left.

Nearby Attractions: Three Chimneys horse farm and Toyota tours (see pages 164 and 165); Buffalo Trace Distillery tour (call 502-223-7641).

See color photos, page 15.

Three Chimneys

1981 Old Frankfort Pike
Versailles, KY 40383
(859) 873-7053
www.threechimneys.com

THREE CHIMNEYS

HORSE-BREEDING FARM

Although a tour of a horse-breeding farm is a slight diversion from the other companies in this book, we decided to include Three Chimneys because the thoroughbred industry is the third-largest industry and the number-one tourist attraction in the state of Kentucky. In fact, Kentucky-bred horses are a majority among winners of the world-famous Kentucky Derby.

As you leave the city of Lexington and drive along the Old Frankfort Pike, you will be calmed by the gently rolling hills, and the black or white ribbons of fencing that zigzag across green pastures dotted with sleek brown horses. Enjoy this scenic drive past other horse farms while watching for the low, forest-green sign that identifies Three Chimneys.

Walk along the red brick walkway to the office, poshly decorated with colonial furniture and Oriental rugs. Further down the red brick path, past the great oaks, is the limestone stallion barn. This five-star equine hotel, lined with oak panels, trimmed with Palladian windows, and topped with a skylight in a cupola, is home to champion racehorses, now studs worth millions of dollars. Each 16-foot-square stall has black bars with black-and-gold engraved nameplates. Grooms attend to the stallions' every need.

These knowledgeable grooms are available to answer all your questions and list each of their charges' accomplishments; for example, Seattle Slew won the Triple Crown in 1977 and has sired eight champion racehorses and almost 100 stakes winners. His foals have won millions of dollars in purse money. Kentucky Derby winner Silver Charm, who retired from the racetrack in 1999 as the third richest racehorse in history, occupies a nearby stall.

Every day, the stallions graze and stretch their legs in their individual one- to two-acre paddocks. They are also ridden or walked daily for exercise. Breeding sessions are twice daily, February through July. To ensure the safety of mares and stallions, the round walls of the breeding shed are lined with foam-rubber-padded vinyl, and the floor is covered with wood chips and a raised cocoa mat. Five grooms assist with the breeding—a brief act, but one that can be worth $100,000 to Seattle Slew's owners.

Cost: Free. Tips to grooms are appreciated.
Freebies: No
Video Shown: No
Reservations Needed: Yes. For tours in April, July, and September–November call 2–3 months in advance; other times of the year, call at least 2 weeks ahead of time.
Days and Hours: Tue, Thur, and Sat 1:00 PM. Closed holidays.
Plan to Stay: 1 hour
Minimum Age: None
Disabled Access: Yes
Group Requirements: Standard bus tours are discouraged.
Special Information: Please respect the grounds and horses. This is neither a zoo nor a public riding stable.
Gift Shop: No
Directions: From Lexington, take Rt. 4 (New Circle Rd.) to Old Frankfort Pike. Drive west for 8 miles, passing a red brick church on your right. The farm is .5 miles ahead on your left. From Cincinnati, take I-75 South to I-64 West to Midway exit. Follow signs on Rt. 62 West through Midway 2 miles to a 4-way stop. Turn left onto Old Frankfort Pike. Farm is 2 miles ahead on your right.
Nearby Attractions: Toyota tour (see page 16); Kentucky Horse Park; Keeneland Racecourse and Calumet Farm tours (organized through Horse Farm Tours Inc. at 859-268-2906).

Toyota

1001 Cherry Blossom Way
Georgetown, KY 40324
(502) 868-3027 / (800) 866-4485
www.toyotageorgetown.com

VEHICLES

Toyota's largest vehicle manufacturing plant outside of Japan is located in this growing community in Kentucky's Bluegrass Region. Toyota Motor Manufacturing, Kentucky (TMMK), covers 7.5 million square feet of floor space, the equivalent of 156 football fields. But don't worry about your legs getting tired on the plant tour, because you'll be riding comfortably in one of their trams.

TMMK employs more than 7,000 team members who build nearly 2,000 quality vehicles each day. A "takt time" of 55 seconds on both of the vehicle assembly lines means that two new Toyota vehicles are built in Georgetown every 55 seconds!

TMMK began production in 1988 with the popular Toyota Camry sedan. The Avalon sedan was added in 1994. The Sienna minivan was produced from 1997 to 2002. Production of the Camry Solara coupe begins in 2003.

Toyota vehicles get their start in Stamping, taking shape from huge coils of cold-rolled steel. The steel is cleaned, straightened, and stamped into sheet-metal components that make up the vehicle bodies. With hundreds of tons of force, the automatic presses shape the steel into doors, hoods, roofs, and many other parts.

The sheet-metal components then move to Body Weld, where team members and computer-controlled robots perform the welding that results in a completed body shell. The new vehicle bodies then travel by overhead conveyors to Paint before moving on to the Trim, Chassis, and Final lines in Assembly.

As you tour TMMK, your guide points out the foundations of the world-renowned Toyota Production System. These will include examples of *kaizen,* or continuous improvement; just-in-time parts delivery; and the *andon* system, where team members can stop the line at any time to address quality concerns or any problems.

In the TMMK Visitor Center, you will see current models of the vehicles and engines built in Georgetown, plus the very first Camry produced by team members in May 1988. The Visitor Center also includes interactive video displays and exhibits on Quality, Teamwork, and the Toyota Production System.

Cost: Free

Freebies: Toyota vehicle (in the form of a refrigerator magnet!).

Video Shown: 10-minute video provides a brief plant overview, including sections not included on the tour.

Reservations Needed: Yes, but walk-ins will be accommodated as space permits.

Days and Hours: Plant tour: Mon–Fri 10:00 AM, 12:00 PM, and 2:00 PM, Thur also 6:00 PM. Closed holidays. *Toyota reserves the right to cancel or reschedule tours at any time.* Visitor Center: Mon–Fri 9:00 AM–4:00 PM, Thur until 7:00 PM.

Plan to Stay: 1.5–2 hours for plant tour, video, and exhibits.

Minimum Age: Plant tour: 1st grade for public tours and 4th grade for school tours. Visitor Center: none.

Disabled Access: Yes

Group Requirements: Maximum group size is 64 adults. Large groups must call several months in advance.

Special Information: Photographs and video and mechanical recordings are allowed in the Visitor Center but not during the plant tour.

Gift Shop: Sells logoed golf shirts, T-shirts, caps, etc. Open same hours as Visitor Center.

Directions: From Lexington, take I-75 North to Exit 126 (Georgetown/Cynthiana). Turn right onto U.S. 62 (Cherry Blossom Way). Drive exactly 2.5 miles and turn left at Visitor Entrance sign.

Nearby Attractions: Three Chimneys horse farm, Rebecca-Ruth Candies, and Old Kentucky Candies tours (see pages 164, 14, and 162); Kentucky Horse Park; Keeneland Racecourse; Calumet horse farm; Georgetown College.

See color photos, pages 17–19.

Wild Turkey

1525 Tyrone Road
Lawrenceburg, KY 40342
(502) 839-4544
www.wildturkeybourbon.com

BOURBON

Wild Turkey Distillery sits on a hill next to the Kentucky River. Water from this naturally filtered limestone riverbed and corn from nearby farmers are the main ingredients in bourbon, a uniquely American whiskey. This tour shows almost all steps in crafting the bourbon named after founder Thomas McCarthy's private stock taken on a wild turkey hunt.

The first surprise is the metal-barred windows on the big, gray, square warehouses throughout the grounds. They provide vital air circulation to the rack houses where the bourbon ages. The tax-hungry government once required installation of the bars to prevent any barrels from leaving without proper fees being paid.

The initial step in producing bourbon is mixing corn, rye, and water. The mix is cooked and cooled, then malted barley is added. With special yeast added, this sour mash ferments in cypress-wood or stainless steel tanks. Watch the slow, gentle swirl of the thick yellow mash in the vats; carbon-dioxide bubbles rise to the surface as the yeast changes sugar to alcohol, called "distiller's beer." Stand next to the 40-foot-high copper still, where the alcohol is separated in a vaporization process.

Charred white-oak barrels then become the colorless whiskey's home. The tour guide explains that the burnt layers of wood inside the barrel give bourbon its distinctive flavor and color (whiskey must be aged in new, charred-oak barrels for two years to be legally called "bourbon"). Inside a cool warehouse amid racks of barrels on wood planks, you'll enjoy the sweet bourbon smell. Wild Turkey calls this the "angels' share" because one-third of each barrel's contents evaporates over the bourbon's eight years of aging. It's not until you walk through the quality control lab and the bottling area that the process seems any different from what it must have been 100 years ago.

Cost: Free

Freebies: Food made with Wild Turkey, such as a bourbon brownie; a barrel bung; lemonade; coffee; and recipes that use Wild Turkey; smells.

Video Shown: In 15-minute video, "a true Kentucky legend," master distiller Jimmy Russell, covers the history of bourbon to Wild Turkey distilling and its products.

Reservations Needed: No, except for groups of 20 or more people.

Days and Hours: Mon–Fri 9:00 AM, 10:30 AM, 12:30 PM, and 2:30 PM. Closed holidays.

Plan to Stay: 45 minutes for tour, plus time for snacks and visitors center. The visitors center is in a restored building with a small display of ceramic Wild Turkey decanters, historical mementos, a scale model of the bourbon production process, and a gift shop.

Minimum Age: No

Disabled Access: Visitors center is fully accessible. Remainder of the facility has gravel paths and flights of stairs to some areas.

Group Requirements: Advance notice requested for groups of 20 or more. No maximum size.

Special Information: Wear comfortable walking shoes. Tour runs all year, but not all areas are in production during certain weeks in July and August.

Gift Shop: Sells wide range of merchandise from T-shirts to barbecue sauce, so you can take a piece of Kentucky tradition home with you. Open Mon–Fri 8:30 AM–4:00 PM. Catalog available from (800) BUY-TRKY.

Directions: From Louisville, take I-64 East to Rt. 151 South to Rt. 127 South. Turn left on Rt. 44, which turns into U.S. 62 East. Bear right onto Tyrone Rd. (Rt. 1510) to distillery. From Lexington, take U.S. 60 West (take Business Route at split) to Versailles to U.S. 62 West to distillery. You're almost there when you see billboards announcing "Bird Sanctuary Ahead" and "Home of Wild Turkey."

Nearby Attractions: Beaver Lake and Taylorville Lake; Ripplewood Estate.

See color photos, page 21.

Blaine Kern's Mardi Gras World

233 Newton Street
New Orleans, LA 70114
(504) 361-7821 / (800) 362-8213
www.mardigrasworld.com

PARADE FLOATS AND PROPS

You know this tour is going to be fun as soon as you arrive. Colorful Mardi Gras props—such as a gigantic jester, alligators, and Marilyn Monroe—perch in front of this fantasy factory. Blaine Kern, known locally as "Mr. Mardi Gras," is the world's largest float builder. His family-run company, begun in 1947, creates 75 percent of Mardi Gras–parade floats. The Kern Companies also build props for casinos and amusement parks, plus floats for up to 60 parades worldwide annually.

After a guide and a video explain the history of Mardi Gras and the company, you can dress up in authentic Carnival costumes. Don sequined headdresses, gowns, and regal coats of armor and imagine yourself as a noble king or queen of the ball! You'll enter a maze of amazing props with a 15-foot torso of Cleopatra standing nearby.

Follow the yellow arrows to the next "den" (float artists' warehouse). It's a big carpentry and paint shop, where workers build sensational floats for each Mardi Gras "krewe" (club). Artists, painters, and sculptors decorate each float with brightly colored themed scenes. Gold and silver foil on the sides of the floats glistens and flutters in the breeze. The floats are as colorful and animated as Saturday morning cartoons, and strings of lights trace their outlines at night.

In den 7, also used as a function room for parties, gigantic King and Queen Kong figures flank the performance stage. Completed tractor-trailer-sized floats constructed of wood, papier mâché, fiberglass, and Styrofoam rest here waiting to be set free along their parade routes. Notice the famed "Bacchasaurus" float, with stairs under its belly to assist the krewe members in climbing onto the float. It's the Trojan Horse meets *Jurassic Park!*

The Mardi Gras floats come alive when krewe members dance, sing, throw kisses, wave their arms, and toss beads, doubloons, stuffed animals, and cups from their floats.

Cost: Adults, $13.50; seniors, $10; children under 12, $6.50; under 3, free.

Freebies: Mardi Gras Jester Bead King Cake sample and coffee.

Video Shown: 11-minute video covering Mardi Gras and company history.

Reservations Needed: No, except for groups over 25 people.

Days and Hours: Mon–Sun 9:30 AM–4:30 PM. Closed Mardi Gras, Easter Sunday, Thanksgiving, and Christmas. Depending on the season, time, and day, you will see differing amounts of float-building activity.

Plan to Stay: 1 hour for introductory talk, video, costume try-on, and tour, plus time for the gift shop.

Minimum Age: None

Disabled Access: Yes

Group Requirements: During Carnival Season (January 6 to the day before Ash Wednesday), groups of 10 or more people should call 2 weeks in advance. Otherwise, 1 day is sufficient. Group discounts available.

Special Information: King Cake and coffee included (the King Cake tradition is that whoever eats the piece containing a baby figure must host the next party). Excellent site for parties, complete with miniature parades and lit floats. Call (800) 362-8213.

Gift Shop: Sells Carnival paraphernalia including beads, cups, and doubloons, plus T-shirts, books, and posters. Ships King Cakes. Open same hours as tour.

Directions: From New Orleans, cross Crescent City Connection to Westbank. Take General De Gaulle Dr. East exit. Turn left onto Shirley Dr. Follow signs to Mardi Gras World. From downtown/French Quarter, take free Canal St. ferry and then free shuttle bus. Future plans for paddle-wheel steamboat directly to Mardi Gras World dock.

Nearby Mardi Gras–Related Attractions: New Orleans Mint, Arnaud's Restaurant, and Musee Conti Wax Museum.

Kliebert's Turtle and Alligator Tours

41067 West Yellow Water Road
Hammond, LA 70403
(985) 345-3617 / (800) 854-9164

TURTLE AND ALLIGATOR FARM

Harvey Kliebert knows a good business opportunity. After raising turtles for 35 years and alligators for 25 years, in 1984 he decided to turn the farm into a tourist attraction. This example of agritourism has not only added to his income but also turned the colorful Harvey and his farm into celebrities. While you're there, you can check out the airboat used in the Burt Reynolds' movie *Gator*. Harvey himself appears occasionally in MTV interviews.

It's still an authentic turtle and alligator farm, dotted with duckweed- and clover-covered ponds that the breeding turtles and alligators call home. Over 17,000 laying turtles produce more than 1 million eggs per year. Once the turtles lay their eggs, which they do up to three times between April and August, Harvey and his crew dig up the eggs from the dirt nests on the pond banks. They then dip the eggs in a pressure machine that removes salmonella. All of the hatchlings are sold outside the U.S.A. for aquariums, children's pets, or food.

The gator breeding pond provides the most excitement for visitors, with gators lounging at the water's edge. Egrets and herons nest in trees overhead. Harvey has about 250 breeder alligators, all born in 1957. The big ones grow to 14 feet long and 1,200 pounds. If you watch the workers throw the gators dead chicken, fish parts, or ground nutria, you can happily assume that they're not too hungry during your visit.

Around June 1 of every year, the female gators start building their nests, piling dirt and grass in mounds two feet high. They then lay eggs just once per year, sometime between June 15 and July 1. As the tour guides/alligator farm workers glibly explain, the female will attack any animal or person that comes around the nest. Fortunately, Harvey and his crew have developed methods of chasing the female away so they can grab her eggs. After incubation, the gators live in pens until they are sold for their meat and hides, or sold to breeders in Florida.

Cost: Adults, $6; children, $3; children under 2, free.

Freebies: Recipe sheets

Video Shown: No

Reservations Needed: No, but recommended for groups over 20 people.

Days and Hours: Open March 1–October 31: Mon–Sun 12:00 PM until dark. Call ahead. The farm is open only during the afternoon so visitors don't scare nesting turtles. No tours during extreme cold or storms. Closed holidays.

Plan to Stay: 45 minutes for tour, plus time for gift shop.

Minimum Age: None

Disabled Access: Yes

Group Requirements: Groups over 20 people should call 1 week in advance. No maximum group size. Group discount of 25 percent off for 10 or more people. School groups receive 50 percent discount.

Special Information: Turtles lay eggs April through July; alligators lay eggs June 15–July 1. Annual Alligator Day the third Saturday of August, although may be moved up 1 month.

Gift Shop: Sells alligator heads, fingers, teeth, jewelry, turtle-foot back-scratchers, and just about any gift or food you can imagine that can be made and sold out of alligator or turtle parts. Open March 1–October 31: Mon–Sun 11:00 AM until dark. Call for additional days and hours. Closed holidays. List of products available from above number.

Directions: From New Orleans, take I-10 West to I-55 North to the Springfield exit. Take LA 22 West, which crosses over I-55. Turn right onto the frontage road that runs parallel to I-55. Turn left onto Hoffman Rd. Turn right on Yellow Water Rd. and follow signs. From Baton Rouge, take I-12 East to I-55 South. Take Springfield exit. Take LA 22 West and follow directions above.

Nearby Attractions: Abita Brewing Company tour in Abita Springs (call 504-893-3143); Global Wildlife Center in Folsom.

Konriko

309 Ann Street
New Iberia, LA 70560
(800) 551-3245
www.conradricemill.com

RICE AND CAJUN SEASONINGS

The best place to start a tour of the Konriko Rice Mill is in the Konriko Company Store, a replica of an old plantation company store next to the mill. While you wait for a tour to begin, the friendly Cajun staff offers you a cup of strong, flavorful South Louisiana–style coffee. Something is always cooking for visitors in the store, too: one day it might be Konriko red beans and rice; another day, Konriko's jambalaya mix with rice. Once you've sampled some good Cajun coffee and cooking, the tour officially begins.

After watching an informative slide presentation, you move next door to America's oldest rice mill. Konriko's mill was built by founder Philip Conrad in 1912, and has been in continuous operation ever since. Made of wood and corrugated tin, the mill is loud and rickety when in operation. But it has great character and is on the National Register of Historic Places.

Before entering the mill, you'll see the outdoor scale and dryer that weighs and dries the unmilled rough rice local farmers deliver. An average truckload of rice is about 30,000 pounds. Next to the dryer is a bin that stores the rice before it is processed. When full, the bin holds 1 million pounds of rice—about $100,000 worth. And don't overlook Konriko, the company's "guard" dog, sometimes sleeping in the sun.

Inside, your guide uses a scale model of a mill as a visual aid to explain how different varieties of rice are milled. Walk on the wooden floors between boxes of rice, piles of cardboard containers, burlap bags, and packaging machines. You'll enter several aromatic rooms where workers mix and package Konriko rice and seasonings. Peek into the rice-cracker production room. If you're lucky, your tour guide will give you a hot rice cake fresh from the oven to top off the tour.

Cost: Adults, $3.25; seniors 62 and over, $2.75; children under 12, $1.75.

Freebies: Fresh, hot coffee; cooked Konriko products; and recipes.

Video Shown: 20-minute "historically correct" slide presentation on Cajun culture and Konriko's development.

Reservations Needed: No, except for groups over 15 people.

Days and Hours: Mon–Sat 10:00 AM, 11:00 AM, 1:00 PM, 2:00 PM, and 3:00 PM. No production on Saturdays, holidays, and during factory repairs, but tours usually run.

Plan to Stay: About 40 minutes for video and tour, plus time for gift shop.

Minimum Age: None

Disabled Access: Full access to Konriko Company Store. 4 steps lead to mill.

Group Requirements: Groups over 15 people should call 2 weeks in advance. Maximum group size is 50. Group rates available for 30 or more. Special tour times can be arranged.

Special Information: Mill can be loud. Hot in the summer.

Gift Shop: Konriko Company Store sells local foods and crafts, complete assortment of Konriko rice cakes, brown rice crackers, famous Wild Pecan Rice, mixes, T-shirts, novelty items, even Cajun dance video and music tapes. Open Mon–Sat 9:00 AM–5:00 PM. Closed Thanksgiving, Christmas, New Year's, and July 4th. Catalog available at above number.

Directions: From I-10, take Lafayette/U.S. Hwy. 90 exit (Exit 103), and follow U.S. 90 through Lafayette toward New Iberia. At LA 14 (Center St.) in New Iberia, exit and turn left. Turn right on St. Peter St., then right on Ann St. Rice mill is on left.

Nearby Attractions: McIlhenny Tabasco sauce tour (see page 22); Shadows-on-the-Teche; Rice Museum in Crowley; Delcambre Shrimp Boat Landing; Vermilionville, Acadian Village, and Jean Lafitte National Historical Park/Acadiana Cultural Center in Lafayette.

McIlhenny Company

Avery Island, LA 70513
(337) 365-8173 / (800) 634-9599
www.tabasco.com

TABASCO®
BRAND PEPPER SAUCE

TABASCO BRAND PEPPER SAUCE

This concentrated hot pepper sauce, first created after the Civil War on an exotic 2,200-acre island in the South Louisiana bayou country, has such a lively flavor that it is now sold in more than 110 countries and territories around the world and its labels are printed in 21 languages and dialects. McIlhenny Company grows the *Capsicum frutescens* peppers (tabasco peppers) in several countries to ensure a good harvest. But there is only one Tabasco sauce factory, and you'll recognize this modern redbrick building as soon as you open your car door and catch a whiff of the piquant pepper aroma.

A film explains that McIlhenny planted hot pepper seeds from Mexico or Central America. He created his sauce (brand-named Tabasco, a Mexican-Indian word) by mashing the peppers with Avery Island salt, aging the mash in wooden barrels, adding vinegar, and then straining the mixture.

Along a corridor in the modern factory, observe four lines of Tabasco sauce bottling from behind a long glass wall. The smell here isn't nearly as strong as it must be inside the packaging room. Some lines produce more than 300 bottles of Tabasco sauce a minute, helping the factory produce about 600,000 bottles a day.

After the bottles are spun around in the carousel and injected with the hot red pepper sauce, they journey naked down the assembly line. Machines automatically clothe the bottles with the familiar bright red octagonal caps, green foil neckbands, and diamond-shaped labels. The dressed bottles are then mechanically packed in boxes, ready to travel. Their final destination will be dining tables from Pennsylvania to Peking, where their red caps will be removed and they will "drop in" to spice up a meal.

Cost: Free

Freebies: Miniature Tabasco sauce bottle, recipes, and other McIlhenny products.

Video Shown: 11-minute overview of McIlhenny's history and operations, as well as Tabasco sauce origins and the full processing, including harvesting of peppers, mashing, aging, mixing with vinegar, and bottling.

Reservations Needed: No, except for groups over 20 people.

Days and Hours: Mon–Sun 9:00 AM–4:00 PM. Last tour 30 minutes before closing. May not see production Fri–Sun. Closed holidays and long weekends.

Plan to Stay: 25 minutes for video and tour, plus time for gift shop and grounds.

Minimum Age: None

Disabled Access: Yes

Group Requirements: Groups larger than 20 people should make advance reservations; 1 week's notice appreciated.

Special Information: Some production process details are in photos and captions above the viewing window.

Gift Shop: Tabasco Country Store sells a wide variety of Tabasco specialty foods and novelty items, from pepper earrings to lithographs, toys, cookware, ties, cookbooks, and spices. Open same hours as tour. Gift shop at Jungle Gardens entrance open until 5:30 PM (sells similar items). Catalog available at (800) 634-9599.

Directions: From New Orleans, take I-10 West to Exit 103A. Follow U.S. 90 through Lafayette toward New Iberia. Exit at LA 14 and turn left. At LA 329 junction, turn right. Stay on LA 329 approximately 6 miles. The road dead-ends at Avery Island, where the toll road has a nominal charge per vehicle. Signs will direct you to factory.

Nearby Attractions: Konriko tour (see page 169); Jungle Gardens and Bird City on Avery Island.

See color photo, page 23.

Motivatit Seafoods

412 Palm Street
Houma, LA 70364
(985) 868-7191
www.motivatit.com

OYSTERS, BLUE CRAB, AND CRAWFISH

Louisiana is known for its tasty seafood, and few factories process more of it than Motivatit. The Voisin family, owners of the company, has been involved in the seafood industry since their ancestors arrived in Louisiana from France in 1770. The oyster plant shucks 400 to 500 burlap sacks (40,000 to 50,000 pounds) of oysters daily. The nearby blue crab and crawfish plant processes 25,000 to 30,000 pounds of blue crabs daily, in addition to 5,000 to 6,000 pounds of crawfish between February and June.

Most food-processing plants you visit seem highly automated. Workers appear to spend their hours monitoring or assisting the computerized, fast-moving machines. But this is not so at seafood-processing plants. The removal of the shells and the meats from oysters, crabs, and crawfish is too gentle and dexterous a motion for machines to handle. Sure, you'll see half-shelled oysters move down an assembly line; modern refrigeration units; big, steaming vats for crabs; and what looks like a giant kaleidoscope of metal rods to sort crab leg sizes; but human hands do the real work of getting the meat from the shell.

You enter what looks like the world's largest raw-oyster bar. If you close your eyes, you can easily imagine that you're next to the ocean listening to carpenters build a house. Rows of rubber-aproned workers stand in front of metal tables piled with fresh, salty-smelling oysters. These professional shuckers, working on one oyster at a time, use hammers to crack the hinge holding the shells together. They pry open the oyster, scoop out the meat with a small knife, and toss the meat and shells into separate buckets. The best shuckers can repeat this rhythmic hammering, prying, and tossing at a rate of almost 500 oysters per hour.

At the crab and crawfish plant, the tour often begins in front of big colanders filled with reddish-colored steamed crabs. In an adjoining room, thousands of cooked crabs are piled high on a table, with the workers grabbing them to pull off the backs and claws. Once the crabs are debacked, it's much easier to get at the lump meat. In the picking rooms, the workers' speedy, careful hands manipulate small paring knives to pluck out all the meat from the crab (or crawfish, in season). It reminds you of an old-time sewing bee. Nothing seems to go to waste at this plant, as even the crab shells are decorated for re-use as Christmas-tree ornaments.

Cost: $5 per person

Freebies: Occasionally, a dirty-colored Louisiana oyster.

Video Shown: No

Reservations Needed: Yes. Individuals need to either join a scheduled group tour or form a group.

Days and Hours: Mon–Fri 8:00 AM–5:00 PM. Before 11:00 AM is best time to see production. Closed holidays.

Plan to Stay: 30–45 minutes for tour of each plant. Visitors pick one factory to tour.

Minimum Age: None, but children must be supervised.

Disabled Access: Yes

Group Requirements: 1 week's advance notice; longer during peak travel seasons.

Special Information: Floors are wet. Oyster production busiest, as the locals say, in the "months with the Rs" (September–April).

Gift Shop: No

Directions: From New Orleans, take Hwy. 90 West to Houma. Turn left at Gum St. Oyster plant and corporate headquarters are at the corner of Gum and Palm Sts. Directions to crab and crawfish plant available upon request.

Nearby Attractions: Southdown Plantation Home/Terrebonne Museum; swamp tours; Louisiana Universities Marine Consortium (LUMCON)-Marine Research Facility tour in Chauvin (call 504-851-2800). Annual Breaux Bridge Crawfish Festival (first full weekend in May) 2 hours away.

Tony Chachere's

519 North Lombard Street
Opelousas, LA 70570
(800) 551-9066
www.tonychachere.com

CREOLE SEASONINGS AND RICE MIXES

We love stories about people who start new businesses at the age most people focus on retirement. The late Tony Chachere started his third career at the age of 67. Having retired from successful stints in pharmacy and insurance, he decided to fulfill a lifelong desire to write and publish a cookbook. While a member of Cooks Unlimited, a men's cooking club, he had developed a "secret" spicy seasoning mix that he used in many of the book's recipes. The popularity of the seasoning recipe in his cookbook encouraged Tony to start manufacturing the blend for consumers. Today the seasoning is the number-one-selling spice mix in the Cajun/Creole category.

After a brief talk about Tony's and the company's histories, your tour guide leads you into the refrigerated ingredients room. It's piled high with boxes and burlap bags filled with spices. Smell the pungent aromas emanating from the boxes of ground red pepper and oregano. The company uses more than 8.5 million pounds of ingredients each year, and it all begins here.

Because of the overwhelming smell on the second floor, you can't observe the actual mixing together of the spices. Even on the first floor, you'll notice that workers wear portable air units that filter the pungent air around them. Next, your guided factory-floor tour takes you into the packaging area. The spices drop down through overhead pipes to several different fast-moving assembly lines. Each day, the auger processor fills 2,000 cases of eight-ounce "little green cans" with the seasoning mix. On another line, gumbo and jambalaya mixes are automatically sealed between two sheets of foil (creating bags) and inserted into boxes.

During the current tour, you walk through the warehouse. Here, finished products of all types and sizes wait in large brown boxes for shipment to stores and distribution points worldwide. As you pass by the food scientists' kitchen, you may smell the product being tested. In the UPS shipment area, used for smaller orders, you'll be surprised to see a popcorn popper. The company uses popcorn as a more environmentally conscious packing material than Styrofoam. A true indicator of where you live may not be the zip code on your UPS package, but rather the size of the can of Tony Chachere's Creole Seasoning you order—locals always keep 17-ounce cans on their kitchen tables.

Cost: Free

Freebies: Bag of souvenir items, including catalog, pamphlet cookbook, and product samples.

Video Shown: No, but one is planned.

Reservations Needed: No, except for groups larger than 10 people.

Days and Hours: Mon–Fri 9:30 AM–11:00 AM and 1:30 PM–3:30 PM. Closed limited holidays.

Plan to Stay: 30 minutes for tour

Minimum Age: 7

Disabled Access: Yes

Group Requirements: Groups over 10 people should call 2 weeks in advance. Special times can be arranged. No maximum group size.

Special Information: No photography

Gift Shop: Sells all of their seasoning and rice mixes, including Original Creole Seasoning, and both of Tony's cookbooks. *Cajun Country Cookbook* and *Tony Chachere's Second Helping* contain mouth-watering recipes accumulated through a lifetime steeped in Cajun culture and Southern hospitality. Free catalog available at number above.

Directions: From I-10, take I-49 North to U.S. 190 West. Turn right onto Lombard St. Factory is 5 blocks ahead on left.

Nearby Attractions: Opelousas Museum and Interpretive Center; Opelousas Museum of Art; Opelousas Vieux Village; Chretien Point Plantation.

MeadWestvaco

35 Hartford Street
Rumford, ME 04276
(207) 364-4521
www.meadwestvaco.com

PAPER

Deep in the heart of Maine's Western Mountains you'll find MeadWestvaco paper mill. Papermaking at the Rumford facility began in 1901. Some of the mill still works much as it did over 100 years ago. while other areas have advanced into more modern technological systems. Many workers today follow in the footsteps of their great-grandparents in the long and proud tradition of papermaking.

Papermaking begins with wood chips that are cooked in digesters (large cooking vats) to make pulp. The pulp, resembling Cream of Wheat, is blended with additives to make the stock. The stock, 99.5 percent water, jets from the head box of the paper machine onto a mesh screen called a "wire." Here, water drains and is suctioned off. You'll need to climb upstairs to see the wire of the enormous No. 15 paper machine, which is as long as a football field.

The stock, now called a "paper web," moves to the press section of the machine. The web rumbles through, over, and under a series of rollers. Try to follow the actual course of the speeding paper. The heavy rollers press even more water out of the paper web. A granite roller on the No. 15 paper machine weighs over 4 tons. After going through the presses, the web is much smoother but still contains 60 percent of its water.

The dryer section looks similar to the press section, but here the rollers are hollow cans heated with steam. The intense heat evaporates almost all of the remaining water. The paper can be uncoated, coated on one side (like a Campbell's soup label), or coated on both sides (like the pages of *Oprah, Vanity Fair,* and *Marie Claire*). A series of rollers transfers the coating—made of clay, latex, and starches—onto the paper. The paper then rolls across a very sharp blade that removes the excess coating.

At this point the paper, although coated, does not look glossy. It moves to the super-calender, a vertical alignment of steel and cotton rolls. At the "nip point," where the rolls meet, the paper is subject to such intense heat and pressure that the coating melts and is pressed flat for a high gloss.

At the lighting booth, see how paper is inspected for visual defects and how paper is tested for optical and strength properties as well as various functional properties.

Cost: Free

Freebies: Brochure detailing how paper is made; pen or pencil.

Video Shown: 20-minute video explains papermaking process, history of the mill and safety rules.

Reservations Needed: Yes

Days and Hours: Mid-June–mid-September only. Days and times are subject to change, please call (207) 369-2589 for current schedule.

Plan to Stay: 2 hours

Minimum Age: 14

Disabled Access: Yes

Group Requirements: Group tours offered to educational groups only. Call at least 2 weeks in advance.

Special Information: No open-toed shoes or photography in mill. Tours may become more limited. Summer forestry tours can be arranged by calling (207) 369-2098.

Gift Shop: No

Directions: From Portland, take I-95 (Maine Tnpk.) North. Take Exit 12 for Rt. 4 North. Tun left on Rt. 108 North (stay on Rt. 108 for approximately 22 miles). Turn right on Canal Street. Mill Administration Building is directly ahead at end of road.

Nearby Attractions: Sunday River Ski Resort; Western Mountains; Rangeley Lake Tour Region 1 hour away; Portland 1.5 hours away.

Thos. Moser Cabinetmakers

72 Wright's Landing
Auburn, ME 04211
(207) 784-3332 / (800) 862-1973
www.thosmoser.com

THOS. MOSER
CABINETMAKERS

FURNITURE

Woodworking tours can provide a feast for all your senses with the sound of the saws, the smell of the wood and the finishes, and the touch of the wood grains at different stages of production. The Thos. Moser workshop tour lets you see everything involved in making their natural-finished heirloom furniture, including laminating, rasping, machining, sanding, routing, milling, planing, dovetailing, making mortises and tenons, and assembling. This tour also provides a bountiful lesson in wood selection and its role in furniture making. While we all enjoy the beauty of natural solid wood, we may not realize how it expands and contracts, playing a key part in its design. As you walk on the factory floor, the guide explains all of this and more.

The process begins with rough mill panel making, where they make the tabletops and panels that become parts of their furniture. You see many different size saws, jointers, and panel glue racks. With the table saws buzzing in the background, observe how carefully the craftspeople marry the American black cherry woods by grain and color to create the panels. Throughout the process notice the unique techniques to join pieces where grains do not match completely and to allow movement.

Chair making involves lots of wedging, fitting, and grinding to create their signature Thos. Moser Continuous Arm Chair. To form the gently curving back brace and arms, 11 knife-cut slices of the same tree, each one-tenth-of-an-inch thick (called a flitch), are laminated together and held in tension for superior strength. Notice how each "continuous arm" is carefully rasped, filed, and sanded to perfect smoothness. The natural tension in the wood ensures it will keep its shape for generations, and the flexibility of the northern ash spindles bend and conform to your back.

You will be delighted by the aromatic finishing area. Here the boiled linseed oil is sprayed onto the furniture, then wiped in; afterward, the furniture is sanded and given a hand-rubbed wax finish. You leave the tour appreciating what it takes to custom-build furniture of truly lasting value.

Cost: Free

Freebies: Beautiful catalog upon request, which includes production and product pictures.

Video Shown: No

Reservations Needed: Yes

Days and Hours: Fri 1:00 PM, except for holidays.

Plan to Stay: 1.5 hours or longer, depending on your interest in woodworking.

Minimum Age: 10

Disabled Access: Yes

Group Requirements: Group over 20 should call 1 month in advance, will be split into smaller groups.

Special Information: Must wear closed-toe shoes. Wear your eyeglasses or company will provide protective eyewear.

Gift Shop: Does not directly sell the furniture, although if you ask after tour you can meet with a customer service representative to place an order. May have limited items in inventory at the workshop, but most of their products are made-to-order. Showroom in Freeport, Maine, at 149 Main Street (207-865-4519) about 30 minutes away, does have some special-priced items (seconds, consignment items, returns) in the "Must-Be-Seen Room." Catalog available by calling (877) 708-1973 or on website. Also showrooms in Chicago, Charleston, New York, and San Francisco.

Directions: From Maine Tnpk. (I-495) take Exit 12. Turn right from the exit ramp. At the first light, take right onto Kitty Hawk Ave. (follow airport sign), continue straight through blinking red light. Shop is on the right.

Nearby Attractions: Tom's of Maine tour (see page 175); Bates College and Lost Valley Ski Area; Shaker Village; The Center for Furniture Craftsmanship about 1 hour away; Freeport's outlet stores and Portland about 30 minutes away in different directions. Maine Wood Product Assoc. brochure lists woodshop tours (call 207-767-0188).

Tom's of Maine

Trackside Drive
Kennebunk, ME 04043
(207) 985-2944 / (800) FOR-TOMS
www.tomsofmaine.com

NATURAL TOOTHPASTE

Over 30 years ago, Kate and Tom Chappell moved to Maine to live a simpler life and to create a company committed to developing all-natural personal hygiene products, such as toothpaste, mouthwash, soap, and deodorant. While we don't know if they found a simpler life, they have created a successful, socially conscious, environmentally committed company. In fact, their tasty toothpaste—made without artificial preservatives, sweeteners, or coloring—is the top-selling brand in many major stores.

Almost all Tom's of Maine products are made in a restored railroad station, a very different setting from most successful companies' plants. On the first floor, toothpaste ingredients are mixed in a 3,000-pound vat. Ingredients for liquid products such as mouthwash or shampoo have a second mixing area.

As you walk upstairs to the second floor, you'll know what products the toothpaste and liquid lines are packaging. If you smell cinnamon, they're packaging that flavor toothpaste or mouthwash. An intense coriander smell usually means deodorant. You cannot miss the machine that pumps the still-warm toothpaste into recyclable tubes and clamps the backs closed. Notice how the company tries to reduce the amount of product packaging. For the mouthwash, the outer paper carton has been replaced with a thin leaflet that folds into the back of the recyclable plastic container.

What's most interesting about this tour isn't so much the production process, but the sense that the workers enjoy their jobs and take seriously their responsibility for quality control. The smiles you see aren't just to show off good teeth. Every hour, most workers on the packaging line switch positions. A worker who just put the tubes into the filler machine now boxes toothpaste. While you may be bored brushing your teeth, the people who make your toothpaste aren't!

Cost: Free

Freebies: Just-finished product sample

Video Shown: 2-minute *Sesame Street* video, "How Does the Toothpaste Get into the Tube?"

Reservations Needed: Yes

Days and Hours: Call for hours since the tour dates and times may vary. Closed holidays. When tours not available, you can watch video of production in the nearby outlet store.

Plan to Stay: 1 hour for the tour and a talk about the company and its philosophy, plus time for video and outlet store.

Minimum Age: 5

Disabled Access: Flight of stairs leads to factory. Can view video in fully accessible outlet store.

Group Requirements: Groups larger than 8 people should call 1 month ahead. Groups larger than 15 people may be split into smaller ones (some groups go to the outlet store before the tour).

Special Information: No photography.

Outlet Store: Located about 1 mile away on Storer St. (call 207-985-3874). Sells all Tom's natural personal-hygiene products, including discounted factory seconds. Open Mon–Sat 9:30 AM–5:00 PM. Closed holidays.

Directions: Tours meet at the Tom's of Maine factory. From I-95, take Exit 3. Turn left onto Rt. 35. At fork just past school, bear left. Turn left at stoplight (Rt. 1) and right onto Rt. 35. Go over railroad bridge (you can see factory on right). Make immediate right onto unmarked street.

Nearby Attractions: Thos. Moser Cabinetmakers tour (see page 174); Kennebunkport Brewing Co. tour (call 207-967-4311; larger plant gives tours in Portland, call 207-761-0807); Wedding Cake House; Brick Store Museum; Kennebunkport resort area, beaches, and former President George H.W. Bush's residence.

Baltimore Museum of Industry

1415 Key Highway
Baltimore, MD 21230
(410) 727-4808
www.thebmi.org

CANNED GOODS, TEXTILES, AND PRINTING

Every American student learns about how industrialization changed our society. The Baltimore Museum of Industry takes you back in time, letting you stroll down the streets of Baltimore during the city's 19th-century industrial dominance. Formerly the Platt & Company Oyster Cannery (circa 1865), the museum now houses hands-on canning, garment, machine shop, and printing exhibits.

Drive onto the museum's 6-acre campus. You immediately see an enormous red crane, donated by Bethlehem Steel, that stands twice as high as the museum's main building. Directly ahead of you is the Port of Baltimore, home to the only remaining steam tug on the east coast, the 1906 S.T. *Baltimore*. Enter the main green brick building and walk down the street passing a turn-of-the-century-style bank, bakery, and pharmacy. Your first major stop is at the "Shucking Shed," where workers of all ages and races filled their buckets with oysters in exchange for tokens. Next, learn about the canning process. As you walk past the wall of familiar labels and conveyer belts, look toward the middle of the room and focus on the enormous circular pot. The Steam Retort Closed Cutter Steamer, invented in 1874, holds four rusted baskets of 1,150 cans and steams out the bacteria in all of the oysters.

Your next stop is a typical machine shop of the early 1900s. Tools hang on the walls. Walk on the warped 1865 wood floor. First, imagine all of the belts and pulleys moving around the cast iron pipes and metal machines. Then see the mechanisms come alive as your tour guide revs up the steam engine.

Moving from metal machines to garment machines, enter the world of quality clothing. Fabric patterns are strewn across two long wooden tables. Huge shelves stand in the middle of the exhibit, while sewing machines and irons line the sides. See the difference between cutting patterns with heavy iron shears versus an electric silver cutting machine. If scheduled in advance, groups can participate in a pocket-making production line.

Next, journey through the evolution of printing. Tour guides explain how tedious the original typesetting process was until the invention of the Linotype by Baltimore's Ottmar Mergenthaler. Witness printing move through the Portable Wheel Press, Proof Press, and Platen Press all the way through current-day computers. Samples are given out along the way.

Cost: Adults, $6; seniors/students, $4.50; family, $20; children under 6, free.

Freebies: Printing samples

Video: 11-minute video, "Maryland Manufacturing," in an art deco movie theater.

Reservations: No, except for groups of 10 or more.

Days and Hours: Mon–Sat 10:00 AM–5:00 PM; Sun 12:00 PM–5:00 PM. Closed Thanksgiving, Christmas Eve, and Christmas Day.

Plan to stay: 1.5 hours

Minimum Age: None

Disabled Access: Yes

Group Requirements: Groups of 10 or more should book 10 days in advance, adults, $4.50; seniors/students, $3.50. No maximum size.

Special Information: Birthday parties and school groups can make cardboard moving vans down an assembly line or sew pockets in the garment factory.

Gift Shop: The Emporium offers unique gifts that promote learning for kids, as well as books for adults, T-shirts, and handicrafts made by Museum volunteers. Open same hours as museum.

Directions: From I-83 South, take Lombard St. West. Turn left on Light St. Continue south past Inner Harbor. Turn left on Key Hwy. The Museum is on the left. From Baltimore Bltwy., I-695, take I-95 North. Take Key Hwy, Exit 55. Turn at light, go under overpass, turn left onto Key Hwy. Museum is on your right.

Nearby Attractions: Moore's Candies and Pompeian Olive Oil tours (see pages 178 and 179); Baltimore Inner Harbor; Fort McHenry.

Bartley Collection

65 Engerman Avenue
Denton, MD 21629
(800) 787-2800
www.bartleycollection.com

**WOODEN FURNITURE
REPRODUCTIONS**

Have you ever yearned for a magnificent Queen Anne sideboard or an 18th-century Chippendale night stand? If you are at all handy with woodworking, you can use Bartley antique reproduction kits to make your own highboys, four-poster beds, dining tables, chairside tables, jewelry boxes, and more. With the plant manager as your guide, you can tour the one-acre factory where these antique reproductions are designed, created, and packed.

Pass the hardware department, where you may see a worker assemble each kit's perfectly reproduced brass fittings. When Bartley designers find desirable antiques to reproduce, they make rubberized castings of the original hardware and intricate moldings. These castings become the foundations for brass pourings and guide workers in reconfiguring their machines.

As you enter the rough mill, the scent of lumber and sound of ripsaws prevail. Bundles of 8- to 16-foot-long rough-cut boards crowd the aisle. Workers plane the rough-cut lumber, revealing the grain and color. Different saws cut the boards to the proper dimensions. Despite a dust collection system, a faint film of sawdust clings to everything in the plant, an unavoidable mark of the woodworker's craft.

The wide sections of wood are matched by grain and color; edges are aligned (or recut) and glued. Notice the radio-frequency gluer: it sends energy through the wood, activating a catalyst in the glue that cures it. The wide belt sander's five sanding heads, with progressively finer grades of sandpaper, then smooth the surfaces.

Amid conventional routers, bandsaws, drill presses, and shapers are two computerized routers. A vacuum sucks air through holes in the tabletop, holding the board in place. The router's patterns are programmed by a designer in the main office, and it runs automatically, without a worker's intervention. The table moves forward and back as the six router heads spin. Before seeing the showroom, watch the cabinetmakers in the sample shop create prototypes, following the designers' sketches and building reproductions from scratch.

Cost: Free

Freebies: No

Video Shown: No

Reservations Needed: Yes, since tours not often given.

Days and Hours: Tours given during spring and fall sales. Calls for details and dates.

Plan to Stay: 20 minutes for tour, plus additional time in showroom.

Minimum Age: 12

Disabled Access: Limited aisle space and sawdust on floors makes it unsuitable for wheelchairs and walkers.

Group Requirements: Groups should call 1 week in advance. No more than 6 people can be accommodated at a time.

Special Information: Wear sneakers and clothing that will not be harmed by sawdust. Parts of plant can be noisy.

Showroom: Most reproductions are on display. Kits can be purchased or ordered. Open Mon–Fri 9:00 AM–5:00 PM, Sat 10:00 AM–3:00 PM. Catalog available from above number.

Directions: From Annapolis, MD, and points west, cross the Bay Bridge and take Rt. 50 South to Easton. Turn left on Rt. 404 East. In Denton, turn left into the Denton Industrial Park. The Bartley Collection is the second factory on the left. From Norfolk, VA, take Rt. 13 North toward Salisbury. Continue on Rt. 13 to Bridgeville, DE. In Bridgeville, take Rt. 404 West toward Denton. Turn right into industrial park.

Nearby Attractions: St. Michaels and Oxford, old ship-building towns with antique shops, restored buildings, and boat-builders; Black Water Wildlife Refuge, Wild Goose Brewery tour (call 410-221-1121), and Brooks Barrel Company tour (410-228-0790) in Cambridge 20 minutes away; Atlantic Ocean beaches 1 hour away.

Moore's Candies

3004 Pinewood Avenue
Baltimore, MD 21214
(410) 426-2705
www.moorescandies.com

CHOCOLATES

Since 1919

How often have you been on a tour where the company owner accompanies you, introduces you to the employees (many of whom are immediate family members), and lets you make your own candy? Here's the place! Don't look for a factory or industrial park—this plant is in the 1,500-square-foot basement of the family residence. The company has produced treats from this same space since 1929. In fact, one employee has been dipping Moore's chocolates since the 1920s.

Owner Jim Heyl grew up in the house's upper level. When young Jim needed to raise money for his Cub Scout pack, his parents worked for and eventually bought Moore's Candies, known for helping groups with fund-raising. These fund-raising sales are still important to Moore's Candies' business. Recently Jim's son, Dana, came into the business to take it into the third generation. In August 2000, the Food Network picked Moore's as one of America's best chocolate makers.

The tour is an informal look at this small, hands-on candy-making operation. Tour guide Jim enthusiastically describes the chocolate "waterfall," the home nut-roaster, and the fillings prepared by all of the candy makers. Rich aromas draw you from one table to the next, where caramel or vanilla buttercream fillings are prepared for their chocolate bath, or special-order chocolate swans are filled with home-dry-roasted cashews.

Watch one worker hand-dip chocolates while another uses a wooden paddle to stir bubbling caramel in a copper cauldron. Cherries roll around in rotating kettles, getting a sugar coating before their journey through the enrober, which workers call the "I Love Lucy" machine, for a chocolate cover. This chocolate coating seals in the cherries, whose natural acid reacts with the coating to form the liquid inside a chocolate-coated cherry. Before you leave, be sure to run your own pretzel through the enrobing machine and eat the rewards of your efforts.

Cost: Adults $3; children $2.

Freebies: Sample chocolate right off the packing line; Official Candymaker Certificate.

Video Shown: 2-minute video of production process.

Reservations Needed: Suggested for individuals. Required for groups over 10 people. Call ahead to see if in production.

Days and Hours: Mon–Thur 10:00 AM and 1:00 PM. Closed holidays and between Christmas and New Year's. No tours 6 weeks before major candy holidays.

Plan to Stay: 20 minutes, plus time in gift area.

Minimum Age: 10; 6 for school groups.

Disabled Access: Yes

Group Requirements: Minimum group size is 10; maximum is 40; 3–5 days' notice required. Special tours may be arranged. For groups larger than 15, with 5 days' advance request, 10-minute slide presentation covers origins of the cocoa bean, harvesting, roasting, and how chocolate is made.

Special Information: Most production in fall through early spring. No photography.

Gift Area: Assorted candies include Maryland chocolate and confection specialties (Crabs by the Bushel, Crab Pop, Chesapeake Chocolates, and Maryland honey caramel). Open Mon–Fri 9:00 AM–4:00 PM and Sat 10:00 AM–3:00 PM. Closed holidays and Saturdays in August. Mail-order price list available.

Directions: From Baltimore Beltway (Rt. 695), take Exit 31A. Take Rt. 147 South for 2 miles. Turn left onto Pinewood Ave. Factory is the first building on the left, a brick house that looks like a residence. Park in rear and use building's rear entrance.

Nearby Attractions: Pompeian Olive Oil and Baltimore Museum of Industry tours (see pages 179 and 176); Seagram's tour (call 410-247-6019); GM Minivan tour (call 410-631-2111); White Marsh Shopping Mall; Fire Museum; Baltimore's attractions include Fort McHenry, Inner Harbor Area, Lexington Market, and National Aquarium.

Pompeian Olive Oil

4201 Pulaski Highway
Baltimore, MD 21224
(410) 276-6900 / (800) 638-1224
www.pompeian.com

**OLIVE OIL AND
RED WINE VINEGAR**

IMPORTED
POMPEIAN
OLIVE OIL

Did you know that it takes 2,000 olives to make one quart of olive oil? Or that olive oil was one of the earliest products traded internationally? Do you know the differences between types of olive oil, the recommended way to toss a salad, or the uses of olive oil (even in desserts)? Discover these and other interesting historical, gastronomical, and international business facts on a tour of Pompeian, headquartered in East Baltimore. The company is America's oldest and largest importer, bottler, and distributor of olive oil and red wine vinegar.

Pompeian prides itself on tailoring its educational tour to each group's specific interests. Though there is no "typical tour," the basic tour includes the tank storage system, quality control, and bottling process. The 200-year-old, 22-ton granite mill in front of the plant was found in pieces in Spain, restored, and shipped to Baltimore for permanent display at Pompeian. Although earlier mills were human-powered, this mill was originally steam-operated to produce olive oil, a natural fruit juice. Notice the four cone-shaped grinding stones on a 15-foot-wide base. This mill is the only one of its kind in America.

The tour highlight is going underground to see the extensive storage tank system, which covers the length of a football field. The 18 tanks hold 1.5 million gallons of extra-virgin olive oil. The underground temperature naturally maintains itself around 64°. In Spain, the oil is pressed from olive fruit within 72 hours after picking; it's then shipped to Baltimore for storage in these tanks. In the quality control area, learn about the different types of tests performed, the chemical composition of olive oil, and the fundamentals of general nutrition. In the bottling areas, you may see oil pouring into four-ounce bottles or gallon jugs. From another bottling line, smell the pungent aroma of red wine vinegar aged in casks in Spain for 15 years. The tour ends with a culinary treat, ranging from light snacks to an olive oil tasting.

Cost: Free

Freebies: Nutrition literature and recipes.

Video Shown: 17-minute video, "Olive Oil: From Tree to Table," sent out to groups in advance. Provides overview of olive oil production in Spain and at Baltimore plant.

Reservations Needed: Yes. Provides group tours only (individuals and families join scheduled group tours).

Days and Hours: Third week of each month 10:30 AM and 2:30 PM. Closed holidays.

Plan to Stay: 1 hour

Minimum Age: 9. Because of the high level of tour's educational content, company's recommended minimum age is 12.

Disabled Access: Limited to main floor

Group Requirements: Minimum group is 10 people; maximum is 30. Groups should call 2 weeks in advance for reservations.

Special Information: Vinegar aroma can be strong. For a tour of an olive processing company, see the feature on Graber Olive House, Ontario, CA (page 68).

Gift Shop: No, but can purchase cases of 16-ounce bottles at a discount.

Directions: From I-695 (Beltway), take Rt. 40 West toward Baltimore (Rt. 40 is Pulaski Hwy.). Pompeian is on the left at their billboard.

Nearby Attractions: Moore's Candies and Baltimore Museum of Industry tours (see pages 178 and 176); GM Minivan tour (call 410-631-2111); Seagram's tour (call 410-247-6019); Fells Point; Inner Harbor area; Fort McHenry; National Aquarium; Camden Yards; B&O Railroad Museum.

Salisbury Pewter

2611 North Salisbury Boulevard
Salisbury, MD 21801
(410) 546-1188
www.salisburypewter.com

PEWTER TABLEWARE, ORNAMENTS, AND GIFTS

SALISBURY PEWTER

Although Salisbury Pewter was founded in 1979, its craftspeople follow the same production process used 200 years ago. Pewter spinning is one of the oldest crafts in American history. During your guided tour of Salisbury Pewter, you'll learn the components of their lead-free, non-tarnishing pewter and the history of pewter (did you know that during the Civil War, pewter tableware was melted down for bullets?), and observe pewter-smithing from behind Plexiglas walls.

In the spinning department, watch an apprentice or master spinner, trained for up to ten years, clamp a flat disk (or "blank") onto a lathe. As the disk spins on the lathe, the craftsman sways back and forth. Using a steel rod—which each spinner designs personally—the spinner gently urges the pewter into shape around the brass mold (or "chuck") to form a bowl, coffeepot, or serving tray. During detailing (or "kurling"), a worker uses a tool resembling an architect's compass to add lips and curved bases. The pewter shavings flying into the air are later remelted to avoid waste.

As you walk down the hall, notice raw materials, tools, and pewter cups in various stages of production. In the back, craftspeople wearing white gloves sit in front of rapidly spinning polishing wheels. To polish a large serving tray, a worker must always keep it moving against the cotton-compound spinning wheel. With the tray on their knees, they rock their bodies from side to side and swing their arms back and forth—it's a rigorous workout. During the three-step polishing process, different grades of compound polish the pewter to high-bright or satin finishes. A worker proudly stamps the trademark on the bottom of the finished piece.

Cost: Free
Freebies: No
Video Shown: 6-minute optional video covers the history of pewter and Salisbury Pewter's production process.

Reservations Needed: No, except for groups over 20 people.
Days and Hours: Mon–Fri 9:30 AM–4:00 PM. No production week between Christmas and New Year's, and July 4th week, but can watch video and view equipment and display cases. Closed holidays.
Plan to Stay: 15 minutes for tour, plus time for the video and outlet.
Minimum Age: None
Disabled Access: Yes
Group Requirements: Groups over 15 people should call 1 day in advance.
Special Information: This new Salisbury location was built with tours in mind. Other outlet store in Easton has limited tour opportunities (call 410-820-5202).
Showroom: This 3,000-square-foot store sells Salisbury Pewter's 600 items, including jewelry and jewelry boxes, wedding and decorative gifts, picture frames, and Maryland crab gift items. First-quality items sold at outlet prices (20 percent off) and factory seconds discounted up to 75 percent. Open Mon–Fri 9:00 AM–6:00 PM and Sat 10:00 AM–5:00 PM. May 1–December 31: also open Sun 11:00 AM–4:00 PM. Closed holidays. Catalog available from above number.
Directions: From Ocean City, take Rt. 50 West. Take Rt. 13 North. Salisbury Pewter will be on your right in approximately .5 miles. You'll be greeted by the "Watch Our Craftsmen Work" sign. From Washington/Baltimore area, take Rt. 50 East. Take Rt. 13 North. Follow directions above. (Alternately, from Rt. 50 East, turn left onto Naylor Mill Rd. Turn left onto Rt. 13 North. Salisbury Pewter will be immediately on your right.)
Nearby Attractions: Salisbury Zoo; Ward Museum of Wildfowl Art; Ocean City beaches 30 miles away; Chincoteague and Assateague Islands, VA, are 1 hour away.

American Textile History Museum

491 Dutton Street
Lowell, MA 01854
(978) 441-0400
www.athm.org

AMERICAN
TEXTILE
HISTORY
MUSEUM

CLOTH

In 1814, Lowell became America's first factory town when Frances Cabot Lowell, a Boston merchant, learned the secrets of the power loom from England. Thanks to nature's abundance and this early act of espionage, textile production in America grew swiftly from a necessary domestic craft into one of the country's primary industries. The American Textile History Museum traces this technological revolution and its effect on the lives of American people.

The American Textile History Museum is housed in a redesigned 1850s mill. Two floors are dedicated to the museum's permanent exhibit, "Textiles in America." The display features re-created scenes from 200 years of textile production, beginning with an 18th-century farmhouse kitchen, where a spinning wheel takes pride of place, and ends at a working 1940s weave room.

In the weave shed, watch cloth being woven. The museum manufactures new cloth using vintage looms and the classic overshot design and patterns. The antique looms, some of the oldest power looms still in operation, re-create the rich beauty of traditional fabrics made in America during the 18th and 19th centuries. The finished products include coverlets, runners, decorative pillows, and throws.

The first floor offers changing exhibits. As you walk up the ramp to the second floor, look at spinning wheels through floor-to-ceiling glass windows. There are around 250 spinning wheels among the exhibits! Behind a flax processing window exhibit, hear recorded sounds of flax breaking, wooden knives beating flax, and stems breaking apart. Ask a guide to point out tools such as swifts, niddy-noddies, teasels, and spinning jennies. A range of fabrics is also on display, from hand-woven bedcovers to the upholstery of the 1926 Ford; there is machinery from an 1870s woolen factory and period clothing.

Cost: Adults, $6; children under 17, seniors, and students with ID, $4; children under 6 and museum members, free.

Freebies: No

Video Shown: 5-minute video covering flax making

Reservations Needed: No, for self-guided tours. Yes, for all programs, guided tours, and groups of 15 or more people.

Days and Hours: Tue–Fri 9:00 AM–4:00 PM (Thur until 8:00 PM), Sat, Sun, and Mon holidays 10:00 AM–5:00 PM. Closed Mon, Thanksgiving, Christmas, and New Year's.

Plan to Stay: 2 hours

Minimum Age: None, but 6 is recommended minimum.

Disabled Access: Yes

Group Requirements: Groups of 15 or more people call (978) 441-0400, ext. 245, for reservations and group discounts.

Special Information: Museum features Osborne Textile Research Library, Textile Conservation Center, Webster Education Center, and Gazebo Café. For information on their changing calendar of public programs and special events, visit website. School programs available.

The MuseumStore: Sells textiles including hand-woven fabrics, handcrafted artisan's wares, jewelry, textile and fashion books, and textile artifacts. Also sells pillows, tablecloths, placemats, napkins, and blankets made from the traditional raised weave patterned fabrics woven in the museum's 1940s weave room on vintage looms (known as the museum's own collection of heirlooms).

Directions: From I-495, take the Lowell Connector to Thorndike St. After the 4th traffic light, bear right onto Dutton St. and the Museum's red brick building with green and yellow banners will be on the left. Museum is adjacent to Lowell's National Historic Park.

Nearby Attractions: Harbor Sweets tour (see page 186); Lowell's National Historic Park Service offers many guided tours, walks, exhibits, mill and canal tours, etc. (call 978-970-5000); New England Quilt Museum (call 978-452-4207); Boott Cotton Mills Museum (call 978-970-5000); Whistler House Museum of Art; Brush Art Gallery and Studios; Tsongas Industrial History Center; New England Sports Museum; July Lowell Folk Festival (largest free folk festival in U.S.).

Boston Beer

30 Germania Street
Boston, MA 02130
(617) 368-5080
www.samadams.com

SAMUEL ADAMS BEER

In 1984 founder Jim Koch revived his great-great-grandfather's beer recipe and launched the Boston Beer Company. Almost immediately, the company's full-bodied Samuel Adams beers started winning awards. To ensure freshness, Samuel Adams brews most of its beer at other breweries that are located nearer to retailers nationwide. It develops its new beers in a part of this urban development park that once housed the Haffenreffer Brewery. Lining the walls of the beer museum are lithographs tracing the history of this urban brewery site, plaques describing the history of beer, and other beer memorabilia.

The tour guide, often a brewer, begins by handing out tastes of barley malt and hops. As you chew on barley malt, which tastes like Grape Nuts cereal, your guide explains that the use of only these ingredients (plus yeast and water) makes Samuel Adams one of the few beers to pass Germany's purity laws; thus, it can be sold and brewed in Germany.

All the shiny tubs, vats, and kettles of the brewhouse are viewed in one small area, providing a good introduction to the steps involved in brewing beer. Each vessel is labeled so you can identify the mash tub, copper brew kettle, or glass-lined stainless-steel aging tank. The custom-made "Jules Verne Tank" resembles a submarine standing on end, complete with portholes and interior lights. If fermentation is beginning, you can see the sudsy froth from the top porthole. Although Samuel Adams makes only a small percentage of its output at this Boston site, you'll leave with the full story of the company and its beer.

Cost: $2, which is donated to Youth Enrichment Services and the restoration of Granary Graveyard, final resting place of Samuel Adams.

Freebies: 7-oz. logoed tasting glass, for 21 years old and over. Free postage for Samuel Adams postcard to friends or family. In the tap room, glasses of beer and perhaps a taste of seasonal ale brewed only at this location.

Video Shown: In the tasting room, a short video tells why Jim Koch, a sixth-generation brewer, started the company and how it operates.

Reservations Needed: No, except for groups larger than 25 people.

Days and Hours: Thur and Fri 2:00 PM, Fri also 5:30 PM, Sat 12:00 PM, 1:00 PM, and 2:00 pm, May–August: also Wed 2:00 PM. Call above number for schedule changes. No beer production during Saturday tours. Closed holidays.

Plan to Stay: 1 hour for tour and tasting, plus time for gift shop and beer museum.

Minimum Age: None. Children are welcome. Root beer is available for minors.

Disabled Access: Yes

Group Requirements: Groups larger than 25 people should call 2 weeks in advance for reservations (call 617-368-5232).

Gift Shop: Sells logoed mirrors, glasses, hats, T-shirts, and baseball jackets. Open during tour.

Directions: Take I-93 just south of downtown Boston to Exit 18 (Massachusetts Ave.). Bear left off the ramp onto Melnea Cass Blvd. Continue straight on Melnea Cass Blvd. to the eighth traffic light. Then take a left onto Tremont St. (note: Tremont St. eventually becomes Columbus Ave.). Continue straight on Tremont to the 11th traffic light, then turn right onto Washington St. Take your 4th right onto Boylston St. Continue straight on Boylston St. for 2 blocks, then turn left onto Bismark St. Watch for the "Samuel Adams" signs.

Nearby Attractions: National Braille Press and Wm. S. Haynes flutes tours (see pages 188 and 190); Mass Bay Brewing Co. tour (call 617-574-9551); Doyle's restaurant, a nearby pub full of Irish family history, has all Samuel Adams beers fresh on tap; *Boston Globe* newspaper tour (call 617-929-2653); Phillips Candy House tour (call 617-282-2090); Franklin Park Zoo; Arnold Arboretum.

Cape Cod Potato Chips

100 Breed's Hill Road
Hyannis, MA 02601
(508) 775-7253 (recording) / (888) 881-CHIP
www.capecodchips.com

CAPE COD. Potato Chips

Cape Cod Potato Chips still follows the company's original intent—"to make the best potato chip possible." Just as when Steve Bernard founded it in 1980, the company still kettle-cooks its potato chips one batch at a time. Cape Cod's production, which started in 1980 at 200 bags per day, is now 150,000 to 200,000 bags a day, using 28 million pounds of potatoes each year.

From the plaques in the entranceway, you'll learn that four pounds of potatoes yield one pound of potato chips and that, depending on the month, the potatoes come from different Eastern Seaboard states. Each truckload of 45,000 to 50,000 pounds of potatoes is unloaded into its own silo, since the potatoes must be inspected for solid mass (or "gravity"), external defects, size, and color before farmers receive payment. Different rollers and brushes, depending on the skins' thickness, wash and peel the inspected spuds, which then tumble down to the trim table for further inspection and halving of large potatoes.

Through glass windows, you watch sliced potatoes feed into one of the three production lines, each with six gas-fired cooking kettles. Raw potatoes sizzle in hot oil, creating clouds of steam. In the midst of this steam, workers rake the potatoes back and forth in the eight-by-three-foot vats with stainless-steel rakes. The steam subsides as the cooking cycle ends. A worker tilts a scoop into the kettle for the cooked batch of potato chips. Oil drips back into the kettle through the scoop's screen bottom. The worker tilts the scoop back to its original position, allowing the potato chips to slide into a white basket with holes. This centrifuge spins for four minutes, allowing excess oil to drain through the holes. Other workers pour the drained chips onto a long cooling conveyor belt.

As you walk along the production line, read the plaques that describe potato-chip making. Along the opposite wall of the corridor, a schematic diagram explains how popcorn is produced. Further down the corridor, workers inspect the cooled chips along a vibrating table that moves them forward without breaking them. The chips pass under the salter box and are transported by "bucket elevator" to the next room for packaging. On each packaging line a carousel of 14 hoppers weighs and releases the correct amount of chips into the bagging machine. Workers hand-pack bags into cardboard boxes, which are shrink-wrapped for shipment or storage in the warehouse.

Cost: Free

Freebies: Sample bag of potato chips.

Video Shown: No

Reservations Needed: No, except for groups over 25 people.

Days and Hours: Mon–Fri 9:00 AM–5:00 PM. Closed holidays.

Plan to Stay: 15 minutes for self-guided tour, plus time in gift shop.

Minimum Age: None, except small children will need to be picked up to see activity beyond cooling chip conveyor.

Disabled Access: Yes

Group Requirements: Groups over 25 people should call 2 weeks in advance.

Special Information: No photography. On rainy summer days, allow for waiting time to enter the tour.

Gift Shop: Sells all Cape Cod potato chips, popcorn, logoed caps, golf balls, and T-shirts. Open same hours as tours. Closed holidays.

Directions: From Rt. 6, take Exit 6 for Rt. 132 South. At 4th traffic light, turn left into Independence Park. Take 2nd right onto Breed's Hill Rd. Factory is on the left.

Nearby Attractions: Pairpoint Crystal tour (see page 189); Cape Cod Mall; JFK Museum; Hyannis waterfront and beaches; Thornton Burgess Museum.

Cranberry World at Edaville USA

7 Eda Avenue
Carver, MA 02330
(508) 866-8190
www.edaville.com

CRANBERRY JUICE AND RELATED PRODUCTS

Cranberries were named because the plant's blossom resembles a crane's head—a "craneberry," which eventually became "cranberry." This native North American fruit is grown primarily in Massachusetts, Wisconsin, New Jersey, Oregon, Washington, and parts of Canada. Cranberry World offers these and other "berry" unusual facts, along with exhibits and interactive audiovisual displays tracing cranberry cultivation from pre-Pilgrim times to the present. You'll also get a taste of Ocean Spray juice drinks.

Once inside, look for the "rocker" scoop, a wooden cranberry-harvesting implement used from the late 1800s to 1950s. On hands and knees, a grower-harvester put the scoop into the cranberry vines. The scoop's long wooden teeth gently tugged the berries off the vine, then the farmer rocked the scoop and the berries rolled back. At best, the scoop method yielded an average of 400 pounds per day; today's mechanical picking machines average 5,800 pounds daily.

Other highlights include the wooden one-third-scale model of the "bounce machine," a quality control device that tests "bounce-ability." Ask a guide to put wooden beads into this machine to simulate cranberries. Good berries bounce and are sold as fresh fruit; bad berries are discarded.

Push buttons to activate brief videos on cranberry sauce and cranberry juice production, as well as television commercials dating back to 1955.

Cost: Edaville USA family theme park admission is $15; children under 3, free. Special events may have higher charge.
Freebies: Tastes of Ocean Spray juice drinks, recipe leaflet.
Videos Shown: Brief videos throughout the museum on harvesting and sauce and juice production; old commercials.
Reservations Needed: No
Days and Hours: November–January, Mon–Fri 4:00 PM–9:00 PM, Sat and Sun 2:00 PM–10:00 PM; July–August, Fri–Sun 11:00 AM–6:00 PM; September–October Harvest Festival: Sat–Sun 10:00 AM–5:00 PM.
Plan to Stay: 45 minutes–1 hour for museum, videos, and gift counter.
Minimum Age: None
Disabled Access: Yes
Group Requirements: None; Call for special rates.
Special Information: Edaville USA family theme park offers the following attractions: train ride through Cranberry Country (steam or diesel), children's rides, antique fire engine rides, Transportation Museum, climbable trains, BBQ Pavilion, and Freight House Café. Plan to stay 3–4 hours for entire park.
Gift Counter: Sells cranberry-related products and more. Open same hours.
Directions: From I-495 take Exit 2. Follow Rt. 58 North 4 miles. Make left onto Rochester Rd., where you will see an Edaville sign. Take your 2nd right onto Pine St. Edaville will be on your right. From Rt. 3 take Exit 6 (Rt. 44 West) to Rt. 58 South. Follow for 7 miles. Make a right onto Rochester Rd. and follow above directions.
Nearby Attractions: The Massachusetts Cranberry Harvest Festival held Columbus Day Weekend features operation of harvesting equipment, historical displays, and cranberry-related cooking and crafts demonstrations; Plymouth Rock; *Mayflower II*; Whale-Watch Cruises; Plymouth National Wax Museum; Plymouth Plantation; beaches.

Crane

Crane Museum
Routes 8 and 9
Dalton, MA 01226
(413) 684-6481
www.crane.com

PAPER

Crane's fine papers are used worldwide for stationery and by the Bureau of Engraving and Printing for currency (see page 100). Since 1801 Crane has produced 100 percent cotton paper that offers strength, durability, and surface texture unsurpassed by paper made from wood. The company uses denim scraps from Levi Strauss jeans and worn dollar bills to make recycled paper. This family-owned company's mills are in Dalton, in western Massachusetts. The Crane Museum, housed in the company's Old Stone Mill (built in 1844), has welcomed visitors since 1930.

The museum sits on the banks of the Housatonic River, which supplied water to wash the rags and drive the machines of the early Crane paper mills. This ivy-covered stone building has a completely different feel from the modern, multimedia-filled company museums built recently. The museum's interior resembles the Old Ship Church in Hingham, Massachusetts, with rough-hewn oak beams, colonial chandeliers, many-paned windows, and wide oak floorboards. The ceiling looks like an upside-down ship's hull.

After you watch the video on Crane's modern paper-production techniques, walk through exhibits on the history of the company and of papermaking since the Revolutionary War. A scale model of the vat house in the original Crane mill shows the laborious process of hand-making paper one sheet at a time. This process, used by company founder Zenas Crane, contrasts with the modern method of making long continuous rolls of paper.

Among the many different kinds of paper displayed in glass cases are those used for currency, American Express checks, stock certificates, and the stationery of presidents and movie stars. One exhibit of corporate innovation features Crane's paper collars, which the company made after the Civil War. Although they are rarely seen today, at the time these disposable collars were fashionable and very profitable.

Cost: Free

Freebies: Crane writing pad

Video Shown: 20-minute video on company's history and papermaking methods.

Reservations Needed: Yes

Days and Hours: Open June–mid-October only: Mon–Fri 2:00 PM–5:00 PM. Closed major holidays.

Plan to Stay: 30 minutes for exhibits, plus time for video.

Minimum Age: None

Disabled Access: Museum is all on one ground-level floor. However, there are a couple of steps to reach it.

Group Requirements: With 1 week's notice, Crane can handle groups up to 50 people.

Special Information: Can visit museum before 2:00 PM if call a few days ahead. Company retirees run museum; they answer questions and offer interesting anecdotes.

Gift Shop: No

Directions: From I-90 (Mass Pike), take the Lee Exit. Follow Rts. 7 and 20 North through Pittsfield. Take Rts. 8 and 9 East about 5 miles. Turn right onto Housatonic St. At bottom is Pioneer Mill. Museum is on the right at the end of Mill.

Nearby Attractions: Berkshire attractions include Clark Art Museum, Mt. Greylock, Berkshire Museum, and Tanglewood.

Harbor Sweets

Palmer Cove
85 Leavitt Street
Salem, MA 01970
(978) 745-7648 / (800) 234-4860
www.harborsweets.com

While Salem is known for its witches' potions, Harbor Sweets brews only the sweet variety. The company's key players are its 150 part-time/flex-time employees (many disabled, elderly, or foreign-born) and its innovative founder, Ben Strohecker, the former Schrafft's Candy marketing director, who launched Harbor Sweets in 1975.

While the company has expanded into three connected brick buildings, visitors see only the first room. From the slightly raised gift-shop platform, you can observe the labor-intensive production of Sweet Sloops, one of Harbor Sweets' most popular nautical New England-theme candies; you can also see molded candies at the far end. Even though you don't enter the production areas, workers will gladly answer your questions. The air smells of caramel, toffee, and chocolate.

Notice the home-style, four-burner gas stove in the back. Leaning over copper cauldrons, workers stir batches of almond butter crunch and caramel with wooden paddles. The butter crunch is poured onto a cooling table and then smoothed. With a bladed metal rolling pin, a worker scores the crunch into squares and then triangles. A helper breaks the triangles apart. The triangles proceed through the enrober for a coating of white chocolate. With a long metal ice-cream spoon, a worker draws lines representing the mast and jib. After the cooling tunnel, workers hand-dip the Sweet Sloops into melted chocolate and chopped pecans, often a tough job—they must eat their mistakes.

All other candies are molded. Depending on the candies being made, melters contain milk or dark chocolate, some with crushed orange or peppermint crunch. A worker holds a 16-cavity plastic mold, while the "depositor" drops a specially timed amount of chocolate into each cavity. Another worker inserts dollops of raspberry/cranberry ganache and white chocolate from a hand-held funnel. After they have been chilled, the candies are individually foil-wrapped before being beautifully gift-boxed.

Cost: Free

Freebies: Chocolate sample from a silver serving platter

Video Shown: No

Reservations Needed: No, except for groups over 6 people.

Days and Hours: Mon–Fri 8:30 AM–4:30 PM. Call about Saturday hours before candy-giving holidays. Closed holidays and 2 weeks in July. Limited production May through August.

Plan to Stay: 10–15 minutes for self-guided viewing, plus time in gift shop.

Minimum Age: None

Disabled Access: Yes

Group Requirements: Groups larger than 6 people should call 1 week in advance to arrange a tour guide. Groups over 12 will be split into smaller groups. No maximum group size.

Special Information: Best time to see production is September–Easter.

Gift Shop: Sells Harbor Sweets' 6 varieties of nautical New England–theme candies in a variety of gift box sizes. Open Mon–Fri 8:30 AM–4:30 PM, Sat 9:00 AM–3:00 PM, with extended hours before holidays and shorter hours in summer. Catalog available from (800) 243-2115.

Directions: From Rt. 128, take Rt. 114 East to Salem. Turn left onto Leavitt St. Harbor Sweets is the last building on the left. From 1A North (follow Rt. 1A as it meanders to Salem), turn right onto Leavitt St.

Nearby Attractions: American Textile History Museum tour (see page 181); Saugus Iron Works, first integrated ironworks in North America, with reconstructed blast furnace, 17th-century iron mill, and working waterwheel (call 781-233-0050); Salem's attractions include Pickering Wharf, Salem Witch Museum, House of Seven Gables, and Peabody/Essex Maritime Museum.

Other Eastern Massachusetts Candy Tours: Stowaway Sweets candy tour in Marblehead (call 800-432-0304); Phillips Candy House tour in Dorchester (call 617-282-2090).

Hebert Candies

575 Hartford Turnpike
Shrewsbury, MA 01545
(800) 642-7702
www.hebertcandies.com

CHOCOLATES

With events such as weekly summer "Thursday Night Cruising" charity family fun nights, "Chick Cliques" birthday parties with ice cream sundaes, and special school vacation-week tours and activities, you know this fifth-generation candy company (started in 1917) prides itself on giving back to the local community. So now that we know this place is fun, let's find out how they make chocolate.

First don a hair net before your tour guide takes you into the Geneva room. Geneva candies, their signature candies, start with chocolate from 10-pound blocks of solid chocolate, broken with a hammer. A worker tosses pieces of white, dark, milk, or dietetic chocolate into corresponding 110° vats. The Geneva chocolate machine dispenses liquid chocolate into clear plastic trays containing 50 squares. If needed, a worker hand-places almonds individually in each of the 10 rows of five squares. The chocolate hardens in the 55° cold room.

In another area, a few workers may hand-place white cardboard sticks at an angle into chocolate lollipops. To make hollow molded chocolates, such as soldiers, a workers pours just the right amount of liquid chocolate up to the soldier's belly button, then clamps the clear plastic molds shut with heavy-duty paper clamps. The worker rolls the mold to distribute the chocolate inside. After letting the chocolate stand to stiffen, the worker turns it again to coat the mold.

Walk downstairs to the kitchen. The Dayton ball beater turns in circles making cream centers. The extruder squeezes out rows of nine centers, such as peanut butter, which march side by side along the big white enrober. Once coated in chocolate, they receive a swirl design on top designating the type of center, perhaps peppermint.

In the packing area, rubber-gloved ladies put individual chocolates into paper cups and fill boxes as they move along the conveyor belt. The last woman brushes the candies to maintain their sheen and weighs the candy boxes. Next pass through the warehouse adjacent to the huge overhanging funnel full of Styrofoam packing pieces.

Walk down the ramp to the noisy candy bar department. In this maze-like three-stage process, liquid chocolate flows into empty clear plastic molds. The resulting chocolate shells wind their way around the bend. Spigots pour fillings such as peanut butter into shells. Chocolate covers it and the bars drop out when flipped over. Daily two machines can make 130,000 candy bars—most become fundraiser candies, a mainstay of Hebert's business.

Cost: Free
Freebies: Chocolate samples during the tour
Video Shown: Plans for 25-minute video
Reservations Needed: No, except for groups over 10 people.
Days and Hours: Tue–Thur 10:30 AM–2:30 PM.
Plan to Stay: 45 minutes, plus additional time for video and candy store.
Minimum Age: None
Disabled Access: Yes, tour route altered slightly.
Group Requirements: Groups over 10 people should call 1 week in advance. Groups enjoy special discounts. Maximum group size is 20.
Special Information: Hebert Candies was America's First Roadside Candy Store. Mascot is Geneva man.
The Hebert Candy Mansion: Sells Geneva candies and assorted boxes such as Mansion Fancy. Sells kosher candies and ice cream. Open Mon–Fri 9:00 AM–8:00 PM (9:00 AM–9:00 PM during the holidays), Sun 10:00 AM–8:00 pm. Directions: From I-90 East, take Rt. 20 West. On your left in 2.5 miles, drive between the stone fence to Hebert Candies stone Tudor-style mansion. From I-90 West, take Exit 11. At light, make left onto Grafton St. Take Rt. 20 East. Drive 5 minutes. Hebert's will be on your right.
Nearby Attractions: Green Hill Farm maple sugaring in March (call 508-842-2588); National Plastics Center & Museum (call 978-537-9529); Ecotarium; Higgins Armory Museum; Worcester Art Museum; Sturbridge Village 30 minutes away.

National Braille Press

88 Saint Stephen Street
Boston, MA 02115
(617) 266-6160
www.nbp.org

National Braille Press

National Braille Press, founded in 1927, is one of only five companies in the U.S.A. that mass-produce Braille materials, and the only one that publishes original self-help books for the blind. The company prides itself on its leading-edge position in computer-assisted production of Braille publications and on hiring people with disabilities (almost half of its 35-person in-house staff).

The company produces approximately 23 million Braille pages per year from this four-story converted piano factory on a tree-lined street in the Northeastern University area. Specialized translation software helps workers transcribe the written word into Braille pages. To find any errors in the transcription, blind proofreaders listen to an audio tape of what should be written while following the Braille version with their hands. The proofreading room chatters with the sound of the Braille typewriters that proofreaders use to note mistakes.

Once the pages are corrected, a software version of the publication to be printed directs the computerized plate-embossing machines, which punch the raised dots of the Braille alphabet onto zinc printing plates. For any new errors, a small hammer knocks dots out or in on the zinc plates. In the cluttered printing area, you'll watch and hear reconditioned Heidelberg cylinder presses spin out up to 8,000 Braille pages per hour. Workers then hand-collate Braille versions of well-known magazines such as *Parenting* and *Book World,* computer manuals for Microsoft, or popular children's books, before stitch-binding completes the production process.

Cost: Free, but donation requested.
Freebies: Samples of Braille materials
Video Shown: No
Reservations Needed: Yes, call 1 week in advance.

Days and Hours: Mon–Thur 10:30 AM and 2:00 PM. Closed holidays.
Plan to Stay: 1 hour
Minimum Age: While there is no official minimum age, children should be at least 6 to appreciate the tour. The company tries to make the tour more interactive for children. Watching blind people and those with disabilities working at productive jobs provides kids with a lasting impression.
Disabled Access: Yes; enter from bottom floor.
Group Requirements: Can handle groups up to 12 people with 5 days' advance notice.
Special Information: Carefully supervise children around the printing presses. Tours also available at the American Printing House for the Blind in Louisville, KY, the largest and oldest (1859) publishing house for the blind (see page 153).
Gift Shop: No
Directions: By subway, take the "E" train on the Green Line to the Northeastern University stop on Huntington Ave. Cross Huntington onto Opera Pl. and turn right onto St. Stephen St. The building is 1 block ahead on your right. By car, take the Massachusetts Ave. exit on I-93 (Southeast Expwy.). Turn right on Massachusetts Ave. and go straight until you cross Huntington Ave. At Symphony Hall (on your left), turn left on St. Stephen St. National Braille Press is ahead on your left.
Nearby Attractions: Wm. S. Haynes flute and Boston Beer (Samuel Adams) tours (see pages 190 and 182); *Boston Globe* newspaper tour (call 617-929-2653); Phillips Candy House tour (call 617-282-2090); Boston's museums and attractions include Symphony Hall, Christian Science Center, Museum of Science, Back Bay.

Pairpoint Crystal

851 Sandwich Road
Sagamore, MA 02561
(508) 888-2344 / (800) 899-0953
www.pairpoint.com

GLASS

Since Pairpoint's philosophy is "made in America the old-fashioned way," it utilizes the same hand tools and processes as when Deming Jarves founded the company in 1837. Pairpoint makes cup plates (many are collectors' items), limited editions, and other fine pieces for such museums as New York City's Metropolitan Museum of Art and Boston's Museum of Fine Arts.

Though the observation window shields you from the furnaces' 2,500° heat, you know the factory below is hot—the artisans wear shorts year-round. Watch a gaffer, the most experienced glassblower on the five-person team, fill his cheeks with air and blow into the blowpipe. Once the glass at the other end of the pipe reaches the desired size, he twirls the rod like a baton to elongate the glass.

Using another rod, a team member gathers glass from the furnaces and brings it to the gaffer, who attaches it to the original piece, snips it with shears, then shapes the piece with wooden and metal hand tools. Eventually the piece is transferred to the pontil rod and cracked off from its original blowpipe. The gaffer inserts the work, perhaps a vase or a flask, into a reheating furnace called a "glory hole" and then shapes its opening.

Cup plates, widely used in the mid-1800s as plates for handle-less cups of hot tea, have increased in popularity since Pairpoint started pressing them in the early 1970s. A gob of 34-percent lead crystal glass is placed in a mold, and an artisan pulls on a lever to exert just the right amount of pressure. While the standard patterns on these three-and-one-half-inch-diameter cup plates include endangered species, birds, and geometric shapes, you will also want to see the gift-shop display of collector's cup plates commissioned by companies, clubs, and towns.

Cost: Free
Freebies: Product brochures
Video Shown: No
Reservations Needed: No
Days and Hours: May–December: Mon–Fri 9:00 AM–12:00 PM and 12:30 PM–4:00 PM. February–April: Mon–Fri 10:00 AM–5:00 PM with limited production. Closed holidays. No weekend glass-blowing.
Plan to Stay: 20 minutes for self-guided tour, plus time for gift shop.
Minimum Age: None
Disabled Access: Yes
Group Requirements: Maximum group size is 40.
Special Information: Call to find out about production January–April.
Retail Store: Sells works by the artists, including museum reproductions, vases, candlesticks, and cup plates. Open May–December: Mon–Fri 9:00 AM–6:00 PM, Sat 10:00 AM–6:00 PM, Sun 11:00 AM–6:00 PM. Open January–April: Mon–Sat 10:00 AM–5:00 PM and Sun 11:00 AM–5:00 PM. Closed holidays. Catalog available from (800) 899-0953.
Directions: From Boston, take I-93 South to Rt. 3 South to Sagamore Bridge. After bridge, take first exit onto Rt. 6A. Pairpoint is on your left. From Hyannis, take Rt. 6 West. Take last exit before bridge. Turn left onto Adams St. and left onto 6A. Pairpoint is on your right.
Nearby Attractions: Sandwich Glass Museum; Thornton Burgess Museum; Sandwich Boardwalk (look for nearby plaque designating site of original Boston and Sandwich Glass Co., also founded by Jarves); Yesteryears Museum; Old Grist Mill.

Wm. S. Haynes

12 Piedmont Street
Boston, MA 02116
(617) 482-7456
www.wmshaynes.com

THE HAYNES FLUTE
MFD BY
WM. S. HAYNES CO
BOSTON, MASS

FLUTES AND PICCOLOS

Flutists from all over the world travel to Boston just to visit this famous flute factory. Since 1888, when William S. Haynes opened his flute-making shop in the heart of downtown Boston, legendary artists like Jean-Pierre Rampal have refused to play anything but Haynes flutes.

After viewing the dozens of autographed photos of famous musicians in the front office, you will be guided to the first floor of the factory. Every part of a Haynes flute is made by hand on the premises, except for the hollow silver tube body, purchased prefabricated from a precious-metal supplier. If the diameter of this tube is off by more than one one-thousandth of an inch (less than the thickness of a human hair) it is returned.

The first stages of flute-making begin in this downstairs workshop, where artisans learn the basics of their craft in what looks more like a machine shop than the birthplace of these beautiful instruments. Drill machines line the walls in a corner where your guide explains Haynes' method of drop forging, which is more precise and laborious than the casting process used by other flutemakers. The craftsmen hunch over their tables, laboring on the precise placement of the tone holes on the body.

The upstairs workshop resembles a jewelry shop, where trained artisans work with tiny silver keys. Each craftsman serves a five-year apprenticeship next to a 20-year veteran in order to learn precisely the craft of handfinishing the keys. Behind a glass window, watch an artisan polish the flutes to their shiny final appearance with the delicacy and accuracy of a surgeon. You understand why artists around the world proudly send the company records and CDs on which they play their beloved Haynes instruments.

Cost: Free

Freebies: Catalog, price list, and literature.

Video Shown: No. However, "The Haynes Story," a brief video on flute-making and Haynes' history, is for sale.

Reservations Needed: No, except for groups of 6 or more people.

Days and Hours: Mon–Fri 9:00 AM–3:00 PM. Closed holidays.

Plan to Stay: 30 minutes. Flutists should allow extra time at the end of the tour to try out the gold flutes.

Minimum Age: No minimum age, but to best appreciate the tour, a child should be of high-school age or play the flute.

Disabled Access: Yes

Group Requirements: Groups of 6 or more should call 1 week in advance.

Special Information: Best time to tour is Tue or Thur 11:00 AM–2:00 PM, when the tester plays the flutes to check their quality. Parts of the tour can be loud.

Gift Area: Videos, posters, and Haynes logo T-shirts available in the front office. Open Mon–Fri 8:00 AM–4:00 PM.

Directions: By subway, take the Green Line to the Arlington stop. Walk in the direction of traffic down Arlington St. Piedmont St. is the third street on the left. By car from the west, take I-90 (Mass Pike) East to Prudential Center exit. Go toward Copley Square. Follow ramp onto Stuart St. Turn right onto Arlington St. and left onto Piedmont St. Check before you go for Big Dig traffic rerouting.

Nearby Attractions: National Braille Press and Boston Beer (Samuel Adams) tours (see pages 188 and 182); *Boston Globe* newspaper tour (call 617-929-2653); Phillips Candy House tour (call 617-282-2090); downtown Boston's attractions include Boston Symphony Hall, Carl Fisher Music Store, Berklee School of Music, Fanueil Hall, Boston Common, Public Garden, and the Back Bay.

Yankee Candle

Route 5
South Deerfield, MA 01373
(413) 665-2929
www.yankeecandle.com

CANDLES

If you've ever made candles by melting wax and crayons, you have something in common with Mike Kittredge, founder of Yankee Candle. While you can no longer tour the factory, you can see historical storyboards depicting the beginning of Yankee Candle, and the original Queen Atlantic gas stove Mike used to melt wax in his parents' cellar at age 17 in 1969. Adjacent to the candle museum, where you see candle-making demonstrations, the walls display a pictorial history of the company's development from Mike's parents' house to a renovated paper mill in 1974 to the current Yankee Candle Complex.

Watch videos at four different locations in the Candle Emporium to discover all the steps performed at the nearby factory to make taper, jar, pillar, and sampler candles. Yankee Candle's workers describe the factory, which has piped-in music, as a huge craft studio that smells like a spice rack. The automatic taper-candle-dipping machine, resembling a chandelier with wicks instead of light bulbs, dips up to two miles of wicks per day. To create the standard seven-eighths-inch taper candle, the machine dips braided cotton wicks into liquid wax as many as 30 times, alternating with dips into a cooling water bath. Workers then hand-dip the final, harder wax layers to create smooth, dripless candles.

Textured pillar candles start as colorful solid-wax cylinders. Workers place four smooth pillar candles on pedestals to begin their transformation. The candles, pushed up through 300° grooved rings, emerge from the top of the press as ionic (vertically grooved) or twist (spirally grooved) pillars. The making of jar candles will remind you of Jell-O molding: a machine fills eight glass containers at a time with hot, colorful, fragrant wax.

The Candlemaking Museum is designed as an 1810 chandler's workshop. Workers dressed in period garb give continuous live demonstrations, hand-dipping bayberry and beeswax candles. After you watch the candle making, you'll want to dip your own candles and test-sniff some of the 175 fragrances of Sampler's votive candles in the Candle Emporium. Fragrances include the traditional (vanilla), the unexpected (gingersnaps), the delicious (chocolate truffle), and the inspirational (stargazer lily).

Cost: Free

Freebies: No

Video Shown: Continuously running video provides close-up shots of the production processes.

Reservations Needed: No, except for bus tours.

Days and Hours: Mon–Sun 9:30 AM–6:00 PM. Extended hours from November–Christmas. Closed Thanksgiving and Christmas.

Plan to Stay: 20 minutes for video and Candlemaking Museum, plus 1–2 hours for retail stores and any special events on the grounds.

Minimum Age: None

Disabled Access: Yes

Special Information: Chandler's restaurant has fine dining (call 413-665-1277 for reservations), Candlewick Café and Coffee Haus offer casual dining.

Group Requirements: Bus tours call (413) 665-2929 for special parking and to reserve space in museum for 20-minute demonstration.

Retail Store: Sells thousands of different styles, varieties, and fragrances of candles, including Country Kitchen and House-warmer jar candles, and aromatic samplers. Seconds Room has overruns and flawed candles at marked-down prices. Open Mon–Sun 9:30 AM–6:00 PM; extended hours during holiday season. Catalog available from (800) 243-1776. Entire 80,000-square-foot complex includes Candle Shop, Bavarian Christmas Village, Kringle Market, Candle Emporium, the Black Forest, Enchanted Castle, and Santa's Workshop.

Directions: Take I-90 (Mass Pike) to I-91 North to Exit 24. Turn right on Rtes. 5 and 10. Yankee Candle will be on the left.

Nearby Attractions: Mt. Sugarloaf State Reservation; Historic Deerfield; Mohawk Trail Autoroad; Magic Vines Butterfly Conservatory.

Alticor (formerly Amway)

7575 Fulton Street East
Ada, MI 49355
(616) 787-6701
www.alticor.com

Alticor, parent company of Amway, Quixtar, and Access Business Group, is a global enterprise committed to helping people live better lives.

The entrance to the Visitor Center features a global map of key markets, a list of core values, and a tribute to company cofounders. Watch a welcome video about the entrepreneurial spirit of Alticor, hosted by Chairman Steve Van Andel and President Dick DeVos. The video screen then rises to the ceiling, revealing doorways into the heart of the exhibit. A 24-foot wall of backlit photographs introduces you to some of Amway's independent business owners (IBOs), representing varied markets around the world. Amway and Quixtar IBOs distribute more than 450 products manufactured by Access Business Group—including personal care and cleaning products, water treatment systems, Artistry skin care and cosmetics, and Nutrilite vitamins and food supplements.

In contrast to a photo display highlighting Nutrilite's farming and production practices, step onto a simulated metal factory floor as you enter the Access Business Group exhibit. Take a virtual tour of three production lines to see how Access makes powder, toothpaste, and printed products. Access delivers 30 million orders each year to global destinations, and you'll see a busy conveyor moving overhead, carrying some of these products. Watch a lively video on distribution logistics, accompanied by a distribution center diagram that lights up during each process step. The research and development section features interactive displays on thermal imaging and magnification.

In the Artistry section, you can evaluate how much your skin has been exposed to the sun, or use a color wheel to select different eye shadows or foundations to match your skin tone. From different computers,

log onto the Quixtar visitor site, and browse through products available from this popular online shopping service and business ownership opportunity.

At the end of your visit, you will have a new appreciation for the spirit of free enterprise that has inspired people to build this American-made venture into a global business.

Cost: Free

Freebies: Travel-size product samples

Videos Shown: 8-minute video introduces the global nature of the enterprise.

Reservations Needed: No, except for groups of 10 or more people.

Days and Hours: Mon–Fri 8:30 AM–12:00 PM, 1:00 PM–5:00 PM. Call ahead for holiday schedules.

Plan to Stay: 45 minutes, depending on your use of the interactive exhibits.

Minimum Age: None, although children under 16 must be accompanied by an adult.

Disabled Access: Yes

Group Requirements: Groups of 10 people or more must call at least 2 weeks in advance. Maximum group size is 50 people.

Gift Shop: No. Catalog available (call 800-544-7167).

Directions: From Grand Rapids, take I-196 East, which becomes I-96, to Exit 39 for M-21. The exit road becomes Fulton St. In about 5 miles, turn left into the Amway World Headquarters Building. Look for the row of international flags in front.

Nearby Attractions: Wolverine World Wide tour (see page 203); Public Museum of Grand Rapids; Grand Rapids Art Museum; Gerald R. Ford Museum; Grand Rapids Symphony Orchestra; Frederik Meijer Gardens and Sculpture Park; John Ball Park Zoo.

Amon Orchards

8066 U.S. 31
Acme, MI 49610
(800) 937-1644
www.amonorchards.com

CHERRIES AND CHERRY PRODUCTS

Northern Michigan calls itself the cherry capital of the world. The roads in and around Traverse City are lined with bright red cherry trees during the summer. Stands selling the juiciest, freshest cherries you've ever tasted appear along most roads.

David Amon accurately predicted a sharp drop in the price of cherries and added tourism and specialty products to Amon Orchard's agriculture business. The company also branched out to other types of fruit production and now enjoys taking visitors through the fields to see and learn about it all.

Relax as you ride in a shaded, canvas-topped, open-sided trolley that meanders through rows of eight- to ten-foot-tall trees on this 200-acre, family-run orchard. Your driver (perhaps David himself) spouts interesting facts you probably never knew about cherries. You learn that the "fresh" cherries with stems in your supermarket were probably handpicked in Oregon or Washington long before they were ripened.

The driver stops the trolley to let you pull a ripe fruit from a tree, perhaps one of the three different apricot or nectarine varieties or seven different types of peaches they grow. From the trolley you can also reach some red tart, light, or dark sweet cherries. The juice from these fresh, ripe fruits will squirt into your mouth and, if you're not careful, onto your shoes!

One of Amon's missions through the tour is to teach people about the changes in agriculture, such as integrated pest management systems that use "good" bugs to eat "bad" bugs, thus requiring less pesticide. Another proudly pushed theme is that cherries aren't just for dessert anymore. Creative uses of cherries include many of the specialty products you'll want to sample in the retail store before or after the tour.

Cost: $1 donation for trolley ride
Freebies: Ripe fruit from trees, cherry juice, gourmet product samples, recipe brochure.
Video Shown: No

Reservations Needed: No, during National Cherry Festival (first or second week in July). Advance notice required for motor-coaches.

Days and Hours: Mid-July and during Cherry Festival week and weekends in October. Arrangements can be made for motorcoach groups year-round.

Plan to Stay: 1 hour for trolley tour, petting farm, u-pick (call for the Ripe and Ready Report and map, telling you what months the different fruits are best for picking), and retail store. In October wander around the maze carved through 8-foot-tall cornstalks.

Minimum Age: None

Disabled Access: Yes

Group Requirements: Call at least a few days in advance for motorcoach group tours year-round. Call for group tour rates.

Special Information: Orchard is particularly scenic during spring blossom season, with special tours available. Family Fall Festival on October weekends features u-pick pumpkins.

Retail Store: Grandma Amon's Country Market and gift shop sells fresh-picked fruit from orchard, jams, gourmet cherry products including "Fudgie" sauce, cherry hot-pepper jelly, cherry Mexican salsa, dried cherries, and baked goods. Daily in-store specials. Mid-June–October: Mon–Sun 10:00 AM–6:00 PM. November–December: Tue–Sat 10:00 AM–5:00 PM. Catalog available from above number.

Directions: From Traverse City, take U.S. 31 North. Orchard is about 8 miles ahead on your right. From Mackinaw City, take I-75 South to U.S. 31 South. Orchard is on your left 10 miles south of Elk Rapids.

Nearby Attractions: National Cherry Festival week (first or second week in July) events include cherry pie-eating contests, Cherry Royale Parade, and Taste of Cherries. Kilwin's Chocolates tour (see page 199); Good Harbor Vineyards tour (call 231-256-7165); the Music House; Grand Traverse Bay.

Chelsea Milling

201 West North Street
Chelsea, MI 48118
(734) 475-1361
www.jiffymix.com

"JIFFY" *mixes*

"JIFFY" MIXES

You recognize "JIFFY" mixes by their little blue-and-white boxes and low prices, not by any supermarket coupons or fancy advertising campaigns. Chelsea Milling Company, founded in 1887, prides itself on this and has been producing its all-purpose JIFFY Baking Mix in a low-key fashion since 1930. Grandma Mabel Holmes named the famous biscuit mix (archrival of General Mills' Bisquick) after hearing her father's housekeeper say, "The muffins will be ready in a jiffy." Howdy Holmes, ex-racecar driver, is now at the helm of this family-run business.

The family feeling extends to the tour program. The head tour guide has been conducting tours for more than 25 years—following in the footsteps of her mother, who also led tours for nearly 20 years. After watching the slide show, you walk upstairs into the factory to watch the packaging process.

The dark blue, heavy, well-oiled, vintage 1950s and '60s machinery hisses as it works hard 24 hours a day. As you walk next to the circular box-making machine, a stack of flat boxes (or "shells") feeds into the machine. Simultaneously, a roll of waxed paper threads through and is cut and shaped around a metal block. The cardboard boxes form around the waxed paper.

As you walk to the filling area, notice the floor vibrating under your feet! For corn muffin mix, the number-one prepared food mix in the U.S.A., maize-colored powder funnels down from the second floor to fill each box, one at a time. Along each of the 16 small box lines, funnels fill the boxes in a two-step process. The boxes march single file along a conveyor belt over a scale and to the box topsealer. At this circular machine, each station around the wheel performs one step toward sealing the waxed paper and then the box.

Workers hand-pack 24 small boxes into each case, and two cases of like product are glued together to form a piggyback carton. These piggyback cartons travel along a roller-coaster conveyor belt to the warehouse. And, if the boxes are not dizzy enough already, a driver will release two double-stacked pallets onto the Lanwrapper, which spins the cartons around as they are covered with heavy-duty shrink-wrap.

Cost: Free

Freebies: Recipe booklet; small box of "JIFFY" mix (2 boxes for people 13 years old or older).

Video Shown: 15-minute slide show covers company history, flour-milling process, and packaging.

Reservations Needed: Yes

Days and Hours: Mon–Fri 9:00 AM–1:30 PM. Closed holidays. Closed between Christmas and New Year's.

Plan to Stay: 1.5–2 hours

Minimum Age: Prefers 1 adult for every child under 6.

Disabled Access: Some accessibility. Call for more information.

Group Requirements: Groups should call at least 1 week in advance for reservations. Regular group maximum is 45 people; however, special arrangements can be made for larger groups.

Special Information: No photography inside factory.

Gift Area: Guests can purchase 24-pack variety tour case containing an assortment of mixes and a recipe booklet. Also, individual products can be purchased by the case.

Directions: From I-94, take M-52 North (Exit 159). As you roll into Chelsea's Main Street, go through 4 traffic lights. As you cross the railroad tracks, notice white, 120-foot-high silos with blue "JIFFY Mixes" lettering to your left. Take 1st left onto North St. and park on right.

Nearby Attractions: The Walter P. Chrysler Museum tour (see page 202); Jeff Daniels' Purple Rose Theater; Stagecoach Stop U.S.A.; Ann Arbor's attractions, including University of Michigan, are 20 minutes away.

DeKlomp/Veldheer

12755 Quincy Street off U.S. 31
Holland, MI 49424
(616) 399-1900
www.veldheer.com

WOODEN SHOES AND DELFTWARE

Holland, Michigan, is full of Dutch re-creations, at least one of which you'll feel enticed to visit. The Tulip Time Festival (usually the second or third week of May) will pleasantly overwhelm you with the dazzling colors of millions of tulips in full bloom. At DeKlomp, the only delftware factory in the U.S.A., watch delftware and wooden shoes being made through windows in the back of the large retail store. Also enjoy Veldheer's tulip farm and show garden.

Delftware originated with pottery brought to the Netherlands from the Orient in the thirteenth century. In 1310 Dutch artists in the village of Delft adapted the Oriental patterns, giving birth to the familiar blue-and-white hand-painted floral designs and Dutch scenery. Much of what passes for delftware in this country is actually mass-produced and stencil-decorated. However, DeKlomp's small staff of artisans paints each individual piece with the blue-and-white designs.

Dressed in traditional Dutch costume during Tulip Time, the artisans happily discuss each step of the production process, from molding the clay to decorating the final product. All materials—clay, molds, and machinery—are imported from the Netherlands. Walk by the paint room, where pottery is hand-painted and signed on the bottom.

At the next window, notice the unique machines used to create wooden shoes; ask to see them in action. Using a dual-action shaper machine and a pattern, a worker makes the left and right shoes simultaneously. By rotating a block counterclockwise, the machine traces a mirror image, thus producing a matched pair. The narrow shelves along the wall contain wooden shoe patterns. A worker places one of these patterns on the center rod of the dual-action carving machine. The right rod carves the right shoe, and the left rod, the left shoe. You will also see the only automated wooden shoe carving machine in the U.S. and a shaper machine that makes souvenir 3.5- to 12.5-centimeter shoes—sometimes as many as five in a row, resembling a totem pole.

Cost: Production viewing: free. Gardens: adults, $5.

Freebies: No

Video Shown: No

Reservations Needed: No

Days and Hours: June–December: Mon–Fri 8:00 AM–6:00 PM, Sat and Sun 9:00 AM–5:00 PM. January–April: Mon–Fri 9:00 AM–5:00 PM. Tulip Time Festival (10 days in May, starting the week before Mother's Day): Mon–Sun 8:00 AM–dusk. Closed Thanksgiving, Christmas, and New Year's. Wooden shoes not carved January–March. Painting and shoes sometimes not in production at other times during the year.

Plan to Stay: 45 minutes for self-guided tour of production through windows in the back of the retail store, plus time for gift shop and Veldheer's Tulip Gardens.

Minimum Age: None

Disabled Access: Yes

Group Requirements: Groups over 20 should call in advance to arrange a guided tour. No maximum group size.

Retail Store: Large gift shop carries all of the shoes and delftware made in the factory, including delft canister sets and Christmas ornaments, miniature wooden-shoe souvenirs, and a wide variety of Dutch gifts and foods. A separate store sells tulip bulbs. Open same hours as tour. Price list available from above number.

Directions: From Grand Rapids, take I-196 West to Exit 55 (Business Rt. 196 West). Then exit at U.S. 31 North and follow it to Quincy St. The factory is at the corner of Quincy St. and U.S. 31.

Nearby Attractions: Downtown Holland's art galleries; Dutch Village; Holland State Park Beach; Windmill Island; Saugatuck, an artists' colony.

Henry Ford Museum and Greenfield Village

20900 Oakwood Boulevard
Dearborn, MI 48121
(313) 271-1620 / (800) 835-5237
www.hfmgv.org

U.S. MANUFACTURING AND CARS

It's getting difficult to take a car-factory tour in Michigan. Fortunately, Michigan has a good substitute with the constantly improving Henry Ford Museum (not affiliated with the Ford Motor Company or the Ford Foundation). The "Made in America" exhibit inside this sprawling, high-ceilinged museum should be a favorite of factory-tour lovers.

You'll be attracted to the entrance of the football field-size exhibit area by the clanking machine that assembles electrical switches and by the swinging robotic arm that sprays paint on a farm-tractor chassis. Encircling the exhibit area is a constantly moving, overhead conveyor belt with chairs, propellers, wheels, bike frames, sinks, and more hanging from it. Full-size displays, along with videos (many with historic footage), photographs, talks, and hands-on activities, offer a creative look at U.S. manufacturing history and processes.

While you'll be fascinated by the machines, such as the one that made light bulbs from ribbons of molten glass, take time to read the text descriptions and watch the videos scattered throughout. Displays explain the workers' roles and the positive and negative impact of machines on them. For example, the display of the "clean room" used in fabricating computer chips tells how workers in this controlled environment suffer stress-related injuries.

"Made in America" has a few historical displays on car manufacturing, such as the area devoted to Ford's Highland Park plant of the 1920s that revolutionized mass production with its moving assembly line. Car buffs will want to visit another area of the museum for the exhibit called "The Automobile in American Life." It's filled with big, intriguing, and a seemingly overwhelming number of artifacts. These include the actual 1961 Lincoln in which President Kennedy was assassinated and the experimental automobile (quadricycle) that Henry Ford invented in 1896.

Greenfield Village features the original buildings and homes of famous American inventors and industrialists, such as Thomas Edison, the Wright brothers, and Henry Heinz.

Cost: Museum: adults, $13.50; senior citizens 62 and over, $12.50; children 4–12, $8.50; children under 4, free. Greenfield Village: adults, $15; seniors, $14; children 4–12, $10; children under 4, free. Combination tickets: adults, $20; seniors, $19; children 4–12, $14. Imax: adults, $10; seniors and children 4–12, $8.50, children under 4, free.

Freebies: Drawings made by rubbing crayons over brass etchings.

Videos Shown: In the museum, video clips and features appear everywhere.

Reservations Needed: No, except for groups of 15 or more people.

Days and Hours: Both open Mon–Sat 9:00 AM–5:00 PM., Sun 12:00 PM–5:00 PM. Closed Thanksgiving and Christmas. Village building interiors closed January–March.

Plan to Stay: Full day for both museum and Village.

Minimum Age: None

Disabled Access: Yes

Group Requirements: Groups of 15 or more people should call 2 weeks in advance for reservations and group discounts. Educational programs for school groups: calling 2 weeks in advance.

Special Information: Special events throughout the year; call the above number for schedule.

Gift Shops: 5 stores offer books, souvenirs, crafts, toys, and logoed items related to exhibit themes. At least 4 cafés and cafeterias. Open same hours as museum.

Directions: From I-94, exit northbound on Oakwood Blvd. (Exit 206), then follow signs. From I-75, exit Southfield (M-39) north, drive 8 miles, then exit northbound on Oakwood Blvd. (Exit 4) and follow signs. From I-96, exit Southfield (M-39) south, drive 11 miles; exit northbound on Oakwood Blvd. (Exit 4) and follow signs.

Nearby Car-Related Attractions: The Walter P. Chrysler Museum tour (see page 202); Henry Ford Estate—Fair Lane tour (call 313-593-5590).

Hoegh Industries

317 Delta Avenue
Gladstone, MI 49837
(906) 428-2151
http://hoegh.abka.com

PET CASKETS

Hoegh Industries is the world's largest manufacturer of pet caskets, cremation urns, and memorial plaques. Dennis Hoegh began the business in 1966, after meeting a dog owner who could not find a casket worthy of his beloved sled dog. The company now produces more than 30,000 caskets annually in eight sizes and 22 styles, ranging from a hamster-sized 10-inch case to a 52-inch box fit for the grandest Great Dane. Molded of high-impact styrene plastic and equipped with a padded cloth interior, the caskets are made by a crew of eight workers.

Your tour starts near the computerized ovens; each one heats and softens four pieces of plastic simultaneously. Plastic sheets in different sizes—some pink, some blue, most buff—line the corridor waiting their turn in the ovens. Entering the oven as a rigid sheet clamped into a metal frame, the plastic undergoes a startling transformation. The rigid sheets become flexible, cloth-like membranes, vibrating and jiggling as they're pulled out of the oven. As a plastic sheet hovers in the air, a mold rises up to meet it. Vacuum pumps suck all the air from the space between plastic and mold, and a pet casket is formed.

Once cool, molded bottoms are lifted out of the frame so a worker can cut off the flashing and scrape the edges. One worker collects this excess plastic and feeds it into a waist-high grinder, creating tiny plastic pebbles. Beyond the grinder machine you can see where the polyurethane foam is added. The casket bottom sits in a wooden support, while a worker sprays a thin stream of superheated chemicals along the bottom inside edge. The worker must quickly insert, brace, and clamp down the interior wall, since the chemicals immediately begin to expand like exploding meringue. Confined by the interior and exterior casket walls, the foam expands within the cavity into a sturdy insulation, creating a double-walled eternal vessel. Home workers sew the cloth interiors for the caskets.

Step outside to admire the model pet cemetery. Most intriguing is a wall of remembrance plaques. A pet's photograph can be engraved onto a durable metal plaque, along with a name, dates, and a brief comment. Look for the plaques for Chuck the lizard, Fruit Loops the toucan, and the pet turkey who would walk on a leash, who died at age 13.

Cost: Free

Freebies: Postcards, brochures, rulers, pencils, pens, occasionally calendars.

Video Shown: Optional 17-minute video highlights the production process and shows a model pet cemetery. Video usually shown in winter or bad weather; also can be sent to groups, upon request.

Reservations Needed: No, however preferred for groups larger than 10 people. Individuals and families may want to call ahead (same day) to give the factory notice.

Days and Hours: Open Mon–Fri 8:00 AM–4:00 PM. Lunch break from 12:00 PM–12:30 PM. Closed holidays.

Plan to Stay: 30–45 minutes

Minimum Age: No minimum if accompanied by a parent. Children in groups should be 10 years old.

Disabled Access: Yes

Group Requirements: Groups larger than 10 people should call at least 1 day in advance.

Special Information: Umbrella tables are available for picnicking in the outdoor area.

Gift Shop: No

Directions: Take I-75 North. At the Mackinac Bridge, follow U.S. 2 West. When you reach Gladstone, turn left on Delta Ave. The factory is on the right.

Nearby Attractions: Iverson Snowshoes tour (call 906-452-6370); DeLoughary's Sugar Bush maple syrup and cream tour (call 906-466-2305); Fayette State Park; Seney National Wildlife Refuge; Hiawatha National Forest.

Kellogg's Cereal City USA

171 West Michigan Avenue
Battle Creek, MI 49017
(616) 962-6230
www.kelloggscerealcityusa.org

BREAKFAST CEREAL

Twelve years after Kellogg Company discontinued its popular plant tours in 1986, the Heritage Center Foundation opened Kellogg's Cereal City USA. Tony the Tiger welcomes you inside the 45,000-square-foot extravaganza, named by the Discovery Channel as the second best factory tour for kids on the planet, and into the history of breakfast cereal, which all started in Battle Creek, Michigan.

At the simulated Cereal Production Line, Jill and Mr. Grit describe how a grit—the heart of the corn—becomes a golden corn flake. The video tour replicates every facet of the production process.

In the simulated production line, the aroma of the grain at each processing step is reproduced. Every few minutes an overhead car full of kernels of corn and flavoring travels the rail and stops to release its contents into the cooking tank. See the corn pass through on metal screens as it dries. Learn that tempering equalizes the moisture in the grain and is therefore the single most important step in the process. A large, loud re-creation of a separator divides the tempered corn into single kernels before the pressing units roll them into flakes. You can even try some warm corn flakes right off the line.

Step into the Historical Timeline's old-time nickelodeon theater and listen as Duff, a local historian, brings to life the early history of Battle Creek, the Battle Creek Sanitarium, and the cereal boom. At the '50s and '60s exhibit, learn how the Kellogg Company developed Saturday morning television programming and reminisce about shows like *Arthur Godfrey, The Beverly Hillbillies, Rin Tin Tin,* and *The Monkees.*

In the Cereal City cinema, "A Bowl Full of Dreams," watch Bob Keeshan, better known as Captain Kangaroo, narrate a film on Kellogg Company marketing campaigns and reminisce during the vintage commercials that follow. Finish the day with a Froot Loops sundae at Sullivan's ice cream counter.

Cost: Adults, $7.95; seniors 65+, $6.50; children 3–12, $4.95; children under 2, free. Annual individual and family passes available.

Freebies: Single-serving box of cereal.

Videos Shown: The Bijou Theater shows a 15–20-minute video, "Best to You Revue," on the cereal industry, Kellogg brothers, and Kellogg characters. You feel as though you've been shrunk to the size of a salt shaker while viewing oversized spoons, bowls, and cereal boxes. Videos in each exhibit area.

Reservations Needed: No, except groups over 20 people.

Days and Hours: Open year-round. Times vary by season. Call ahead or check website.

Plan to Stay: 2.5 hours plus time for shopping and eating.

Minimum Age: None

Disabled Access: Yes

Group Requirements: Discounts for groups of 20 or more people. Call 2 weeks in advance. Educational group tours available.

Special Information: Battle Creek festivals include: The World's Largest Breakfast Table, the second Saturday in June; Team USA Hot Air Balloon Championship in July; and the International Festival of Lights, late November–December. Call the visitor center at (800) 397-2240 for information.

Gift Shop: Factory Store sells more than 500 items, including Ron Lee collectible Kellogg character figurines, clothing, kitchen items, and souvenirs. Become a "Famous Flake!" by getting your photo on a commemorative 18 oz. box of Kellogg's Corn Flakes. Also shop online at above website.

Directions: From I-94 take exit 98B to Downtown Battle Creek. Continue about 5 miles to the second light and turn left onto Michigan Ave. Kellogg's Cereal City USA is located about 4 blocks on the left.

Nearby Attractions: Binder Park Zoo; Full Blast Family Center; Kalamazoo Air Museum; Kalamazoo Valley Public Museum; Gilmore Car Museum.

Kilwin's Chocolates

355 North Division Road
Petoskey, MI 49770
(231) 347-3800
www.kilwins.com

Kilwin's

FUDGE, CHOCOLATES, AND ICE CREAM

Among its popular tourist attractions, Northern Michigan and Mackinac Island have an abundance of candy and fudge shops, with few more respected than Kilwin's. At most of its 44 retail stories in Michigan and Florida, you can watch them make creamy fudge. All of the store's chocolate candies and brittle are made and shipped from this small factory on the outskirts of Petoskey, the resort town where Don and Katy Kilwin opened their first shop in 1947 as a sideline to their bakery business.

What we like about tours of small to mid-size candy companies is how close you get to the action. In the production area you may see candies boxed, cream centers mixed, peanut brittle poured, chocolate blocks warmed in melters, liquid chocolate funneled into molds, or pecans marching through the enrobing machine. Making peanut brittle is at least a two-person operation that requires more muscle than you might expect. Two workers pick up a copper kettle and pour its dense, hot mixture of mostly peanuts, sugar, and butter onto a cold steel table. Once the brittle is partially cool, the rubber-gloved workers slice the 9-foot slabs into three pieces. They then hover over the pieces, flipping and stretching out each part so it's not too thick with peanuts.

To make the solid milk chocolate tool kits and ice-cream-cone suckers, liquid milk chocolate is poured into molds, which cool on metal trays in a nearby room. A worker then adds the decorations to create the ice-cream effect. Watch a worker gently dip the top part of the sucker into white chocolate. It's a real skill to get just the right amount of white chocolate onto the candy so that the cone-looking part stays dry. Sprinkling jimmies (sprinkles) on top completes this production feat.

Cost: Free

Freebies: Sample of one of their popular chocolates, such as the tuttle (caramel, pecans, and chocolate).

Video Shown: No

Reservations Needed: No, during summer season, except for groups over 10 people. Yes, for remainder of year.

Days and Hours: June, July, August (sometimes September): Mon–Thur 10:30 AM, 11:00 AM, 2:00 PM, and 2:30 PM. Tours only by special request other months of year. Closed holidays and unscheduled plant shutdowns.

Plan to Stay: 20 minutes for tour, plus time in retail store.

Minimum Age: None

Disabled Access: Yes

Group Requirements: Motorcoach tours can visit all year with 1 week's advance notice. Call (231) 347-4831.

Special Information: Production changes daily, so call ahead if you have favorites. Limited ice-cream production on tour.

Retail Store: Sells full line of 300 confectionery products, including fudge, tuttles, truffles, and sugar-free chocolate. Open year-round Mon–Fri 9:00 AM–5:00 PM. Closed holidays. Catalog and franchise information available at above number.

Directions: From the south, take I-75 North to Gaylord Exit 282. Turn left on Rt. 32 West to Rt. 131 North. Turn right to Petoskey. Turn left onto Division Rd. Kilwin's is immediately on left. From the Upper Peninsula, take I-75 South and exit at Indian River Exit 310. Turn right onto Rt. 68 West. Take Rt. 31 South to Petoskey. Turn left onto Division Rd. Kilwin's is on the right at top of hill.

Nearby Attractions: Amon Orchards tour (see page 193), Boyer Glassworks (call 231-526-6359); Petoskey's Gas Light District; Lake Michigan's beaches; Mackinac Island (self-proclaimed fudge capital of world), 35 miles away.

Lionel

26750 Twenty-Three Mile Road
Chesterfield, MI 48051-2493
(586) 949-4100, ext. 1211
www.lionel.com

MODEL TRAINS AND ACCESSORIES

Just about every American over 35 recognizes the Lionel brand name. Back in 1949, people of all ages used to stop by the company's showroom on East 26th Street in New York City to see the famous miniature railroad display. Store buyers and collectors would come to watch as small locomotives pulled freight cars through pretend towns and over imitation mountains. In 1964 the showroom closed its doors. But today, thanks to the hard work, dedication, and volunteer efforts of the employees at Lionel's Michigan headquarters, you can once again enjoy seeing Lionel trains in action and learning the story behind the company that started in 1900.

Your visit begins with a video about Lionel, its heritage, and its manufacturing. Then you enter the showroom. Lights rise slowly over the 14-by-40-foot railroad display, illuminating a fascinating arrangement of trains, tracks, and scenery that will remind kids (and kids at heart) why they love collecting model trains.

This classic display features multiple levels of tracks with many different rail lines. Buttons around the display allow visitors to operate accessories themselves, including trains on a smaller layout just for young kids.

The design of the main display's bottom level includes elements from the original 1949 layout, such as the underground passenger platform and the yard and roundhouse area. The next level reveals more modern-era trains, including more freight cars and diesel- or steam-powered engines. The top, overhead level uses the American Flyer line, which, although different in size from the other model trains, fits in perfectly with the rest of the display.

While watching the chugging, rumbling trains, don't forget to enjoy the impressive scenery of a small, semi-real city. The workers who created this extraordinary display thought of every detail, right down to the park statues, rail yard workers, and store signs. Also notice the company timeline on the wall, illustrating more than 100 years of model train history. It includes rare and unique prototype train models, artifacts, historic ads, and photos.

Cost: Free

Freebies: Souvenir pin and product catalog

Video Shown: 10-minute video on company history and manufacturing process.

Reservations Needed: Yes

Days and Hours: Wed and Thur 10:00 AM, 3:00 PM, and 4:00 PM; Fri 10:00 AM, 1:30 PM, and 2:30 PM; Sat 9:00 AM, 10:00 AM, 11:00 AM, and 12:00 PM. Times change seasonally, so call for recording. Closed holidays.

Plan to Stay: 1 hour for video and tour of visitors center, plus time for gift shop.

Minimum Age: None

Disabled Access: Yes

Group Requirements: For groups of 20 or more people, additional visitors center tour times may be available. Maximum group size is 60 people.

Special Information: Information available about Railroader Club membership.

Gift Shop: Sells the Visitors Center Boxcar (available only at this store), other trains, starter sets, train accessories, and logoed items including T-shirts, signs, and clocks. Discount for Railroader Club members. Open Tue–Fri 1:30 PM–4:30 PM, Sat 10:00 AM–12:30 PM. (Call ext. 1443 for seasonal hours.)

Directions: From I-94, take Exit 243 (Twenty-Three Mile Rd./New Baltimore exit). Veer left at exit if coming from Detroit and stay on Twenty-Three Mile Rd. Turn left at 3rd light onto Russell Schmidt Rd. (You'll see "Lionel" sign.) Turn right into visitor parking.

Nearby Attractions: The Walter P. Chrysler Museum tour (see page 202); Morley Candy factory tour (groups only, call 586-468-4300); Yates Cider Mill; Anchor Bay Aquarium; Military Air Museum; Detroit's attractions about 30 minutes away.

Simplicity Pattern

901 Wayne Street
Niles, MI 49121
(616) 683-4100
www.simplicity.com

SEWING PATTERNS

Simplicity Pattern Company has been synonymous with sewing since 1927. The Niles facility, built in 1931 and expanded in the 1970s, covers 750,000 square feet. Retiree-led tours are generally for groups. During September open houses, the public can take tours.

Over the noise of the paper mill, a supervisor or worker describes the production of the tissue paper upon which one of Simplicity's 800-plus current patterns will be printed. Simplicity recycles paper from various sources by mixing it with water and then running the pulp through a papermaking machine that steams the water out. The paper is wound around a cardboard core. The resulting tissue-paper roll, weighing in excess of 4,000 pounds, is then cut into various widths for use on the pattern presses.

In the prepress area, another supervisor or worker explains that the corporate office in New York sends clear, big rolls of film for patterns, instruction sheets, and envelopes. A step-and-repeat process makes envelope-printing plates. High-intensity lights burn an image or pattern into an aluminum plate.

Your guide takes you to the envelope manufacturing area to watch a Miehle press print envelopes on a sheet of 48-by-55-inch flat stock paper using black, blue, red, and yellow inks. A guillotine blade cuts the envelopes, stacked in quantities of 2,450 sheets, into 21 rectangular sections. A die-cutter trims them to the exact envelope shape.

The Stevens press prints, cuts, and folds instruction sheets from a continuous roll of newsprint that is over 48,000 feet long. Clauberg presses print the pattern, requiring 2 to 30 pieces depending on the level of detail, on tissue paper received from the mill area, then cut and fold the tissue into individual patterns.

In the pattern finishing area, machines fold the envelopes and glue the sides together. The inserting machine utilizes a separate hopper for the finished envelopes, instruction sheets, and pattern tissue. Vacuum pulls a pattern tissue and an instruction sheet in between belts where they are electronically timed to come together. Vacuum also pulls the envelope into a Ferris wheel pocket where air is used to open the envelope. The pattern and instruction sheet drop into the envelope and the flap tucks in. A small hydraulic press compresses and bundles pattern packets for shipping worldwide.

Cost: Free
Freebies: Pattern and booklet
Video Shown: No
Reservations Needed: Yes, groups over 12 people should call 1 month in advance. Individuals occasionally can join group tour. By reservation, open houses in September are best opportunities for individuals to tour facility.
Days and Hours: Mon–Thur 10:00 AM. Closed holidays. No tours December 15–January 15.
Plan to Stay: 1.5–2 hours
Minimum Age: 12
Disabled Access: Yes, although a lot of territory is covered.
Group Requirements: Groups over 12 people should call 1 month in advance. No maximum group size.
Special Information: Sometimes strong smells in the mill. September open houses coincide with National Sewing Month.
Gift Shop: No
Directions: From I-80/90 in Indiana, take IN-933 North (becomes M-51 in Michigan). In Niles, turn right onto Main St. Turn left onto 13th St. Turn left onto Wayne St. Turn right onto 12th St. Simplicity is on the left. From U.S. 31, take U.S. 12 East to M-51 North. Follow above directions.
Nearby Attractions: Four Flags Museum; Fernwood Botanical Gardens. Attractions in Elkart, IN, including Walter Piano tour (see page 147), are 45 minutes away.

Walter P. Chrysler Museum

One Chrysler Drive
Auburn Hills, MI 48326
(888) 456-1924
www.chryslerheritage.com

WALTER P CHRYSLER MUSEUM

AUTOMOBILES

When you step into this 55,000-square-foot polished red granite and black glass modern building, modeled after the adjacent DaimlerChrysler Technology Center, the futuristic 35-foot tower in the two-story atrium catches your eye. Three spectacular Chrysler cars rest on platforms jutting out from the tower. As you stare up at the vehicles—including the striking red 1989 Viper prototype and a 1962 Chrysler experimental turbine car—you are startled by the fact that the tower slowly rotates, allowing you to view each of the cars without moving an inch. Next on your heritage tour, get a feel for the early days of the company's history when you step into a realistic diorama of Walter P. Chrysler's 1908 workshop, where Chrysler stands by his toolbox, examining his handiwork.

On the first and second floors, cars are displayed chronologically. Each is accompanied by advertisements and photos from the period with informative labels that allow you to compare the price of the car to the price of bread that year, or contrast each model with the first Chrysler. With 75 vehicles exhibited, you'll examine everything from the 1924 Chrysler, a sleek black touring car prototype, to the big-engine muscle cars of the 1960s and '70s. Did you know that Chrysler was the first to develop an aerodynamically efficient design? Compare the aerodynamic Airflow to its squarish predecessors: you'll notice that most cars were vertically designed before the futuristic 1934 Airflow introduced the sloping windshield and front, and the tapering tail.

Nowadays Chrysler cars are designed by a platform design team that comprises representatives from all parts of the company, from marketing to engineering. Each person gives input into a model's design. Now you can be part of this team at one of the interactive exhibits. Select the shape, color, equipment, and other features of the model. You get feedback on your design via the cover of a virtual auto magazine: if the cover reads "Smash Hit" your model design was a success; the headline "What Went Wrong?" means it's back to the drawing board. Either way, you can print out your design and take it with you.

Cost: Adults, $6; children 6–12, $3; seniors, $3; DaimlerChrysler retirees and children under 6, free.

Freebies: No

Video Shown: Three 10-minute films: "Inside DCTC," shows how DaimlerChrysler develops cars; "The Early Years," on Walter P. Chrysler and the early history of the company; and "Speed and Power," on Mopar muscle cars. Plus interactive video stations on specialized topics.

Reservations Needed: No

Days and Hours: Tue–Sat 10:00 AM–6:00 PM, Sun 12:00 PM–6:00 PM. Closed Easter, July 4th, the day before Thanksgiving, Thanksgiving, Christmas Eve, Christmas, New Year's Eve, and New Year's.

Plan to Stay: 1.5 hours for tour and films, plus time for store.

Minimum Age: None

Disabled Access: Yes. Most videos are closed-captioned.

Group Requirements: Groups of 15 or more should call 24 hours in advance. Group rate $3 per person.

Gift Shop: Sells world's greatest collection of Chrysler Heritage Brand items, such as apparel, books, magazines, and a wide selection of die-cast Chrysler-related model automobiles.

Directions: From I-75, take the Chrysler Dr. exit. Turn right at the first light onto Chrysler Dr. Proceed on Chrysler Dr. for 1.3 miles. Follow the signs to the museum parking lot. From M-59, take the Squirrel Rd. exit. Proceed north on Squirrel Rd. to Featherstone Rd. Turn right onto Chrysler Dr. and follow the signs to the museum parking lot.

Nearby Attractions: Chelsea Milling, Henry Ford Museum, and Lionel tours (see pages 194, 196, and 200); Marvin's Marvelous Mechanical Museum (248-626-5020); Meadowbrook Hall Museum, a house built in 1929 by the widow of one of the Dodge brothers; Great Lakes Crossing mall.

Wolverine World Wide

465 Wolverine Street
Rockford, MI 49341
(616) 866-5514
www.wolverineworldwide.com

**HUSH PUPPIES SHOES AND
WOLVERINE WORK BOOTS**

HUSH PUPPIES®

Few American shoe brands are better known than Hush Puppies. With foreign competition accounting for 80 percent of the men's and women's shoes sold in the U.S.A., it's a good feeling to visit Wolverine World Wide, which supplies millions of pairs of shoes annually from 11 domestic factories. The company was founded in 1883, but Hush Puppies weren't introduced until 1957. They were named after hush puppies, the fried corn-dough balls used by farmers to quiet their barking dogs. Extremely popular in the 1950s and '60s, these casual suede shoes were recently revamped and revitalized in Day-Glo shades of green, purple, and pink.

One of the best aspects of this tour is that you walk right onto the busy factory floor, close to all the action. You hear the stammering and hissing of the different machines, and smell the glue used in cement construction. Shoes in progress chug along the line like sitting ducks in a shooting gallery. At each station, a worker takes them off the line and performs the next step in the process of building a pair of shoes.

Trays with two pairs of upside-down ivory-colored lasts (the plastic molds around which the shoes are constructed) move down the four-row production line. An insole is tacked onto each last. The flange machine heats a counter (thermoplastic insert that reinforces the heel) to 450° to soften it before it is shaped around an ice-cold mold. When the worker steps on the foot pedal of the toe-laster machine, pinchers stretch the pigskin leather upper around the toe.

One worker places the sides and heels into the automatic machine that seals and flips them over into the heat-set oven. Another worker oversees the machine that automatically applies cement to the bottom of the shoe. While these steps may not appear very automated, they replace the previous elbow, wrist, and paintbrush system of applying the glue. Further down the assembly line, a worker matches already-sewn uppers with soles, places them upside down in the sole-lay

machine, and clamps it shut under 550 pounds of pressure. Once the shoes are cleaned, several workers pop out the lasts, insert shoelaces, and inspect and box the shoes to be shipped to 80 countries worldwide.

Cost: Free

Freebies: No

Video Shown: No

Reservations Needed: Yes, 2–3 weeks in advance.

Days and Hours: Tour availability has become very limited, please call ahead. Closed holidays, 1–2 weeks around Christmas and New Year's, and usually first 2 weeks of July.

Plan to Stay: 30 minutes for a tour of either the Hush Puppies or Wolverine work boot plants, plus time in the nearby outlet store.

Minimum Age: 18

Disabled Access: Yes

Group Requirements: Not interested in standard bus groups.

Special Information: High noise level; can be hot; strong smells.

Outlet Store: Nearby retail outlet sells small stuffed Hush Puppies animals and apparel with company logos, and has big clearance area for discontinued styles. Small historical display shows antique miniature shoes, oversized Hush Puppies statue, and early company photographs. Open Mon–Fri 9:00 AM–8:00 PM, Sat 9:00 AM–6:00 PM, and Sun 12:00 PM–5:00 PM. Closed holidays. Call (616) 866-9100 for more details.

Directions: From Grand Rapids, take I-131 North to 10 Mile Rd. exit. Turn right onto 10 Mile Rd. Turn left onto Main St. In 1 mile, turn left onto Wolverine St. Plant is 1 block ahead on left.

Nearby Attractions: Alticor household and personal-care products visitor center (see page 192); Squire Street Square; Rockford Area Historical Museum (open May–October, limited hours); Grand Rapids attractions, including Gerald R. Ford Museum, about 15 miles away.

3M Birthplace Museum

203 Waterfront Drive
Two Harbors, MN 55616
(218) 834-4898 (also answer for B&B)
www.lakecountyhistoricalsociety.org

Every great company has humble beginnings. The famous 3M company began in this small, green, square building in 1902, with the original goal of mining corundum. The five businessmen who founded Minnesota Mining and Manufacturing signed the articles of incorporation here, and it served as the original office and headquarters. In 1991 the Lake Country Historical Society purchased the building (phone number above is for the LCHS) and renovated it, and it now showcases both the past and present of 3M. If you like corporate history, as well as the nearby lighthouses, original big old trains just down the street, and other Lake Superior attractions, then this museum is worth a visit.

The building, which pays tribute to the birthplace of 3M, its early struggles, and its current successes, has different exhibit areas packed neatly into the small space. The displays include a re-creation of the company's first office, with original artifacts and documents, a history of the company in photos, a "lab" area showcasing 3M's commitment to research and development and product diversification—featuring a hologram wall that displays old and new products— and a few hands-on technology applications.

Sandpaper is a product that fueled 3M's original growth. The museum pays tribute to this product with a jumbo roll of sandpaper, before it is cut into smaller pieces, and a colorful sandpaper mosaic. Another well-known company product, Scotch Tape (invented in 1925), is featured in a timeline that shows how this product has evolved. The story behind Post-its, a big winner for 3M, is also revealed.

Innovation is at the heart of 3M. You may be surprised by all the products you see that you might not have known the company had developed. These diverse products on display range from the synthetic rubber used in astronauts' space boots to labels used to tag monarch butterflies. When the company says that one out of four people in the world use a 3M product every day, this museum brings to life the reality of this statement.

Cost: Adults, $2.50; age 9–17, $1; children under 8, free.

Freebies: No

Video Shown: Some of the displays have accompanying interactive kiosk with videos.

Reservations Needed: No, except for groups over 10.

Days and Hours: Open late May–October only. Mon–Fri 12:30 PM–5:00 PM, Sat 9:00 AM–5:00 PM, and Sun 10:00 AM–3:00 PM. Closed November–April. Guided tours given by request, otherwise self-guided.

Plan to Stay: 30 minutes

Minimum Age: None

Disabled Access: Entire museum display area on first floor.

Group Requirements: Groups over 10 must call a few days in advance. Groups can request guided tour. Bus groups can combine tour with visits to other area historical attractions.

Special Information: The local Two Harbors lighthouse offers bed and breakfast accommodations with reservations through the number above.

Gift Shop: Located down the street at the Lake County Historical Society Depot Museum, 520 South Ave. Sells variety of Lake Superior, lighthouse, and other local gifts and souvenirs. Mon–Sat 9:00 AM–5:00 PM and Sun 10:00 AM–3:00 PM.

Directions: From Duluth area, take Rt. 35 North to Hwy. 61 North into Two Harbors. Turn right onto Waterfront Dr. Building at corner of 2nd Ave.

Nearby Attractions: Lake County Historical Society Depot Museum, which features in front of the building the wood-burning Three Spot, the first engine train used in the area, and a Mallet, one of the world's most powerful steam locomotives; Two Harbors lighthouse; and Gooseberry Falls State Park. Duluth attractions include Stora Enso paper tour (see page 211), S.S. *William A. Irvin* cargo boat tour, and Great Lakes Aquarium about 30 minutes south. The Split Rock Lighthouse is 30 minutes north.

Arctic Cat

601 Brooks Avenue South
Thief River Falls, MN 56701
(218) 681-8558 / (800) 279-0179
www.arcticcat.com

ARCTIC CAT®

**SNOWMOBILES AND
ALL-TERRAIN VEHICLES**

The Arctic Cat snowmobile has often set the standards for the North American snowmobile industry. In 1962 the Arctic Cat was the first front-engine snowmobile ever produced in this country; in the early 1970s it was the top-selling snowmobile. Tough times for the industry and the U.S. economy in the late 1970s halted production. During the early 1980s the "Boys from Thief River" restructured the company; now, once again, it manufactures award-winning racing and touring snowmobiles. The company also produces Arctic Cat ATVs, which now account for at least a third of their business.

Depending on the month, your tour shows what's involved in making the Arctic Cat snowmobiles or ATVs (although not in sequential assembly order) and numerous subassembly steps. The first thing you see is a line hanging with parts that have been through the powder paint shed, on their way to an oven that bakes the paint into the metal parts. Throughout the tour, you often see parts on conveyors moving in and out of cleaning, priming, and painting booths.

Robots and workers weld together the chassis. Workers put the parts in the jig, a frame that holds them together during assembly. With sparks flying, a robotic arm moves from spot to spot welding the chassis. Down the line, workers bolt some parts and robotic arms weld others to the chassis, including the skis.

The foam cushion seats start as liquid chemicals, with the mix determining the desired plushness. This mixture is squirted into preheated molds and, within a few minutes, out pops a cushion. After the vinyl is stretched around it, the seat is ready for the silk-screened logo. In the main assembly area, each chassis moves down the line with a parts cage that contains all its pieces; workers pull out parts as needed. When they test the engine, you think about the fun of riding the machine on the nearby Thief River.

Cost: Free

Freebies: May give out balloons, bumper stickers, decals, product literature.

Video Shown: No

Reservations Needed: No, except for groups larger than 10 people.

Days and Hours: Mon–Fri 1:00 PM. Closed holidays and usually the week of July 4th. Special arrangements possible for other tour times. Occasional shutdowns when waiting for parts, so call ahead about the day you want to visit.

Plan to Stay: 45 minutes for tour, plus time for gift counter.

Minimum Age: None

Disabled Access: Yes

Group Requirements: 1 week's advance notice for groups larger than 25 people so that additional tour guides will be available.

Special Information: No photography.

Gift Shop: Sells logoed items, including T-shirts, caps, mugs, and scale-model Arctic Cats and trucks. Open Mon–Fri 1:00 PM–4:00 PM or after tour, if earlier. Catalog with full line of clothes and accessories available at above number. Information about Cat's Pride, the world's largest organized snowmobile owners club, available from (800) 279-8558 (800-461-1987 in Canada).

Directions: From Hwy. 2, take Hwy. 59 North through center of Thief River Falls. Turn left onto Brooks Ave. (Bowling Center on the corner). Arctic Cat is on your right. From Hwy. 32, turn left at Brooks Ave.

Nearby Attractions: Christian Brothers hockey stick factory tour in Warroad (see page 207); Polaris snowmobile tour (see page 209) in Roseau; Red Lake River; Pioneer Park; Agassiz Wildlife Reserve.

Blandin Paper

115 S.W. First Street
Grand Rapids, MN 55744
(218) 327-6682
www.upm-kymmene.com

PAPER

UPM

Since pioneer days, northern Minnesota has depended on the forest products industry. Today sophisticated machinery replaces late-1800s logging camps. Blandin Paper specializes in making coated paper for such magazines as *Time, Forbes,* and *Sports Illustrated,* and Spiegel catalogs.

The huge, new No. 6 paper machine—375 feet long, 35 feet wide, and 60 feet high—fills your view as the guided tour begins. It produces 4,500 feet of paper per minute with only a few people operating it. The pulp, 99.3 percent water, flows in at the machine's "wet end." Paper is initially formed on a wire screen; suction, gravity, and presses decrease the water content. The paper then enters the dryer, where it takes a roller-coaster ride through 40 heated cylinders that reduce the moisture content to less than 3 percent. Look for the electronic hole-detectors that find flaws in the paper as it runs around the cylinders. The machine marks the edge of the web with blue dye where it senses holes, which are patched when the paper is rewound.

The 24-ton rolls (45 miles of paper) then go through the coater machine for a thin layer of coating formula, consisting mostly of clay. The running web is immersed in a coating bath, and excess is scraped off with blades. Airfoils, steam-heated dryer cans, and gas-fired infrared burners dry the coating on one side, then the other side goes through the same processes.

Next, the roll goes through the supercalenders to receive its glossy shine. The paper spins rapidly between vertical stacks of fiber and metal rolls to polish the coated surface. The space between the rollers determines the amount of gloss. Winder machines cut the jumbo rolls and rewind them into smaller-diameter rolls, though each still averages the size of two men. This process produces up to 1,400 tons per day.

Cost: Free

Freebies: Brochure illustrating the paper-making process and a seedling.

Video Shown: 8-minute video about the company, its commitment to quality, the foresting of trees, and the mill.

Reservations Needed: No, except for groups larger than 10 people.

Days and Hours: Tours from the first Monday in June through the Friday before Labor Day. Wed–Fri 10:00 AM–4:00 PM. Last tour at 3:00 PM. Closed July 4th. Call (218) 327-6302 about tours at other times of the year.

Plan to Stay: 45 minutes for video and tour.

Minimum Age: 12

Disabled Access: Mostly accessible, although a few steps lead to the control room and tour involves a lot of walking.

Group Requirements: Groups larger than 10 people need advance notice; call (218) 327-6302.

Special Information: No photography. No open-toed shoes allowed. Temperature in mill is very warm, and machines are loud. The chemically produced kraft pulp needed for paper production is not manufactured at the mill, so there's none of the sour odor that bothers some people at paper mills.

Gift Shop: No

Directions: From the intersection of Hwy. 169 and Hwy. 2 (at Central School), go 1 block south on Pokegama Ave. Turn right at 3rd St. N.W. Tour information center is 1 block ahead on the left.

Nearby Attractions: Forest History Center; Gunn Park; Judy Garland Museum. Other Minnesota paper industry tours include Stora Enso (see page 211) and Boise Cascade in International Falls (call 218-285-5011).

Christian Brothers

Highway 11
Warroad, MN 56763
(800) 346-5055
www.hockeystick.com

III CHRISTIAN
America's Stick

HOCKEY STICKS

Who is better equipped to make hockey sticks than a former hockey star and Olympic Gold medalist, or two? Brothers Roger and Billy Christian combined their hockey acumen—honed during the 1960 (U.S.A.'s first Olympic gold in hockey) and 1964 Winter Olympics—and their carpentry skills to found Christian Brothers in 1964 with Hal Bakke. Today the company is one of the world's best-known hockey-stick manufacturers, only two of which are in the U.S.A. Your tour guide explains some of the company history.

Particularly during winter, you can follow along as workers create sticks for National Hockey League (NHL) professional hockey players and silk-screen the famous players' names onto the shafts. Whether the sticks are for a schoolyard team or the NHL, they start as ash and elm blanks, cut to the general length and width of a handle. A grader, using a specially designed bending machine, tests the wood for strength and integrity. (In fact, all of the factory's machines were custom-designed for the Christians; several are one-of-a-kind inventions.) Workers then add a block of wood to the handles, slice the block, and glue the blade form together. A carousel-like machine heats the sticks two by two, setting the glue and bonding blade and handle together. Each time the machine turns, workers add two more sticks.

After going through a sander machine so powerful that its operation shakes the ground around it, the sticks enter the steamer for softening. Workers hand-press the curve into the blades. Each NHL pro who uses a Christian stick has sent the factory a sample stick with a blade curve that lies on the ice just the way he likes. New sticks are made with the exact dimensions of this template.

Christian Brothers' best playmaker is a machine that forces a fiberglass-like tube over the blade and cuts it off, edge-free, with air scissors. After another hand smoothing and an epoxy bath, 1,200 sticks per hour pass through the silk-screener, which affixes the company's name (and, for custom orders, the player's name) to three sides of each handle.

Cost: Free

Freebies: Posters, brochures, sometimes miniature hockey sticks (drink stirrers).

Video Shown: No

Reservations Needed: No, except for groups over 40 people.

Days and Hours: Mon–Thur 10:30 AM and 3:00 PM. Closed holidays, week between Christmas and New Year's.

Plan to Stay: 20 minutes

Minimum Age: None

Disabled Access: Yes. A few aisles may be too narrow for wheelchairs.

Group Requirements: Groups larger than 40 people should call 1 week ahead. Large groups will be split into groups of 15.

Special Information: No photography. Factory filled with sawdust. Winter visits are the best time for seeing NHL pros' custom orders. Plant busiest with retail stock orders April–June. Company also manufactures protective equipment for hockey and in-line skating but at other plants.

Gift Shop: Christian Brother's hockey sticks and athletic wear are available at retail stores in Warroad.

Directions: From the east, take Hwy. 11 West to Warroad, which lies 6 miles south of the U.S./Canada border. Christian Brothers sits prominently on your left. From I-29, take Hwy. 11 East to Warroad.

Nearby Attractions: Polaris snowmobile tour (see page 209) in Roseau; Arctic Cat snowmobile tour in Thief River Falls (see page 205); Marvin Windows tour (call 218-386-1430); Warroad Library & Heritage Center; Lake of the Woods Recreational Area.

Faribo Woolen Mills

1819 N.W. Second Avenue
Faribault, MN 55021
(507) 334-1644
www.faribowool.com

WOOL BLANKETS AND THROWS

Long ago, 800 central-U.S. mills made woolen blankets. Today only three carry on, the largest being Faribo Woolen Mills. Faribo produces more than half the wool blankets made in the United States. It is one of the few "fully vertical" mills left (a soup-to-nuts mill, starting with raw wool and ending with a finished blanket). Although automated machines help with the weaving, the process is still labor-intensive. Workers handle fibers, comb batting, spin yarn, and finish and bind woven pieces—human touches that machines cannot replicate.

In the wool stock area, huge bales of raw wool await your inspection. You may catch the scent of wet wool. Touch Faribo blankets' three component fibers: domestic wool, merino wool, and acrylic. Each fiber feels softer than the next. Scouring and blending operations clean the wool stock before the dyeing vats color it. In carding, the fibers are combed into huge fluffy sheets of batting. Workers card the wool into ends of roving. Your tour guide may let you feel how soft and weak the roving is, easily torn by the gentlest tug. Then try tearing the spun yarn apart—you'll hurt your hand before you succeed!

In the weaving room, elephantine computerized looms transform the yarns into blankets. Shuttles fly from side to side on the looms so rapidly that the human eye cannot follow. Horizontal "packing bars" move back and forth to pack in the just-woven yarns. Faribo's 26 automated looms can create over 2,000 items a day. Watch the careful inspectors at the burling station, where each woven piece is backlit and inspected, inch by inch, for snags, flaws, and finished quality, then measured and sized.

The final stop is the finishing area. Massive presses pull the blankets and throws, squaring them, truing the edges, and preparing them for the sewers. Using yarn as thread, the sewers add silken tapes to bind blankets' edges or overstitch the edges with sergers. These laborious personal touches continue as the final products are carefully prepared for shipment worldwide.

Cost: Free

Freebies: Logoed souvenir

Video Shown: 15-minute video runs continuously in the retail store. Features a mother sheep describing the blanket-making process to her lamb.

Reservations Needed: Yes

Days and Hours: Mon–Fri 10:00 AM and 2:00 PM. Closed New Year's, Easter, last week in June, and the first 2 weeks in July, Thanksgiving weekend, and 2 weeks around Christmas. Plan to arrive 15 minutes before tour.

Plan to Stay: 40 minutes for tour, plus time for retail store.

Minimum Age: None, for families; 12, for groups.

Disabled Access: Only to the first floor of the factory (can see everything except the first and last production steps).

Group Requirements: Groups larger than 10 people should make reservations at least 1 or 2 weeks in advance. Large groups will be split into groups of 12–14.

Special Information: Automated looms in the weaving area are loud, and portions of the tour can be hot during summer.

Retail Store: Sells Faribo first-quality blankets and throws as well as discontinued lines and irregulars, various manufacturers' all-season clothing for men, women, and children, and one-of-a-kind antique bobbins. Open Mon–Sat 9:00 AM–5:30 PM, Sun 12:00 PM–4:00 PM (until 5:00 PM in summer). Closed holidays. Catalog available from (800) 448-WOOL.

Directions: From Minneapolis, take Rt. 35 South to Faribault. Then follow billboards directing you to factory and store.

Nearby Attractions: Rice County Historical Museum; Alexander Faribault Park; Cannon River Dam.

Polaris

301 5th Avenue, S.W.
Roseau, MN 56751
(218) 463-2312
www.polarisindustries.com

SNOWMOBILES, ALL-TERRAIN VEHICLES, PERSONAL WATERCRAFT

Polaris is the world's largest manufacturer of snowmobiles and also a major producer of all-terrain vehicles (ATVs) and personal watercraft, as well as the new Victory motorcycle. Its resurgence is somewhat similar to that of Harley-Davidson (see page 218), which regained competitiveness after its management buyout from AMF. Polaris was a division of Textron, a multinational conglomerate, before its own management buyout in 1981. At that low point in Polaris' history, the company had about 100 employees and the Roseau plant was shut down. Now it has more than 2,500 workers and over $1 billion in annual sales.

Even with the company's big investment in labor-saving technology and robotics, this huge plant in rural northwestern Minnesota, 10 miles from the Canadian border, has become one of the biggest employers in the region. The tour lets you see firsthand how Polaris assembles snowmobiles and ATVs (all the parts are made in other Polaris plants in Osceola, Wisconsin; Spirit Lake, Iowa; and a Hudson, Wisconsin, engine plant jointly owned with Fuji Heavy Industries). You can walk between the two snowmobile and two ATV lines, observing the subassembly, preassembly, final assembly, and testing areas of the line.

In the snowmobile subassembly area, workers and robots put the parts together and prepare the skis and frame. Most of the metal parts are E-coated, submerged in black liquid paint primer, for corrosion resistance, then sprayed with a powder-coat finish. Preassembly adds the chain case, suspension, and tracks. Heading over to the final assembly area, notice the finished hoods hanging from the monorail on their way from the plastics area. A visitor favorite is watching the motor being hoisted, lowered, and quickly fastened into place.

After all the final parts, tubes, and wires are connected, finishing touches such as the reflector tape and Polaris nameplate are added. Finally, the snowmobile or ATV travels to the test shacks that sit near the ends of each line. The workers give them a little gas, start the engines, and test all the parts and critical features.

After watching production in action, walk through the Experience Center and see Polaris' product lines from the very beginning to present day.

Cost: Free

Freebies: Small packet with decals, stickers, and pin.

Video Shown: Yes, theater shows DVD movies featuring athletes using various Polaris products.

Reservations Needed: No, except for groups over 15 people.

Days and Hours: Mon–Fri 4:00 PM. Open holidays and week between Christmas and New Year's.

Plan to Stay: 2 hours

Minimum Age: None, but quite noisy for young children.

Disabled Access: Yes

Group Requirements: Headphones available only to groups smaller than 10 people. Large groups should call at least 2 days in advance. No maximum group size, but ratio is 10 people per guide.

Special Information: Noisy; groups receive headphones or earplugs depending on number of people on tour. No photography. Tours also available of the Polaris Spirit Lake, IA, plant that manufactures personal watercraft, ATVs, and Victory motorcycles (call 712-336-6702).

Gift Shop: Sells snowmobiles, logoed clothing, and other accessories. Located in Experience Center.

Directions: From the west, take Hwy. 11 East. At the first traffic light in Roseau, turn right at Hwy. 89 (also 5th Ave., SW). Polaris will be on your right. From the east, take Hwy. 11 West and turn left at Hwy. 89 in Roseau. Polaris will be on your right. From the north, take Hwy. 310, which becomes Hwy. 89 in Roseau; plant is a few blocks ahead on right.

Nearby Attractions: Christian Brothers hockey stick and Arctic Cat snowmobile tours (see pages 207 and 205); Marvin Windows tour (call 218-386-4222); Roseau River Wildlife Area; Lake of the Woods; Roseau City Park and Museum.

SPAM Museum

1101 North Main Street
Austin, MN 55912
(800) 588-7726
www.spam.com

Processed meat never had it so good—the SPAM Museum features SPAM and Hormel Foods milestones from the 1930s to the present day. The museum is 16,500 square feet, with 16 exhibit areas where you discover the invention of SPAM luncheon meat, how SPAM is canned, and other Hormel Foods history.

In the lobby, notice the large photomosaic on the wall—it appears to be photographs of the 1937 and 2001 SPAM cans, but actually consists of more than 1,200 historic photographs. On the wall opposite the photomosaic, more than 3,390 SPAM cans are assembled around a globe, depicting SPAM's global presence.

Walk up to a huge, unlabeled SPAM can. Before the entrance, pause at the 1920s telephone switch board, slip on a headset, and listen to "party line" conversations concerning Hormel Foods-related stories, such as employee Cy Thompson's embezzlement of over $1 million in 1921. When you've had your fill of corporate gossip, enter the can and watch a puppet play called "SPAM Is BORN," all about the invention of SPAM and how it got its name. As you exit the can, notice that it now features the SPAM label, a testament that you truly witnessed the product's birth.

Move on to the Marketing exhibit, which features the KSPaM radio station, the Hormel Foods Girls Theater, Hormel Foods print advertising, and Hormel Foods television commercials. Listen as the KSPaM booth broadcasts remote, live radio from around the world and 1940s radio commercials. Next door at the Hormel Foods Girls Theater, you hear what it was like to be a Hormel Foods Girl from three former Girls.

Next, get ready to see how SPAM is canned. You won't be able to enter an actual production plant, but you can watch a video of the entire process. Afterwards, you can practice canning SPAM yourself at an interactive area where you stuff the "meat," a pliable pink beanbag, into a can.

After you attach the lid and cook the can in a mock oven, you slap on a label and pack the can into a cardboard carton. At the push of a button, a screen displays your production time as well as the number of cans produced at the Austin plant, so you can have an idea of the rate of speed necessary during production.

Like SPAM luncheon meat, the new museum features a little bit of everything and teaches the public why SPAM's appeal both as a food item and a souvenir generator just might last as long as the product's shelf life!

Cost: Free

Freebies: No

Videos Shown: 18-minute film dedicated to people who love SPAM and various video presentations that include interviews, commercials, chef demonstrations, and production.

Reservations Needed: No, except for guided tours.

Days and Hours: Mon–Sat 10:00 AM–5:00 PM, Sun 12:00 PM–4:00 PM. Closed Thanksgiving, Christmas, and Easter.

Plan to Stay: 1.5 hours, plus time for SPAM store.

Minimum Age: None

Disabled Access: Yes

Group Requirements: Guided group tours for museum and SPAM café can be arranged through the Austin Convention and Visitors Bureau (800-444-5713, ext. 300).

SPAM Retail Store: Sells logoed T-shirts, hats, and other merchandise. Open same hours as museum. Hormel Foods gift catalog available (call 800-588-7726).

Directions: From I-90, take Exit 178B. Bear to the right and follow signs.

Nearby SPAM/Hormel Foods Attractions: Jay C. Hormel Foods Nature Center (hiking, canoe rentals, skiing); SPAM Merchandise Shop; George A. Hormel Foods Home; annual SPAM Jam.

Stora Enso North America

Duluth Paper Mill
100 North Central Avenue
Duluth, MN 55807
(218) 628-5100 / (218) 722-6024 (summer reservations)
www.storaenso.com/na

PAPER

After waiting in the entrance area of the mill tower, you walk upstairs past individual offices. In this massive brown complex, the only ribbon of windows is along the walkway to the offices. From a video and your tour guide's introduction, you learn that Stora Enso, domiciled in Helsinki, Finland, is one of the leading forest products manufacturers in the world. Each year, the Duluth mill can manufacture 240,000 tons of supercalendered paper used for four-color printing in magazines, newspaper advertising inserts, and catalogs. Users include *Better Homes and Gardens* magazine, and J.C. Penney and Target catalogs and newspaper inserts. Approximately 45 truckloads of logs arrive each day, allowing this mill to be the largest producer of this high-quality, glossy paper in the United States.

Your guide explains the blue paper machine model, just a portion of the $1.5 million scale model paper mill. Wearing headphones and safety glasses, follow your tour guide downstairs to the "wet end" where pulp slurry, 99 percent water and 1 percent pulp, jets between two wire screens. In the press section, water is squeezed out of the paper sheet. Acting as a sponge, felt absorbs 40 percent of the water.

Walk alongside the long steel Northern Star train-like paper machine. The paper travels at about 53 miles per hour from the wet end to the dry end of the machine. It takes approximately 45 minutes to make a 24-foot-wide, 9-foot-diameter reel of paper weighing 30 tons. In the dryer section, the paper weaves between 53 steam-heated drying canisters. Number 53 canister, at 275°, sucks out the last bit of the moisture.

The remote-controlled, yellow overhead crane system transports the paper rolls to the massive supercalender machines. Here, the paper weaves in and out of 12 calendar rolls. Steam, heat, and pressure smooth the surface of the paper. The supercalender polishes the paper to give its shine.

Cranes transport the huge supercalendered paper reels to the winders. The paper runs under the floor in a single sheet. Slitters, resembling saw blades, cut the reels into smaller rolls based on customer orders. After the paper is rewound onto a cardboard core, each roll slowly glides by on the in-ground, orange conveyor system to an elevator that delivers it downstairs to the rollwrap and shipping area.

Cost: Free

Freebies: Brochures about forestry

Video Shown: 6.5-minute video provides company information and shows paper-making process.

Reservations Needed: Yes, pick up tour tickets at Duluth Visitor Information Office on Harbor Drive by the Vista Boats. Groups of 10 or more people, see below.

Days and Hours: Public tours Memorial Day–Labor Day only. Mon, Wed, Fri 9:00 AM, 10:30 AM, 1:00 PM, 3:00 PM. Closed July 4th and occasional maintenance shutdowns.

Plan to Stay: 1 hour

Minimum Age: 10

Disabled Access: Yes

Group Requirements: Maximum group size is 25 people. Group tours also offered during the summer months by appointment. Call (218) 628-5312.

Special Information: No cameras, high heels, or open-toed shoes permitted. Expect warm temperatures and to walk approximately .5 mile. Call (218) 628-5312 at least 48 hours in advance if need special accommodations. Paper mill tour in Wisconsin Rapids, WI (see page 363). Stora Enso also gives recycling tour in Wisconsin Rapids (call 715-422-3789).

Gift Shop: No

Directions: From Duluth, take I-35 South to Central Ave. exit. Turn left at bottom of ramp. Parking lot will be on your left. Tour begins at the mill's entrance tower. From Minneapolis/St. Paul, take I-35 North. Take Central Ave. exit in West Duluth. Turn right at bottom of ramp. Follow above directions.

Nearby Attractions: 3M Museum tour (see page 204); Lake Superior Gardens Center; S.S. *William A. Irvin* Ore Boat floating museum; Great Lakes Aquarium; North Shore Scenic Drive; Munger Trail.

Peavey Electronics

Peavey Visitors Center and Museum
4886 Peavey Drive
Meridian, MS 39305
(601) 486-1460
www.peavey.com

MUSIC AMPLIFIERS AND ELECTRIC GUITARS

LISTEN TO THIS™

Hartley Peavey, founder of the world's largest music and sound equipment manufacturer, grew up in this eastern Mississippi railroad town. As a teenager in 1965, he constructed his first guitar amp in his parents' basement. Today his company employs 2,000 workers in Mississippi, Alabama, and England, and markets amplifiers, guitars, keyboards, and sound systems in 103 countries. Every form of music—from punk to polka, from country to classical—has been touched by Hartley Peavey's products.

Though its factories are not open for tours, the company celebrates its history—research and development and manufacturing—at the Visitors Center. In its first life, the building was a U.S. Department of Agriculture research facility, specializing in sugar-producing crops. Peavey lovingly restored the exterior to its original Federalist style. But the interior is now strongly postmodern, with splashes of chrome, teal, yellow, and black—colors found on many Peavey's products.

Called the Peavey World Tour, the center presents exhibits and video programs and has become a mecca for musicians of all types who trust their stylings only to equipment bearing the Peavey logo. The first-floor galleries provide a personal view of the company's founder. Look for a 1901 photograph of Hartley Peavey's grandfather and the original lightning-bolt logo drawn on notebook paper. One room re-creates the basement where Hartley made his first amplifier, complete with tools and old issues of *Popular Mechanics* and *Popular Science*. Upstairs galleries chronicle the company's growth from this basement workshop to 19 facilities.

Follow the yellow banister downstairs to today's "world of Peavey" and make your own music on some of the world's most sophisticated and coveted sound systems. Test the full Peavey line, including electric guitars, electronic keyboards, amplifiers, and complex studio mixing equipment. Peavey

Electronics designed this hands-on space for visitors of all ages. Several guitars are mounted on the floor, giving toddlers a chance to pluck away at the taut steel strings.

Cost: Free

Freebies: Copy of *Monitor,* the company magazine, and guitar picks.

Videos Shown: 18-minute video on company history and goals; 7-minute video on media matrix computer sound system.

Reservations Needed: Yes

Days and Hours: Closed temporarily for remodeling. Call ahead for appointment.

Plan to Stay: 1 hour for museum and playing instruments, plus time in gift shop.

Minimum Age: None

Disabled Access: 5 steps to first-floor historical exhibits. Staircase down to video theater and hands-on equipment display.

Group Requirements: Groups of 50 or more need reservations. Call (601) 484-1460.

Special Information: Set up for self-guided tours, but guided visits can be arranged.

Gift Shop: Gear shop sells logoed items from key chains, T-shirts, and coffee mugs to $100-plus satin tour jackets. Open center hours. Catalog available from (800) 752-7896 or above website.

Directions: From Jackson, take I-20 East through Meridian as it changes to I-20/59. Take Exit 157B for Hwy. 45 North. Take the first exit (for Sonny Montgomery Industrial Park). At bottom of ramp, turn right onto Marion Russel Rd. After you cross railroad track (about 1 mile), turn right into the center's parking lot.

Nearby Attractions: The Jimmie Rodgers Museum (Meridian is the birthplace of Jimmie Rodgers, the father of country music); Annual Jimmie Rodgers Country Music Festival; Grand Opera House of Mississippi (tours of "The Lady" are available; call 601-693-LADY); Merrehope Mansion; Dunn's Falls Water Park; the Dentzel Carousel!.

Viking Range

111 Front Street
Greenwood, MS 38930
(662) 455-1200
www.vikingrange.com

VIKING RANGE CORPORATION

COOKING EQUIPMENT

What might you find in the homes of many rich and famous people, on the set of *Friends,* or in the White House? A Viking Range, manufactured in the heart of the Mississippi Delta. On the tour, it's hard to determine which is more surprising—the vast array of products, colors, and sizes available or the fact that such a big company manufactures the majority of its parts right at this local, small-town plant. In 1983 founder Fred E. Carl Jr. developed the first commercial-type range for home use when he wanted a heavy-duty range for his new house. The cooktops, ovens, ventilation products, dishwashers, and waste disposers the company added to its line in recent years can be found in the homes of celebrities and professional cooks alike.

In the receiving area, forklifts heave large quantities of raw materials such as sheet steel and wiring into the factory. The Vipros turret punch press, one of the company's newest, most powerful, and most impressive machines, loads the sheet metal mechanically onto the press table. Silver shavings drop soundlessly to the floor as the machine's sharp prongs drill screw holes. Intricate software allows the Vipros to seem as if it runs on its own. Once the Vipros makes enough of one part, it automatically makes the required number of another part. Hydraulics keeps this giant press running more quietly than you would expect.

After the drilling stage, other machines fold the shiny metal with ease. You'll recognize the oven bases as the shaped pieces move down the assembly line. Because they're built from the bottom up, each oven part fits into the next: the sides into the base, the windows into the front door panel, the cut-outs for the burners and knobs into the stove top.

The expertise required by the workers themselves, who wire the ovens for their features, is as impressive as the machines. Reaching into the cavity of a nearly completed oven, the workers intricately connect wires of different shapes and sizes. With the insides in place, workers add the exteriors. Since they are custom-made, the assembled appliances vary from one to the next. In vibrant shades such as stainless steel, cobalt, eggplant, and lemonade, the ovens resemble sculptured works of art inspiring enough to make you want to fire up the burner and cook something!

Cost: Free
Freebies: No
Video Shown: 1-hour video, "Range Project," by request.
Reservations Needed: Yes. Call 1 week in advance.
Days and Hours: Second and third Thursday of the month, 1:00 PM–4:00 PM. Closed holidays. No production during the weeks of Christmas and July 4th.
Plan to Stay: 45 minutes
Minimum Age: 18
Disabled Access: Yes
Group Requirements: Groups over 10 people should call 2 weeks in advance. Maximum group size is 20 people.
Special Information: No photography
Gift Shop: No
Directions: From Memphis, take I-55 South to Grenada. Take Hwy. 7 South to Greenwood, and turn right on Hwy. 82. Take Main St. exit. Bear right onto Main St. and turn right on Market St. Bear left at traffic light onto Viking Rd. Factory is on left in about 1 mile. From Jackson, take I-55 North to Winona. Take Hwy. 82 West to Greenwood, and take Main St. exit. Bear right onto Main St. Turn right on Market St. and bear left at traffic light onto Viking Rd. Factory is on your left in about 1 mile.
Nearby Attractions: Historic Cotton Row District of Greenwood; Mississippi Delta; Cottonlandia Museum; Florewood Plantation State Park.

Anheuser-Busch

12th and Lynch Streets
St. Louis, MO 63118
(314) 577-2626
www.budweisertours.com

BUDWEISER BEER

The tour of the St. Louis brewery (founded 1852), located next to the Anheuser-Busch World Headquarters, puts a face on the world's largest brewer. As the tour guide leads you from the tour center to the Budweiser Clydesdale paddock and stable, lager cellar, Brew House, Lyon's Schoolhouse, and Bevo packaging plant, a sense of history and the smell of hops surround you.

The Budweiser Clydesdales tradition began in 1933 when August A. Busch Jr. presented his father with the first team of Clydesdales to celebrate the repeal of Prohibition. Today the gentle giants make more than 500 appearances annually with their bright red beer wagon. See where the beer is actually made in the historic six-story Brew House. Built in 1891, the Brew House is a tour favorite with its clock tower, ornate wrought-iron railings, and hop vine chandeliers from the 1904 World's Fair. The Lyon School House, built in 1868, is the oldest structure in the Anheuser-Busch complex. It served as the company's headquarters from 1907 until 1981.

Visit the beechwood aging and fermentation cellars and Bevo Packaging Plant. Anheuser-Busch is the only major brewer that still uses the famous beechwood aging process to age and naturally carbonate its beers. In the lager cellar, stainless steel lager tanks are lined with a layer of beechwood chips, providing additional surface area to attract and retain yeast. Beechwood aging is part of the secondary fermentation. Each of the lager tanks holds enough beer to fill approximately 200,000 six packs.

The Bevo Packaging Plant was constructed in 1917 and stands eight stories tall and houses 27 acres of floor space and over 25 miles of conveyor belts. You will see fast-paced action as bottles and cans are filled. Whimsical fox sculptures are perched on each corner of the building, all munching on chicken legs and holding a mug of Bevo, a non-alcohol cereal-based beverage that Anheuser-Busch produced during the Prohibition era.

Cost: Free

Freebies: For guests 21 or older, beer samples, soda, and snacks.

Videos Shown: Brew House: 7-minute multimedia presentation tells story of brewing process. Bevo Packaging Plant: 3-minute video tells how bottles and cans are filled with the world's favorite brews.

Reservations Needed: No, except for groups of 15 or more.

Days and Hours: September–May: Mon–Sat 9:00 AM–4:00 PM, Sun 11:30 AM–4:00 PM. June–August: Mon–Sat 9:00 AM–5:00 PM, Sun 11:30 AM–5:00 PM. Call for holiday hours.

Plan to Stay: 1.25 hours for tour, plus additional time for gift shop.

Minimum Age: Under age 18 must be accompanied by adult.

Disabled Access: Yes

Group Requirements: Groups larger than 15 should call 1 week ahead. No maximum group size.

Special Information: Anheuser-Busch also gives tours in Merrimack, NH; Jacksonville, FL; Fort Collins, CO; and Fairfield, CA. For general information on all tours, call (314) 577-2626 or see above website. See page 225 for feature on Merrimack, NH, tour.

Gift Shop: BUD WORLD sells clothing, hats, glassware, beach gear, framed pictures and Budweiser and other Anheuser-Busch logoed items. Open same hours as tour.

Directions: Take I-55 to Arsenal St. exit. Follow signs to Tour Center (on 12th and Lynch Sts.).

Nearby Attractions: St. Louis area attractions include Boeing Museum (see page 215), Grant's Farm, St. Louis Zoo, Gateway Arch, Union Station, Botanical Gardens, St. Louis Science Center, and National Bowling Hall of Fame and Museum. Tour Center front desk has information sheet with directions and hours for nearby attractions.

Boeing

James S. McDonnell Prologue Room
McDonnell Boulevard and Airport Road, Building 100
St. Louis, MO 63134
(314) 232-5421
www.boeing.com/prologueroom

AIRPLANES, MISSILES, AND SPACECRAFT

The Boeing Company in St. Louis calls its company museum the Prologue Room, after William Shakespeare's comment that "what is past is prologue." To Boeing, past achievements are not history but the beginning of each new technical advancement. As you stand on the steps overlooking the museum room, you'll realize Boeing's part in aviation's past, present, and future. Models of commercial planes, missiles, spacecraft, and fighter jets of all sizes and colors seem to be everywhere.

Boeing aircraft built in St. Louis downed every enemy fighter shot down during Operation Desert Storm. With this track record, the display of military planes will pique your curiosity. A wide, oval glass case shows the evolution of Boeing military planes from aviation's golden age in the 1930s to the most current technology. In the center of the oval are one-seventh-scale models of the F/A-18 Hornet, F-15 Eagle, and AV-8B Harrier combat fighters, and the AH-64 Apache helicopter. A glass oval in the back of the museum has a similar display for the generations of the company's commercial aircraft, from the DC-1 (the first successful commercial passenger plane) to the Boeing 777.

Although the museum does not show how Boeing builds its products, displays do provide a complete history of its aviation products. Aviation buffs can study aircraft and fighter plane lineage charts and display cases depicting Boeing's numerous firsts, such as building the first planes to land at the North and South Poles. The center of the museum contains full-size engineering mock-ups of the Mercury and Gemini spacecraft that carried America's early astronauts into space. In the era before computer-aided design, engineers had to build these full-scale models to test the practicality of their hand-drawn designs.

Notice the aviation-art gallery, which features oil paintings by several artists whose work is also displayed in the National Air and Space Museum in Washington, D.C.

You leave understanding how since 1916 Boeing products have affected wars' outcomes, made worldwide travel possible, and helped explore the universe.

Cost: Free

Freebies: No

Video Shown: Optional video in gallery area runs for 2 hours. Consists of shorter videos presenting company history, building of jet fighters, and Boeing planes in flight accompanied by music. Can watch 5 minutes of it or the entire video.

Reservations Needed: Yes

Days and Hours: June–August only, except for school programs. Mon–Sat 9:00 AM–4:00 PM. Closed July 4th.

Plan to Stay: 45 minutes for museum, plus time for video.

Minimum Age: None, but 6 years old recommended to appreciate displays.

Disabled Access: Yes

Group Requirements: Groups larger than 20 should call ahead to arrange a guided tour. During school year, programs available for 4th, 5th, and 6th graders, with maximum group size of 40.

Special Information: The Boeing Company in Everett, Washington also gives tours (see page 341).

Retail Store: Located 5 minutes away at 5900 N. Lindbergh Blvd. (314-895-7019), corner of Lindbergh and McDonnell Blvd. Sells aviation posters, photos, and models, plus Boeing-logoed items including T-shirts, caps, jackets, mugs, and key chains. Open Tue–Fri 10:00 AM–6:00 PM and Sat 10:00 AM–3:00 PM year-round.

Directions: From downtown St. Louis, take I-70 West to I-170 North. Turn left onto Airport Rd. Enter through Boeing Executive Offices gate 2 blocks ahead on the left. Look for large black glass building.

Nearby Attractions: St. Louis' downtown attractions, including Anheuser-Busch (Budweiser) brewery tour (see page 214), are 20 minutes away.

Chrysler

1050 Dodge Drive
Fenton, MO 63026
(636) 343-3360 / (636) 349-4040
www.daimlerchrysler.com

MINIVANS AND PICKUP TRUCKS

Since Chrysler introduced the minivan to the market in 1984, its minivans have earned many awards and the number-one position in sales. The Dodge Caravan was *Motor Trend* magazine's 1996 "Car of the Year." Since 1987, Chrysler's St. Louis Assembly Plant II has built the long-wheelbase minivan. In 1992 this factory became the first North American assembly plant to successfully initiate a three-shift schedule, operating three seven-hour production shifts five days a week and two nine-hour shifts on Saturday. (Plant I builds the Dodge Ram pickup truck.)

Building the skeleton frame in the metal shop starts the production process. Parts arrive by train and truck from the stamping plant. Fenders, doors, and roofs are attached on the assembly line to create the gray frame. Chrysler is proud of its extensive use of robotics. The plant underwent a $578 million renovation to launch a new generation of minivans in January 1995 and increased the number of robots to more than 400. Look for the robotic arm that uses large suction cups to pick up the roof panel and, with workers' guidance, place it precisely. The minivan then heads through a tunnel that automatically welds the roof joints.

Sparks fly when the entire frame heads down a row of robots, each with an assigned place to spot-weld the body frame. Once the frame is assembled and its dimensions tested, it receives a primer-coat bath. The entire frame is immersed in 73,600 gallons of paint (resembling a whale as it's lowered into the vat), then moved through the rinsers. By negatively charging the body and positively charging the paint, the primer bakes into the frame's smallest corners.

From the paint area, the shiny frame travels through the assembly lines that bring the minivans to life. Some lines install the interior electric systems; others, the engine and axles; and ergonomic robot arms help with steps such as seat and windshield installation. Ask the tour guide to explain the Joint UAW/Chrysler Product Quality Improvement Partnership and point out worker suggestions that have been successfully implemented. Notice the overhead signs at different assembly stations that say "Critical Buzz, Squeak, and Rattle Operation." At the tour's end, peek into the test booth where the minivan "travels" (on rollers) up to 65 miles per hour, while a worker analyzes the electrical systems, transmission, and engine.

Cost: Free

Freebies: Brochure with production pictures and statistics.

Video Shown: No

Reservations Needed: Yes, call 2 weeks in advance. Company prefers that individuals and families join a scheduled group tour.

Days and Hours: Mon–Fri based on tour guides' schedules. Closed holidays, Christmas week, and one week in summer, usually at the end of July.

Plan to Stay: 1.5 hours for tour

Minimum Age: 13

Disabled Access: Wheelchairs and walkers not allowed on factory floor. Special arrangements can be made for physically challenged if a cart is available.

Group Requirements: Groups of 10 or more get a plant retiree as a guide. No maximum group size with 2 week's advance notice.

Special Information: You'll walk at least 1 mile on tour. No photography.

Gift Shop: The Ram Store sells logoed apparel and mugs. Hours vary.

Directions: From I-44 West, take Exit 275 onto North Highway Dr., which runs parallel to I-44. Turn right before overpass onto Marez Ln. Plant entrance is last driveway on left.

Nearby Attractions: St. Louis attractions, including Anheuser-Busch (Budweiser) brewery tour (see page 214), about 25 minutes away. Limited tours at Ford plant in Hazelwood (call 314-731-6365).

Hallmark Visitors Center

Crown Center Complex
2501 McGee
Kansas City, MO 64141
(816) 274-5672
www.hallmarkvisitorscenter.com

Hallmark's slogan, "When You Care Enough to Send the Very Best," applies to its visitors center. You will walk through 14 exhibits that tell the story of the world's largest greeting-card company. See a 40-foot historical timeline and learn how Hallmark started when a man named Joyce C. Hall began selling picture postcards from his fourth-floor room at the Kansas City YMCA. The timeline has memorabilia from Hallmark's history intertwined with world events.

During the six-minute multimedia film presentation on the essence of creativity, listen and watch Hallmark artists explain how the creative process works. Did you know that Winston Churchill was an artist? One of his paintings hangs in the visitors center along with other originals by Norman Rockwell, Grandma Moses, and Saul Steinberg.

Another area is devoted to the craft and technology of card production. You can watch a technician make engraving dies—the metal plates that raise the three-dimensional designs on paper—or cutting dies, which work like steel cookie cutters to make unusually shaped cards. Two presses churn out the cards you might purchase 10 months from now. At the touch of a button, you can watch a machine turn ribbon into a miniature star bow and take one home with you.

View clips from Hallmark commercials and Hallmark Hall of Fame television dramas. Costumes, props, and a real Emmy award are on display. Hallmark employees' affection for company founder Hall shows in a display of Christmas trees that employees gave Hall from 1966 to 1982. Each tree's decorations reflect a theme of importance to the company during that year. To experience Hallmark's international appeal (cards sell in more than 100 countries), rub the sheep dog's nose on the handrail of one of the cards to hear birthday greetings in 12 languages. One of the newest exhibits features the Hallmark Keepsake Ornament collection. You can see some of the most popular Keepsake Ornaments, like the Starship Enterprise, the 1957 Corvette, Peanuts characters, and sports heroes.

Cost: Free

Freebies: Postcard and a bow

Videos Shown: Short videos on topics related to the exhibits are shown throughout the visitors center.

Reservations Needed: No, except for guided tours for groups of 10 or more.

Days and Hours: Mon–Fri 9:00 AM–5:00 PM and Sat 9:30 AM–4:30 PM. Closed Thanksgiving, Christmas Eve, Christmas, and New Year's. Also usually closed the first 2–3 weeks in January for yearly renovations.

Plan to Stay: About 1 hour, but can spend any amount of time for self-guided tour.

Minimum Age: None

Disabled Access: Yes. Call (816) 274-3613 for information.

Group Requirements: Escorted tours available for groups of 10 or more people. Groups should make reservations 2 to 4 weeks in advance. School/youth groups need 1 adult for every 7 children. Call (816) 274-3613.

Special Information: Hallmark Cards tour in Topeka, KS (see page 151). Some Hallmark Production Centers in other cities conduct tours by advance reservation; check with visitors center for information.

Gift Shop: Not in visitors center. The closest of the 47,000 independent retail outlets is in Crown Center.

Directions: Located in Crown Center Complex, about 1 mile south of downtown Kansas City. Take Grand Ave. to 25th St. and park in the Crown Center Parking Garage. Proceed to third level of Crown Center shops. The visitors center is located outside Halls department store.

Nearby Attractions: Ford Motor plant tour (call 816-459-1356); Kaleidoscope children's interactive exhibit (call 816-274-8301); *Arabia* Steamboat Museum; Toy and Miniature Museum.

See color photos, page 25.

Harley-Davidson Motor Company

11401 North Congress
Kansas City, MO 64153
(816) 270-8488 / (888) 875-2883
www.co.platte.mo.us/harleytourinfo.htm

MOTORCYCLES

The Harley-Davidson motorcycle has come a long way from the 10-by-15-foot shed where, a century ago, the Davidson brothers and William S. Harley handcrafted their first motorcycle. Now thousands of Harley motorcycles are built each year, including the V-Rod, Sportster, and Dyna Glide models made in Kansas City.

As you approach the plant, note the hundreds of employees' Harleys parked out front. In the tour center, notice models of bikes made here, including the second bike ever produced at this plant, covered with employee signatures.

On the plant tour you'll see the fabrication area, where a four-foot roll of steel goes into a huge press. The press lowers and a fender, a gas tank, or an oil tank appears. Next, a laser cuts off the excess steel from the fender and cuts holes in it for wiring. In the polish area, a robot arm with a buffer wheel buffs the fender.

On the frame line, see machines bend stainless steel tubes into the shape of a frame. Then, behind a big orange weld curtain, watch workers weld pieces of frame together. The frames hang off an ergonomic carrier that the welders can adjust to a comfortable position. The finished frames pass through quality check and are taken to a paint line. At the wheel line watch a worker lacing (putting spokes into) a rim. The wheel is tightened, a tire is mounted on it, and it joins the assembly line.

Every Sportster put together on the assembly line has to be done in two minutes or less. But if there is ever a question of quality, Harley-Davidson employees can stop the line. The assembly line moves at four miles an hour, and a new piece is added at each station, from the kickstand to the oil tank. At one station, a hook lifts the power train (engine and transmission). Two workers lower it into the frame and tighten the bolts. It must be a perfect fit, with parts fitting properly into each of the holes in the frame.

After the last assembly line station, the assembled Sportster is ready for a roll test. It's taken into a compartment with two steel wheels on the floor. A tester rides the bike to check that everything functions, from the engine to the horn. Finally, the motorcycle is wrapped up in plastic and crated by a robot. Next, you see the line where the V-Rod motorcycle is assembled and, finally, the area where Revolution engines (engines used in the V-Rod) are built.

Cost: Free

Freebies: Copy of *Enthusiast* magazine

Video Shown: 15-minute film on the history of Harley-Davidson Motor Company.

Reservations Needed: Yes

Days and Hours: Mon–Fri 8:00–11:30 AM. Closed New Year's Eve, New Year's, Memorial Day, Labor Day, Thanksgiving, day after Thanksgiving, week between Christmas and New Year's, and the month of July.

Plan to Stay: 1.5 hours for tour, including film.

Minimum Age: 12

Disabled Access: Yes

Group Requirements: Groups of 10 or more call 1 day ahead

Special Information: No plant tours during month of July and other periods, due to special production needs. Call ahead for schedule. Protective eyewear (provided) and shoes that completely enclose the feet required for plant tour. No photographic equipment allowed in plant. York, PA, plant tour (see page 285) and Milwaukee, WI, engine and transmission tour (call 414-535-3666) available.

Gift Counter: Sells T-shirts, hats, coffee mugs, and other logoed items. Open same hours as tour.

Directions: Take I-29 to the 112th St. Exit. Go east on 112th St. to end of street. Turn left on Congress. Harley is the first drive on the right.

Nearby Attractions: Ford tour (call 816-459-1356); Union Station.

Purina Farms

Nestlé Purina PetCare Company
200 Checkerboard Drive
Gray Summit, MO 63039
(314) 982-3232
www.purina.com

PET FOOD

From its 1894 beginnings as a horse- and mule-feed store to its position today as the world's largest producer of pet food, Nestlé Purina PetCare Company remains focused on animal care and nutrition. Located on the grounds of the oldest and largest animal nutrition center in the world, Purina Farms wants visitors to gain a greater appreciation and understanding of their pets. While the Visitor Center has a few displays about Nestlé Purina PetCare and its products, the complex resembles a family-oriented petting zoo more than a promotion-laden company museum.

A timeline traces the company's 100-year-plus history and product development. You can see classic Purina commercials for products such as Dog Chow, the nation's leading dry dog food. A hands-on exhibit lets you experience the sights and sounds of a pet food factory. Interactive displays teach the basics of pet nutrition and the remarkable sensory and physical abilities of domestic animals. Scent boxes help you experience how a dog smells things, while other displays show the differences between your vision and that of dogs and cats.

The Farm Animal Barn contains sheep, cows, horses, hogs, rabbits, and turkeys. Roll up your sleeves here to romp in the hayloft, pull a rope to determine your "horsepower," pet piglets, or milk a cow. Inside the Pet Center, home for different breeds of dogs, cats, puppies, and kittens, you'll see cats lounging and climbing on a five-story Victorian mansion, complete with special windowsills, stairways, and mantelpieces. Petting windows and outdoor areas for dogs let you cuddle and play with them. The Pet Center also features videos and newsletters with tips on pet care, and next door are two areas for canine competition. You leave having learned more about your favorite pets and about Nestlé Purina PetCare's efforts to keep them well fed.

Cost: Free, except for some special events.

Freebies: Brochures on pet care and the company's products are available by request from front desk.

Videos Shown: 2 videos shown in a converted 48-foot grain barn: 1 provides a brief history of Ralston Purina; the 2nd captures the special role animals play in human lives. Short videos shown at selected exhibits.

Reservations Needed: Yes, although they can usually accommodate a large number of visitors.

Days and Hours: Open mid-March–mid-November only. Spring and fall: Wed–Fri 9:30 AM–1:00 PM, Sat–Sun 9:30 AM–3:00 PM. Summer: Tue–Sun 9:30 AM–3:30 PM. Closed holidays.

Plan to Stay: 2 hours for displays in main building, videos, Farm Animal Barn, animal demonstrations, and Pet Center, plus additional time for wagon rides, dog shows, children's play areas, and gift shop.

Minimum Age: None

Disabled Access: Yes

Group Requirements: No maximum group size. Requests 1 week's advance notice for large groups.

Special Information: Special events scheduled throughout the year include "Easter Village," "Country Time," and the very popular "Haunted Hayloft." Hosts more than 60 canine events yearly: All Breed Shows, National Specialties, Herding Trials, Agility Trials, and Lure Coursing, among others. Call for schedule.

Gift Shop: Sells animal-decorated items including mugs, cards, pencils, and banks; also logoed clothes and hats. Open same hours as visitors center.

Directions: From St. Louis, take I-44 West. Pass Six Flags Over Mid-America. Take the Gray Summit exit and turn right onto Hwy. 100. Turn left on Country Road MM. Follow signs to Purina Farms.

Nearby Attractions: Shaws Arboretum; Six Flags Over Mid-America.

Kool-Aid

Hastings Museum of Natural and Cultural History
1330 North Burlington Avenue
Hastings, NE 68901
(402) 461-2399 / (800) 508-4629
www.hastingsmuseum.org

FRUIT DRINKS

Many of today's business leaders may remember starting down the road to financial success setting up a front-yard stand selling Kool-Aid for a nickel. Since 1927, Kool-Aid has provided young children with fun, fruity relief from summer's thirst, creating some of childhood's fondest memories along the way. In the summer of 2002, the city of Hastings celebrated the 75-year-old birthday of both Kool-Aid and the Hastings Museum by opening "Kool-Aid Discover the Dream." Located downstairs in the Hastings Museum, this 3,300-square-foot exhibit pays homage to Edwin Perkins, the inventor of Kool-Aid, the official soft drink of Nebraska.

As you enter the museum, the Kool-Aid kid draws you downstairs to the exhibit. You first walk into DM Perkins General Store, Edwin's father's store. In this turn-of-the-20th-century storefront, you can play store clerk selling merchandise behind the counter. In the next room, a display shows the birth of an entrepreneur. Starting as a kitchen chemist, Edwin invented many products before he hit upon Kool-Aid.

Next door, the Hastings Room shows the introduction of Kool-Aid. Print up a Kool-Aid packet, measure out the powder, and hand-fill up a packet like it was done 75 years ago. In 1931, the Perkins family moved to Chicago. Underneath your feet, follow the flowing, undulating ropes of fiber optics creating a river of green, orange, purple, and red Kool-Aid.

The Chicago Room shows other products Kool-Aid produces, such as bubble gum, ice cream mixes, and soda. Notice the display of premiums including the plastic pitcher produced in the summer of 1963 when the packages were redesigned to show the smiling pitcher. Try selling Kool-Aid at a 1940s stand offering "Kool-Aid 5¢ a glass." In a small theater, watch five-year segments of commercials spanning 40 years. Generation Xers remember 1970s commercials when the ground would rumble as the jovial Kool-Aid man would break through the nearest wall shouting "Oh yeah!" and provide pitchers of thirst-quenching Kool-Aid.

The General Foods room (Perkins sold his company to General Foods in 1953, which ultimately merged with Kraft in 1988) features an original red, 50-pound fiberglass Kool-Aid man costume. In a diorama, learn how the ad agency art director's son's traced patterns on a frosty windowpane led to the designer's doodles, which became the Pitcher Guy, the friendly, smiling Kool-Aid pitcher inviting young children to quench their thirst.

You leave this exhibit with a true understanding of the history behind Kool-Aid and Perkins' business prowess. And, of course, you'll want to find the nearest ice-cube-filled glass of your favorite Kool-Aid flavor—especially if you visit in the summer.

Cost: Museum: Adults, $5; seniors, $4.50; children 3–12, $3.

Freebies: No

Videos Shown: Various DVD interactives show Perkin's early business years and nostalgic TV commercials.

Reservations Needed: No

Days and Hours: Mon 9:00 AM–5:00 PM, Tue–Sat 9:00 AM–8:00 PM, Sun 10:00 AM–8:00 PM. Closed Thanksgiving and Christmas.

Plan to Stay: 30 minutes in exhibit, 3 hours in entire museum including Super Screen Theatre, Planetarium, and the Museum Store.

Minimum Age: None

Disabled Access: Yes

Group Requirements: Groups over 15 people should call 2 weeks in advance for discount.

Special Information: During second weekend in August, Kool-Aid Days in various locations in Hastings features entertainment, children's activities, and Kool-Aid man.

Gift Shop: Sells Kool-Aid logoed memorabilia. Open similar hours to museum.

Directions: From I-80, take Rt. 281 South (becomes Burlington Ave.) Turn left on 14th St. Turn right into parking lot.

Nearby Attractions: Stuhr Museum of Prairie Pioneer in Grand Island; Pioneer Village in Minden; The Arch and MONA (Museum of Nebraska Art) 1 hour away in Kearney.

Weaver's

1600 Center Park Road
Lincoln, NE 68512
(402) 423-6625
www.weaversnacks.com

SNACK FOOD

Since 1932 Weaver's Potato Chips has used homegrown potatoes to produce some of the most popular potato chips in its area of the Midwest. It started on Ed Weaver Sr.'s stove with a scrub brush, knife, and kettle. More than 90 percent of Weaver's potato-chip ingredients come straight from Nebraska. Every day 100,000 pounds of these potatoes are trucked into the factory, where they are dumped into large bins and sent on a short trip through the plant, then a longer trip to stores in 14 states as potato chips.

Unlike most snack-food companies, Weaver's currently allows you to view the process up close, sometimes only five feet away from the machines, instead of seeing it from an observation deck or overhead walkway. You can watch as the whole, uncooked potatoes jump into the washers for a hot bath and scrub-down (they always scrub, rather than peel, the potatoes to retain the vitamins). The clean potatoes are then sent to the slicers, where razor-sharp blades quickly slice the potatoes into pieces one one-hundredth of an inch thin. A spiked roller pierces little holes in the chips to prevent blistering while they cook. The slices move to the 35-foot fryer and cook until crispy. You and the cooked chips then move ahead to the packaging room.

The potato chips enter a very modern, high-tech piece of chip-making machinery: an optic sorter. Although you will not be able to see this particular process up close, your tour guide will explain it to you. The optic sorter takes photographs of the chips as they move past the camera's lens. Dark brown, green, and other imperfect potato chips are actually blown off the conveyor by air jets. The rest of the chips move on to the packaging room. Chips are gently conveyed to the sophisticated packaging equipment that automatically weighs, fills, and seals bags. Workers inspect the bags and then hand-pack them into cardboard boxes for storage in the warehouse. Delivery trucks pick them up and deliver them to stores all across the Midwest. Be sure to taste your free sample on the way out.

Cost: Free

Freebies: Half-ounce bag of potato chips

Video Shown: No

Reservations Needed: Yes, call at least 1 week in advance.

Days and Hours: Mon–Wed 10:00 AM–11:00 AM and 11:30 AM–1:30 PM. Closed holidays.

Plan to Stay: 30–40 minutes

Minimum Age: None

Disabled Access: No

Group Requirements: Groups larger than 20 people will be split into smaller groups.

Special Information: Wear comfortable shoes, since there is a lot of standing and walking on the factory floor.

Gift Shop: No

Directions: From I-80, exit at Hwy. 2 in Lincoln. Follow Hwy. 2 West to Rt. 77 South. Take second left into the industrial park. Plant is red, white, and blue building on the left.

Nearby Attractions: Sugar Plum Candies tour (call 402-420-1900); Christian Record Services Braille Printer tour (call 402-488-0981); State Capitol; University of Nebraska; Chet Ager Nature Walk; Star City Shores; Pioneer Park; Folsom Children's Zoo; Children's Museum.

Ethel M Chocolates

Two Cactus Garden Drive
Henderson, NV 89014
(702) 433-2500
www.ethelm.com

CHOCOLATES

Only in Las Vegas would a candy factory identify its product lines with flashing red neon signs. Thousands of people come here daily as a diversion from Las Vegas' casinos. Ethel M began in 1981 with one shop and now has around 20 in three states. A tour of the facility not only shows you how premium chocolates are made, but also offers you relaxation in its cactus garden.

Stroll along pathways that meander through the Ethel M cactus garden's 350 varieties of shrubs, succulents, and cacti. Species collected from South Africa, the Red Sea, South America, and Japan are up to 60 years old. The garden blossoms with red, orange, and purple flowers from late March to May, but the stone benches soothe visitors year-round.

The Living Machine, located adjacent to the cactus gardens, purifies the chocolate factory's wastewater. Visitors view over an acre of waste-consuming ecologies in tanks, marshes, and reed beds transforming wastewater into water clean enough to be used for landscape irrigation.

Start your self-guided factory tour at the kitchen. From a corridor, observe the chocolate-making through glass windows. Depending on when you visit, you'll see different production steps. Batches of toffee bubble in copper kettles, then workers pour this Almond Butter Krisp onto cooling tables. Buttercreams (maybe raspberry or chocolate) or liqueur creams (perhaps Amaretto) swirl slowly in shallow, round mixers. Metal blades stir these candy centers until they're smooth.

Further along the corridor, notice the two massive pale-yellow machines. An overhead video explains the processes occurring inside the machines. Empty plastic coin-shaped molds, patterned after U.S. 1904 Series coins, methodically move along the conveyor belt through the long machine. Liquid milk or dark chocolate pours through spigots to fill the molds. Some even get mint cream centers. The molds are vibrated to shake out air bubbles, conveyed through a cooling tunnel, and then flipped over to release the chocolate coins. You exit into the retail store, where you are greeted with a sample chocolate of the day.

Cost: Free

Freebies: Sample chocolate of the day

Videos Shown: Short overhead videos explain chocolate-making.

Reservations Needed: No

Days and Hours: Mon–Sun 8:30 AM–7:00 PM. Closed Christmas. No production for 1 week in July, but can visit cactus garden and view videos.

Plan to Stay: 15 minutes for self-guided tour and videos, plus cactus garden and shops.

Minimum Age: None

Disabled Access: Yes

Group Requirements: Can accommodate very large groups; those larger than 200 people need to call (702) 435-2641 in advance for special tour times.

Special Information: Best times to see production are Mon–Sun 9:00 AM–2:00 PM. Guided cactus garden tours for groups of 10 or more with 1 day's advance notice to (702) 435-2641. Special Christmas season cactus garden display.

Gift Shops: Chocolate Shop sells entire Ethel M line—more than 60 varieties of chocolates. Offers 1-pound assortment gift boxes, the popular 29-ounce "Taste of Las Vegas" assortment, with a photograph of Las Vegas's neon lights on the cover, and silver "Las Vegas slot machines" filled with chocolate coins. Open same hours as tour. Closed Christmas and shorter hours on Thanksgiving. Catalog available from (800) 4-ETHELM. Cactus Shop offers cactus plants, books, and T-shirts.

Directions: From Las Vegas strip, drive east on Tropicana. Turn right onto Mountain Vista. Turn left onto Sunset Way (Green Valley Business Park) and follow signs. From Hoover Dam, take Boulder Hwy. to Sunset Rd. Turn left onto Sunset Rd. Turn right onto Sunset Way. Follow above directions.

Nearby Attractions: National Vitamin and Ron Lee's World of Clowns tours (see pages 26 and 224); Sunset Station Casino.

National Vitamin

7440 S. Industrial Road
Las Vegas, NV 89139
(702) 269-9600 / (888) 346-6848
www.nationalvitamin.com

VITAMINS

You may take vitamins daily, but you probably never imagined the sophisticated machines that manufacture tablets like vitamin C. Raw materials such as ginseng and echinacea are inspected by Quality Control, weighed and then taken to the blending room. There, a huge stainless steel V-shaped blender mixes precise amounts of these ingredients.

Once blended, some formulas are made into hard-shell capsules, while others become tablets. In the tablet manufacturing area, a tablet press forms dry powders into various shapes: round, oval or even dinosaur shape. The tablet press has an upper punch and a lower punch, and a die that forms the tablet's shape. The blended formula is loaded into each die cavity. The punches then apply up to five tons of pressure to form the tablets. The machine can produce up to 2,000 tablets per minute! It's so fast that, even looking at it directly, all you will see is a blur and the tablets leaving the machine. Fortunately a video monitor shows the process in slow motion. In the next room, watch as a large dryer-like machine coats tablets to keep them fresh or to disguise unpleasant tastes, then move to the Quality Control Lab, where chemists carefully test the final products and raw materials to meet strict quality standards of potency and purity.

In the next area, soft gel capsules like vitamin E take shape. Water, glycerin, and gelatin are heated to form a viscous, honey-like liquid that will make up the outside of the soft gels. The liquid is loaded into warm tanks, where it must remain heated until production begins. Next, these tanks are hooked up to the production machine, which forms and fills the golden capsules. The soft gels emerge on a conveyor, and then tumble inside long drying tubes along with special lint-free towels.

Next, a worker wheels trays of them into a drying tunnel in which humidity, air, and temperature are constantly regulated. The capsules dry there for 18 to 30 hours. Finally, workers inspect trays full of the yellow capsules and discard those that are deformed or leaking. The perfect capsules travel to the packing room, where the vitamins and supplements are loaded into bottles, capped, and labeled for shipment all around the world.

Cost: Free

Freebies: Choice of samples of vitamins, skin care products, or chewable vitamin C.

Videos Shown: 2-minute introductory video on nutrition and vitamins and video monitors throughout the tour.

Reservations Needed: No, except for groups over 30 people.

Days and Hours: Mon–Sun 6:00 AM–6:00 PM. Closed Easter, Thanksgiving, Christmas, and New Year's.

Plan to Stay: 25 minutes for self-guided tour and video, plus time for retail outlet.

Minimum Age: None

Disabled Access: Yes

Group Requirements: Guided tours available for groups of 15 or more. Groups of 30 or more should call a day in advance.

Retail Outlet: Sells vitamins, supplements, and botanicals, as well as health and body care products. At the smoothie bar you can add vitamins to a fresh fruit smoothie. Open same hours as tour.

Directions: From I-15 North, take the Las Vegas Blvd. Exit. Turn right on Las Vegas Blvd. After .5 miles, turn right on Warm Springs Rd. After .5 miles take a left on Industrial Rd. From I-15 South, exit at Blue Diamond Rd. West and go .25 miles. Take a right on Industrial Rd. The entrance is .75 miles on the right.

Nearby Attractions: Ron Lee's World of Clowns and Ethel M Chocolates tours (see pages 222 and 224); Shelby American Automobiles tour and museum (call 702-643-3000); casinos.

See color photos, page 27.

Ron Lee's World of Clowns

330 Carousel Parkway
Henderson, NV 89014
(702) 434-1700 / (800) 829-3928
www.ronlee.com

CLOWN AND ANIMATION FIGURINES

Ron Lee has come a long way since 1976, when he started sculpting animal figures in his garage and playing accordion in a band to support his family. The designer of "Hobo Joe" and other clowns now creates 1.25-inch to 18-inch pewter sculptures of Bugs Bunny, Popeye, Superman, the Flintstones, and other popular animated characters.

When you enter the 30,000-square-foot building, you will notice the clown and circus memorabilia. Display cases feature 600 goose eggs dressed up as faces of famous Clown Hall of Fame–inductee clowns, such as Emmett Kelly Sr. Notice the 5-by-11-foot miniature amusement park sculpted by Ron Lee.

On the self-guided tour, look through glass windows at nine stations to see the making of figurines by hand. Even though the windows are not presented in the chronological order of the process, videos help you understand the steps. In the hand-painting department, 20 artisans apply colorful acrylic paints to tiny clowns, Looney Tunes characters, and Flintstones. At another window, a worker deburrs the metal casting with a tool that resembles a jeweler's grinding bit on a drill. This process removes the imperfections in the casting.

Walk further down the hallway to see the casting of the pewter sculptures. Watch as two workers pour molten metal into the opening of a spinning, round blue machine that contains the mold for a sculpture. The force of the spinning packs the metal more tightly into the mold. A craftsman hand-cuts molds out of rubber and cooks them in a Vulcanizer at yet another window, while in the spray-booth room, a worker applies a high-gloss clear finish to the figures with a spray gun. In the finishing room, you may see Betty Boop, Snow White, and Bugs Bunny lined up, waiting to be mounted on onyx or to be shipped or numbered. End your tour in the Gallery, where on most days Ron Lee himself greets visitors and signs autographs amid his numerous colorful creations.

Cost: Free, includes museum and tour.
Freebies: None
Videos Shown: Videos explain the process taking place behind each window.
Reservations Needed: No, for self-guided tours.
Days and Hours: Mon–Fri 8:30 AM–3:30 PM. Closed holidays.
Plan to Stay: 20 minutes for tour, plus time for gallery and Carousel Café.
Minimum Age: None
Disabled Access: Yes
Group Requirements: No maximum group size. Groups of 20 or more should call 1 day in advance.
Special Information: Members of the Ron Lee Collectors Club receive discounts and enjoy the 3-day Ron Lee Convention.
Gallery: Sells Ron Lee figurines. Call (702) 434-3920 for information. For Carousel Café, call (702) 434-1847. Both open same hours as tour.
Directions: From Las Vegas, take Las Vegas Blvd. south. Turn left onto Warm Springs Rd. and take it into Henderson. Turn right onto Carousel Pkwy. The factory is at the end of the road. From I-95 North, turn left onto Lake Mead Dr. Turn right onto Gibson St. and left onto Warm Springs Rd. Then turn left onto Carousel Pkwy.
Nearby Attractions: Ethel M Chocolates and National Vitamin tours (see pages 222 and 26); Shelby American Automobiles tour and museum (call 702-643-3000); Las Vegas; Lake Mead.

Anheuser-Busch

221 Daniel Webster Highway
Merrimack, NH 03054
(603) 595-1202
www.budweisertours.com

BUDWEISER BEER

One of every two beers consumed in America is made by Anheuser-Busch, with this brewery serving all of New England. Of Anheuser-Busch's 12 U.S. breweries, this brewery is in the prettiest setting, located in the picturesque Merrimack Valley. It can package 8 million 12-ounce servings in 24 hours.

Your tour guide will lead you to the brewery, built in 1970, past a life-size replica of a Clydesdale horse. In the brewhouse, a mixture of water and rice or corn fills three stainless-steel mash tanks. Malt enzymes break the starch in the corn or rice into fermentable sugars. Once strained, the remaining liquid ("wort") is boiled and hops are added. After cooling, the liquid is pumped into 45° fermentation cellars. On the ground floor of this four-story cellar, you may see a worker place a layer of beechwood chips in the stainless-steel tanks. These chips provide a surface area on which yeast settles during secondary fermentation.

On your way to the packaging area, notice the eight-foot carved mahogany mural of the Anheuser-Busch corporate trademark. Through glass windows, watch the tightly woven maze of filling lines. Once rinsed, bottles proceed to the rotating bottle-filler. They then speed through capping and labeling to packaging. After the brewery tour, don't miss the Old World–style Clydesdale Hamlet, modeled after an 18th-century German Bauernhof. This stable and courtyard are home base for the traveling East Coast Clydesdale eight-horse show hitch. This close-up look at the Budweiser Clydesdales (special photo opportunities first Saturday of each month) is a highlight of the tour.

Cost: Free

Freebies: Beer, soda, and snacks.

Video Shown: If packaging line isn't operating, 2 6-minute films show packaging and brewing processes.

Reservations Needed: No, except for groups larger than 15.

Days and Hours: January–April: Thur–Mon 10:00 AM–4:00 PM; May, September–December: Mon–Sun 10:00 AM–4:00 PM; June–August: Mon–Sun 9:30 AM–5:00 PM. Call to see if bottling on weekends or holidays. Generally closed day before and day of Thanksgiving, Christmas, and New Year's.

Plan to Stay: 1.25 hours for tour, hospitality room, and Clydesdale Hamlet, plus time for shopping and tour assembly room displays.

Minimum Age: Under age 18 must be accompanied by adult.

Disabled Access: Yes

Group Requirements: Groups larger than 15 should call 1 day in advance. Groups of more than 35 people will be split into smaller groups. No maximum group size.

Special Information: No photography inside brewery. First Saturday of each month is Budweiser Clydesdale Camera Day (1:00 PM–3:00 PM), when you can pose with one of the Clydesdale horses. Tour includes indoor and outdoor walking, and some stairs. See page 214 for St. Louis, MO, feature and information about other Anheuser-Busch brewery tours.

Gift Shop: Tour Center Store sells logoed items, including T-shirts, bathing suits, steins, and jackets. Closes 1 hour later than tours.

Directions: From Boston, take I-93 North to I-495 South to Rt. 3 North. In New Hampshire, Rt. 3 becomes Everett Tnpk. Get off at Exit 10. At end of ramp, go right. At the next set of lights, turn left onto Daniel Webster Hwy. At the next traffic light, turn right into the brewery. Park in second lot on right. From Rt. 101, take Everett Tnpk. South to Exit 10 in Merrimack. At end of ramp, turn left. At the second set of lights, turn left onto Daniel Webster Hwy. Follow to next traffic light and turn right into brewery.

Nearby Attractions: Stonyfield Farm Yogurt tour (see page 228); Currier Gallery of Art (call 603-669-6144); New England Quilt Museum (call 978-452-4207); American Textile History Museum (see page 181).

Castle Springs

Route 171
Moultonborough, NH 03254
(603) 476-2352 / (800) 729-2468
www.castlesprings.com

BOTTLED SPRING WATER AND BEER

You know this isn't your typical factory tour when you drive into the main entrance of this 5,200-acre estate and the road winds you near the "Falls of Song" 50-foot cascading waterfall. When retired RJR Nabisco chairman and CEO J. Paul Sticht bought the property in 1992, he sensed a good tourism and manufacturing opportunity. The company is proud of its 100 percent environmental control and for being selected to produce commemorative bottles with a papal label for the 1995 U.S. visit of Pope John Paul II.

From the visitors center, a short tram ride takes you to the Castle in the Clouds (the one on the label really exists!) nestled in the Ossipee Mountains above Lake Winnipesaukee. Built in 1913 as a retirement home for Thomas Plant, a former shoe-factory owner, the castle was a wedding present for his second wife. Enjoy the self-guided tour of the castle's interior and back patio. Notice that the kitchen's hard rubber floor tiles adhere together like a jigsaw puzzle.

Ride through the woods to one of the natural spring sites. A green roof shades a two-foot-deep swimming pool–sized spring enclosed with arched Plexiglas. Water is gravity-fed one mile away from the source through an underground pipe to the bottling plant 220 feet below the spring.

Another scenic ride takes you to the bottling plant for a quick peek through glass windows at the filling line. A circular machine rotates clockwise, turning empty bottles upside down and rinsing them. For sparkling water, carbon dioxide is added first. Natural spring water fills 325 small bottles or 175 large bottles per minute. The bottles then pass through the blue capping machine. Caps appear to be magically airlifted and placed onto each bottle.

In 1996 the company opened a microbrewery in a new bottling plant that adjoins the water bottling facilities. Handcrafted premium beers are bottled under the brand name LuckNow, which was Plant's original name for his castle.

Cost: Adults, $12; seniors, $10; children 7–17, $7; children 6 and under, free. Horseback riding, $35 per person.

Freebies: 12-oz. bottle natural spring water, LuckNow beer samples.

Video Shown: Short video shows bottling processes and advertising clips.

Reservations Needed: No, but suggested for horseback riding.

Days and Hours: Mid-May–mid-October: Mon-Sun 9:00 AM–4:00 PM. Call for specific open/close dates.

Plan to Stay: 2 hours for tours, longer for hiking trails.

Minimum Age: None

Disabled Access: Yes

Group Requirements: Groups of 15 people or more should call at least 1 day in advance. No maximum group size. Group rates available. Private function room available for luncheons, receptions, and banquets.

Special Information: Grounds are particularly scenic during foliage and lilac seasons.

Gift Shop: Sells logoed T-shirts, mugs, and hats, plus novelties such as soda-bottle bird feeders. Snack bar. Open same days and hours as above.

Directions: From I-93, take Rt. 104 East to Meredith. Take Rt. 25 East to Moultonborough. Take Rt. 109 South to Rt. 171 South. Main entrance is 2 miles ahead on left.

Nearby Attractions: Hampshire Pewter tour (see page 227); Science Center; Washington Cruise Ship; Mt. Washington Cruises.

Hampshire Pewter

43 Mill Street
Wolfeboro, NH 03894
(603) 569-4944
www.hampshirepewter.com

hampshire pewter company

PEWTER TABLEWARE, ORNAMENTS, AND GIFTS

Wolfeboro is the oldest summer resort in the U.S.A., making it a fitting home for Hampshire Pewter. In fact, current owners Jenine and Bob Steele left their computer-industry jobs for this distinctly small-town setting. Using skilled craftspeople and modern machines, the company has revived the craft of colonial pewter-making. As high-tech manufacturers strive to develop lighter, stronger, and more durable metals, it's good to know that pewter is still valued.

On your guided tour, watch through glass windows as craftspeople mix pure tin with other fine metals to create Queens Metal Pewter. Hampshire Pewter is the only U.S. company to use this special alloy, which consists mostly of tin. Unless you remember your high-school chemistry, you probably don't think of metal as a liquid. But to combine the metals, a worker liquefies them at over 1,900° in a big pot in the back of the small foundry, "cools" the mixture to 600°, then carefully pours it into specially designed, heavy bronze molds to form shapes.

When the temperature cools to 450°, the liquid becomes a solid. The crafter judges when the pewter has solidified enough to be carefully knocked from the mold. The different castings that make up an item, such as the stem and bowl of a goblet, must be soldered together quickly—otherwise the flame's heat may melt or scorch the joined pieces.

In the workshop area, craftspeople called finishers then turn the pewter piece on a lathe, using chisels to chip away all the rough, gray metal. As a piece spins, the finishers artfully and gently carve the fine details of traditional designs. Delicately holding the pewter pieces, a crafter buffs them on cotton wheels to obtain the soft pewter luster. When you see workers finish the process by stamping each piece with the distinctive "touchmark" that identifies a Hampshire Pewter original, you know that the trademark is well deserved.

Cost: Free

Freebies: No

Video Shown: 8-minute video on history of pewter and close-up views of the Hampshire Pewter production process.

Reservations Needed: No reservations needed June–mid-October, except for groups of 15 or more people. Reservations are needed mid-October–May.

Days and Hours: Memorial Day–Columbus Day: Mon–Fri 10:00 AM, 11:00 AM, 1:00 PM, 2:00 PM, and 3:00 PM. Labor Day–Columbus Day: same schedule except no 1:00 PM tour. Call for hours and reservations mid-October through May. Closed holidays.

Plan to Stay: 20 minutes for tour and video, plus time for gift shop.

Minimum Age: None, but viewing windows start 4 feet up from the ground.

Disabled Access: Yes, but viewing windows start 4 feet up from the ground.

Group Requirements: 10 days' advance notice for groups of 15 or more people.

Special Information: No photography

Retail Store: Tabletop Shop sells full selection of 200 hand-cast pewter items, ranging from teddy bear birthday-candle holders to flower vases and classic goblets. Personal engraving available. Open Mon–Sat 9:00 AM–5:00 PM. Closed Memorial Day, Thanksgiving, Christmas, and New Year's. Downtown store nearby on Main St. has longer hours and is open Sun and holidays. Catalog available from (800) 639-7704.

Directions: From Boston and southern New Hampshire, take I-95 North. Exit at Rt. 16 North. From Rt. 16, exit at Rt. 11 North. At the traffic circle, take Rt. 28 North. Stay on this road into Wolfeboro. Soon after the center of town, turn right on Mill St. Hampshire Pewter is in a red barn-like building on your right.

Nearby Attractions: Castle Springs bottling plant and castle tour (see page 226); Pepi Herrman Crystal tour (call 603-528-1020); Annalee Dolls Museum (call 800-43-DOLLS); Lake Winnipesaukee; Libby Museum.

Stonyfield Farm

10 Burton Drive
Londonderry, NH 03053
(603) 437-4040
www.stonyfield.com

YOGURT

As the name suggests, Stonyfield Farm Yogurt began on a farm. But meteoric growth forced this award-winning company to its present location in Londonderry. Developed in 1983 by two environmentalists, the all-natural yogurt can now be found in grocery stores nationwide. Their original mission hasn't changed—to demonstrate that a company can do well in the world and still be profitable. The tour shows you how they work their "magic" and live their corporate mission, despite selling 40 percent ownership to Dannon.

Your tour begins in a mini-theater, where you see a lively video about the company's beginnings at the Wilton, New Hampshire, farm. Pass Stonyfield's Memory Lane, which chronicles many of the company's memorable "mooments." These notable milestones highlight the successes and failures of Stonyfield innovations—such as the short-lived Garden Salad Yogurt.

The windowed viewing area reveals different areas of the bustling Yogurt Works. Look into the research and development lab, where new ideas for flavors and products take form. Peek inside quality control and discover a science lab with petri dishes, test tubes, and the quality control team checking the incoming ingredients and the yogurt as it is being made. You may catch a glimpse of one of the shiny tanker trucks delivering a load of fresh farm milk as you pass the receiving bay. Your tour guide will explain the yogurt-making process: how Stonyfield mixes its special concoction of healthy yogurt bacteria (or "culture") into the milk and then provides the right environment for this "good bacteria" to turn the milk into yogurt (via the "magic of science").

Watch through large windows as empty cups are stacked in the filler, then drop onto the conveyer belt. First, a dollop of fruit goes into the bottom of each cup, then yogurt sprays out of spouts that look like showerheads, filling the containers. Next the cups travel under a roll of plastic where special cutters—similar to cookie cutters—chop and then melt a circle of plastic (the safety seal) to the top of the cup. Lastly, the lids latch onto the

cups and head down to the packing machine at the rate of 240 cups per minute. Once the cups are sealed in cases, the yogurt elevator takes the cases up to the overhead tracks that carry them to the incubator. The containers may appear ready to ship to the stores, but the "magic" yogurt process has just begun.

Cost: $1.50; children under 4, free.

Freebies: Various yogurt samples

Video Shown: 10-minute video covers company history and close-up views of production process.

Reservations Needed: No, except for groups larger than 10 people.

Days and Hours: Mon–Sat 10:00 AM–4:00 PM on the hour. Closed holidays and special Stonyfield days. Call (603) 437-4040 ext. 4326 for current schedule.

Plan to Stay: 1 hour for tour, video, and sampling, plus time for gift shop.

Minimum Age: Recommended minimum age is 4; however, strollers welcome.

Disabled Access: Yes

Group Requirements: Groups of more than 10 people should call in advance. Maximum group size is 40 people. Group rate is $1 per person.

Special Information: No production on Saturdays; video shown.

Gift Shop: Logoed and cow-motif products, country gifts, books, and kids' stuff; all Stonyfield Yogurt flavors and types at factory price. Open Mon–Sat 9:30 AM–5:00 PM.

Directions: From Boston, take I-93 North to North Londonderry (Exit 5). Turn left onto Rt. 28 North. After 2 miles, turn left onto Page Rd. Take left onto Webster Rd. Turn left at stop sign. Turn right onto Burton Dr. Stonyfield Farm will be on your right. From Nashua, take Everett Tnpk. North. Take Rt. 101 East to S. Willow St. Turn right onto Rt. 28 South. Bear left at the fourth set of lights. Turn right onto Harvey (follow as it turns right in 1 mile). Turn right onto Burton Dr.

Nearby Attractions: Anheuser-Busch Brewery tour (see page 225); Redhook Brewery tour in Portsmouth (call 603-430-8600); Currier Gallery of Art; Canobie Lake Park; The Met Children's Museum.

Edison National Historic Site

Main Street and Lakeside Avenue
West Orange, NJ 07052
(973) 736-0550, ext. 42
www.nps.gov/edis/home.html

ELECTRONICS

Most people think of Thomas Edison as the inventor of the light bulb, but after touring his laboratory, you'll realize that the simple bulb was only one of hundreds of inventions. Edison developed the disc phonograph, the motion picture system, and improved electrical generators and meters here.

The laboratory is a quad of brick buildings resembling a campus. Entering it you feel as if you've stepped into the early 20th century—it's full of objects actually used by Edison and his colleagues. Enter Edison's office and library, where the tour interpreter may play a tune on an old wax-cylinder phonograph.

Next is the stockroom where you'll find tools and natural materials—like elephant hide and tortoiseshell—that were used in the development of Edison's inventions. In searching for filament materials for the light bulb, Edison experimented with both human hair and coconut hair. In the heavy machine shop, Edison's "muckers" (his nickname for the people who worked for him) built prototypes that were sent to the patent office.

Edison's first love was chemistry, and in the chemistry lab you'll examine remnants of the work he was doing when he died. Searching for a domestic source of rubber for his friend Henry Ford, Edison grew and made rubber from 14-foot goldenrod plants. Unfortunately, the resulting material was coarse and didn't last long.

Next, look inside a replica of Black Maria, the first structure built as a motion-picture studio, to see what a film set looked like in Edison's day. The Black Maria predates electric lighting of film sets—all light had to be obtained from the sun. The roof opens up to let the sun in, and the building itself is built on a track so it can move to follow the sun around. After touring Edison's workplace, you can visit Glenmont, the Victorian mansion where this ingenious man lived with his family.

Cost: Adults, $3; children 17 and under, free.
Freebies: No

Video Shown: "The Invention Factory," an 18-minute video about the site, and *The Great Train Robbery,* a 10-minute Edison film.
Reservations Needed: No. Special tickets are required for Glenmont tour.
Days and Hours: Call for information, as plans to undergo restorations. Shorter winter hours. Closed Thanksgiving, Christmas, and New Year's.
Plan to Stay: 2 hours for both tours, plus time for store.
Minimum Age: None
Disabled Access: Laboratory: yes. Glenmont: no. Notify ranger at desk, who will install wheelchair ramps in laboratory. Call ahead if possible.
Group Requirements: Call ahead for reservations.
Special Information: Hot days are not a good time to visit: there is no air conditioning. Tours are abbreviated on hot days. Special tickets required for Glenmont tour. Starting in 2002 the Laboratory & Glenmont will be undergoing renovation—visitors should call ahead to find out what is open.
Bookstore: Sells items such as books, sound recordings, posters, and postcards related to Thomas Edison. Mon–Sun 9:00 AM–5:00 PM.
Directions: From the east, take the New Jersey Tnpk. Take Exit 15-W onto I-280 westbound. Follow I-280 to the West Orange/South Orange/Montclair exit. Make right at end of exit ramp. Go to end of street and make a left onto Main St. Follow Main St. for about .75 miles. Parking is on left. From the west, take I-280 eastbound to the Mount Pleasant Avenue/West Orange/Montclair exit. Make a left at end of ramp. At the second traffic light, make a left onto Main St. Follow Main St. for .5 miles. Parking is on left.
Nearby Attractions: Ford Ranger plant tour (see page 230); Turtleback Zoo; Newark Museum; Montclair Art Museum.

Ford

Edison Assembly Plant
939 U.S. Highway 1
Edison, NJ 08818
(732) 632-5930, ext. 5306
www.fordvehicles.com

RANGER PICKUP TRUCKS

The Big Three auto companies owe part of their resurgence to the mushrooming popularity of non-car cars: pickups, minivans, and sport-utility vehicles. Classified as "trucks" for purposes of energy and safety regulations, this is one of the few vehicle segments that Japanese manufacturers were slow to exploit. The Ford Ranger compact pickups made at this plant are ranked as one of the most popular vehicles sold in the U.S.A.

As Ford's second-smallest assembly plant, the Edison facility produced only cars from the 1947 Lincoln up to the Ford Escort in the late 1980s. In 1990 Ford switched the plant to making pickups, extensively retooling the factory and retraining the workers. Production went from 85 percent manual to about 85 percent robotic, so here you'll see the latest in automation and robotics. The tour begins on the final trim lines, where workers install small pieces like the mirrors, instrument panel, and back windshield as the pickups move by on the ubiquitous conveyors.

Robots do more than 90 percent of the body welding. No people seem to be nearby as the steel body shell moves down the line in a synchronized pattern, allowing the robotic welding arms to do their jobs hundreds of times the exact same way every day. If you're not too startled or amazed by the waterfall of sparks generated by each weld, study the different role each robot plays in building the body.

Another part of the plant constructs the frame that supports the engine, cab, and other truck parts. Watch how the engine is "decked" to the frame and, later, how the frame (at this point resembling a giant go-cart more than a pickup) is decked with the body cab. "Pit" workers test the pickup's features such as brake and gas lines. More robots help with the front windshield and seat installation. Giant praying mantis–like arms pick up the glass and slap it into place. With all the advanced technology you'll encounter during the tour, you'll enjoy debating your fellow visitors about what was the coolest thing you saw.

Cost: Free

Freebies: No

Video Shown: No

Reservations Needed: Yes. Individuals and families are either joined with a scheduled group tour or formed into a group.

Days and Hours: Thur 10:00 AM. Closed holidays, 2 weeks around Christmas, and month of July. Because of limited tour times, it is difficult to book a tour.

Plan to Stay: 1.25 hours

Minimum Age: 15

Disabled Access: Yes

Group Requirements: Minimum group size is 15 people; maximum, 35. Call 4–6 weeks in advance to schedule tour.

Special Information: No photography. Tour does not visit paint department, although tour guide explains the process. About every year or so the plant has an open house that offers tours all day, a look at new pickup models, and food.

Gift Shop: No

Directions: From the New Jersey Tnpk., take Exit 10. Take 287 North to Hwy. 1 South. Plant is on right.

Nearby Attractions: Edison National Historic Site tour (see page 229); American Labor Museum in Haledon tells the story of American workers, their unions, and their diverse ethnic heritage (call 973-595-7953); Delaware and Raritan Canal State Park.

Wheaton Village

1501 Glasstown Road, Route 55
Millville, NJ 08332-1566
(856) 825-6800 / (800) 99-VILLAGE
www.wheatonvillage.org

WHEATON VILLAGE

GLASS AND OTHER CRAFTS

In 1888 Dr. T. C. Wheaton, interested in making medicine bottles, purchased a Millville glass factory, which burned down in 1889. A working replica of this original factory is the centerpiece of Wheaton Village. Established in 1968, Wheaton Village focuses on the art and heritage of American glassmaking, regional craft, and folk life.

At set times, workers demonstrate traditional glassblowing. One worker narrates as another gathers molten glass onto a long rod (a "punty"). To make a paperweight, the gaffer inverts the gob of glass onto a mold, perhaps flower-shaped. The gob absorbs colored powdered glass from inside the mold. At other times, you can also observe these workers without narration.

Sharing the floor are glassworkers on fellowship from all over the world, making contemporary sculptures. While casting, workers wear protective outfits and face protection. With a saucepan-size ladle, a worker pours 30 to 50 pounds of molten glass into a sandcasting (made in sand) mold.

The Museum of American Glass houses the largest collection of entirely American-made glass. Its 7,500-plus objects include paperweights, chandeliers, prisms, and the nearly-nine-foot-tall, 193-gallon *Guinness Book of World Records'* largest bottle. The museum covers the glass industry from the first factory (1739), through the 1800s, when South Jersey was a major glassmaking center, to today. The glass whimsy exhibit contains objects such as walking canes that workers made from leftover glass.

The Crafts and Trades Row building contains several studios and historical exhibits. Two potters transform clay into pots as pottery wheels spin. Over a torch, a lampworker manipulates glass rods of various colors and diameters to create marbles. Each colored swirl requires a separate rod. You may see a worker forming miniature animals or people at a tiny tea table. Afterwards, enjoy the peaceful, 60-plus-acre grounds' picnic tables, shrubs, shady pine trees, scampering squirrels, and flocks of birds and Canada geese— or browse the unique museum shops.

Cost: Adults, $8; seniors, $7; students, $5; under 5, free.

Freebies: No

Video Shown: No

Reservations Needed: No. Groups, see below.

Days and Hours: Village hours: January–March: Fri–Sun 10:00 AM–5:00 PM (Crafts and Trade Row closed); March also: Wed–Thur, Sun 10:00 AM–5:00 PM.; April–December: Mon–Sun 10:00 AM–5:00 PM. Glass demonstrations: 11:00 AM, 1:30 PM, and 3:30 PM, when village is open. Closed Easter, Thanksgiving, Christmas, and New Year's.

Plan to Stay: 3.5 hours, plus time in shops.

Minimum Age: None

Disabled Access: Yes

Group Requirements: Groups of more than 25 adults or 10 schoolchildren need reservations 1 month in advance. Craft Sampler Days (provide hands-on crafts participation for school groups) must be arranged only on the first Monday in November for March programs. Other hands-on programs available year round.

Special Information: Make Your Own Paperweight Program available to individuals and groups over age 18 with 1 week's advance notice. Call (800) 998-4552 for special events calendar or more information.

Gift Shops: Shops sell works made at Wheaton Village and those by other American glassmakers; also, crafts, books, and penny candy. Open same hours as Village.

Directions: From Philadelphia, take Walt Whitman Bridge (follow signs to Atlantic City) to Rt. 42 South. Take Rt. 55 South to Exit 26. Signs lead to main entrance. From Atlantic City, take Atlantic City Expwy. West to Exit 12. Take Rt. 40 West. Turn left onto Rt. 552 West. At first traffic light in Millville, turn right onto Wade Blvd. Follow the signs.

Nearby Attractions: Parvin State Park; Atlantic City's beaches and casinos 35 miles away; Cape May's beaches and Victorian homes 40 miles away.

Heart of the Desert

Eagle Ranch
7288 Highway 54/70
Alamogordo, NM 88310
(505) 434-0035
www.eagleranchpistachios.com

PISTACHIOS

Pistachios

According to ancient Turkish legend, young lovers walked through moonlit pistachio groves to test their love. If they heard pistachios splitting open on the trees, they knew their love was indeed true. Centuries later, in another desert thousands of miles away, the Schweers family may have had this romantic legend in mind when they chose Heart of the Desert Pistachios as their trademark. As owners and operators of Eagle Ranch Pistachio Groves, New Mexico's first and largest pistachio farm, the Schweers have put years of love and hard work into producing these delicious nuts.

Tours are offered year-round, but if you visit Eagle Ranch in September, you can watch the mechanical shaking machines harvest the pistachios. The shakers clasp and vibrate the trees, releasing showers of nuts that are then transported into bins by conveyor belt. The pistachios move past a group of "gals" who remove blemished or deformed nuts. The good pistachios enter a needle sorter, a 6-foot-diameter barrel open at both ends. The needles that line the inside of the barrel hook into the split nuts' green meat, leaving the unsplit pistachios to roll out the bottom. The unsplit nuts are shelled, and these nutmeats are flavored, roasted, and packaged.

The split nuts, meanwhile, flow across a sloped, vibrating sizing machine composed of flat plates with various size holes. As the pistachios jump along the vibrating plates, the smaller nuts fall through the tiniest holes into bins underneath. The remaining nuts continue along the machine, dropping into openings of increasing size until each bin along the way holds larger-sized pistachios.

In another process, pistachios move downhill on a hopper that feeds into a seemingly benign color-sorting machine. Suddenly you may hear a machine gun–like blast as nuts shoot out of the color sorter. A jet of air kicks out those nuts whose hue does not match the machine's prescribed color standards. The remaining pistachios are either sprayed with chili flavors or salted, then roasted in a huge oven. Workers insert and remove 40-pound trays of nuts from the 10-foot-tall roaster in a nonstop workout. Meanwhile you can take a relaxed stroll into the gift shop, where you can sample and "go nuts" over Heart of the Desert pistachios.

Cost: Free

Freebies: Pistachio nut and candy samples

Video Shown: No

Reservations Needed: No, unless groups larger than 10 people want different tour times.

Days and Hours: Memorial Day–Labor Day: Mon–Fri 10:00 AM and 1:30 PM. Labor Day–Memorial Day: Mon–Fri 1:30 PM. Closed Thanksgiving and Christmas.

Plan to Stay: 45 minutes for tour, plus time for gift shop, visitors center, and art gallery.

Minimum Age: None

Disabled Access: Yes

Group Requirements: Groups larger than 10 people should call 1 week in advance for alternative tour times. No maximum group size.

Special Information: Adjacent to gift shop is a visitors center with background information on the farm and pistachios, and an art gallery.

Retail Store: Sells pistachios, Southwestern Indian jewelry, gourmet items, gift baskets, pottery, and T-shirts with Southwestern themes. Open Mon–Sat 8:00 AM–6:00 PM; Sun 9:00 AM–6:00 PM. Mail-order brochure available from (800) 432-0999.

Directions: From I-25 or I-10, take Hwy. 70 North. Eagle Ranch is 4 miles north of Alamogordo on Hwys. 54/70.

Nearby Attractions: Apache Trail attractions include White Sands National Monument, Space Hall of Fame, Ruidoso Downs Race Track, Lincoln National Forest, Hubbard Museum of the American West, Valley of Fires State Recreation Park, and Lincoln Historical District (Billy the Kid Museum and Lincoln Heritage Center).

Babcock

36 Delaware Avenue
Bath, NY 14810
(607) 776-3341 / (800) 840-9705

LADDERS

Babcock presents a nice American small business, small-town (population 6,000) story of struggle and success in making and marketing a core product found in every home and business in this country. The business started in 1905 and positions itself as one of the country's premier manufacturers of wooden step and extension ladders. It has innovatively developed a new business line in producing gift crates, planters, and other special-purpose boxes from the scrap wood left over from making ladders. It has many old-time employees, sometimes with fathers, sons, and grandsons from the same family involved in the woodworking.

It takes different types of wood to make a ladder: southern yellow pine, basswood, hemlock, and ash. You will see all the steps involved in turning these into wooden ladders of all sizes from 2 to 30 feet high, recognized as the "World's Tallest Ladder." You experience production from the time wood arrives to when the finished product is shipped out the door. You're surrounded by air tools and riveting guns, plenty of saws and other woodworking machines for cutting, mooring, and milling.

Walk through a few of the 10 gray sheds. The first one you walk by has stacks of "profiled" wood that has already been planed. Slide the door open to go into the next shed. The royal blue drill presses designed by the company have 15 motors. The Rabbiter makes grooves in the wood at 69-degree angles, which are a feature of the ladder's steps. Shrill sounds fill the air. You may even want to cover your ears as you walk by the new assembly line where air guns shoot in solid steel rivets. You'll walk through the warehouse next to ladders of all different heights, closed and standing tall, and even see them laid flat being wrapped in large cardboard sheets for shipping. The next time your feet touch the rungs of an extension ladder or the steps of a stepladder, they will have new appreciation for all the work involved in making it.

Cost: Free
Freebies: No
Video Shown: No
Reservations Needed: Yes
Days and Hours: Mon–Thur 8:00 AM–3:00 PM. Closed major holidays and week between Christmas and New Year's.
Plan to Stay: 45 minutes
Minimum Age: No
Disabled Access: Yes
Group Requirements: No minimum or maximum.
Special Information: Must wear safety glasses that they provide. No sandals. Can be loud. Plans to turn small white house next to parking lot into a museum.
Gift Shop: Located in the office. Sells full line of products at 50 percent off list price, including wooden ladders, fiberglass ladders, wooden crates, hanging planters, and CD boxes. Open Mon–Fri 8:00 AM–4:30 PM.
Directions: From Corning, take I-86 West or Rt. 17 West. Take Bath Exit 39. Turn right on Rt. 415 North. When in Village of Bath, make left on East Morris St., and then turn left on Delaware Ave. Located at end of street in the dead end. Look for the round blue and yellow logo on the side of the building.
Nearby Attractions: Historic downtown Bath; Corning Museum of Glass (see page 234); Keuka Lake Wine Trail (call 800-440-4898 for brochure) with tours of 8 wineries in the area; Glenn Curtiss Museum.

Corning Museum of Glass

One Museum Way
Corning, NY 14830
(607) 937-5371 / (800) 732-6845
www.cmog.org

Like a glass prism, a visit to the Corning Museum of Glass is multifaceted. The experience of the Glass Innovation Center, the Art and History Galleries, the Sculpture Gallery, the Steuben Factory, and the Hot Glass Show illuminates the history of glass, optical fiber communications, and glassmaking. The Museum's world-famous collection of more than 35,000 glass objects traces 35 centuries of human experience with glass, starting in ancient Egypt's 18th Dynasty, when the search for perfectly clear crystal began.

Learn how light transmits information through optical fibers in the Glass Innovation Center's interactive educational exhibits. The spherical mirror alters your perception. The float glass exhibit explains the production process of large panes of glass. An overhead monitor lets the audience look through the flameworker's lens as he melts glass rods over a single gas-flamed jet and forms tiny glass animals in an on-the-spot demonstration.

The real fascination is watching the Hot Glass Show. Walk along a frosted glass bridge and around to the Hot Glass Stage. In this intimate setting, with the Steuben Factory as a backdrop, you feel the heat from the furnace. Gaffers, whose cheeks as they blow into the long blowpipes resemble Louis Armstrong's when he's playing the trumpet, collect gobs of red-hot glass from a furnace containing molten glass. A narrator and master glassblower explain and demonstrate glassmaking before a walk downstairs offers a look into the working Steuben factory, the only place in the world where Steuben glass is made.

During this walk, look through the glass windows to see the engraving process that makes Steuben glass so unique and valuable. The engraver first coats the glass with protective shellac, then transfers an image onto its surface with India ink. To cut the design, the engraver presses the glass upward against as many as 50 different fine copper wheels on a rotating lathe. Intricate designs may take 300 hours to engrave.

Across the parking lot, at the Museum's Walk-in Workshop, you can make a glass flower, bead, picture frame, or magnet using a variety of glassworking techniques, for a nominal fee. Even the youngest visitors can sandblast a design on their own drinking glass.

Cost: Adults, $12; youth (6–17), $6; children and members, free; families (2 adults with dependent children), $36.

Freebies: No

Video Shown: 13-minute award-winning "Glass into Dreams" film and a variety throughout the galleries.

Reservations Needed: No, but recommended for groups larger than 20 people.

Days and Hours: Open Mon–Sun 9:00 AM–5:00 PM, July–Labor Day: Mon–Sun 9:00 AM–8:00 PM. Closed Thanksgiving, Christmas Eve, Christmas, New Year's Eve, and New Year's. Best time to see Steuben factory production is Mon–Fri 9:00 AM–5:00 PM. Hot Glass Shows all day, every day. Outdoor stage in summer.

Plan to Stay: 2 hours minimum

Minimum Age: None

Disabled Access: Yes

Group Requirements: Groups of 20 or more should call 2 weeks in advance for special group rates and reservations (call 607-974-2000). No maximum group size.

Special Information: No photography in Steuben factory visitor's gallery.

Gift Shop: Sells Steuben and other glass objects, glass-related books, souvenirs, and Corning tabletop and cookware products. Open same hours as Museum.

Directions: From New York City, take Rt. 17 West. Take Corning exit and follow signs. From Rochester, take I-390 South to I-86/Rt. 17 East. Follow above directions.

Nearby Attractions: Corning Historic Market Street shopping district; Finger Lakes Wine Country Visitor Center in CMoG Lobby; Babcock ladder tour (see page 233); Watkins Glen International Race Track; various wine trails; Rockwell Museum of Western Art; Benjamin Patterson Inn Museum; National Soaring Museum.

See color photo, page 29.

George Eastman House

900 East Avenue
Rochester, NY 14607
(585) 271-3361
www.eastman.org

In the 1980s Eastman-Kodak stopped giving public plant tours. While we wouldn't normally include a company founder's home, the exhibits and videos on George Eastman and Kodak provide a personal look at the company's roots. America's great companies begin and grow with individuals, and Kodak owes its existence to this hardworking inventor and businessman. (He probably would also have loved this book.)

George Eastman lived in this house from 1905 to 1932. The 50-room mansion and grounds have been authentically restored. Your guide's amusing gossip and anecdotes give you a sense of this great American entrepreneur, inventor, and marketer. In the conservatory, stand under a huge replica of an elephant's head and tusks while you listen to the story about why Eastman stood his ground to take a photo of an onrushing rhino. It provides a lesson on how he built his successful business.

Colorful displays in two second-floor rooms capture his personality, lifestyle, philanthropy, management techniques, and marketing strategy. Kodak's early history is intertwined with George Eastman's life, so the displays also show the company's development. You'll learn many tidbits, including why Eastman named his company "Kodak," why he gave away 500,000 "Brownie" cameras—one to every child who turned 12 in 1930—and see early Kodak advertising campaigns featuring themes still used today. You'll leave with a taste of how Eastman turned new scientific inventions into enormously popular products—a trait American companies have relearned.

Cost: Adults, $8; seniors, $6; students, $5; children 5–12, $3; children under 4, free.

Freebies: No

Videos Shown: A second-floor room continuously screens videos about George Eastman and Kodak. The Kodak video shows manufacturing process and overviews company's new products and direction.

Reservations Needed: No, except for groups larger than 30 people.

Days and Hours: Museum: Tue–Sat 10:00 AM–4:30 PM, Sun 1:00 PM–4:30 PM, Thur open until 8:00 PM. Closed holidays. During May (Lilac Festival in Rochester), open Mon–Sun 10:00 AM–4:30 PM. Tours: Tue–Sat 10:30 AM and 2:00 PM, Sun at 2:00 PM.

Plan to Stay: 2 hours for house and gardens tour (which can be self-guided), watching most of both videos, visiting second-floor exhibits. You'll even have time for the excellent International Museum of Photography and Film attached to the house (one of the world's greatest collections of photography, film, technology, and literature). All are included in the admission fee above.

Minimum Age: None

Disabled Access: Yes

Group Requirements: Groups larger than 30 people must schedule tours in advance by calling (585) 271-3361, ext. 238. Group rates available.

Gift Shop: Books, posters, collectors' items, and other photography-related gifts available in museum's gift shop. Open same hours as museum.

Special Information: Devices available to assist hearing-impaired.

Directions: Take New York State Thrwy. to Exit 45. Take Rt. 490 North toward Rochester. At Exit 19, go north on Culver Rd., then left on East Ave. The museum is on the right.

Nearby Attractions: Jell-O Gallery (see page 236); Memorial Art Gallery; Strong Museum; Rochester Museum and Science Center; Highland Park (annual May Lilac Festival); Seneca Park Zoo; Susan B. Anthony House.

Jell-O Gallery

23 East Main Street
LeRoy, NY 14482
(585) 768-7433
www.jellomuseum.com

DESSERT

The famous American dessert was born in this small town in upstate New York. While the Jell-O Gallery is not a factory tour or a company-owned museum, it's around the corner from the original factory site. Fans of U.S.A.-made products, their quirky early history, merchandising, and advertising will pay homage here to "America's Most Famous Dessert."

LeRoy, New York, has a long history with Jell-O, although production stopped here in 1964. The Genesee Pure Food Company purchased the rights to produce it for $450 in 1899. Renamed the Jell-O Company in 1925, the company eventually merged into what was known as the General Foods Company. Today it is part of the even bigger Kraft Foods Company. As the largest selling prepared dessert in the U.S.A., approximately 13 boxes of Jell-O are bought every second (strawberry is the overall best seller). Salt Lake City, Des Moines, and Milwaukee rank as the top cities in per capita Jell-O consumption.

It's not just these fun facts that make the Gallery worth visiting, it's the cute displays, many of which showcase collectibles. The Gallery, run by the local nonprofit historical society, regularly acquires collectibles over eBay and or by donation. Notice the display of gelatin boxes from around the world, the Jell-O molds in various shapes, such as a NASCAR set, and the recipe book covers. Gracing the walls are 19 original oil paintings used in advertising in the 1920s, created by famous illustrators of the era.

In the late 1990s, over 3,000 spoons appeared on a Jell-O billboard on Times Square, with 100 of them now found at the Gallery. Examine the Geleometer, the machine that tests the jiggleness of the gelatin. Before you leave, be sure to have your picture taken as the Jell-O girl from the early advertising or in the Jell-O delivery truck.

Cost: Adults, $3; children ages 6–11, $1.50.
Freebies: No. Occasionally free Jell-O boxes.
Video Shown: 5-minute video on Jell-O advertising.
Reservations Needed: No, except for groups.
Days and Hours: Open all year Mon–Fri 10:00 AM–4:00 PM. May–October: also Sat 10:00 AM–4:00 PM, Sun 1:00 PM–4:00 PM.
Plan to Stay: 45 minutes
Minimum Age: No
Disabled Access: Stairs to get into building.
Group Requirements: Recommend groups of 12 or more people call at least 2 days ahead. Rates $2 per person for groups.
Special Information: Gallery has kids' play area.
Gift Shop: Sells Jell-O items, including shirts, golf balls, magnets, recipe books. Open same hours as Gallery.
Directions: From New York State Thrwy. (I-90) take Exit 47 (Rt. 19). Turn left on Rt. 5 (Main St.). Gallery is a few blocks ahead on the left.
Nearby Attractions: George Eastman House (see page 235); Historic LeRoy House; Underground Railroad driving tour (leaflet available from Historical Society).

NBC Studios

30 Rockefeller Plaza
New York, NY 10112
(212) 664-3700
www.shopnbc.com/nbcstore

TELEVISION PROGRAMS

NBC prides itself on being the first radio network (1926), the first coast-to-coast television network (1951), and the first to broadcast a series in color (1953, *Kukla, Fran & Ollie*). This tour of the network headquarters (NBC employees call it 30 Rock) reflects that spirit. After seeing the behind-the-scenes hardware that helps edit, select, and broadcast shows to millions of homes, you appreciate what's involved when you flick on your TV.

While you will see neat technical TV hardware, the tour's highlight is visiting the sets of well-known shows or possibly meeting a TV star in hallways lined with NBC promotional posters and interactive exhibits. With your guide you may explore the versatile Studio 3K, used for several NBC sports and entertainment programs. Examine the imitation wood, plants, and other background materials that look so realistic on television.

Up to 12 different sets appear simultaneously in *Saturday Night Live* Studio 8H, with the band and monologue sets the only two "permanents." During the show, actors jump between stages, and workers move walls and props preparing for upcoming skits. If you're here the week a new *SNL* is taped, you can briefly watch a rehearsal through glass walls, with the casually clothed director, guest host, camera operators, and production assistants going over segments. But don't let the relaxed dress fool you. As employees walk briskly by, you can feel the pressures and deadlines of live television. You'll also have a hands-on experience with the news and weather in the mini-studio at the end of the tour.

Cost: Adults, $17.50; children 6–16, seniors, and groups of 4 or more, $15 per person.
Freebies: Small "NBC Studio Tour" button and the possibility of meeting a TV star.
Video Shown: 10-minute video explains NBC history and the television production process. During the introductory time period, you can also participate in an old-time radio show. In NBC Experience Store, the globe-shaped, high-definition theater shows 8-minute history of NBC programming.
Reservations Needed: No, except for groups larger than 10 people.
Days and Hours: Mon–Sat 8:30 AM–5:30 PM, Sun 9:30 AM–4:30 PM, every 30 minutes. Call about extended hours during busy December and summer seasons. Closed Christmas. Purchase tickets early in the day; they can sell out by mid-morning.
Plan to Stay: 1 hour for video and tour, plus time for NBC Experience Store.
Minimum Age: 6
Disabled Access: Yes
Group Requirements: Groups larger than 10 people need at least 1 week's advance reservations (call 212-664-7174). Maximum group size is 80. Group rates available.
Special Information: No photography. Tour varies with fast-breaking news or broadcast schedule changes. For show tickets, write NBC Tickets at the address above. At corner of 49th St. and Rockefeller Plaza, look through the glass walls at the street-level *Today Show* studio. NBC Burbank, CA (see page 78), also gives tours.
NBC Page Program: Tour guides are part of the NBC Page Program that gives people an opportunity to break into broadcasting. For more information, contact NBC Page Program, Employee Relations, at above address.
NBC Experience Store: Sells clothing, CDs, videos, caps, mugs, and other novelty items, many with logos of your favorite shows and NBC Sports. Sweet Shop sells chocolates and bulk bin candy. Open Mon–Fri 8:00 AM–7:00 PM, Sat 9:00 AM–6:00 PM. Extended hours in summer.
Directions: Located on corner of 49th St. between 5th and 6th Aves. Take B, D, or F subway to 47–50th St./Rockefeller Plaza. Walk up a few flights to building lobby.
Nearby Attractions: Radio City Music Hall and Sony Wonder Technology Lab (see pages 242 and 243); Rockefeller Center; Madison Square Garden tour (call 212-465-5800); Museum of Television and Radio.

New York Stock Exchange

20 Broad Street
New York, NY 10005
(212) 656-5165
www.nyse.com

NYSE

While the New York Stock Exchange (NYSE) isn't a factory, it is the place many companies in this book rely on to raise money. More than 1.2 billion shares are traded on an average day at the world's leading equities marketplace. Even if you have no background in finance, the video, architecture, and action on the trading floor give you an enlightened view of our economic system.

At your first look through the visitor gallery's glass windows, there seems to be nothing but confusion on the trading floor below. But once you concentrate on the activities at the individual trading posts, listen to the continuously playing audiotaped explanation, and look at the diagrams, the trading begins to make sense.

The 48,000-square-foot trading floor covers five rooms. From Visitor Center Gallery, you see the largest, the Main Room. More than 2,800 listed companies trade at each of the 20 trading posts on the trading floor. Overhead high-definition flat panel display screens flash the most current trading data for the stocks traded at that location.

The brokers and specialists buy and sell stock in a continuous auction process. Orders to buy and sell originating from anywhere in the world are fully executed in seconds. Before you leave the gallery, examine the room's beautiful architecture, with its ornate gilded ceiling, marble walls, and famous wall of windows.

Displays describe the NYSE's function, workings, and development since it was founded in 1792 to trade New York State bonds that covered Revolutionary War debts. The exhibits teach financial neophytes about stock and bond trading and answer common questions. Other displays show more experi-

enced investors how to retrieve computerized information on stocks, bonds, futures, and options. The newspaper's stock price tables will have new meaning after your visit.

Cost: Free

Freebies: NYSE literature at information desk.

Video Shown: 10-minute video in the Presentation Theater, "It All Starts Here," features some historical footage and close-ups that take you onto today's trading floor.

Reservations Needed: No, except for groups of 10 or more people.

Days and Hours: *For security reasons, Visitor Center Gallery is temporarily closed.*

Plan to Stay: 40 minutes for trading-floor viewing gallery, video, and displays, plus time for gift counter.

Minimum Age: None

Disabled Access: Yes

Group Requirements: Groups of 10 or more people need reservations at least 1 month in advance. Maximum group size is 30 people. Call (212) 656-5165.

Special Information: No photography. Tight security. Taped explanation in viewing gallery available in major foreign languages.

Gift Shop: Marketplace Gift Shop sells NYSE publications and logoed items, including caps, T-shirts, mugs, and key rings. Mon–Fri 8:45 AM–4:30 PM.

Directions: Take the No. 2, 3, 4, or 5 subway to Wall St. stop. Look for the six-Corinthian-column facade of building's Broad St. entrance.

Nearby Financial Attractions: Museum of American Financial History (call 212-908-4110); Commodities Exchange Visitors Gallery (call 212-748-1000); New York Federal Reserve Bank tour (call 212-720-6130). South Street Seaport also nearby.

Original American Kazoo Company

8703 South Main Street
Eden, NY 14057
(716) 992-3960
www.kazooco.com

KAZOOS

"If you can hum...you can play the kazoo" is the motto of the Original American Kazoo Company, the only metal-kazoo factory in the world. The kazoo is truly an American instrument, invented in the U.S.A. in the 1840s. Since kazoos are made the same way today as when the company started in 1916, we can say some things never change.

Pass through the toy and gift shop into the museum and factory. Wander around the small museum area looking at exhibits of kazoo trivia, history, and memorabilia. Learn that "Kazoo" was once a brand name for underwear and that the U.S. Navy ship U.S.S. *Kalamazoo* was nicknamed "the Kazoo"—its sailors owned kazoos printed with the ship's real name. Display cases show a variety of creative kazoos. Look for the liquor bottle–shaped kazoo (made in 1934 to "Kazelebrate" the end of Prohibition) and even a Woody Woodpecker model.

An 18-step process transforms sheets of metal into the classic submarine-shaped kazoo, without soldering, welding, or gluing. Pieces are joined by shaping and crimping metal. From behind a railing, you watch as workers operate individual presses (built in 1907) that flange edges, curve bottoms and tops, and stamp out the air hole. Parts are "seamed" together over a sword-shaped mold, then workers hand-insert the resonator and screw on the cap. Notice the single ten-horsepower motor that drives all of the presses, as you listen to the rhythmic thump of the metal blanks being transformed into kazoos.

Don't blow off this place because the manufacturing steps sound confusing—posters describe how the company makes kazoos to the tune of about 35,000 per week. In fact, you'll probably leave playing your favorite song on a kazoo.

Cost: Free
Freebies: No

Video Shown: 10-minute video in the museum shows news clips about the company.

Reservations Needed: No, except for groups larger than 15 people.

Days and Hours: Mon–Sat 10:00 AM–5:00 PM, Sun 12:00 PM–5:00 PM. Production takes place Tue and Fri 10:00 AM–5:00 PM. Call ahead to check days and times. No tour on weekends, video only. Closed holidays, week between Christmas and New Year's, and inventory days.

Plan to Stay: 20 minutes for self-guided tour, video, and the museum displays, plus time for gift shop.

Minimum Age: None, for families; 6, for school groups.

Disabled Access: Yes

Group Requirements: Reservations required 2 days in advance for group tours given Mon–Fri 10:15 AM–2:30 PM. Minimum group size is 20. Groups larger than 35 people are split into shifts. Minimum age is 6 for school groups. Groups receive a discount on one kazoo per customer.

Special Information: The tour does not take you onto factory floor. As you stand behind the viewing area railing, a worker describes the manufacturing process and answers questions. You can make your own metal kazoo during tour.

Gift Store: Sells kazoos of all kinds, toys, wind chimes, cards, hand-crafted instruments, and children's books. Also sells jewelry, glassware, and other gift items. Open Mon–Sat 10:00 AM–5:00 PM, Sun 12:00 PM–5:00 PM. Closed holidays.

Directions: Take New York State Thrwy. to Exit 57A. Turn left onto Eden-Evans Center Rd. When you reach the first traffic light, turn right onto Main St. (Rt. 62). The company is 2 blocks ahead on the left.

Nearby Attractions: Leon, NY, an Amish community, is 20 minutes away. Perry's Ice Cream (see page 240) and Buffalo's attractions, including QRS Music tour (see page 242), are about 45 minutes away.

Perry's Ice Cream

One Ice Cream Plaza
Akron, NY 14001
(716) 542-5492 / (800) 8-PERRYS
www.perryicecream.com

ICE CREAM

When H. Morton Perry started his business in 1918, he bottled milk for dairy farmers in the Akron area. Every so often he made small batches of ice cream for his family and friends—to rave reviews. By 1932 he began selling his ice cream to the public, and Perry's Ice Cream Company was born. H. Morton's grandchildren now run the business. You'll see that modern freezers have taken the place of ice-cooled storerooms, and a fleet of trucks has replaced horse-drawn wagons. You'll view an impressive manufacturing facility that makes millions of gallons of ice cream and related frozen treats every year.

After watching a video that covers Perry's proud history and the production of its quality ice cream, you'll walk up to a mezzanine area and peer through glass walls that survey the production floor. To your right are vats that hold the base mixes for ice cream and yogurt. In the center are the ever-moving machines that make ice cream and "novelty items," what they call treats like ice-cream sandwiches and cones. In this area, up to eight movable production lines may be in action. To the left are freezers for the finished products. While you're taking in the view, you'll munch on a delicious novelty item.

The various ice-cream flavors start as base mixes and then journey through enclosed machines and pipes that add goodies like pecan halves, caramel sauce, chocolate chips, or strawberries. Look for the line that makes ice-cream sandwiches. The vanilla ice cream is piped in and squirted between two traveling chocolate wafers. The ice cream and wafers come together in a continuous stream that makes and packages 120 sandwiches per minute.

Perry's can make cones a lot faster than your local ice-cream parlor. The cones are loaded into one end of the production line. Ice cream is shot inside, then chocolate sauce and nuts drop on top. Quicker then you can say "another scoop, please," the cones are packaged and off to the massive freezer.

Cost: $1; children under 3, free.

Freebies: Ice-cream novelty item of your choice.

Video Shown: 10-minute video on Perry's history and production process.

Reservations Needed: Yes

Days and Hours: Mon–Fri 9:00 AM–1:00 PM. Hours vary seasonally. Closed holidays.

Plan to Stay: 30 minutes for video and tour.

Minimum Age: No

Disabled Access: Yes

Group Requirements: Maximum group size is 40 people. Should call 1 month in advance.

Special Information: No photography of production floor.

Gift Counter: Sells logoed T-shirts, mugs, and key chains, etc. Open same hours as tour.

Directions: From the east, take I-90 West to Exit 48A (Pembroke). Take Rt. 77 South. Turn right onto Rt. 5 West, then right onto Rt. 93 North. Follow Rt. 93 as it turns and curves through Akron. Turn right at Ice Cream Plaza. From the west, take I-90 East to Exit 49 (Depew). Turn left on Rt. 78, then right on Rt. 5 East. Turn left on Rt. 93 North to Ice Cream Plaza.

Nearby Attractions: Original American Kazoo Company museum and factory (see page 239); Erie County Park; Octagon House; Niagara Falls is 35 miles away.

QRS Music

1026 Niagara Street
Buffalo, NY 14213-2099
(716) 885-4600
www.qrsmusic.com

PLAYER-PIANO ROLLS

At the world's oldest and largest mass manufacturer of player-piano rolls, you see how computer technology now makes a product whose prime was in the Roaring Twenties. You've gotta love a tour that begins by letting a nostalgic visitor play a popular tune on a player piano. Next to this old-fashioned roll-playing piano sits a baby grand equipped with Pianomation, a contemporary piano-playing system run from CDs.

Enter the memorabilia-filled waiting area, where old ads and letters from Jackie Gleason and Princess Grace of Monaco adorn the walls. In the corner sits a 1912 QRS "marking piano," which produces master rolls by recording an actual performer. The modified piano keys are pneumatically connected to a stylus that makes small markings on a roll of paper in the recorder.

Upstairs, look through glass windows at the predecessor of today's high-tech recording studio. To make the master roll, the "arranger" played a song beat-by-beat on a "recording piano" that put holes directly on a master sheet. With this time-consuming process (eight hours to make a three-minute song) the roll could not be played back until the recording was finished. Now, a computerized process produces the master roll. Watch the arranger enter keystrokes on the computer and instantly play them back for accuracy. The floppy disk, not holes in paper, creates the master.

In the manufacturing area, a worker feeds the disk into a perforator machine that cuts a pattern on sheets of paper according to computer code. Nearby, another worker handles the printer that puts song lyrics and other information onto the rolls. Look for the device that slurps up the sheets into finished piano rolls. As the tour ends, you're happy that our world of CD players and digital audio tapes still has room for player-piano music.

Cost: Adults, $2; children under 11, $1.
Freebies: No

Video Shown: 12-minute historical slide show on company history and how player-piano music is created. Tour guide explains more recent developments.

Reservations Needed: No, except for groups larger than 8 people.

Days and Hours: Mon–Fri 10:00 AM and 2:00 PM (2 tours daily). Closed holidays.

Plan to Stay: 1 hour for slide show and tour, plus time to look at items in waiting area and seconds area.

Minimum Age: None

Disabled Access: Small flight of stairs to the exhibits in the waiting area. However, most of tour is not wheelchair accessible.

Group Requirements: Groups larger than 8 people should call 2 weeks in advance. Maximum group size is 20.

Special Information: The tour is a mecca for people with player pianos and will be most interesting for those with some player-piano experience.

Sales Desk: Sells 3,500 QRS rolls in stock, including children's music, Broadway and movie musicals, country and western hits, and rock 'n' roll hits. Seconds are half-price, but you must sift through individual boxed and unboxed rolls for the song titles. Also sells audiocassettes and CDs of player piano music. Tour admission is redeemable toward purchase. Open Mon–Fri 8:00 AM–4:00 PM. Catalog available from above number.

Directions: From Rt. 33, take Rt. 198 West to Rt. 266. Turn left on Rt. 266, which is Niagara St. QRS 1 mile ahead on the right.

Nearby Attractions: Original American Kazoo museum and factory (see page 239); Rich Products History Exhibit in Rich Renaissance Niagara building (call 716-878-8422); Buffalo area attractions include Buffalo Museum of Science and Albright Gallery. Niagara Falls is about 20 miles away.

Radio City Music Hall

1260 Avenue of the Americas
Rockefeller Center
New York, NY 10020
(212) 247-4777
www.radiocity.com

LIVE ENTERTAINMENT

No, this isn't a factory. But they do create the Radio City Rockettes here and produce some of America's best-loved entertainment, such as the Radio City Christmas Spectacular. This behind-the-scenes tour of a New York landmark, built in 1932, combines architecture with a glimpse of what it takes to put together a U.S.-made show that's famous worldwide.

While standing in the art deco Grand Foyer, your theatrical tour guide expounds on the history of Radio City Music Hall, which gained National Historic Landmark status in 1978. Many of its original features have been restored, including the 24-karat gold leaf ceiling, which rises 60 feet over the Grand Foyer. In the Grand Auditorium, sit in the ocean of nearly 6,000 red velvet seats. Inspired by an ocean sunrise, rays of yellow, red, and orange theatrical lights can shine down from the coves between the Grand Auditorium's 60-foot-high arches. Four 70-foot-wide hydraulic elevators divide the stage's floor into sections that allow for many special effects. For example, the front "pit" elevator can descend 27 feet for loading an ice-skating rink.

Peek into the costume shop to see a variety of unique costumes and the original sewing machines and tables. Walk through the private apartment used by Roxy, Radio City's famed impresario. Visit one of the two rehearsal studios. The worn wooden floors resemble an old high-school gymnasium floor. Instead of basketball court markings, painted lines designate the stage elevators. Even numbers along a line denote where the Radio City Rockettes stand.

While you may not see a Radio City Rockette practice her legendary "eye high" kicks, you will meet a member of the world's most famous precision dance troupe. Wearing a custom costume, she talks about the history of the Rockettes.

Cost: Adults, $16; children under 12, $10.
Freebies: Grand Tour button, opportunity to take a photo with a Radio City Rockette.
Video Shown: No
Reservations Needed: No, however tickets sold on first-come, first-served basis in the Radio City Avenue Store. Tour content and prices may change. Groups, see below.
Days and Hours: Mon–Sat 10:00 AM–5:00 PM, Sun 11:00 AM–5:00 PM. Open 365 days a year. Tours depart approximately every 30 minutes.
Plan to Stay: 1–1.25 hours for tour, plus time in Radio City Avenue Store.
Minimum Age: None
Disabled Access: Yes
Group Requirements: Groups of 25 or more people should call (212) 465-6100 for reservations and discount information. Call at least 2 months in advance for Christmas and spring season.
Special Information: Photography allowed, except during rehearsals. No video cameras.
Gift Shop: Radio City Avenue Store sells the popular Radio City Rockette doll, coffee mugs, postcards, and magnets featuring the colorful Radio City marquee and other New York scenes. Open Mon–Sat 10:00 AM–6:00 PM; Sun 11:00 AM–6:00 PM.
Directions: Accessible by 5th and 6th Ave. bus lines. Subway stops below building, so take B, D, Q, or F subway to 47–50th St./Rockefeller Plaza station. When you walk upstairs, you'll see the bright marquee lights. Buy tickets at the Radio City Avenue Store.
Nearby Attractions: NBC Studios and Sony Wonder Technology Lab tours (see pages 237 and 243); Madison Square Garden tour (call 212-465-5800); NASDAQ Stock Market in Times Square.

Sony Wonder Technology Lab

550 Madison Avenue
New York, NY 10022
(212) 833-8100
www.sonywondertechlab.com

ELECTRONICS

After your high-tech greeting by b.b.wonderbot, Sony Wonder's telepresence robot, you ride up an elevator to a black room dotted with tiny, star-like lights. You hear computer screens beckon "Come here!" "Over here!" You approach a screen where your photo is taken, and you type in your name and record your voice—this information is all stored on your new Sony Wonder Card, which you use to interact with the exhibits.

On your way to the Technology Workshop, read, watch, and listen to the history of communication technology, from early phonographs to the 21st century's newest gadgets. Curious about how digital sound is stored? Have you ever seen the inside of a Sony video camera? Swipe your card at one of the Signal Viewer stations—here, CD players, video cameras, and other everyday Sony devices that record and project signals, images, and audio are explained. Learn how a TV screen works—and that the average American watches 1,825 hours of TV a year!

At the Processing Signals station, you can add an echo to your own voice, or play your voice backward. In the Audio Lab, produce a jazzy tune using a baby's wail, a cow's moo, and other odd sounds in place of instruments—the computer mixes the sounds for you and plays back your composition. In the Image Lab, "point" a laser tracking device at an electronic canvas several feet away to create a silly "painting"—you can even paste in your own face. There are plenty of hands-on exhibits where you can learn how technology is used in industries like TV production, medicine, and meteorology. You may want to be an ultrasound trainee, performing a simulated ultrasound on a pregnant woman. At another station, search for a "leak" in the area by manipulating an infrared camera on the end of a huge red robotic arm in the center of the room. You can even edit a Billy Joel video, splicing together live concert footage with other images to create a clip worthy of MTV. You may leave Sony Wonder wanting to become a television producer, an imaging specialist, or a computer artist!

Cost: Free

Freebies: Certificate of Achievement with your name and photo.

Videos Shown: Several 15-minute videos demonstrating high-definition technology. Videos change, but the subject is always natural wonders like fish swimming underwater or an aerial view of different regions of the U.S.

Reservations Needed: No, except for groups.

Days and Hours: Tue–Sat 10:00 AM–6:00 PM, Thur 10:00 AM–8:00 PM, Sun 12:00 PM–6:00 PM. Closed Mondays and major holidays.

Plan to Stay: 1 hour

Minimum Age: None. Children under 8 years old may need adult assistance at some exhibits.

Disabled Access: Yes

Group Requirements: Groups of 8 to 35 people can reserve space 2 weeks in advance.

Special Information: Last admission 30 minutes before closing.

Gift Shop: None

Directions: Located in Sony Plaza on 56th St. between Madison and 5th Aves. Take E or F subway to 5th Ave./53rd St. and walk up 3 blocks to 56th St., or take the N or R subway to 5th Ave./60th St. and walk down 4 blocks to 56th St.

Nearby Attractions: NBC Studios and Radio City Music Hall tours (see pages 237 and 242); Madison Square Garden tour (call 212-465-5800); NASDAQ Stock Market in Times Square; Museum of Modern Art; St. Patrick's Cathedral; Central Park; Rockefeller Center.

Steinway & Sons

1 Steinway Place
Long Island City, NY 11105
(718) 721-2600
www.steinway.com

STEINWAY & SONS

A piano mecca exists inside a four-story building in urban Queens, New York. Part lumberyard, woodshop, fine-cabinet studio, music-playing room, and back-office operation, Steinway & Sons is a world microcosm, with 33 different nationalities of workers. More than 500 craftspeople, trained by apprenticeship, hand-build 2,800 pianos each year. Since it takes one year and approximately 12,000 parts to make a Steinway piano, you will be amazed by the number of pianos in progress.

One tour highlight is the rim bending. Six men carry a laminated, rock-maple board (often with 18 layers) to one of the piano-shaped presses, the same ones invented 100 years ago by the founder's son. They wrestle the wood, bending it around the press, then hammer, screw, and clamp the wood into place. Each rim stays one day on the press. Once removed, rims rest calmly for at least six weeks in a sauna-hot, dark room. Here you appreciate the range of piano sizes, as the rims stand from five to nine feet tall.

The belly department is rumored to be named after the original German-American beer-drinking craftsmen whose bellies hung over the pianos as they worked here. Soundboards are custom-fit into each piano. Workers hammer in the bridge to which strings will be attached. Saws hiss and the floors vibrate with the rhythmic banging and drilling. Cast-iron plates suspended in air wait for installation into rims. In the stringing department, you'll watch with fascination as a worker attaches each metal string to the plate (or "harp"), loops it tightly around the bridge, and then clamps it around the tuning pin. This process is skillfully repeated until all strings are installed.

The final stage is tuning. Master voicers in soundproof rooms regulate the "action," which is how piano-makers refer to the key-and-hammer mechanism. To ensure that all hammers rise to the same height, voicers hit each key and watch the corresponding hammer bob like a woodpecker's head. Once the action is regulated, the voicer inserts it into the front of the piano and tests its musical quality, adjusting its tuning and brightness before the piano's first performance in Carnegie Hall, or your living room.

Cost: Free

Freebies: No

Video Shown: No, but can purchase 15-minute video that alternates between factory and pianists' performances.

Reservations Needed: Yes

Days and Hours: Alternating Thur 9:00 AM. No tours July and August. Closed holidays and week between Christmas and New Year's.

Plan to Stay: 2.5 hours

Minimum Age: 16

Disabled Access: Yes, via freight elevators.

Group Requirements: Maximum group size is 15 people. Call several weeks in advance for reservations.

Gift Area: Can order books, videos, posters, and logoed items including mugs, T-shirts, and pens, with delivery in 7–10 days. Product listing available at above number.

Special Information: Since factory covers 450,000 square feet and 4 floors that may have sawdust, wear comfortable walking shoes.

Directions: From LaGuardia airport, take Grand Central Pkwy. West. Take first exit and turn right onto Steinway St. to 19th Ave. Steinway & Sons is on your left. From Manhattan, take Triboro Bridge toward Queens. Take first exit in Queens. Stay in right lane to get onto Astoria Blvd. Turn left onto Steinway St. Follow above directions. Call for subway directions (N train to Ditmars Blvd.).

Nearby Attractions: Shea Stadium; Manhattan's music attractions include Radio City Music Hall tour (see page 242), Lincoln Center, Carnegie Hall, Steinway Hall (company's piano showroom and museum—call 212-246-1100).

Furniture Discovery Center

101 West Green Drive
High Point, NC 27260
(336) 887-3876
www.furniturediscovery.org

FURNITURE-MAKING

While most of High Point's famous furniture factories no longer give public tours, you'll experience the furniture manufacturing process from A to Z at this unique interactive museum. The displays in the main exhibit area, set up to simulate the "flow of production" in an ideal furniture factory, offer a comprehensive look at the detailed production involved in crafting dressers, china cabinets, highboys, and upholstered chairs.

Approach a designer's studio desk, where manufacturing always starts, and pick up the drafting tools and wood samples. Mascots "Joe" and "Josephine"—life-size blueprints detailing the measurements of an average-size man and woman—stand upright as a reminder of the human dimensions of furniture design.

Visit Harvey Hardwood, a 500-pound solid red oak that gives a two-minute lesson about forestry and the use of hardwood. His animated face and motion-triggered presentation entertain children and adults alike.

A giant blueprint of a Queen Anne highboy greets you in the case goods section, where your "factory tour" officially begins. Displayed (although not running) are the machines used to shape, carve, sand, and assemble. You can grip the handles of band saws, lathes, and drills. The multi-spindle carver is fascinating; follow the contours of a model and see how spinning blades produce 16 identical matches.

Grab an air-powered nail gun in the upholstery section and begin simulating the assembly of a frame for a loveseat. A large blueprint outlines the furniture's design. Touch more than 15 samples of fabric and then select your favorite on the interactive computer, which allows you to design your own sofa by picking a style and watching it come together frame by frame on the screen. Sit on an upholstered chair and you'll appreciate the sturdy craftsmanship and design.

In the special exhibit area, the Serta Miniature Bedroom Collection contains reproductions of famous bedrooms, such as King Tut's and Kublai Khan's (whose round, moon-shaped, carved bed is a favorite among visitors). Crafting large or small furniture requires precise measurements, a steady hand, and an eye for detail—all of which are comprehensively explained in the heart of High Point, the furniture-making capital of the world.

Cost: Adults, $5; seniors, students, and children over 15, $4; children 6–15, $2; under 6, free.

Freebies: No

Video Shown: No

Reservations Needed: No, except for groups of 15 or more people.

Days and Hours: Mon–Fri 10:00 AM–5:00 PM, Sat 9:00 AM–5:00 PM, Sun 1:00 PM–5:00 PM. Closed holidays and Mondays November–March. Call for extended hours during April and October International Home Furnishings Market.

Plan to Stay: 1 hour, plus time for gift shop.

Minimum Age: None

Disabled Access: Yes

Group Requirements: Groups of 15 or more people should make reservations 2 weeks in advance for a guided tour. Discounts available for groups over 15 people.

Gift Shop: Sells a wide selection of furniture books, furniture-shaped chocolate, jewelry, logoed T-shirts, and bookmarks. Open same hours as museum.

Directions: From I-85, take downtown High Point exit. Head 2 miles north. Turn left on West Green Dr. Discovery Center is 1 half block on left in the back of the Convention & Visitors Bureau. From Hwy. 68, turn left on Hwy. 311. Head south and turn right on West Green Dr. Discovery Center is 1 half block on left.

Nearby Attractions: Young/Spangle furniture factory tour (see page 249); Krispy Kreme doughnut tour (call 336-885-8081) Angela Peterson Doll and Miniature Museum; High Point Museum and Historical Park.

Pillowtex (formerly Fieldcrest Cannon)

Cannon Village Visitors Center
200 West Avenue
Kannapolis, NC 28081
(704) 938-3200
www.cannonvillage.com

SHEETS AND TEXTILES

You can't help noticing the tall, red brick smokestack bearing the Fieldcrest Cannon name; it towers against the background as you drive into Kannapolis. (Appropriately, the town's name combines two Greek words meaning "City of Looms.") You'll pass some of the 1,600 "mill houses" constructed for employees in the early 1900s. Here, on land that was once a 600-acre cotton plantation, farming and textiles are interwoven with the history of the land.

The museum, with its old wooden looms and textile artifacts, is located in the Cannon Village Visitor's Center and provides an introduction to the textile industry. The museum includes a photographic history of the plant, early to modern towels made by Pillowtex, other displays, and a video about the process of producing towels and sheets.

You will learn that when bales of fresh cotton are received, the dirty cotton is cleaned to remove lumps and alien fibers. Enormous barrels of spun, coiled cotton ropes wait to be processed. In the card room, large, noisy card machines align webs of soft cotton side by side.

To make the famous cotton/poly 50/50 blend, a drawing machine processes four barrels each of cotton and polyester. More than 550 looms in the nearby plant weave threads into muslin and percale sheeting; another plant bleaches, prints, and dyes it. At a Concord, North Carolina, facility, the sheet is cut, hemmed, labeled, and packaged.

Cost: Free

Freebies: Coupon booklet for discounts at various Cannon Village shops, including a coupon for a complimentary item from the Pillowtex outlet store.

Video Shown: 20-minute video covers history of the town and company. Shows towel-manufacturing process.

Reservations Needed: No

Days and Hours: Mon–Sat 9:00 AM–5:00 PM, Sun 1:00 PM–6:00 PM. Closed Thanksgiving, Christmas, New Year's, and Easter.

Plan to Stay: 1 hour for museum, plus time for Cannon Village shops.

Minimum Age: None

Disabled Access: Yes

Group Requirements: None

Special Information: For insurance reasons, plant tour was discontinued.

Outlet Store: Pillowtex Bed & Bath is in Cannon Village (call 704-939-2869). Open Mon–Sat 9:00 AM–7:00 PM, Sun 1:00 PM–6:00 PM, with extended hours around Christmas. Closed Christmas.

Directions: From I-85 North, take Exit 58 for Kannapolis. Take Hwys. 29 and 601 North. Travel under bridge. Take first right, onto 1st St. and into Village. Go to Cannon Village Visitors Center. From I-85 South, take Exit 63. Follow Lane St. into Kannapolis.

Nearby Attractions: Cannon Village has many specialty shops, factory outlet stores, and restaurants; Charlotte Motor Speedway.

Replacements, Ltd.

1089 Knox Road
Greensboro, NC 27420
(336) 697-3000 / (800) REPLACE (800-737-5223)
www.replacements.com

REPLACEMENTS, LTD.

CHINA, CRYSTAL, FLAT-
WARE, AND COLLECTIBLES

For a special dinner party, you carefully set the table with the fragile bone china Aunt Millie willed you. But a guest accidentally dropped a precious teacup while helping clear the table. Once you see Replacements, Ltd.'s rows of shelves (62,000, to be exact!) stacked 16 feet high with 160,000 different patterns of china and crystal, you will feel confident about matching Aunt Millie's teacup. Replacements, the world's largest supplier of obsolete, active, and inactive china, crystal, and flatware, receives 15,000 pattern requests every month.

In the research department, "detectives" identify discontinued china, crystal, and flatware patterns for desperate customers, who send pictures, photocopies, or pencil rubbings of their treasures. The researchers use old catalogs (one prize possession is a 1936 Fostoria Catalog) and pictures to identify patterns. Antique dealers and a 2,000-buyer network receive Replacements' 1,000-page bimonthly wish list of customer requests. Buyers scour auctions, estate sales, and flea markets worldwide in search of specific patterns.

Wearing goggles that protect their eyes, skilled restoration-area workers carefully smooth out small (less than one-eighth of an inch) chips in crystal. Besides restoring crystal to its original beauty, workers reglaze and fire certain china pieces to remove scratches. Paintbrushes in hand, these artists expertly dab special paint onto the gold and platinum trim on ornate, elegant porcelain.

One tour highlight comes when your guide leads you down an aisle of the 3.2 million–piece warehouse. Looking without touching is difficult—but required—as you peer at towering shelves and spot anything from the elegant stem of a Baccarat crystal to a Limoges dessert plate. Equally impressive is the flatware department. Here you see gleaming silver serving spoons and shiny butter knives being inspected, identified, and inventoried. Workers polish precious pieces on high-speed buffing machines,

then seal them in their own plastic bags to retard tarnishing. You leave with a true appreciation of the effort and dedication involved in researching, restoring, and replacing the "irreplaceable."

Cost: Free

Freebies: Logoed magnet

Video Shown: No

Reservations Needed: No, except for groups larger than 25 people.

Days and Hours: Mon–Sun 8:30 AM–8:30 PM, every 30 minutes. Closed Thanksgiving and Christmas.

Plan to Stay: 20–30 minutes, plus time in showroom and museum.

Minimum Age: None

Disabled Access: Yes

Group Requirements: Groups larger than 25 should call 2 days ahead; will be split into smaller groups.

Special Information: Wear comfortable shoes. Museum adjacent to showroom focuses on Ohio River Valley's early-20th-century glass industry.

Retail Store: 12,000-square-foot showroom displays porcelain, crystal, and metal collectibles in antique mahogany, oak, and walnut showcases (some dating back to the 1800s, and many with their original glass!). Also, Masons' lamps (Wedgwood), crystal perfume bottles, and jewelry. Open Mon–Sun 8:00 AM–9:00 PM.

Directions: Take I-85/40 and exit at Exit 132. Go north (left if coming from Greensboro, right from Burlington) on Mt. Hope Church Rd. and turn left on Knox Rd. Replacements is on left.

Nearby Attractions: Seagrove Area Potteries tours about 40 miles away (see page 248); Thomas Built Buses gives limited tours (call 336-889-4871); Greensboro's attractions include Colonial Heritage Center, Greensboro Arboretum, Greensboro Cultural Center at Festival Park; Burlington Factory Outlets; Winston-Salem's attractions are 25 miles away.

Seagrove Area Potteries

Museum of North Carolina Traditional Pottery
122 Main Street
Seagrove, NC 27341
(336) 873-7887 / (336) 873-7300
www.tourseagrove.com

FRIENDS OF THE
POTTERY CENTER

POTTERY

More than 100 pottery studios scattered across the countryside make up the Seagrove pottery community. Within a 20-mile radius of the tiny, rural town of Seagrove (population approximately 357), the potteries are located along Route 705, Potters' Row, and its snaking secondary roads. Hand-painted 12-foot wooden signs point up different roads toward clusters of studios. At the Museum of North Carolina Traditional Pottery, you can obtain a map marking all the locations, find help focusing your exploration, and view a sampling of the pottery styles made in the area.

Starting in the 1750s, English potters migrated to the Seagrove area for its good clay and its location on a major commercial road. Despite the influx of 20th-century mass production, several potteries have persevered; some are now in their eighth and ninth generations. Now the largest community of potters in the U.S.A., Seagrove maintains the feeling that its people have been making pots for a long time.

In this laid-back, Old World–style community, many of the potteries are small family operations. Some are in backyards; some have dirt or brick floors, covered with clay dirt. Many use North Carolina native clay, which fires up to a light orange/brown terracotta color.

In a low-ceilinged log building with an earthen floor, Vernon Owens, owner of Jugtown Pottery, and his wife make salt-glazed crocks, milk churns, molasses jugs, and other traditional pieces. They throw salt onto the pots during the firing inside the 2,300° wood-burning kiln. The salt melts, bonds with the silica in the clay, and leaves a clear, bumpy, orange-peel texture. At Holly Hill Pottery, one of the area's larger potteries, you'll see up to four potters transforming mounds of clay into tea glasses or dinner plates. Another potter may be loading the 1,000-cubic-foot gas-fired kiln. As you visit many potteries, you'll recognize their distinctive characteristics. In fact, by looking at the shapes and silhouettes of each potter's antique-like pitchers, experienced eyes can classify them not only as North Carolina pots, but also specifically as Seagrove pots.

Cost: Free
Freebies: Potteries of the Seagrove Area map available at the Museum of North Carolina Traditional Pottery and at all the potteries.
Video Shown: No
Reservations Needed: No, unless motorcoach groups want a guide (see below).
Days and Hours: Generally Mon–Sat 9:00 AM–5:00 PM. Call the above numbers regarding schedules.
Plan to Stay: 1–2 days, although it's impossible to visit every pottery shop.
Minimum Age: None
Disabled Access: Yes, for most studios.
Group Requirements: Call 1 week in advance (336-873-7300) to arrange for a motorcoach step-on guide.
Special Information: Kilns are especially hot in the summer. The Seagrove Pottery Festival, held the weekend before Thanksgiving, features pottery demonstrations and sales.
Gift Shop: At Sells annual Seagrove Area Pottery Shop Guide. Open Mon–Fri 10:00 AM–2:00 PM, Sat 9:00 AM–3:00 PM. Reduced winter hours.
Showrooms: Sell each studio's wares, including face jugs, grape pitchers, Seagrove traditional and functional stoneware, and contemporary stoneware with pastel designs. Open generally Mon–Sat 9:00 AM–5:00 PM. Closed holidays.
Directions: From Greensboro intersection of I-85 and I-40, take I-73/I-74 South (old Rt. 220). After sign for area potteries, take Seagrove Exit 45. Turn left onto Rt. 705. Museum of North Carolina Traditional Pottery is in an old brick building on right.
Nearby Attractions: North Carolina Zoological Park; Southern Pines and Pinehurst golf communities.

Young/Spangle

1150 Tryon Road
High Point, NC 27260
(910) 884-4535 / (800) 962-3694

FURNITURE

North Carolina is known for furniture-making, and High Point is the furniture capital of the world. The large factories do not give public tours. However, Young/Spangle, a small family-owned and -operated business that has been manufacturing custom furniture since 1941, graciously opens its doors to visitors. Instead of the hustle-bustle and noisy atmosphere of many manufacturers, you hear the steady hum of sewing machines and intermittent hammering and stapling. Roll upon roll of different colored and patterned fabric catches your eye.

Seated at sewing machines, several women stitch together hand-cut pieces of upholstery fabric. The common work area is one large open space that has a folksy, informal feeling. In one spot a worker staples or hammers fabric to a wooden frame, carefully matching the fabric to make sure all the petals of a flower, for example, align correctly. In another space a worker fills a cushion with fiberfill, feathers, or down.

Since the company specializes in custom pieces (they can even reproduce something from a magazine photograph!), you will see different types of furniture. The introductory video and your tour guide, one of the company owners, explain processes that you may not see. Furniture pieces, such as overstuffed mauve chairsleepers, receive final touches before being shipped. For the company's regular line of leather furniture, workers cut hides according to patterns and sew cushions and other upholstery parts.

The guide turns over a chair and explains the quality craftsmanship that goes into making each piece. She points out the double-dowel and corner block joint frame construction, which is sturdier than stapling. Eight-way hand tying, a manual process of tying string in eight different directions around the furniture's springs and frame, makes furniture more durable and prevents sagging springs. In addition to manufacturing comfortable and sturdy made-to-order furniture that can be passed down and reupholstered through generations, the company restores original furniture. Upon personally testing one of their chairs, you will agree that Young/Spangle deserves its reputation.

Cost: Free

Freebies: No

Video Shown: 14-minute video on how company makes furniture.

Plan to Stay: 30 minutes

Reservations Needed: Yes. Individuals can call for same-day reservations. Groups, see below.

Days and Hours: Mon–Fri 9:00 AM–2:30 PM. Closed holidays and week between Christmas and New Year's.

Minimum Age: None

Disabled Access: Yes

Group Requirements: Groups larger than 20 people should call 1 week in advance; will be split into smaller groups.

Special Information: Groups larger than 15 people can arrange tours of other furniture factories and showrooms by calling High Point Convention & Visitors Bureau 1 month in advance (call 910-884-5255).

Retail Store: No, but can place catalog or custom orders. Open for ordering Mon–Fri 9:00 AM–3:30 PM.

Directions: From I-85, look for High Point sign and take Business I-85. Take West Green Dr. Turn left onto Tryon Ave. Look for brick building on the right at the end of street. From I-40, take Hwy. 68 South. Turn left onto Ward St. Turn left onto Prospect St. and right onto Courtesy Rd. Young/Spangle is at corner of Courtesy Rd. and Tryon Ave.

Nearby Attractions: Furniture Discovery Center (see page 245); Krispy Kreme doughnut tour (call 336-885-8081); Atrium Furniture Mall.

Pipestem Creek

7060 Highway 9
Carrington, ND 58421
(701) 652-2623
www.pipestemcreek.com

SunFeeders
by Pipestem Creek

SUNFLOWER BIRD-FEEDERS AND WREATHS

Named for the beautiful, pristine stream that flows through the nearby prairie, Pipestem Creek makes an unusual natural product. Ann Hoffert, a former nurse practitioner, established Pipestem Creek in 1991 at her dad's 7,500-acre farm. Her wreaths and bird-feeders are made of homegrown sunflowers, millet, barley, ornamental corn, burgundy amaranths, and everlasting flowers. The plants are carefully dried, preserved, and hand-fashioned into large and small edible wreaths, suitable for bird feeders or home decorations. The wreaths, called Sun Feeders, and the home decorations, called Sun Florals, sell through national mail-order catalogs as well as in specialty shops and direct orders.

The drive to Pipestem Creek takes you past acres of planted fields, towering grain elevators, and rumbling tractor/combines, which service the feed business run by Ann Hoffert's father and her husband on the family farm. Several red, wooden, old-fashioned granary buildings and a train depot house Pipestem Creek's drying, shipping, and gift-shop facilities. In the white production building, bedecked with vines in the summer and surrounded by flowering beds, workers at large tables carefully assemble the sweet-smelling sunflower heads, corn husks, amaranths, and sheaths of millet or green barley. It can take a worker up to an hour to create one of the largest wreaths.

The head gardener comes and goes with armfuls of dried materials, distributing fragrant supplies to the workers. Some assemblers are neighborhood farmwives, who take home raw materials and return later with finished components. One wall is covered with pictures and informational materials spelling out Pipestem Creek's history and illustrating its varied marketing methods.

If you visit during summer, your tour guide (probably Ann herself, perhaps accompanied by one of her daughters) will walk you past a big farmhouse and through the private gardens to admire the 1,500 feet of rainbow-colored beds planted in everlastings. One of the tall, red granary buildings houses edible crops while they're drying. Cast your gaze upward at the ceiling—you'll see a cornucopia of sunflower heads, each one bound with wire and hung separately to dry, head-down, free from destructive mold and hungry critters. Other edible grains, along with sparkling burgundy amaranths and colorful heads of Indian corn, fill every blank space.

Cost: Self-guided tours: free. Guided tours: adults, $3; children, free.

Freebies: No

Video Shown: No

Reservations Needed: No, except for groups over 10 people.

Days and Hours: Mon–Fri 8:00 AM–4:00 PM, weekends by appointment or chance.

Plan to Stay: 1 hour, plus time for gift shop.

Minimum Age: None

Disabled Access: Grounds and gift shop accessible. Stairs in production areas.

Group Requirements: Groups larger than 10 people should call 1 week in advance. No maximum group size.

Special Information: August is the best month for viewing sunflower fields. To also see the everlasting flower fields, specialty crops, and gardens tour from May–October.

Gift Shop: Features sunflower-based products, Sun Feeders, Sun Florals, and dried flower arrangements. Housed in a 10-sided wooden granary. Open same hours as tour. Free catalog available at above address.

Directions: From I-94, take Hwy. 281 North. Turn right onto Hwy. 9 East. Pipestem Creek is about 1 mile ahead on the right.

Nearby Attractions: Arrowwood National Wildlife Refuge; Foster County Museum; Hawksnest Ridge; McHenry Railroad Loop.

Airstream

419 West Pike Street
Jackson Center, OH 45334
(937) 596-6111 (ext. 7401)
www.airstream-rv.com

AIRSTREAM

**RECREATIONAL
VEHICLES**

Wally Byam invented the Airstream back in 1932 because his wife refused to go camping unless she could take her kitchen. He decided to build a trailer with built-in comforts that copied the sleek, bullet-shaped design of an airliner, which could travel the roads like a "stream of air." Little could he have imagined that it would become the Rolls-Royce of RVs, one of the finest examples of American industrial design, and be used as television and movie stars' offices and dressing rooms on studio backlots.

The tour at this Thor Industries subsidiary (Thor is the second-largest RV manufacturer in the U.S.A.) shows you what makes these trailers and motor homes so unique: aircraft-style manufacturing. To build the shiny aluminum shell, the individual sheets of aluminum are laid up and measured for the curved roof and side walls, drilled, and then riveted together and connected to the end cap and interior metal ribs. Approximately 4,000 rivets are used. Spaces for the doors and windows are cut out of this aluminum shell.

In another area the chassis rails are laid down. A high-grade aluminum skin seals the underbelly from beneath. Fiberglass insulation is inserted before workers put down the tongue-and-groove plywood floor that seals the chassis, from above. Hoists lift the aluminum shell and place it gently on the chassis, which sits on special leveling jacks. Workers then bolt the chassis and shell together.

Once the exterior shell is sealed and married to the chassis, it's thoroughly checked for water leaks. In the water check, huge pumps spray hundreds of gallons of water on the top and sides of the RV body. Meanwhile, workers inside the RV use flashlights to help search for any leaks at the seams and rivet holes. Any needed additional caulking and weather sealing is done from the inside.

With the outside and chassis completed, the workers turn to the RV's inside. The toi- lets are always the first interior objects installed. Although the interiors can be highly adjustable, the toilet has to go over the septic-tank hole, and everything else goes in around it. Workers then rivet on the interior skin. Electrical wiring, carpeting, plumbing, and furniture are installed. All cabinets and furniture, built at the plant, are anchored to the interior metal frame. When complete, the RVs go to the mechanics building, where they are inspected.

Cost: Free

Freebies: No

Video Shown: No

Reservations Needed: No, except for groups over 20 people.

Days and Hours: Mon–Fri 2:00 PM. Closed holidays, weeks around Christmas and New Year's, and usually at beginning of July.

Plan to Stay: 1.5 hours for tour and gift shop.

Minimum Age: 16

Disabled Access: Yes

Group Requirements: Groups over 20 people should call 2 days in advance. No maximum group size. Special tour times can be arranged.

Special Information: No photography. Wally Byam Caravan Club International headquarters in town (call 937-596-5211 about Airstream company and WBCCI rallies).

Gift Shop: The Wally Byam Store at the Factory Service Center sells full collection of logoed items and accessories, including T-shirts, caps, and scale-model RVs. Open Mon–Fri 8:15 AM–4:45 PM. Closed holidays, but not during factory shutdown periods.

Directions: From I-75, take the Indian Lake/Jackson Center Exit 102. Take SR 274 East and head into Jackson Center. Plant is on left.

Nearby Attractions: Wally Byam Memorial Park; Neil Armstrong Space Museum; Dayton's attractions, including Wright-Patterson Air Force Base, 50 miles away.

Airborne Express

145 Hunter Drive
Wilmington, OH 45177
(937) 382-5591
www.abxair.com

AIR FREIGHT

The nationwide sort hub of Airborne Express probably ranks as the hottest nightlife spot in Wilmington, Ohio. But its luminaries—the 1 million packages flown in from across the country each weeknight—do not sit in First Class, and the treatment they receive is not so much red carpet as it is black conveyor belt. Two thousand workers hover over almost 16 miles of conveyor belts in Airborne's sprawling facility, unloading, sorting, and reloading all of this freight in just 4 hours. Visitors who brave the lengthy late-night tour here learn a bundle about Airborne's freight operation and view the activity from some prime vantage points.

The first stop on the tour, following an introductory video, is the maintenance hangar, where you'll see crews performing heavy repair work on one of the DC-8, DC-9, or Boeing 767 aircraft that make up the company's fleet. Discover why Airborne buys used planes from passenger airlines and converts them to handle cargo, rather than purchasing new aircraft. Then, cross the tarmac—or "ramp"—on your way to an Aircraft Rescue and Fire Fighting station. Here, see the vehicles used in airport emergencies, which are painted a bright chartreuse color called safety yellow.

By now, planes are arriving on the ramp and the nightly sorting operation begins in earnest. In one of Airborne's six Sort Center buildings, stand an arm's length away from moving conveyors in what feels like a massive three-story machine. Workers here send packages on different conveyors depending on their particular sort code, a cryptic dilution of ZIP codes, geographic regions, and airport abbreviations. You find out that seven different people must make the same mistake for a package to get misdirected, one reason for Airborne's high rate of fulfillment.

Next, get a bird's-eye view of the action on the ramp from the Ground Operations Tower. Most nights you will also be able to climb aboard a gutted airplane. Inside this cavernous space, see how Airborne's specially developed cargo containers are secured to the plane's fuselage. These containers (shaped like a capital "D" or its mirror opposite) maximize use of a plane's interior space while still utilizing its original doors. If only your method of unpacking groceries were this efficient!

Cost: Free

Freebies: Company fact sheet

Video Shown: 9-minute video gives an overview of Airborne's sorting operation.

Reservations Needed: Yes, 2 weeks advance notice is recommended. Individuals are added to existing groups.

Days and Hours: Night tours: Mon–Fri 11:30 PM. Day tours: Mon–Fri by appointment, for special groups only. Closed holidays. Generally no tours given between Thanksgiving and Christmas.

Minimum Age: Night tour: 12; day: 8.

Plan to Stay: 2–3 hours

Disabled Access: Yes, but tour route will be altered.

Group Requirements: Maximum group size is 30. Subgroups of 6–8 people tour together.

Special Information: Tours are strenuous, with about 2.5 miles of walking and 10 flights of stairs, so wear comfortable shoes. No open-toed shoes or shorts permitted. Tours spend up to one hour outside, so dress appropriately; however, no tours in severe weather. No photography.

Gift Counter: Sells logoed items such as caps, key chains, and stuffed airplanes. Open at end of each tour.

Directions: From Cincinnati, take I-71 North to Exit 50. Turn right onto Hwy. 68, left onto Hwy. 22 East, and right onto Hwy. 73. Turn right onto Airport Rd. From Columbus, take I-71 South to Exit 50 and follow above directions.

Nearby Attractions: Cowan Lake State Park; Caesar Creek State Park; Fort Ancient Indian Burial Mound; Kings Island amusement park is 30 miles away.

▲ Specially developed cargo containers are unloaded from a DC-8 aircraft at Airborne Express's Wilmington, Ohio, hub.

▼ A DC-8 taxis in.

American Whistle

6540 Huntley Road
Columbus, OH 43229
(614) 846-2918
www.americanwhistle.com

"How does that little ball get into the whistle?" is the question asked by most curious children (and adults) who tour the American Whistle Corporation. The answer is, "The corking machine does it." You'll have to go on the tour to find out what that means.

The corking machine is just one of the many whistle-making steps you'll see at the only metal-whistle manufacturer in the U.S.A. As you journey through the factory's work stations, with the din of the press in the background, you'll be amazed to learn from your tour guide that more than 1 million whistles are manufactured each year in this neat, compact facility. Watch whistles being cut, stamped, soldered, baked, bathed, polished, and packaged.

The press is your first stop, after an initial briefing by your tour guide. Here, in rapid succession, a 37-ton press fitted with a die (a piece similar to a cookie cutter) stamps down on each small brass square. One after another, brass cutouts resembling miniature sets of Mickey Mouse ears are punched out. In a later process, the ears fold upward to become the sides of the whistle.

During another part of the tour, you are privileged to view the whistles in their own private bathing area-a tiny room off the main factory floor. Here, in a large, open, circular trough called a vibratory, the whistles take a stone bath. The stones resemble rough jade pieces and are placed in with the whistles and a tiny bit of liquid. Then the trough vibrates for seven hours to smooth any rough edges off them. The finished, bright, shiny whistles, lined side-by-side for inspection and packaging, are the same whistles you see being tooted by policemen at busy traffic intersections or by referees at the Super Bowl.

Also learn how to use a whistle as a safety tool. American Whistles are four decibels louder than their nearest competitors, and the company sponsors a Whistle Defense Program to encourage safety awareness. While a piercing whistle can scare away attackers and bring help, it cannot be used against the victim.

Cost: $3 per person

Freebies: New "American Spirit" chrome whistle.

Video Shown: No

Reservations Needed: Yes. Individuals and families must join scheduled group tour.

Days and Hours: Mon–Fri 9:00 AM–4:00 PM. Closed holidays.

Plan to Stay: 1 hour for tour

Minimum Age: None

Disabled Access: Yes

Group Requirements: Minimum group size of 15 people, or $45. Call at least 1 week in advance. Maximum 65 people per group.

Special Information: Photography restricted in parts of the factory.

Gift Counter: Display case is located in the factory at the end of the tour. Whistles (metal, plastic, and even 24-karat gold), lanyards, and mouthpiece covers available in many colors. Catalog available from above number.

Directions: From I-71, exit for Rt. 161 (Dublin-Granville Rd.). Go west on Rt. 161 to Huntley Rd. Turn right onto Huntley Rd. Factory is on the right in about 1 mile—roughly halfway between Rt. 161 and Schrock Rd.

Nearby Attractions: Krema Peanut Butter tour (call 614-299-4131); Anthony Thomas Candy tour (group tours only, call 614-272-9221); other Columbus attractions include State House, Columbus Zoo, and Center of Science and Industry.

Carousel Magic!

44 West Fourth Street
Mansfield, OH 44902
(419) 526-4009
www.carouselmagic.com

Ah, the beauty and wonder of a carousel. Who among us does not stand back and gaze at the colorful animals as they bring smiles and happiness to children and adults alike? Enter a world where these animals come to life. Your tour guide, dressed in an early 1900s plaid suit with a long skirt and a high-collared white blouse, leads you onto the carving floor through large, glass-paneled, wooden double doors in the back of the gift shop. Carousel Magic!, one of only two carousel-carving factories in the U.S.A., and the only major U.S. producer of full-size carousel horse carving kits, dedicates itself to preserving and fostering the tradition of carousel-making, through building, restoring, and repairing carousels.

Begin by seeing a kiln-dried, 12-inch-high block of basswood, made of several layered boards. Not yet completely glued together, your tour guide "opens" the block into its two halves and, to your surprise, it is hollow! This construction method makes the body stronger than a solid block would, permits expansion and contraction of the wood, prevents considerable cracking or warping, and reduces the animal's weight by 25 to 30 percent.

Nearby, small and large chunks of wood soar through the air as mallet meets gouge (chisel) to remove excess bulk from a larger block of wood. On another workbench, the apron-clad master carver firmly places the bottom of the gouge's wooden handle in the palm of his right hand, wraps the four fingers of his left hand around the middle of the tool, supports its underside with his left thumb, and delicately applies pressure as the curved, U-shaped blade carves detail into a horse's mane. The thin sliver of wood curls up and gently falls to the shaving-covered, hardwood floor. Touch the smoothness of the resultant groove.

Proceed up a flight of steps to the art department, where the tip of a painter's thin brush, covered in bright red, colors an intricate rose carved on the horse's saddle. Run your fingers along the shiny body of a finished animal, examine its trappings, and be dazzled by the glass eyes and jewels. Inspired by this process, you can order a carving kit, start creating, and become a part of this magical tradition.

Cost: Adults, $4; children 5–12, $1; children 5 and under, free when accompanied by an adult.

Freebies: No

Video Shown: No

Reservations Needed: No, except for groups of 10 or more people.

Days and Hours: Tue–Sat 10:00 AM–4:00 PM. Closed holidays and December 22nd–April 2nd.

Plan to Stay: 30–45 minutes, plus time for gift shop.

Minimum Age: None

Disabled Access: Yes

Group Requirements: Groups of 10 or more people should call a few days in advance. Maximum group size is 47 people. Special rates for school groups and home school groups.

Gift Shop: Sells carousel-related music boxes, stickers, jewelry, and books. Open Mon–Sat 10:00 AM–5:00 PM. Call to check for special holiday hours.

Directions: From the north, take I-71 South to Rt. 30 West (Exit 176). Take SR 13 South. Turn right onto Fourth St. Carousel Magic! is on the right. From the south, take I-71 North to SR 13 North (Exit 169). In Mansfield, SR 13 becomes Diamond St. Turn left onto Fourth St. Carousel Magic! is on the right.

Nearby Attractions: Carousel District in downtown Mansfield, which includes the Richland Carousel Park (contains a working carousel of 52 animals and 2 chariots, the first hand-carved wooden carousel built in the U.S. since 1930), boutiques, art galleries, and bookstores; Richland Discovery Center and Academy (technological discovery zone).

Creegan

510 Washington Street
Steubenville, OH 43952
(740) 283-3708
www.creegans.com

ANIMATED FIGURES AND COSTUME CHARACTERS

The coal- and steel-industry problems in this tri-state area of West Virginia, Pennsylvania, and Ohio may have left a void in Steubenville. However, few places have more vigor than the family-owned and -operated Creegan Company, the nation's largest manufacturer of animated and costume characters. You may recognize Beary Bear, Plentiful Penguin, or Strawberry Bunny from your local retail store windows and seasonal mall displays. Creegan also designs characters for Sea World, Hershey's Chocolate World, and Walt Disney World. Inside the former Montgomery Ward department store, Creegan employees bring an array of characters to life.

Your guide leads you into a virtual craft heaven containing what must be thousands of spools of ribbon of every color, pattern, and texture. Puppet heads, scenery, and props lurk behind silk flowers and craft paraphernalia. A large, lifelike white gorilla stands beside three rosy-cheeked elves. During some tours, an employee dressed as Beary Bear wanders around. Up a wide staircase is the art shop, where workers make costumes and paint faces on molded plastic heads. On the main floor, a huge vacuum-form machine presses out the puppets' faces. Here you may see sheets of stark white plastic being pressed over molds into various facial configurations.

Downstairs in the sculpting area, one woman sculpts all of the character-head molds. Shelves contain hundreds of plaster molds shaped like heads, feet, hands, and animals. Further along is the mechanics/electronics department, full of workbenches laden with toolboxes, handsaws, lathes, vises, and drill presses. Peek inside some headless mechanized bodies to discover some figures' detailed electronic insides and to see how the parts unite to produce a character's body movements. After a tour of the Creegan Company, you will agree with its motto: "We make things move."

Cost: $1

Freebies: Cake, candy, or cookie samples from Fancy Food section of the store.

Video Shown: No, but some are for sale, including "Strawberry Bunny Visits the Creegan Company."

Reservations Needed: Preferred

Days and Hours: Mon–Fri 10:00 AM–4:00 PM, Sat 10:00 AM–2:00 PM (tours by request on Saturdays from November 1st–Christmas). Call for extended tour hours November 1–December 31. Closed Easter, Christmas, and New Year's.

Plan to Stay: 30 minutes, plus time for shops.

Minimum Age: None

Disabled Access: Yes

Group Requirements: 1 day's advance notice is requested for groups larger than 10 people. Inquire about group discounts on store merchandise.

Special Information: Individuals not part of a group may walk through the factory on their own, or may join a group led by one of the entertaining tour guides.

Retail Stores: Showroom displays and sells Creegan's most recent animated figures and scenery. Year-round Christmas shop offers ornaments, gifts, and novelties. Retail store carries a variety of items, including cake-decorating and candy-making supplies and seasonal decor items. Open Mon–Fri 10:00 AM–5:00 PM, Sat 10:00 AM–2:00 PM, Sun by appointment; November 1–December 31, Mon–Thur 9:00 AM–6:00 PM; Fri–Sun 10:00 AM–5:00 PM. Catalog available.

Directions: From I-70, take SR 7 North to Steubenville. Turn left on Washington St., then left on 5th St. Creegan's is on the corner of Washington and 5th Sts.

Nearby Attractions: Brooke Glass, Hall China, Homer Laughlin China, and Senator Heinz History tours (see pages 349, 258, 351, and 294); Weirton Steel Mill tour (call 304-797-8597); Welsh Jaguar Classic Car Museum. Steubenville is the "City of Murals," with 21 beautifully painted historic murals throughout the city.

Goodyear World of Rubber

Goodyear Tire & Rubber Company
1144 East Market Street
Akron, OH 44316
(330) 796-7117
www.goodyear.com

GOODYEAR

Akron, Ohio, is so closely identified with the beginnings and growth of the rubber industry that it is acknowledged as the rubber capital of the world. Most of the rubber and tire factories have moved out of Akron, however, so the closest you can get is to visit the Goodyear World of Rubber. This traditional company museum's exhibits trace the history of the company and the rubber industry.

Enter the museum through a small grove of rubber trees that creates the ambience of a rubber plantation. When you look up at the lush tree leaves and down at the rubber trunk, you'll imagine yourself in a tropical setting. Now that you have gained respect for nature's role in rubber production, bounce through the other exhibits, which describe synthetic rubber, the evolution of tires, the history of the blimp (with models), rubber-making and tire-building processes, and the interstate trucking industry. Short, informative videos accompany many exhibits.

The museum includes a replica of Charles Goodyear's workshop, where he discovered a process for vulcanizing rubber to give it elasticity. The workshop looks like a kitchen because it really was one. Legend has it that Goodyear accidentally discovered his rubber-curing process when he stuck the rubber recipe in the oven to hide it from his wife. The Goodyear Memorial Collection features paintings and many personal mementos acquired from heirs of this famous inventor. You'll also be surprised to learn that the Goodyear Tire & Rubber Company is connected to Charles Goodyear by name only. Frank A. Seiberling founded the company in 1898, 38 years after Charles Goodyear's death.

The museum displays many Goodyear products, including the intriguing artificial heart and moon-tire displays. Finally, two Indianapolis 500 race cars with Goodyear tires illustrate the company's strength: making world-class, high-quality tires.

Cost: Free

Freebies: No

Videos Shown: Optional 25-minute video on tire production process shown in theater. If not playing, ask museum staff to start it. Other short videos throughout museum complement the displays.

Reservations Needed: No, except for groups of 20 or more people.

Days and Hours: Mon–Fri 9:00 AM–4:30 PM. Closed holidays.

Plan to Stay: 1 hour for museum and main video.

Minimum Age: None, but children should be at least 6 to appreciate the displays.

Disabled Access: Yes

Group Requirements: Groups of 20 or more need to call for reservations; special guided tours available by calling 1 month in advance.

Special Information: No photography

Gift Shop: Gift Center sells Goodyear-logoed items, including miniature blimps, jewelry, and clothing. Open same hours as museum.

Directions: From I-76 West, take Exit 24 (Kelly Ave.). Follow signs to Goodyear World of Rubber. From I-76 East, take Exit 25A (East Market St.) Turn left onto East Market St. Proceed to Goodyear World of Rubber parking lot.

Nearby Attractions: Stan Hywet Hall; Hale Farm and Village; Akron Art Museum; John Brown Home; Quaker Square.

Hall China

1 Anna Avenue
East Liverpool, OH 43920
(330) 385-2900
www.hallchina.com

CHINA

What seems to be a small cluster of red brick buildings on the outskirts of East Liverpool is actually 11 acres of production, retail, and office space for Hall China, founded in 1903. Since its early years, Hall has been recognized as an industry leader in hotel and restaurant china production. Hall produced the first lead-free glazed chinaware, which requires only one firing at 2,400°.

Walk up the steps into the 1940s-style foyer, and the receptionist will point you in the direction of yellow arrows that lead you into the factory and on your way through the self-guided tour. Immediately you see stacks of bowls and pitchers as you hear the clinking of china being hand-packed. Next you're surrounded by tall, freestanding, wheeled racks loaded with unfinished gray clay pottery pieces ranging from pasta bowls to mugs, waiting to be glazed and fired.

The facility's ambience is friendly and easygoing. When asked questions, workers eagerly explain the pottery-making process. Some workers sit at potter's wheels, while others, bent over wooden workbenches, hand-sponge and trim away seams to smooth the just-formed mugs and bowls.

Glance over into the plant's interior to see workers making bowls out of hunks of raw clay. A long, stout log of gray clay is mechanically sliced into thick rounds. A worker places each slice into a bowl-shaped mold. Two new automatic casting machines dry these molds continuously.

The jiggering machines mechanically spin and shape each hunk of raw clay into a bowl. The inverted wet clay bowls are placed on conveyors fitted with 149 horizontal shelves, which rotate upward into a dryer for 11 hours and 15 minutes. A new massive computerized jigger machine transforms logs of clay into dried ware without human touch.

As you near the tour's end, you smell the wax and glaze mixtures that will coat the clay pieces. You may see a woman stirring a large cauldron of glaze with a long wooden pad-dle. Before each piece is glazed, a worker air-sprays it to remove any dust or particles. Watch as a worker places both hands inside two crocks to lift them, then simultaneously dips them into the pot of glaze. Slowly and carefully, she twists her wrists to uniformly cover each piece with glaze. The two crocks are then set upon a grate to dry. Kiln firing at 2,400° fuses the clay with the glaze and gives each piece its shiny color.

Cost: Free

Freebies: No

Video Shown: No

Reservations Needed: No, except for groups larger than 10 people.

Days and Hours: Mon–Fri 10:00 AM. Closed holidays. Minimal production week between Christmas and New Year's.

Plan to Stay: 20 minutes for self-guided tour, plus time in Hall Closet.

Minimum Age: None. Children must be accompanied by adult.

Disabled Access: Yes

Group Requirements: Call at least 3 weeks ahead to reserve guided tour for groups of 10 or more people.

Special Information: Wear comfortable shoes and lightweight clothing, since factory is warm.

Gift Shop: Hall Closet offers overruns of first-quality Hall China products, such as cookware and bowls, at slightly discounted prices. Open Mon–Sat 9:00 AM–5:00 PM.

Directions: Take Rt. 7 North, which becomes SR 39. Follow it east until it takes a sharp, 90-degree turn. Immediately after the turn, look for Boyce Church sign and make a left onto Anna Ave. At the cluster of redbrick buildings, turn right into parking lot.

Nearby Attractions: Brooke Glass, Creegan Animation, Homer Laughlin China, and Senator Heinz History Center tours (see pages 349, 256, 351, and 294); Sterling China tour (call 330-532-1544) in Welsville, OH; East Liverpool Museum of Ceramics; Beaver Creek State Park; Thompson Park.

Harry London Candies

5353 Lauby Road
North Canton, OH 44720
(330) 494-0833 / (800) 321-0444
www.harrylondon.com

CHOCOLATES

A triangular glass portico entrance, a classy maroon awning, and the meticulously landscaped grounds welcome you to Harry London Candies. Before the tour, a friendly white-smocked tour guide offers you a mocha meltaway or chocolate peanut butter "buckeye," and your taste buds come alive!

Stroll through the Chocolate Hall of Fame. Old photographs and memorabilia show how Harry London first started manufacturing his quality chocolates out of his Ohio home in 1922. Gleaming white tanks and large vats swirl, mix, and heat up to 80,000 pounds of the rich, smooth brown confection a day. Foot upon foot of tubing starts here and transports the warm, liquid "food of the gods" (from the Latin meaning of "cacao") to the state-of-the-art candy-making processes you witness along the rest of your tour.

Floor-to-ceiling glass walls separate you from the fast-paced and efficient world of mass-producing quality chocolate. Look down on four 80-foot-long enrobing lines. Workers hand-place cookies, marshmallows, cherry cordials, or cream centers at the beginning of the line. Once the centers are coated with chocolate, workers hand-decorate them. Using a pastry bag, workers draw Zs with hot liquid dark chocolate onto "zebras," named for their chocolate cream centers with white chocolate on top.

The candies proceed through the cooling tunnel and then on to packaging. Videos and signs explain as you watch employees operate the wrapping machine (it wraps 72 to 100 pieces per minute) and the centrifugal-force table, where chocolate is spun into every conceivable shape. After this spellbinding trip through the world of Harry London candy-making, you'll agree that "any sane person loves chocolate."

Cost: Adults, $2; children 3–18, $1; children under 3, free.

Freebies: Chocolate samples on arrival and at end of tour. Fudge and caramel pecan popcorn samples while they are being made in the store.

Videos Shown: 7-minute video covers history of Harry London Candies and of chocolate manufacturing, plus 1-minute videos along tour path describing various candy-making procedures.

Reservations Needed: Yes

Days and Hours: Mon–Sat 9:00 AM–3:30 PM. Tours run every half hour. Closed major holidays. Call for seasonal Sunday hours.

Plan to Stay: 1 hour for tour, plus time for retail store.

Minimum Age: None

Disabled Access: Yes

Group Requirements: Groups should call at least 1 month in advance for reservations. No maximum group size. Call for special tours to be given to groups with a specific interest (such as marketing students or small children).

Special Information: No photography or recording devices.

Directions: Take I-77 to Exit 113 for Akron-Canton Airport. Turn right onto Lauby Rd. Turn right at the second entrance and "Harry London Candies" sign.

Retail Store: The 2,400-square-foot retail store features over 500 varieties of chocolate and gourmet candy, including pretzel joys, chocolate peanut butter buckeyes, and Hawaiian Gold. The store is designed with a lot of natural light, a large brick fireplace, and an authentic candy kitchen for making fudge and caramel corn as you watch. Catalog is available to order directly. Open Mon–Sat 9:00 AM–6:00 PM, Sun 12:00 PM–5:00 PM.

Nearby Attractions: Hoover Historical Center tour (see page 260); I-77 is known as the "Hall of Fame Highway," including Rock and Roll Hall of Fame, Inventors Hall of Fame, and NFL Football Hall of Fame.

Hoover Historical Center

1875 Easton Street NW
North Canton, OH 44720-3331
(330) 499-0287
www.hoover.com

VACUUM CLEANERS

Surrounded by elegant decor and antique furnishings, you tour nine rooms and see as many as 75 vacuum cleaners exhibited in a Victorian Italianate-style farmhouse, once the boyhood home of William Henry "Boss" Hoover, founder of the Hoover Company. The Center is now home to the "Sweeping Changes" display, which chronicles the history of the Hoover family and company and the evolution of the vacuum cleaner.

See antique cleaning devices and manual cleaners from the late 1800s to the current Hoover Self-Propelled WindTunnel upright. Inspect the 1908 Hoover Model "O," the world's first commercially successful, portable, electric vacuum cleaner. "Take a ride" on a replica of the 1910 manual Kotten suction cleaner. Step up onto the oval platform and rock side-to-side. Watch as the bellows on each side of the platform activate, and cause the attached nozzle to sweep up the sand on the floor. Push a button to hear a recording of Hoover salesmen singing "All the Dirt, All the Grit," the company theme song of the 1920s and 1930s. On the second floor, touch products that were made by Hoover for WWII to aid the war effort.

Read the history of the Hoover family and company while you look at family photographs housed in elaborate frames. View four generations of Hoovers in one photograph. Learn about the business relationship that began between William and janitor James Murray Spangler, upon Spangler's creation of the "electric suction sweeper," a device made from a tin soap box, a fan, a motor, a sateen pillowcase, and a broom handle.

If you visit during the summer, enjoy a pleasant walk through the Center's fragrant and colorful herb and flower gardens. Don't forget to stop in Bitzer Park, in the center of town, which holds a life-sized bronze statue of William walking and talking with a young boy. It represents his reputation as a gifted mentor, and is a tribute to his entrepreneurship and philanthropy.

Cost: Free

Freebies: No

Video Shown: 6-minute video that covers the background of the Hoover business.

Reservations Needed: No, except for groups of 10 or more people.

Days and Hours: Tue–Sun 1:00 PM–5:00 PM, with tours conducted on the hour; last tour at 4:00 PM. Morning reservations are available for groups. Closed major holidays.

Plan to Stay: 1 hour for tour and gift shop.

Minimum Age: None

Disabled Access: Yes, for first floor. No, for second floor. For those unable to climb the steps, a video shows what is displayed on the second floor.

Group Requirements: Groups of 10 or more people should call at least 2 weeks in advance, but notice of 1 month or more is preferred. Maximum group size is 60.

Special Information: No video cameras.

Gift Shop: Sells vacuum-shaped chocolates, toy Hoover vacuums, key rings, pens, postcards (one of a vintage Hoover ad), and baseball hats and T-shirts with the Hoover logo. Open same hours as museum.

Directions: From I-77, take Portage St. East past Whipple Ave. and turn right at the next light onto Wise Ave. At the 4-way stop, turn left onto West Maple St., which turns into Easton St. The Center is located about 2 miles past the Hoover Company on the left side of the street, opposite Walsh University.

Nearby Attractions: Harry London Candies tour (see page 259); Bitzer Park; Canton Museum of Art; National McKinley Birthplace Memorial; National First Ladies' Library; Canton Classic Car Museum.

International

6125 Urbana Road
Springfield, OH 45502
(937) 390-5848
www.internationaldelivers.com

TRUCKS

Springfield, Ohio, is home to numerous International-manufacturing facilities; the company's roots in the community date back to 1806. However, the company's vehicles, which become utility trucks, rental trucks, pickup and delivery trucks, and tow trucks, are seen everywhere—delivering farm produce to market, transporting school children to classes, and moving freight. In Springfield, you'll learn how these massive vehicles are made in the Assembly Plant, which features the main tour, the Cab Assembly and Stamping Facility, Paint Facility, and Body Plant.

One of the largest plants in the country, the Assembly Plant comprises 33 acres under roof. In the Assembly Plant, you'll see the complete assembly process of International trucks, beginning with a steel frame rail and ending as a completed truck rolls off the line. Highlights of the tour include the frame inverter, cab mount, and new cab trim line. The process of inverting frames is fairly new in the large truck industry. Key processes like u-bolt tightening, prop-shaft installation, and axle squaring and pinning can be completed while the frame is inverted, thus making them more ergonomic and ensuring quality. On the plant's new cab trim line, a glass bonding cell installs the front and rear windows of the cab using a robotic glue-dispensing station, air cylinders, and suction cups to aid in lifting and installing the glass. Also on the cab trim line, the driver control module and the instrument panel are combined and inserted through the cab door.

Upon request, you can also tour the adjacent Cab Assembly and Stamping Facility (CAS), opened in 2001, and the Paint Facility. Watch cabs for the new trucks being stamped and assembled using state-of-the-art robotic equipment, tooling, and processes.

Completed cabs move on to the Paint Facility, where colors of all varieties are applied using electric paint robots. Then, they are ready to be sent to the Assembly Plant, where they are added to chassis traveling down assembly lines. After seeing the full assembly, stamping, and paint process, you'll understand what makes these high-performance trucks.

Cost: Free

Freebies: Educational brochures about the company and Springfield operations.

Video Shown: No

Reservations Needed: Yes

Days and Hours: Mon–Fri 8:00 AM–3:00 PM. Closed holidays, week between Christmas and New Year's, the first 2 weeks of July and the last week of August.

Plan to Stay: 1.5 hours for Assembly Plant, plus 1 hour for additional facilities.

Minimum Age: 14

Disabled Access: Yes

Group Requirements: Must call in advance.

Special Information: No photography, open-toed shoes, shorts, or personal radios. Safety goggles provided. Can be hot in summer and noisy any time. Cab Assembly and Stamping tours as well as Paint Facility tours available upon special request.

Gift Shop: Eagle's Nest sells logoed T-shirts, hats, pens, and model trucks. Open Mon–Fri 12:00 PM–12:30 PM, 3:30 PM–4:30 PM. Hours subject to change (call 937-390-4118).

Directions: Take I-70 to Rt. 68 North. Follow Rt. 68 to County Line Rd. Exit. Turn right. At 1st traffic light, turn right onto Urbana Rd. At traffic light by the large company sign, turn right. Park in visitor's section and proceed to main lobby.

Nearby Attractions: Dayton's attractions, including Wright Memorial Air Force Museum, are 15 miles away.

Lee Middleton Original Dolls

1301 Washington Boulevard
Belpre, OH 45714
(740) 423-1481 / (800) 233-7479
www.leemiddleton.com

BABY DOLLS

Lee Middleton began creating dolls at her kitchen table in 1978, using her children as the first models. While the kitchen table may have given way to a 50,000-square-foot "dollhouse" factory (hidden behind a pastel-colored Victorian gingerbread facade), the same detailed, labor-intensive production process continues. Today, Lee Middleton Original Dolls is the nation's largest domestic doll factory. The tour shows the intricacy involved in making her vinyl collectible baby dolls.

All dolls start with molds for heads, forearms, and lower legs. A measured amount of liquid vinyl fills metal mold trays. The vinyl cures to a solid state in rotational molding ovens. After the molds cool, workers pull a small plug from each one. Then they use pliers to magically yank warm, hollow vinyl parts from each mold's tiny opening.

Stencils are used in painting vinyl doll faces. One head may require different stencils for eyebrows and lips, while blush on the cheeks is done freehand. Air is pumped into the head, temporarily expanding it like a balloon and enlarging the eye sockets. Workers then insert eyes into the openings and focus them, before delicately applying eyelash strips. When the heads, arms, and legs are attached to polyfill-stuffed bodies to complete the dolls, you appreciate the "labor" involved in their birth. The doll makers include a Bible with each of their "babies" because Lee Middleton wanted to thank God for giving her the talents that make her collectible dolls so special.

Cost: Free
Freebies: No
Video Shown: No
Reservations Needed: No, except for groups over 10 people. Scheduled tours take precedence over walk-ins.

Days and Hours: February 1–December 31: Mon–Fri 9:00 AM, 10:15 AM, 11:00 AM, 12:30 PM, 1:15 PM, and 2:15 PM. January tours by appointment only.

Plan to Stay: 25–30 minutes for tour, plus time for gift shop.

Minimum Age: None

Disabled Access: Yes

Group Requirements: Groups of 10 or more people must call in advance. Maximum group size is 60 people.

Special Information: No photography during tour.

Gift Shop: Sells limited-edition first quality Lee Middleton Original Dolls, store edition dolls, Small Wonder Play Babies, designer doll accessories (including clothing and nursery furnishings), and other gift and souvenir items. Store has an Adoptable Nursery. Baby receives a birth certificate for the trip home. Open January: Mon–Fri 12:00 AM–5:00 PM, Sat 9:00 AM–5:00 PM; February–April: Mon–Sat 9:00 AM–5:00 PM; May–December: Mon–Fri 9:00 AM–6:00 PM, Sat 9:00 AM–5:00 PM, Sun 12:00 PM–4:00 PM.

Directions: From I-77, take Parkersburg, WV, exit for Rt. 50 West. Head west across Ohio River. Once over the bridge, road becomes Washington Blvd./Rt. 618. Look for a large dollhouse-like building .75 miles ahead on left. From the east, take Rtes. 7 & 50. Take Belpre exit onto Main St. Turn right onto Washington Blvd./Rt. 618. Factory is on the right.

Nearby Attractions: Fenton Art Glass tour (see page 350); Stahl's Christmas Shop; Children's Toy and Doll museum; Doll Showcase store; Historic Marietta, OH; Blennerhassett Island and Museum.

Longaberger

5563 Raiders Road (State Route 16)
Frazeysburg, OH 43822
(740) 322-5588
www.longaberger.com

The Longaberger® Company

BASKETS

Tree-lined streets and beautifully restored Victorian houses create historic charm in Dresden, Ohio, also home to Longaberger Baskets. A short drive from Dresden's center is the world's largest basket-making plant—six-and-a-half acres under one roof! Upon entering Building A, you are struck with the beauty of all the product displays in the Gallery. Here you can see the products Longaberger has offered over the years and watch a video explaining the history of the company, the manufacturing process, and the Hartville plant.

After leaving the Gallery, look down to a view of hundreds of weavers from a quarter-mile mezzanine. Guides along the way explain the different processes. The maple logs used to make the baskets are first "cooked" for eight hours, then cut and measured into wood strips of the proper length for each style of basket. Weavers' fingers nimbly maneuver the moist, flexible maple strips to create the mosaic of the weave. The basket gradually takes shape as the craftsperson weaves, then taps the weave with a hammer to ensure a secure, tight, durable result.

Near the end of the process, the basket receives a "haircut" to trim away excess upsplints (the basket's vertical strips of wood). The weaver wraps the last band of wood around the circumference of the basket, hand-tacks it into place, then dates and signs the completed artwork.

Take a shuttle bus to Building B to see the staining, quality assurance, and Collectors Club Miniatures areas. One of the few automated processes you'll see at Longaberger occurs in the staining chamber. Here, baskets are hooked onto circular overhead racks called "spinners." As the spinners rotate them, the baskets move down a conveyor belt through the chamber where they are doused with stain. You leave with the image of row upon row of wooden baskets waiting to be filled with strawberries, fresh-baked bread, just-picked daisies, or even today's newspaper.

Cost: Free

Freebies: No

Video Shown: 18-minute optional video gives company history, describes the basket-making process, and discusses the Hartville plant. Shown in the Gallery.

Reservations Needed: No, except for groups larger than 15 people.

Days and Hours: January–March: Mon–Sat 9:00 AM–5:00 PM, Sun 11:00 AM–5:00 PM. April–November: Mon–Sat 8:00 AM–6:00 PM, Sun 11:00 AM–6:00 PM. December: Mon–Thur 9:00 AM–5:00 PM, Fri–Sat 9:00 AM–8:00 PM, Sun 11:00 AM–8:00 PM. To see weaving, tour the plant Mon–Fri before 2:00 PM. No weaving on Sat or Sun. Weaving demonstration in the Gallery 7 days a week. Closed holidays.

Plan to Stay: 2 hours for Gallery, Building A, Building B, and Just for Fun Shop.

Minimum Age: None

Disabled Access: Yes

Group Requirements: Groups larger than 15 people should call 3 days in advance to arrange tour. No maximum group size.

Special Information: On-site shuttle bus provides transportation to and from parking and in between buildings.

Gift Shop: Just for Fun Shop, at the end of the tour in Building A, sells select Longaberger baskets—the only baskets available without contacting a Longaberger independent sales associate. Logoed T-shirts, gifts, and basket accessories are available. Open same hours as tour. "Wish List" catalog with entire Longaberger basket and pottery line is available from an independent sales associate at (800) 966-0374.

Directions: Take I-70 to Zanesville, then Maple Ave./SR 60 North. Turn left onto SR 16. Plant is ahead 2.8 miles on your right. Stop at gatehouse for directions.

Nearby Attractions: Longaberger Homestead; Longaberger Golf Club; The World's Largest Basket; Triple Locks and Side-Cut Canal.

Malley's Chocolates

13400 Brookpark Road
Cleveland, OH 44135
(216) 362-8700
www.malleys.com

Malley's

CHOCOLATES

You cannot miss the enormous ice-cream sundae that adorns the top of Malley's Chocolates' 60,000-square-foot building. This landmark commemorates Malley's first ice cream and chocolate shop, opened in 1935. Like all the best candy-factory tours, this one begins with a sample, great chocolate smells, and a brief introduction to chocolate making. To put you in the right mood, they pipe in sounds of the tropical rainforest. The immediate landscape is festooned with banana and cacao trees hand-painted in lively pastels. Temporarily you return to the very origins of chocolate—to the tropics where cocoa beans grow.

As you gaze out over the expansive, modern candy kitchen, your tour guide describes chocolate's journey from its birth in the cocoa plantations to the creamy liquid that you see swirling and churning in the 500-pound chocolate melter. This is Malley's secret chocolate recipe, which is kept under lock and key. Meanwhile, in the center's kitchen, anything from strawberry to caramel centers may be bubbling away in copper kettles on gas stoves. Amid all this modern equipment, look for the antique gas stove dating back to the company's inception.

Your attention is drawn to the center of the room, where the automated kettle-lift pours 60 pounds of chewy, gooey hot caramel onto one of several cooling tables. Like a construction worker hurrying to smooth out a layer of concrete before it hardens, a chocolatier uses a huge spatula to quickly spread and smooth the thick caramel. A large rolling-and-cutting instrument is used to cut the still-soft caramel into pieces.

In another area, you see the enrober automatically coating the candy centers with chocolate. Before your tour concludes, you pass by the design center to glimpse some of Malley's specialty items.

Cost: $3; children under 2, free.
Freebies: Samples at beginning and end of tour, and a take-home treat.

Video Shown: 3-minute video describes hand-packing process.
Reservations Needed: Yes. Individuals and families must join scheduled group tour.
Days and Hours: Mon–Fri 10:00 AM–3:00 PM. Call for weekend hours. Closed holidays. Plant shutdowns are unusual and unpredictable.
Plan to Stay: 1 hour for tour, plus time in retail store.
Minimum Age: None
Disabled Access: Yes
Group Requirements: Minimum group size is 15 people; maximum is 45. Reservations needed 2 weeks in advance (4 weeks during holiday seasons).
Special Information: No photography. Best days to see production are before major holidays.
Retail Store: Sells full selection of Malley's chocolates including assorted chocolate creams, molded chocolate dinosaurs, and, of course, Grandpa Malley's Favorite Almond Crunch. Look in rear of store for Sweet Slips, bags of chocolates discounted due to minor flaws. Hand-painted walls and floral prints add to the flavor of a real sweet shop. Open Mon–Sat 10:00 AM–6:00 PM. Catalog available from (800) ASK-MALL.
Directions: From the east, take I-480 West to West 130th St. exit. Turn left onto West 130th. Turn right on Brookpark Rd. Malley's is on the right. From the west, take I-480 East to West 130th St. exit. Turn left at end of exit ramp. Malley's is on the left.
Nearby Attractions: *Cleveland Plain Dealer* newspaper tour (call 216-999-5665); Great Lakes Brewing Company tour (call 216-771-4404); NASA-Lewis Research Center (call 216-433-2000); Cleveland's attractions include Cleveland Zoo, Tower City, The Flats, Rock and Roll Hall of Fame, Great Lakes Science Center, and Cleveland Museum of Art.

Mosser Glass

9279 Cadiz Road
Cambridge, OH 43725
(740) 439-1827
www.mosserglass.com

MOSSER GLASS
M
CAMBRIDGE, OHIO

A beautiful country landscape is the backdrop for the little red farm cottage located conveniently just off the road. The front porch framed in white columns beckons you in. As you enter Mosser's "Little Red House" showroom, the sparkle of glass from every corner catches your eye. In this glass menagerie you see glass of all colors and shapes. Walls are decorated with everything from miniature punchbowls to figurines of clowns and frogs—samples of what you will see made in the factory downstairs.

The first part of the tour takes you through the shipping area. After viewing hand packing, your guide points out a display case of colored particles. These are the various chemicals used in Mosser's recipes for coloring glass. What really catches your eye, however, is stacks of over 200 intricately designed cast-iron molds, used in creating all of the hand-pressed glass shapes.

As you move past the batch room, you see machines that resemble inverted cement mixers forming an initial mixture of silica sand and soda ash. Large furnaces that heat the mixture to about 2,500° then come into view as you enter the open, high-ceilinged, cement block factory. From this point on, the pressing of each piece of glass is done by a four-person human assembly line. While you watch glass being made, you are facing a furnace and its four-person team; beyond is an enormous factory window fitted with huge exhaust fans. The window is wide open to a panoramic view of the Ohio countryside.

Watch the glassmaking team in action as the glowing molten mixture is removed from the furnace by the "gatherer." Another person cuts and then presses the hot material into the mold. A third worker removes the hot piece of glass from the mold and puts it onto the fire polisher, which smoothes any rough edges or mold marks left from pressing. Finally, the last worker places the glass piece onto a slow conveyor belt for the "lehr," or cooling oven, where it undergoes a gradual, three-and-a-half-hour cooling process.

As your tour ends at the lehr, you see the warm finished shapes being removed from the conveyor belt. Along one wall you observe glass figures receiving an acid rinse in a large tub to produce the soft, brushed effect of frosted glassware.

Cost: Free

Freebies: No

Video Shown: No

Reservations Needed: No, except for groups larger than 15 people.

Days and Hours: Mon–Fri 8:00 AM–3:00 PM. Lunch break from 11:00 AM–11:45 AM. Closed holidays, 2 weeks in July, and last week of December.

Plan to Stay: 15 minutes for tour, plus time to browse Little Red House showroom.

Minimum Age: None

Disabled Access: Yes, for factory; 4 steps into showroom.

Group Requirements: Groups larger than 15 should call a few days in advance for reservations. No maximum group size, since large groups will be split into groups of 8.

Special Information: No sandals or open-toed shoes. Factory can get quite warm in the summer.

Gift Shop: Little Red House showroom offers everything from glass candlesticks, paperweights, and miniatures, to antique reproductions. Open Mon–Fri 8:00 AM–4:00 PM. Closed holidays.

Directions: From I-77, take Exit 47. Take SR 22 West. Mosser Glass is .5 miles ahead on the right.

Nearby Attractions: Boyd's Glass tour (call 740-439-2077); Degenhart Paperweight & Glass Museum (call 740-432-2626); Salt Fork State Park and Lodge; Cambridge's antique shops and glass museums.

Robinson Ransbottom Pottery

Ransbottom Road
Roseville, OH 43777
(740) 697-7355
www.ransbottompottery.com

STONEWARE POTTERY

There is something heart-warming, appealing, and even patriotic about being in the deep Midwestern interior of Ohio, winding your way through beautiful expanses of countryside and heavily vegetated landscape, and finally encountering a business that blends so inextricably with its surroundings that you do not realize you've reached a manufacturing facility. The country you have just driven through is the earth from which Robinson Ransbottom mines the clay for its timeless stoneware. The raw materials used in the pottery are all obtained within a five- to 10-mile radius of this rustic plant.

As you embark on your self-guided tour, you enter one of a series of warehouses and production facilities. A dark earthiness surrounds you, as arrows direct you to various stops. At Stop One you may view any of a variety of glazing and hand-decorating techniques, such as pottery being hand-dipped (the procedure is called "slipping"), rolled, or mechanically spray-glazed.

One of the plant's most interesting areas is the beehive kilns. These two kilns were built in the mid-1800s, and they literally look like enormous beehives. You may see the kilns being loaded ("set") or unloaded. Each kiln holds about 30 tons, or 20,000 pieces, of pottery, and reaches a temperature between 2,300° and 2,400°.

As you exit the plant through the stock area, pass stack upon stack of stoneware birdbaths, vases, urns, and crockery. Robinson Ransbottom Pottery is such a down-to-earth operation that it's hard to believe the company processes about 700 tons of clay per month. Since it was founded in 1900, Robinson Ransbottom boasts that its products are "Old as yesterday, modern as tomorrow."

Cost: Free
Freebies: No

Video Shown: 10-minute video on pottery-making process, shown at Pot Shop.

Reservations Needed: No, except for groups larger than 25 people.

Days and Hours: Mon–Fri 9:00 AM–2:00 PM. Production stops at 2:00 PM. Closed holidays and for 2 weeks around the beginning of July.

Plan to Stay: 20 minutes for self-guided tour, plus time for video and Pot Shop.

Minimum Age: None

Disabled Access: Yes

Group Requirements: Groups larger than 25 should call 1 week in advance for guided tour. No maximum group size.

Special Information: No photography. At Stop Two, safety laws prohibit any conversation with employees. You are asked to be silent while watching at this stop so as not to distract the workers.

Gift Shop: Pot Shop offers housewares, gardenware, and novelties. Seconds shop located at back of store. Open Mon–Sat 9:00 AM–5:00 PM, Sun 12:00 PM–5:00 PM. May be closed weekends January–March.

Directions: From I-70, take SR 22 South to Rt. 93 South. Turn left onto CR 102 and right on Zanesville Rd. Turn left onto Elm St. Take Elm St. to end and turn left on Ransbottom Rd. Robinson Ransbottom Pottery is 1 mile ahead on the left.

Nearby Attractions: Roseville-Crooksville pottery-communities attractions include Alpine Pottery tour (call 740-697-0075), Beaumont Bros. Pottery tour (call 740-982-0055), Ohio Ceramic Center (Crooksville), Cope Gallery, and July pottery festival featuring tours of other pottery factories; Zanesville's attractions, including Zane Landing Park, Zanesville Art Center, Historic Freight Station, and Shultz Mansion, are within a 10-mile radius.

Velvet Ice Cream

State Route 13
Utica, OH 43080
(740) 892-3921
www.velveticecream.com

ICE CREAM

A picturesque farm-country landscape welcomes you to Velvet Ice Cream's 20-acre site. The scene is complete with a mill stream, pond, ducks, and an 18-foot antique water-powered grist mill, taking you back in time to another century. Ye Olde Mill, whose original hand-cut stone foundation dates back to 1817, is featured on the company's ice-cream cartons. It's hard to imagine that adjacent to it is Velvet Ice Cream's modern, state-of-the-art ice cream factory, capable of producing over 2,000 gallons of ice-cream products each hour!

The company has been owned and run by the Dager family since 1914. A stroll through their ice-cream museum reveals some of the antique ice cream–making equipment used throughout history—and lots of fun facts about America's favorite dessert. You can just picture the workers slowly and laboriously turning cranks by hand in what must have been a tedious, painstaking process. The museum also tells the history of milling, the world's oldest industry.

Your guided tour starts in the barn-like visitor center. Walk to the factory. A sign near the viewing windows proudly boasts: "Welcome to Ohio's Ice Cream Capital." Your attention is drawn to hundreds of feet of stainless-steel tubing, which seems to outline every corner and angle of the factory. The cold mixture of cream, milk, and sugar is pumped through this labyrinth of tubing to the processing machinery.

You might see juicy red strawberries being dumped into the mix at the flavor vats. The filling operation follows, as the ice cream is pumped into carton after carton. A maze of conveyor belts transports the filled containers as they are lidded and wrapped in polyethylene for shipping. They finally disappear into freezer storage where, within a few hours, they are frozen. Look for the novelty machines making ice cream sandwiches, pushups, or the 1817 gourmet ice cream bar—vanilla and peanut-butter ice cream coated in chocolate—yum!

Cost: Free

Freebies: No

Video Shown: 12-minute video shows ice cream–making process.

Reservations Needed: No, except for groups larger than 10 people that want a guide.

Days and Hours: May–October: Mon–Fri 11:00 AM–3:00 PM hourly for guided tour. Self-guided viewing from factory gallery during museum hours. Sometimes no production on Fridays. See Gift Shop section below for museum days and hours. Closed November–April.

Plan to Stay: 1 hour for guided tour and self-guided visit to museum, plus time for Ye Olde Ice Cream Parlor and scenic grounds.

Minimum Age: None

Disabled Access: Yes

Group Requirements: Groups larger than 10 people that want a guided tour should call 1 week in advance. School groups receive ice-cream sample.

Special Information: Arrive before 3:00 PM to see production. No photography allowed in viewing gallery. Annual Memorial Day Weekend Ice Cream Festival, Buckeye Tree Festival (second Sunday in September), and other special events throughout the summer.

Gift Shop: Ye Olde Mill contains a replica of an old-fashioned early-1800s ice-cream parlor, restaurant, and gift shop. Restaurant offers homemade food and, of course, ice cream. Gift shop sells nostalgic gifts, Ohio-made handcrafted items, Ohio food products, and Olde Mill souvenir items. Hours for museum, restaurant, ice-cream parlor, and gift shop are May–October: Mon–Sun 11:00 AM–8:00 PM (June–August until 9:00 PM).

Directions: Take SR 62 to Utica. Turn onto Rt. 13 South and go 1 mile. You're there when you see Ye Olde Mill.

Nearby Attractions: Dawes Arboretum; Mound Builders Park (Indian burial grounds).

Frankoma Pottery

2400 Frankoma Road
Sapulpa, OK 74067
(918) 224-5511
www.shopfrankoma.com

POTTERY

The name "Frankoma" combines founder John Frank's name with that of Oklahoma, a source of rich clay deposits. In 1927 Frank left Chicago to teach art and pottery at the University of Oklahoma. Five years later, equipped with one small kiln, a butter churn for mixing clay, a fruit jar for grinding glazes, and a few other crude tools, he started his own pottery studio. Several fires, expansions, and a generation later, Frankoma Pottery has grown to 70,000 square feet.

As your guide leads you through this facility, you will observe Frankoma's two methods of forming pottery. In the casting department, "slip" (liquid clay) is poured into plaster molds. The molds absorb water from the slip, leaving harder clay against the mold's walls. Excess slip is poured out. After four hours of drying, the piece is removed from the mold and allowed to dry overnight. The second, more interesting method is pressing, which is used for plates and flat pieces. A 50-ton hydraulic press slams down on a solid slab of clay to form each object. It smashes the clay around a mold, pushing excess clay out the sides. Regardless of how it is formed, each piece is taken to the trim line, where rough edges are hand-trimmed with a paring knife and smoothed with a wet sponge.

After the pottery is fired, it is ready for glazing. A hand-held air gun sprays glaze on flat pieces. Deep pieces are dipped in glaze to coat the inside and then sprayed on the outside. The brushing department "dry-foots," or removes the glaze from the pieces' bottoms, so they do not stick to the kiln.

Look through the continuously firing tunnel kiln, which is open on both ends. Long, pottery-filled kiln cars enter one end. Each kiln car reaches a maximum temperature of 2,000° at the center, allowing the clay to solidify and the glaze to melt and change color. The car emerges from the other end at 350°. You will leave with a new appreciation for the hands-on nature and collectibility of Frankoma pottery.

Cost: Free

Freebies: No

Video Shown: No

Reservations Needed: No, except for groups larger than 10 people.

Days and Hours: April–December: Mon–Sat 9:00 AM–5:00 PM, Sun 1:00–5:00 PM. Call to confirm times.

Plan to Stay: 30 minutes, plus time in gift shop.

Minimum Age: None

Disabled Access: Yes

Group Requirements: Advance reservations preferred for groups of 10 people or more. Groups larger than 25 will be split into smaller groups. School groups get free clay to take back to their schools.

Special Information: Since kilns fire constantly, it can get hot in the summer.

Gift Shop: Sells full line of microwavable, ovenproof, and dishwasher-safe Frankoma dinnerware and accessories. Look for baking pans, relish dishes, and bean pots shaped like Oklahoma, Texas, Louisiana, and Arkansas. Seconds sold at discount. Open Mon–Sat 9:00 AM–5:00 PM, Sun 1:00 PM–5:00 PM. Closed holidays. Catalog available from above number.

Directions: Take Turner Tnpk. to Exit 215 (Sapulpa exit). Turn left on Hwy. 97, then right onto Hwy. 166 East to Old Hwy. 66 (Frankoma Rd.). Turn left; Frankoma is on your right .5 miles down the road.

Nearby Attractions: Keepsake Candles tour (see page 269); Mr. Indian store; Tulsa's attractions, including Philbrook and Gilcrease Museums, are about 20 minutes away.

Keepsake Candles

Route 3
Bartlesville, OK 74003
(918) 336-0351
www.keepsakecandles.com

Keepsake Candles®
Traditional
Handcrafted Quality

DECORATIVE CANDLES

It's known as the "church fund-raising project that got out of hand." In 1969 Ed Ririe agreed to make candles molded in the shape of his mother's antique glassware for the church Christmas Bazaar. The color for the candles came, despite protest, from his daughters' crayons. Now Ed's wife, Alice Ririe, manages the company, and the candles are sold in all 50 states and around the world. Built in the 1950s by the government as part of a radar station, the factory was once a half-court gymnasium. You'll find other equipment of unique origin on your tour, such as worktables made from hospital gurneys, a melting vat that was once a dairy tank, and a storage cabinet that was formerly an analog computer.

Enter this unique structure and you're confronted with a huge stack of wax slabs. The slabs are melted in a vat that can hold 1,400 pounds of liquid wax. The wax for the candles' outside shell is mixed with other substances in order to raise the melting point so the shell holds its shape as the candle burns down.

A shell maker takes a bucketful of melted wax and adds a wax-based dye. The shell maker then carefully pours some colored wax into a pliable silicon rubber mold. The worker hand-twists the mold to make sure all sides have an even coating of wax. After about four layers, the shell will be thick enough to stand on its own. Similar to a process the Romans used to make lead pipes 2,000 years ago, this is called slush molding.

A worker splits apart the flexible mold to reveal a brightly colored shell that resembles a piece of antique pattern glass. The shell is polished using pantyhose, the same way you would use sandpaper on wood.

The worker uses an old coffeepot to pour the clear, scented, liquid wax into the shells. Depending on the day, peppermint, strawberry, or cinnamon may permeate the air around you. After it cools, each candle is tagged with its color, scent, date, pattern, and style.

Cost: Free

Freebies: No

Video Shown: 4-minute video covers manufacturing, shown in retail store.

Reservations Needed: No, except for groups over 10 people.

Days and Hours: Mon–Fri 9:30 AM, 10:30 AM, 11:30 AM, 1:00 PM, 2:00 PM, 3:00 PM.

Plan to Stay: 15 minutes for tour, plus time in the Country Store.

Minimum Age: 4

Disabled Access: Yes

Group Requirements: Groups should call 1–2 weeks in advance. Maximum group size 45 people. Large groups will be split into groups of 10–12 people.

Special Information: Factory is not air-conditioned; it can be very hot in summer. Grounds have antiques, including farm equipment and buggy. Railroad cars and caboose in front of store.

Country Store: Shop has 5 rooms, each with its own theme. Candles are displayed on antique stoves, cupboards, and sewing machines. Seconds sold at discount. Also sells baskets, gourmet foods, candleholders, and seasonal items. Open Mon–Sat 9:00 AM–5:30 PM and Sun 1:00 PM–5:00 PM. Closed most holidays. Catalog available from above number.

Directions: From U.S. Hwy. 75, take U.S. Hwy. 60 West through Bartlesville; 2 miles past Phillips Research Center, turn right onto CR 3235. Keepsake Candles is at the top of Radar Hill.

Nearby Attractions: Frankoma Pottery tour (see page 268); Phillips' Mansion; Wild Horse Refuge; Woolaroc Museum and Game Refuge; Tallgrass Prairie; Frank Lloyd Wright's Price Tower; June Oklahoma Mozart Festival; Red Dirt Soap Company.

Franz Family Bakery

340 N.E. 11th Avenue
Portland, OR 97232
(503) 232-2191, ext. 365
www.franzbakery.com

BREADS, BUNS, AND DOUGHNUTS

Since its 1906 beginnings in a simple two-story frame home, Franz Bakery has fed millions of people in the Pacific Northwest. Franz's plant now covers six city blocks and turns out over 85 million pounds of baked goods each year. Your tour guide provides many impressive statistics, such as the company's daily production of 75,000 loaves, 684,300 buns, and 45,000 doughnuts from 250,000 pounds of flour. Yet, until you see the dough marching in and out of the ovens, it sounds impossible.

To create baked goods in these huge quantities, the process is highly automated with constant movement of dough and bread everywhere you look. Even with machines 100 times bigger than those you use at home, it takes 17 steps to make Franz bread, from the sifting of the flour to the loading of it on delivery trucks. You'll stare at dough being kneaded in mixers that work it into 1,200-pound pieces. The divider and rounder machines turn this hunk of dough into softball-size pieces that relax in the overhead proofer before being molded into loaf shapes and dropped into pans.

After the proof box, which allows the dough to rise to its proper size, the pans enter 100-foot-long ovens. Bread stays inside for 19 to 21 minutes, while buns only need a seven- to nine-minute experience. You'll enjoy the heat from these ovens on chilly, rainy Portland days. Once the pans move out of the oven, vacuum-suction cups gently lift the bread from the pans and place the hot bread onto a 4,000-foot-long cooling rack. After one hour and 18 minutes of cooling, the bread moves through machines that slice it, slip it into plastic bags, tie the ends, and code the packages. In the time it takes you to eat one slice of bread, 75 to 100 loaves are packaged.

Cost: Free

Freebies: Apple juice and bread; take-home Franz sack with bread miniloaf and goodies.

Video Shown: No

Reservations Needed: Yes. Tours for school and scout groups only.

Days and Hours: Mon and Fri 9:00 AM–11:00 PM, Tue–Thur 9:00 AM–4:00 PM. Closed holidays, and July and August.

Plan to Stay: 1 hour for tour and tasting, plus time in thrift store.

Minimum Age: 7

Disabled Access: Yes, for most of tour.

Group Requirements: Minimum group size is 10 people; maximum is 60. Tours scheduled 4–6 weeks in advance.

Special Information: No photography. Sneakers or walking shoes required. The intense smells may bother some people. Snyder's Bakery in Spokane, WA, another United States Bakery subsidiary, also gives tours (call 509-535-7726).

Outlet Store: Thrift store sells excess breads, buns, pastry, and muffins at discount. Open Mon–Fri 9:00 AM–5:30 PM, Sat 9:00 AM–5:00 PM. Closed holidays.

Directions: Company requests that you call above number for directions.

Nearby Attractions: Oregon Convention Center; Lloyd Center; Holladay Park; Portland's downtown attractions, including Rose Test Gardens and Japanese Gardens, are about 15 minutes away.

Harry and David

1314 Center Drive
South Gateway Center
Medford, OR 97501
(541) 864-2277 / (877) 322-8000
www.harryanddavid.com

Harry and David®

**ROYAL RIVIERA PEARS
AND GIFT BASKETS**

Since brothers Harry and David Holmes began mailing succulent Royal Riviera pears around the country in the 1930s, their company has grown into a mail-order business whose gift baskets are an institution at holiday time. From an overhead balcony, watch workers hand-pack these beautiful baskets. Each packer receives a wooden box containing all of the components that go into the basket (which may include fruit, preserves, nuts, and candies), the basket itself, and a Styrofoam form that resembles a cowboy hat. After the packer fills the basket, it is transported by conveyor belt to workers who cover it with cellophane and send it to the shrink-wrap machine.

Around Christmas, you see the packing and wrapping of the Tower of Treats—five boxes, each containing a different product such as fruit, cookies, or cheese, stacked in a tower and wrapped with a ribbon. Each worker fills a box and passes it to the next person, who covers the box with a lid and adds another box on top. Once all five boxes are stacked, one member of a two-person team holds the ribbon, while the other wraps the ribbon around the tower and adds a pre-made bow and baubles on top. You see the ribbons flying as each team assembles up to 1,500 towers a day.

In the bakery, watch as fruit galettes, cookies, and cheesecakes are prepared by hand and placed into and removed from the ovens. Enter the candy kitchen, where the smell of chocolate wafts from vats that stir the brown liquid with rotating blades. Here you'll see the chocolate poured into molds and put through the enrober, the cooling chamber, and the cool room before being packed and frozen for later use in gift boxes.

Cost: $5

Freebies: Fruit galettes and chocolate samples; coupon for $5 off any $35 purchase in Harry and David store.

Videos Shown: On bus ride: 5-minute company history video. In bakery and kitchen area: 3-minute operations video. In packing house: 3-minute videos on gift production.

Reservations Needed: Recommended for individuals, required for more than 10 people.

Days and Hours: Mon–Fri 9:15 AM, 10:30 AM, 12:30 PM, and 1:45 PM. Closed holidays, July 4th week, and Christmas week.

Plan to Stay: 1 hour for tour, plus time for Harry and David's Country Village and Jackson & Perkins Rose Garden.

Minimum Age: 7

Disabled Access: Yes

Group Requirements: Groups over 10 people should call 1–2 months in advance. Maximum group size is 60.

Special Information: October through mid-December is the best time to see production. While the candy kitchen and bakery operate year-round, during the spring and summer you'll see less packing of gift boxes.

Gift Shop: Harry and David's Country Village comprises a gift shop, pantry, and produce department. It carries many of the same gourmet gifts found in the Harry and David catalog. Open Mon–Sat 9:00 AM–8:00 PM, Sun 10:00 AM–6:00 PM. Closed holidays. Catalog and Fruit-of-the-Month Club information available (call 800-547-3033).

Directions: From Portland, take I-5 South. Take Medford Exit 27 onto Barnett Rd. Turn left at second light onto Center Dr. Store is on right. From San Francisco or Sacramento, take I-5 North to Medford Exit 27. Turn left after exiting and go over freeway. Turn left onto Stewart Ave., then left onto Center Dr. Store is on right. You will be transported to the plant, 1 mile away, by van.

Nearby Attractions: Peter Britt Summer Music Festival in Jacksonville; the Oregon Shakespearean Festival in Ashland.

Luhr-Jensen

400 Portway Avenue
Hood River, OR 97031
(541) 386-3811 / (800) 366-3811
www.luhrjensen.com

FISHING LURES

LUHR·JENSEN™
"Where Legends Live."

Established in 1932 in an unused chicken coop on a Depression-ridden fruit ranch, Luhr-Jensen has become the largest manufacturer of fishing lures in the United States, and possibly the world. The family-owned company manufactures each lure, from raw metal to a jewelry-finished product ready for the dealer's tackle department. The plant is located in one of the country's best fishing areas—about 50 feet away from the Columbia River that separates Oregon from Washington.

A guided tour through the plant reveals all of the steps involved in creating Luhr-Jensen fishing lures, from stamping out the basic metal blade to plating, painting, assembling, and final packaging. Even before entering the punch-press area, you can hear these big machines stamping lure blades from long ribbons of brass. Literally millions of varying sizes, shapes, and thickness are punched out each year. One day you may see the popular Krocodile lures stamped out, while another day it may be spinner blades for the Willy Wobbler. The nearby plating room is a bustle of activity as chromium, nickel, copper, and even 24-karat gold and pure silver are coated onto the brass lure blades.

Nearby, in the paint room, watch workers with airbrushes carefully applying red, chartreuse, green, and other brightly colored fish-attracting patterns to the metal blades. In the main assembly area, hear the sounds of pneumatic wire-twisting machines and the rattle of blades, beads, clevises, and metal bodies. Spinners, lake trolls, and other wire-shafted lures are assembled by hand. In an adjacent area, the steady hum of printing presses signals preparation of the packaging material for the final step in preparing the lures for shipment to dealers throughout the world. You'll want to head directly for the nearby Columbia River and use your free lure to land steelhead and salmon.

Cost: Free

Freebies: Fishing lure

Video Shown: No

Reservations Needed: No, except for groups larger than 15 people.

Days and Hours: Mon–Fri 10:30 AM and 1:00 PM. Closed holidays.

Plan to Stay: 45 minutes

Minimum Age: None

Disabled Access: Yes

Group Requirements: Groups larger than 15 should make reservations at least 1 week ahead. No maximum group size.

Special Information: No photography.

Gift Shop: No

Directions: From Portland, take I-84 East to Exit 63. Turn left, back over freeway, and follow Frontage Rd. (Portway Ave.) toward river. Luhr-Jensen is on the riverfront, adjacent to a large boardsailing-event parking area. From I-84 West, take Exit 63, turn right and follow Frontage Rd. toward river.

Nearby Attractions: Catch the Wind Kites tour (call 541-994-7500); Mt. Hood; river rafting, fishing, boardsailing, mountain biking, hiking, and enjoying Hood River area scenery. Hood River is the "Windsurfing Capital of the World." Companies such as Da Kine Hawaii, makers of windsurfing and other sports accessories, offer limited tours (call 800-827-7466).

Oregon Connection / House of Myrtlewood

1125 South 1st Street
Coos Bay, OR 97420
(541) 267-7804
www.oregonconnection.com

WOODEN TABLEWARE AND GOLF PUTTERS

The myrtle tree is a broadleaf evergreen found in a small area of the Pacific Coast. The wood looks yellow and brown when finished, and its fine grain makes it more durable than well-known redwood. At House of Myrtlewood, videos and guided tours reveal all the mysteries of this beautiful hardwood and how it's turned into everything from salad bowls to patented golf putters.

If you like the smell of freshly cut wood, you'll enjoy walking through the small sawmill area where logs are sliced into six- to eight-foot sections of varying thickness. Watch the workers use disks of various sizes as patterns to draw circles on the wood slabs, trying to avoid knotholes or other flaws. They cut out these circles, called "blanks," and drill holes in the center to prepare them for the initial "rough out" on the lathe. Large, wet wood chips fly off the lathe during the rough-out turning. Next the pieces go to the drying room, where it takes about nine weeks to dry the wood down from about 50 percent moisture to a 6.5 percent moisture content.

On the main factory floor, watch the "finish turning" of the dried rough-out. Turners do not use a pattern to shape bowls and trays. Instead, each piece is individually turned; no two pieces are exactly alike. Look up at the humming overhead drive line (whose design dates back to the 1850s and the Industrial Revolution), which powers the lathes. The pieces are then sanded and receive an oil finish. When workers burn in the company name, you appreciate the effort that went into that finished piece.

Cost: Free

Freebies: Homemade fudge samples in gift shop; coffee or tea.

Video Shown: 12-minute video describes myrtle tree, sawmill, and processing of myrtlewood products.

Reservations Needed: No, except for groups larger than 50 people.

Days and Hours: Mon–Sat 9:30 AM–5:00 PM, Sun 11:00 AM–4:00 PM. Factory operates Mon–Thur, but tours run every day. Closed Christmas, New Year's, Thanksgiving, and Easter. Call ahead to verify tour times.

Plan to Stay: 20 minutes, plus time for gift shop.

Minimum Age: None

Disabled Access: Yes

Group Requirements: Groups larger than 50 people should call a day ahead.

Special Information: Limits on flash photography, for safety reasons. You may not see all 15 steps involved in making products.

Gift Shop: Carries full range of myrtlewood wares, from bowls, trays, cutting boards, and candleholders to Wooden Touch golf putters. (Putting green available for testing patented, handcrafted putter.) Also sells other gift items, homemade fudge, and Oregon gourmet foods. In the hobby room, craftspeople will find myrtlewood for turning and carving. Open same hours as tour. Catalog available from (800) 255-5318.

Directions: From Portland, take I-5 South to Hwy. 38 West. Then go south on Hwy. 101. Company is just off Hwy. 101 in South Coos Bay, in a wood building with large myrtle tree–shaped sign and American flag on top. From California, take I-5 North to Dillard-Winston exit and go west. Follow directions to Hwy. 42 West. Then go north on Hwy. 101. In approximately 5 miles, billboard will direct where to turn.

Nearby Attractions: The Real Oregon Gift myrtlewood factory tour (call 541-756-2582); Tillamook Cheese factory tour, about 4 hours up the Oregon coast (see page 276); Oregon coast beaches; Shoreacres State Park.

Pendleton Woolen Mills

Blanket Mill
1307 S.E. Court Place
Pendleton, OR 97801
(541) 276-6911
www.pendleton-usa.com

WOOL PROCESSING AND WEAVING

Beginning with Indian blankets in 1909, Pendleton Woolen Mills has grown to include 13 plants producing men's and women's sportswear, blankets, and fabrics. The company operates on the "vertical" system of manufacturing, which means that it performs all the steps in processing raw wool all the way into finished products. In Pendleton, Oregon, you can tour the original Pendleton plant, which began as an Indian trading post. Pendleton does 95 percent of its manufacturing in the U.S., in contrast to 30 percent for others in the apparel industry.

Once the wool is graded and washed in the Portland, Oregon, scouring plant and dyed in the Washougal, Washington, mill, it's shipped to this facility as big bales. Upstairs, the carding machines transform the loose wool into thin, straight, round strands called "roving." The spinning machines convert the roving to yarn by drawing out and twisting the fiber strands. The twisting gives the yarn its strength.

The first floor vibrates under your feet as you walk into the weaving room. The eight- to ten-foot-wide electronic looms pound as their harnesses move up and down. The 19 Jacquard looms produce complex patterns, such as Indian designs. A tape that carries a pattern of punched holes (similar to that of a player-piano roll) controls the sequence in which the yarns are raised and lowered. Depending upon the warp that was wound onto a loom (could weigh over 1,000 pounds), it may require more than a month of weaving time.

Once completed, blankets and fabric are inspected before shipment to the Washougal Mill for finishing. Finished blankets are ready for distribution. The fabric may be shipped to the Milwaukee, Oregon, plant to be made into men's Pendleton "damn good wool shirts," icons of the Northwest lifestyle.

Cost: Free

Freebies: No

Video Shown: No

Reservations Needed: No, except for groups larger than 8 people.

Days and Hours: Mon–Fri 9:00 AM, 11:00 AM, 1:30 PM, and 3:00 PM. Closed holidays, 2 weeks in summer (usually August), and week between Christmas and New Year's.

Plan to Stay: 20–25 minutes, plus time for video and Sales Room.

Minimum Age: None, except difficult to keep ear protection on young children.

Disabled Access: Yes, for first floor. No, for second floor carding and spinning.

Group Requirements: Groups larger than 8 people should call 1 week in advance.

Special Information: Company most interested in giving tours for local community. No photography. Pendleton's Washougal (WA) Weaving Mill (in Portland area) gives tours of the dyeing and fabric- and blanket-finishing process (call 360-835-1118). Near the Washougal mill is a seconds store open Mon–Sat 8:00 AM–4:00 PM. In Portland, OR, watch spinning and weaving of wool at the Foundation plant (call 503-226-4801).

Sales Room: Carries full line of Pendleton menswear, fabric, plus Indian bed and baby blankets, shawls, and robes. Offers seconds and discontinued items. Sells logoed T-shirts and sweatshirts. Open Mon–Sat 8:00 AM–5:00 PM. Closed holidays.

Directions: From Portland, take I-84 East to Exit 210. Turn left under Frwy. Turn left at stop sign at bottom of hill. Turn right under bridge (viaduct). Turn right at "Yield" sign onto S.E. Court Place. Pendleton will be on your left.

Nearby Attractions: Pendleton Underground Tours; Umatilla County Historical Society Museum; Wildhorse Gaming Resort.

Rodgers Instruments

1300 N.E. 25th Avenue
Hillsboro, OR 97124
(503) 648-4181
www.rodgersinstruments.com

ELECTRONIC AND ELECTRONIC-PIPE COMBINATION ORGANS

Next time you're in New York's Carnegie Hall or Philadelphia's Academy of Music, listen for beautiful music from an organ made by this leading builder of classic electronic and pipe organs. Rodgers prides itself on technical innovation in organ-building, whether by making the first transistorized organ amplifier (1958) or by introducing Parallel Digital Imaging Technology to create warmer, more authentic pipe-organ sounds. The technology and craft of organ-building resonate throughout the manufacturing area.

This guided tour shows all the steps involved in organ-making. Regardless of your interests—woodworking, electronics, or music—you'll find the process appealing. Don't expect huge machines or speeding assembly lines here; it takes weeks to make an organ. Instead you'll see skilled workers painstakingly laboring over each piece. Be sure to look for the Shoda machines in the cabinet shop area, where all the organ's wood parts begin their journey. The Shoda drills, saws, and shapes the wood according to a computerized program, while a vacuum seal holds the wood to the cutting table. This vacuum is so strong that a dollar bill placed on the worktable cannot be pulled across the surface!

Cut parts from such woods as Sitka spruce, American black walnut, oak, and mahogany are assembled in the case-up area. Here, sides, feet, key deck, back rails, and other support pieces are glued and clamped together, ensuring a dimensionally correct case. A "white sanding" process utilizes fine-grit sandpaper to give the wood a white flour-like surface. In the finishing department, instrument cases, benches, and pedalboard frames are stained, lightly sanded, and given a lacquer top coat. Notice that, despite all the sanding, the area is dust-free: air curtains outside the white-sanding room and finishing area prevent the dust from migrating.

It's often the multiple ranks of 61 pipes each that give organs their powerful presence. Look for pictures of one of the largest organs Rodgers ever designed and built—the 194-rank (11,000 pipe) organ at Houston's Second Baptist Church, which took one and a half years to build. Throughout the tour you'll see and hear the roles that traditional external pipes and internal electronics (now mostly computer surface-mount circuit boards) play in organ music. This contrast of technology and traditional craftsmanship makes the tour diverse: in one room an artisan hand-sands wood cases, while a computer technician next door tests circuit boards.

Cost: Free

Freebies: Demonstration CDs and literature

Video Shown: 12-minute video covering company history, organ construction, and sound technology, shown upon request.

Reservations Needed: Yes. No drop-in tours accepted.

Days and Hours: Tue and Thur 9:00 AM–12:00 PM. Closed for 1 week mid-August.

Plan to Stay: 45 minutes–1 hour

Minimum Age: No, but children must be able to wear safety glasses. Kids will enjoy the tour more if they're interested in music.

Disabled Access: Yes

Group Requirements: Groups must call 10 days in advance to make reservations. Maximum group size is 100 people.

Special Information: Photography in showroom only. Tours can be customized to your interests.

Gift Shop: No

Directions: From Portland, take I-5 South to Rt. 26 West. Get off at Cornelius Pass Rd. exit and turn right. Turn right onto Cornell Rd. Immediately after Hillsboro airport, turn right onto 25th Ave. Rodgers is on the right. Can also take the MAX rapid transit line from downtown Portland to the Hillsboro Fairgrounds exit. Rodgers is across the street, about .25 mile walk.

Nearby Attractions: Shute Park; Fairgrounds events; wine-tasting scenic route (Hillsboro to Salem); Hillsboro Blimp Factory at Hillsboro Airport Facility. Portland's attractions, including Oregon Zoo, Rose Test Gardens, and Japanese Gardens, are about 15 miles away.

See color photos, page 31.

Tillamook Cheese

4175 Highway 101 North
Tillamook, OR 97141
(503) 815-1300
www.tillamookcheese.com

CHEESE

Tillamook may be the largest and most automated cheese maker in the Northwest, but its tour begins by showing respect for the raw material that underlies its success: a plastic life-size cow with attached milking machine. The 176-member Tillamook County Creamery Association turns one of the finest milk supplies in the U.S.A. into 50 million pounds of cheese yearly. A self-guided tour and accompanying videos show you what's involved in making and packing its famous Tillamook Cheddars.

On the cheese-making side of the plant, peer through glass windows at the shiny enclosed cooking vats, each the size of an oval swimming pool. Notice the electronic control panels that direct the heating, thickening, and stirring of each vat's 25,000 quarts of milk. When the cooking is complete, the curds and whey are pumped to the Cheddarmaster machine, which looks like the side of a silver ocean liner with its screen-covered portholes. Inside this machine, the curd is drained of the whey, matted together, turned and tested for proper body, milled by cutting into finger-sized pieces, salted, and stirred.

Then the curd travels to the pressing towers, where pressure and vacuum remove any remaining whey. Watch the 40-pound cheese blocks eject from the tower into clear, vacuum-sealed bags for their stay in the aging room. About four months of aging or curing at 40° is required for medium-flavored cheese, and nine months for sharp.

While most of the cheese making happens inside the machines, you see more action on the packaging side of the plant. The properly aged 40-pound blocks are transformed into five-pound loaf, two-pound baby loaf, nine-ounce random cut, and snack-bar sizes. The spinning assembly-line machines, with help from paper-hatted workers, do all the cutting, weighing, wrapping, sealing, and packaging at a mesmerizing pace. The colorful Tillamook label moves past too quickly for reading, but you know there's tasty cheese inside.

Cost: Free

Freebies: Tillamook Cheese and Curd samples. School groups may call to arrange ice cream cone discounts.

Videos Shown: Throughout self-guided tour, continuously running videos cover Creamery's history, dairy workings, and an inside view of cheese-making machines.

Reservations Needed: No, unless group wants lunch service in café.

Days and Hours: Summer: Mon–Sun 8:00 AM–8:00 PM; Labor Day–mid-June: 8:00 AM–6:00 PM. Closed Thanksgiving and Christmas. Not always in full production on weekends and holidays.

Plan to Stay: 30 minutes for self-guided tour and historical and dairy displays, plus time for gift shop.

Minimum Age: None

Disabled Access: Yes

Group Requirements: Bus groups and groups larger than 20 people should call 1 week in advance to schedule an on-bus presentation.

Gift Shop: Sells all varieties of Tillamook Cheese, logoed shirts, hats, other cow-emblazoned items, and Oregon specialty foods. Special sales offer cheeses at 99 cents per pound. Open same hours as tour. Call (800) 542-7290 for catalog. Café offers sandwiches, burgers, soups, and salads, and Ice Cream Counter features nearly 30 flavors of Tillamook Ice Cream.

Directions: From Portland, take Rt. 6 West and go north on Hwy. 101. Factory is on your right about 2 miles north of town of Tillamook.

Nearby Attractions: Oregon Connection/House of Myrtlewood tour, down the coast about 4 hours (see page 273); Pioneer Museum; Oregon Air Museum; Three Capes Scenic Driving Loop; Oregon coast.

Weyerhaeuser

785 North 42nd Street
Springfield, OR 97478
(541) 741-5478
www.weyerhaeuser.com

PAPER Weyerhaeuser

We make paper in many forms in the U.S.A., with much of it coming from the abundant forests of the Pacific Northwest. This Weyerhaeuser mill makes the ubiquitous brown paper that forms the smooth inside and outside layers of corrugated boxes. As in most paper mills, this one surrounds you with new sights, sounds, and smells.

To produce "linerboard," as it's called in the paper industry, Weyerhaeuser starts with a combination of wood chips from local sawmills and recycled paper. Before the plant opened in 1949, sawmills incinerated the chips as waste. Today these chips are a precious resource. In addition, recycled paper has become an important source of fiber. Weyerhaeuser uses more than 450 tons of recycled paper per day while producing linerboard with up to 40 percent recycled content. You'll notice hills of wood chips surrounding the mill buildings, with whole trucks being lifted skyward to unload more chips. The wood chips' density makes them look like a desert of light brown sand.

On your tour, you'll see stacks of huge bales of recyclable paper—corrugated boxes, office paper, and more. The bales are dropped into a massive blender that whirls the fiber into slurry. Nonpaper materials, such as adhesives, plastic liners and dirt, are removed through a sophisticated screening process.

In the pulp mill, the chips are cooked to separate out the pulp (for safety reasons you do not see that process). Once cooked, the fibers are washed, refined, and blended with the recycled paper slurry. The mixture then enters a 500-foot-long machine that turns the pulp into paper at speeds of up to 2,250 feet per minute. Make sure you feel the pulp that the tour guide takes from the front of the machine. To some, it feels like thick applesauce.

Follow the pulp's path through the noisy machine, as it is transformed from slurry (99.5 percent water) into a finished sheet (8 percent water). It travels over and under rows of rollers, which press and dry out the water to make the paper that is then wound onto 30-ton reels. A new reel is produced about every 30 minutes. The reels, each holding 15 miles of linerboard, are cut into one- to two-ton rolls, banded, and shipped to Weyerhaeuser box-manufacturing plants via waiting trucks and boxcars.

Cost: Free

Freebies: Brochures and pamphlets

Video Shown: No

Reservations Needed: No, except for groups.

Days and Hours: Mon and Fri 9:00 AM. Other times may be available. Closed holidays and week between Christmas and New Year's. Semi-annual closings for maintenance during selected days in April and October.

Plan to Stay: 1.5 hours

Minimum Age: Children must be able to walk and wear earplugs and hardhats. No strollers.

Disabled Access: No, stair-climbing and extensive walking inside and outside the mill.

Group Requirements: Groups should call 1 week ahead. No maximum group size.

Special Information: As with all paper mills in the Northwest, this one can be hot, humid, and noisy, while outdoor weather may be cold and damp. Dress appropriately and wear sturdy shoes. No open-toed footwear.

Gift Shop: No

Directions: From I-5, take Hwy. 126 East to 42nd St. exit. Go south on 42nd St. Mill complex is about 1 mile ahead. Turn left at 3rd traffic light. Visitors must check in at main gate.

Nearby Attractions: Willamette Pass ski area; Lively Park Wave Pool; Lane County's Covered Bridges; Mt. Pisgah hiking trails and arboretum; University of Oregon.

Anderson Bakery

2060 Old Philadelphia Pike
Lancaster, PA 17602
(717) 299-2321
www.andersonpretzel.com

 ANDERSON

PRETZELS

Although you may not have heard of Anderson pretzels, chances are you've eaten them. Besides their own brand of pretzels, Anderson makes most of the generic and store-brand pretzels in the U.S. For more than 100 years, Anderson has been baking pretzels in almost every flavor, shape, and size imaginable, including unsalted ("baldies") and peanut-butter-filled pretzels.

This self-guided tour begins with a walk past a photo display of the company's impressive history, from its beginnings in 1888 in Lancaster, in the heart of Pennsylvania Amish country, to its latest building and warehouse expansion. The pictures also illustrate the history of pretzel-making in the U.S.A. In 1946, for example, a one-day shift produced 500 pounds of pretzels, compared to the 80,000 pounds each Anderson shift turns out today.

Farther down the observation walkway is a glass-enclosed corridor, where you can watch Anderson's employees and the huge pretzel-making machines. The pretzels' ingredients wait patiently in several huge storage tanks before being piped directly into four large mixers. Batches of pretzel dough are mixed, weighed, and sent to the extruders.

The dough pretzels move to the ovens by way of the proof belt. Here, intense heat forces the pretzels' yeast to rise, or proof. The proofed pretzels are sent to the cooker, which bakes them brown, and then the salter, where salt rains down on the still-moist dough.

In another area, watch extruders force fresh dough slabs through openings in a die plate and slice the strands with moving knife blades. Suddenly, thousands of long, thin pretzel sticks are born. You can see highways of pretzel twists, gems, rods, logs, and "minis" travel by conveyor to the cooker and the baking room, where enormous ovens bake them crispy brown. Their final destination is the packaging room where the pretzels, each shape on its own route, dive into boxes, cartons, tins, and bags for their journeys to stores all over North America.

Cost: Free

Freebies: Dutch pretzel sample.

Video Shown: No

Reservations Needed: No

Days and Hours: Mon–Fri 8:30 AM–4:00 PM. Closed most major holidays. *Factory tour discontinued.*

Plan to Stay: 30 minutes for tour, plus time in factory outlet.

Minimum Age: None

Disabled Access: Yes (there is an elevator to the second floor).

Group Requirements: Groups should call in advance to verify dates and times.

Special Information: The soft-pretzel shop offers a pretzel sample fresh from the oven and a cold drink, April–October.

Factory Outlet: All Anderson products available, plus T-shirts, hats, and other company souvenirs. Special deals on large cartons of broken pretzels. Catalog available from above number. Open year-round: Mon–Fri 8:30 AM–5:00 PM; April–December: also open Sat 8:30 AM–3:30 PM.

Directions: From Pennsylvania Tnpk., take Exit 21 (Reading/Lancaster) to Rt. 222 South. When highway ends, take Rt. 30 East to Rt. 340 East exit. Turn right onto Rt. 340 and drive through 1 traffic light. Anderson is on the right.

Nearby Attractions: Sturgis Pretzel tour (see page 297); Jam and Relish Kitchen viewing window in Kitchen Kettle Village (call 800-732-3538); Pennsylvania Amish attractions; Dutch Wonderland Amusement Park; dozens of factory outlet stores; James Buchanan House.

Asher's Chocolates

80 Wambold Road
Souderton, PA 18964
(215) 721-3000 / (800) 223-4420
www.ashers.com

Approaching Asher's 125,000-square-foot state-of-the-art facility, the aroma of chocolate greets you. Enticed to come inside, you pass through the entranceway, turn left, and proceed up a ramp. Shortly, you enter a 168-foot corridor, not more than four feet from the factory floor.

To the right, a colorful, oil-painted mural extends the length of the corridor. It includes a depiction of Asher's original store window in Center City Philadelphia, as well as painted plaques exhibiting facts about Asher's. One plaque tells you that Asher's is the oldest family-owned and -operated candy manufacturer in the U.S., dating back to 1892, and is currently run by the third and fourth generations. At four stations along the corridor, a video explains in detail what you see through windows to the left, as the machines and employees work in unison during your self-guided tour.

Crispy buttercrunch toffee asserts its beginning in a large copper kettle sitting atop a gas fire. The cook, wearing a shower cap and elbow-length black rubber gloves, pours thick corn syrup into the mixture of sugar and butter. In a circular motion, with much effort and speed, he mixes the ingredients. Lifting the kettle from the fire, he pours the gooey substance onto a cool metal table and spreads it one-quarter-inch thick.

Before it cools, he uses a hand-operated rotary knife, which looks like a rolling pin fit with 12 pizza cutter blades, and scores the toffee to make a square pattern. He then breaks the toffee along the scores and places it on a traveling wire-mesh bed. Liquid chocolate falls from above and rises from below to enrobe the toffee in chocolate majesty. For the crowning final touch, nuts pass through a chute, scatter, and cover the toffee waiting below.

Nearby, the depositor machine drops measured amounts of tempered chocolate onto a bed of yellow, pink, blue, and white sugar beads, which stick to the surface of the chocolate. Pretty nonpareils are in the making.

After your tour, browse the old-fashioned Victorian candy store, with a cobblestone road beneath your feet. Admire the ticket booth and the charming trolley. Sample a chocolate-covered pretzel, for which Asher's is famous, or try a sugar-free, low-sodium chocolate. Take home a box of Rocky Road Fudge or French Mint Truffles, and each time you take a bite into one of these delectable confections, remember your trip to Asher's.

Cost: Free
Freebies: Chocolate samples.
Videos Shown: 5-minute videos shown at each station explain in detail the candy-making process.
Reservations Needed: No, except for groups of 10 or more.
Days and Hours: Mon–Fri 10:00 AM–3:30 PM; Sat 10:00 AM–4:00 PM. Closed holidays.
Plan to Stay: 30 minutes, plus time for candy store.
Minimum Age: None
Disabled Access: Yes
Group Requirements: Groups of 10 or more, call (215) 721-3276 to make reservations.
Special Information: Tours also in Lewiston, PA, about 2–3 hours away. Call (717) 248-8613.
Gift Shop: Candy Store offers a variety of candy, stuffed animals, baskets, and seasonal items. Open Mon–Fri 9:30 AM–5:00 PM; Labor Day to Memorial Day, also open Sat 10:00 AM–4:00 PM. Closed holidays.
Directions: From Philadelphia, take Rt. 76 West to I-476 North to Rt. 63 (Lansdale Exit) on the Pennsylvania Tnpk. Turn right at Rt. 63 (Sumneytown Pike). Turn right onto Wambold Rd. Asher's is on the left. From points west, take I-276 East to I-476 North. Proceed as above.
Nearby Attractions: Byers' Choice tour (see page 282); Philadelphia attractions, including the Philadelphia U.S. Mint tour (see page 298), are 15 miles away; Mennonite historical area; Family Heritage Restaurant; King of Prussia Mall (largest mall on the East Coast); Valley Forge.

Benzel's Bretzels Bakery

5200 6th Avenue
Altoona, PA 16602
(814) 942-5062 / (800) 344-4438
www.benzels.com

Whether you love trains, pretzels, or factory outlet shopping, Benzel's Bretzel Bakery offers all of the above, plus a bit of nostalgia. In 1911 Adolf Benzel stepped off a boxcar at the Altoona, Pennsylvania, train station with his family and all his worldly belongings and started the Benzel tradition. Railroad buffs will enjoy the caboose parked on the grounds and the massive train mural along the Outlet Store's back wall. The mural depicts the railroad's influence on the Altoona area, including an unusual look at the Horseshoe Curve.

An in-store video captures the history of Adolph Benzel's arrival in Altoona and the beginnings of Benzel's Bretzel Bakery. The video, a visual factory tour, walks you step by step through the baking process that now generates 50 million pretzels daily. Benzel's is one of the few companies in the U.S.A. that still produces pretzels from the flour-malt-yeast-and-salt concoction first used by Catholic monks. You will come to understand what is involved in mixing the dough, shaping it into various pretzel forms from extruders, and baking and bagging the finished pretzels.

At a rapid rate, pretzels travel the conveyor belts, where they rise, steam, and are salted before they reach the 100-foot ovens. You can almost feel the heat as the pretzels are baked by intense flames from the gas-fired ovens. While Grandpa Benzel didn't make his "bretzels" like this in 1911, his grandchildren's products and factory still utilize his basic recipe, continuing the family's traditions and heritage.

Cost: Free
Freebies: Fresh pretzels hot off the line and 1-ounce sample bag.
Video Shown: 25-minute video explains Benzel family's pretzel-making history and process.

Reservations Needed: No, except for groups larger than 40 people.
Days and Hours: Mon–Fri 10:00 AM–5:00 PM, Sat 10:00 AM–1:00 PM. Holiday hours vary; call above number.
Plan to Stay: 25 minutes for video, plus time in factory store.
Minimum Age: None
Disabled Access: Yes
Group Requirements: Groups larger than 40 should call a few days ahead. No maximum group size.
Special Information: Benzel's has seasonal activities and promotional giveaways throughout the year.
Factory Outlet: Sells all Benzel's and Pennsylvania Brand pretzel products as well as decorated gift tins, gift baskets, candies, nuts, and various snack food items at discounted prices. Open same hours as above. Pretzel catalog available from above number.
Directions: From Pennsylvania Tnpk., exit at Rt. 220 North. Follow Rt. 220 North to Altoona, then take Rt. 764 North. Benzel's is one-quarter mile past 58th St., on the left across from 52nd St. Look for old train caboose in front. From I-80, exit at Milesburg. Follow Rt. 220 South to Altoona, then to 17th St. bypass in Altoona. Turn right onto 17th St. Turn left onto 7th Ave., which joins 6th Ave. Continue on 6th Ave. Benzel's is on the right across from 52nd St., 1 block past traffic light at the corner of 51st St.
Nearby Attractions: Horseshoe Curve National Historic Landmark; Altoona Railroaders Memorial Museum (call 888-425-8666); Mishler Theatre (call 814-944-9434); Baker Mansion (call 814-942-3916); Boyer's Candy Outlet; Lakemont Park.

Cannondale

172 Friendship Village Road
Bedford, PA 15522
(814) 623-9073 / (800) 245-3872
www.cannondale.com

BICYCLES AND CLOTHING

Cannondale started in a crowded loft above a pickle factory in 1971, building the industry's first bicycle trailer. It later added cycle apparel and accessory lines, then made its first bicycle in 1983. Its lighter aluminum bicycle revolutionized the industry at a time when steel models dominated. Widely regarded as the bike industry's leading innovator, Cannondale is the leading manufacturer of aluminum bicycles, selling more than 80 models in over 60 countries worldwide. It now even manufactures its own brand of off-road motorcycles and high-performance sport ATVs.

Headquartered in Connecticut, Cannondale manufactures virtually all of its products at two factories in Bedford, Pennsylvania. This tour of its bicycle and clothing plant gives you an opportunity to observe parts of a patented, state-of-the-art production system. You may have glimpses of the welding, decaling, and painting areas, along with the wheel-building room. Look at posters on a bulletin board that illustrate how the paint line runs. In the stitching room, see stitching of logoed jerseys and shirts. In the assembly room, parts such as cranks, derailleurs, and handlebars are attached onto the frame.

When Cannondale decided to become a major player in the worldwide bicycle business in 1988, it wanted to prove that it could economically produce a large number of award-winning bikes in the U.S.A.—not overseas. To do this, it had to convert its factory, change production methods, and maintain less inventory. Computer-instructed laser cutters and electric arc plasma cutters precisely miter each frame tube, and cut water-bottle holes and seat slots at the same time. Other efficient methods include those used for heat-treating the rack of frames and quenching them in their own bath, as well as for frame alignment, painting, and quality testing. Whether you are a bike rider or factory tour enthusiast, you will enjoy the combination of sights and processes.

Cost: Free
Freebies: No
Video Shown: No
Reservations Needed: Yes
Days and Hours: Wed and Fri 10:00 AM–1:00 PM. Closed major holidays, last week of December, and first week of January.
Plan to Stay: 30–45 minutes
Minimum Age: 12
Disabled Access: Yes; however, tour is on factory floor.
Group Requirements: Maximum group size is 10 people.
Special Information: No photography. Safety glasses provided. Motorcycle plant at 2 Corporate Dr. in Bedford does not give tours.
Gift Shop: No. Products sold through authorized dealers.
Directions: From the Pennsylvania Tnpk. (I-76), take the Bedford exit. Turn right onto Business 220. Follow as road goes into North Richard St. Turn right onto Hwy. 30 West. Follow Hwy. 30 West for approx. 3 miles. Make a right onto Friendship Village Rd. (you will see a sign for Friendship Village Campground). Cannondale will be on your right.
Nearby Attractions: Benzel's tour (see page 280); Friendship Village Campground; Shawnee State Park; Old Bedford Village; Fort Bedford Museum; Espy House National Historic Landmark; Bedford Fall Foliage Festival (occurs usually the first 2 weekends in October); Bedford Springs; Bison Corral (call 814-733-4908); Gravity Hill; Blue Knob Four Seasons Resort; Lake Raystown Resort and Lodge; Bedford County's 14 covered bridges.

Byers' Choice

4355 County Line Road
Chalfont, PA 18914
(215) 822-6700
www.byerschoice.com

CAROLERS FIGURINES

As you step onto the cobblestone floor entranceway of family-oriented Byers' Choice, you are transported back in time to the streets of Victorian England. Tall, blazing street lamps and quaint Victorian storefronts line the walls, beckoning you onward.

You first stop at the St. James Theatre, where you watch a short video that explains the history of family-run Byers' Choice and previews the production of its handcrafted Christmas Carolers figurines. The video details how Joyce Byers' simple hobby of creating cheerful clay and fabric figurines of Christmas carolers, whose heads are uplifted and mouths are open wide as if in song, grew to a nationwide business. Compliments from friends and family encouraged Joyce to sell her homemade figurines at local women's exchanges. The Victorian carolers, representing a simpler time and way of life, were a hit when introduced at the New York Gift Show in 1978.

Upon returning to the Victorian street, peer into life-size versions of Victorian storefronts. View a dining room whose decorations change with the seasons, and walk into a dressmaking and tailoring shop to have a picture taken in Victorian attire.

Then, turn a corner into Ye Olde Curiosity Shoppe—everything is changed! Suddenly, you are like giant Gulliver in the land of the Lilliputians. The life-size Victorian street scenes that you previously viewed are meticulously reproduced to the 13-inch scale of the Carolers figurines. Other nearby rooms contain miniature, picturesque tableaus of Victorian England heavily populated by joyful, singing Byers' Choice Carolers figurines. All of the heartwarming Carolers vignettes were created by owner Joyce Byers.

Finally, wind your way to the factory workshop. Through a wall of one-way glass, view the complete production of the Byers' Choice Carolers, from body building to dressing. The 80,000-square-foot workshop appears remarkably calm. Artisans wearing headsets listen to books on tape provided by Byers' Choice, as they handcraft Carolers figurines at wooden tables. Some artisans shape clay heads and paint candid faces on them; others create wire body frames wrapped in tissue paper. A few craftswomen skillfully stitch the delicate fabrics and fur that will become the Carolers' clothing, which other craftswomen painstakingly pin on the figurines.

For most styles, only one hundred figurines of each design are produced, thereby creating an endless selection of figurines. An opportunity to purchase a Byers' Choice Carolers figurine awaits you in the gift shop at the conclusion of the tour.

Cost: Free

Freebies: Christmas Gallery and Byers' Choice sculpture garden brochures.

Video Shown: 10-minute video of company history and figurine-making process.

Reservations Needed: No, except for groups over 20 people.

Days and Hours: Mon–Sat 10:00 AM–5:00 PM, Sun 12:00 PM–5:00 PM. Closed Easter, Thanksgiving, Christmas, and New Year's.

Plan to Stay: 1 hour for video and self-guided tour, plus time for gift shop, outdoor sculpture garden, and international crèche collection.

Minimum Age: None

Disabled Access: Yes

Group Requirements: Reservations for groups over 20 people.

Special Information: No photography of figurine workshop.

Gift Shop: Primarily sells vast array of Byers' Choice Carolers. Open same hours as tour.

Directions: From Philadelphia, take I-76 West to Pennsylvania Tnpk. East. Get off at Fort Washington (Exit 26). Take Rt. 309 North toward Montgomeryville. Pass Montgomeryville Mall on left. Turn right onto Rt. 202 North. Continue to second traffic light. Turn left onto County Line Rd. Byers' Choice is one-half mile on your right.

Nearby Attractions: Asher's Chocolates tour (see page 279); Moravian Pottery and Tile Works tour (call 215-345-6722); Henry Mercer Museum; James A. Michener Art Museum.

▲ The popular Carolers figurines are warmly displayed in homelike settings and festive villages, while production can be viewed from the workshop observation deck.

In Chalfont, Pennsylvania, Byers' Choice Christmas Gallery and Visitors Center features heartwarming ▼ sculpture, award-winning landscaping, and a 22,000-square-foot Winter Greene strolling area.

The Crayola FACTORY

Two Rivers Landing
30 Centre Square
Easton, PA 18042-7744
(610) 515-8000
www.crayola.com

Crayola®

CRAYOLA CRAYONS AND MARKERS

You can't help feeling like a kid again when you visit The Crayola FACTORY at Two Rivers Landing, the discovery center built in 1996 by Binney & Smith, makers of Crayola products. In fact, don't be surprised if the experience raises many childhood memories. You may remember when the now-classic 64-crayon box with built-in sharpener was introduced in 1958; or you may remember your tenth birthday, by which time you, like the average American child, had probably worn down 730 crayons.

The "Factory Floor" level of the discovery center features crayon manufacturing and marker assembly, using machinery transferred from the nearby production plant. Behind a glass wall is the flatbed molder that makes a small percentage of the company's crayons. Watch a worker pour a mixture containing melted paraffin wax and powdered pigment from a bucket onto a long table with thousands of small holes. Bright yellow wax seeps into the holes. After four to seven minutes of cooling, 1,200 crayons magically appear as they are pushed up and out of the molds! The worker also demonstrates and explains the labeling and packaging machines.

In the marker assembly area, the marker machine has actually been slowed down so you can follow the process of mating the barrels, cylinders, and marker caps. At normal speed, this machine can make 42,000 markers in one eight-hour shift.

Follow the ramp down to the "Creative Studio," which begins the playful, interactive portion of your visit. Draw on clear glass walls with special glass-writer markers. Step into "Cool Moves," where a computer captures your image on a huge video screen.

In the "Easton Press and Bindery," you can practice printmaking. In the "Light Zone," mix up different colored rays of light or lie on your back daydreaming under the "Dreamscapes" exhibit. At the end of your colorful experience, you can use Crayola Model Magic to create three-dimensional art.

Cost: Adults and children, $8; seniors 65+, $7.50; under 3, free. Includes admission to National Canal Museum, located in same building.

Freebies: Box of 4 crayons and a marker from the assembly lines, and art projects you create while there.

Videos Shown: 10-minute video covers products made by the company, including Silly Putty, chalk, paint, and crayon production. Another video shows TV clips.

Reservations Needed: No, with walk-ins accommodated on a first-come, first-served basis until day is sold out. Groups over 10 people, see below.

Days and Hours: Tue–Sat 9:30 AM–5:00 PM, Sun 12:00 PM–5:00 PM. Closed Mondays, except federal holidays. Closed Easter, Thanksgiving, Christmas, and New Year's. Call for summer hours.

Plan to Stay: 1.5–2.5 hours, plus time in gift shops.

Minimum Age: None

Disabled Access: Yes

Group Requirements: Groups over 10 people should call 2 weeks in advance. Groups over 70 people will be split.

Gift Shops: Magic Forest Gift Shop sells logoed clothing, candy, and toys. Open same hours as Crayola Factory. The 7,200-square-foot Crayola Store, next door, sells a range of Binney & Smith products, from mini to large boxes of crayons, and from posters to teddy bears wearing logoed sweatshirts. Open Mon–Sat 9:00 AM–6:00 PM, Sun 12:00 PM–6:00 PM. Closed holidays.

Directions: From Philadelphia, take Northeast Extension of Pennsylvania Tnpk. to Allentown Exit onto Rt. 22 East. Get off at the 4th St. exit (last exit in PA). At traffic light, turn left on Buskill St. Turn right onto N. 3rd St. Follow signs to "The Crayola FACTORY."

Nearby Attractions: Martin Guitar and Mack Trucks tours (see pages 34 and 290); Allen Organ Company tour (call 610-966-2202); canal boat ride and walking tour of Easton; Lehigh Valley attractions, including Dorney Park and Wildwater Kingdom.

Harley-Davidson Motor Company

Final Assembly Operations
1425 Eden Road
York, PA 17402
(717) 852-6590 / (877) 746-7937
www.harley-davidson.com

MOTORCYCLES

The company that Bill Harley and the Davidson brothers started in 1903, when they motorized a bicycle to drive through Milwaukee, now produces one of the U.S.A.'s most recognized and respected products. Evident at rallies that draw thousands of people, Harley-Davidson stirs passion in its riders, dealers, and employees. See firsthand what sparks this passion by touring the company's final assembly plant in York, Pennsylvania.

The factory tour takes visitors on a mile-long walk through the shop, past many stages of motorcycle assembly. Except for the robots that weld and polish some of the parts, workers and machines labor together to build the motorcycles. See how presses transform sheets of metal into fenders, teardrop gas tanks, and tailpipes. Behind Plexiglas, you may see sparks flying as lasers trim the fenders and tanks. Inside one workstation, a robot twists around to polish fused-together gas tanks. Walk by colorful, painted gas tanks and various sub-assembly processes.

As the motorcycle is assembled, it journeys by overhead conveyor down an assembly line to different stations where workers drill, screw, and attach parts.

Following the assembly process, the cycle cruises into the roll test booth, where it is placed on rollers and "driven" at speeds up to 75 miles per hour. While the engine rumbles, the stationary rider checks every electrical component, plugging in different devices to test the bike's performance.

Although you can't buy a new Harley at tour's end, you do get to check out a variety of the newest models on display at the tour center.

Cost: Free

Freebies: Copy of *The Enthusiast,* Harley owners' and fans' magazine; product catalog.

Video Shown: Continually running short video in waiting area shows the history of Harley-Davidson, some production areas not on the tour, and information about the various models of motorcycles.

Reservations Needed: No, except for groups of 10 or more. Recommend calling, since plant tour times and availability may change.

Days and Hours: Mon–Fri 9:30 AM, 10:30 AM, 12:30 PM, and 1:30 PM. Harley-Davidson recommends calling in advance; taped message explains changes in hours and availability. Closed major holidays and week between Christmas and New Year's.

Plan to Stay: 1 hour for factory tour, plus time for video and gift shop.

Minimum Age: 12

Disabled Access: Yes

Group Requirements: Groups of 10 or more must be scheduled in advance.

Special Information: Must wear safety glasses (provided) and closed-toe shoes. No photography. Annual 3-day open house at end of September. Kansas City, MO, plant tours (see page 218) and tours of Milwaukee, WI, engine and transmission plant (call 414-535-3666) available. Status of Milwaukee Harley-Davidson museum and "experience center" uncertain at press time.

Gift Shop: Souvenir shop in tour center sells clothing and novelty items. Open Mon–Fri 9:00 AM–3:45 PM.

Directions: From I-83, take Exit 21A (Arsenal Rd./Rt. 30 East). Turn onto Eden Rd. at "Harley-Davidson" sign. Visitors' parking available. From Rt. 30, take Eden Rd., then follow above directions.

Nearby Attractions: Pfaltzgraff Pottery and Wolfgang Candy tours (see pages 292 and 301); York Barbell Museum (call 717-767-6481); Industrial and Agricultural Museum (call 717-846-6452); York County Historical Museum; Gates House and Plough Tavern; outlet stores and antique shops; Gettysburg, Hershey, and Lancaster nearby.

Herr's Snack Factory Tour

Visitors Center
Routes 1 and 272
Nottingham, PA 19362
(800) 63-SNACK
www.herrs.com

Herr's snack food production has come a long way from when the company used a small, old-fashioned cooker in a barn. It now has an advanced and highly automated plant that makes tens of thousands of potato chips, corn chips, tortilla chips, popcorn batches, cheese curls, and pretzels every day. The comfortable, specially designed visitors center and café, creative video, and extensive guided tour provide a tasty education in how Herr's makes its products.

While watching the action through glass walls, you'll "ooh" and "aah" at the panoramic views. In the pretzel area, gaze at a 100-yard stretch of pretzel twists, in rows of 20 to 24 across, marching to massive ovens. In the corn chip, cheese curl, potato chip, and popcorn production sections, your vista overlooks the entire process. Follow the raw ingredients—either corn or potatoes—as they tumble in by the truckload at the beginning of the production line; travel along a conveyor belt through a series of machines that wash, slice, cook, or season them; then head out on bucket lifts to a sorting and bagging area. Other memorable images include machines and workers bagging and boxing together in almost symphonic unison, and the cavernous warehouse filled with snack-food boxes.

Except for the boxing of bags, machines do most of the work. Notice how only a few people oversee production in most areas. Smart machines can even sense discolored potato chips and use air jets to blow these rebels off the line. The guides salt and pepper the tour with interesting facts and figures about the company, including Herr's recycling efforts. But the best thing the guides do is grab samples of warm potato chips directly from the quickly moving conveyer belt. Bagged chips will never again taste the same!

Cost: Free

Freebies: Warm potato chips during the tour; small sample bag at end of tour.

Videos Shown: 10-minute video on company history, narrated by Herr family members; short videos throughout tour show unique view of snacks being made.

Reservations Needed: Yes, but can take walk-ins if space permits.

Days and Hours: Mon–Thur 9:00 AM–3:00 PM on the hour; Fri 9:00 AM, 10:00 AM, and 11:00 AM. Closed holidays.

Plan to Stay: 1.5 hours, including video, tour, gift shop, and café.

Minimum Age: None

Disabled Access: Yes

Group Requirements: With advance notice, can handle any size group, which will split into smaller ones for tour. Video shown in 140-seat auditorium.

Special Information: If you are interested in particular products, such as tortilla chips or cheese curls, call ahead for production schedule on day of your visit.

Gift Shop: Sells Herr's food products; logoed clothing items; Nottingham, PA, T-shirts; scale model of Herr's delivery truck; and Chipper the Chipmunk doll. Open Mon–Fri 8:00 AM–5:00 PM. Call for extended holiday hours. Catalog available from above number.

Directions: From Philadelphia, take I-95 South to Rt. 322 West exit. From Rt. 322, turn left onto Rt. 1 South. Turn left onto Rt. 272 South and right at light onto Herr Dr. Factory and Visitors Center at end of road. From Baltimore, take I-95 North to Exit 100. Take Rt. 272 North. Turn left at light onto Herr Dr.

Nearby Attractions: DaimlerChrysler and Hagley Museum tours (see pages 98 and 99), about 1 hour away; Longwood Gardens; Plumpton Park Zoo; Franklin Mint Museum; Brandywine River Museum; Lancaster County attractions about 30 miles away.

See color photos, page 33.

Hershey's Chocolate World

Visitors Center
Park Boulevard
Hershey, PA 17033
(717) 534-4900
www.hersheychocolateworld.com

CHOCOLATE

This visitors center dedicated to chocolate features a wall display of the Hershey's chocolate story and a 12-minute journey through a simulated chocolate factory. The entire chocolate-making process, from harvesting the bean to packaging the bar, will be revealed to you with true-to-life machines, overhead speakers, and videos. You will find new respect for "The Great American Chocolate Bar."

As you stand in line for the ride, take some time to read the company history displayed on the wall; watch the video describing how cocoa beans are cultivated and harvested in South America and Africa before their trek to Hershey, Pennsylvania. Enjoy the indoor tropical garden at the center of Chocolate World. The exotic plants and palm trees displayed here come from regions of the world where cocoa beans are harvested.

Riding inside a cocoa-bean-shaped cart, you pass scenes depicting the chocolate-making process. Glance at the initial process of cleaning and sorting the beans. You'll understand the true cocoa-bean experience as you enter the roaster and feel the air temperature suddenly rise. Ride past the extractor, which removes the center "nibs" from the bean. Smell the luscious aroma of liquid chocolate as it flows by to be mixed with milk and sugar. Toward the end of your ride, an impressive display of Hershey's products will confront you, as recorded children's voices sing "It's a Hershey's Chocolate World!" You'll see how Hershey distributes its products worldwide and know why, at Chocolate World, they say, "Wherever you go, no matter how far, you'll always be near a Hershey bar."

Cost: Free

Freebies: Samples of Hershey's Miniatures, Hershey's Kisses, or other chocolate products.

Videos Shown: Continually running video in waiting area explains cocoa-bean harvesting and initial processing. Videos throughout ride provide close-up view of the real production process.

Reservations Needed: No

Days and Hours: Mon–Sun 9:00 AM–5:00 PM; some extended hours—best to call in advance. Closed Christmas.

Plan to Stay: 12-minute ride, plus time for displays, gift shops, and restaurants.

Minimum Age: None

Disabled Access: Yes

Group Requirements: None

Special Information: Expect long lines during summertime, although they tend to move quickly. During the 1970s, the company had to close well-known tour of Hershey plant because of overwhelming crowds and safety concerns. Visitors center in Oakdale, CA (see page 69).

Gift Shops: Gift shops and food court sell Hershey's products, ranging from T-shirts and mugs to the more unusual Hershey's Kisses–shaped cap with silver foil and pull string, and a hollow Kisses-shaped piñata that can hold up to 10 pounds of Kisses. Open same hours as ride. Catalog available from (800) 544-1347.

Directions: From the west, take I-83 to Rt. 322 East. Exit at Rt. 39 West to Hersheypark Dr. Chocolate World is the first "Hershey Attraction" on the right. From the east, take Pennsylvania Tnpk. to Exit 20. Follow Rt. 72 North to Rt. 322 West, then follow above directions. From Lancaster, take Rt. 283 West to Rt. 743 North and follow signs to Hershey. Call (800) HERSHEY for recorded directions.

Nearby Attractions: Hersheypark entertainment complex (87-acre amusement park); ZooAmerica North American Wildlife Park; Hershey Gardens; Hershey Museum; the Hotel Hershey; Hersheypark Arena, with concerts, sports, and special events year-round.

Martin Guitar

510 Sycamore Street
Nazareth, PA 18064
(610) 759-2837 / (800) 345-3103
www.martinguitar.com

GUITARS

Ever since C. F. Martin Sr. started making guitars in 1833, Martins have been widely recognized as one of the top U.S.-made products. The company has received highest accolades from the Buy America and Made in the USA foundations. Many popular musicians use Martins, including Paul McCartney, Willie Nelson, and Eric Clapton. The craftsmanship you'll see on this tour demonstrates why these famous musicians are among more than 800,000 satisfied Martin owners.

The guitar-making area resembles a large woodshop. Only recently have power tools and machines appeared, although most of the approximately 300 separate steps that go into making a Martin are done by hand. With so many things to see (including string-making), the guided tour moves quickly.

Stand beside workers as they diligently bend, trim, shape, cut, glue, fit, drill, finish, sand, stain, lacquer, buff, and inspect the different woods that will become Martins. Look for the station where a craftsman uses ordinary clothespins as clamps. These distinctly low-tech devices help secure for drying a glued, serrated strip of wood along the interior edge of the guitar's curvaceous sides. This lining provides additional surface area for attaching the front and back of the body.

Craftsmen use a variety of files, carving knives, and rasps to shape, finish, and attach the neck. Notice how the dovetail neck joint is meticulously trimmed and then checked to ensure a proper fit with the body. When you view a historic Martin or play a modern one in the museum after the tour, you'll really appreciate the three to six months of craftsmanship required to convert rough lumber into a Martin acoustic guitar—a true American classic.

Cost: Free. Group tours, nominal charge.
Freebies: Sound-hole cut-outs; product literature.
Videos Shown: Optional videos show production process, including interviews with C. F. (Chris) Martin IV, the sixth-generation family member who over-

sees the company. Request showing in Martin Museum.
Reservations Needed: No, except for groups.
Days and Hours: Mon–Fri 1:15 PM, best to arrive early. Closed holidays, week between Christmas and New Year's, and July 4th. Small lobby-area museum is open Mon–Fri 8:00 AM–5:00 PM.
Plan to Stay: 1.5–2 hours, including tour, video, gift shop, and museum.
Minimum Age: None, for families; 12, for groups.
Disabled Access: Yes
Group Requirements: Group tours must be arranged in advance. Will split larger groups into groups of 10.
Special Information: Photography permitted without flash. No video cameras.
Gift Shops: 1833 Shop sells Martin guitars, antique and used Martins on consignment, strings, supplies, books, clothing, and other memorabilia. Nearby in the old Martin factory (10 W. North St.) is Guitarmaker's Connection, which sells acoustic guitar tonewoods, kits, parts, instrument-making supplies, strings, and construction/repair books. Both open Mon–Fri 8:30 AM–5:00 PM. Combined catalog available from (800) 247-6931.
Directions: We suggest contacting Martin Guitar for directions from New York City and other points, and for their detailed map, "Navigating Nazareth." From Northeast Extension of Pennsylvania Tnpk., take Exit 33. Take Rt. 22 East to intersection with Rt. 191 North. In Nazareth, Rt. 191 turns left onto Broad St. Stay on Broad St. even though Rt. 191 turns right. Pass the Nazareth Boro Park, turn right onto Beil Ave., then right onto Sycamore St.
Nearby Attractions: Crayola FACTORY and Mack Trucks tour (see pages 284 and 290); Old Martin Homestead (call 610-759-9174); Allen Organ Company tour (call 610-966-2202); Lehigh Valley's attractions include Bushkill Falls, Dorney Park, and Wildwater Kingdom.

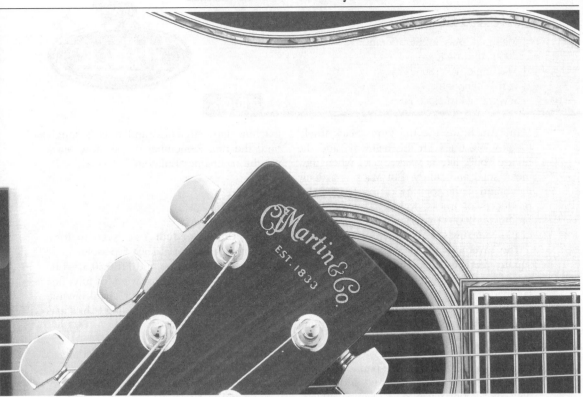

▲ Martin acoustic guitars, considered the world over to be the finest you can play, are handcrafted in Nazareth, Pennsylvania.

▼ It takes cedar ribbons and a lot of clothespins for this important step in the building of a Martin guitar.

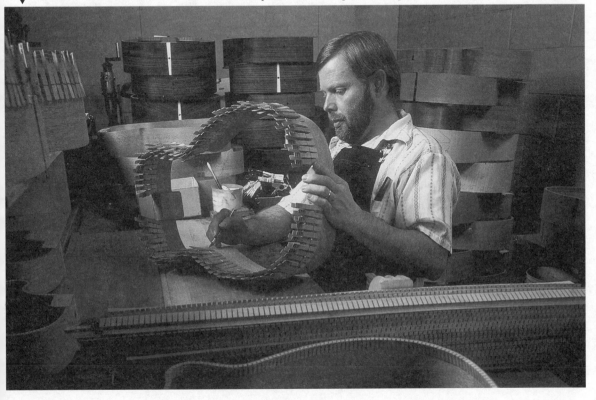

See color photos, pages 1 and 35.

Mack Trucks

Macungie Assembly Operations
7000 Alburtis Road
Macungie, PA 18062
(610) 709-3566
www.macktrucks.com

TRUCKS

Many Americans use the term "Mack truck" for any big truck on the highway, and the phrase "built like a Mack truck" when they mean solid and sturdy. But Mack is actually the brand name for one of the largest U.S. producers of trucks, founded by the Mack brothers in 1900. This plant makes all but four of the company's heavy-duty truck models.

The cavernous plant (just under 1 million square feet) is filled with all the sights, sounds, and smells that make factory tours fascinating. The tour guide, often a Mack retiree, enjoys explaining how the manufacturing process is constantly going through extensive quality improvements. Every step you see, from workers bolting on side-view mirrors to their guiding an 80-pound fuel tank into place, has been videotaped and studied with the scrutiny given to an Olympic athlete.

From the cab assembly line, you stroll through the warehouse and the chassis prep area, walk down the final assembly lines, and peek into the painting booths. Everywhere you look, it seems that air hoses and drills hang from the rafters. Different things may catch your attention. It could be the huge steel-frame rails that form the chassis of each truck, the moving assembly line that workers stand beside to build the cab, the massive engines, or the process used to lower and bolt the engine or the cab to the chassis.

The dynamometer is every visitor's favorite when it is in operation. To simulate road conditions, the trucks are placed on rollers that spin around at 65 miles per hour. A worker sitting in this moving-but-stationary truck tests the drive train, gauges, and electrical systems. Meanwhile, workers at another station inspect the truck's brakes, lights, and other systems.

The process for putting the tires on the rims demonstrates how truck-building has changed. In earlier times, workers used a sledge hammer to pound the tire onto the rim. Today, a worker guides the tire while a machine lifts, stretches, and rolls it snugly onto the rim. Remember to ask how Mack got the nickname "Bulldog."

Cost: Free

Freebies: No

Video Shown: No

Reservations Needed: Yes. Need to form or join a group of at least 5 people.

Days and Hours: Tue and Fri 8:30 AM–1:00 PM. Closed holidays, last week of July, first week of August, week after Thanksgiving, and 2-week period including Christmas and New Year's.

Plan to Stay: 1.5 hours

Minimum Age: 7; specific ratios of adults to children required.

Disabled Access: Tight spaces on factory floor and in museum.

Group Requirements: 5-person minimum, with no maximum. Appreciates 3 weeks' advance notice for large groups.

Special Information: Plant can be warm during summer months. No open-toed shoes.

Gift Shop: Macungie Mack Shop sells hats, toy trucks, T-shirts, belts, pins, and more, all with the famous Mack Bulldog logo (stuffed bulldogs, too). Open Tue–Fri 9:00 AM–3:00 PM. Usually also open after tour. Mack Shop also in company's headquarters in Allentown; open Mon–Fri 10:00 AM–4:00 PM. Call (610) 709-3459 for more information.

Directions: From I-78, take Rt. 100 South. After Laidlaw school-bus parking facility on right, turn right at next street, which is Alburtis Rd. (unmarked). Factory is ahead on left.

Nearby Attractions: Mack Museum, featuring 14 antique trucks and 80,000 photographs (call 610-266-6767); Allen Organ Company tour, almost next door (call 610-966-2202); Martin Guitar tour and Crayola FACTORY visitor center (see pages 288 and 284).

QVC

Studio Park
West Chester, PA 19380-4250
(800) 600-9900
www.qvctours.com

QVC

ELECTRONIC RETAILING

While QVC (Quality, Value, Convenience) does not manufacture products, QVC is all about products—in fact, it sells them via live television, 24 hours a day, seven days a week, including some products made by companies featured in this book. The largest electronic retailer in the world, QVC welcomes you to its headquarters at Studio Park, a state-of-the-art broadcast facility on 80 wooded acres.

You'll enter a lobby that includes the 3,000-square-foot Studio Store. A tour guide will give you a brief history of this multibillion company, including the fact it was founded in 1986 by Joseph Segel, also founder of the Franklin Mint. As you follow the tour guide, you learn that QVC is really two businesses: QVC the merchandiser that searches for, tests, and prepares thousands of different products each year for the other business, and QVC the Network, a round-the-clock live television production.

Follow your tour guide on a route above and around the main studio, designed to demonstrate products in their natural habitats. The 20,000-square-foot studio includes the Home set, made up of a living room, a sun room, a kitchen, a garage, bedrooms, a home office, and a working fireplace. Along the way, the guide will show and tell you about some of the various areas you will see, including Sets and Props, a Quality Assurance lab, backstage areas, and the live control room. You will also see an interactive display showing how orders are taken, processed, and shipped right to you in just a few days. The product Hall of Records includes some of the best-sellers and company favorites.

The climax is the Observation Deck that juts out into the studio. Here you can watch the live show in progress and check out some up-to-date statistics on incoming calls and product sales.

By the end of the tour, you'll understand how the whole thing works, from product selection and testing to on-the-air sales,

order processing, and shipping. Millions of calls come in, and millions of products are shipped out each year. You will learn about shopping on the Internet via QVC Online and about the company's ventures around the world, including Germany, the U.K., Mexico, and Japan. You might even spot one of QVC's hosts or guests, or have a chance to be part of a studio audience.

Cost: Adults, $7.50; children 6–12, $5.

Freebies: No

Videos Shown: 3-minute video covers what QVC is and 5-minute video shows how a product gets on the air.

Reservations Needed: No, except for groups of 10 or more. Yes, for participation in studio audiences.

Days and Hours: Mon–Sun 10:00 AM–4:00 PM, every hour on the hour.

Plan to Stay: 2 hours

Minimum Age: Not recommended for children under 6, but they are welcome.

Disabled Access: Yes

Group Requirements: Groups of 10 or more people should call for discounts.

Studio Store: Sells logoed products and a sampling of on-air merchandise, including jewelry, furniture, cosmetics, kitchen products, gourmet food, toys, and more. Open Mon–Sun 9:30 AM–6:00 PM.

Directions: From Philadelphia, take I-76 West to Rt. 202 South. Exit at Boot Rd. Turn left at light onto Boot Rd. At third light, turn right onto Wilson Dr. Go straight, cross Airport Rd., and follow the signs to the QVC Studio Tour entrance.

Nearby Attractions: Anderson Bakery and Sturgis Pretzel tours (see pages 278 and 297); Simon Pearce on the Brandywine restaurant and glassblowing (call 610-793-0948); American Helicopter Museum; Longwood Gardens; Franklin Mint Museum; Brandywine River Museum; Lancaster, Philadelphia, and Wilmington attractions are about 20 miles away.

Pfaltzgraff

Bowman Road
Thomasville, PA 17364
(717) 792-3544
www.pfaltzgraff.com

POTTERY

PFALTZGRAFF

The Pfaltzgraff family name has been connected to pottery for centuries. George Pfaltzgraff began creating fire-glazed crocks and jugs in rural York County, Pennsylvania, in the early 1800s. Your guided tour takes you through the modern pottery-making process, from the preparation of the clay to the firing, decorating, and glazing of each piece of pottery. As you walk between machines, the retiree tour guide fills the tour with many details and production statistics.

At the cup-forming machines, "pugged" (solid) clay is placed on a pedestal and spun rapidly to form a cup or mug. The new piece journeys through a dryer before being sponged to remove small particles of excess clay. After handles are attached with slip (liquid clay), workers methodically and laboriously hand-paint cups or mugs using a sponge-rubber stamp and small brush to create one of Pfaltzgraff's dozens of different designs.

Odd-shaped pottery pieces, squares or ovals, are made in a special station. Instead of molds, ram presses form each piece. Two plaster dies (called "male" and "female") exert 2,200 pounds of pressure on a piece of clay, squeezing out excess water. Suddenly, what was a lump of clay becomes a piece of pottery. The piece joins others like it on shelves waiting for the carousel glaze machines or hand-applied decorations.

As you walk past the enormous kiln, you will feel its heat. The temperature near the entrance is "only" about 500°, rising to 2,200° in the center of the kiln! This allows the glaze to achieve its glassy appearance as the clay hardens. Each piece spends about 12 hours in the kiln, until it "cools down" to 400°. Pieces are then shelved for inspection later.

Since Pfaltzgraff pottery comes in many styles and shapes, including special holiday and seasonal lines, different decorating methods are used. Some pieces are hand-decorated with decals that, when soaked in water, come off the paper and stick to the once-fired piece. The pieces are sent back to the kiln and fired one more time, sometimes for up to eight hours, to ensure that the decals adhere.

While a plate made on a plate roller is handled by workers an average of 32 times before completion, only one person handles items made in the dry-press facility, from forming through firing and sorting. Even the transporting process, which removes and shelves the plates, is mechanical.

In the lobby, learn about Pfaltzgraff history. The new museum includes historical photographs, old crockery, artifacts, and a timeline.

Cost: Free
Freebies: Small pottery piece.
Video Shown: No
Reservations Needed: Yes, at least 2 days in advance.
Days and Hours: Mon–Fri 10:00 AM. Closed holidays, week of July 4th, and Christmas week.
Plan to Stay: 1.5 hours
Minimum Age: 7
Disabled Access: Yes
Group Requirements: Reservations required 1 week in advance.
Special Information: No photography. Floor can be slippery from clay. No open-toed or open-heeled shoes. Audio headsets and safety goggles provided. President's Day weekend and June Manufacturers Days offer the opportunity to tour many York-area factories.
Outlet Store: Pfaltzgraff Factory Store in Village at Meadowbrook (2900 Whiteford Road, York, PA, 717-757-2200) sells all Pfaltzgraff stoneware, including holiday collections, factory seconds, and discontinued lines. Tent sale late September. Map to outlet store available at factory.
Directions: From York, take Rt. 30 (Lincoln Hwy.) West to Thomasville. Turn right onto Bowman Rd. at Pfaltzgraff sign. Park in visitors lot at left.
Nearby Attractions: Harley-Davidson factory tour, Utz Quality Foods potato chip tour, Hershey's Chocolate World visitors center, and Wolfgang Candy Company tour (see pages 285, 299, 287, and 301); Martin's Potato Chips tour (call 800-272-4477); York County Historical Museum.

▲ Visitors to Pfaltzgraff get a close-up view of how stoneware dinnerware pieces are made in the Thomasville, Pennsylvania facility.

▼ Pfaltzgraff workers at the factory circa 1915 in York, Pennsylvania, still in operation today.

Senator Heinz History Center

1212 Smallman Street
Pittsburgh, PA 15222
(412) 454-6000
www.pghhistory.org

SENATOR JOHN HEINZ PITTSBURGH REGIONAL
HISTORY CENTER
IN ASSOCIATION WITH THE SMITHSONIAN INSTITUTION

WESTERN PENNSYLVANIA PRODUCTS

Vaulted ceilings, red brick walls, steel posts connected by iron braces, a 1949 trolley, a robotic tour guide, an intricate mural of Pittsburgh life—this and plenty more greet you as you walk into the Great Hall of the 160,000-square-foot Senator John Heinz Pittsburgh Regional History Center, located in Pittsburgh's historic Strip District. Home of the Chautauqua Lake Ice Company a century ago, where a piece of track remains on which a railroad car brought ice into the building, the Center houses multiple attractions on six floors.

Learn all about Henry J. Heinz and his company, business philosophy, and marketing genius in the "Heinz 57" exhibit, dating back to the company's beginning in 1869. See the original jars that contained horseradish—the company's first product. Note that the bottles are clear. Henry purposely packaged his products in transparent bottles so customers could witness the ingredients' purity. Competitors were using sawdust and other filler items, disguised in green bottles. Henry was determined to show that he was committed to quality.

View silver chafing dishes and cardboard spoons that well-groomed employees used to offer product samples to customers at the markets. Read an 1888 entry from Henry's diary: "Very busy—we are boiling at the rate of 1,000 bushels tomatoes for catsup daily and 300 bushels of apples for apple butter." Put on an apron and race to pack pickles into a jar, imitating the workers in the early factories.

Next, enter the "Glass: Shattering Notions" exhibit and be intrigued by what appears to be a cracked wall of glass facing you. Discover how glass is formed and the pivotal role that Western Pennsylvania played in the nation's glass industry. Enjoy countless varieties—creamers, vases, cake plates, glass doorknobs—and colors—ruby red, yellow, light blue, dark purple—of glass items surrounding you. Guess whether four particular items are glass, then flip up plastic panels to uncover the answers and a description of each product.

Before you leave the Strip District, visit the unique shops and try the ethnic foods. Stop at a club and dance for a few hours. Above all, look north over the Allegheny River. Sight the friendly neon Heinz Ketchup bottle pouring its glory over the city.

Cost: Adults, $6; senior citizens 62+ and students, $4.50; children 6–18, $3; children 5 and under, free; special group rates.

Freebies: No

Videos Shown: 13-minute video introduces the 2nd-floor "Points in Time" exhibit. Additional video showing old Heinz commercials will bring back memories.

Reservations Needed: No, except for guided tours.

Days and Hours: Mon–Sun 10:00 AM–5:00 PM. Closed Easter, Thanksgiving, Christmas, New Year's.

Plan to Stay: 2.5 to 3 hours for self-guided tour, plus time for Museum Shop.

Minimum Age: None

Disabled Access: Yes

Group Requirements: Make reservations 2 to 3 weeks in advance; call (412) 454-6304.

Special Information: Self-guided or guided tours. Variety of guided tours, plus classes and teacher programs; call for information. An expansion of the Center is planned to be complete in 2004.

Gift Shop: Museum Shop sells books, toys, jewelry, and glassware. Open same hours as Center.

Directions: From north, take I-79 South to I-279 South to I-579. Cross Veterans Bridge. Follow signs for 7th Ave. Turn right on Grant St., left on 11th St., right on Smallman. From east (Pennsylvania Tnpk.), take Pittsburgh/Monroeville exit. Follow signs to Pittsburgh via I-376. Take Grant St. exit. After 7th Ave., turn left on 11th St., right on Smallman.

Nearby Attractions: Brooke Glass, Creegan, Hall China, and Homer Laughlin China tours (see pages 349, 256, 258, and 351); Carnegie Museums.

Sherm Edwards

509 Cavitt Avenue
Trafford, PA 15085-1060
(412) 372-4331 / (800) 436-5424

Sherm Edwards
⊒[CANDIES]⊏

CHOCOLATES

"Good Chocolate Is Not Cheap. Cheap Chocolate Is Not Good." The sign greets you as you embark on your tour of this 50-plus-year-old, family-owned candy manufacturer. The inescapable aroma of rich chocolate fills your nostrils as you witness Sherm Edwards' very own special blend of chocolate being mixed in 500-pound melters on the factory floor. Dark, light, and white chocolate blends are then pumped into molds of everything from gourmet chocolate spoons (that really enhance a cup of coffee!) to three-foot-tall Easter bunnies.

As you progress through the 3,600-square-foot plant whose walls are stacked high with huge bars of raw chocolate, you notice workers, hands awash in chocolate, coating the bottoms of fruit-and-nut eggs. Conveyer belts then transport the eggs through enrobers, where chocolate cascades envelop each egg before it travels into the cooling tunnel to solidify the coating.

Another corner of the factory is the candy kitchen, packed with equipment such as 80-quart mixers, enormous copper pots for caramel making, and marble slabs for cooling fudge and jellies. Award-winning Sherm Edwards' Pecan Crisp is created here, with lots of real butter and pecans and just enough crunchy-sweet brittle to hold all the pecans together. You'll discover just how they make chocolate-covered cherries and strawberries. The liquid filling around the fruit of these cordials is produced in the panner, a machine resembling a miniature cement mixer, which spins the fruit to coat it with sugar. The fruit is then dipped in chocolate and the sugar coating liquefies, producing the syrup inside the chocolate cordials.

Cost: Free
Freebies: Various candy samples

Video Shown: No

Reservations Needed: Yes. Prefers that individuals and families join group tours.

Days and Hours: Mon–Fri 9:00 AM–3:00 PM. Closed major holidays. Easter–mid-September, production slows to 1 or 2 days per week.

Plan to Stay: 30 minutes for tour, plus time for retail outlet store.

Minimum Age: None

Disabled Access: Retail store is accessible. Stairs lead from retail store down to factory floor.

Group Requirements: Can handle groups from 10–45 people with 1 day's advance notice. Local Radisson Hotels arrange bus tours for groups staying at hotels. Group discounts on purchases.

Special Information: Candy production depends on holidays; for example, chocolate hearts produced before Valentine's Day and molded chocolate bunnies and eggs before Easter.

Retail Store: Sells chocolates, fudges, and nut brittles made on the premises, over 300 varieties of molded chocolate novelties, and hard candies and jellybeans. Slightly imperfect factory seconds available. Open Mon–Sat 9:00 AM–5:00 PM. Call about holiday hours. Price list available.

Directions: Take I-376 East to Exit 16A. Take Rt. 48 South to Rt. 130 South to Trafford. Cross over bridge into Trafford. Take first left, then immediate right, then another right onto Cavitt Ave. Sherm Edwards Candies is on the right. From Pennsylvania Tnpk., take Exit 6 to Business Rt. 22 West to Rt. 48 South, then follow above directions.

Nearby Attractions: Westinghouse Airbrake Museum (call 412-823-0500); Pittsburgh's attractions about 30 minutes away.

Snyder's of Hanover

1350 York Street
Hanover, PA 17331
(717) 632-4477, ext. 8592
www.snydersofhanover.com

PRETZELS AND POTATO CHIPS

Pennsylvania is the snack-food capital of the U.S.A. Small family businesses that hand-twist pretzels and mega-companies that churn out over 400,000 pounds of pretzels and potato chips a day cover the state, particularly in the area surrounding York and Lancaster Counties.

Now best known for its Sourdough Hard Pretzel, Snyder's of Hanover actually began as a potato-chip company in 1921, when the Snyder family started chipping potatoes in their home. It wasn't until 1970 that Snyder's produced a full range of pretzel items, and now it can produce 420,000 pounds of pretzels each day.

When you tour Snyder's state-of-the-art facility, your tour guide gives a brief introduction full of interesting facts—but can't divulge top-secret baking times, oven speeds, and formulas. Since this is a reverse-chronology tour, first follow your guide down the corridor overlooking the shipping warehouse. At the palletizer, pretzel boxes travel down the conveyor single-file and line up to make rows of three boxes, with four of these rows (12 boxes) filling each case.

Further down the corridor, look through windows at what is probably the most automated packaging system in the snack-food industry. Machines build boxes from flat cardboard cutouts, machines fill the bags, and more machines close the boxes. Notice the two new auto case-packers in the far corner. These machines perform all the packaging steps, except for sealing the cartons.

To your left, pretzels shake along conveyor belts on their way to the form- and fill-machines. To your right, potato chips vibrate along a conveyor highway to their own set of form- and fill-machines. These stainless steel, circular machines each consist of 14 buckets that weigh and release the appropriate amount into bags that are just being formed below.

The most impressive sight on the tour is the oven room, with seven of the largest ovens in the world. As you keep walking down the hall, it seems like you'll never reach the end of these 150-foot-long, massive gray ovens. Silver exhaust stacks rise through the ceiling. Feel the heat through the windows. Pretzels travel through the upper half of each oven for baking, slide down to reverse direction, and dry or become hard and deliciously crunchy during their journey in the lower half of the oven.

Cost: Free

Freebies: Product samples

Video Shown: 15-minute video covers company history and pretzel twisting, along with close-ups of production steps.

Reservations Needed: Yes

Days and Hours: Tue–Thur 10:00 AM, 11:00 AM, and 1:00 PM.

Plan to Stay: 1 hour, plus time in outlet store.

Minimum Age: None

Disabled Access: No, for factory tour. Yes, for outlet store.

Group Requirements: Groups of 15 or more people should call 1 day in advance.

Special Information: No photography

Outlet Store: Sells 1-oz. vending machine bags to bulk 6-lb. cartons of pretzels, potato chips, and tortilla chips. Also sells decorative gift tins and logoed clothing. Open Mon–Sat 9:00 AM–6:00 PM and Sun 12:00 PM–5:00 PM. Closed holidays. Catalog available by calling (800) 233-7125, ext. 1410.

Directions: From Pennsylvania Tnpk., take I-83 South to Rt. 30 West. Take Rt. 116 West. Snyder's will be on your left. Check in for tour at outlet store counter.

Nearby Attractions: Utz Quality Foods potato chip tour in Hanover (see page 299); Harley-Davidson motorcycle tour (see page 285) and Wolfgang Candy (call 717-843-5536) both in York, about 1 hour away. Lancaster and Pennsylvania Dutch attractions about 1–1.5 hours away.

Sturgis Pretzel House

219 East Main Street
Lititz, PA 17543
(717) 626-4354
www.sturgispretzel.com

PRETZELS

Pennsylvania has many large pretzel manufacturers whose tours will "wow" you with massive machines, fast-moving conveyor belts, and mind-boggling production numbers. At Sturgis Pretzel House, though, pretzel making is more of a participatory art. The workers, many of whom are fifth- and sixth-generation relatives of the founder, proudly explain that Sturgis is the first commercial pretzel bakery in the U.S.A. (opened in 1861). Housed in a restored 200-year-old building, with displays of old pretzel-making equipment as well as modern mixers, extruders, and oven, the company makes the tour an integral part of its business.

Playing pretzel-maker is the most fun on the tour. As you stand in front of a rolling table, your tour guide will give you a small ball of dough. You'll roll the dough into a thin pencil, pick it up from both ends, cross it to form rabbit ears, then twist the ends and pull them back to rest on the loop. As you twist your pretzel, the guide explains that the monk who invented the pretzel in A.D. 610 wanted to make from dough the sign of prayer, which involved crossing both arms with hands on the opposite shoulders. The three holes in a pretzel represent the Father, Son, and Holy Ghost.

You won't get rich after you receive an "Official Pretzel Twister" certificate. In the days before automation, founder Julius Sturgis paid twisters about 25 cents per thousand pretzels. Now the company manufactures most of its hard pretzels by machine. You can stand near the machine that automatically shapes the dough into pretzels and then bakes and salts them. While contemporary pretzel making seems so easy, it doesn't compare to the dexterity shown by the Sturgis family member who hand-twists a soft pretzel as the tour ends.

Cost: $2. Children under 2, free.
Freebies: Small hard pretzel that doubles as your tour ticket, paper hat that you must wear during tour, and well-earned "Official Pretzel Twister" certificate.

Video Shown: No
Reservations Needed: No, except for groups of 12 or more people.
Days and Hours: Mon–Sat 9:30 AM–4:30 PM, every 15–30 minutes. Closed Thanksgiving, Christmas, and New Year's.
Plan to Stay: 20 minutes for tour, plus time for gift shop.
Minimum Age: None
Disabled Access: Yes
Group Requirements: Groups of 12 or more should call ahead. Groups also receive free soft pretzels.
Special Information: It can be hot standing near the pretzel-baking machine.
Gift Shop: Tour ends at small gift shop. You enter the pretzel house through larger store that sells gift items and pretzels, including their unique horse-and-buggy-shaped pretzels. Special prices on multiple bags and large bags. Look for book titled *The Pretzel Story,* which includes photographs, company history, and explanation of evolving pretzel-making process. Open Mon–Sat 9:30 AM–4:30 PM. Catalog available.
Directions: From Lancaster, take Rt. 501 North to Lititz. Turn right on Main St. (Rt. 772). Sturgis Pretzel House is on left, with big pretzel in front. From the east, take Pennsylvania Tnpk. (I-76) to Exit 21. Go south on Rt. 222 and turn right onto Rt. 772 into Lititz. Follow above directions.
Nearby Attractions: Wilbur Chocolate Candy Americana Museum (interesting exhibits, including handmade candy demonstrations and video on chocolate-making, plus factory outlet; call 717-626-3249); Johannes Mueller House; Lititz Springs Park; Pennsylvania Dutch sites and Lancaster attractions all within short drive.

U.S. Mint

5th and Arch Streets
Philadelphia, PA 19106-1886
(215) 408-0114
www.usmint.gov

COINS

We all know that money doesn't grow on trees, but do you know where 50 percent of U.S. coins come from? A tour of the Philadelphia U.S. Mint, which currently strikes approximately 10 million quarters, 4.4 million dimes, 2.6 million nickels, and 20 million pennies each weekday, will show you just that. Encompassing an entire city block, the world's largest mint also houses a museum of rare coins, historic medals, and antique mint machinery.

In the lobby area, see all commemorative coin designs issued since 1892 and notice the 1901 Tiffany mosaics on the walls. Press on past the displays to the glass-enclosed observation gallery above the mint factory floor. From this 300-foot-long vantage point, you witness mere strips of metal and blanks being turned into money. An awesome array of machines heats, washes, dries, sorts, edges, stamps, inspects, counts, and bags the coins that are punched out of the metal strips.

You will better understand what you see on this self-guided tour if you refer to the diagram in the free pamphlet distributed at the beginning of the tour and press the buttons to hear the taped explanations. A new video system gives visitors a close-up view of coinage production, of the designing and engraving processes, and of a special ceremony held in the mint's vault. From another area you can see medals and special collectors' coins produced by a process similar to that used for regular coins.

In the mezzanine area, additional displays of coins and artifacts include the original coining press used at the first mint in 1792. These displays appear more interesting than the earlier ones, probably because you just saw how such coins are made. Then hurry down to the gift shop to purchase your own coins and begin your collection. Or, of course, you can just admire your spare change with your newfound knowledge.

Cost: Free

Freebies: Brochure

Videos Shown: 7 videos show close-ups at each production stage.

Reservations Needed: No

Days and Hours: *For security reasons, public tours have been discontinued until further notice. Please check their website as it is kept very current regarding changes in policy.*

Plan to Stay: 45 minutes for self-guided tour and coin gallery, plus time for gift shop.

Minimum Age: None, but smaller children may not be able to see or understand all the displays.

Disabled Access: Yes

Group Requirements: None

Special Information: Read pamphlet before beginning self-guided tour. It also explains the sculptor-engravers' and die-makers' work not seen on public tour.

Gift Shop: Sells commemorative coins and medals, as well as books on money, American history, and U.S. presidents. Mint your own souvenir medal in gift shop for $2. Open same days and hours as tour. For catalog information, call (800) USA-MINT.

Directions: From Pennsylvania, take Schuylkill Expwy. (Rt. 76 East) to Vine St. Expwy., exit right at 6th St. Go south 2 blocks and turn left onto Market St. Go 1 block and turn left onto 5th St. Go 1 block north to Arch St. Mint imposingly occupies entire right side of 5th and Arch Sts. From New Jersey, take Benjamin Franklin Bridge to Philadelphia. Take 6th St./Independence Hall exit on right, follow signs to 6th St. Turn left onto Market St. and follow above directions.

Nearby Attractions: Asher's Chocolates and Byers' Choice tours (see pages 279 and 282); downtown Philadelphia attractions include Independence Hall, Liberty Bell, Betsy Ross' House, Christ Church, and Benjamin Franklin's grave.

Utz Quality Foods

900 High Street
Hanover, PA 17331
(717) 637-6644 / (800) 367-7629
www.utzsnacks.com

UTZ QUALITY FOODS, INC.

POTATO CHIPS

The Hanover Home brand potato chips made by Salie and Bill Utz in 1921 at a rate of 50 pounds of chips per hour has evolved into a large regional snack-food company that produces up to 14,000 pounds of award-winning chips per hour. This self-guided tour allows you to view the entire 30-minute process that transforms a raw spud into a crunchy chip. An overhead observation gallery equipped with push-button audio and video stations lets you view the entire factory floor.

Potatoes roll and tumble like marbles past you into the peeling machine, which tosses them until the skin is removed. Peeled whole potatoes move along to the slicer, which is programmed to chop them into slices 55/1000ths of an inch thick. The slices are bathed in 340° cooking oil, showered with salt, and dried on long conveyors while being inspected for discoloring. Flavorings (such as barbecue or sour cream and onion) are added just before packaging.

Notice the pipes running throughout the factory, along walls and over workers' heads. These pipes carry water and oil to and from the production floor. Utz's innovative in-house recycling program uses water to eliminate most of the discarded product waste, such as unused potatoes, skins, and damaged returns. The "waste" is then sold to local farmers for animal feed, while the oil is used to make soap.

As you walk through the observation gallery, you see several Utz products traveling in different directions until they reach the packaging area. Chips are poured into giant funnels, which dump precisely measured amounts into bags of all sizes. Workers pack the bags into boxes, and Utz's almost 300 trucks transport them all over the eastern U.S. Although your potato chip trip ends above the loading area, don't forget to grab a "souvenir" bag on your way out.

Cost: Free

Freebies: Snack-size bag of potato chips.

Video Shown: 2 stations on tour show live camera shots.

Reservations Needed: No, except for groups larger than 10 people.

Days and Hours: Mon–Thur 8:30 AM–4:30 PM. If factory is in production on Fri, tours will be offered. Call above number in advance for Fri schedule. Closed holidays.

Plan to Stay: 20 minutes for self-guided tour, plus time for nearby outlet store.

Minimum Age: None

Disabled Access: Flight of steps to observation gallery; however, all visitors are accommodated, so call ahead for assistance.

Group Requirements: Groups of 10 or more should call 2 days in advance to schedule tour guide.

Special Information: Brochure available on recycling program.

Outlet Store: Located a few blocks east on the corner at the corporate offices, 861 Carlisle St. (Rt. 94). All Utz products, including chips, pretzels, and popcorn, available in several sizes; chips and pretzels in cans up to 96 ounces; also, decorator cans with Christmas and other designs. Look for special "Grandma Utz" Pennsylvania Dutch–style hand-cooked chips, and gourmet hand-dipped chocolate-covered chips and pretzels. Open Mon–Sat 8:00 AM–7:00 PM, Sun 11:00 PM–6:00 PM. Catalog available.

Directions: From Harrisburg, take I-15 South to PA 94 South into Hanover. Turn right onto Clearview Rd. (outlet store is on corner). Utz potato-chip factory is straight ahead at intersection of Clearview Rd. and High St. Tour entrance is on left side of building. From Maryland, take MD 30 North (becomes PA 94) to Hanover. Turn left onto Clearview Rd. and follow directions above.

Nearby Attractions: Snyder's of Hanover and Pfaltzgraff pottery tours (see pages 296 and 292); Martin's Potato Chips tour (call 717-792-3565); Gettysburg about 20 minutes away.

Wendell August Forge

620 Madison Avenue
Grove City, PA 16127-0109
(724) 458-8360 / (800) 923-4438
www.wendellaugust.com

METAL AND CRYSTAL GIFTWARE

Wendell August Forge is the oldest and largest hand forge in the country. The company that Wendell August started in 1923 with making hand-forged architectural pieces (such as railings and gates) now makes beautiful metal giftware. This self-guided tour shows you the steps in producing their individually handcrafted products, from the cutting of sheet metal to the final hammering and polishing of finished pieces.

Die engraving is the most intricate and time-consuming step. Master die engravers use only a hammer, chisels, and their own creative talents to engrave designs into steel slabs. The carved die design, sometimes taking eight weeks to complete, is the reverse of the actual image. Try to find the engraver's initials on the die; they're cleverly hidden in the design.

Your ears alert you to the hammering area. Watch craftspeople carefully clamp down a blank piece of aluminum or bronze over the design. They use specially designed hammers to force the metal into the die's carved-out portions, creating a raised image on the other side. One moment it's a flat piece of metal, and the next you see the detailed image of an eagle soaring gracefully over a rocky canyon.

After this initial hammering, the piece moves to an anvil to be flattened, anviled, and edged before the remarkable "coloring" process occurs. Each metal piece is placed face down onto a specially grated screen and held over an open fire in an early-1930s forge. The fire's black smoke bakes onto the piece. After cooling, special polishing removes 97 percent of the baked-on smoke, leaving just enough color to highlight the design. Although Wendell August artisans never produce two identical pieces of giftware, their hallmark and company logo on the back of each item attest to its quality.

Cost: Free

Freebies: Brochure and map; catalog available upon request.

Video Shown: 7-minute video provides close-up view of production steps.

Reservations Needed: No, but recommended for groups of 15 or more.

Days and Hours: November–January: Mon–Fri 9:00 AM–8:00 PM, Sat 9:00 AM–6:00 PM, Sun 11:00 AM–5:00 PM. January–November: Mon–Fri 9:00 AM–2:30 PM. When not in production, see manufacturing process video in gift shop; may be able to view work area.

Plan to Stay: 20 minutes for self-guided tour, plus time for video and gift shop.

Minimum Age: None for families, above elementary-school age for groups.

Disabled Access: Yes

Group Requirements: Welcomes any size group. Recommends 1 week's advance notice for groups larger than 15. Insurance prohibits tours by groups of elementary-school-age children.

Special Information: You may talk with the craftspeople but, for your own safety, do not touch any metal in production. During busy seasons, Wendell Bear may greet you with a hug. In heart of Amish Country, Berlin, OH, plant tour (call 330-893-3713) features production tours, museum, and theater.

Gift Shop: Store and showroom display all Wendell August handmade items, including intricately designed coasters, plates, serving pieces, trays, and Christmas ornaments. Engraved crystal and glass, plus other unique gift items. Open same hours as above except January–November: Mon–Thur 9:00 AM–6:00 PM, Fri 9:00 AM–8:00 PM. Catalog available from numbers above. Gift shop also has LGB model train suspended overhead on 200 feet of track and authentic nickelodeon.

Directions: From I-79, take Exit 31. Follow blue and white signs. From I-80, take Exit 3A. Follow signs.

Nearby Attractions: Daffin's Chocolate Factory tour (call 724-342-2892); Troyer Farms Potato Chips tour (call 800-458-0485).

Wolfgang Candy

50 East 4th Avenue
York, PA 17404
(717) 843-5536 / (800) 248-4273
www.wolfgangcandy.com

CANDY

The English Tudor Das Sweeten Haus Center provides your first flavor of Wolfgang Candies. Inside, you get a true sense of family history and involvement in the business. Started in 1921, this fourth-generation family business makes most of its candies for fundraisers. The brown 1926 Model T parked inside the Tudor structure runs on chocolate instead of gas. Notice old company invoices as well as a soda fountain.

Walk on a quiet residential street past R. Wolfgang's house. You enter Building 3 and don a hair net to watch their popular peanut butter marshmallow candies being made. Mixers swirl and stir peanut butter or marshmallow. First, marshmallow drops into molds made from cornstarch. Next the peanut butter drops over the marshmallow. Chocolate coats the whole delicacy. Walk by the taffy pull machine. Four rollers twist peanut butter swirls into peanut butter kisses candies. Walk downstairs and next to the long white enrober machine that covers fillings with a chocolate waterfall followed by a 10 to 15 minute journey through the 55° to 65° cooling tunnel.

In the kitchen, two workers pour boiling peanut brittle mixture from a big copper kettle onto a cooling table. The workers, using bendable spatulas, spread the peanut brittle mixture across the table. One of the workers runs a sword underneath the mixture to prevent it from sticking to the table. Water running inside this metal table cools the mixture. Another worker rolls a metal rolling pin with blades to score the candy so that it will break into even pieces.

Corn syrup is stored in tanks above Building 3. Inside, a 40,000-gallon tank stores chocolate at 110° to 115°. Much of the candy is hand packed. Along the assorted line, candies are placed in proper order on a grid. Computer sorting provides efficiencies for fundraiser candies. Before Easter, you may see them making their famous chocolate-covered peanut butter eggs.

Cost: Free

Freebies: Small bag of chocolates and hard candies

Video Shown: 25-minute video covers candy production.

Reservations Needed: No, except groups larger than 10.

Days and Hours: Visitor Center: Mon–Fri 8:00 AM–5:00 PM, Sat 9:00 AM–4:00 PM. Factory tours: Mon–Fri 10:00 AM. Closed some holidays.

Plan to Stay: 40 minutes, plus additional time for Das Sweeten Haus and Wolfgang Sweet Shoppe.

Minimum Age: None for families, 1st grade for school groups.

Disabled Access: Yes for Das Sweeten Haus Center and Building 2's first floor, 16 steps for Building 3.

Group Requirements: Groups over 10 people should schedule appointment 2 weeks in advance by calling (717) 764-8479. Maximum group size is 50 people.

Special Information: Full production September–Easter. President's Day weekend and June Manufacturers' Day offer the opportunity to tour many York-area factories.

Gift Shop: Wolfgang Sweet Shoppe sells hand-dipped raisin clusters (watch as they are made Mon–Fri 7:00 AM–3:30 PM), peanut butter petals, chocolate-covered pretzelettes, nonpareils, and more. Open same hours as the Visitor Center.

Directions: From I-83, take North George St. exit. Turn right onto North George St. Turn left onto 4th Ave. From I-30 West, turn left onto North George St. Turn left on 4th Ave.

Nearby Attractions: As "factory tour capital of the world," many York-area factories offer tours or museums including Harley-Davidson motorcycles and Pfaltzgraff pottery (see pages 285 and 292); York Barbell Museum (call 717-767-6481), Martin's Potato Chips tour (call 717-792-3565), and Naylor Wines tour (call 800-292-3370); Industrial and Agricultural Museum (call 717-846-6452); Central Market House.

Zippo/Case Visitors Center

1932 Zippo Drive
Bradford, PA 16701
(814) 368-1932 / (888) 442-1932
www.zippo.com/about/zcvc

ZIPPO LIGHTERS AND CASE KNIVES

Located in the wooded hills of northwestern Pennsylvania, the Zippo/Case Visitors Center commands attention from the moment you enter the curving drive flanked by 14 custom made Zippo street lighters. Your eye is drawn first to an enormous three-bladed Case Canoe pocketknife topping the entrance of the building, and then upward to an imposing 40-foot Zippo lighter with a flickering neon flame.

The doors open directly into the Zippo/Case store. Straight across the store, two massive reproductions of chrome Zippo lighters beckon you into the museum, with its open ceiling and colorful exhibits. Take a few minutes to study the time line on the wall to your left, which contains photographs, video clips, and interesting factoids about Zippo, Case, Bradford, and the world. Next to the time line you'll see the famous Zippo lighter American flag, consisting of 3393 red, white, and blue Zippo lighters.

Begin your self-guided tour by watching the introductory video in the theater on your right. The maze of exhibits leads through an interactive station full of information about US and Canadian geography as shown on the surface of Zippo lighters. A WWII exhibit features a tableau of a military foxhole and a wall display of letters to George Blaisdell, the founder of Zippo, from commanders including Eisenhower and MacArthur. "Zippo in the Movies" highlights more than 1,000 documented appearances of Zippo lighters on the big screen. The largest exhibit is framed by a huge glass wall, where you can observe the Zippo Repair Clinic in operation. Zippo technicians repair approximately 1,000 lighters per day, follow the process of these repairs and you will truly appreciate Zippo's legendary guarantee: "It works, or we fix it free."

Continue through striking displays of rare historic Case knives, including a mesmerizing "knife in motion" hologram. The grand finale of the tour is *ZAC* ("Zippo And Case"), a 7-foot-high audio kinetic sculpture. Colorful, pool-size balls plop, ting, bang, and ring their way through a dynamic obstacle course, delighting adults and children alike.

Cost: Free

Freebies: No

Video Shown: 9-minute video on Zippo/Case history and products, and shorter clips at exhibits.

Reservations Needed: No, except for groups over 12 people.

Days and Hours: Visitors Center: Mon–Sat 9:00 AM–5:00 PM; June–December also Sun 12:00 PM–4:00 PM. Repair Center: Mon–Fri 9:00 AM–3:30 PM. Closed major holidays.

Plan to Stay: 1 hour for video, museum, and Repair Center, plus time for gift shop.

Minimum Age: None, for families; 5th grade, for groups.

Disabled Access: Yes

Group Requirements: Groups of 12 or more should call 1 week in advance (call 814-368-2711). Maximum group size is 65. Groups receive gold Zippo lighter lapel pin and collectors' guide.

Special Information: The 1947 Zippo Car "lives" at the Visitors Center when it's not traveling; its travel schedule is accessible via the website. Each year, members of the Case Collectors Club are offered exclusive limited-edition knives. Zippo/Case Swap Meet every other July.

Gift Shop: The Zippo/Case Store carries the full line of Zippo and Case products, including sunglasses and watches, as well as T-shirts, hats, and other items unavailable anywhere else. Open same hours as Visitors Center.

Directions: Take I-86 to U.S. 219 South, follow to Bradford. When U.S. 219 South ends, turn right. Proceed to intersection (4-way stop). Yield to right. After a quarter-mile, bear right at fork. Follow the signs to the Visitors Center.

Nearby Attractions: Northern Lights Candles Factory tour (call 800-836-8797); Willamette Industries Paper Factory tour (call 814-965-2521); Allegheny National Forest; Kinzua Bridge State Park; Knox Kane Railroad; Allegheny Arms and Armor Museum; Penn Brad Oil Museum.

See color photos, pages 37–39.

Vanguard Racing Sailboats

200 High Point Avenue
Portsmouth, RI 02871
(401) 683-0960
www.teamvanguard.com

RACING SAILBOATS

VANGUARD

As one of the leading builders of racing boats between eight and 16 feet, Vanguard supplied watercraft for the 1992 and 1996 Olympics. The Barcelona games marked the first time in 25 years that a non-host country won the job of building them. So that no sailor has an advantage, precision manufacturing drives Vanguard's boat-building process to ensure that the boats are identical. If you can tolerate the strong glue smell, you can walk along the plant floor, stand next to the workers, and observe all the stages in making the different Vanguard models.

Fiberglass boats are built from the outside in, starting from separate molds of the hull and deck. The molds are mirror images of these boat-body parts. The precision begins in the room where a bandsaw cuts stacks of fiberglass sheets according to an exacting pattern. In the spray booth, the bright gel coat that's sprayed into the mold provides the boat's color.

In a process called "laying up fiberglass," workers use paint rollers to glue the strips down into the molds. You'll see them hand-lay the resin-soaked fiberglass sheets, reminding you of making papier-mâché dolls. To ensure that each boat weighs the same, the resin and fiberglass are carefully weighed before being laid into each boat; the hulls are specially measured against a template. The separately made hull and deck are also cored with PVC foam and vacuum-bagged.

In a nearby area, workers add hardware such as the cleats and mast step. Hanging from the ceiling are decks and hulls joined by glue and married together with huge pterodactyl clamps. As these flying dinosaurs are lowered, you realize that hidden inside is a sleek racing boat. Even if you're only an occasional sailor, you'll appreciate what's involved in building a high-performance racing boat.

Cost: Free
Freebies: Stickers
Video Shown: No
Reservations Needed: Yes
Days and Hours: Mon–Fri 9:00 AM–2:30 PM. Closed holidays.
Plan to Stay: 1 hour for tour
Minimum Age: 10
Disabled Access: Yes
Group Requirements: No maximum group size as long as 5 days' advance notice is given.
Special Information: As with any fiberglass-boat manufacturing plant, there is a strong glue smell.
Gift Shop: No
Directions: From Rt. 114 North, turn right into Portsmouth Business Park (Hedly St.) and follow signs to production offices. From Rt. 114 South, turn left into Portsmouth Business Park and follow signs.
Nearby Attractions: Thames Glass tour in Newport is less than 1 hour away (call 401-846-0576); Herreshoff Marine Museum in Bristol; Colt State Park; Haffenreffer Museum of Anthropology; Newport's beaches, mansions, Naval War College Museum, Museum of Yachting at Fort Adams, Tennis Hall of Fame, and other attractions are 20 minutes away. (This area of Rhode Island has many sailboat manufacturers, but very few give public tours. However, if you own a boat made by a company in this region, or are considering the purchase of one, a tour probably could be arranged by calling the company or your local dealer directly).

American Classic Tea

Charleston Tea Plantation
6617 Maybank Highway
Wadmalaw Island, SC 29487
(843) 559-0383 / (800) 443-5987

On a small island 25 miles south of Charleston, the last 11 rural miles along a dead-end road, lies the only commercial tea plantation in the U.S.A. Charleston Tea Plantation is a tea farm rather than an Old South plantation with white columns. Its entrance, however, through a seven-foot-high chain-link fence (bearing only the number 6617) and long rows of perfectly manicured five-foot-wide tea hedges, is just as enchanting. The Charleston Tea Plantation offers visiting hours for its plantation grounds.

Park between the tea hedgerows near the gazebo and live Spanish moss–covered oak tree. In the gazebo, watch a video on tea history, harvesting, and processing. The video explains the processes that harvested tea leaves undergo in the factory: in a five-foot-high bin, a fan blows air through them to reduce their moisture content. After 18 hours, the flaccid leaves are ground and spread out to oxidize in open air. The green leaves turn coppery orange. Next, in a 250° dryer, the leaves tumble back and forth among seven conveyors and turn from copper to black tea, which is then tasted, sorted, graded, and packaged.

Next, stroll along the paved walkway to the 20-foot-long by 12-foot-high mechanized harvester, a big green monster whose wheelbase straddles a tea row. The efficiency of this hybrid cotton picker and tobacco harvester allows the plantation to compete with inexpensive Far East manual-harvesting costs. Mack Fleming, co-owner and president (in alternating years), designed it when he was Director of Horticulture for Lipton. Lipton operated a research facility at this site from 1963 until 1987, when Mack Fleming and Bill Hall purchased it. While Mack got his taste of the tea industry at Lipton, Bill Hall, a third-generation tea taster, earned his tea experience through an apprenticeship in England, tasting 800 to 1,000 cups of tea five days a week for four years.

At the end of your visit, enjoy American Classic Iced Tea and benne sesame wafers while relaxing under the white latticework gazebo.

Cost: Free

Freebies: Tea samples with benne wafers.

Video Shown: 8-minute video overviews entire production process, from harvesting to factory.

Reservations Needed: No

Days and Hours: Call ahead for hours.

Plan to Stay: 45 minutes to one hour

Minimum Age: None

Disabled Access: Yes

Group Requirements: None

Special Information: Wear comfortable shoes and clothing for the outdoor walk.

Gift Shop: Awning-stripe tent offers tea bags, loose tea, ready-to-drink tea beverages, logoed T-shirts, and Charleston sweet grass baskets. Open visiting hours. Catalog available from 800 number above.

Directions: From Charleston, take Hwy. 700 (Maybank Hwy.) South directly onto Wadmalaw Island. Plantation entrance is 11 miles from Church Creek Bridge.

Nearby Attractions: Atlantic Littleneck Clam Farm tour (call 843-762-0022), 25 miles away; Angel Oak Park, 11 miles away; Kiawah Island Resort, 22 miles away.

BMW

1400 Highway 101 South
Greer, SC 29651
(888) TOUR-BMW (888-868-7269)
www.bmwusfactory.com

BMW Zentrum

The bright new BMW Zentrum Visitors Center seems to appear out of nowhere as you approach it. The Zentrum (German for "center") sits in front of BMW's first manufacturing facility outside of Germany. Ten white flags wave in front of the white horseshoe-shaped building nestled on BMW's 1,039 acres. Opened in 1996, the 28,000-square-foot Zentrum gives you views of famous BMW race and art cars and a sneak preview of the experimental BMW cars of the future.

Follow a covered walkway from the Zentrum into the quiet factory that produces the sporty Roadsters, Coupes, and X5s. In the Communications Plaza, the plant's "town center," the three main manufacturing areas—body, paint, and assembly—physically intersect.

In the body shop, workers in green fire-resistant jackets weld the steel parts together at a marriage station, while bursts of sparks fly into the air. The paint shop is seven stories high (only three stories above ground), protected by a glass wall, and highly pressurized to keep debris from contaminating the paint environment. Cars pause at each station to be cleaned and coated with a sealant to reduce noise and water leakage before being primed, color-coated, and clear-coated.

In assembly, the painted bodies are placed on a rotating conveyor and tilted 90 degrees so workers can install the parts in the car's underbody without bending or stooping. Each car travels along the oval assembly line on an AABV (Automated Assembly Body Vehicle), a small platform run by electronic monorail under the floor. Associates install the interior parts, such as the engine, fuel lines, gas tank, dashboard, seats, and radio.

Finally the cars are rigorously tested. New cars are driven straight off the line onto a rough cobblestone road to check the handling, shifting, and braking. Afterwards, an eight-minute water test simulates heavy rain hitting at highway speeds.

Cost: Zentrum, free; plant tour, $5.

Freebies: No

Video Shown: 17-minute movie "Ride the Line," virtual factory tour following the assembly line of a BMW Z3 Roadster. Shown every half hour in the surround-sound theater.

Reservations Needed: No, for Zentrum; yes, for the plant tour.

Days and Hours: Zentrum: Tue–Sat 9:30 AM–5:30 PM. Closed holidays. Plant tours: Tue–Thur 10:00 AM and 2:00 PM. Plant tours may be abbreviated or canceled due to new model development and unreleased automobile designs.

Plan to Stay: 1.25 hours for Zentrum, 45 minutes for tour, plus time in gift shop and café.

Minimum Age: None, for Zentrum; 12, for plant tour.

Disabled Access: Yes

Group Requirements: Groups over 20 people should fax request 1 month in advance to (864) 989-5527, or write BMW Manufacturing Corp., P.O. Box 11000, Spartanburg, SC 29304. Maximum group size: 20 people. BMW confirms reservations up to 90 days ahead. Group discounts available.

Special Information: No photography in plant.

Gift Shop: Sells BMW memorabilia and BMW model cars. European-style café serves German beer, pretzels, and cappuccino. Open same hours as Zentrum.

Directions: From I-85, take Exit 60 for Hwy. 101 South. Turn left after 300 yards at 1-mile-long driveway. Follow signs for "BMW Visitors Center."

Nearby Attractions: Biltmore House in Asheville, NC, and Blue Ridge Mountains are 1 hour away.

Mt. Rushmore Jewelry

2707 Mt. Rushmore Road
Rapid City, SD 57701
(605) 343-7099 / (800) 658-3361
www.mtrushmorejewelry.com

JEWELRY

Black Hills Gold jewelry first appeared after the Black Hills Gold Rush of 1876. By law, in order to use the name "Black Hills Gold," companies must manufacture the jewelry in the Black Hills of South Dakota. To produce Black Hills Gold's characteristic green tint, 12-karat gold is alloyed with silver; alloying gold with copper creates a pink tint. This tour shows you the ancient lost wax method of casting used to manufacture all Black Hills jewelry.

Imagine a golden leaf, precise in form and detail and smaller than a contact lens. At Mt. Rushmore jewelry such minuscule foliage is commonplace. See workers with soldering needles tack tiny leaves and grapes onto the shanks of rings. At the "wriggling" station, watch a craftsperson wiggle a tool back and forth to etch ridges and veins into a leaf one-third the size of a corn flake. Artisans sit at rows of workstations equipped with small drills, jeweler's loupes, and plenty of tweezers.

All jewelry originates in the Design Room. Artists fashion rubber molds into which hot wax is shot. After the wax sets, the mold is pried apart, and the wax ring joins others on a wax "tree" about the size of a centerpiece. The tree is then dipped in plaster, and this plaster cast slides into a kiln. The wax melts, and liquid gold is injected into the resulting hollow cavity. When the metal has set, the hot cast is dunked in cold water. The plaster shatters, revealing an exact duplicate of the original wax model. This gold tree of rings is pruned, and each ring is ground, buffed, frosted, and polished. During busy holiday seasons, the company's 125 employees produce over 1,000 pieces of jewelry per day.

Cost: Free

Freebies: No

Video Shown: 7-minute video on company history, legend and history of Black Hills Gold, and production shown in showroom.

Reservations Needed: No, except for groups larger than 30 people.

Days and Hours: May–September: Mon–Fri 8:00 AM–4:00 PM, tours generally on the hour; October–April: tours by walk-in or reservation. Closed holidays and week between Christmas and New Year's.

Plan to Stay: 30 minutes, plus time in factory showroom.

Minimum Age: None

Disabled Access: Yes

Group Requirements: No maximum group size. Large groups will be split. Requests 1 day's advance notice for groups larger than 30 people.

Special Information: This family-run business is one of the few jewelry manufacturers' tours that allows visitors directly onto the production floor.

Factory Showroom: Sells entire 3,600-style line of Black Hills Gold jewelry and 2,000 non–Black Hills Gold diamonds, rubies, emeralds, and sapphires. Rings are arranged in velvet cases among elegant watches, dishes, and crystal bowls. Open May–September: Mon–Sat 8:00 AM–8:00 PM, Sun 9:00 AM–4:00 PM; October–April: Mon–Fri 8:30 AM–5:00 PM. Closed Christmas, Thanksgiving, and Easter.

Directions: From I-90, take Exit 57. Turn left onto Omaha St. Turn right onto Mt. Rushmore Rd. Mt. Rushmore Jewelry is at intersection of Fairmont Blvd. and Mt. Rushmore Rd. From Hwy. 79, travel west on Fairmont Blvd. to Mt. Rushmore Rd.

Nearby Attractions: Sioux Pottery and Crafts tour (see page 307); video and observation booth at Landstrom's Black Hills Gold Creations (call 800-843-0009 or 605-343-0157); Mt. Rushmore; Reptile Gardens; the Ranch Amusement Park; Geology Museum at South Dakota School of Mines; the Journey Museum; Crazy Horse Mountain Carving.

Sioux Pottery and Crafts

1441 East Saint Joseph Street
Rapid City, SD 57701
(605) 341-3657 / (800) 657-4366
www.siouxpottery.com

POTTERY

The red clay used at Sioux Pottery comes from Paha Sapa, the Black Hills area, and is considered sacred. This clay is carefully fashioned into vases and pots whose exteriors are then graced with Sioux Indian designs symbolizing the Sioux culture, environment, activities, and dealings. For example, crossed arrows represent Friendship, a zigzag of lightning stands for Swiftness, and a diamond wedged between two backward Es connotes Horses Killed in Battle.

Along with the red clay, the craftspeople at Sioux Pottery also utilize a more secular variety from Kentucky. This white, elastic clay is used for certain pieces, such as those with handles, which are too delicate to withstand the pronounced shrinkage inherent in firing red clay. About ten artists can be seen working at any one time, each one seated at an old kitchen table. The floors of their workspace are powdered with dust; boot-prints lead to a dank back room where the red clay exists as "slip" (earthy red liquid). From outside, the slip is piped into concrete vats, where it is mixed and strained, then turned into clay.

The artists employ three different methods for turning clay into pots: casting, wheel throwing, and jiggering. In casting, slip is poured into plaster molds. The plaster absorbs the excess liquid, and the clay takes the shape of the mold. In wheel throwing, potters bend over spinning pottery wheels, hand-forming original pieces from balls of clay. The third method, jiggering, is used for flat plates and bowls. As the wheel spins, a potter lowers a blade that cuts out the shape. White or red, all unfired pottery is called "greenware." You'll see shelves of greenware, all dull and smooth. The Indian artists paint freehand designs and proudly sign their names on each piece.

Cost: Free
Freebies: No

Video Shown: No

Reservations Needed: No, except for groups larger than 12 people or to arrange tours outside regularly scheduled times.

Days and Hours: Self-guided tours: Mon–Fri 8:00 AM–5:00 PM. Best viewing days Tue–Fri. Guided group tours available upon request. Closed holidays and week after Christmas.

Plan to Stay: 20 minutes, plus time in gift shop.

Cost: Free

Minimum Age: None

Disabled Access: Yes

Group Requirements: Call 2–3 days in advance for groups larger than 12 people. Groups larger than 20 will be split into smaller groups.

Special Information: A lot of clay dust in the back rooms' air.

Gift Shop: Sells handmade pots, bowls, and dishware, as well as mandalas, dance shields, painted cattle skulls, and sacred medicine wheels, all created locally by members of Sioux nation. Factory seconds available at 50 percent off. Open May–August: Mon–Fri 8:00 AM–5:00 PM, Sat 10:00 AM–4:00 PM, Sun 12:00 PM–4:00 PM; September–April: Mon–Fri 8:00 AM–5:00 PM, Sat 10:00 AM–2:00 PM (in September, Sat 10:00 AM–4:00 PM. Catalog available by mail for $5.

Directions: From I-90 bypass, take Exit 59 and go south on LaCrosse St. Turn left (east) on East North St. to Cambell St. Turn right (south) on Cambell to St. Patrick St. Turn right again (west) on St. Patrick to East Saint Joseph St. Sioux Pottery is 2 blocks ahead on your right.

Nearby Attractions: Mt. Rushmore Jewelry tour (see page 306); Black Hills National Forest; Mt. Rushmore; Geology Museum at South Dakota School of Mines; Reptile Gardens; the Ranch Amusement Park.

Gibson

145 Lt. George W. Lee Avenue
Memphis, TN 38103
(901) 543-0800 (ex. 101)
www.gibson.com

Whether you are a music lover or a wood worker, or fascinated by an American business success story, the tour lets you experience the making of this world-famous electric guitar. The company started in 1894 when Orville Gibson created a whole new family of guitars and mandolins. Through the years the company has had different owners, each facing successes and challenges. The Gibson Corporation of today, dedicated to both its history and innovation in wood technologies, has grown a long way from when it was purchased from bankruptcy for $5 million in 1986.

You walk on the factory floor, within nose length of 16 different workstations in making electric guitars. Although guitar making involves many steps that require hand workmanship, this facility, completed in late 2000, showcases state-of-the-art guitar manufacturing. You see millions of dollars of guitars in various stages of production, from bare woods to finished products. The tour begins with the initial body building from maple and mahogany woods and goes all the way to the last steps when they put on the strings to tone it for final inspection.

Each step has its unique process that combines handwork and machines. For example, the binding process puts a white plastic trim around the outside rim of the guitar to both protect it and make the instrument more attractive. A limber five-foot piece of plastic is put through the glue pot and then wrapped around by hand. A harness is then used to "mummify" it until dried. In a later stage, after the guitar is sprayed with a solvent-based paint, they scrape off the excess so you can still see the shiny white trim.

Notice the special care that goes into the neck fitting, as it is slid into a slot on the body. Hand scrapers are used to make it smooth and straight. At the very end, the electronic parts are put on, including the two pickups, the control pod assembly, the tuner knobs, and the machine heads for the strings. These are used for the sound to resonate through the amplifier. Next time you hear the B.B. King Lucille, the Les Paul Classic, or the Flying V, you will know all about its birth.

Cost: $10 per person
Freebies: No
Video Shown: No
Reservations Needed: Recommended
Days and Hours: Mon–Wed and Sun 1:00 PM and 2:00 PM; Thur–Sat 11:00 AM, 12:00 PM, 1:00 PM, and 2:00 PM. Closed Thanksgiving, Christmas Eve, Christmas, and New Year's.
Plan to Stay: 30 minutes, plus time for Memphis Rock 'n' Soul Museum and gift shops.
Minimum Age: 12, unless can be ensured one-to-one ratio of adults to children. No minimum for museum.
Disabled Access: Yes
Group Requirements: Groups broken into 15 people per group. $2 per person discount available.
Special Information: No video cameras allowed. Factory is part of a manufacturing and expanding entertainment complex. The same building is the home of the Smithsonian's exhibition "Rock 'n' Soul: Social Crossroads," which has a separate admission charge, and a lounge. Plans for a dedicated Gibson Museum in future.
Gift Shops: Gibson Store sells logoed merchandise, plus selected guitar models. Open Mon–Sat 10:00 AM–6:00 PM. Memphis Rock 'n' Soul Museum store sells items related to history of local music and rock and roll musicians. Open Mon–Sun 10:00 AM–7:00 PM. Both stores closed same holidays as tour.
Directions: Located downtown, about 1 block south of Beale St.
Nearby Attractions: Sun Studios (birthplace of rock and roll, where Elvis recorded his first song); National Civil Rights Museum; Mississippi River; Graceland is about 8 miles away.

Jack Daniel's Distillery

Lynchburg, TN 37352
(931) 759-6180
www.jackdaniels.com

WHISKEY AND BEER

In the heavily vegetated, woodsy, hilly terrain of south-middle Tennessee, you feel like you're visiting a national park rather than the world's oldest registered distillery (1866) when you tour Jack Daniel's. A babbling brook follows you through the entire tour. You learn from the tour guide that the water is no coincidence, that Jasper Newton (Jack) Daniel chose this property because of Cave Spring's iron-free water. This pure limestone water flows at 56° year-round and is one secret of Jack Daniel's fine whiskey.

Your tour begins with a short minivan ride up the hill to one of 45 aging houses. The large wooden structure's air is thick and musty with the smell of whiskey and wood. Your eyes take in only a small fraction of the 20,164 barrels of aging whiskey lined up seven stories high. Four years of warm days and cool nights inside these white-oak barrels gives Jack Daniel's whiskey its flavor and color.

In the rick yard, land marked by a black smokestack, Moore County hard sugar-maple wood is burned to make charcoal. In charcoal mellowing vats the distilled, fermented whiskey seeps through ten feet of charcoal and a wool blanket at a rate of less than six gallons an hour.

You'll see another interesting whiskey-making step in the hot, noisy mash room. Here, in large tanks called mash tubs, corn, rye, barley malt, water, and yeast ferment for four days. A panel measures the liquid's progress toward becoming 140-proof whiskey.

A wooden structure that resembles an old Southern country farmhouse is actually Jack Daniel's original office, which dates back to 1878. Still in its natural setting, it is filled with period furniture, old file cabinets, and ledgers that documented the company's financial transactions.

Cost: Free

Freebies: Ice-cold glass of lemonade in White Rabbit Saloon after tour.

Video Shown: Video at tour's beginning explains Jack Daniel's and whiskey making.

Reservations Needed: No, except for groups larger than 30 people.

Days and Hours: Mon–Sun 9:00 AM–4:30 PM. Closed Thanksgiving, Christmas Eve, Christmas Day, New Year's Eve, and New Year's. During 2-week July shutdown, you follow standard tour route, even though distillery isn't in production.

Plan to Stay: 1 hour for videos and tour.

Minimum Age: None

Disabled Access: Yes. Specially designed van tour for people in wheelchairs.

Group Requirements: Groups larger than 30 should call on Thursday of week before visit.

Special Information: Lots of walking, so wear comfortable shoes. Tour booklets available in major foreign languages. Distillery is designated a National Historical Landmark.

Gift Shop: Just about every store in Lynchburg sells Jack Daniel's souvenirs but no whiskey. Lynchburg Hardware and General Store has largest selection, including old-time saloon mirror, wooden whiskey chest, stoneware jugs, and playing cards. Catalog available at above number.

Directions: From Nashville, take I-24 South to Exit 111 (Hwy. 55 West). As you enter Lynchburg, visitors center parking lot entrance is off Hwy. 55 next to Mulberry Creek Bridge. From Chattanooga, take I-24 North to Exit 111. Follow above directions.

Nearby Attractions: Lynchburg is filled with Southern charm and hospitality. Visit courthouse and Miss Mary Bobo's Boarding House (Southern-style food served).

MasterCraft

100 Cherokee Cove Drive
Vonore, TN 37885
(800) 443-8774
www.mastercraft.com

MasterCraft

WATER-SKI BOATS

Knoxville, Tennessee, is to boats what Detroit, Michigan, is to cars. More boats are made in Knoxville than anywhere in the world. MasterCraft, the largest inboard boat manufacturer in the world, builds about 3,500 boats per year. Their boats are in high demand, especially by water skiers—more world records have been shattered behind MasterCraft ski boats than any other boats.

Unlike cars, which are painted last, boats are spray-painted first. In the 72,000-square-foot lamination building, workers spray gel coat into each boat mold. Afterwards, they peel the masking tape off and then spray colored stripes. Fiberglass is hand-laid into the mold. After unfurling each cloth-like layer of fiberglass, the worker uses a hand roller to pop out the air bubbles. For each boat, a worker repeats this laying out and rolling process for up to 22 layers of fiberglass. During your tour, you see 40 to 50 boats in different stages of production. Each day, 16 boats start the cycle and 16 boats finish. Notice that most of the process is done by hand—there's hardly any automation, another difference between boat and car assembly.

After lamination, each boat is pushed outdoors on its dolly to the adjacent 72,000-square-foot rigging building. Pass by the sewing department. Rolls of upholstery are cut and sewn. On dollies, boats move along the rigging line for assembly. Decks are attached. While the boat is hoisted up, the engine slides in and a mechanic tightens the bolts. After the steering wheel is inserted, the upholstery is set over the seat bracing.

Once assembled, each boat is water-tested for 15 to 20 minutes to ensure optimal performance, testing out the RPMs and turning radius. As you watch the water test on beautiful Lake Tellico, located in front of the factory, you'll wish you were skiing or wakeboarding behind the boat.

Cost: Free

Freebies: Commemorative tour T-shirt.

Video Shown: Planned

Reservations Needed: Recommended

Days and Hours: Mon–Thur 2:00 PM. No production Fridays. Closed between Christmas and New Year's and during model changes for 1–3 weeks in July.

Plan to Stay: 40 minutes, plus time in the gift area.

Minimum Age: None, however small children must be able to wear the supplied safety glasses.

Disabled Access: Yes

Group Requirements: Maximum 10–12 people. Call at least one week in advance.

Special Information: No photography. Noisy in lamination building.

Gift Shop: Sells license plates and logoed merchandise, including logoed life jackets. Located in sportswear coordinator's office. Open Mon–Thur 9:00 AM–5:00 PM.

Directions: From Knoxville, take Rt. 129 South, which runs into Hwy. 411 South. Travel through Vonore. Turn right onto Hwy. 72 West. Turn into Tellico West Industrial Park. Follow signs. From the south, take I-75 North. At Exit 72, turn right onto Hwy. 72. Travel 17 miles. Turn left into Tellico West Industrial Park. Follow signs. From the north, take I-75 South. At Exit 72, turn left onto Hwy. 72. Follow above directions.

Nearby Attractions: Sea Ray boat tour (call 423-884-6631); Great Smoky Mountain National Park; Knoxville attractions 50 minutes away include University of Tennessee.

Nissan

983 Nissan Drive
Smyrna, TN 37167
(615) 459-1444
www.nissandriven.com

CARS AND PICKUP TRUCKS

Imagine 89 football fields side-by-side and back-to-back, all under one roof! That would be an unfathomable size for a sports complex, but it is the size of Nissan's first U.S. manufacturing plant. Since the plant began production in 1983, the unemployment rate in Rutherford County has been cut in half. On your tour, you are shuttled through an enormous facility, where 6,300 Nissan employees build Frontier trucks, Xterra sport utility vehicles, and Altima sedans.

Zigzagging through the massive welding operation, you feel as if you are on a movie set. Look up at the conveyor systems suspended from the ceiling as sparks fly from tentacle-like robot arms welding together the main body parts of the vehicle shell. The Intelligent (or "smart") Body Assembly System (IBAS) is a mixture of automation and computerization. IBAS robots replace the conventional jigs that hold steel panels together as the Altima body is welded. The computerized capabilities of the system allow for more than one model of vehicle to be assembled in the system before lasers check the accuracy of the welds.

As your tour guide maneuvers the shuttle along the maze of aisles, the unmistakable smell of fresh paint begins to fill your nostrils. While in the paint facility, gaze through glass that encloses the paint lines. Here, in a precise and lengthy process, robots and humans apply layers of protective coatings, primer, and paint. Employees carefully check each vehicle's finish as part of the quality control system. You can feel the heat as you pass the enclosed paint-bake ovens, where the paint finish is baked onto each vehicle.

In the final assembly areas, you see the human touch. With heads bowed in concentration and fingers flying, people install the hundreds of parts that transform the painted vehicle shells into dynamic machines. It's fun

to witness the finishing touches in the final production stages as workers put in seats or install tires on the moving production line, where 400,000 vehicles are produced each year.

Cost: Free

Freebies: No

Video Shown: 10-minute overview of Nissan and manufacturing at Smyrna vehicle assembly plant and nearby Decherd engine plant.

Reservations Needed: Yes. Maximum of 50 people per tour, whether individuals, families, or groups. Occasional last-minute reservations, so it's worth a call to see if you can fit into tour.

Days and Hours: Tue 8:30 AM, 10:00 AM, and 1:00 PM. Closed holidays, week between Christmas and New Year's, and 2 weeks in summer.

Plan to Stay: 1.5 hours for video and tour.

Minimum Age: 10 (5th grade)

Disabled Access: Yes

Group Requirements: Maximum of 55 people per time period. Reservations accepted up to 3 months in advance.

Special Information: No photography or shorts.

Gift Shop: No

Directions: From Nashville, take I-24 East toward Chattanooga. Take Exit 70 (Almaville Rd.) and turn left toward Smyrna (Almaville Rd. becomes Nissan Dr.). Nissan is about 3 miles ahead on right. Enter Gate 1.

Nearby Attractions: Sam Davis Home; attractions in Murfreesboro (geographic center of Tennessee) include Stones River Battlefield, Oakland Mansion, and antique stores. Nashville's attractions, including Purity Dairies tour (see page 312) and Grand Old Opry, are 20 miles away.

Purity Dairies

360 Murfreesboro Road
Nashville, TN 37224
(615) 244-1900
www.puritydairies.com

ICE CREAM AND DAIRY PRODUCTS

A cheery ice-cream parlor welcomes you to Purity Dairies' ice-cream plant. In the tour room, the 75-year-old company shows a film about milk and the manufacturing of their dairy products. Then the big blue curtain opens, revealing a huge window with a panoramic view of the ice-cream factory.

Seeing the production of ice-cream sandwiches is almost like watching a live theater performance, with each player taking a specific role. The show is a continuous interaction of machinery, humanity, and ice cream. In the foreground, two women handle the sandwich machine. One feeds chocolate wafers into the machine, which squirts out the exact amount of vanilla ice cream filling for each sandwich. The other worker boxes the sandwiches after they have been automatically wrapped. A complicated labyrinth of overhead piping, frosty and dripping with condensation, runs throughout the plant. A milk-based mixture is pumped to various stainless-steel machines, where it is flavored, transformed into ice cream, and shot into individual cartons. The cartons are automatically shrink-wrapped and sent to the freezer for hardening.

A short walk outside takes you to the milk plant, with more overhead pipes everywhere. The daily production of 10,500 pounds of cottage cheese causes a natural sour odor in the room where Purity makes Little Miss Muffet's curds and whey. An enormous stainless-steel tub filled with the white lumpy stuff comes into view, and your guide explains the intricacies of separating curds and whey to produce cottage cheese.

In another part of this facility, Purity manufactures its own plastic milk containers. It takes 7,754 plastic beans to make a gallon jug. At the end of the tour, visitors convene at the weigh station and the group is collectively weighed. Here the Purity trucks are also weighed before heading out to make deliveries. The loud moo you might hear is the horn on one of Purity's special home-delivery trucks, painted white with large black spots that resemble a...guess what? (The horn is a hint.)

Cost: Free

Freebies: Children receive ice-cream sandwiches; adults receive frozen yogurt, premium ice cream, sherbet, and gift pack of cottage cheese and other items.

Video Shown: 17-minute movie about Purity's milk and other products.

Reservations Needed: Yes. Individuals and families must join scheduled group tour. Tours may fill years in advance, but individuals or families should ask about available space on existing group tours.

Days and Hours: Tues, Thur, Fri: Children's tours, 10:00 AM, 11:15 AM, and 12:30 PM. Adult tours, 10:00 AM–12:00 PM.

Plan to Stay: 1.5 hours for video and tour.

Minimum Age: 4

Disabled Access: 20 steps lead up to plant entrance.

Group Requirements: Adult tours need at least 4 months' advance reservations; children's tours, 8 weeks ahead. At press time, company said group tours are booked far in advance. Maximum group size is 40.

Special Information: Because company has expanded marketing territory, tour is very popular. Book as far ahead as possible.

Gift Shop: No

Directions: From the south, take I-65 to Fesseler's Lane exit. Turn right at end of exit, then take first right on Elm Hill Pike. Purity is at intersection with Murfreesboro Rd. From the north, take I-65 to Murfreesboro Rd. exit. Turn left at end of exit. You'll see signs and Purity logo.

Nearby Attractions: Nissan tour (see page 311); Grand Old Opry; Opry Mills.

Saturn

Welcome Center
100 Saturn Parkway
Spring Hill, TN 37174
(931) 486-7787 Welcome Center / (800) 326-3321 Plant Tour
www.saturn.com

CARS

To many Americans, the Saturn car represents the rebirth of U.S. automobile manufacturing. Since the first General Motors Saturn rolled off the line in 1990, these import-fighting cars have earned a reputation for their high quality, the no-haggle sales approach by retailers, and enthusiastic customers. The manufacturing plant began offering regular public tours in the summer of 1997. A horse barn has been renovated into the new Saturn Welcome Center. The Welcome Center's theme is the "Saturn Difference" and consists of interactive displays and exhibits on the Saturn story.

This highly integrated manufacturing complex includes the power train, general assembly, and body systems buildings. Saturn's Spring Hill site sits on some 2,400 acres of what was previously farmland—in fact, the company currently farms approximately 1,200 acres of land, raising corn, wheat, soybeans, and hay. The Saturn manufacturing plant has been designed to blend into the countryside, so very little of the plant can be seen from the highway or the Welcome Center. To see the manufacturing plant, you will need to register for a plant tour and take a ten-minute bus ride from the Welcome Center to the plant.

Near the entrance to the Welcome Center is a kiosk that gives you a short introduction to the company. The displays are arranged in eight horse stalls that can be viewed by starting at either end of the barn. The history stall contains mementos from the site and the founding of Saturn. Other stalls contain videos and memorabilia on teamwork, owner's letters, and community activities. Three of the stalls are dedicated to the manufacturing story, where you can see the polymer beads that make up Saturn body panels and view a display that explains the lost-foam process used in making Saturn engines.

Cost: Free

Freebies: Saturn Welcome Center brochure and product brochures.

Video Shown: 15-minute video entitled "One Car at a Time" covers Saturn production.

Reservations Needed: No, for Welcome Center; yes, for plant tour. Occasional last-minute cancellations allow walk-in visitors to take a plant tour. Call (800) 326-3321 for information and reservations.

Days and Hours: Welcome Center: Mon–Fri 8:00 AM–5:00 PM. Plant Tour: Mon, Tue, Thur, Fri 8:30 AM, 10:00 AM, 1:00 PM, 2:30 PM; Wed 10:00 AM, 1:00 PM, 2:30 PM. Plant closed holidays, including the day after Thanksgiving, the week between Christmas and New Year's, Good Friday, and 2 weeks in July. Call Welcome Center for hours during holiday weeks.

Plan to Stay: 2 hours for Welcome Center and plant tour, plus time for gift shop.

Minimum Age: 6, for plant tour; none, for Welcome Center.

Disabled Access: Yes, for Welcome Center. Call above number for accommodations on plant tour.

Group Requirements: No maximum for Welcome Center, although advance notice appreciated. Maximum 30 people per plant tour time period. Reservations accepted up to 3 months in advance.

Special Information: No photography in plant. Visitors must wear safety glasses on tram tour. No shorts.

Gift Shop: Saturn Stuff Store sells Saturn-logoed items, including shirts, hats, key chains, jackets, and videos. Hours are same as the Welcome Center.

Directions: From Nashville, take I-65 South. Exit at Rt. 396, Saturn Pkwy. West. Take Hwy. 31 South. Watch for sign.

Nearby Attractions: Natchez Park; Nashville's attractions, including Purity Dairies tour (see page 312) and Grand Old Opry, about 40 minutes away. Local area around Spring Hill and Columbia includes many antebellum homes and Civil War sites.

American Airlines
C. R. Smith Museum

4601 Highway 360 at FAA Road
Fort Worth, TX 76155
(817) 967-1560
www.crsmithmuseum.org

You'll recognize the American Airlines C. R. Smith Museum, named after the man who served as company president for most of the years between 1934 and 1973, by the fully restored DC-3 (the *Flagship Knoxville,* which flew for American from 1940 to 1948) housed in a glass hangar in front of the museum. The Grey Eagles, a group of mostly retired American pilots, bought the *Knoxville,* and a team of American mechanics restored it to its current glistening condition. This 35,000-square-foot corporate museum contains informative interactive displays and video presentations.

The circular glass History Wall in the center of the open floor plan highlights company developments and memorabilia from the first airmail service (1918) to today, including a 767 maintenance manual on CD-ROM. Some of the oldest items, including a letter Charles Lindbergh carried on his first airmail flight from Chicago to St. Louis, bring American's heritage to life. Beyond this section is an "American Family" display, with lifelike mannequins representing American employees and videos describing their jobs and teamwork.

"Working in the Air," "Working on the Ground," and "Maintaining the Fleet" exhibits detail the equipment and procedures used in airline operations. You'll also get an up-close look at a jet engine, aircraft landing gear, and an air traffic control system. The "Flightlab" has a wind tunnel, test equipment, and simulators that teach the basic principles of flight. Near these more technical displays are brass-plate etchings of four different American Airline planes. Put a piece of paper on your chosen plate and rub it with a crayon to make a souvenir. If only flying a real plane and running an airline were this easy!

Cost: Free

Freebies: Brass rubbings (see above).

Videos Shown: 14-minute film, "Spirit of American," runs every half-hour. Theater's all-around sound system and panoramic screen give you the feeling of flying on an American Airlines jet. Also, touch-screen videos throughout museum.

Reservations Needed: No, but recommended for groups larger than 20 people. Inquire about scavenger hunt.

Days and Hours: Tue–Sat 10:00 AM–6:00 PM, Sun 12:00 PM–5:00 PM. Call for holiday hours.

Plan to Stay: 1.5–2 hours for displays, videos, and film, plus time in gift shop.

Minimum Age: None

Disabled Access: Yes

Group Requirements: Reservations requested for groups larger than 20 people for self-guided tour and film.

Special Information: Special-event rental of museum available (call 817-967-5910). Summer educational program, "Eagle Aviation Academy" (call 817-967-5993). With the museum's open floor plan, the Map and Guide provide a helpful overview of the numerous displays.

Gift Shop: The Museum Store sells aviation-related items, such as models, crystal and porcelain eagles, clocks, mobiles, toys, and books. Also, museum and American Airlines–logoed items. Closes half-hour before museum.

Directions: From Dallas/Fort Worth Airport (3 miles away), take south exit and follow signs for Hwy. 360 South. Exit at FAA Rd. Turn right at stop sign. Museum is on right. From Hwy. 183 East, take FAA Rd./Hwy. 360 South exit. Turn right at stop sign. Museum is on right.

Nearby Attractions: Mrs Baird's Bakery, Mary Kay museum, and Studios at Las Colinas tours (see pages 323, 322, and 325); Dr Pepper Bottling Plant tour (call 972-721-8112); Six Flags over Texas; Fort Worth Zoo and Fort Worth Museum of Science and History about 20 miles away; Downtown Dallas attractions, including JFK Museum, about 15 miles away.

Blue Bell Creameries

1101 South Horton Street
Brenham, TX 77833
(979) 830-2197 / (800) 327-8135
www.bluebell.com

Blue Bell Ice Cream

ICE CREAM

This "Little Creamery in Brenham" maintains its small-town image through its advertising and girl-and-cow logo. At its headquarters, the 19th-century red brick schoolhouse offices, 1930s-replica refrigerated delivery truck, country store, and ice cream parlor further that country feel. In the visitors center, see photos of Blue Bell and Brenham, and the company's original wooden time clock.

In the plant, look down through glass windows at the production floor's maze of stainless-steel pipes and various shaped tanks. Almost everything happens inside the tanks, so your tour guide explains the process. Base-mix ingredients are blended, homogenized, and pasteurized, then cooled and piped into refrigerated holding tanks. The tanks' huge round doors resemble ship portholes. Liquid flavorings are added in the rectangular flavoring tanks.

The mailbox-shaped freezer barrels whip and freeze the mixture to milkshake consistency. The ice cream and "dry" ingredients (fruit, cookie chunks, cookie dough, etc.) meet in the white pipes before traveling into containers. If the flavor of the day is banana split, workers peel and slice bananas in the behind-the-scenes kitchen. In the filler machine, empty, open, half-gallon round cartons spin to mix ice cream and ingredients as they flow into the cartons. Colorful lids slide down to cover the filled cartons.

Another room offers more movement as three-ounce Dixie cups are filled. Cups resting in a circular disk are filled two at a time; the disk rotates after every two are filled. You will be mesmerized by the repetitive spin-fill, spin-fill process. Nearby, ice cream sandwiches start as chocolate wafers sliding down a V-shaped holder. Two wafers converge, and a hardened ice cream slice drops between them. Paper quickly wraps around the sandwich and helps maintain its shape. The sandwiches travel single-file until

they're mechanically pushed into cardboard boxes. All this whets your appetite for the samples you'll enjoy in the ice cream parlor.

Cost: Adults, $2.50; children 6–14 and seniors 55 and older, $2; under 6, free.

Freebies: Ice cream serving in the parlor; logoed paper hat.

Video Shown: Short video at beginning of tour covers company history.

Reservations Needed: No, except for groups of 15 or more people. Everyone must make reservations for spring break and Easter tours.

Days and Hours: Summer: Mon–Fri 10:00 AM, 11:00 AM, 1:00 PM, 1:30 PM, 2:00 PM, 2:30 PM. Fall and winter tour schedule varies; call for exact tour times and days. Closed holidays.

Plan to Stay: 40–45 minutes, plus time in visitors center, ice cream parlor, and Country Store.

Minimum Age: No

Disabled Access: Modified tour available.

Group Requirements: Groups of 15 or more should call at least 2 weeks in advance. Call 1 month ahead for spring and summer tours. Maximum group is 45 people.

Special Information: March and April are busiest tour months because bluebonnets, the Texas State Wildflower, are in bloom. No photography in plant. Allow some waiting time during summer.

Gift Shop: Country Store sells logoed items, Texas handicrafts and cookbooks, jellies, and hot sauces. Items gift-wrapped in ice cream containers. Open year-round Mon–Fri 8:00 AM–5:00 PM. March–December, also open Sat 10:00 AM–4:00 PM. Closed holidays.

Directions: Take U.S. 290 to FM 577 North. Blue Bell is 2 miles ahead on right.

Nearby Attractions: Monastery of St. Claire; Rose Emporium; Historic Downtown Brenham; annual Maifest; Washington County Fair.

Collin Street Bakery

401 West 7th Avenue
Corsicana, TX 75110
(903) 874-7477 / (800) 504-1896
www.collinstreetbakery.com

COLLIN STREET BAKERY

FRUITCAKE

Collin Street Bakery (1896) is the oldest fruitcake bakery in the U.S.A. The family-owned company's history is as colorful as the cherries, pineapples, papaya, and pecans on its cakes. The Deluxe Fruitcake has circled the earth aboard an Apollo spacecraft and adorned the tables of royalty, famous entertainers, sports legends, and politicians.

A glass-windowed, metal door opens from the lobby onto a small elevated platform. (Tell someone in the Bake Shop that you want a tour; they'll admit you to the baking area and explain the action. Otherwise, you can watch through the window—minus the aroma and sounds.) From October to mid-December, what you see is one of the most memorable sights of any in this book. A sea of workers, standing in small stalls on both sides of at least three production lines, hand-decorate fruitcakes' tops with pecans and candied fruit. The cakes, at this point only dough in round baking pans, flow in from the left. Each worker grabs a cake, decorates it with pecans, and then places it back on the line headed for the ovens.

Another worker races about with a big scoop, keeping each decorator's holding bin filled with pecans. During this busy period the staff increases from around 80 employees to over 650, and workers decorate over 30,000 Original Deluxe Fruitcakes each day, making more than 1.5 million each year. Workers have been known to burst into their own classic holiday song—"I've Been Working on the Fruitcake."

From the platform, look toward the back of the production area at a highly automated bakery operation. To the left, pecan-filled batter is mixed in vats, and dough is automatically deposited into baking tins and leveled by hissing machines. To the right, an oven consumes long trays of up to 2,800 cake pans in one swallow. The dough-filled tins travel a precisely timed journey through the long oven and cooling tunnel. As a testament to the fruitcake's quality, flags from some of the 200 countries to which Collin Street ships hang from the back of the production area (Japan is the top fruitcake importer).

Cost: Free

Freebies: Small samples and 10-cent coffee; postcards.

Video Shown: Optional 10-minute video on production process, shown in lobby area.

Reservations Needed: No, except for groups of 8 or more.

Days and Hours: Mon–Thur 9:00 AM–11:00 AM and 1:00 PM–3:00 PM. Closed holidays. October 1–mid-December, you watch fruitcake production from small landing just inside production area. Other times, take guided tour through baking machinery. Any time of year, need to ask for tour in adjoining Bake Shop.

Plan to Stay: 10 minutes for viewing, plus time for video and Bake Shop.

Minimum Age: None

Disabled Access: Yes

Group Requirements: Requests 1 week's advance notice for groups of 10 or more. No maximum group size, although only 10 people can watch from landing at one time.

Special Information: No photography in plant.

Bakery Shop: Sells over 136 different baked items, including Deluxe Fruitcake, rum cake, pecan pie, and pecan bread. Ask about unboxed factory-second fruitcakes. Also sells logoed T-shirts, caps, and baskets. Open Mon–Thur 7:00 AM–5:30 PM, Fri–Sat 7:00 AM–6:00 PM, and Sun 12:00 PM–6:00 PM. Fruitcake catalogs available from (800) 248-3366 and Cryer Creek Kitchens food items available from (800) 468-0088.

Directions: From I-45, take exit for Hwy. 31 West; becomes 7th Ave. in Corsicana. Bakery is on your left.

Nearby Attractions: Navarro Pecan Co. group tours available through Chamber of Commerce (call 903-874-1503); Pioneer Village; Richland-Chambers Lake.

Dublin Dr Pepper Bottling

Old Doc's Soda Shop and Museum
221 South Patrick
Dublin, TX 76446
(254) 445-3939
www.dublindrpepper.com

BEVERAGES

In 1885 Wade Morrison named his newly developed soft drink after his former sweetheart's father, Dr. Pepper. Opened in 1891, this is the World's Oldest Dr Pepper Bottling Plant, and it still cranks out returnable bottles of Dr Pepper with 1960s machinery. The late Bill Kloster, employee of the plant since 1933 and owner from 1991 to 1999, spent the better portion of 60 years amassing one of the largest collections of Dr Pepper memorabilia. The plant remains in the Kloster family, with grandson Mark overseeing the business.

On Tuesdays, when the plant bottles, a fruity fragrance fills the air as reusable bottles slowly and noisily shake, rattle, and roll past on the old machinery. Gears shift and bottles rise, drop, and turn like amusement park carousel horses, then do-si-do and waddle single file down the conveyor belts. Since parts are no longer available, many of these vintage machines are held together with ingenuity and baling wire. The bottles file past at what may seem like slow motion (32 per minute) compared to today's speedier bottling lines (1,500 per minute).

The filling process begins as bottles clatter through the 37-foot-long 1965 Miller Hydro Bottle Washer. Once washed, the bottles receive a squirt of syrup and then are filled with pure carbonated water. Once filled, the bottles rotate to the capper and then are mixed. Bottles turn over in three somersaults, then a worker grabs two bottles in each hand and sets them into bottle-shaped cutouts on a lightboard for inspection. After twirling each bottle to ensure consistent color (indicative of proper mixing) and crack-free bottles, the worker places 24 bottles into the pockets of each red or yellow wooden crate. People travel great distances to see this process and load their cars with these wooden crates of Dr Pepper, made with Imperial pure cane sugar (other bottlers use corn syrup).

In the museum rooms, Bill's artifacts trace Dr Pepper's heritage from its beginnings in an 1885 Waco, Texas, drugstore to the present. His extensive collection includes Dr Pepper signs, billboards, advertisements, calendars dating back to 1944, clocks, and various treasures. His prized possessions were a life-size cardboard cutout of the red, white, and blue saluting Patriotic Girl, and attention-grabbing motion displays like the carousel with three airplanes bearing the numbers 10, 2, and 4 (representing the times you should drink Dr Pepper for some extra "pep").

Cost: Adults $2; senior citizens $1.50, children 6–12 $1; children under 6, free.

Freebies: Ice-cold Dr Pepper

Video Shown: No

Reservations Needed: No, except for groups larger than 10 people.

Days and Hours: Mon–Fri 9:00 AM–5:00 PM. Sat 10:00 AM–5:00 PM. Sun 1:00 PM–5:00 PM. No tours 12:00 PM–1:00 PM. Closed Thanksgiving, Christmas, and New Year's. Bottling is on a weekly basis. When not bottling, a simulation is shown.

Plan to Stay: 30 minutes for tour and museum area, plus time in gift shop.

Minimum Age: None

Disabled Access: Yes

Group Requirements: Groups larger than 10 should call 1 week in advance. Groups over 20 will be split.

Special Information: Dr Pepper Museum located in a 1906 bottling plant in Waco, TX (call 254-757-1024). Dr Pepper Bottling in Irving, TX, offers tours of high-speed bottling plant (call 972-721-8112).

Gift Shop: Old Doc's Soda Shop sells logoed items including T-shirts, kitchen accessories, clocks, and memorabilia with vintage Dr Pepper logos and designs. Vintage soda fountain serves up Dr Pepper and ice cream and sandwiches. Purchase Dr Pepper by the case. Open same hours as above.

Directions: From Fort Worth, take Hwy. 377 South to Dublin. Plant 1 block past town.

Nearby Attractions: Dublin Historical Museum; Hoka Hey Foundry; Proctor Dam and Parks.

Imperial Sugar

198 Kemper Street
Sugar Land, TX 77478
(281) 490-9805
www.imperialsugar.com

IMPERIAL SUGAR COMPANY
A DIVISION OF IMPERIAL HOLLY CORPORATION

SUGAR

Imperial has refined sugar in Sugar Land (a small town just outside Houston) for over 150 years, making Imperial the oldest continuing commercial enterprise in Texas. The original site of the 1843 mill and surrounding sugarcane fields now features a large industrial complex that produces more than 3.5 million pounds of refined cane sugar a day. This video tour and visit to the packaging room shows you what's involved in making all that sweet stuff.

Your video tour starts in the warehouse, which can store 40 million pounds of raw sugar. Watch workers use small front-end loaders to remove the raw sugar from open boxcars. A conveyor-belt system carries the raw sugar to the top of the warehouse, where it rains down to form light-brown hills on the floor below.

The video shows the refining process in the Melt House, where centrifugal machines noisily spin and wash the raw sugar to remove molasses and impurities. Overhead pipes then move the washed raw sugar to large, enclosed melt tanks, where it is mixed with warm syrup and hot water to form sugar liquor. The guide's explanations throughout the video helps you better understand what you see.

The sugar goes through many more refining steps than you might expect before you visit the packaging room with your tour guide. In the packing room, you'll stand next to machines that fill, weigh, and package sugar into containers from single-serving packets to 100-pound bags. The sweet-smelling air, the rhythmic machines, and the constant movement of colored bags and boxes have an almost hypnotic effect.

Cost: Free
Freebies: Brochure explains processing of raw sugar into refined cane sugar.

Video Shown: 25-minute video takes you through sugar processing steps.
Reservations Needed: No, except for groups of 10 or more.
Days and Hours: Mon–Fri 10:00 AM and 2:00 PM. Closed holidays. Calling first is recommended; refinery occasionally operates on 4-day work schedule.
Plan to Stay: 1.25 hours for presentation, video, and tour of packaging department, plus time in gift shop.
Minimum Age: 3rd grade for school groups. No minimum for children with their parents.
Disabled Access: Refinery has old buildings with steps throughout.
Group Requirements: Groups of 10 or more should call 2 weeks in advance. Maximum group is 60 people.
Special Information: No open-toed or open-heeled shoes. No photography. Any jewelry above waist (including watches and rings) must be removed, along with all items from top shirt pocket.
Gift Shop: Sells logoed items including caps, T-shirts, mugs, aprons, and golf items. Also sells Imperial Sugar cookbooks, a company tradition since 1915. Open after tours.
Directions: Take I-59 South to Hwy. 6 exit in Sugar Land. Turn right (north) onto Hwy. 6. At Alt. 90, turn right and then left onto Ulrich. Tour center is in 2-story building between silos and 8-story building in front of security office. Park in employee lot or on street.
Nearby Attractions: Frito-Lay tour (call 281-342-0951); George Ranch; Confederate Museum; Fort Bend Museum. Houston's attractions, 15–30 miles away, include Space Center Houston tour (call 281-244-2100).

318 | **Texas**

Jardine's Texas Foods

1 Chisholm Trail
Buda, TX 78610
(512) 295-4600
www.jardinefoods.com

TEXAS-STYLE FOODS

After touring Austin and Texas Hill Country sites, Jardine's authentic Texas-style foods round out a Texas gastronomic experience. The graceful live oak trees, restored chuck wagon, wisteria-covered gazebo, and oak rocking chairs on the wide front porch of the company's headquarters all welcome you to the Jardine ranch and invite you to "set a spell."

The "Jardine Outfit," the company's nickname for itself, immediately makes you feel at home. A visit to Jardine's combines ranch relaxation, a warm homey feeling, and an opportunity to view the bottling and packaging of hot sauce, barbecue sauce, chili, and jalapeño peppers through windows in the limestone ranch-house "factory."

Legend has it that after many years of cooking for cowboys on trail drives, D. L. Jardine settled in Texas Hill Country. As a chuck wagon "cookie," he added various combinations of chilis, peppers, and spices to beans, meat, and cornbread. Since 1979, the Jardine Outfit has produced foods based on these early recipes—initially packaging them in the family's garage and now on this peaceful 30-acre ranch. To develop new recipes, the Jardine R&D Outfit (Rowdy & Dangerous) researches the history and culture of foods that characterize Texas heritage.

As you stroll outdoors under the sloped, ridged-tin roof and awning, look through several windows into a small section of the factory. If they're making Jardine's popular Chisholm Trail Texas Chili Bag O' Fixin's, watch hair-netted workers hand-fill reusable cloth bags with cellophane-wrapped spice packets. Seated at a long table, they grab packets from red plastic bins, insert them into the cloth bags, and pull a string to tighten each bag shut.

In the next area, items are hand-packed. Workers stuff jalapeños, olives, or pickles into glass jars. Through the last window, you'll see the horseshoe-shaped automatic filling line. Sauces, such as barbecue and picante, simmer in the three kettles to the left. The sauce passes through a pipe and a funnel into the bottles, which are capped, suction-sealed, labeled, and sent along a conveyor belt to the shipping warehouse. You leave craving the nearest Texas-style restaurant or your own kitchen so you can whip up some of these specialties.

Cost: Free

Freebies: Bottle of Texas Champagne brand hot pepper sauce only if you mention this book; mail order catalog.

Video Shown: No

Reservations Needed: Preferred; required for groups larger than 15 people.

Days and Hours: Mon–Fri 8:00 AM–5:00 PM. Closed holidays.

Plan to Stay: 15 minutes for tour, plus time for grounds, historic graveyard, and gift display case.

Minimum Age: None

Disabled Access: Yes

Group Requirements: Groups larger than 15 should call 2 days in advance. Food tastings are arranged for groups.

Special Information: Picnic tables and open-pit barbecue available on request.

General Store: Sells Jardine's authentic Texas-style foods, including salsas, condiments, spices, and other ranch-style recipes. Open Mon–Fri 8:30 AM–4:30 PM. Closed holidays. Catalog available from (800) 544-1880.

Directions: From I-35, take Exit 221 for Loop 4 toward Buda. Travel 1.1 miles and turn right just past the D. L. Jardine's sign. Turn right onto Chisholm Trail, which leads to the offices. Park on left.

Nearby Attractions: Manny Gammage's Texas Hatters tour (see page 321); Austin's attractions, including the State Capitol, Lyndon B. Johnson Library & Museum, and 6th Street, are 11 miles away.

JCPenney Museum

6501 Legacy Drive
Plano, TX 75024
(972) 431- 5128
www.jcpenney.net

JCPenney

RETAIL STORES AND CATALOGS

In 1902 James Cash Penney opened "The Golden Rule" cash-only dry-goods store in the small mining town of Kemmerer, Wyoming. With 36 stores in 1913, the company was renamed J. C. Penney Company, and the "Penney Idea," seven mission-statement principles that guide the company today, was formulated. Now the company has over 1,050 stores nationwide and a thriving catalog, ecommerce, and drugstore business. You can visit its state-of-the-art home office and also the company's historical museum.

In the central rotunda at the heart of this 125-acre complex is a larger-than-life bronze sculpture of Mr. Penney. A replica of the first Golden Rule store is carved into his desk. A small, open museum area displays well-worn, yellowed early advertisements through recent catalog covers. A replica of the first Kemmerer store—including shopkeeper, dry goods, and original wooden counter—lines one wall. Other displays illustrate company development, including credit cards (1957) and the first electronic point-of-sale system (1960s).

You will be most impressed with the expansiveness of this three-story glass-atriumed megastructure. With a portion of the profits from selling its 45-story New York City skyscraper (company headquarters from 1964 to 1987), Penney purchased 429 acres in rural Plano, Texas. This 1.9-million-square-foot office unites over 3,300 corporate "associates," Mr. Penney's name for his first employees, who worked "with" rather than "for" him.

The open floor plan and walkway seating areas facilitate communication between associates. Company day-care services and fitness facilities promote employee morale.

A robotic mail-delivery system and on-site direct video broadcast system connecting all the over 1,050 stores enhance productivity. After seeing many of its features, you'll agree that this futuristic home office—located on Legacy Drive—is a legacy to the founder and to the company's associates.

Cost: Free

Freebies: Museum brochures

Videos Shown: Small theater shows short nostalgic films, including 1950s interviews with Mr. and Mrs. Penney.

Reservations Needed: No

Days and Hours: Mon–Fri 8:00 AM–5:00 PM.

Plan to Stay: 20 minutes for museum plus time for lunch in company cafeteria, where curved glass walls frame a water-pool with fountain.

Minimum Age: None

Disabled Access: Yes

Group Requirements: None

Gift Shop: JC's, down the escalator from museum, sells logoed clothing and other items. Open Mon–Fri 8:00 AM–3:00 PM.

Directions: From Dallas, take Dallas Tollway North to Legacy Dr. exit. Turn left onto Legacy Dr., then right onto Communications Pkwy. Turn left onto Headquarters Dr. Park in North or South garage.

Nearby Attractions: American Airlines C. R. Smith Museum, Mary Kay factory and museum, and Studios at Las Colinas tours (see pages 314, 322, and 325); Dr Pepper Bottling Plant tour (call 972-721-8112); Dallas' downtown attractions, including Dealey Plaza and JFK Sixth Floor Museum, are 20–30 miles away.

Manny Gammage's Texas Hatters

15755 Interstate Highway 35 South
Buda, TX 78610
(512) 295-4287 / (800) 421-4287
www.texashatters.com

WESTERN-STYLE HATS

By such titles as "Dr. of Mad Hattery," "Wizard of Lids," and "A 'Manny' of Many Hats," you know that Manny Gammage was no ordinary hat maker. One of the few custom Western-style U.S. hat makers left, he hatted such personalities as Ronald Reagan, Howard Cosell, Jerry Jeff Walker, Burt Reynolds, and Willie Nelson. Now his wife and daughter carry on his legacy. Photographs, many autographed by the famous people wearing Manny's hats, form a collage on the shop walls. Baseball caps, each with its own story, hang from the ceiling's wooden beams.

Once inside the small store, make your way over to the wooden counter and take a stool. Ask Joella, Manny's daughter and third-generation hat-maker, to guide you through the wooden saloon door marked "Employees Only," into the small production area. Be careful not to touch anything as you work your way through the cramped quarters to the back.

Hats start as unshaped hat bodies made of beaver and hare's hair. From cubbyholes lining the walls, a worker selects the correct solid wooden block for the desired hat style and the wearer's head shape. After steam-heating the hat, he uses his muscles to stretch it over the heavy block. With an iron that weighs 15 pounds in the morning but feels like 45 pounds by evening, the worker irons and hand-sands the brim in circular stroking motions. He also irons out the crown as it slowly rotates on a contraption clamped to the wooden worktable. These processes are repeated and fine-tuned to correctly shape each hat.

As you squeeze your way into the next area, Joella explains that there are "too damn many steps" involved in making a hat. Study the well-worn poplar-wood disks, or "flanges," stored in slotted shelves. Look for the LBJ flange—you'll recognize it by the letters LBJ on the side. Sandbags are lowered onto a wooden flange to flatten the hat's brim. In the next small area, an old Singer sewing machine puts bindings in the brim; leather sweatbands and satin linings are sewn in by hand. More personality comes from the hatband—elephant hide, snakeskin, lizard, leather, and feathers. Even if you don't buy a hat, you'll leave with some great stories.

Cost: Free

Freebies: A token souvenir

Video Shown: No

Reservations Needed: Yes, must call 1 month in advance. Tours can be difficult to schedule since small family business.

Days and Hours: Tue–Sat 9:30 AM–5:30 PM. Closed holidays and 1st week of August.

Plan to Stay: 20 minutes

Minimum Age: None. Children require adult supervision.

Disabled Access: Retail area only.

Group Requirements: Groups larger than 5 will be split into smaller groups and need to call at least 1 week in advance.

Special Information: Best time to watch workers is in the morning. Hot in summer. Very tight quarters with strict safety rules.

Retail Store: Sells custom-made hats for 1-week delivery. Most popular styles are high roller and hunter, both in black. Open same hours as above. Catalog available from 800 number.

Directions: Take I-35 to Exit 220. Exit puts you on Overpass Rd. Look for 45-foot-high hat sign.

Nearby Attractions: Jardine's Texas Foods tour (see page 319); Austin's attractions, including Sixth Street, Lyndon B. Johnson Library and Museum, and Capitol Building, are 11 miles away.

Mary Kay

16251 Dallas Parkway
Addison, TX 75001
(972) 687-5720
www.marykay.com

&* MARY KAY

COSMETICS AND SKIN-CARE PRODUCTS

Inscribed at the entrance to the company museum is the late Mary Kay Ash's motto: "You can do anything in the world that you want to do if you want it badly enough and you are willing to pay the price." This determination and Mary Kay's ability to motivate and reward her (mostly female) sales force made Mary Kay, Inc.—founded in 1963 by Mary Kay and her son Richard—into one of America's most admired companies.

Drive from corporate headquarters to the aromatic manufacturing facility, where 40 lines fill and package over 200 Mary Kay products. On the eye-shadow line, gray plastic bottoms, clear tops, and eye-shadow refills merge on a freeway system that, together with human hands, packages approximately 38,000 per ten-hour shift. Once mascara and lip-gloss tubes are filled, workers manually insert applicators with a gentle twist. In another line, watch as a highly automated process adds the applicators to these products. It's fun to follow a bottle through the fragrance line—filling, manually inserting pumps, stamping down lids, and hand-packing perfume bottles.

The tour highlight, however, is the waxy-smelling lipstick line. Liquid lipstick is pumped into oblong metal molds, which are stacked onto an iced cooling table to solidify. Workers manually insert each lipstick bullet into its tube. Upright tubes march into a glass-enclosed oven, where flames caress the outer layer to give the lipstick a brilliant shine. The next time you apply (or watch someone apply) lipstick, you'll appreciate this labor that enhances women's beauty.

The corporate tour's highlight is the late Mary Kay's personal office at the corporate headquarters, with its crescent-shaped pastel sofa and her desk. Afterwards, take a self-guided tour of the Mary Kay Museum: Dreams Come True in the corporate office lobby (reservations not required). Its art deco white, pink, and black granite floors and brass-trimmed dark wood cases display mannequins wearing the director's suits since 1963, Mary Kay product lines, and many photographs and awards.

Cost: Free

Freebies: No

Video Shown: Several videos in museum cover company history, manufacturing process, company career opportunities, and annual seminars.

Reservations Needed: No, for museum. Yes, for corporate and manufacturing facility tours. Individuals, call (972) 687-5720 at least 2 days in advance. Groups, see below.

Days and Hours: Museum: Mon–Fri 9:00 AM–5:00 PM. Manufacturing headquarters tours: Mon 2:00 PM, Tue–Thur 10:30 AM and 2:00 PM, Fri 10:30 AM. Corporate tours: Mon–Fri 9:00 AM–4:30 PM. Closed holidays.

Plan to Stay: 45 minutes for museum and corporate tour; 1 hour for factory tour.

Minimum Age: None

Disabled Access: Yes, for corporate building and most of factory tour (call ahead for arrangements for 1 flight of stairs).

Group Requirements: Groups larger than 25 must call at least 1 week in advance for reservations. Groups larger than 15 will be split into smaller groups.

Special Information: Photography allowed in museum and office, but not in plant.

Gift Shop: No

Directions: To corporate headquarters: From Lyndon B. Johnson Frwy. (I-635), take Dallas Tollway North exit at Westgrove/Keller Springs. Follow service road through Keller Springs and turn left at Westgrove. Turn left back onto service road going south. Mary Kay is first big building on right. To manufacturing facility: from Stemmons Frwy. (I-35), take Regal Row exit. Head south on Regal Row. Plant is 2 blocks ahead on left.

Nearby Attractions: American Airlines C. R. Smith Museum, JCPenney Museum, and Studios at Las Colinas tours (see pages 314, 320, and 325); Dr Pepper Bottling plant tour in Irving (call 972-721-8112); Cavanaugh Flight Museum; Downtown Dallas attractions include JFK Museum, Dallas Museum of Art, Museum of the Americas, and West End Marketplace.

Mrs Baird's Bakery

7301 South Freeway
Fort Worth, TX 76134
(817) 293-6230
www.mrsbairds.com

BREAD

Discover the bakery that introduced sliced bread to Texas. Now one of the most modern bread bakeries in America, Mrs Baird's started as a home-kitchen operation in 1908. Although the Baird children once delivered bread to the neighbors in baskets, a fleet of delivery trucks now journey the vast highways of Texas and the surrounding region. One thing has not changed since Mrs. Baird began baking in her home five generations ago: "Family pride" is still the final ingredient.

After donning a hairnet, embark on a voyage into the bakery. Notice the smell of yeast permeating the air around you. Compare your own pantry to this fantastic food warehouse. Bags stacked high on metal shelves around you contain up to 2,000 pounds of ingredients, such as salt and powdered milk. Each of these "super sacks" of ingredients will eventually end up sifted together in the 25-foot-tall sifter and then moved to the mixers to become part of the bread dough. The company uses 100,000 pounds of flour each day to make up to 140,000 loaves of bread.

As you move out of the ingredient area and closer to the ovens, the aroma changes to that of fresh-baked bread. Machines drop fistfuls of dough for hamburger buns into baking pans. Turn around to see larger portions of dough for making loaves of bread fall into place. In the afternoon, witness Mrs Baird's specialty, hand-twisted white bread, the only exception to full automation in the plant. Watch the baker twist two long ropes of dough together like a braid to form one loaf. The dough is then placed in the pans and taken by conveyor to rise.

Gaze upward at a bumper-to-bumper highway of bread and hamburger buns traveling by on cooling tracks above your head. The depanner machine removes the fresh-baked bread from the pans with rows of suction cups. Blades, sharpened every five minutes, slice the 107° bread. Then the fresh bread is popped into the bags you see in the store.

Cost: Free

Freebies: Hot slice of bread, pencil, activity pamphlet for children, and a sweet baked goodie, freshly baked at the cake plant next door (cake plant is not open for tours).

Video Shown: 5-minute video on the nutritional importance of bread, the company history, and the baking process.

Reservations Needed: Yes, reservations should be made at least 3 weeks in advance. Call (817) 293-6230 and ask for the tour coordinator or call (817) 615-3050 to leave a voice-mail message.

Days and Hours: Mon, Wed, and Fri 10:00 AM–4:00 PM. Closed holidays.

Plan to Stay: 45 minutes

Minimum Age: 6

Disabled Access: Yes

Group Requirements: Maximum group size is 50 people. Larger groups will be divided. One adult is required for every 10 children.

Special Information: No photography. It's warm in the bakery, so dress comfortably. No shorts, sandals, or jewelry. Hand twisting can be seen only on afternoon tours.

Gift Shop: No

Directions: From downtown, take I-35W South to Sycamore School Rd. Turn left under the highway overpass. Take an immediate left onto the service road. Turn right into the bakery and follow "Tour Visitors" signs.

Nearby Attractions: American Airlines museum, Mary Kay, and Studios at Las Colinas tours (see pages 314, 322, and 325); Dr Pepper Bottling plant in Irving tour (call 972-721-8112); *Ft. Worth Star-Telegram* newspaper tour (call 817-390-7400, ext. 2240).

Nocona Athletic

208 Walnut Street
Nocona, TX 76255
(940) 825-3326
www.nokona.com

Nokona

BASEBALL GLOVES AND FOOTBALL EQUIPMENT

Nocona, Texas, is the leather goods capital of the Southwest. Nocona Athletic Goods Company started making Nokona baseball gloves and other sporting goods during the Depression. While U.S. sporting-goods companies began shifting labor-intensive baseball-glove production overseas in the early 1960s, Nocona proudly stayed at home. (Currently, imports represent 98 percent of glove sales nationwide.) The Nokona ball glove is one of three glove lines still made in the U.S.A., and the plant tour gives you the chance to see all of the production steps. While workers have some help from machines, you'll notice that the process is far from automated.

Making baseball and softball gloves begins with selecting the correct leather, which Nocona does on site, not overseas. The tour guide passes around pieces of cowhide and kangaroo leathers so you can feel the contrasting textures, and explains the differences between leather used in today's gloves compared to that of previous decades. Each glove's 14 to 18 leather pieces are die-cut from big leather sheets. Workers lay a metal frame in the shape of a hand on the correct spot and use a press to cut out a piece. They use experience gained from guiding patterns here for the past 50 years.

After stamping the name and logo on the leather, workers meticulously sew the pieces together. Up to this point the glove has been built inside out, so it's turned right side out one finger at a time on a hot iron. Workers then weave a long needle in and out of the glove to lace the leather together before stretching it on hot irons and applying leather-conditioning oils. You'll be tempted to pick up a glove and play catch in the middle of the factory.

From the aroma of leather, move to the smell of glue in the department that assembles football equipment, such as shoulder pads and helmets. Workers construct this equipment mostly from pre-molded plastic parts and shock-absorbing pads. Don't forget to visit the company's small collection of old leather baseball mitts and football helmets, conjuring images of Ty Cobb and Knute Rockne in the years of day games, grass gridirons, and U.S.A.-made sporting goods.

Cost: Free
Freebies: Product catalogs used for wholesale trade.
Video Shown: No
Reservations Needed: Preferred
Days and Hours: Mon–Fri 8:00 AM–12:00 PM and 1:00 PM–4:00 PM. Closed holidays, 2 weeks at Christmas, and 2 weeks around July 4th.
Plan to Stay: 1 hour
Minimum Age: None
Disabled Access: Yes
Group Requirements: No minimum. Maximum group size is 30 people with 1 day's advance notice.
Special Information: Glue smell may initially bother some people.
Gift Shop: Nocona Boot Company Factory Outlet (6 blocks away on Hwy. 82) sells first- and second-quality Nokona gloves.
Directions: From Dallas, take I-35 to Hwy. 82 West exit in Gainesville. Stay on Hwy. 82 West into Nocona, turn right at Clay St., and left on Walnut. Company is in big red brick building on right.
Nearby Attractions: Nocona Belt Company tour (call 940-825-3271); Justin Park; Lake Nocona.

Studios at Las Colinas

6301 North O'Connor Road
Building One
Irving, TX 75039
(972) 869-FILM (7752)
www.studiosatlascolinas.com

TELEVISION/MOVIE STUDIO

You do not have to visit Hollywood to get your fill of movies—on the outskirts of Dallas, Texas, you can tour the birthplace of movies like *Robocop* and *JFK,* and one-time home of popular TV shows *Barney* and *Walker: Texas Ranger.*

Begin your tour in the Foley room, where Foley artists are responsible for adding the sound effects to movies. In this dimly lit room, see examples of how early Foley artists created sounds—coconut shells clapped together for clip-clopping horses, a grid of loosely hanging wooden blocks tapped against a table for a column of marching soldiers. Then volunteer to re-create the sound for an *Addams Family Values* clip using a modern sampler filled with pre-recorded music and sound effects.

Upstairs, get a closer look at models hanging overhead including the F14 Tomcat from *Top Gun,* the airplane from *Airplane,* and the submarine from *Hunt for Red October.* Then move on to the extensive Costume Museum. Highlights include the complete set of original costumes from *The Sound of Music,* Dorothy's dress from *Wizard of Oz,* Michael Keaton's *Batman* costume, uniforms from *The Natural,* and Christopher Reeve's *Superman* suit. Other famous costumes belonged to Harrison Ford, Eddie Murphy, John Travolta, Sean Connery, Robin Williams, and Julia Roberts.

Move downstairs to Studio A, the 15,000-square-foot sound stage. This massive room is soundproof, so much so that *Walker: Texas Ranger* could be filmed here while Garth Brooks rehearsed at full volume in the next room. To accomplish this feat, 30-inch-thick walls have insulation as well as a six-inch separation from one 30-inch wall to the next, almost as if each studio were its own building. Grids for lights cover the entire ceiling with enough power to light up two apartment buildings.

Take a moment to take pictures in front of the Oval Office set from *JFK.* Learn how the set was constructed in the 1950s, only to be put into storage until Oliver Stone discovered it. Stone spent $70,000 renovating the life-like set for only one and one half minutes of black and white film.

End your tour in the visual effects theater where volunteers, young and old, will dodge falling rocks, avoid booby traps, and escape the bad guys, all unscathed as they test their acting skills in front of a green screen.

Cost: Adults, $12.95; seniors, $10.95; children 4–12, $8.95; children under 3, free; disabled half price due to limited access.

Freebies: No

Video: 15-minute video on the history of the movie-studio system.

Reservations Needed: No, except for groups of 15 or more. Tickets available 30 minutes before tour.

Days and Hours: May 5–September 1: Mon–Sat 10:30 AM, 12:30 PM, 2:30 PM, and 4:00 PM. Sun same hours except 10:30 AM. September 3–May 4: Mon–Fri 12:30 PM and 2:30 PM. Sat same above hours.

Plan to Stay: 1.5 hours

Minimum Age: None

Disabled Access: Yes, except for Costume Museum, viewable on video.

Group Requirements: Groups of 15 or more qualify for group discount. Call (972) 869-7703 at least 1 week in advance.

Special Information: Private parties and events can include studio tour plus a few movie star look-alikes and rolling out the red carpet for a Night at the Oscars starring your guests. Call (972) 869-7770.

Gift Shop: Sells T-shirts, audio tapes and CDs, pencils, magnets, ice cream treats, and beverages. Open Mon–Fri 12:00 PM–3:00 PM, Sat 10:00 AM–4:30 PM.

Directions: From I-35 East go south to 635 West. Take the Valley View exit. Turn left onto O'Connor Rd. south. Pass through Royal Lane. Make 1st right into company driveway. From 183 East take 161 North. Take O'Connor Rd south. Pass through Royal Lane. Make first right into company driveway.

Nearby Attractions: American Airlines museum, JCPenney museum, and Mary Kay museum each about 30 minutes away (see pages 314, 320, and 322); Dr Pepper Bottling Plant tour (call 972-721-8112); Mrs Baird's Bakery about 1 hour away (see page 323).

Kennecott Utah Copper

Kennecott's Bingham Canyon Mine Visitors Center
128 South Highway 111
Bingham Canyon, UT 84006
(801) 569-6287
www.kennecott.com

Ⓚ Kennecott

COPPER MINE

If you moved Chicago's Sears Tower to the bottom of the Bingham Canyon Copper Mine, it wouldn't even reach halfway to the top of the mine. In fact, at over two-and-one-half miles across and one-half mile deep, this mine is the deepest human-made excavation on earth. In 1906 steam shovels began eating away at a mountain that divided Bingham Canyon. Today huge rotary drills and electric shovels have replaced steam shovels, and an open pit has replaced the mountain. Kennecott is still mining copper from Bingham Canyon, which has yielded over 14 million tons of copper—more than any other mine in history.

Your visit begins with an unbelievable view of the mine from an overlook. The view encompasses hundreds of millions of years of the earth's history and lots of brown dirt in a circular pattern. Look down at the workers and machines who remove about 300,000 tons of material daily, knowing that soon you will learn exactly how miners remove the copper ore from this canyon.

Inside the Visitors Center, eight exhibits teach you everything from the mine's history to the daily uses of copper and how Kennecott protects the environment through reclamation and revegetation projects. For those especially interested in history, one exhibit tells how the surrounding area of Utah developed and prospered along with the copper industry. You will also learn about the people of Kennecott and the company's community efforts.

In the center's 80-seat theater, watch a video, which provides a condensed explanation of the entire copper-mining process, as well as some of the history behind the mine and its neighboring communities. As you drive away from the Bingham Canyon Mine, be sure to glance back at the mountainside you saw as you drove in; you now have a new appreciation of the mining industry, copper, and Bingham Canyon.

Cost: $4 per vehicle, $3 for motorcycles, with all funds going to local charities.

Freebies: Company brochures

Video Shown: 13-minute video explaining mine history and operation.

Reservations Needed: No, but call at beginning and end of season to verify Visitors Center is open.

Days and Hours: Open April–end of October, weather permitting: Mon–Sun 8:00 AM–8:00 PM. Closed holidays.

Plan to Stay: 1 hour

Minimum Age: None

Disabled Access: Yes

Group Requirements: None. $40 entrance fee for tour buses. Free for school buses. Booklet available for educators and tour guides.

Special Information: Tour does not permit you to go down into the mine. However, observation deck and exhibits offer views of it.

Gift Shop: Sells souvenirs, T-shirts, and postcards, as well as educational books, small rocks, and minerals. Shop is operated by local Lions Club, and is not part of Kennecott. Open same hours as Visitors Center.

Directions: From Salt Lake City, take I-15 South to 7200 South exit, and turn right. Turn right onto 7800 South, which turns into Bingham Hwy. Take Bingham Hwy. toward Copperton. Mine is visible on mountainside ahead. Follow signs to Kennecott's Bingham Canyon Mine.

Nearby Attractions: Salt Lake City's attractions, including Salt Lake Temple, Great Salt Lake, and ski resorts, are about 25 miles away; Mormon Church headquarters.

Ben & Jerry's

Route 100
Waterbury, VT 05676
866-BJTOURS
www.benjerry.com

BEN&JERRY'S
VERMONT'S FINEST • ICE CREAM & FROZEN YOGURT™

ICE CREAM AND
FROZEN YOGURT

Nestled in the heart of the Green Mountains, the Ben & Jerry's ice cream factory sits on a rolling pasture. The grounds are filled with whimsical interactive displays and games, like the interactive timeline, to ease the waiting time for this popular tour. Given Ben & Jerry's down-home image, you'd expect to see hundreds of workers using individual churns to make its ice creams and yogurts. Instead, from a glass-enclosed, temperature-controlled mezzanine area you look down at a state-of-the-art ice cream factory that can turn out 180,000 pints per day.

The tour starts in the Cow over the Moon Theater. In the movie, you'll find out how two childhood friends, Ben Cohen and Jerry Greenfield, turned a five-dollar correspondence course on ice cream making into a business that shares its success with its employees and the community—and has fun while doing it!

Afterwards, follow the enthusiastic tour guide up to the mezzanine. Ice cream and frozen yogurt begin as an unflavored base mix stored in the 36° tank room. The mix travels to the flavor vat, to the freezer (where it gets the consistency of soft-serve), into the fruit and chunk feeder, to the automatic pint-filler that handles "chunk intensive" flavors, to the pint bundler, and finally to the spiral hardener. In this last step, the ice cream freezes solid at a temperature of -60°. When in production, watch live-feed, real-time videos showing ice cream pints emerging from the spiral hardener, then groups of eight are shrink-wrapped or "bundled."

Then it's off to the Flavoroom for two delicious samples. After you've had a taste, make sure you peek into the Quality Assurance Lab. Every hour a quality control worker grabs pints off the production line, freezes them, and slices them open, inspecting the ice cream for the proper amount of chunks and swirls.

After passing by the QA Lab, enter the Ben & Jerry's Hall of Fame, full of pictures, posters, and paraphernalia that humorously document the company's proud, offbeat history.

Cost: Adults, $2; senior citizens, $1.75; children 12 and under, free. Portion of proceeds donated to KABOOM!, a nonprofit organization that builds playgrounds for children.

Freebies: Two ice cream samples and a Ben & Jerry's button.

Video Shown: 7-minute movie about founders.

Reservations Needed: No, except for groups of 10 or more people. Reservations not accepted for July, August, and holidays.

Days and Hours: November–May: Mon–Sun 10:00 AM–5:00 PM. June: 9:00 AM–6:00 PM. July–August: 9:00 AM–8:00 PM. Late August–October: 9:00 AM–6:00 PM. Tours every 30 minutes, with tickets sold on a first-come, first-served basis. No production Saturdays, Sundays, holidays, or company celebration days, although production video shown. Call for up-to-date schedules.

Plan to Stay: 30 minutes for tour and movie, plus time for grounds, displays, and gift shop. Grounds are a low-key family activity park.

Minimum Age: None

Disabled Access: Yes

Group Requirements: Groups of 10 or more call (802) 882-1240, ext. 2289.

Special Information: Afternoon tours fill quickly, particularly in summer.

Gift Shop: Scoop Shop features variety of Ben & Jerry's flavors. Gift shop offers Vermont gifts, logoed clothes, memorabilia, and other fun stuff. Open same hours as tour, except November–May: Mon–Sun 10:00 AM–6:00 PM. Catalog available from (802) 846-1500

Directions: Take I-89 to Exit 10. Go north on Rt. 100 toward Stowe. Factory is about 1 mile ahead on left.

Nearby Attractions: Rock of Ages, Vermont Teddy Bear, and Cabot Creamery tours (see pages 332, 335, and 328); Cabot Creamery Annex Store; Stowe and Sugarbush ski areas; Cold Hollow Cider Mill; Mt. Mansfield.

Cabot Creamery

2878 Main Street
Cabot, VT 05647
(800) 837-4261
www.cabotcheese.com

CHEESE

On a hillside in Vermont, sparkling white 130,000-gallon milk silos emblazoned with the red-and-green Cabot Creamery logo overlook the entrance to the visitors center and plant, where some of the nation's best sharp cheddar cheese is made (winner of U.S. Championship Cheese Contest). This guided tour shows you how the cooperative creamery converts milk from local farms into famous Vermont cheddar cheeses, and also how it packages its yogurts, cottage cheese, and sour cream.

You'll peer through glass windows into the packaging and processing rooms, where workers fill large cooking vats with quality-tested, heat-treated milk and a starter culture. The curd that forms is cut with stainless-steel knives that help separate the curd from the whey. Once the whey is separated and drained off, workers vigorously mix the curd on huge metal finishing tables to "cheddar" it until the correct pH level is reached.

In overhead towers, the curd is then pressed into 42-pound blocks or round stainless-steel frames to create cheese wheels. Every 90 seconds another block emerges from a tower and enters an airtight cellophane bag for proper aging (nine months for sharp cheddar, 14 months for extra-sharp). With the cheese-making process in various stages of production, your ten-minute walk captures the five hours needed for every vat of milk to become cheese (33,000 pounds of whole milk in each vat yields approximately 3,500 pounds of cheese).

Cost: $1; children under 12, free.

Freebies: Cabot cheese and dip samples under the "Grazing Encouraged" sign in gift shop. Cabot Critters coloring book, 1 per family.

Video Shown: 10-minute video on history of Vermont farming and dairy industry, development of Cabot Cooperative Creamery in 1919, and highlights of processes used to make different Cabot products.

Reservations Needed: No, except for groups larger than 20 people.

Days and Hours: June–October: Mon–Sun 9:00 AM–5:00 PM; November–May: Mon–Sat 9:00 AM–4:00 PM. Tours run every 30 minutes. Last tour 30 minutes before closing. Call ahead for cheese-making days. Closed January.

Plan to Stay: 30 minutes for tour and video, plus time to nibble in the gift shop.

Minimum Age: None

Disabled Access: Yes

Group Requirements: Groups larger than 20 should call at least 1 week in advance.

Special Information: Cabot Creamery Annex store (near Ben & Jerry's factory on Rt. 100) shows cheese-making video and sells Cabot products, Vermont specialty foods, beer, and wine.

Gift Shop: Sells all Cabot products, including such specialty cheddars as salsa or garlic & herb. Offers selected factory specials and other Vermont-made food products and gifts. Open same hours as tour. Cheese catalog available from (800) 639-3198.

Directions: From I-89, take Exit 8 for Montpelier. Head east on Rt. 2 and turn left onto Rt. 215 East in Marshfield Village. Cabot Creamery is 5 miles ahead on right. From I-91, take St. Johnsbury exit. Head west on Rt. 2 and turn right on Rt. 215 to Creamery.

Nearby Attractions: Maple Grove Farms, Ben & Jerry's, and Rock of Ages tours (see pages 331, 327, and 332); Goodrich's Sugarhouse (call 800-639-1854); Vermont Cheese Council (www.vtcheese.com) for other Vermont cheese tours.

Crowley Cheese

Healdville Road
Healdville, VT 05758
(802) 259-2340 / (802) 259-2210
www.crowleycheese-vermont.com

CHEESE

When most cheese factories call their cheese "handmade," they usually mean that machines did the processing with a little human involvement. At the U.S.'s oldest still-operating cheese factory (established 1882), "handmade" means what it says. Except for modern sanitation and refrigeration techniques, Crowley's cheese-making tools are from the 1800s.

The outside of this three-story brown clapboard building, a National Historic Place, looks more like a house than a cheese "factory." But inside, the solo cheese-maker proudly enjoys showing visitors how to make old-style Colby cheddar using 19th-century techniques. You can stand near the 1,000-gallon sterile vat that looks like a large bathtub filled with milk. Steam flows through the hollow walls to heat the milk.

The cheese-maker adds the culture and, later, rennet (a milk-coagulating enzyme). Once the mixture has a yogurt texture, it is "cut" into small cubes, which separate from the whey and become the curd. Watch how the cheese-maker uses the cheese rake to gently stir the curd. This keeps curd particles separate and helps them cook evenly.

Once the whey is drained, the curds look like mounds of popcorn. The cheese-maker works the curds by hand, rinsing them with fresh spring water before placing them into cheesecloth-lined metal hoops. Overnight, old crank presses remove excess whey. Then the cheese wheels age at least two months for mild and over a year for extra-sharp. After looking at the pictures on the walls, listening to the cheese-maker's explanation, and watching traditional cheese-making techniques, you leave saying the Little Miss Muffet nursery rhyme.

Cost: Free
Freebies: Cheese
Video Shown: 9-minute video on history of company and cheese-making process, usually shown when not in production.

Reservations Needed: No, except for groups over 25 people.
Days and Hours: Mon–Fri 8:00 AM–4:00 PM. Closed holidays. Since small operation, call ahead about cheese production schedule.
Plan to Stay: 15 minutes for tour, plus time for gift shop and duck pond.
Minimum Age: None. Tour is very popular with young children; *Sesame Street* filmed feature on cheese-making at Crowley.
Disabled Access: Yes
Group Requirements: Groups larger than 25 should call a few days ahead.
Special Information: Best time to see production and talk to cheese-maker is 11:00 AM to mid-afternoon. When no one is in factory, calls to above number may not always be answered. Don't despair, just call back or try contacting gift shop at (800) 683-2606.
Retail Store: Located 1.5 miles away on main Rt. 103; sells mild, medium, and sharp Crowley Cheese in 8-oz. bars, 2.5- and 5-pound wheels, smoked bars, and spiced (caraway, dill, garlic, hot pepper, onion, and sage) bars; Vermont specialty foods and gifts. Open Mon–Sat 10:30 AM–5:30 PM, Sun 11:00 AM–5:30 PM (suggest calling to check if open). Closed Christmas and New Year's. Call above number for order form.
Directions: From I-91, take Rt. 103 North. At split with Rt. 100, stay on Rt. 103 for 3 miles. Pass Crowley Cheese Shop, turn left onto Healdville Rd. for factory. From Rutland, take Rt. 7 South to Rt. 103 South. Then go approx. 10 miles to flashing yellow light at Belmont Rd. in Mt. Holly. Continue on Rt. 103 South for about 3 miles and turn right onto Healdville Rd.
Nearby Attractions: Cerniglia Winery tour (call 800-654-6382); Vermont Marble Exhibit (call 802-459-3311 ext. 436); Weston (a lovely small New England village); Coolidge Family Homestead; Okemo ski area.

Grafton Village Cheese

533 Townshend Road
Grafton, VT 05146
(802) 843-2221 / (800) 472-3866
www.graftonvillagecheese.com

CHEESE

Grafton Village Cheese Company
Premium Vermont Cheddar

Cheese making has long been a part of Vermont life, with grazing dairy cows a familiar sight. The state has cheese factories off all sizes, from the large Cabot Creamery (see page 328) to the very small Crowley Cheese (see page 329). They often sit in picturesque locations and you discover them just when you're hungry for a small snack.

Grafton, Vermont, is likely the prettiest home of any of the state's cheese factories. Cheese-making traditions in this historic village date from the 19th century (started in 1892) when dairy farmers gathered together in a cooperative to make their surplus milk into cheese. The town's preservation has retained much of the character from that century.

Grafton Village Cheese, now owned by the nonprofit Windham Foundation, has won numerous awards, especially for its Classic Reserve and Premium cheddars. It owes much of its fame to Scott Fletcher, Grafton's master cheesemaker, who has been with the company for more than 30 years. He is one of the deans of Vermont cheese making and gives his personal touch to each step of the process. As with most cheese factories, you can watch production through big glass windows. You see long metal tables and vats, with cheese in various stages of its creation.

The process, almost eight hours long, requires close monitoring. It begins with fresh Vermont Jersey cow milk that is pumped into the cheese vats. Depending on the time of day and Grafton's production schedule, you will gather glimpses of cheese makers adding rennet to separate the milk solids from the whey, stirring the heated milk, testing the mixture for flavor and acidity, squeezing whey from the coagulated curd, and then packing the curd into hoop molds for aging. Look for the critical step called "cheddaring," when the curd is cut into slabs, then stacked and pressed together several times until most of the whey is drained off. Grafton naturally ages its cheeses: one year for a sharp cheddar

and up to four years for a mature Vermont cheddar. In another area, big blocks of properly aged cheddar are cut into different sizes, before waxing and perhaps smoking.

Cost: Free

Freebies: Plentiful samples in the retail store

Video Shown: 9-minute video that shows closeups of the production process and history of the company. Video continually shows even when not in production.

Reservations Needed: No.

Days and Hours: Mon–Fri 8:00 AM–4:00 PM, Sat and Sun 10:00 AM–4:00 PM. Closed Thanksgiving, Christmas, and New Year's. Most production occurs Mon–Sat 8:00 AM–1:00 PM, depending on the season and demand. Call for current production schedule.

Plan to Stay: 15 minutes, plus time for gift shop.

Minimum Age: None

Disabled Access: Yes

Group Requirements: Large bus groups call ahead to break into groups of 15–20 people. Guide available.

Special Information: In summer, see Vermont Jersey cows pet and feed, next to the covered bridge.

Gift Shop: Sells all of the company's cheeses, include the Classic Reserve, Premium, Yankee Thrift, and flavored cheddars in bricks, blocks, and wheels of different sizes. Offers other Vermont-made specialty foods, including jellies and mustards, and crafts. Catalog available from above number. Open same hours.

Directions: From I-91, take Exit 5. Take Rt. 121/US 5 West. Turn left at the Old Tavern onto Townshend Rd.

Nearby Attractions: Grafton Ponds cross-country skiing, snow shoeing, ice skating, and mountain biking; Nature Museum; The Old Tavern; Okemo and Stratton Ski Mountains about 1 hour away; Vermont Cheese Council (www.vtcheese.com) for other Vermont cheese tours.

Maple Grove Farms

1052 Portland Street
St. Johnsbury, VT 05819
(802) 748-5141 / (800) 525-2540
www.maplegrove.com

**MAPLE SYRUP AND
SALAD DRESSING**

The company that two women started in 1915 is now one of the world's largest packagers of maple syrup and manufacturers of maple products. Maple Grove Farms has also developed a full line of natural fruit syrups and gourmet salad dressings, with its honey-mustard dressing a top-selling New England gourmet dressing.

This guided factory floor tour has a small-town feeling. You'll watch bottles of pure maple syrup or salad dressing filled, labeled, and packed on the assembly line. Downstairs in the "kitchen," workers on one side boil and mix maple syrup for making candy; on the other side, it's salad dressing or fruit syrup. Your nostrils will battle over the conflicting smells, with fruit syrups (especially raspberry) usually the clear winner.

A vintage 1930s candy depositor pours the maple candy mix into rubber sheet molds. The mixture cools for about an hour before the "ladies," as the tour guide calls them, shake the candy out onto padded mats. The candies are placed into metal baskets for an overnight bath in a crystallizing mixture of sugar and syrup, a natural preservative. Look through the glass window at carts filled with candy air-drying on metal trays, and at the quick-moving hands that individually pack the maple candies into boxes (3,000 to 4,000 pounds per day).

Cost: $1; children under 12, free.

Freebies: Small sample bag of maple candies. Gift shop offers free tastes of different maple syrups and the salad dressing of the day.

Video Shown: Tour begins with 8-minute video highlighting maple syrup–making process, company history and manufacturing. When factory tour not operating, this video plays in Cabin Store

Reservations Needed: No, except for groups of more than 40 people.

Days and Hours: Mon–Fri 8:00 AM–11:45 AM and 12:30 PM–4:30 PM, year-round. Tour runs about every 12 minutes. Closed holidays.

Plan to Stay: 45 minutes, including tour, video, Maple Museum, and gift shop. Maple Museum is an authentic sugarhouse with all tools and equipment used by Vermont sugar-makers, and complete explanation of evaporation process.

Minimum Age: None

Disabled Access: Only on bottom floor of factory, but company does not encourage it because floor can be slippery.

Group Requirements: Tours for groups of more than 40 people require reservations.

Special Information: Production stops around 3:30 PM. While syrup and dressing are filled and packed daily, candy not made every day during winter.

Gift Shop: Cabin Store sells many maple products, such as maple butter, maple crunch, and maple drops. Also offers company's gourmet dressings and fruit-flavored syrups, along with standard Vermont tourist items. Look for factory seconds in seconds area. Cabin Store and Maple Museum open Mon–Sun 8:00 AM–5:00 PM, from beginning of May until late October. During winter, store is in factory and open same hours as tour. Catalog available from (802) 748-3136.

Directions: From I-91, take Exit 20 for Rt. 5 North. Take Rt. 2 East. Factory is about 1 mile from center of town. From I-93, take Exit 1 in Vermont, turn onto Rt. 18 toward St. Johnsbury, then turn left onto Rt. 2 West. Factory is a few miles ahead on left.

Nearby Attractions: Cabot Creamery tour (see page 328); Goodrich's Sugarhouse (call 800-639-1854); Fairbanks Museum and Planetarium; New England Maple Museum, about 1.5 hours away in Pittsford.

Rock of Ages

773 Graniteville Road
Graniteville, VT 05654
(802) 476-3119
www.rockofages.com

GRANITE QUARRY, MEMORIALS, AND SCULPTURES

Rock of Ages Corporation was founded in 1885 by native Yankees and immigrants looking for a better life. The company has grown to become the largest quarrier, manufacturer, retailer of finished granite memorials, and wholesaler of granite blocks for memorial use in North America, with 13 active quarry properties and 10 manufacturing and sawing facilities. Rock of Ages has conducted narrated tours of its quarrying operations since 1924, currently letting you experience the world's largest-dimension granite quarry located in Graniteville, part of Barre, Vermont, the self-proclaimed "Granite Center of the World."

The narrated shuttle bus tour of the E. L. Smith Quarry offers expansive views of the 50-acre, 600-foot-deep active quarry. From behind a wire fence at the edge of the quarry, look down at the process of mining granite by man and machine. The walls form deep canyons of Barre gray granite. Slot-drilling machines cut huge blocks of granite off the walls (you may also hear controlled explosions that split the bottom of the block). Notice the powerful, tall derricks towering above the quarry that lift the blocks. At the nearby saw plant, these blocks are sliced into slabs.

After the outdoor tour, with its views of Vermont's Green Mountains in the background, journey inside for a self-guided tour of the manufacturing plant that spans two football fields. From one end of the cavernous plant, look over a wood railing from an observation deck as granite artisans labor to make enduring tombstones and other memorials and sculptures. The process of cutting, polishing, and sculpting involves both craftsmanship and the latest technology to produce precision surface plates and machine bases accurate to 25,000,000th of an inch.

Cost: Visitor Center and manufacturing: Free. Quarry tour: Adults, $4; seniors, $3.50; children 6–12, $1.50.

Freebies: Small samples of granite in bins behind Visitors Center.

Video Shown: 18-minute video in the Visitors Center on geology and history of the quarry, and modern granite quarry methods.

Reservations Needed: Groups over 20 people that want step-on guide should book tour 1 week in advance, longer in advance in fall.

Days and Hours: Visitor Center: May 1–October 31: Mon–Sat 8:30 AM–5:00 PM, Sun 12:00 PM–5:00 PM (Fall: Sun 8:30 AM–5:30 PM). Closed July 4th. Quarry tour: June–mid-October: Mon–Fri 9:15 AM–3:00 PM approx. every 45 minutes or more frequently in the fall. Closed July 4th. Manufacturing: all year, Mon–Fri 8:00 AM–3:30 PM. Closed major holidays and usually the first 2 weeks of January.

Plan to Stay: 1.5 hours for all tours and visitor center, plus time for gift shop.

Minimum Age: None

Disabled Access: Yes, except for few steps leading to manufacturing observation area.

Group Requirements: Special rate of $2.50 per person for adults. Step on guides available for bus groups.

Special Information: Noisy tour for young children. The Visitors Center houses geological displays and exhibits, manufacturing displays, sculpture, and memorials outside.

Gift Shop: Features fine-quality granite gifts, including penholders and clocks. Also carries stone-related gifts from all over the world. Open same months and hours as Visitors Center.

Directions: From I-89, take Exit 6. Follow Rt. 63 to bottom of hill. Go straight through light. Follow signs. From Rt. 302 West, in East Barre turn left onto Rt. 110. Follow signs to "quarries/Graniteville."

Nearby Attractions: Ben & Jerry's and Cabot Creamery tours (see pages 327 and 328); Porter Music Box Museum; Bragg Farm Sugarhouse (call 800-376-5757); Morse Farm Sugar Works (call 800-242-2740); Vermont Marble Exhibit (call 802-459-3311) in Procter, VT, about 70 miles away.

▲   A titan block of Barre granite is pulled from E. L. Smith Quarry.

A master sculptor transforms Barre granite into an enduring masterpiece at Rock of Ages Manufacturing
▼   Center in Graniteville, Vermont.

Simon Pearce

Route 5, Windsor, VT 05089
(802) 674-6280
The Mill, Quechee, VT 05059
(802) 295-2711
www.simonpearce.com

GLASS AND POTTERY

Simon Pearce, originally trained as a potter, apprenticed in Sweden before opening a glassblowing factory in Ireland in 1971. Because of high energy costs, Simon moved his business to the U.S. in 1981. Simon housed his first U.S. factory in a historic, 200-year-old red brick woolen mill next to the Ottauquechee River in Quechee, Vermont. In 1993 Simon designed a brand-new manufacturing facility 9 miles away in Windsor, Vermont.

Both facilities offer self-guided tours. From Windsor's raised catwalk viewing gallery, you can observe the entire glassblowing process. The doors of the large furnace in the room's center open automatically when a worker steps on a floor mat to gather glass from the furnace. Workers may appear to be wandering around, but each has a specific mission as part of a two- or three-person team.

The glassblower chooses a blowpipe from the warmer, gathers the appropriate amount of glass from the center furnace, and blows it into a wooden mold. The apprentice opens the mold and gathers glass onto a pontil iron, which holds the piece during hand finishing of the rim. The cross underneath each piece, made by this pontil iron, has become the Simon Pearce trademark.

In Quechee, you can watch glass and pottery production. Stairs at the back of the extensive, well-displayed showrooms lead you down to a smaller, more intimate operation. From behind a wooden railing, you observe a glass-blowing team only a few feet in front of you.

Feel free to ask about the processes as a potter hand-throws pottery on a wheel. Both facilities will impress you with the skill and craftsmanship involved in handmade pottery and glass.

Information below applies to both facilities unless otherwise noted.

Cost: Free
Freebies: No
Video Shown: No

Reservations Needed: No, except for groups.
Days and Hours: Windsor: Mon–Sun 9:00 AM–5:00 PM. Quechee: Mon–Sun 9:00 AM–9:00 PM. Both closed Thanksgiving and Christmas.
Plan to Stay: 30 minutes each, plus time in gift shops and Simon Pearce Restaurant in Quechee (802-295-1470 for reservations).
Minimum Age: None
Disabled Access: Yes, at Windsor. No wheelchair access to production in Quechee, but gift shop and restaurant are accessible.
Group Requirements: Windsor easily accommodates buses. Groups larger than 50 should call 1 month in advance.
Special Information: Facilities can get warm because of furnaces. Similar to the Quechee facility, Simon Pearce on the Brandywine in West Chester, PA, includes gourmet restaurant and glassblowing (call 610-793-0948). From catwalk, at former Bausch & Lomb facility in Mountain Lake Park, MD, can watch glassblowing (call 301-334-5277).
Retail Shops: Sell first- and second-quality Simon Pearce pottery and glass. Windsor open Mon–Sun 9:00 AM–5:00 PM. Quechee open Mon–Sun 9:00 AM–9:00 PM. Catalog available from (800) 774-5277. Retail shops at all four facilities as well as stand-alone stores throughout New England.
Directions: To Windsor: from western Massachusetts, take I-91 North to Exit 9, bear right onto Rt. 5. Simon Pearce is 1 mile ahead on left. From New Hampshire, take I-89 to I-91 South. Follow above directions. To Quechee: from western Massachusetts, take I-91 North to I-89 North to Exit 1. Take Rt. 4 West. Turn right at first blinker after Quechee Gorge. Follow signs. From New Hampshire, take I-89 North to Exit 1 in Vermont. Follow above directions.
Nearby Attractions: For Windsor: Harpoon Brewery (call 802-674-5491); American Precision Museum (call 802-674-5781); Vermont State Craft Center; Constitution House. For Quechee: quaint town of Woodstock; Billings Farm; Killington Ski Resort.

Vermont Teddy Bear

6655 Shelburne Road
Shelburne, VT 05482
(802) 985-3001 / (800) 829-BEAR
www.vermontteddybear.com

TEDDY BEARS

A plain little teddy belonging to a boy named Graham was the inspiration for Vermont Teddy Bears. When Graham's father discovered that none of Graham's stuffed animals—not even that most American of toys, the teddy bear—were made in the U.S.A., he decided to make an American teddy bear. Since the company is located on a 57-pastoral-acre site, you'll drive down its long, winding drive toward the airport hangar-shaped shipping building, the hexagonal retail store (each panel a different color), and the multicolored barn silo topped with a beanie—complete with propeller.

After visiting the company museum in the lobby, you head for the workshop, a magical place that enchants young and old. Moving through the brightly painted workshop, you'll expect Santa's elves to appear at any moment. The enthusiastic tour guides ("Bear Ambassadors"), workers, and bears do everything in their power to make sure you have fun.

Stand behind a railing as your guide uses props to theatrically explain the processes you see. At the cutting area, watch a hydraulic press, with cookie-cutter dies, stamp out bear parts from 12 to 14 layers of soft fur. Workers at several stations sew together bear limbs, torsos and heads, inside-out so seams are hidden. Bears are then turned right side out and pumped full of stuffing with 130 pounds of air pressure. Limbs are joined to torsos, and eyes are placed.

Bears are dressed as everything from artists to veterinarians and carefully packed in a box with an air hole to make sure the bear will not have to hold his breath the whole trip. Each bear has a board game (so he won't be bored while traveling), some bear food (so he doesn't get hungry), and a personalized message.

After the tour, you'll want to go back to the Make a Friend for Life cub house to help stuff your own teddy bear. Select your fat-free (that is, unstuffed) bear. Spin the dial to choose the bear's filling—dreams, happiness, love, giggles. After the teddy is stitched up, you'll receive its birth certificate.

Cost: Tour: Adults, $2; children under 12, free. Make a Friend for Life (stuff your own bear): $19.95–$24.50.

Freebies: Fuzzy little "Button Bear" that fits over shirt button.

Video Shown: No

Reservations Needed: No, except for groups of 10 or more people.

Days and Hours: Mon–Sun 10:00 AM–5:00 PM. Limited weekend production; however, tours are still fun. Closed holidays. Call 800 number for extended summer hours.

Plan to Stay: 25 minutes for tour, plus time for Bear Shop and Make a Friend for Life cub house.

Minimum Age: None (but must bring the kid inside you).

Disabled Access: Yes

Group Requirements: Groups over 20 people should call (802) 985-3001 in advance, if possible. Maximum group size is 40 people.

Gift Shop: Bear Shop is stocked with bears waiting to go home with you. All are handcrafted and guaranteed for life. Carries logoed T-shirts, fleece pullovers, and sweatshirts. Open Mon–Sat 9:00 AM–6:00 PM, Sun 10:00 AM–5:00 PM. For more information on Bear-Grams and catalog, call (800) 829-BEAR.

Special Information: National American Teddy Bear Day celebrated on November 14, the day the American Teddy Bear was born. Private birthday parties available.

Directions: From I-89, take Exit 13 onto I-189 West. When I-189 ends, turn left onto Rt. 7 South through town of Shelburne. Factory located .5 miles past Shelburne Museum.

Nearby Attractions: Ben & Jerry's ice cream tour (see page 327); Lake Champlain Chocolates viewing window (call 802-864-1807); Shelburne Farms (call 802-985-8686); Shelburne Museum.

The Candle Factory

Williamsburg Soap & Candle Company
7521 Richmond Road
Williamsburg, VA 23188
(757) 564-3354
www.candlefactory.com

CANDLES AND SOAP

In 1964 the Barnett's of Williamsburg opened a gift shop along busy Richmond Road. They soon added candle making as a tourist attraction, and the scent of their ten-inch bayberry tapers lured visitors inside. While the Candle Factory now produces over 13 million candles a year in more than 70 different shapes, colors, and scents, the fragrant aromas of rose, pine, lemon, jasmine, and bayberry still beckon travelers.

The process begins when paraffin is brought to the factory in a specially designed truck. The truck's holding tank is surrounded by steam coils that keep the paraffin hot. Steam coils also keep the paraffin in liquid form in the holding tanks behind the factory and in the pipes that bring it to the production area.

Most of the Candle Factory's production area, where candles are made by dipping, pouring, and molding, is visible through the large observation-booth window. Scents and dyes are stirred into the 180° wax, and parallel rows of hanging wicks are dipped over and over into the bubbling vats. To ensure that the candles are evenly shaped, they are dipped 42 times. Although a machine does the dipping, dexterous workers must then trim the wicks, put the candles in a die-cut mold to shape the bases, and polish and box them. The factory can produce over 1,000 of these tapers in two hours. Each year the factory uses 1 million pounds of wax and 6 million feet of wick.

Poured candles are made by pouring hot wax into a ceramic or glass container with a wick inside. Since the wax shrinks as it cools, a second pouring is needed to fully fill the container. For molded candles, wax is poured twice into a cylindrical mold. Once removed from the mold, the new candles must be trimmed, straightened, polished, and boxed. The largest molded candles must be shaped by hand.

Cost: Free

Freebies: No

Video Shown: A button in observation booth starts informative 9-minute video that describes candle and soap making and Candle Factory history. Shows processes not seen from booth.

Reservations Needed: No

Days and Hours: Mon–Fri 9:00 AM–5:30 PM. Candle Factory is in production Mon–Fri; video in observation room is available same hours and days as gift shop. Closed Thanksgiving, Christmas to New Year's, and July 4th week.

Plan to Stay: 20 minutes for self-guided tour from observation room, plus time for gift shops.

Minimum Age: None

Disabled Access: Yes

Group Requirements: No advance reservations needed. Tour buses welcome. No maximum group size; however, only 30 people can fit in room at one time.

Retail Store: Candle Factory sells wide selection of candles and soaps, candle accessories (such as holders and sconces), factory seconds, and market test runs. Open Mon–Sun 9:00 AM–5:00 PM. Call for extended summer and fall hours. Closed Thanksgiving, Christmas, and New Year's. Other shops on premises include Barney's Country Store, Quilts and Needlework Shop, Emporium, and Christmas House.

Directions: From I-64, take Exit 231A (Norge exit). Take Hwy. 607 in the direction that exit lets you off. Turn left onto Richmond Rd. (Rt. 60). Candle Factory is on right. From I-95, take I-295 South to I-64 East. Follow above directions.

Nearby Attractions: Williamsburg Pottery Factory and Williamsburg Doll Factory tours (see pages 339 and 338); Anheuser-Busch (Budweiser) Brewery tour (call 757-253-3600); Colonial Williamsburg; Busch Gardens; James River Plantation; Richmond Road, "the Discount Boulevard of Virginia."

Rowena's

758 West 22nd Street
Norfolk, VA 23517
(800) 627-8699
www.rowenas.com

POUND CAKES, JAMS, JELLIES, COOKING SAUCES, AND GIFTS

For a taste of Southern hospitality and mouth-watering pound cake, stop by Rowena's in Norfolk. Rowena's began in 1983, when friends and family urged Rowena Fullinwider to sell her jams and cakes, which were already favorite gifts and charity-bake-sale items. Today, Rowena's is a million-dollar business that ships its foods nationwide and overseas.

Your tour begins in Rowena's retail store. Within the maze of its compact operation, you'll see every stage of production. As you enter the kitchen, enjoy the sweet smell of Carrot Jam (a Rowena's specialty) or the zesty scent of Heavenly Curry Sauce. Watch a cook drain jam from the mixing bowl by turning a faucet at the bottom, or stir up a Lemon Curd Sauce with a three-foot whisk.

Your appetite will be further whetted in the next room, where cakes are made. Most of the equipment will be familiar to anyone who cooks, but on a grander scale. You could curl up in one of the two extra-large mixers (originally they belonged to the cruiseship U.S.S. *United States*), and you could make a meal licking one of their huge beaters. Rowena's cooks are especially proud of the two enormous six-shelved rotating ovens. Look inside the window and watch 25 large cakes or 250 small loaf cakes take an hour's ride on the Ferris-wheel racks.

After baking and cooling, the cakes are hand-wrapped and decorated with ribbon. Workers also label all sauce and jam jars with flowery stick-on labels. While this room may be quiet when you visit, it's a scene of round-the-clock action during the busy holiday season. Finally you'll be able to taste any of Rowena's foods available. As you savor pound cake with Raspberry Curd or sample Peach Orange Clove Jam, you will appreciate the TLC that goes into Rowena's products.

Cost: Free

Freebies: "I toured Rowena's" paper hat and lots of samples.

Video Shown: No

Reservations Needed: Yes

Days and Hours: January–September only: Mon–Wed 9:00 AM–3:00 PM. Closed holidays.

Plan to Stay: 30 minutes, plus time in gift shop and tearoom.

Minimum Age: Rowena's prefers that children be of school age.

Disabled Access: Yes

Group Requirements: Maximum group size is 25 people. Call 1 week in advance.

Special Information: Factory gets hot during warm months.

Gift Shop: Sells Rowena's entire line, including Almond, Lemon, and Coconut Pound Cakes, Lemon Curd Sauce, and Heavenly Curry Sauce. Look for seasonally updated recipe leaflets and two children's story cookbooks, *The Adventures of Rowena and the Wonderful Jam and Jelly Factory* and *The Adventures of Rowena and Carrot Jam the Rabbit*. Open year-round Mon–Fri 8:30 AM–5:00 PM. Catalog and information available at above number.

Tea Room: Charming English tea room serves Rowena's treats on silver-tiered trays with perfectly brewed tea. Open Tue–Fri 11:00 AM–4:00 PM, Sat 11:00 AM–3:00 PM.

Directions: Since street names change frequently, please pay close attention to directions. From Virginia Beach Expwy., take I-64 or I-264 to Waterside Dr. (becomes Boush St.). Turn left on 22nd St. Rowena's is on right at the end of the street. From Richmond, take Granby St. exit. Pass the Virginia Zoological Park on the left and follow Granby St. when it veers to the right. Take a right on 22nd St. Rowena's is at the end of 22nd St. on right.

Nearby Attractions: Chrysler Museum of Art; Waterside; Nauticus Maritime Museum; Norfolk Botanical Garden; Virginia Zoological Park; Hunter Victorian and Hermitage Museums; Virginia Beach and Colonial Williamsburg are less than 45 minutes away.

Williamsburg Doll Factory

7441 Richmond Road
Williamsburg, VA 23188
(757) 564-9703
www.dollfactory.com

Lady Anne, doll

PORCELAIN DOLLS

Williamsburg Doll Factory's showroom instantly transports you to a fanciful world of Victorian weddings and Civil War–era Southern teas. This is the world of Margaret Anne Rothwell and her Lady Anne porcelain dolls.

Margaret Anne's mother taught her to make doll clothing as a child in Belfast, Ireland. When she moved to the U.S., she made dolls for her own daughters. Friends and family urged her to go into business and, in 1977, she began making dolls in her home. Her first business milestone came when her dolls were accepted by theme parks such as Busch Gardens and Walt Disney World. In 1980 she began making porcelain dolls that became very popular; to meet the demand, she moved to her present location. A deal with the QVC shopping network has led to even more success.

Margaret Anne designs each doll's concept. The dress is most important because it determines the doll's complexion, hair color, and style. In the porcelain department, Margaret Anne's son David and other artists create molds, mix porcelain slip, paint, and kiln-fire heads and body parts. Through an observation window, you'll watch them carefully paint doll faces. Completed doll parts are strung with elastic to allow joint-like movement.

Some dolls have porcelain bodies as well as heads and limbs, while others have a "composite" body of latex and clay (a modern version of the glue-and-papier-mâché composite of antique dolls). Every material used in Lady Anne dolls, except some wigs and eyes, is made in the U.S.A.

You can also observe the finishing department operations. Watch a craftsperson glue individual eyelashes onto a doll's face, fit a doll's dress, or crown a doll with a wig of golden curls. After being dressed and inspected, these enchanting dolls are matched with a certificate of authenticity and shipped to a collector who will treasure their quality and beauty.

Cost: Free

Freebies: No

Video Shown: No

Reservations Needed: No, unless groups larger than 30 people want guided tour.

Days and Hours: Mon–Fri 9:00 AM–5:30 PM except during 12:00 PM–1:00 PM lunch. Factory does no weekend production; however, you can view workstations. Closed Thanksgiving, Christmas, and New Year's.

Plan to Stay: 20 minutes for self-guided tour through observation windows, plus time in retail store.

Minimum Age: None, but children must be kept off doll displays.

Disabled Access: Yes

Group Requirements: Groups larger than 30 should call 1 week in advance to arrange for tour guide, maybe even Margaret Anne herself.

Special Information: No photography

Retail Store: Sells limited edition Lady Anne and other collectible dolls, and doll parts for hobbyists. Open Mon–Fri 9:00 AM–5:30 PM (6:00 PM in summer), Sat 9:00 AM–6:00 PM, Sun 10:00 AM–5:00 PM. Closed Thanksgiving, Christmas, and New Year's.

Directions: From I-64, take Exit 231A (Norge exit). Take Hwy. 607 in the direction that exit lets you off. Turn left onto Richmond Rd. (Rt. 60). Doll Factory is on right. From I-95, take I-295 South to I-64 East. Follow above directions.

Nearby Attractions: Williamsburg Pottery and the Candle Factory tours (see pages 339 and 336); Colonial Williamsburg; Busch Gardens; James River Plantations; Richmond Road, "the Discount Boulevard of Virginia."

Williamsburg Pottery Factory

Route 60
Lightfoot, VA 23090
(757) 564-3326
www.williamsburgpottery.com

POTTERY, WOOD, FLORAL DESIGN, AND PLASTER

Williamsburg Pottery Factory is a sprawling, 200-acre monument to America's love of discount shopping, annually attracting over 3.5 million visitors—more than Colonial Williamsburg and Busch Gardens combined. Within the 32 buildings and outlet stores you'll find everything and anything: jewelry, gourmet foods, Oriental rugs, furniture, shoes, plants, imports from around the world, lawn Madonnas, cookware, and pottery. You can also tour the four main factories—pottery/ceramics, woodworking, floral design, and cement/plaster.

The Pottery's nearly 2 million square feet of factory and retail space took nearly 60 years to complete—and it's still growing. It all began in 1938 when James E. Maloney, still active in the business, bought the first half-acre of land, dug a well, built his kiln and a one-room shack for his young wife and himself, and set up his roadside pottery stand. "Jimmy," as he's always been known in these parts, is first, last, and always a potter. He worked closely with Colonial Williamsburg's archeologists and ceramics experts during that colonial capital's restoration by John D. Rockefeller. In 1952 The Pottery became licensed to make and sell replicas of CW's 18th-century salt-glaze and redware. This helped The Pottery grow.

In the pottery/ceramics factory, potters create thousands of pots and decorative home accessories by hand and with molds. Eighteenth-century-style salt-glaze and slipware is made, glazed, and fired here in the giant kiln. Highlights include seeing old-fashioned clay tavern pipes and the famous Williamsburg "Bird Bottle" birdhouses being made. Although signs posted in the workshop provide the basics, the craftspeople are happy to explain their work.

While The Pottery was once known mostly for its pottery, many other things are now made here. In floral design production, designers create arrangements of native Williamsburg dried flowers and plants grown right at The Pottery. At the cement/garden-ware factory building, you can watch fabrication of lawn and garden benches, birdbaths, and fountains. A tour of the plaster factory takes you from mold making through the drying and trimming of plaster wall plaques, statues, containers, and other decorative objects. Among the numerous retail stores are greenhouse, potpourri, cactus, silk-flower arranging, and lamp production areas. You leave feeling that you've had a potpourri of experiences.

Cost: Free

Freebies: No

Video Shown: No

Reservations Needed: No

Days and Hours: Pottery/ceramics factory: Mon–Fri 9:00 AM–3:00 PM with short breaks at 10:00 AM, 12:00 PM, and 2:00 PM. Grounds: Mon–Sun sunup to sundown. Closed Christmas.

Plan to Stay: 1 hour for 4 self-guided tours, plus hours for shopping.

Minimum Age: None

Disabled Access: Yes

Group Requirements: Group tours available by advance arrangement with Marketing Department.

Special Information: Wear comfortable walking shoes and watch where you walk.

Outlet Shops: Pottery's shops sell nearly everything. Shops rustic, but prices are great. Open Sun–Fri 9:00 AM–6:30 PM, Sat 9:00 AM–7:00 PM. Shorter hours January–April. Closed Christmas.

Directions: From I-64, take Exit 234A for Lightfoot. Turn right on Hwy. 199. Turn right at first traffic light. After first stop sign, go through back entrance to grounds. Follow driveway around. Pass nursery. After second stop sign, ceramic factory will be on your right. From I-95 South, take I-64 East; follow above directions.

Nearby Attractions: The Candle Factory and Williamsburg Doll Factory tours (see pages 336 and 338); Colonial Williamsburg; Busch Gardens; James River Plantations.

Boehms Chocolates

255 N.E. Gilman Boulevard
Issaquah, WA 98027
(425) 392-6652
www.boehms.com

CHOCOLATES

A visit to Boehms tells a story, taking you through Julius Boehm's artifact-filled Austrian Alpine home, the candy factory he founded, and the chapel dedicated to mountain-climbers. A climber himself, Boehm was lured to Washington's Cascade Mountains, "America's Alps." He was considered the oldest man, at age 80, to climb 14,000-plus-foot Mt. Rainier. A lover of art and music, he filled his home with such items as a marble replica of Michelangelo's *David,* a wind-up music box, and a potpourri of Bavarian Old World artifacts.

Downstairs from Boehm's home is the candy factory. The pungent chocolate smell fills the air. Depending on the day, different sweets simmer in the kitchen. Mixers' metal blades stir Victorian creams. A worker with a wooden paddle stirs a truffle or peanut-brittle mixture in a copper cauldron before pouring it onto a steel cooling table and spreading it to the thickness of the steel bars at the long table's edges.

Women, trained in the art of hand-dipping chocolate, roll out the day's soft filling into round strips. With one hand they pinch off a portion, gently tossing it to the other hand, which continuously swirls the chocolate around on a marble slab to maintain the desired temperature. This process coats the filling and decorates the top. Other varieties of centers pass through the enrober's chocolate waterfall to get their chocolate coating. After traveling through a cooling tunnel, all chocolates are hand-packed into gift boxes for distribution to Boehms' retail stores.

Next visit the Luis Trenker Kirch'l, a replica of a 12th-century Swiss chapel near St. Moritz. Boehm built this masculine church with a boulder inside as a dedication to mountain climbers who died attempting to reach their mountains' summits. Current Boehms owner Bernard Garbusjuk, trained as a pastry chef in his German homeland, proudly boasts that your tour isn't too commercialized since it ends in the chapel and not at the gift shop.

Cost: Free

Freebies: Chocolate samples

Video Shown: No

Reservations Needed: Yes, for guided tour; no, for self-guided tour.

Days and Hours: Factory floor guided tours available for individuals and families mid-June–end of August only. Mon–Fri (except Wed) 10:30 AM, 1:00 PM, and 2:15 PM, Sat–Sun 1:00 PM. Self-guided viewing through windows available year-round including weekends. Closed holidays.

Plan to Stay: 45 minutes for factory, home, and chapel tour, plus time for gift shop and grounds.

Minimum Age: None, for families. Children in groups must be 6 years or older with one adult for every 5 children.

Disabled Access: Yes, for factory and chapel. Difficult for home.

Group Requirements: Minimum group size is 15; maximum is 50. Groups should call 1 month in advance.

Special Information: Limited production on weekends. Foreign-language tours arranged with advance notice. Chapel available for rental.

Gift Shop: Sells all 160 luscious Boehms candies including Boehms' specialties, Mozart Kugeln (marzipan and filbert paste center double-dipped in chocolate) and Mount Rainier (caramel fudge and cherry center dipped in chocolate). Open year-round Mon–Sat 10:00 AM–6:00 PM, Sun 11:00 AM–6:00 PM. Closed some holidays. Call ahead to check. Mail-order brochure available.

Directions: From I-90, take Exit 17. Follow Front St. to Issaquah. Turn left onto Gilman Blvd. Two candy canes mark entrance.

Nearby Attractions: Boeing, Microsoft Museum, and Redhook Ale Brewery tours (see pages 341, 344, and 345); Lake Sammamish State Park; Snoqualmie Falls; Gilman Village; Salmon Days Festival in October. Seattle's downtown attractions, including Pike Place Market and the Space Needle, 13 miles away.

Boeing

Tour Center
Highway 526
Everett, WA 98206
(800) 464-1476
www.boeing.com

COMMERCIAL AIRCRAFT

Touring Boeing's 747, 767, and 777 aircraft plant is like visiting the Grand Canyon. You oversee the assembly areas from a third-story walkway, marveling at the size of the facility (it's the world's largest-volume building;—11 stories high, 98 acres) while attempting to grasp the details of the process. As with the Grand Canyon, it's best to just take in the vastness, listen to your tour guide, and be awed by it all.

A short bus ride from this 1,000-acre complex's visitor center, a long brisk walk though an underground tunnel, and an elevator ride take you to the open-air mezzanine observation deck. Gaze out over the subassembly floor as different airplane parts slowly come to life. The loud rivet-guns' spattering fills the air, as earmuffed workers assemble plane wings, passenger bays, and nose cones. Overhead, cranes zigzag back and forth with plane parts.

You may see up to thirteen 747s, 767s, or 777s on the final assembly floor at any one time. Don't expect to watch an entire plane created before your eyes. A new 747 rolls out about every five days, helping Boeing capture nearly 60 percent of the global commercial aircraft market. Notice the true colors of the jumbo jet's shiny metals and materials, the miles of wiring, the electronic components, and the other plane innards you take for granted at 30,000 feet. As the bus travels back to the tour center, you'll pass the paint hangar. Sitting nearby on the runway waiting for flight tests are freshly painted jets headed for airlines around the world.

Cost: Adults, $5; children under 15 and seniors 62 and older, $3.

Freebies: Brochure

Video Shown: All tours begin with one of several short videos.

Reservations Needed: Recommended Memorial Day–Labor Day. Groups larger than 10 people should always call in advance.

Days and Hours: Mon–Fri 9:00 AM–11:00 AM, and 1:00 PM–3:00 PM, on the hour. Call (800) 464-1476 for additional tour times during peak season (May through October). Closed holidays, week between Christmas and New Year's, and for special events. Same-day tickets available from 8:30 AM and may sell out by 12:00 PM.

Plan to Stay: 90 minutes for video and tour, plus time for gift store and wait.

Minimum Age: Children must be 50 inches tall.

Disabled Access: Yes

Group Requirements: Groups of 10 or more people should make advance reservations. Maximum group is 50 people. Reservation fee, $10 per person. Call (800) 464-1476 for group reservations.

Special Information: No photography allowed on Boeing property. GrayLine of Seattle also offers tour with guaranteed entrance. The Boeing company museum in St. Louis, MO, also gives tours (see page 215).

Gift Store: The Flight Line Gift Store sells souvenir and gift items with Boeing logo, including clothing, miniature airplanes, postcards, and aviation books and posters. Open Mon–Fri 9:00 AM–5:00 PM. Closed holidays. Call (425) 342-8500 for special events.

Directions: Located 25 miles north of Seattle. Take I-5 to Exit 189. Go west on State Hwy. 526 and follow signs to Boeing Tour Center.

Nearby Attractions: Boehms Chocolates, Microsoft Museum, and Redhook Ale Brewery tours (see pages 340, 344, and 345); *Seattle Times* North Creek tour (call 425-489-7015); Everett Center for the Arts; Animal Farm; Firefighters Museum; Kasch Park; Walter E. Hall Park and Golf Course; Silver Lake Park. Museum of Flight at Boeing Field in Seattle (call 206-764-5700). Tour Center desk has Everett Visitor's Guide, which includes all local attractions, accommodations, restaurants, and map.

Frito-Lay

4808 N.W. Fruit Valley Road
Vancouver, WA 98660
(360) 737-3000
www.fritolay.com

In 1932 two entrepreneurs unaware of each other set out on similar paths that would eventually lead to Frito-Lay, Inc. In Texas, Elmer Doolin and his mother, Daisy, cooked Fritos brand corn chips in her kitchen at night. By day, he sold them from the back of his Model-T Ford. Meanwhile, in Tennessee, Herman W. Lay sold potato chips from the back of his Model A. In 1945 the two companies began selling each other's products; they merged in 1961 and became part of PepsiCo in 1965.

After your guide shows you the color-coded oil- and corn-holding tanks behind the plant, peek through the entranceway into the Fritos, Doritos brand, and Tostitos brand tortilla chips "kitchen" area. Corn is ground between large milling stones to form masa, a golden dough. An extruder flattens ribbons of masa, and whirling blades cut them. These raw Fritos fall into a precisely heated blend of oils, where they curl up as they cook. For Doritos and Tostitos, masa is pressed into a thick sheet and fed through rollers. Large cutters then stamp it into triangles or circles. As the shapes flash-bake in large, 700° toaster ovens, flames create golden flecks and small "bubbles" in them. The proofer equalizes their moisture content, and then all three products are salted and seasoned.

At least 7 million pounds of potatoes arrive daily at 40 Frito-Lay plants across the nation. Employees hand-inspect the washed, peeled potatoes, which then drop into a round, spinning tub. Centrifugal force helps straight blades slice Lays brand potato chips; blades shaped like tambourines with rippled edges cut Ruffles brand potato chips. After the slices cook in hot oil, they're salted or seasoned and cooled in a rotating drum. Before packaging, they pass through the potato-chip sizer, which sorts out small chips for small bags and large chips for large bags.

Visit the Cheetos brand cheese-flavored snacks area. Stone-ground cornmeal is kneaded into a smooth, hot, elastic dough, which is then pressed through an extruder's tiny holes. The change of pressure and temperature when the bits of hot dough leave the extruder causes them to expand and begin to pop and bounce. A sharp blade cuts these nuggets of popped cornmeal before oven baking or frying. You'll be amazed by the giant, hollow, spinning cylinder in which the pale-yellow Cheetos bounce around to receive a real cheese coating, emerging bright orange.

See the highly automated packaging process before visiting the large warehouse, which can store only one-and-a-half days' output. You'll leave filled with tastes of all the freshly made Frito-Lay products—and you'll know how Ruffles got their ridges.

Cost: Free
Freebies: Fresh samples during tour
Video Shown: No
Reservations Needed: Yes. Individuals and families must join scheduled group tour.
Days and Hours: Mon and Tue by reservation only. No summer tours. Closed holidays.
Plan to Stay: 1 hour
Minimum Age: 5
Disabled Access: Yes, limited to lower level.
Group Requirements: Minimum group is 5 people; maximum is 40. Call at least a month in advance.
Special Information: No photography. No jewelry, shorts, or open-toed shoes. Can be quite warm in summer. Frito-Lay once had national tour program; now only a few factories still give tours, mostly to local groups.
Gift Shop: No
Directions: From I-5, take 4th Plain exit. Go west on 4th Plain Blvd. Turn right onto Fruit Valley Rd. Factory is about 1 mile ahead on left.
Nearby Attractions: Fort Vancouver; Officer's Row.

Liberty Orchards

117 Mission Street
Cashmere, WA 98815
(509) 782-4088 / (800) 231-3242
www.libertyorchards.com

LIBERTY ORCHARDS CO. INC.
CASHMERE, WASHINGTON 98815, U.S.A.

FRUIT CANDIES

The story of Liberty Orchards is the story of two Armenian immigrants striving to succeed in the U.S.A. After failed attempts at running a yogurt factory and an Armenian restaurant, in 1918 they purchased an apple orchard, which they called Liberty Orchards to honor their new homeland. Aplets and Cotlets fruit candies, originally known as "Confections of the Fairies," grew out of a use for surplus fruit.

A guided tour of Liberty Orchards, now in its third generation, shows you how they create these natural fruit-flavored candies. Start your tour in the nut-sorting room, where California walnuts and Hawaiian macadamia nuts are sorted. Visit the Old-World kitchen where concoctions of fruit juices, fruit purees, pectin, sugar, and cornstarch cook at 230° in stainless-steel kettles large enough to produce 256 pounds of candy. As the candy boils, steam emerges from the kettles, and a fruity, perfumed aroma fills the air. With long metal paddles, the cook stirs the bubbling concoction and then tastes it for correct consistency—a tough job, but someone has to do it. The cook's helpers pour the hot candy into smaller kettles and add nuts and natural flavoring. Then they pour the candy into long, plastic-lined wooden trays, roll it flat, and cover it for a day's rest in the cooler.

In the factory, workers flip the slabs of cooled candy out of their trays and coat the candy with cornstarch, which acts as a natural preservative to keep moisture inside. Candy-cutters cut the candy into bite-size cubes. Tumblers coat the sides of the cubes with cornstarch and then cover them with powdered sugar. Nimble-fingered packers hand-pack the candies into plastic trays at a rate of 4,000 to 5,000 per hour per packer. Fortunately the tour guides pass out free samples of these chewy treats, or you would be tempted to reach into the packing bins.

Cost: Free

Freebies: 3 different flavors of candies.

Video Shown: No, but you can purchase colorfully illustrated 20-page booklet called "The Story of Aplets & Cotlets," which covers family history, product and packaging development, and production process.

Reservations Needed: No, but preferred for groups larger than 12 people.

Days and Hours: April–December: Mon–Fri 8:00 AM–5:30 PM, Sat–Sun 10:00 AM–4:00 PM. Occasional weekend production. No production during 11:00 AM–11:30 PM lunch break and after 4:00 PM. January–March: Mon–Fri 8:30 AM–4:30 PM. Tours run every 20 minutes, stopping half hour before closing. Closed New Year's, Christmas, Thanksgiving, President's Day, and Easter.

Plan to Stay: 15 minutes, plus time for Country Store.

Minimum Age: None. Children under 16 must be accompanied by adults.

Disabled Access: Yes

Group Requirements: Groups larger than 12 people will be split into smaller groups. Call 2 days in advance.

Special Information: Floor can be slippery. Production generally Mon–Fri, plus occasional weekends. Liberty Orchards is in heart of Washington's apple industry, which produces 5 billion apples per year—half of all the apples eaten in America.

Gift Shop: Country Store sells all Liberty Orchards fruit and nut candies (such as Aplets and Cotlets), apple gifts, and Northwest products. Open same hours as tour. Catalog available from (800) 888-5696.

Directions: From Seattle, take U.S. 2 East. Take Cashmere exit, which puts you on Aplets Way. Follow Aplets & Cotlets signs. Turn left onto Mission St. Liberty Orchards is on left.

Nearby Attractions: Boeing Everett plant tour (see page 341); October Apple Days festival; Nearby Cascade loop attractions include Leavenworth Bavarian Village, Ohme Gardens, and Rocky Reach Dam.

Microsoft Museum

4420 148th Ave. NE
Redmond, WA 98052
(425) 703-6214
www.microsoft.com/museum

PERSONAL COMPUTERS AND SOFTWARE

At the Microsoft Museum, you won't find Monet, but you will be able to touch the exhibits. This highly interactive museum offers a journey through the vision, technology, history, and culture of the Microsoft Corporation. Microsoft's original mission to have a personal computer in every home once seemed farfetched. However, today it is close to reality. Take a self-guided exploration into the past, present, and future of Microsoft at the Microsoft campus in Redmond, Washington.

As you walk through the entrance, see an overview and display of Microsoft's vision, products, and services beginning with Microsoft's first software. Although they were only designed in the mid-1970s, some of the items are already considered archaic. Once you appreciate the origin of technology, prepare to experience present-day technology and look to the future.

Enter the first of four interactive exhibit areas: "Inside Microsoft." Explore the nearly history of Microsoft by looking at a timeline highlighting company milestones, a Bill Gates exhibit, the world's first personal computer (the Altair 8800—Microsoft wrote its first piece of software for this machine), and other important company artifacts. Get a feel for Microsoft's corporate culture by looking at daily life. Next, move into the "Living Zone." Discover how technology is changing and shaping our everyday lives as you focus more on the desires of individual consumers. Here you can try out the latest PC games, the Xbox, MSN, WindowsXP, OfficeXP, and other products for home.

Once you feel like you've played enough, walk into the "Learning Zone." The "Learning Zone" focuses on how methods of teaching and learning are being transformed by technology. Learn about Microsoft's vision for a Connected Learning Community, a vast computer network for the purpose of sharing ideas and education. Also, test Microsoft's educational programs like Encarta and the Magic School Bus Series. Your last stop is the "Working Zone." Experience how continuous technological innovations at Microsoft have transformed the business world. Workplace products, such as mobile computing, the Tablet PC, and small business products are featured.

With so many interactive exhibits, the Museum really engages its visitors and provides hands-on entertainment that is as informative as it is fun. With facts, history, and humor, the Museum thoroughly captures Microsoft's distinctive culture, revealing the personalities behind the scenes.

Cost: Free

Freebies: Microsoft Museum pencils and activity brochures for school groups.

Videos Shown: Corporate videos highlight new Microsoft products and historical milestones.

Reservations Needed: No, except for groups of 10 or more.

Days and Hours: Mon–Fri 9:00 AM–7:00 PM. Call ahead if you want to visit after 5:00 PM; Museum sometimes closes for special occasions.

Plan to Stay: 1 hour or more for self-guided tour.

Minimum Age: None

Disabled Access: Yes

Group Requirements: Groups of 10 or more people must call ahead. The museum welcomes school field trips and community groups.

Gift Shop: For employees only.

Directions: Take SR 520 East toward Redmond to the 40th Ave. NE exit and turn left onto 40th Ave. Turn right onto 150th Ave. NE. Continue about 1.5 blocks. Museum is in green building on the left side of street.

Nearby Attractions: Boehms Chocolates, Boeing, and Redhook Ale Brewery tours (see pages 340, 341, and 345); Lake Washington; Seattle's attractions, including Pacific Science Center, Pike Place Market, Boeing's Air and Space museum, and Space Needle, 13 miles away.

Redhook Ale Brewery

14300 NE 145th Street
Woodinville, WA 98072
(425) 483-3232
www.redhook.com

BEER

Founded in 1981, Redhook Ale Brewery has become one of the most respected regional breweries in the Northwest. Redhook blends perfectly the use of modern technology and old-world tradition, to brew its classic pub-style I.P.A. (India Pale Ale) and full, rich Redhook E.S.B. ale (Extra Special Bitter), both of which have a loyal following in the region.

The 24-acre site was modeled after a Bavarian brewery in Andechs, Germany, and includes a Public House, outdoor beer garden, and pub. Enter the steel and concrete main building under the portico. Make your way to the Forecaster's Pub, where the tour guide begins with a brief history of Redhook.

Follow the tour guide to the Tour Gallery, where you are immediately aware of the sweet smell of hops and malt. Press your nose against the windows to look into the brewhouse. You'll notice computer control panels monitoring the amounts of malted barley, hops, yeast, and water. Proceed to the fermentation cellar, which houses numerous stainless-steel tanks—not a copper tank in sight! The rows of polished tanks, with their maze of pipes and valves, have automatic mechanisms to regulate temperature and pressure. The equipment even allows brewers to transfer batches from vessel to vessel without manual labor.

Then prepare your senses for the bottling hall. It's so loud the guide stops speaking and lets the visual process explain itself. From your position on the open-air catwalk, watch the empty bottles get rinsed, filled, crowned, and labeled. You may experience déjà vu—the automated bottling line is reminiscent of the opening sequence in *Laverne and Shirley*. If you can sing the show's theme song, the guide will give you a free pint! Even if you can't, everyone of drinking age samples Redhook beers throughout the tour.

A century-old German company designed Redhook's brewing equipment, making it one of the most technically advanced breweries. However, although high-tech equipment may play a big role in Redhook's beer making, as a "craft" brewery, Redhook follows the German purity law, using only water, malt, hops, and yeast to create beer in the European tradition.

Cost: $1

Freebies: Samples of Redhook ales and tasting glass.

Video Shown: No

Reservations Needed: No

Days and Hours: Winter: Mon–Fri 2:00 PM and 4:00 PM; Sat and Sun 1:00 PM, 3:00 PM, and 5:00 PM. Summer: Mon–Fri 1:00 PM, 3:00 PM, and 5:00 PM; Sat and Sun 12:00 PM–5:00 PM on the hour. Closed Thanksgiving, Christmas, and New Year's. Bottling line runs Mon and Tue.

Plan to Stay: 1 hour for tour and beer sampling, plus time to drink and eat at Forecaster's Pub.

Minimum Age: None, however minors may need supervision.

Disabled Access: Yes

Group Requirements: None

Special Information: The company has an architecturally similar brewery in Portsmouth, NH. Call (603) 430-8600 for tour times.

Gift Shop: Forecaster's Pub sells shirts, beer mugs, and other accessories with Redhook logo or picture of brewery, along with catered menu and full selection of Redhook beers. Open Mon–Thur 11:00 AM–10:00 PM, Fri and Sat 11:00 AM–midnight, Sun 11:00 AM–7:00 PM.

Directions: From I-5, take I-90 East to I-405 North. Take Hwy. 522 East, Exit 23. Take Woodinville Exit and stay to the right. At the second light, turn right onto NE 175th St. At the 4-way intersection, turn left onto Hwy. 202. Continue approximately 2 miles. Redhook Ale Brewery is just past Columbia Winery on the left.

Nearby Attractions: Boehms Chocolates, Boeing, and Microsoft Museum tours (see pages 340, 341, and 344); Columbia Winery (call 425-488-2776); Chateau St. Michelle tours and tasting (call 425-488-3300); Molbaks Nursery (call 425-483-5000).

Seattle's Best Coffee

19529 Vashon Island Highway
Vashon, WA 98070
(206) 463-5050
www.seattlesbest.com

COFFEE

The birth of America's love of gourmet coffee started in the Pacific Northwest, and Seattle's Best Coffee has been a key player. Founded by James Stewart in 1970, Seattle's Best Coffee has sprouted into a national retail store chain and mail-order operation. You can visit SBC's small specialty and certified organic-roasting facility (one of two the company uses to roast its coffee) on bucolic Vashon Island.

Before you enter this two-story 1914 converted country store (originally a dance hall over a dry-goods store), relax on the porch chairs. Inside the tasting room, your tour guide explains that roasting, the hands-on art that unlocks the coffee's flavor, is the most important process in coffee making. Learn that the longer coffee beans are roasted, the darker they become.

You may be lucky enough to observe a professional tasting in action. Seated at the heavy granite cupping table, which spins like a lazy Susan, master roaster Peter Larsen, founder Jim Stewart, and director of quality assurance Dave Wickberg taste and evaluate different coffees. Observe them as they sample a small spoonful of coffee, rapidly inhaling the coffee, forcing it to spray over their tongue while drawing in air. They swirl the coffee in their mouths and discard it into the two-foot high aluminum spittoons positioned at their feet. The cuppers evaluate each coffee for its aroma, acidity, body, and flavor.

Walk along the weathered wooden floor to the museum area. Illuminate an interactive world map showing the world's coffee-growing regions, and see coffee packages from Japan, Germany, and Saudi Arabia. Notice the collage of unusual items SBC has found over the years in the burlap bags of coffee beans it receives—soccer and lottery tickets, cigarette packages from Indonesia, belt buckles, and other common objects (coins, nails, etc.)—all screened out during the production process.

Look down over the balcony railing at the red German Probat Roaster. Several times a week, it roasts 132-pound batches of organic coffee for approximately 20 minutes. Afterwards, they cool in a stainless-steel pan at the lower side of the roaster. You'll leave with a new appreciation for the cup of coffee you drink every morning.

Cost: Free
Freebies: 4-oz. sample of the day. On front porch, coffee available for 50 cents per cup.
Video Shown: No
Reservations Needed: Yes. Call the day you plan to visit to see if they will be roasting.
Days and Hours: Mon–Fri 10:00 AM–3:00 PM. Closed major holidays. Since tours are rather informal here, you'll need to ask the person working behind the retail counter to give you a tour.
Plan to Stay: 15 minutes, plus time in store.
Minimum Age: None
Disabled Access: Yes, for retail store and museum area. Tight quarters for tasting room.
Group Requirements: Groups over 4 adults should call 1 week in advance. Groups over 12 people will be split into smaller groups.
Special Information: Roasting process is loud.
Retail Store: Sells SBC bulk and pre-packed coffees, coffee and espresso makers, thermoses, logoed ceramic and plastic tumblers, as well as latte bowls. Open Mon–Fri 7:00 AM–6:00 PM, Sat 9:00 AM–4:00 PM. Also open Sun 10:00 AM–3:00 PM, in summer. Catalog available from (800) 962-9659.
Directions: Take ferry from Seattle or Tacoma to Vashon Island. Vashon Hwy. is the main street off ferry. SBC is in the center of town.
Nearby Attractions: Vashon Island beaches and peaceful biking roads.

Washington's Fruit Place Visitor Center

105 South 18th Street
Yakima, WA 98901
(509) 576-3090
www.fruitplace.com

FRUIT

Never had the opportunity to walk through an apple or cherry orchard? Well, the Washington's Fruit Place Visitor Center offers the next best thing: a life-sized photomural of these orchards. Experience not only harvest time, but also the winter and spring orchard months—all at once! See an apple tree, its branches devoid of fruit, but covered in pretty, glistening snow. Gaze at a cherry tree, in bloom, dressed in blossoms of pink and white. Regard both kinds of trees heavy with fruit, so real that you are tempted to reach up, pluck a piece, and take a bite. On the photo wall, view ripe pears, apricots, and peaches. A spotlight shines on them, highlighting their beautiful green and orange colors.

From here, with photographs and step-by-step descriptions, learn the process that apples pass through, from orchard to shipping. Note that Washington's hot days and cool nights are the ideal conditions for the apples to thrive. As part of this exhibit, look through the window of a miniature controlled-atmosphere storage room. Observe the little bins of apples stacked one upon the other. Open the front door and listen to the revving of a forklift's engine. In this airtight room, the oxygen level is greatly reduced, the carbon dioxide is removed, and the temperature stays just above freezing. Essentially, the apples "take a nap" and remain as fresh as the day they left the orchard.

Next, join a crowd of many ages gathered around a large wall map. Watch as a curious child presses a button corresponding to a picture of a red apple. As she does so, the country of Spain lights up, instantly revealing where in the world Washington-grown red apples are shipped. Press the button corresponding to Italy, and discover what fruits are exported there. Keep pressing buttons, and be amazed at the areas of the world where Washington's apples, cherries, pears, plums, nectarines, peaches, and apricots travel.

For extra fun, tour the Visitor Center while the Cherry Harvest Festival or Apple Harvest Festival is taking place. Listen to live music. Shake hands or have your picture taken with Crispy Apple or Mr. Cherry Man, complete with his cherry head, top hat, and tuxedo. Watch as a red-haired clown paints a plum on a child's face. Sample many varieties of cherries and apples. Best of all, feast on wonderful sweets, such as chocolate-covered cherries and caramel-dipped apples.

Cost: Free

Freebies: Fruit samples, can of Tree Top Apple Juice, and recipes.

Video Shown: 5-minute video overviews the fruit process, from orchard to shipping.

Reservations Needed: No, for self-guided tours. Yes, for guided tours and groups of 20 or more.

Days and Hours: Mon–Fri 10:00 AM–5:00 PM. May–December: also Sat 10:00 AM–4:00 PM. Closed holidays.

Plan to Stay: 45 minutes, plus time for the gift shop.

Minimum Age: None

Disabled Access: Yes

Group Requirements: Groups of 20 or more must make reservations.

Special Information: Cherry Harvest Festival occurs during June/July. Apple Harvest Festival occurs during October. Call for exact dates and times.

Gift Shop: Sells fruit-themed items, including preserves, apple butter, cider, clothing, toys, jewelry, and books. Open same hours as tour.

Directions: Take I-82 to Yakima Ave. Terrace Heights exit. Follow the signs to Terrace Heights. Turn right onto South 18th St. Visitor Center is on the left.

Nearby Attractions: Sarg Hubbard Park; Yakima Greenway trail system; Yakima Arboretum; McGuire Youth Playground; Washington Apple Commission Visitor Center in Wenatchee (approx. 2 to 3 hours from Yakima; call 509-663-9600 for more information).

Blenko Glass

Fair Grounds Road
Milton, WV 25541
(304) 743-9081
www.blenkoglass.com

GLASS

BLENKO GLASS COMPANY, INC.

At Blenko Glass, you will see a three- to four-inch diameter "gob" of molten glass transformed into a foot-high water vase or pitcher right before your eyes. This self-guided tour allows you to stand behind a wooden railing and observe glassmaking for as long as you want. Only a few yards away workers hold yard-long blowpipes, or "punties," with red-hot glass at the end. You'll feel the heat gushing out of the furnaces. Although there are no signs to explain the glassblowing process, you will quickly figure out the steps by their artful repetition.

It takes six people and about five minutes to initially shape each item. A "gatherer" delivers a glass gob to a blower seated at a workbench. The blower, who has at least eight years of experience, rolls the punty along the arms of his workbench with his left hand and cups the glass into a wooden scoop-shaped block held in his right. The blower constantly twirls the punty to keep the glass from sagging. Then he lowers it into a hand-carved cherry wood mold and blows air into the punty's opposite end so the glass fills up the mold. Another craftsperson then gently kicks the mold's clamps open and, with a two-pronged pitchfork, carries the translucent object to the finisher. After several more steps, which require reheating, the finished piece is allowed to cool.

Walk through the museum on the second floor as you make on your way to the observation area, and learn about Blenko's history. The company started in 1893 to manufacture stained glass for windows but has since diversified. Exhibits include some of Blenko's custom products, such as green and crystal glass buttons made for Miss West Virginia in the 1960s, a paperweight commemorating George Bush's inauguration, and the Country Music Award Trophy. In the Designer's Corner, stained-glass windows made by nine leading American studios glow in the sunlight.

Outside, the "Garden of Glass" affords a relaxing stroll along a gravel walkway lined with stone benches and a menagerie of glass animals. Walk over the wooden footbridge, alongside a fountain, to a peaceful three-acre lake. You'll want to end your tour at the adjacent outlet store, which offers great values on Blenko glass.

Cost: Free

Freebies: No

Video Shown: No

Reservations Needed: No, except for groups larger than 50 people.

Days and Hours: Mon–Fri 8:00 AM–12:00 PM and 12:30 PM–3:00 PM to watch craftspeople. Plant is closed for 2 weeks beginning around July 1 and week between Christmas and New Year's.

Plan to Stay: 30 minutes for self-guided tour and museum, plus time for outlet store.

Minimum Age: None, but children must be supervised.

Disabled Access: Yes, for outlet store and "Garden of Glass." However, flight of stairs leads to museum and observation gallery.

Group Requirements: Groups larger than 50 should call ahead to avoid time conflicts with other groups.

Special Information: Due to furnaces, observation deck is hot in summer.

Factory Outlet/Museum: Store's tables are crammed with various colored vases, seconds, discontinued items, and bargains. Store and museum hours: Mon–Sat 8:00 AM–4:00 PM and Sun 12:00 PM–4:00 PM. Catalog available at above number.

Directions: Take I-64 to Exit 28, then Rt. 60 West. Turn left at traffic light onto Fair Grounds Rd. Follow signs to Blenko Glass Visitor Center.

Nearby Attractions: Gibson Glass, makers of multicolored paperweights, offers self-guided tour (call 304-743-5232); October West Virginia Pumpkin Festival; Camden Park; Berryhill House and Gardens & Craft Center.

Brooke Glass

130 6th Street
Wellsburg, WV 26070
(304) 737-0619

Brooke

GLASS

Brooke Glass is the last surviving glass factory in a town that once had many. The company's buildings have been used by glassmakers since 1879, originally by Riverside Glass. Primarily making pressed-glass products through the years, the company adapted its product lines to the times. In the 1930s and '40s, it made taillights for cars and railroad lantern globes. Today it makes popular Victorian-style and art deco lamp and lighting fixture parts, candle glass, and other giftware items.

The video part of the tour begins in the mold room, where various sizes of cast-iron molds are repaired and cleaned, awaiting their use. These intricate molds can cost thousands of dollars and become the temporary home for molten hot glass. In the main production area, the two ovens glow from the tremendous heat needed to melt together the components that form glass. A worker uses an iron rod with a ceramic or stainless steel ball on the end to gather an orange glob of glass, which is then placed into the mold. The excess molten glass is snipped off. Sometimes the mold is then put into a machine that spins it at such a high speed that the glass pattern seems to grow out of the mold.

Quickly the mold is placed under an air compressor, where it cools enough to solidify the glass. The mold is then opened. What was glowing orange molten glass only a few seconds earlier is now a clear-colored light fixture or vase. A second worker gently removes the piece from the cast-iron mold and puts it into the fire polisher for a few seconds before it heads off for cooling. This two-person process continues at a rapid, mesmerizing rate.

After the video, you'll hear drills putting holes into the tops of the solid glass lighting fixtures and notice workers dipping the clear glass pieces into a special acid bath that frosts them. In the art department, the cool, peaceful artistry contrasts nicely with the other parts of the factory. The artists sit around a big wooden table, with racks of glass pieces waiting for their decoration. Each artist gracefully dips her brush into a paint palette wheel before applying the colors of a floral pattern or nature scene, or perhaps customizing a glass giftware item for a wedding party.

Cost: Free

Freebies: No

Video Shown: 15-minute video available for viewing in gift shop upon request or when factory not in production.

Reservations Needed: Yes

Days and Hours: Mon–Fri 10:00 AM and 2:00 PM. Extra times available for groups. Closed holidays and first 2 weeks in July.

Plan to Stay: 25 minutes for tour, plus time for gift shop.

Minimum Age: No, but could be hot and noisy for young children.

Disabled Access: A few steps lead up to the factory and gift-shop buildings.

Group Requirements: Groups of 15 or more people should call at least 3 days in advance. No maximum group size.

Special Information: No photography. Occasionally do glassblowing, but mostly pressed and, sometimes, spun glass.

Gift Shop: Sells first-quality Brooke Glass items, including lamp and lighting fixtures, candleholders, and bells. Can etch names and other designs to personalize glass pieces. Matching and restoration of antique glass shades available. Open Mon–Sat 9:30 AM–5:00 PM. Closed major holidays.

Directions: From I-70, take West Virginia Rt. 2 North toward Wellsburg. Turn left at Sixth St. in Wellsburg. Park in gift shop parking lot. Tour starts in store.

Nearby Attractions: Creegan Company and Senator Heinz history tours (see pages 256 and 294); Weirton Steel tour (call Weirton Transit at 304-797-8597 to arrange tour); Brooke County Museum; Wheeling's attractions, including Oglebay, 15 miles away.

Fenton Art Glass

420 Caroline Avenue
Williamstown, WV 26187
(304) 375-7772
www.fentongiftshop.com

FENTON
Handcrafted Glass Artistry Since 1905

THE HISTORIC
RIVER CITIES
OF OHIO AND WEST VIRGINIA

West Virginia
Wild and Wonderful

GLASS

In western West Virginia, rich in mountains, sand, and natural gas, the ancient art of glassmaking is kept alive by a handful of artisans and factories. Fenton Art Glass began in 1905, when two Fenton brothers pooled $284 to start their business. Now in its fourth generation of family ownership and management, Fenton Art Glass continues this art in the U.S.A. The tour takes you from the extreme heat and speed of the glassmaking shops to the decorating area's exacting calm.

After a brief chemistry lesson (sand is glass's main ingredient), follow your guide onto the blow/press shop floor. Gatherers, handlers, and carriers dodge around you with gobs of red-hot glass, handles, and freshly blown or pressed pieces. Each worker, trained by apprenticeship, has a specific function in the team effort of creating each item. To produce a bowl, the "gatherer" rolls the long pole ("punty") inside the 2,200° furnace to gather a gob of glass, which is put into a bowl-shaped mold. The presser, one of the most experienced craftsmen in the shop, lowers a lever with exacting pressure, squeezing molten glass into a decorative bowl.

Downstairs, in an enclosed room, fresh-air-masked artisans paint crushed 22-karat gold onto glass items of all kinds. Elsewhere in the decorating area, artists paint designs on glass using crushed-glass pigments. When applying floral designs, an artist first paints the flowers' blossoms on a dozen pieces, returning later to add leaves and stems. You gain an appreciation for the steps involved in producing tomorrow's heirlooms.

Cost: Free

Freebies: Brochure on glassmaking

Video Shown: "Experience Fenton," 22-minute video in Museum Theater, covers production, how specific glass items are made, company history, and hand carving of cast-iron molds.

Reservations Needed: No, except for groups larger than 20 people.

Days and Hours: Mon–Fri 8:30 AM–9:30 AM and 11:00 AM–2:00 PM. Call for late-afternoon tour times, as factory work schedule changes. Closed holidays. No factory tours for 2 weeks starting end of June or beginning of July.

Plan to Stay: 2 hours, including tour, video, and museum, plus time for gift shop. Museum emphasizes first 75 years of Fenton Glass (1905–1980), and other Ohio Valley companies' glass. Museum has same hours as gift shop.

Minimum Age: 2. Supervise children carefully, since you get very close to the hot glass.

Disabled Access: Blowing/pressing area, gift shop, and museum are accessible. Stairs to decorating department.

Group Requirements: Groups of 20 or more need advance reservations.

Special Information: Wear closed-toe, thick-soled shoes. Glassblowing area is well ventilated but hot during summer. Watch where you walk.

Gift Shop and Factory Outlet: Sells Fenton's first-quality line at suggested retail, as well as retired, first-quality and preferred seconds at reduced prices. Also carries other fine gift and home décor items. Museum sells glassmaking history books. Annual February Gift Shop Sale and Summer Tent Sale. Open Mon–Sat 8:00 AM–5:00 PM, Sun 12:00 PM–5:00 PM. Additional hours April–December: Mon–Fri open until 8:00 PM. Closed New Year's, Easter, Thanksgiving, and Christmas. Catalog available from above number.

Directions: From I-77, take Exit 185; follow blue-and-white signs to gift shop. From Rt. 50, take I-77 North. Follow directions above.

Nearby Attractions: Lee Middleton Original Doll factory tour (see page 262); Blennerhassett Island; Historic Marietta, Ohio, across Ohio River.

See color photos, page 41.

Homer Laughlin China

6th and Harrison Streets
Newell, WV 26050
(304) 387-1300 / (800) 452-4462
www.hlchina.com

Since its beginnings in 1871, Homer Laughlin has grown into the nation's largest manufacturer of restaurant china. Its bright-colored Fiesta tableware, introduced in 1936, is the most collected china pattern in the world. On this tour of one of the most automated pottery factories in the U.S.A., you observe three ways of shaping clay, plus the glazing, firing, and decorating processes.

Your tour starts with a talk in the museum room. Glance at the displays on the walls showing discontinued patterns, including Virginia Rose scalloped-edge plates.

As you walk through this mile-long factory, notice the maze of pipes along the ceiling, the tracks along the floor on which the kiln cars travel, and the row upon row of gray stacked plates, cups, and bowls waiting to enter the kiln. Hear the sounds of dishes rattling together. Watch as automatic jiggers form round plates at a rate of 400 to 500 dozen per day. Ram presses squeeze slabs of clay between two plaster dies to create such irregular shapes as slanted sides, squared corners, and ovals. The top die is pressed into the bottom die under 2,200 pounds per square inch of pressure. In the casting process, liquid clay known as slip is poured into plaster molds. The slip dries in the shape of the mold. Cup handles are formed in tree molds of six to eight handles. A machine trims and prepares them for individual hand attachment to each cup.

A spray machine showers liquid glaze onto the dry pottery called "greenware." Once glazed, each piece is loaded by hand onto the shelves of a kiln car. Robotics is used to stack a filled kiln car automatically into the largest fast-fire kiln in the industry.

After the short 11-hour journey (it used to take 48 hours) through this 2,400°, 350-foot-long tunnel kiln, the computer directs each kiln car back to its initial workstation. Presses stamp the Homer Laughlin trademark onto the bottom of each piece. In the decorating department, pattern decals are hand-applied. Workers slide the water-soaked decals onto individual cups and plates and push out air bubbles with small hard-rubber squeegees. Decorative lines are painted on by hand or machine, using a silk-screen pattern, before another firing in the decorating kiln, this time for only 59 minutes. Pieces are shipped out as soon as they're finished, to the tune of 500,000 pieces of china per week.

Cost: Free

Freebies: Souvenir ceramic tray

Video Shown: No

Reservations Needed: Yes

Days and Hours: Mon–Thur 10:30 AM and 12:30 PM. Closed holidays.

Plan to Stay: 1 hour, plus time in outlet store.

Minimum Age: None

Disabled Access: Yes, for most of tour.

Group Requirements: Groups larger than 20 people should call 1 week in advance. No maximum group size.

Special Information: Photography allowed in museum only. Areas near kilns are quite warm in summer.

Outlet Store: Sells first- and second-quality of entire product line, including Fiesta dinnerware and flatware and Lyrica dinnerware. Also offers closeout patterns and colors. Open Mon–Sat 9:30 AM–4:50 PM, Sun 12:00 PM–4:50 PM. Closed major holidays.

Directions: From Pittsburgh, take Rt. 30 West to Chester, WV. Turn left at end of exit ramp and then left onto Rt. 2 South for 2 miles; factory is on right. From Youngstown, take Rt. 11 South to East Liverpool. Follow signs to Newell Toll Bridge. Once on bridge, follow signs to Homer Laughlin.

Nearby Attractions: Brooke Glass, Creegan Company, Hall China, and Senator Heinz History Center tours (see pages 349, 256, 258, and 294); East Liverpool Museum of Ceramics; Mountaineer Park Racetrack and Resort.

Allen-Edmonds

201 East Seven Hills Road
Port Washington, WI 53074
(262) 235-6000
www.allenedmonds.com

Allen Edmonds

SHOES

Allen-Edmonds shoes some of the most famous feet in the world. Visitors to Allen-Edmonds Shoe Corporation will see the inaugural shoes worn by three U.S. presidents and the size 24 EEEEEEs handcrafted for a teenager in Seattle. On display are a pair of alligator golf shoes with gold-plated spikes. For added fun, step into the red, white, and blue clown shoes worn by Oscar- and Emmy-winning actor Ernest Borgnine.

Walk into the atrium gallery of Allen-Edmonds Corporate Centre in Port Washington, Wisconsin, and you'll see the Allen-Edmonds Shoe Revue, a distinctive collection of men's footwear worn by presidents, kings, sports celebrities, and film stars. There is even a pair of brown cordovan loafers presented to the Pope by Allen-Edmonds' president and owner, John Stollenwerk. Along the atrium-viewing gallery are movie posters with displays of the Allen-Edmonds shoes featured in major films and highly rated television shows.

From glass windows along the atrium walkway, notice how shoes progress along a conveyor belt that winds through the Lasting and Bottoming departments. Workers pull unfinished shoes off the conveyor to perform various procedures. One worker guides a shoe through a machine that stitches around the insole. This 360-degree welting process has been a tradition since the company was founded in 1922. Visitors may see worn Allen-Edmonds being recrafted into almost-new condition (they recraft more than 1,000 pairs each week).

Between a video and what you can see from the atrium windows, you will learn the entire handcrafting process. Each pair of Allen-Edmonds shoes requires 212 production steps—from the inspection of the leather to the final shine. Willie Bittner, a 60-year veteran and the firm's master craftsman

(they say he can do all 212 production steps himself), has been featured in magazine articles and television news stories.

In the finishing department in the back, each new pair is blanketed in soft burgundy flannel and tucked into an elegant black and gold box. They await shipment to a major department store, high-end specialty store, shoe salon, or the Shoe Bank, a 75,000-pair on-site shoe store that will undoubtedly be your final destination.

Cost: Free
Freebies: Catalog
Video Shown: 12-minute video includes shoe production and clips of Allen-Edmonds in the news.
Reservations Needed: No, except if groups over 6 people want a tour guide.
Days and Hours: Mon–Fri 7:00 AM–9:00 PM, Sat 9:00 AM–9:00 PM, Sun 9:00 AM–6:00 PM. No production on weekends.
Plan to Stay: 25–30 minutes for atrium gallery and video, plus time in Shoe Bank.
Minimum Age: None
Disabled Access: Yes
Group Requirements: Must call in advance.
Outlet Store: The Shoe Bank offers full line of Allen-Edmonds first-quality men's shoes (some brand-name women's shoes also) at 25 percent off standard price. Open Mon–Fri 7:00 AM–9:00 PM, Sat 9:00 AM–9:00 PM, Sun 9:00 AM–6:00 PM. Recrafting services available. Annual July Tent Sale is a big event. For catalog and dates of July Tent Sale, call (800) 235-2348.
Directions: From Milwaukee, take I-43 North to Exit 100. Look for big American flag at Allen-Edmonds entrance.
Nearby Attractions: Kohler design center and tour (see page 357); Lake Michigan; Cedarburg.

Carr Valley Cheese

S3797 County G
La Valle, WI 53941
(608) 986-2781 / (800) 462-7258

CHEESE

Named after its location, Carr Valley Cheese is one of the few companies that produce cheddar cheese the old-fashioned way. Many Wisconsinites remember the 1930s and 1940s, when, as kids, they snacked on fresh curd from cheese factories that dotted Wisconsin's countryside every few miles. Here, you can taste fresh, warm curd that squeaks against your teeth and observe how it is turned into cheese.

In the retail store, a glass wall runs the length of the production area, where you may see owner Sid Cook, a fourth-generation cheese-maker, clad in bib overalls. Since each of the four 19-foot-long stainless-steel vats is at a different production stage, it helps to review the picture board and audiotape before taking your self-guided tour. Each day 52,000 pounds of pasteurized milk are filtered from holding tanks into cheese vats, which resemble single-lane lap-swimming pools. A large agitator twists and turns as it travels the length of a vat and back. A culture (which begins the ripening process and tastes like sour milk) and rennet (which causes milk to solidify) are added, and a wire harp cuts the mixture into small curds. As the whey (liquid) is removed, a separator extracts the cream. The cheese remains in the vat.

Once solid, the cheese is cut into 20-by-2-inch slabs. While they're stacked like slices in a loaf of bread, excess moisture drains from the slabs. The curd mill chops them into small chunks, and workers fill small black metal buckets with 25 pounds of curd. You can see curds weighed, poured into forms, and pressed into wheels.

Walk around to the back of the plant to see wheels waxed and packaged. In the wax room, a rack of cheese wheels is lowered into a two-foot-deep vat of 200° clear, red, or black wax (color depends on the cheese's age). The wax seals out air and protects the cheese from mold as it cures in the warehouse for up to two years (longer aging means sharper cheddar).

Cost: Free

Freebies: Samples of curds and cheeses.

Video Shown: No, however picture board and 4-minute audiotape in retail store explains cheese making.

Reservations Needed: No, except for groups larger than 30 people.

Days and Hours: Mon–Sat 8:00 AM–12:00 PM. Best time is 10:00 AM. Closed Thanksgiving, Christmas, and Easter.

Plan to Stay: 30 minutes for self-guided tour and retail store.

Minimum Age: None

Disabled Access: Yes, but difficult to get into wax room.

Group Requirements: Groups larger than 30 should call 1 day in advance to schedule tour guide; will be split into smaller groups.

Special Information: Can watch video and some production of European cheeses at their other facility, Wisconsin Pride, in Mauston, WI (call 608-847-6998).

Retail Store: Sells full line of Carr Valley cheese. Wheel sizes: 3-pound "gem," 5.5-pound "favorite," up to 23-pound "daisy," and 72-pound "cheddar" (once the industry standard). Also sells cut cheese, curds, sausages, and Wisconsin-made jams, jellies, and honey. Sells cheese production video. Open Mon–Sat 8:00 AM–4:00 PM. Catalog available from (800) 462-7258.

Directions: From I-90/94, take Hwy. 12 South. Take Hwy. 33 West through Reedsburg (look for Carr Valley Cheese signs) to La Valle. Go straight onto Hwy. 58 South through Ironton. After 1 mile, turn left onto County G. Brick plant is 2 miles ahead on right.

Nearby Attractions: Wisconsin Dells casinos and boat cruises, about 25 miles away. For complete list of Wisconsin cheese plants, write: Cheese Plants, Wisconsin Milk Marketing Board, 8418 Excelsior Drive, Madison, WI 53717.

CaseNewHolland

7000 Durand Avenue
Mount Pleasant, WI 53555
(262) 636-7818
www.cnh.com

TRACTORS

CaseNewHolland (CNH) was formed by the 1999 merger between Case Corporation and New Holland N.V. CNH manufactures Case-IH and New Holland agricultural equipment as well as Case and New Holland construction equipment, Prior to their merger, each company had been making farm and construction machinery for more than a century. Jerome Increase Case started his company in 1842 in Western Racine County to manufacture threshing machines. Abram Zimmerman founded the New Holland Machine Works in New Holland, Pennsylvania, in 1895.

In 2002, tractor assembly was consolidated with transmission manufacturing to reduce complexity, and the New Holland brand was added. This is the only factory in the world where the highly-rated Case two-wheel-drive Magnum series tractor is built. This guided walking tour shows tractor building from start to finish and awes the uninitiated because of the Magnum's size. It weighs as much as eight tons, with tires as tall as people.

When CNH consolidated tractor assembly and transmission manufacturing, the company installed the most current equipment and procedures. Among the new assembly line's important features are automated handling systems, a robotic wash and paint system, and computerized diagnostic testing. As you move between the subassembly areas, your retiree tour guide points out special production features, such as the bar code identification system. Each tractor and cab is identified and tracked with a bar code from the moment the assembly process starts.

After the cab's metal pieces are welded together, it moves down its own line. Workers add components such as glass, fenders, seat, fuel tank, and roof. When cab and body come together, it finally looks like the well-known bright red Case-IH tractor. Just before the tractor receives its tires, a two-member team determines whether it meets the company's stringent quality standards. If it does, the workers place a decal bearing their signatures on the cab threshold. This certifies that the tractor is ready to begin its working life and symbolizes the commitment of the CNH/UAW Employee Involvement Program.

Cost: Free

Freebies: No

Video Shown: 10-minute video covering company history and preview of tour.

Reservations Needed: Yes

Days and Hours: Mon–Fri 8:00 AM–10:00 AM, 1:00 PM. CNH focuses on customer tours but tries to give public tours when time available. Closed holidays, week between Christmas and New Year's, pilot builds, and plant maintenance shutdowns.

Plan to Stay: 1.5 hours for tour, plus time in gift shop.

Minimum Age: 14

Disabled Access: Yes

Group Requirements: Make reservations 2 weeks in advance. Maximum group is 100 people.

Special Information: No photography. Regularly scheduled tours also available at New Holland, PA, hay and forage plant (call 717-355-1588). Tours at Wichita, KS, construction equipment plant (call 316-941-2235).

Gift Shop: Sells logoed T-shirts and caps, and scale model Case and New Holland tractors and construction machines. Open after tours.

Directions: From I-94, exit at Hwy. 11. Follow Hwy. 11 East to the junction with Durand Ave. Turn left onto Durand Ave., then take first right into the parking lot.

Nearby Attractions: SC Johnson Wax Golden Rondelle Theater and Administration Building tour (see page 362); Racine Zoo; Museum of Fine Arts; Racine County Historical Museum; Engine House No. 3.

General Motors

Truck & Bus Group
1000 Industrial Avenue
Janesville, WI 53546
(608) 756-7681
www.gm.com

SPORT-UTILITY VEHICLES AND PICKUPS

General Motors has been building vehicles in Janesville since the Samson Tractor in 1919. Through the years this plant has produced a range of vehicles including Chevys, Buick Skyhawks, and now the popular Suburban, Yukon, Tahoe, and medium-duty trucks. During WWII the factory made artillery shells. With the factory's long history, it's no surprise that this plant and the retiree who leads your walking floor tour exude a sense of pride. It's also one of the few automotive tours that individuals and families can take without advance reservations.

You'll see plenty of robots assisting the workers. In the Suburban body shop, over 160 robots perform about 70 percent of the welds. These robots, which look more like bird beaks, bend over from their bases to apply spot-welds. The colorful shooting sparks make you realize how much safer it is for robots to perform this task than workers, who mostly program, monitor, and repair this equipment.

Once the steel body-frame is assembled, it moves through a dimensional vision system that uses laser beams to check the frame parts' sizes against their ideal measurements. In other parts of the factory, robots also apply the base-coat paint in enclosed booths, and put the prime and urethane on the window glass before workers pop it into place. While the body frame is being constructed, other lines build the chassis. Workers assemble the underneath part first, and a turnover hoist flips the chassis over like a pancake.

In the final assembly lines, an overhead hoist lowers the vehicle body onto the chassis, and workers bolt them together. To the music of air tools, parts such as fenders and grills seem to arrive from every direction for attachment. You will see the dynamic vehicle-test area, where the vehicles sit on rollers and accelerate to 60 mph so major features can be tested. At this point the assembly process is complete, and you're tempted to hop in and hit the road.

Cost: Free

Freebies: None

Videos Shown: 9-minute pre-tour video, which overviews the plant history and vehicle production. 13-minute video on plant history and components of building an SUV.

Reservations Needed: Yes

Days and Hours: Tour times change with production schedule. Call tour hotline for times at (608) 756-7681. Closed holidays, week between Christmas and New Year's, and 2 weeks in July.

Plan to Stay: 1 hours for video and tour.

Minimum Age: None, although children under 5 may be frightened by noise and sparks. Children under 10 must be accompanied by an adult.

Disabled Access: Yes

Group Requirements: Groups of 10 or more should make reservations as early as possible—tours fill quickly, especially in spring and summer. Maximum group size is 60.

Special Information: No photography. Vehicle painting by robots is not on tour, but you see plenty of robots perform other tasks.

Gift Shop: No

Directions: From I-90, take Hwy. 351 West. Turn right at stop sign and proceed north on Hwy. G (Beloit Ave.). Turn left at Delavan Dr. and left at plant. Enter through doors in center of building, directly under flagpole on roof. From Hwy. 14 West, go straight onto O, which becomes Delavan Dr., then turn left at plant. Call above number for maps to plant from other directions.

Nearby Attractions: Wisconsin Wagon group tours (call 608-754-0026); Rotary Gardens; Palmer Park; Tallman House; Milton House.

Jelly Belly Center

10100 Jelly Belly Lane
Pleasant Prairie, WI 53158
(866) TOUR-JBC / (866) 868-7522
www.jellybelly.com

JELLY BEANS AND GUMMI CANDIES

Since Jelly Belly's Fairfield, California, factory tours (see page 4) have become so popular, the company expanded in 2001, opening a warehouse and distribution center in Pleasant Prairie to supplement the tours in California. Now you can hop on the Jelly Belly Express Train and ride around the new warehouse, stopping to learn about the Jelly Belly Candy Company's production process and sample flavors.

When you arrive, a 30-foot-tall, inflatable Jelly Belly bean with a candy corn hat greets you. Walk into the store and line up next to Jelly Belly Junction—a train station entry to the tour. Inside the warehouse, you will board the Jelly Belly Express, a colorful, four-car electric train with no tracks. Your tour guide drives the train, making commentary between stops.

First, watch the Welcome Video on a large-screen display, which details the company history. After you're on your way, you may be tempted to hop off the train for a moment or two once you see the boxes of candy stacked to the rafters. Be patient—sampling comes later! At the raw materials station, try to count how many sacks of ingredients it takes to produce a day's worth of candies.

Unlike tours of modern factories, you stop at the Candy Kitchen, which displays a mini-museum of reproduced equipment from the company's early days, including old candy machinery and candy kettles. The Panning Process shows off what makes Jelly Belly beans so special—machines add candy shells to intensely flavored centers; non–Jelly Belly beans have no flavoring in the center.

As you pass through Candy Alley, three-dimensional beans fly overhead. While viewing the Jelly Belly bean mosaics, you might recognize some of your favorite presidents, artistically rendered in lemon, cotton candy, and green apple flavors, among others. The dancing chorus line of animated Jelly Belly characters sends you along to the Shipping Department. Reward yourself after the tour with a trip to the tasting bar, where you can create your own Jelly Belly recipes by combining multiple bean flavors.

Cost: Free

Freebies: 3-ounce bag of jelly beans. Sample over 100 candies at tasting bar.

Videos Shown: Large screen videos of production and distribution processes shown during ride on Jelly Belly Express.

Reservations Needed: No

Days and Hours: Mon–Sun 9:00 AM–5:00 PM. Closed New Year's, Easter, Thanksgiving, and Christmas.

Plan to Stay: 40 minutes for train tour and sampling, plus time for retail area and snack bar.

Minimum Age: None

Disabled Access: Yes

Group Requirements: None

Special Information: No photography. Fairfield, CA, factory tour (see page 4).

Retail Store: Sells all Jelly Belly beans and Goelitz Confections, Belly Flops (discounted, irregular beans), gift baskets, jelly bean trinkets, hot dogs, ice cream, and desserts. Open same hours as center.

Directions: From Milwaukee, take I-94 (US 41) South to Exit 347. Turn left (east) onto SR 165 (Lakeview Pkwy). Turn left (north) on SR 31 (Green Bay Rd). In .25 miles, turn left (west) on Jelly Belly Ln. into the Jelly Belly Center. From Chicago, take I-94 (US 41) North into Wisconsin, to Exit 347. Stay on left side of ramp. Turn right (east) onto SR 165 (Lakeview Pkwy) and follow above directions.

Nearby Attractions: Great America Theme Park; McDonald's #1 Store Museum tour (see page 134); Chicago's attractions, including Chicago Mercantile Exchange, Chicago Board of Trade, Eli's Cheesecake World, and U.S. Post Office tours one hour away (see pages 126, 125, 128, and 136); Milwaukee's attractions, including Miller Brewery tour (see page 358), Milwaukee County Zoo, Boerner Botanical Gardens, and Milwaukee Art Museum, are about 45 minutes away.

See color photos, page 43.

Kohler

Design Center
101 Upper Road
Kohler, WI 53044
(920) 457-3699
www.kohler.com

BATHTUBS, WHIRLPOOLS, TOILETS, AND SINKS

A visit to Kohler is more than just a tour of the world's largest plumbingware manufacturer. The factory tour begins and ends at the Kohler Design Center, a three-level showcase of products and bathroom layouts that are so attractive you'll want to move in. The Design Center also houses the company museum, which chronicles Kohler history since 1873, and Kohler's own colorful "great wall of china."

Guided by a company retiree, your tour begins in the pottery building's molding area, a humid place where bare-chested men smooth wet clay toilets with large sponges. Next come the kilns: long, brick ovens that bake glazed clay fixtures into vitreous chinaware. Stroll among glossy stacks of Thunder Grey sinks and Innocent Blush commodes. Watch inspectors "ping" the chinaware with hard rubber balls and listen for cracks.

Next, enter Wisconsin's largest iron foundry. Its electric melt system eliminates the smoke and fumes previously associated with foundries. It's still an imposing place, full of molten metal, warning lights, and hissing machinery—a highly memorable industrial experience. Here you'll discover how they make molds to form cast-iron tubs, sinks, and engine blocks. The concrete floor shudders with the heave and thud of massive presses that create sand molds. You'll feel the heat from the "ladles" of glowing molten iron traveling by on forklifts. Deeper inside the building, an automated production line turns out one bathtub casting every 30 seconds.

In the enamel building, workers gingerly remove red-hot bathtubs, lavatories, and kitchen sinks from ovens. Enamel powder that melts into porcelain is quickly sifted onto each fixture. Finally, pass into the whirlpool-bath section, where up to seven tubs bubble serenely. After three hours of touring this enormous plant, you may be more than a little tempted to flop into the water and relax.

Cost: Free

Freebies: Product-line books in Design Center.

Video Shown: 20-minute video in Design Center shows Kohler history and Kohler Village highlights.

Reservations Needed: Yes, for plant tour. No, for Design Center.

Days and Hours: Factory tour: Mon–Fri 8:30 AM. No tours on holidays, week between Christmas and New Year's, last week of July, or first week of August. Design Center: Mon–Fri 9:00 AM–5:00 PM and Sat, Sun, and holidays 10:00 AM–4:00 PM. Closed Thanksgiving and Christmas.

Plan to Stay: 2–3 hours for factory tour, plus time for video, museum, and Design Center.

Minimum Age: 14, for tour; under 18 must be accompanied by adult. None for Design Center.

Disabled Access: Discouraged for tour, because of stairs. Design Center is fully accessible.

Group Requirements: Kohler requests that you call for complete group information. Groups larger than 8–10 people will be split.

Special Information: No photography on tour. Up to 2.5 miles of walking, including some outdoors. Be careful where you walk. During tour you'll see examples of works produced by artists in the Arts/Industry Residency program.

Gift Counter: Design Center sells postcards, polo shirts, and Kohler-logoed items.

Directions: From Chicago and Milwaukee, take I-43 North to Kohler exit. Follow signs into Kohler—the company is the town. Stop at Kohler Design Center for orientation information and start of plant tour. From Madison, take I-94 East to Milwaukee, then I-43 North. Follow above directions.

Nearby Attractions: Shops at Woodlake Kohler; The American Club "five diamond" resort hotel; Blackwolf Run championship golf courses; Waelderhaus, replica Austrian chalet in style of Kohler family's ancestral home; Kohler Village tour (May–October).

Miller Brewing

Visitor Center
4251 West State Street
Milwaukee, WI 53208
(414) 931-BEER
www.millerbrewing.com

BEER

In 1855, German immigrant Fredrick Miller purchased the Plank Road Brewery. Surrounded by woods, the small brewing operation was no bigger than a Victorian house. Today, a replica of the Plank Road Brewery is just one of the historic highlights in Milwaukee's Miller Valley—the home of the nation's second largest brewer, Miller Brewing Company.

Walk outdoors and upstairs to Miller's packaging-center balcony. A blur of cans roars along conveyor belts that wind through wet machinery, packing up to 200,000 cases of beer daily.

The next stop is Miller's mammoth distribution center that covers the equivalent of five football fields. Typically, you can see half a million cases of beer.

In the brew house, Miller makes its beer, up to eight-and-a-half million barrels annually in Milwaukee alone. Climb 56 stairs to look down on a row of towering, shiny brew kettles where "wort," a grain extract, is boiled and combined with hops. Stroll through Miller's historic Caves, a restored portion of the original brewery where beer was stored before the invention of mechanical refrigeration.

Finish your tour at the Bavarian-style Miller Inn and sample a Miller beer or soft drink. Be sure also to take a few minutes to inspect the impressive collection of antique steins. In the summer, you can enjoy your beverage in an adjoining beer garden enlivened by music.

Cost: Free

Freebies: Beer (for those 21 years of age and older with proper ID), soda, peanuts, and postcards.

Video Shown: 15-minute video shows brewing process and overview of Miller's history.

Reservations Needed: No, but recommended for groups of 15 or more.

Days and Hours: Mon–Sat 10:30 AM–3:30

PM. Closed holidays and week between Christmas and New Year's Day.

Plan to Stay: 1 hour for video and tour, plus time for product sampling and gift shop.

Minimum Age: Under age 18 must be accompanied by adult.

Disabled Access: Plant tour: no. Visitor Center (includes video), Miller Inn, and Caves: yes.

Group Requirements: Groups of 15 or more people should call ahead for reservations. Maximum group size is 90. Limited reservations on Saturdays.

Special Information: Best time to see production is weekdays. Miller Brewing Company also gives tours and has a gift shop in Tumwater, WA (call 360-754-5217), and the Miller Marketplace and Brew Kettle Museum in Ft. Worth, TX (call 817-568-BEER).

Gift Shop: Girl in the Moon Brewery Shop sells clothing, caps, glassware, steins, mirrors, tap handles, and other Miller logoed items. Open Mon–Sat: summer 10:00 AM–5:30 PM; winter 10:00 AM–5:00 PM.

Directions: From Chicago, take I-94 West to 35th St. Turn right (north) on 35th St. Turn left (west) onto State St. Pass through "Miller Valley" (well marked) to last building on left, Miller Visitor Center and Gift Shop. From Madison, take I-94 East to Hwy 41 North to the State St. exit. Follow signs to right, down hill to traffic light. Turn left onto State St. Visitor Center is one block ahead on right.

Nearby Attractions: Quality Candy/Buddy Squirrel factory tour (see page 359); Miller Park (home of Milwaukee Brewers); Milwaukee County Zoo; Mitchell Park Horticulture ("The Domes"); Milwaukee County Museum; Milwaukee Art Museum; Boerner Botanical Gardens; Cedar Creek Winery. Miller Visitor Center front desk has information on and directions to many local attractions.

See color photo, page 45.

Quality Candy/Buddy Squirrel

1801 East Bolivar Avenue
St. Francis, WI 53235
(414) 483-4500 / (800) 972-2658
www.qcbs.com

Buddy Squirrel
THE PREMIER NUT SHOP

CHOCOLATES AND POPCORN

This factory tour is actually two tours in one. In 1916 immigrants Joseph and Lottie Helminiak opened Quality Candy Shoppes in Milwaukee's popular Mitchell Street shopping district. In the early 1950s, Buddy Squirrel combined forces with Quality Candy. Today, the two product lines are housed in a 45,000-square-foot factory and warehouse, and the family-owned company operates more than 15 stores in Wisconsin. This joint tour allows you to see how Quality Candy makes award-winning chocolate candies and how Buddy Squirrel processes popcorn, nuts, and snack mixes.

Your tour begins in the Quality Candy kitchens. Here, candy makers prepare and mix the ingredients for the chocolate candies' centers. Centers, made from scratch in these kitchens, include caramel, creams, toffee, cordials, marshmallow, and nougat. From a viewing corridor, you see the centers embark on a short journey to the enrobing room, where they are engulfed in a fountain of either milk or dark chocolate before going through the cooling tunnel. One of the highlights of the tour is watching over 80 seasonal solid chocolate moldings being made, varying in sizes from 1 ounce to a 67-pound rabbit. All the candies then travel to the packing area to be boxed and sent off to a Quality Candy store or wholesaler.

The Buddy Squirrel segment adds some "pop" to the tour. Tons of corn kernels dive into giant poppers, in which they become popcorn. The popcorn is then seasoned with butter, cheese, caramel, and other flavorings. Once again, your taste buds are tempted by the scents in the air. The popcorn meets up with the nuts (also made by Buddy Squirrel but not seen on tour) in the packing room, and the goodies are prepared for their voyage to candy and nut stores all over the region.

Cost: Adults, $2; children 10–13, $1; children under 10, free.

Freebies: Samples of candy and caramel corn.

Video Shown: No

Reservations Needed: Yes. Individuals and families need to join scheduled group tour or form group of at least 10 people.

Days and Hours: Tue–Thur 10:30 AM and 1:00 PM. No tours on holidays, November and December, 4 weeks before Easter (except for Annual Open House), and 1 week at the beginning of July and August.

Plan to Stay: 45 minutes, plus time for Kitchen Store.

Minimum Age: 10

Disabled Access: Yes

Group Requirements: Groups of at least 10 people should call 4 weeks ahead. Maximum group size is 50 people.

Special Information: Annual Easter Open House (the second Sunday before Easter from 10:00 AM–4:00 PM—call for date) features Mr. & Mrs. Easter Bunny and special factory tours.

Retail Store: Kitchen Store sells all Quality Candy/Buddy Squirrel products, including chocolates, award-winning Butter Almond Toffee, Pecan Caramel Tads, popcorns, and nuts. Open Mon–Sat 9:00 AM–4:30 PM (closes at 2:00 PM on Saturdays in summer). Closed holidays. Catalog available from above number.

Directions: Take I-94 to Layton Ave. exit. Turn left onto Brust, then right on Whitnall. Make a quick left on Kansas St. Quality Candy/Buddy Squirrel factory is on right. Enter under bright red awning on south side of building.

Nearby Attractions: Miller brewery tour (see page 358); Milwaukee County Zoo; Mitchell Park Horticulture ("The Domes"); Milwaukee County Museum; Milwaukee Art Museum; Boerner Botanical Gardens; Cedar Creek Winery.

Natural Ovens

4300 Highway CR
Manitowoc, WI 54220
(920) 758-2500 / (800) 558-3535
www.naturalovens.com

Natural Ovens Bakery

Paul Stitt founded Natural Ovens in 1976, after discovering that many food companies were adding appetite stimulants to their products to increase sales. A biochemist, Paul believes food should be good for you, filling, and satisfying. Now he and his wife, Barbara, supply fresh breads to over 1,200 grocery stores in a handful of states. When you tour the facility, you'll notice that in their employee cafeteria, junk food has been replaced by delicious foods made with fresh vegetables, fruits, and grains, some even grown on company grounds.

Your tour begins in the huge lobby in front of an 11-by-17-foot stained-glass window depicting the farm and museum, as well as the growing and harvesting of flax. In 1986 Paul rediscovered flax, which has been proven beneficial in reducing the risk of heart disease. Flax is used in almost all of the bakery's products.

View the bakery through a series of windows. The bakers arrive at midnight to begin mixing the dough for the bread. The bakery uses three semi-truck-loads of flour a week—60 acres of wheat! After the sponge rises for three hours, it's put into the mixer and the rest of the ingredients are added to make enough dough for 550 loaves. You may gasp as the enormous blob of dough is dumped out of the mixer. After the dough has risen twice and been mixed three times, the huge mass goes through the dough divider, making more manageable 2-pound pieces. The smaller clumps look like little rabbits as they flop from the divider into the molder, where they're kneaded and shaped into loaves.

After rising, the dough moves to the 120-foot-long indirect brick oven. In just one hour 4,000 loaves will travel from one end of the oven to the other. Smell the heavenly aroma as you watch thousands of golden loaves emerge right under your nose. Within 16 hours, those same loaves will be sitting on a grocery shelf somewhere far away from Manitowoc.

Cost: Free

Freebies: Hot samples of baked goods.

Video Shown: 8-minute video provides close-up look at the mixing and baking process. Shown when no production.

Reservations Needed: No, except for groups larger than 10 people.

Days and Hours: Tours: Mon, Wed, Thur, Fri 9:00 AM, 10:00 AM, and 11:00 AM. The baking is completed by 2:00 PM. No baking on Tue. Self-guided viewing of bakery when lobby is open, Mon–Fri 8:00 AM–5:00 PM. Farm and Food Museum: May–October, Mon–Sat 9:00 AM–3:00 PM. Both are closed Thanksgiving, Christmas, and New Year's.

Plan to Stay: 1–1.5 hours for bakery tour, self-guided tour of Farm and Food Museum, including antique buildings and machinery, and friendly animals to pet, including Prince the llama, known for his hugs and kisses.

Minimum Age: None

Disabled Access: Yes, though parts of farm and museum are more difficult to access.

Group Requirements: Groups over 10 people should call at least 4–6 weeks in advance. Maximum group size 55 people.

Special Information: When in season, pick berries on the farm grounds.

Gift Shop: The lobby of the factory sells a complete selection of Natural Ovens products, plus specialty items including books, vinegars brewed locally, almond butter, aprons, T-shirts, and maple syrup. Open Mon–Fri 8:00 AM–5:00 PM, Sat 8:00 AM–3:00 PM. Catalog available from number at top of page.

Directions: From the south, take I-43 North to Exit 144. Turn right on Hwy. C. Turn left on CR. Bakery is 2.5 miles ahead on left. From the north, take I-43 South to Exit 149. Turn left onto Hwy. 151 East. Turn right onto CR. Bakery is 1 mile ahead on right.

Nearby Attractions: Wisconsin Maritime Museum; Rahr West Art Museum; West of the Lake Gardens (open May–October); Lake Michigan Car Ferry.

▲ The beautifully manicured grounds of Natural Ovens in Manitowoc, Wisconsin, include the bakery and the Farm & Food Museum.

This huge blob of dough pouring out of the mixer will make 550 loaves of Natural Ovens bread.

▼

SC Johnson Wax

1525 Howe Street
Racine, WI 53403-2236
(262) 260-2154
www.scjohnsonwax.com

SPECIALTY HOME-CLEANING PRODUCTS

In 1886 S. C. Johnson (at age 53) created and marketed a paste wax formula to sell as a sideline to his parquet flooring business. It became so successful that he expanded his line to introduce wood dyes, dance wax, and paints. In 1939 SC Johnson Wax Company moved into a building designed by Frank Lloyd Wright and eventually branched out to manufacture such familiar products as Glade, Edge Gel, and Raid.

In the company's corporate display room, pictures, products, and descriptions illustrate the company's unique development. The unfaltering dedication to business is depicted in the presented histories of the company's four generations of chairmen. See a display of various SC Johnson Worldwide consumer products. Learn how other countries contribute ingredients to products. In the Golden Rondelle lobby, see some of the prestigious awards presented to the company for marketing environmentally friendly products.

Strolling through the company's world headquarters, you will be dazzled by the interior of the Administration Building. Wright built this massive, futuristic "Great Workroom" using 21-foot columns that shoot up and expand outward as they reach the ceiling, resembling the stem and base of upside-down wineglasses. Illuminated Pyrex glass tubing wraps around the building, giving the impression of natural sunlight, yet not one real window exists! Equally impressive in its shape is the Research Tower, rising over 150 feet into the air. Designed using the cantilever principle, which is similar to the root, trunk, and branch system of a tree, the tower appears to hang suspended in the air.

Although not on the tour, the company's nearby production facility, "Waxdale," covers nearly 43 acres. Waxdale's aerosol lines can fill up to 500 units per minute. As the company's primary U.S. manufacturing plant, it is one of the most modern and efficient production, warehousing, and shipping centers in the world.

Cost: Free

Freebies: Brochures on Frank Lloyd Wright and his architecture.

Films Shown: Golden Rondelle Theater shows changing selection of films.

Reservations Needed: Yes

Days and Hours: Architectural tour: Fri 11:00 AM. Spring to fall 1:15 PM additional tour. Film: Fri 12:00 PM. Closed holidays and week between Christmas and New Year's.

Plan to Stay: 45 minutes for architectural tour, plus up to 2 hours for films.

Minimum Age: None, but children under 14 must be accompanied by an adult.

Disabled Access: Yes

Group Requirements: Groups should call 2 weeks to 2 months in advance. Maximum group size is 40 people.

Gift Shop: No

Directions: Take I-94 to Hwy. 20 East (Washington Ave.). Continuing east for about 8 miles, Hwy. 20 East curves left. Do not take curve but go straight (east) onto 14th St. Golden Rondelle Theater is 3 blocks ahead.

Nearby Attractions: CaseNewHolland tractor tour (see page 354); Wustum Art Museum; Racine Zoo.

Stora Enso North America

Fourth Avenue North
Wisconsin Rapids, WI 54495
(715) 422-3789
www.storaenso.com/na

STORAENSO

PAPER

The forests of the Upper Midwest help make Wisconsin the nation's leading paper producer. In the middle of the state lies Wisconsin Rapids, home of Stora Enso, North America's largest manufacturer of the coated printing papers used in magazines, catalogs, annual reports, and brochures. Set inside a concrete and brick building several stories high and stretching five city blocks, Stora Enso's largest machine produces enough paper to create a 19-foot-wide strip from Chicago to New York City every day.

At the head box, the start of the paper machine, a mixture of 99 percent water and 1 percent wood fiber is sprayed onto a rotating mesh screen. A combination of gravity and suction drain most of the water as the sheet of paper forms on the wire. The remainder of the water is removed by squeezing the sheet between giant rollers and then drying it with steam-heated dryers. Five hundred feet away, the newly formed paper wraps onto giant spools at the end of the paper machine. If you time it right (about every 40 minutes), you can see a "turn-up," where a new reel of paper is started without ever slowing down or stopping the process.

The 20,000-pound reels of paper move on to a 475-foot machine that applies two separate layers of coating to each side of the sheet. The next stop is the supercalenders, which iron and polish the sheet to a high gloss. Finally the reels of paper, now weighing as much as 33,000 pounds, are taken to the rewinder, where they are cut into smaller rolls for shipment to customers or conversion to sheets.

Your guide will then escort you to Stora Enso's converting operations. Computer-controlled automated guided vehicles (AGVs) transport rolls of paper across 7,000 feet of predetermined routes in the floor. At the facility's sheeters, rolls of paper are cut to size, packaged, and labeled. The AGVs take the finished paper to a cavernous warehouse that can store more than 20 million pounds of paper.

Cost: Free

Freebies: Small writing pad, brochure, and postcard.

Video Shown: 10-minute overview of the mill's operation, including pulp-making and forestry program.

Reservations Needed: No, except for groups of 5 or more people.

Days and Hours: Wed, Thur, and Sat at 10:00 AM. Other times by prior arrangement. Closed some holidays.

Plan to Stay: 1.5 hours for tour and video.

Minimum Age: None. Parents are discouraged from bringing infants since noise level in mill may disturb them. Children under 12 must be accompanied by an adult.

Disabled Access: Yes. Advance notice requested, so adequate number of guides can be available.

Group Requirements: Groups should call at least 1 week in advance. For specially arranged tours, minimum group size is 5 people. Maximum group size is 60 people.

Special Information: Wear comfortable, flat, closed-toe shoes. Company also offers forest tour nearby and a recycling tour (call 715-422-3789 for recycling tour). Summer paper mill tour at subsidiary in Duluth, MN (see page 211 or call 218-628-5100).

Gift Shop: No

Directions: From Madison, take I-90/94 West to I-39 North (Exit 108). Take Hwy. 73 West and turn right on Hwy. 13 North. Cross the Wisconsin River. Turn right onto West Grand Ave. Turn left on 4th Ave. Mill tour entrance is 1.5 blocks on right.

Nearby Attractions: Wisconsin Dairy State Cheese tour (see page 365) about 1 hour away; Steven Point Brewery tour (call 715-344-9310). Wisconsin Paper Council publishes a brochure of Wisconsin paper tours (call 920-722-1500).

Trek

801 West Madison Street
Waterloo, WI 53594
(920) 478-2197
www.trekbikes.com

BICYCLES

When does a bike start to look like a bike? At the Trek plant, not until it reaches final assembly. Here the lean frame, little more than a wisp of painted geometry, meets pedals, cables, handlebars, and wheels, which are then boxed together for shipment to bike stores worldwide.

You'll see how Trek, which started in 1975 with four employees building frames for Midwestern bicycle dealers, has innovated bike production. Metal frames take their form in the welding area. Thousands of metal pipes and joints, looking like bins of plumbing fixtures, are arranged precisely on steel tables and soldered together. It's a crackly, clattery region made brilliant with spits and stripes of green flame from the welding torch. Trek's frames of carbon fiber, a lightweight, almost ethereal compound, are built in an adjoining area. Workers hustle around the mounted carbon frames, spreading the fast-drying glue before it stiffens and sets. These newly glued frames are baked in an oven, then sanded smooth.

All frames, metal or carbon—about 1,000 a day—go to the paint department. They hang like coats on conveyor hooks that trundle toward large sheet-metal closets: the painting booths. Meanwhile, robots in a nearby department join rims to hubs, creating the wheels that will eventually meet up with the frames. On the glossy floor, heaps of fresh black tires, with the incarnate odor of a bike shop, are stacked hundreds deep. See the spokes bending and weaving into position and the "hop and wobble" process of computer-monitored "rim truing." On your way out, notice the "Employee Parking" area, an indoor rack some 50 yards long that's crowded with colorful bikes. If you drive your car to Trek, the largest manufacturer of quality bicycles in the U.S.A., you'll find a large gravel lot with plenty of places to park!

Cost: Free
Freebies: No
Video Shown: No
Reservations Needed: Yes
Days and Hours: Wed and Fri 10:00 AM. Closed holidays. Closed for 2 weeks around the end of June and beginning of July. Tour schedule subject to change.
Plan to Stay: 45 minutes for tour.
Minimum Age: None
Disabled Access: Most of tour is wheelchair accessible.
Group Requirements: Groups larger than 12 people must call 1 week in advance. Maximum group size is 15 people. Does not want traditional bus tours.
Special Information: No video cameras. Photography restricted in some areas. Trek factory in Whitewater, WI, also offers tours (call 262-473-8735).
Gift Shop: No
Directions: From I-94, take Marshall/Deerfield exit. Travel north on Hwy. 73 toward Marshall. Turn right at Hwy. 19 (Main St. in Marshall). Trek plant is 4 miles ahead on right.
Nearby Attractions: In Waterloo, inquire locally about tour of local pickle factory; John Deere lawn tractor plant tour in Horicon (call 920-485-4411); Madison's attractions, including Arboretum, Vilas Park Zoo, and State Capital tours, about 40 minutes away.

Wisconsin Dairy State Cheese

Highway 34 & C
Rudolph, WI 54475
(715) 435-3144

The Dairy State Cheese plant, owned for generations by the Moran family, is fronted by a busy little shop. Look through the bank of windows either upstairs or downstairs from the shop, and you'll see a vast room filled with stainless-steel pipes, vats, and tables. A few workers move about in hair nets and rubber boots, but much of the "Stirred Curd Cheddar" process you're watching is highly automated. Given the size of the production room, the near absence of people is conspicuous, a testimony to the efficiency of state-of-the-art cheese-making equipment.

Off to your left rise several immense silos filled with thousands of gallons of pasteurized and cultured milk. Ten pounds of milk are used in producing every pound of cheese. A network of pipes carries the milk from the silos to four vats, each one longer than a school bus. All day the upright enclosed vats are filled and emptied. The curds and whey are pumped over to long tables. A "forker" swirls as it drifts up and down the length of the long narrow vat, beginning the process of separating the liquid (whey) from the milk solids (curd).

When the whey is drained off, what remains is a warm mass of glossy curds. The final step is to salt the curds. The fresh curds are automatically fed into presses, where they are compacted into 700-pound blocks of brand-new cheese. The massive orange or white blocks are then sealed into wooden boxes for aging. After about one month, the cheese is shipped to Kraft for cutting. When your tour ends, be sure to return to the shop and browse among the coolers stocked with 85 varieties of cheese. Buy yourself a bag of curds so fresh they'll squeak on your teeth.

Cost: Free

Freebies: Cheese samples

Video Shown: Optional 23-minute film promotes Wisconsin cheese and details manufacturing process.

Reservations Needed: No, except for groups larger than 25 people.

Days and Hours: Mon–Fri 8:30 AM–4:30 PM. Production ends around 4:00 PM. Sun 9:00 AM–12:00 PM, but no production. Call to confirm holiday hours.

Plan to Stay: 15 minutes for self-guided viewing, plus time for video and cheese shop.

Minimum Age: None

Disabled Access: Yes

Group Requirements: Groups larger than 25 should make reservations 2 days in advance. Ice-cream cones and cheese samples provided for school tours.

Special Information: Guide available by request with 2 days' notice.

Retail Store: Cheese shop sells wide selection of cheeses, sausage, and locally made ice cream. Open Mon–Fri 8:30 AM–5:15 PM, Sat 8:30 AM–5:00 PM. Sun 9:00 AM–12:00 PM. Call about holiday hours. Catalog available from above number.

Directions: Take U.S. 51 North to the Hwy. 73 exit at Plainfield. Turn left (west) on Hwy. 73 to Hwy. 13. Turn right (north) and go through Wisconsin Rapids, following signs for Hwy. 34 North. Enter town of Rudolph, and Dairy State Cheese is on right.

Nearby Attractions: Stora Enso tour (see page 363); Stevens Point Brewery tour (call 715-344-9310); Rudolph Grotto Gardens and Wonder Cave. For complete list of Wisconsin cheese plants, write: Cheese Plants, Wisconsin Milk Marketing Board, 8418 Excelsior Drive, Madison, WI 53717.

Aviat Aircraft

672 South Washington Street
Afton, WY 83110
(307) 885-3151
www.aviataircraft.com

For 85-year-old aviation pioneer Curtis Pitts, an airplane is not only a means of transportation, it's also a piece of sporting equipment. Pitts designs acrobatic airplanes, the kind that dip, flip, and roll through the sky like a roller coaster at 4,000 feet. Aviat Aircraft custom-builds about a dozen Pitts Special planes each year; the aircraft often feature pert model names like Hot Stuff and Super Stinker and regularly rack up awards in aerobatic flying competitions. Aviat also manufactures the versatile Husky airplane, a two-seater renowned for its maneuverability and its STOL (Short Take Off and Landing) ability, especially in difficult terrain. Long a favorite among bush pilots, the Husky can be equipped with skis, floats, or even 31-inch tundra tires, enabling it to land virtually anywhere.

At the Aviat factory, adjacent to Afton Municipal Airport, you will see the entire production process of both Husky and Pitts Special planes. These rough-and-tumble flying machines begin as seemingly fragile steel airframes and gradually take shape as paneling, instruments, wiring, and wings are put in place. After a brief visit to the factory's shipping and receiving area, you'll arrive at "Husky Final" and "Pitts Final." Here, largely by hand, workers nestle a plane's engine into the fuselage and then secure the wings with nuts and bolts. See a plane that's ready to roll out of the factory and tackle its first test flight.

While observing other areas of the plant, like avionics, painting, and the "Fab shop," you'll notice that detailed inspections occur at every stage of production. The rigorous inspection process dates from when Pitts Specials were shipped as home-build kits for amateurs to construct themselves. You sense precision, not massiveness, at this factory. Absent is the din typically associated with airplane construction, since hands, not machines, do most of the work here.

Notice the careful craftsmanship in the factory's wing shop, where workers use an eight-inch needle to stitch Dacron fabric securely over the open spars and ribs of a wing. The wing spars in the Pitts Special are made of spruce and mahogany wood rather than metal to give the plane flexibility and lightness for its aerobatic stunts. Finally, watch as painters use handheld sprayers to coat the plane with a gray, weatherproof epoxy primer, followed by as many as 18 layers of colorful paint. If you're suddenly in the mood to abandon your car and fly home, know that a Pitts Special, wings and all, easily fits into a two-car garage.

Cost: Free

Freebies: Brochures on Aviat's various aircraft.

Video Shown: No

Reservations Needed: Only November–May.

Days and Hours: June–October: Mon–Fri 11:00 AM and 2:30 PM. November–May: by appointment only. Closed holidays.

Plan to Stay: 30 minutes for tour, plus time for gift shop.

Minimum Age: None, but noise and fumes in factory may bother small children.

Disabled Access: Yes

Groups: Groups of 25 or more people should call 1 day in advance.

Special Information: Photographs permitted from safety area. Noise and fumes in factory may bother some people.

Gift Shop: Sells jackets, hats, posters, and other Pitts and Husky aircraft memorabilia. Open Mon–Fri 7:00 AM–3:30 PM.

Directions: From Jackson Hole: Begin at Hoback Junction. Drive to Alpine Junction. Make a left onto Hwy 89 South. Drive for 30 miles, through Afton, WY. Facility located on Hwy 89.

Nearby Attractions: Callair Foundation aviation museum (call 307-886-9881); Star Valley Cheese, about 15 miles north (call 307-883-2510 for the restaurant, 307-883-2446 for the factory); Jackson Hole, 70 miles away.

Caribbean

Tortuga Rum

Tortuga Rum Avenue
George Town, Grand Cayman, B.W.I.
(345) 949-7701 / (345) 949-CAKE
www.tortugarums.com

TORTUGA RUM CO. LTD.

RUM CAKES

After you spend your time scuba diving, lounging on the beaches, and perusing the shops in George Town, you can visit the factory that makes the Cayman Island's #1 export. While rum cakes have a long history in the Caribbean, Tortuga Rum Company is the first to commercially market these delicious treats. The founders, Carlene and Robert Hamaty, first baked them from home in 1987 using a 100-year-old family recipe. Now their growing enterprise features a 10,000-square-foot headquarters with a state-of-the-art bakery. It prides itself on plentiful free samples and big observation windows to see the baking, glazing, and packing process.

This facility is able to produce between 5,000 and 6,000 Tortuga Rum Cakes each day in five flavors and three sizes: the 32-oz. large size, the 16-oz. medium size, and the 4-oz. mini. Listen to the live steel drum band playing in the background, while you admire the big revolving ovens that bake 52 sheet pans at a time. The pans look like they are going on a Ferris wheel ride up and around the oven. Their path in the oven takes one and a half hours at 350°. The bakers gingerly remove the pans, glaze the tops with five-year-old premium rum, turn the cakes upside down, and place them on metal trolleys.

The cakes then spend at least two hours in the sterile cooling room. Notice the vacuum machine used to seal the cakes. Its two chambers force out the air from around the cake, wrap it, and preserve the cake's freshness without using chemicals. This vacuum-sealing process ensures a shelf life of six months (indefinitely if refrigerated or frozen). Quick hands put the cakes into individual boxes before another machine shrink-wraps them. The boxed cakes travel through the tunnel and into even bigger boxes for shipment around the world.

Cost: Free
Freebies: Cake samples and fruit punch.
Video Shown: 3-minute video about the company history, rum making, and cake production.

Reservations Needed: No, except for special groups requesting tour guide.

Days and Hours: Mon–Fri 7:00 AM–5:00 PM and Sat 7:00 AM–2:00 PM. Sunday when cruise ship in port. Closed Cayman Islands' public holidays, unless cruise ship in port.

Plan to Stay: 10 minutes, plus time for the grounds and gift shop.

Minimum Age: None

Disabled Access: Yes

Group Requirements: No maximum group size. Organized tours that want a guide should call 1 week ahead. Bus tours through cruise ships include guide.

Special Information: Eventually may be able to view the mixing area. Landscaped grounds for picnics, with local antique windmills, 300-year-old cannons (from the shipwreck of the *Ten Sails*), tropical birds, and other ancient artifacts.

Gift Shop: Sells Tortuga Rum and other brands (this is largest duty-free liquor business in the Cayman Islands, including specially blended rums made in Jamaica), Tortuga Rum specialty foods, including coffee and sauces. Also sells standard Island souvenirs, "Caribbean Rhythms" music, and rum cakes in all 5 flavors: golden original, chocolate, Blue Mountain coffee, banana rum, and coconut. Prices lower than at airport. Open same hours as tour. Smaller Tortuga bakeries in West Bay near the Turtle Farm and in downtown George Town. Except for the rum, can order from website above.

Directions: On North Sound Rd., follow signs for Airport from Seven Mile Beach. You will see from North Sound Rd. the complex on the right, with ornate wrought iron gates and the big company sign.

Nearby Attractions: Well-known beach and water attractions; Cayman Glassblowing Studio (call 345-949-8312); Stingray Beer (call 345-947-6699); Turtle Farm (call 345-949-3893).

Appleton Estate

Siloah, Jamaica, W.I.
(876) 963-9215
www.appletonrum.com

RUM

Appleton Estate, now owned by Wray & Nephew, is the oldest and most famous of all of Jamaica's sugar estates. This industrial-looking facility sits in the picturesque, fertile Nassau Valley spanning both sides of the Black River in the Southwest of Jamaica. The origins of Appleton Estate date back to 1655, when the English captured Jamaica from the Spaniards. Appleton Estate was an established rum-producing sugar plantation by the year 1749, and it has been in continuous operation for two and a half centuries. From its pot and column stills, the distillery can produce up to 10 million liters of its unique estate rums per year.

As with other distillery tours, this experience provides plenty of smells, tastes, and sights, providing an enjoyable alternative to another day on the beach. You discover the intricate history of the estate and the details of the rum-making process. Plus, in the air-conditioned Appleton Lounge, which is the base for your visit, you will have plentiful opportunities to savor and appreciate the subtle differences in rum flavors and textures. Before this part of your visit, you sample during the tour juice freshly pressed from sugar cane; thick molasses; wet sugar; and "high wine," all by-products of the stages in the transformation of sugar cane to rum.

Look for the production steps that are special to Jamaican rum. For example, the tour starts with a trip to the original cane yard where a donkey walked around a circle path to power a simple press that squeezed the liquid from sugar cane. Pot still distillation is the traditional Jamaican method of separating the alcohol from water in the fermented molasses. It uses copper or copper-lined kettles to hold the "dead wash," and along with steam, concentrates and condenses the alcohol vapors.

On a hot day, the walk through the rack houses where Appleton Rums age provides a cool, energizing experience. The "rum conditioning" results from the rum vapors passing through the pores of the barrel. In another area, workers may be hand assembling the 40-gallon aging barrels in the cooperage. It is filled with the sounds of the coopers hammering the wooden hoops into place. The sound is similar to old-time Jamaican spiritual music, helping you stay in a vacation mode.

Cost: Adults, $12; children under 15, $6.

Freebies: Samples of different types of rums and 2 drinks per person. Small sample bottles.

Video Shown: 12-minute video on history of estate, barrel making, and Jamaican rum production.

Reservations Needed: Recommended. Required for groups over 50 people. Tours are arranged through local tour companies, Caribic Vacations (call 876-953-9878), Tourwise (call 876-974-2323), or Glamour Tours (call 876-979-8207), or from hotel tour desks

Days and Hours: Mon–Sat 9:00 AM–4:00 PM. Closed Christmas, Easter Monday, and Boxing Day.

Plan to Stay: 45 minutes for tour, plus time for tasting and gift shops.

Minimum Age: None

Disabled Access: Steps with some ramps throughout facility.

Group Requirements: Can handle large groups. The bar area seats 200 and they cater events for 250 people.

Special Information: Foreign-language tours available.

Gift Shop: Selection of standard and unusual Jamaican souvenirs from T-shirts to crafts. Also snack bar, lounge, and liquor shop. Open same days and hours as tour.

Directions: From Negril or Montego Bay, there are directional signs to follow, although most people come by tour bus. Last few miles you drive through sugar cane fields and along curvy, bumpy Bamboo Ave., under tunnel created by bamboo trees.

Nearby Attractions: Y.S. Waterfalls; Cashew Ostrich Park; Black River Safaris; Pickapeppa Sauce Factory tour (call 876-603-3441); High Mountain Coffee tour (call 876-963-4411).

Bacardi

Route 165, Intersection Route 888
Cataño, Puerto Rico 00962
(787) 788-1500
www.bacardi.com

BACARDI CORPORATION

RUM

After soaking up the Puerto Rican sun and rum, you'll want to cool off at a tour of the Bacardi Rum Distillery, the largest rum distillery in the world, near Old San Juan. Started in the 1860s by Don Facundo Bacardí, the company remains family-owned. When you drive onto the 127-acre complex along the palm tree–lined road and well-manicured grounds, you feel the presence of a successful company.

Relax and wait for the start of your tour by sipping mixed Bacardi cocktails in the pavilion shaded by the undulating roof shaped like spread bat wings. Since the bat is the company trademark, you'll see it reflected throughout the tour. The first stop on your tram ride is the towering white building known as "The Cathedral of Rum." Enter the cool first floor, stand in the replica of an old rum warehouse (complete with oak barrels), and notice the painted wall mural of Old San Juan.

At each stop a different guide will provide you with information about the company, such as the significance of the bat logo (symbol of good luck, prosperity, and tradition). At the Hall of Rum, displays include the maps and flags of all the distillers and bottlers of Bacardi Rum around the world, advertisements, photographs of the Bacardi family, and a diorama of the buildings on the complex.

While you don't see much of the distilling process, another hostess explains the four-step process of fermentation, distillation, aging, and blending. Board the tram to the bottling facility, where overhead signs explain the bottling process. The uncaser turns cartons upside down to remove empty bottles. The bottles do-si-do under the air cleaner, which cleans them with pressurized air and vacuum. Bottles rattle loudly and spin along five or six bottling lines, where filler machines use a vacuum system to fill them. After the capper machines apply tam-

per-resistant caps at a pre-set torque, the labeler glues on labels and tax stamps. At the end of each line, a worker inspects the bottles as they glide by. You leave the tour with a wealth of company information and an opportunity to sample more of their drinks and stroll the peaceful grounds overlooking Old San Juan.

Cost: Free

Freebies: Mixed rum drinks, sodas and juice for minors.

Video Shown: 3-minute video, in English or Spanish, covers bottling process.

Reservations Needed: No, except for groups larger than 20 people.

Days and Hours: Mon–Sat 8:30 AM–4:30 PM every 30 minutes. No tours if special event, so call ahead. No bottling on Saturdays. Closed during the Christmas holidays and the last 2 weeks of May. Call for schedule of other holidays.

Plan to Stay: 1.5 hours for tour and sampling.

Minimum Age: None, as long as accompanied by adult.

Disabled Access: Yes

Group Requirements: Groups larger than 20 people should call 2 days in advance. Ask for pavilion tour.

Special Information: No smoking during the tour, since highly explosive area.

Gift Shop: Rum 'N' Things sells logoed T-shirts and large assortment of gift packs of Bacardi rum. Open Mon–Sat 9:30 AM–5:30 PM. Closed Christmas and the last 2 weeks of May. Call regarding other holidays.

Directions: From Old San Juan, take ferry at pier #2 to Cataño. Take public bus to distillery. Driving from Old San Juan, take Rt. 1 South to Rt. 22 West. Take Rt. 165 North. Distillery on right at intersection with Rt. 888.

Nearby Attractions: Cabras Island; El Morro Castle in Old San Juan.

Cruzan Rum Distillery

West Airport Road
Route 64
St. Croix, U.S. Virgin Islands
(340) 692-2280
www.cruzanrums.com

RUM

CRUZAN RUM DISTILLERY

Rum tours can be sensory experiences, with the smells and tastes, the sounds and sites involved in both the manufacturing and craft of distilling. The Virgin Islands have been making some of the finest rums in the world since the early 1650s. At this historic location still stands the old windmill used for power before electricity and other remnants of an old plantation. International flags surround the stone fortress-like castle entrance. As you walk the grounds, you may see the centuries-old art of barrel making by coopers, as well as modern bottle machines.

The rum-making process begins with high-quality molasses received from Caribbean sugar plantations at the nearby dock. In what looks like a large, deep above-ground swimming pool, the molasses gets diluted with tropical rainwater pumped from a local aquifer. Cruzan adds its proprietary yeast cultures to begin fermentation of this mix into alcohol. Notice the bubbles rising to the top of the rich, brown, pudding-like mass in the holding tanks.

You might get a chance to talk with the Master Distiller at work with Cruzan's modern, five-column, stainless steel and copper still. You might see the rum flowing through tubes in the top of each column of the still. The rum distillate goes into American oak barrels. Walk into the barrel house where the rum ages for a minimum of two years—or for up to 12 years. Surrounded by barrels from floor to ceiling, with the sweet smell of rum in the air, you'll be surprised to learn that over half of the rum evaporates during this stage. The properly aged rum is then charcoal filtered and diluted to 80 percent proof with more local rainwater. Finally, the bottling building (not always in operation) fills bottles with the self-proclaimed "The World's Finest Rum" and prepares it for shipping.

Cost: Adults, $4; children under 18 (drinking age), $1.

Freebies: Small samples in bar area of different types of mixed drinks, such as a Cruzan Rum Piña Colada.

Video Shown: An illustrated board lights up at each step along production process. Accompanied by audio explanation.

Reservations Needed: Groups over 20 people should call at least 1 day ahead.

Days and Hours: Mon–Fri 9:00 AM–11:30 AM and 1:00 PM–4:15 PM. Closed major holidays.

Plan to Stay: 20 minutes for walking tour, plus time for rum samples.

Minimum Age: None

Disabled Access: Stairs throughout complex

Group Requirements: Reservations requested for large groups.

Special Information: For some visitors the smells can be overpowering.

Gift Shop: Sells duty-free Cruzan rum and rum cakes; logoed items, including T-shirts, golf shirts, caps, pennants, flags, and shot glasses. Can order the logoed items from website above.

Directions: From Christiansted, take Rt. 70 West. Get on Hwy 66 (Melvin Evans Hwy.). Pass airport. Make right onto Rt. 64 West. Distillery is a quarter-mile up the road on the right. There is a Cruzan Rum sign at entrance.

Nearby Attractions: St. George Botanical Gardens (340-692-2874); Whim Sugar Cane Plantation (340-772-0598); Fort Christianvaern; beaches; rainforest; national park.

Resources

Itinerary Planners and Vacation Ideas

Factory tours and company visitors centers/museums are free or inexpensive highlights you can add to a family vacation or business trip. This section helps you plan trips based on your favorite products and regions of the U.S.A. Factory tours allow you to watch workers and machines in action, so you'll see most production Monday through Friday during normal business hours (some companies' tours are offered only on specified days or at certain times of year). Company visitors centers/museums usually also have weekend and holiday hours. Most of the trips listed in this section require minimal advance planning; however, many tours require reservations, so plan accordingly.

Please refer to the full write-ups in the book for more information. Check the Nearby Attractions sections to round out these itineraries. Call the destinations to verify times and directions between locations. We also suggest that you use a detailed map of the region you are visiting and plan your trip carefully. AAA offers members a route-planning service, highlighting the best roads and highways that lead to your destination. Also, www.mapquest.com provides planning assistance including directions, estimated travel time, and rest stops along your route.

Day Trips

Atlanta's Pride
CNN (television news), page 112.
World of Coca-Cola Atlanta (soda), page 114.

Chicago-Area for Fun
Eli's Cheesecake World (cheesecake) in Chicago, page 128.
Haeger Potteries (artwork pottery) in East Dundee, page 131.

Chicago on Business
(Try to squeeze one in during your next trip.)
Chicago Board of Trade (grain and financial futures and options), page125. (See the Nearby Attractions under Chicago Board of Trade for more sites related to finance.)
Chicago Mercantile Exchange (agricultural and financial futures), page 126.
U.S. Post Office (mail), page 136.
Traveling to or from O'Hare International Airport:
McDonald's #1 Store Museum (fast food) in Des Plaines, page 134.

Dallas/Fort Worth Area's Corporate Leaders
JCPenney Museum (retail stores and catalogs) in Plano, page 320.
Mary Kay (cosmetics and skin-care products) in Addison, page 322.
Traveling to or from Dallas/Fort Worth Airport:
American Airlines C. R. Smith Museum (air travel) in Fort Worth, page 314.

Detroit Transportation
Henry Ford Museum and Greenfield Village (U.S. manufacturing and cars) in Dearborn, page 196.
Lionel (model trains and accessories) in Chesterfield, page 200.

Fort Wayne Food
(David Letterman's home state, Indiana)
Coca-Cola Bottling (soda) in Kokomo, page 140.
Perfection Bakeries (bread), page 145.
Sechler's (pickles) in St. Joe, page 146.

Kona Coffee Hawaii
Holualoa Kona Coffee in Holualoa, page 117.
Ueshima Coffee in Captain Cook, page 120.
Kona Coffee County driving tour map available from the Kona-Kohala Chamber of Commerce; see Nearby Attractions under both listings.

Las Vegas—Beyond the Casinos
Ethel M Chocolates (chocolates) in Henderson, page 222.
National Vitamin (vitamins), page 233 and color photos, page 27.
Ron Lee's World of Clowns (clown and animation figurines) in Henderson, page 224

Louisville Charm
American Printing House for the Blind (Braille and large-type publications, audio books, and educational aids), page 153.
Colonel Harland Sanders Museum (fast food), page 156.
Hillerich & Bradsby (Louisville Slugger baseball bats), page 159.
Louisville Stoneware (pottery), page 160.

Minnesota—Winter Sports
Arctic Cat (snowmobiles and all-terrain vehicles) in Thief River Falls, page 205.
Christian Brothers (hockey sticks) in Warroad, page 207
Polaris (snowmobiles, all-terrain vehicles, and personal watercraft) in Roseau, page 209.

New York City on Business
(Try to squeeze in at least one during your next trip)
NBC Studios (television programs), page 237.
New York Stock Exchange (stocks and bonds), page 238. (See Nearby Attractions under NYSE for more sites related to finance.)
Sony Wonder Technology Lab (electronics), page 243.
Traveling to or from LaGuardia Airport:
Steinway & Sons (pianos), Thursday mornings only, in Long Island City, page 244.

Northern Indiana—RV Capital of the World
Coachmen in Middlebury, page 139.
Holiday Rambler in Wakarusa, page 141.
Jayco in Middlebury, page 142.
RV/MH Heritage Foundation Museum and local Convention & Visitors Bureau lists other RV company tours (see Nearby Attractions under Holiday Rambler).

Northern Michigan—Chocolates and Cherries
Amon Orchards (cherries and cherry products) in Acme, page 193.
Kilwin's Chocolates (fudge, chocolates, and ice cream) in Petoskey, page 199.

Oregon Coast
Oregon Connection/House of Myrtlewood (wooden tableware and golf putters) in Coos Bay, page 273.
Tillamook Cheese (cheese) in Tillamook, page 276.
Traveling to or from Portland:
Rodgers Instruments (electronic and electronic-pipe combination organs) in Hillsboro, page 275.

Multiple-Day Trips

Auto Factory Adventure (2–4 days)
Day 1:   Toyota in Georgetown, Kentucky, page 165 and color photos, pages 17–19.
         Ford in Louisville, Kentucky, page 158.
Day 2:   Corvette in Bowling Green, Kentucky, page 157.
or
Day 2:   International (trucks) in Springfield, Ohio, page 261.
Day 3:   Nissan in Smyrna, Tennessee, page 311.
         Saturn tour and visitor center in Spring Hill, Tennessee, page 313.
Day 4:   BMW in Greer, South Carolina, page 305.
or
Day 4:   Mercedes-Benz in Vance, Alabama, pages 50–51.

Boston and Beyond (2–3 days)
Day 1:   Boston Beer (Samuel Adams beer), page 182.
         National Braille Press (Braille publications), page 188.
         Wm. S. Haynes (flutes and piocolos), page 190.
Day 2:   Cape Cod Potato Chips (potato chips) in Hyannis, Massachusetts, page 183.
         Cranberry World at Edaville USA (Ocean Spray products) in Carver, Massachusetts,
         page 184.
         Pairpoint Crystal (glass) in Sagamore, Massachusetts, page 189.
or
Day 2:   American Textile History Museum (cloth) in Lowell, Massachusetts, page 181.
         Stonyfield Farm (yogurt) in Londonderry, New Hampshire, page 228.
Day 3:   Anheuser-Busch (Budweiser beer) in Merrimack, New Hampshire, page 225.
         Castle Springs (bottled spring water and beer) in Moultonborough, New Hamp-
         shire, page 226.
         Hampshire Pewter (pewter tableware, ornaments, and gifts) in Wolfeboro, New
         Hampshire, page 227.

Bourbon Bounty in Kentucky (2 days)
Day 1:   Old Kentucky Candies (bourbon candy) in Lexington, page 162.
         Rebecca-Ruth Candies (chocolates and Bourbon Balls) in Frankfort, page 163 and
         color photos, page 15.
         Wild Turkey (bourbon) in Lawrenceburg, page 166 and color photos, page 21.
Day 2:   Maker's Mark (bourbon) in Loretto, page 161.
         Additional places of interest for bourbon lovers: Heaven Hill Distillery; Oscar Getz
         Museum of Whiskey History; Jim Beam's American Outpost; Annual Bardstown
         September Bourbon Festival. (See Nearby Bourbon-Related Attractions under
         Maker's Mark.)

Central Colorado (3 days)
Day 1:   Denver Area
         Hammond's Candies Since 1920 (candy), page 90 and color photos, page 9.
         Stephany's Chocolates (chocolates and toffee) in Arvada, page 93.
         U.S. Mint (coins), page 94.
Day 2:   Boulder Area
         Celestial Seasonings (teas), page 87.
         Coors (beer) in Golden, page 89 and color photos, page 7.
Day 3:   Aspen
         Compromise and Smuggler Mines (silver), page 88.

or

Day 3: Colorado Springs
        Simpich (dolls), page 92.
        Van Briggle (pottery), page 95.

or

Day 3: Estes Park
        Michael Ricker Pewter (pewter sculptures), page 91.

China, Glass, and Pottery in Eastern Ohio Area (2 days)

Day 1: Senator Heinz History Center in Pittsburgh, Pennsylvania, page 294.
        Brooke Glass in Wellsburg, West Virginia, page 349.
        Homer Laughlin China in Newell, West Virginia, page 351.
        Hall China in East Liverpool, Ohio, page 258.
        Side trip to Creegan (animated characters) in Steubenville, Ohio, page 256.
Day 2: Mosser Glass in Cambridge, Ohio, page 265.
        Robinson Ransbottom Pottery in Roseville, Ohio, page 266.
        Roseville-Crooksville pottery communities attractions and annual July pottery festi-
            val featuring tours of other pottery factories. (See Nearby Attractions under
            Robinson Ransbottom.)
        Side trip to Longaberger (baskets) in Frazeysburg, Ohio, page 263.

Colonial Williamsburg Area (2 days)

Day 1: Rowena's (pound cakes, jams, jellies, cooking sauces, and gifts) in Norfolk, page 337.
Day 2: The Candle Factory (candles and soap), page 336.
        Williamsburg Doll Factory (porcelain dolls), page 338.
        Williamsburg Pottery Factory (pottery, wood, and plaster) in Lightfoot, page 339.

Disney World and Beyond (3 days)

Day 1: The Magic of Disney Animation (animated features) in Lake Buena Vista, page 106.
Day 2: Nickelodeon Studios (television shows) in Orlando, page 108.
Day 3: E-One (fire trucks) in Ocala, page 102.

Food and Festivity in Louisiana (2 days)

Day 1: New Orleans area
        Blaine Kern's Mardi Gras World (parade floats and props) in New Orleans, page 167.
Day 2: Cajun Country
        Konriko (rice and Cajun seasonings) in New Iberia, page 169.
        McIlhenny Company (Tabasco brand pepper sauce) on Avery Island, page 170.
        Tony Chachere's (Creole seasonings and rice mixes) in Opelousas, page 172.

Gastronomic Tours in Texas (4 days)

Day 1: Collin Street Bakery (fruitcake) in Corsicana, page 316.
Day 2: Imperial Sugar (sugar) in Sugar Lane, near Houston, page 318.
        Blue Bell Creameries (ice cream) in Brenham, page 315.
Day 3: Jardine's Texas Foods (Texas-style foods) in Buda, near Austin, page 319.
Day 4: Dublin Dr Pepper Bottling (soda), bottling on Tuesdays, in Dublin, page 317.
        Dr Pepper Museum in Waco (see Special Information under Dr Pepper).
        Mrs Baird's Bakery (bread) in Fort Worth, page 323.

Glassblowing in West Virginia (2 days)

Day 1: Fenton Art Glass in Williamstown, page 350.
        Side trip to Lee Middleton Original Dolls in Belpre, Ohio, page 262.

Day 2:   Blenko Glass in Milton, page 348.
         Gibson Glass factory (see Nearby Attractions under Blenko Glass).

Hawaii—Off the Beaches (2 days)
Day 1:   Oahu
         Maui Divers of Hawaii (jewelry) in Honolulu, page 118.
Day 2:   Hawaii (the Big Island)
         Big Island Candies (chocolate-covered macadamia nuts and cookies) in Hilo, page 115.
         Mauna Loa (macadamia nuts and candy) in Hilo, page 119.
         Holualoa Kona Coffee (Kona coffee) in Holualoa, page 117.
         Ueshima Coffee (Kona coffee) in Captain Cook, page 120.

Milwaukee—Beer and Beyond (4 days)
Day 1:   Miller Brewing, page 358 and color photo, page 45.
         Quality Candy/Buddy Squirrel (chocolates and popcorn) in St. Francis, page 359.
Day 2:   Allen-Edmonds (shoes) in Port Washington, page 352.
         Kohler (bathtubs, whirlpools, toilets, and sinks) in Kohler, page 357.
Day 3:   SC Johnson Wax (specialty home-cleaning products) in Racine, page 362.
         CaseNewHolland (tractors) in Mount Pleasant, page 354.
Day 4:   Natural Ovens (breads and cereals) in Manitowoc, page 360.
or
Day 4:   General Motors (sport-utility vehicles and pickups) in Janesville, page 355.
         Trek (bicycles) in Waterloo, page 364.

Musical Instrument Mecca (3 days)
Day 1:   Wm. S. Haynes (flutes and piccolos) in Boston, Massachusetts, page 190.
Day 2:   Steinway & Sons (pianos) Thursday mornings only, in Long Island City, New York,
              page 244.
Day 3:   Martin Guitar in Nazareth, Pennsylvania, page 288 and color photo, page 35.

Niagara Falls (2 days)
Day 1:   (depending on your direction of travel in New York State to Niagara Falls):
         Babcock (ladders) in Bath, page 233.
         Corning Museum of Glass in Corning, page 234.
or
         George Eastman House (photography) in Rochester, page 235.
Day 2:   Choose two of the following:
         Original American Kazoo Company in Eden, page 239.
         Perry's Ice Cream in Akron, page 240.
         QRS Music (player-piano rolls) in Buffalo, page 241.

Pretzels and Potato Chips in Pennsylvania (2–3 days)
Day 1:   Anderson Bakery in Lancaster, page 278.
         Herr's Snack Factory Tour in Nottingham, page 286 and color photos, page 33.
         Sturgis Pretzel House in Lititz, page 297.
Day 2:   Snyder's of Hanover in Hanover, page 296.
         Utz Quality Foods in Hanover, page 299.
         (On the way to Utz and Snyder's, visit Harley-Davidson Motor Company in York,
              page 285, or Pfaltzgraff in Thomasville, pages 292–293.)
or
Day 2:   Chocolate Diversion
         Asher's Chocolates in Souderton, page 279.
         Hershey's Chocolate World in Hershey, page 287.
Day 3:   Utz Quality Foods in Hanover, page 299.

St. Louis and Kansas City—Bud and Beyond (3 days)

Day 1: Anheuser-Busch (Budweiser beer) in St. Louis, page 214.
Boeing (airplanes, missiles, and spacecraft) in St. Louis, page 215.
Chrysler (minivans and pickup trucks) in Fenton, page 216.

Day 2: Purina Farms (pets and farm animals) in Gray Summit, page 219.

Day 3: Hallmark Visitors Center (greeting cards) in Kansas City, page 217.
Harley-Davidson Motor Company (motorcycles) in Kansas City, page 218.

San Francisco with Kids—Fun for Adults, Too! (3 days)

Day 1: (May need to choose only two):
Basic Brown Bear Factory (teddy bears) in San Francisco, page 59 and color photos, page 3.
Fortune Cookie Factory in Oakland, page 66.
Dreyer's & Edy's Grand Ice Cream in Union City, pages 64–65.
(Consider side trip to Intel in Santa Clara for science-oriented children, page 70.)

Day 2: Jelly Belly Candy Co. (jelly beans, chocolates, and Gummi candies) in Fairfield, page 72 and color photos, page 5.

Day 3: Hershey's Visitors Center in Oakdale, page 69.

Studios of Southern California (2–3 days)

Days 1   Paramount Pictures in Hollywood, page 80.
and 2:   NBC Studios in Burbank, page 78.
Warner Bros. Studios in Burbank, page 86.

Day 3: Universal Studios Hollywood in Universal City, page 85.

Sweet Tooth Tour—East Coast (3 days)

Day 1: Moore's Candies in Baltimore, Maryland, page 178.

Day 2: Hershey's Chocolate World in Hershey, Pennsylvania, page 287.

Day 3: Asher's Chocolates in Souderton, Pennsylvania, page 279.

or

Day 3: Sherm Edwards (chocolates) in Trafford, Pennsylvania, page 295.

Sweet Tooth Tour—West Coast (3 days)

Day 1: Phoenix
Cerreta's Candy in Glendale, Arizona, page 54.

Day 2: Las Vegas
Ethel M Chocolates in Henderson, Nevada, page 222.

Day 3: San Francisco Area (fly to San Francisco). Choose one:
Jelly Belly Candy Co. (jelly beans, chocolates, and Gummi candies) in Fairfield, California, page 72 and color photos, page 5.
Hershey's Visitors Center in Oakdale, California, page 69.

or

Day 3: Seattle Area (fly to Seattle)
Boehms Chocolates in Issaquah, Washington, page 340.

Vermont—Beyond Ben & Jerry's (3 days)

From the South:

Day 1: Simon Pearce (glass and pottery) in Windsor and Quechee, page 334.
Grafton Village Cheese in Grafton, page 330.
Crowley Cheese in Healdville, page 329.

Day 2: Rock of Ages (granite quarry, memorials, and sculptures) in Graniteville, page 332.
Maple Grove Farms (maple syrup and salad dressing) in St. Johnsbury, page 331.
Cabot Creamery (cheese) in Cabot, page 328.

Day 3:   Vermont Teddy Bear in Shelburne, page 335.
         Ben & Jerry's (ice cream and frozen yogurt) in Waterbury, page 327.

Washington State (2 days)
Day 1:   Boeing (commercial aircraft) in Everett, page 341.
         Boehms Chocolates in Issaquah, page 340.
         Microsoft Museum (personal computers and software) in Redmond, page 344.
         Redhook Ale Brewery (beer) in Woodinville, page 345.
Day 2:   Liberty Orchards (fruit candies) in Cashmere, page 343.
or
Day 2:   Washington's Fruit Place Visitor Center (fruit) in Yakima, page 347.

York, Pennsylvania—"Factory Tour Capital" (2 days)
Day 1:   Harley-Davidson Motor Company (motorcycles) in York, page 285.
         Wolfgang Candy (candy) in York, page 301.
         Pfaltzgraff (pottery) in Thomasville, pages 292–293.
Day 2:   Herr's Snack Factory Tour (snack food) in Nottingham, page 286 and color photos,
         page 33.
         Snyder's of Hanover (pretzels and potato chips) in Hanover, page 296.

Company Index

Product Index

About the Authors

Karen Axelrod and Bruce Brumberg traveled across the U.S.A. to "kick the tires of the American economy." This husband-and-wife team journeyed from the massive Boeing plant in Everett, Washington, to the ranch-like factory of Jardine's Texas Foods in Buda, Texas (pictured above). During their travels, Bruce earned an "Official Pretzel Twister" certificate, while Karen was awarded an "Honorary Brewmaster" title and "Official Candymaker's Diploma." Fascinated by how things are made and companies grow, they visit factories for fun, business ideas, and free samples.

Karen and Bruce have been interviewed as factory experts on *Good Morning America* and CNN. Their radio interviews or mentions include NPR, WCBS-New York, and WGN-Chicago. *The Wall Street Journal, The New York Times, Business Week,* and *USA Today* have included them several times.

Having visited so many sites, Karen and Bruce are uniquely qualified to help companies improve their factory tour, visitor center, or company museum. They provide consulting services to companies and local tourist boards on factory tours, visitor centers, and museums. For more information and to reach the authors, check out the website www.factorytour.com.

When not traveling, they live with their young children, Hilary and Gregory, near Boston, Massachusetts. Bruce owns a legal and financial publishing company. He is Editor-in-Chief of myStockOptions.com, the premier provider of educational content and tools on employee stock options and other forms of equity compensation. Before writing this book, Karen was a buyer for 10 years for major retail and catalog companies.